Dating Acts

Dating Acts

*Between the Evangelists
and the Apologists*

Richard I. Pervo

POLEBRIDGE PRESS

Dedication

To many benefactors, known and unknown, during 2001-2002:

αἱ προσευχαί ὑμῶν καὶ αἱ ἐλεημοσύναι ὑμῶν ἀνέβησαν
εἰς μνημόσυνον ἔμπροσθεν τοῦ θεοῦ (Cf. Acts 10:4b)

Cover and interior design by Robaire Ream
Cover illustration by Robaire Ream

Library of Congress Cataloging-in-Publication Data
Pervo, Richard I.
  Dating Acts : between the evangelists and the apologists / Richard I.
Pervo.
     p. cm.
  Includes bibliographical references (p.   ) and index.
  ISBN 0-944344-73-9
  1. Bible. N.T. Acts--Criticism, interpretation, etc. 2. Manuscript
dating. I. Title.
  BS2625.52.P47 2006
  226.6'066--dc22

                                                           2006050256

Contents

Preface

This project grew out of the collaborative work of the Acts Seminar, a program of the Westar Institute. The immediate stimulus was a paper by Joseph B. Tyson, "The Date of Acts: A Reconsideration," prepared for the March, 2002 meeting, and presented in revised form at the October, 2002 session. I am very grateful to Joe and to all the members of the Seminar, in particular its leader, Dennis Smith. In addition to his written contributions, Bill Walker graciously provided much advice and assistance, in addition to his written contributions. Heikki Leppä responded very promptly to a request for a copy of his dissertation. Thanks are also due to Tom Hall for his editorial contributions, and to the Westar staff, as well as to my cat Scipio (1992–2005), who usually identified the book needed next by sitting upon it.

The immediate genesis of this book was my own contribution to the October, 2002 Acts Seminar: "Dating Acts," published Forum N.S. 5.1 (Spring 2002) 53–72. The full manuscript was drafted during 2002, and there has been limited opportunity to make references to more recent work.

There is no shortage of books directed toward both a general and a technical audience. Many, if not most, of these publications fail to satisfy either group of implied readers. Efforts to reach a broader audience frequently achieve condescension without clarity. Scholars who read such books suspect that "general audience" is a dispensation from the requirement to prove one's case. Although this is a scholarly work, I have striven to try to make it intelligible to those who are not at home with academic jargon and philology by translating all non-English words in the body of the text, clarifying the meaning of various terms, and, where it seemed helpful, paraphrasing important arguments and conclusions in the simplest possible language. In addition, I have sought to make my methods clear and to explain the background of several vital controversies and to provide examples and illustrations where I believed them useful.

The footnotes may not always live up (or down) to this standard. Be that as it may, since they often provide information useful to those not technically adept, please give them at least a passing glance. Knowing that all intelligent readers tend to skip some passages and skim others, the author can only plead that such selective reading be deliberate and purposeful.

The burden and thesis of this book is that the general consensus by which Acts has been dated c. 80–90 is not well founded. I do not believe that Acts was written in the first century of our era (which was not, of course, the first century of any ancient era). The principal aim is not so much to establish a particular date as to undermine the widespread view that the dating of (Luke and) Acts has little, if any, importance for the understanding of their texts. In building the case I shall give serious consideration to two currently unpopular notions about the sources of Acts. One is the hypothesis that Luke made use of the letters of Paul. Another is that he consulted the writings of the Jewish historian Flavius Josephus. My arguments about the date of Acts do not, however, stand or fall with the acceptance or rejection of these proposals alone. With regard to the former the burden has always been upon those who must devise arguments to explain why Luke knew nearly everything about Paul except that he wrote letters. As for the latter, I shall argue that knowledge of Josephus is the most reasonable explanation for how Luke acquired certain pieces of information. In both cases the proposals rely less upon new information or fresh methods than upon the evolution of thought about Luke as a writer, evangelist, and historian. I shall argue that, although his use of these sources does little to establish the credibility of Acts, this approach toward sources is quite consistent with Luke's employment of other sources, such as the Greek Bible (LXX), and that it is also typical of the ways in which ancient writers made use of various sources.

Those not familiar with ancient practices should note that modern standards for writing history are quite different from those that prevailed in the larger Greco-Roman world. Ancient historians were not obliged to state their authorities. Not even Thucydides, usually viewed as the greatest of Greek historians, can meet the standards for accuracy often demanded of the author of Acts. No historian, ancient or modern, has been able to avoid the commission of errors, and none have been free from bias.

Formally, this monograph is about the date of the book of Acts. As the subtitle indicates, the exercise is not simply an attempt to overturn a consensus. I am seeking to achieve more than the repositioning of a pinpoint upon a timeline. The purpose of establishing a date for Acts is to illuminate its place in the history of early Christianity and to further the understanding of this singular work. The subject of this book is the *significance* of the date of Acts. That is one explanation for its length; another is that arguing against the grain requires far more effort and evidence than does acceptance of the consensus. Such is the nature of the scholarly beast.

Some Notes on Usages

Among the illustrations used are analogies. Analogies can be important aids to learning; they may also be unhelpful or worse. Technical scholarship tends to find them wasteful or inadequate. Generally speaking, scholars are likely to disapprove of all analogies but their own. Both those who present papers and their auditors are familiar with the objection, "I approve of your thesis but do not like your analogy." Such reproofs are often irrelevant. Analogies seek to illuminate a point. Once the point is grasped, the analogy is a bridge that may be burned after it has been crossed. Those who see the weakness of a certain analogy need not worry, for all analogies have limitations and those who recognize the limits of an analogy have grasped the point it seeks to illustrate.

Although popular usage broadly defines the term "metaphor," technical literary criticism speaks of non-literal images as "tropes," dividing these into two groups: those based upon a proposed *similarity* (simile and metaphor) and those related to *contiguity* (synecdoche and metonymy). The terms may seem imposing, but the devices are in constant use. Anyone who invokes the cliché "It is as hot as hell" is employing the trope of simile (as well as the figure of hyperbole). Synecdoche substitutes part for whole or whole for part, as in "Lend me a hand." Metonymy substitutes cause for effect or effect for cause or utilizes an attribute for the object. The last may introduce overlap with synecdoche. In the expression "I need some bread," "bread" means "money." This is a metonymy, substituting the result of money for the thing itself. Of course, "bread" is also a common synecdoche, for it denotes food by identifying one of its components, and allows nourishment to evoke all of the essentials of life. A contemporary example of the attributive sense is "suits," which characterizes executives or bureaucrats—"the bosses," by their mode of dress.

In the Gospels and Acts both of these tropes assume narrative roles. A single healing, for instance, invites the reader to imagine that Jesus, Peter, or Paul performed many such wonders. Summaries (e.g. Mark 1:32–34) make this explicit. Representative examples are a kind of synecdoche. This practice is essential to narrative, for reports of one exorcism after another would soon weary even the most ardent devotee. Healings exhibit a further dimension of synecdoche: they display but a small part of God's loving care for the entire human race. Similarly, miracle stories amount to metonymies, since they seek to lead observers or readers from admiration of the result to veneration of the cause: God. This is not mere academic gobbledygook. There are important differences between the functions of simile/metaphor on the one hand and synecdoche/metonymy on the other. While the parables of Jesus belong to the general category of metaphorical speech, his exorcisms should not be so classified. (Those who find that this paragraph leads them to long for a taste of the grape may take comfort in noting that "taste" is an indisputable synecdoche, while "grape" serves as a ripe example of metonymy.)

At various times the expression "Hellenistic Judaism" appears in this work. This does not imply a strong dichotomy between the "pure" Judaism of Palestine and the lax or adventurous standards and thought of the Diaspora. "Hellenistic Judaism" is a convenient shorthand for Jewish literature composed in Greek, much of it presumably originating outside of Palestine. At times the concept may embrace translations into Greek, in particular the Greek bible, the Septuagint (LXX), which influenced and was influenced by Jews who thought and worshipped in the common language of the Eastern Mediterranean. Similarly "Gnosticism" and "Gnosis" are shorthand expressions for diverse movements.

For some the term "intertextuality" may be unfamiliar. (Others may regard it as an egregious specimen of academic jargon.) The principal referent of "intertextuality" in this book is the direct use of a source (usually written) by the author of Acts, but I have also included material for further reading. Finally, "Collection" with a capital "C" refers to the offering raised by Paul for believers in Judea. When "Chapter" is capitalized it means a chapter of the current book, rather than a chapter in Acts, etc.

Four appendices follow the main body of this book. The first two are contributions to the history of research and can stand alone. Appendix I attempts to summarize research on the sources of Acts, while Appendix II is a catalogue of the range of dates proposed for Acts by various scholars. Appendix IV treats the Jewish Revolt of c.115–117 as an external factor for consideration in dating Acts. Appendix III, however, is intended as a reference to be consulted in the course of reading, for it gathers in one place the names of early Christian authors and writings discussed here, and the dates to which I assign them, with differing views where appropriate.

All biblical quotations not otherwise attributed are from the *New Revised Standard Version* (NRSV), @1989 by the Division of Christian Education of the National Council of Churches of Christ in the U.S.A. In these citations I have, for the sake of clarity, followed "lectionary practice" by supplying proper names for pronouns. These substitutions are in *italics*. Thus, instead of "He asked him" the quotation will read "*Pilate* asked *Jesus*."

The benefactors to whom this work is dedicated provided financial, spiritual, and moral assistance and support during a period of great personal difficulty. No expression of gratitude could be commensurate with their contributions.

To any who may wonder why an author—especially one who, however wrong-headed, is usually interesting—should have elected to take up such barnacle-encrusted subjects as *sources* and *date*, I offer the final words of Apuleius of Madaura's preface to his famous *Metamorphoses* (*The Golden Ass*): "Pay close attention, dear reader, and you will be surprised."

Note: Among the works that appeared after completion of the ms. is Andrew Gregory, *The Reception of Luke and Acts in the Period before Irenaeus*. WUNT 169. Tübingen: 2003. The idea of a "Collection Source" (Appendix I) was anticipated by Dietrich-Alex Koch, "Kollektenbericht, 'Wir'-Bericht und Itinerar: Neue Überlegungen zu einem alten Problem," NTS 45 (1999) 367-90. In 2005 Gerd Lüdemann (assisted by T. Hall) issued *The Acts of the Apostles: What Really Happened in the Earliest Days of the Church*. Amherst, New York: Prometheus Books. This supplements, but does not replace, his *Early Christianity*.

Abbreviations

// indicate a parallel text or texts, usually when literary dependence is presumed. Jude 10//2 Peter 2:12, for example, points to the verse in Jude and takes note of the parallel in 2 Peter's revision of Jude.

AB	*The Anchor Bible*
ABD	*The Anchor Bible Dictionary*. 6 vols. Ed. D. N. Freedman. New York: Doubleday, 1992.
ABRL	The Anchor Bible Reference Library, also published by Doubleday.
ACNT	Augsburg Commentary on the New Testament, published by Augsburg Fortress, Minneapolis.
ACW	*Ancient Christian Writers*, now published by Paulist Press.
ANRW	*Aufstieg und Niedergang der römischen Welt: Geschichte und Kultur Roms im Spiegel der neueren Forschung*. Edited by H. Temporini and W. Haase. Berlin: Walter de Gruyter, 1972-
ANTC	Abingdon New Testament Commentaries.
ASNU	Acta seminarii neotestamentici upsaliensis.
Barn	*Barnabas*
BDAG	Walter Bauer, *A Greek-English Lexicon of the New Testament and other Early Christian Literature*. 3rd ed. Rev. ed., F. W. Danker. Chicago: University of Chicago Press, 2000.
Beg.	*The Beginnings of Christianity*. Part I. 5 vols. Ed. Frederick J Foakes-Jackson and Kirsopp Lake. New York: Macmillan Co., 1920-33.
BETL	Bibliotheca ephemeridum theologicarum lovaniensium.
BHT	Beiträge zur historischen Theologie
BIFCS	*Book of Acts in Its First Century Setting*. 5 vols. Bruce W. Winter, general editor. Grand Rapids: William B. Eerdmans/Carlisle: Paternoster, 1993-1996. Each volume has its own title and particular editors or author.
CCSA	Corpus Christianorum Series Apocryphorum, published by Brepols, Turnhout.
CPJ	*Corpus papyrorum judaicorum*. Ed V. Tcherikover and A. Fuks. 3 vols. Cambridge: Harvard University Press, 1957–64.
CRINT	*Compendia Rerum Iudaicarum ad Novum Testamentum*. Assen and Philadelphia, 1974-. The individual volumes have different editors.

DDD	*Dictionary of Deities and Demons in the Bible*. 2nd Ed. K. Van Der Toorn et al. Leiden: E. J. Brill, 1999.
Did	The *Didache*
EDNT	*Exegetical Dictionary of the New Testament*. 3 vols. Ed. Horst Balz and Gerhard Schneider. Translated from the German *Exegetisches Wörterbuch zum Neuen Testament*. Grand Rapids: William B. Eerdmans, 1990.
FRLANT	*Forschungen zur Religion und Literatur des Alten und Neuen Testaments*. Göttingen: Vandenhoeck & Ruprecht.
FS	*Festschrift*, celebratory volume. This German abbreviation is commonly used for works honoring a scholar, without regard to nationality.
GLAJJ	Menachem Stern. *Greek and Latin Authors on Jews and Judaism*. 3 vols. Jerusalem: Israel Academy of Sciences and Humanities, 1974-1984.
HDR	Harvard Dissertations in Religion. Minneapolis: Fortress Press.
HermMan	*Shepherd of Hermas, Mandates*
HermSim	*Shepherd of Hermas, Similitudes (Parables)*
HJP	Emil Schürer, *The History of the Jewish People in the Age of Jesus Christ (175 B.C.-A.D. 135)* 3 vols. Rev. and Ed. G. Vermes, F. Millar, *et al*. Three Volumes in four parts. Edinburgh: T. & T. Clark, 1973-1987.
HNT	*Handbuch zum Neuen Testament*. Tübingen: Mohr/Siebeck.
HTK	*Herders Theologischer Kommentar zum Neuen Testament*. Freiberg: Herder.
HTS	*Harvard Theological Studies*. Cambridge: Harvard University Press.
HUT	*Hermeneutische Untersuchungen zur Theologie.*, Tübingen: Mohr/ Siebeck.
ICC	*The International Critical Commentary*. Edinburgh: T. & T. Clark.
IgnEph	Ignatius to the Ephesians
IgnMag	Ignatius to the Magnesians
IgnTr	Ignatius to the Trallians
IgnRom	Ignatius to the Romans
IgnPhd	Ignatius to the Philadelphians
IgnSm	Ignatius to the Smyrnaeans
IgnPol	Ignatius to Polycarp
IRT	Issues in Religion and Theology. Minneapolis: Fortress Press.

Josephus. The following short titles and abbreviations are used, with the conventional Latin terms in parentheses:

Against Apion (*Contra Apionem, C. Ap.*) An apology in two books.

Antiquities: *Antiquities of the Jews* (*Antiquitates*). *Ant.* A history extending from creation to the present time, in twenty books.

Life (*Vita*) An autobiography in one book.

War (*Bellum Judaicum, B. J.*) A history of the First Jewish Revolt, in seven books.

JSNTS	Journal for the Study of the New Testament: Supplement Series. Sheffield: Sheffield University Academic Press. .
KAV	Kommentar zum apostolischen Väter. Göttingen: Vandenhoeck & Ruprecht.
KEK	*Meyers Kritisch-Exegetischer Kommentar über Das Neue Testament.* Göttingen: Vandenhoeck & Ruprecht.
κ.τ.λ. (καὶ τὰ λοιπά)	This Greek abbreviation is the source and exact equivalent of Latin *et cetera*.
Lampe	G. W. H. Lampe, *Patristic Greek Lexicon*. Oxford: Clarendon, 1961.
LCC	*Library of Christian Classics*. Philadelphia: Westminster Press.
LCL	Loeb Classical Library. Cambridge: Harvard University Press.
LEC	The *Library of Early Christianity*, Ed. Wayne Meeks. Philadelphia: Westminster Press.
LXX	The Septuagint, Jewish scriptures in Greek. The LXX was the "Bible" of early Christians. Its contents are not identical to those of the Hebrew Bible.
MPG	The *Patrologia Graeca*, edited by J. P. Migne.
NAC	The New American Commentary. Nashville: Broadman Press.
NCB	New Century Bible, published by Oliphants in the U.K. and Eerdmans in the U.S.
NTD	Das Neue Testament Deutsch. Göttingen: Vandenhoeck & Ruprecht
OBT	Overtures to Biblical Theology. Minneapolis: Fortress Press.
Pastor	The pseudonymous author of the
Pastoral(s)	Pastoral Epistles: 1-2 Timothy, Titus.
ÖTKNT	Ökumenischer Taschenbuch-Kommentar zum Neuen Testament. Gütersloh: Gütersloher Verlagshaus Gerd Mohn.
SANT	Studien zum Alten und Neuen Testaments. München: Kösel.
SBLDS	Society of Biblical Literature Dissertation Series, published by Scholars Press and by the Society of Biblical Literature.
SBLMS	Society of Biblical Literature Monograph Series. Various publishers.
SBLSP	Society of Biblical Literature Seminar Papers, published by Scholars Press and by the Society of Biblical Literature.
SBLSS	Society of Biblical Literature Symposium, published by the Society.
SBLTT	Society of Biblical Literature Texts and Translations, published by Scholars Press and by the Society.
SD	Studies and Documents. Various publishers.
SLA	*Studies in Luke-Acts*. Paul Schubert FS. Ed. L. E. Keck and J. L. Martyn. Nashville Abingdon, 1966.
SNT	Supplements to *Novum Testamentum*.Leiden: E. J. Brill.
SNTSMS	Society for New Testament Studies Monograph Series. Cambridge: Cambridge University Press.
SP	Sacra Pagina, a commentary series. Collegeville, Minnesota: Michael Glazier/The Liturgical Press,

SUNT	Studien zur Umwelt des Neuen Testaments. Göttingen: Vandenhoeck & Ruprecht.
s.v.	*sub vocabulo,* "under the word." This bids the reader to consult that particular word in the designated index or dictionary.
TDNT	*Theological Dictionary of the New Testament.* 10 vols. Ed. G. Kittel and G. Friedrich. Trans. G. W. Bromiley. Grand Rapids, 1964-1976.
TLG	the *Thesaurus Linguae Graecae,* a searchable data base of Greek literature published by the University of California at Irvine.
TU	Texte und Untersuchungen zur Geschichte der altchristlichen Literatur. Berlin: Akadmie Verlag.
WBC	Word Biblical Commentary. Dallas: Word Books.
WUNT	*Wissenschaftliche Untersuchungen zum Neuen Testament 2. Reihe.* Tübingen: Mohr/Siebeck

1 The Date of Acts and Some of its Sources
Issues and Methods

INTRODUCTION

Just prior to the First World War, Hans Wendt issued the final edition of his commentary on Acts in the prestigious KEK series.[1] About one half of the introduction treats the sources of Acts, which includes a substantial discussion of Luke's possible use of both the letters of Paul and the work of the historian Josephus (40–45). In due course (1956–1977) this commentary would be succeeded by that of Ernst Haenchen, who sent reams of source theory up the chimney by showing a generation of scholars and clergy that Wendt had wasted much of his time.[2]

Quite different from Wendt and much more in accord with current interests and methods is Charles Talbert, who efficiently dispenses with questions about the sources and date of Acts before he has completed the first page of his lively and insightful commentary on Acts. In his view possible dates range

> . . . [B]etween the early sixties and the early second century. Although arguments aiming at greater precision have been put forward, they have not been compelling . . . Both source critics and form critics have expended incredible energy on the issue of the sources of Acts with very little to show for their efforts . . . To say that Acts was written by an unknown author between the early sixties and the early second century using unknown sources does not advance the cause of interpretation very far.[3]

This quotation vividly indicates the extent to which concern about the date and sources of particular early Christian texts now stands far enough from the cutting edge to make the subject exciting only to a highly impressionable freshman. Indeed, these matters are so out of fashion that a full-scale treatment of them in relation to a single work could almost pass for a radical enterprise, certainly as an exercise "against the grain." Those who attempt to teach New Testament to contemporary college—or even seminary—students must seek to justify the devotion of any attention to the traditional "introductory questions" (Who? When? Where? Why?), and their success is rarely unqualified.

Several factors explain this relative lack of interest. Primary among them is the recognition that the New Testament texts are, to shift the metaphor, a heavily worked vein. Scholars and others have, with diverse instruments of increasing refinement, excavated and tunneled, mined and shored up, examined, sifted, and sampled these revered and foundational writings for nearly two centuries—or, if one counts the days of mere picks and shovels, for nearly two millenia. Many maintain that all usable ore has been extracted. Others opine that the honeycombed structure has finally collapsed, or in the jargon of the academy, "deconstructed." (Excavation is an apposite image so long as one remembers that the word refers primarily to a *process* and secondarily to the *result* of that process.)

Excursus: The History of Criticism in a Nutshell

From the viewpoint of modernism, all scholarly labors prior to the time of the philosopher Emmanuel Kant (1724–1804) are "pre-critical." Broadly speaking, before Kant content dominated the academic world. Of method there was no lack, but these methods were not "scientific." (The German *Wissenschaftlich* is broader than "scientific" in that it applies not only to "the sciences" , and means "methodologically appropriate and objective"). Critical observation is no modern invention. The third century Christian theologian Origen, for example, can still impress readers with the acuity of his observations and his openness in the face of certain problems and questions. Method, however, was primarily theological in structure and pastoral in orientation. The task of theologians was to systematize the faith of the church and to exegetes went the responsibility of demonstrating that Scripture presented the same faith. From the Reformation era onward the production of complementary but competing systems and expositions had a destabilizing effect upon such "assured results." The Wars of Religion (1618–1714) capsized these unsteady vessels and left substantial skepticism in their wake. In the nineteenth century biblical criticism arose as a challenge to traditional views; by the twentieth century critical tools had become, more often than not, handmaids to proclamation of the Christian faith. Postmodernism, which has done to the assuredness of critical method and consensus similar damage to that done by early criticism to the sureties of the faithful, has greatly reduced the distance between "pre-critical" and "critical." Moreover, much contemporary NT study, especially in the United States, has but tenuous links if any to Christian institutions and people.

Some will appreciate the irony that the orientation of the present book is considerably closer to Wendt's commentary than to those of either Haenchen or Talbert—and this even though the author's scholarly specialization owes much to their influence, and his admiration for them remains undiminished by years of writing and research. But since this is not an exercise in autobiography, it is preferable to assign this reversion to the discipline.

It is further ironic—as the present case will soon demonstrate—that New Testament scholarship tends to represent an "Hegelian model."[4] This developmental construct views movements in terms of actions, reactions, and a subsequent balance. The action is called a "thesis," the reaction an "antithesis," and the resulting equilibrium a "synthesis." In the language of American popular culture these may be described as "movement," "backlash," and "permanent gains/losses." For example, the Civil Rights Movement of the 1960s in the U.S. generated a "white backlash," which contributed to the Republican dominance during 1969–93 and an eventual turning away from "affirmative action." Yet legal segregation is dead, and permanent gains include the general acceptance of equal access and voting rights. This analogy reveals that every "synthesis" represents a delicate and impermanent balance of conflicting theses and antitheses.

Scholarship tends to label any current synthesis a "consensus." But while such an accord does include some permanent gains, it may in large measure represent a truce resulting from exhaustion or a period of false calm between storms. My goal is to disturb the prevailing consensus about the date of the book of Acts and about some of its sources. In theory, at least, projects of this nature are always worthwhile. If conducted in a responsible and rigorous manner, they urge everyone to re-examine fundamental presuppositions. If, after due reflection, the presuppositions are affirmed, so much the better. Included in any such consensus, however, are other implications. Within the Hegelian model resides the assumption that every era has its own characteristic questions and issues. This is why each generation must write the history of past generations anew, with or without fresh data. A related assumption is that the key to the understanding of any particular historical era requires the identification of the questions and issues of that era (rather than those of our own) and of how those matters were addressed.[5]

The preceding postulate was the particular contribution of Ferdinand Christian Baur (1792–1860), who set an agenda for the study of early Christianity that remained operative for a good century and is by no means moribund today.[6] His answers are often rejected, but his questions remain vital and his methods have not been fully superseded. The classical Christian tradition either soft-pedaled or denied intra-Christian conflict during the apostolic era (roughly c. 30–90 CE). Protestant historians, in particular those of the German Lutheran tradition, constituted a partial exception to this dogma, since they saw their disputes with Rome (and others) mirrored in the conflicts of the Apostle Paul. For Baur the fundamental challenge of early Christianity was the relationship of this movement to its Jewish parent. He demonstrated not only that Paul struggled with this issue but that it was still alive in the middle third of the second century (c. 130–160), and from this deduced the existence of two antithetical groups. The writings of one of these movements, that of Marcion of Sinope, are largely lost.[7] One form of its antithesis, "Jewish Christianity" is known through its extant writings, a later edition of which survives in works known as the Pseudo-Clementines.[8] The latter are associated, in missionary settings, with the figure of Peter, whose superior, James, remained at Jerusalem as primate of the Church. Baur concluded that the conflict between "Pauline" ("law-free") and "Petrine" ("Jewish") movements long endured. As he developed his ideas, Baur found in the Hegelian model an apt analytical tool.[9] He discovered a "synthesis" of this conflict in Luke and Acts, which he therefore assigned to the mid-second century. In his day the science of historical criticism was rather young. Indeed, from the New Testament perspective, it was propelled into maturity through efforts to refine and, especially, to refute Baur. Leaders of this "antithesis" included such luminaries as Adolph v. Harnack (1851–1930) and Joseph B. Lightfoot (1828–1889), both of whose works can still be read with profit, as can those of William M. Ramsay (1851–1939) and Theodor Zahn (1838–1933).[10]

DATING ACTS

It is no surprise, therefore, that a century ago the date of Acts remained a matter of considerable contention.[11] When Harnack shifted from a preference for c. 80 (with the possibility of an earlier date) to strong support for c. 62, he caused something of a scholarly sensation.[12] Since 1950, however, the date of Acts has not been the subject of much lively discussion, and for two primary reasons:

1. Fresh evidence, new theories, and innovative methods pertinent to the subject have not come forth.
2. Current scholarship, as indicated at the beginning, has shown relatively limited interest in the issue.

New method and theory, while hardly lacking, have not been of the sort that promote detailed philological and historical analysis. Probably the most notable pertinent development over the last half-century has been a gradual erosion of support for an early date. Whereas more conservative commentators once pressed for a date in the 60s, they are now inclined to place the book in the 80s. In the first (1951) edition of his commentary upon the Greek text, the widely respected Frederick F. Bruce (1910–1990) argued for 62; a year later, he was more vague: "toward 70." The final (1990) edition concludes the discussion with these words: "If, then, a date in the late 70s or early 80s of the first century (say, in the principate of Titus [79–81] or early in that of Domitian [81–96]) is assigned to Acts, most of the evidence will be satisfied."[13] Gregory Sterling is but one of a number who now speak of ". . . [a] general consensus that Luke-Acts was written between 80–90 CE."[14]

It is remarkable that few scholars devote much space or effort to the question. Barrett expends rather less than two pages on the discussion,[15] Schneider less than three.[16] Fitzmyer may be more candid than most: "In the long run, it is a matter of little concern when or where Luke-Acts was composed, since the interpretation of it, especially of Acts, depends little on its date or place of composition."[17] This statement would have astonished Ramsay or Harnack far more than any particular proposal about a specific date. Those with a literary orientation may be relatively indifferent to questions of provenance and date, but Fitzmyer is not to be enrolled in their number. Consensus notwithstanding, a date of c. 100, long espoused by Conzelmann, continues to have its adherents.[18] At stake is whether Acts derives from a representative of the second or of the third generation. As a member of the second generation, the author of Acts could still be, however senior, a former companion of Paul and in first-hand touch with some of the personalities of the narrative. Raymond Brown says just this, in so many unenthusiastic words: ". . . [I]n order to preserve the possibility that there is truth in the tradition that the author was a companion of Paul, the best date would seem to be 85, *give or take five to ten years.*"[19] Since one cannot determine a best date on the basis of "preserving a possibility," one must conclude that Brown means that his suggestion will not offend those who wish to view the author as a companion of Paul. This is tantamount to an announcement that the argument has become utterly stale. One could also appeal to Brown in support of a date c. 95. The only hawser holding the Lucan ship to the dock labeled 80–90 is its possible connection to Paul, more specifically, its use of "we." The grounds are thus *internal* to Christian history—or better, to Christian tradition. I do not consider it methodologically sound to date anonymous works primarily by reference to traditions about their authorship. From the scholarly perspective traditions are at best no more than hypotheses; and as Cadbury noted many years ago,[20] Luke and Acts can claim no *demonstrably* early external tradition about authorship.

Consensus is not unanimity. It may emerge for a number of reasons and in response to varying pressures and processes. Ideally, it is the result of lengthy discussion that yields widespread acquiescence or at least tolerance. The current consensus that Acts is to be dated c. 85 (+/-5) is not the product of such a discussion. It is rather the result of a mixture of nearly equal portions of pragmatism and indifference. Not that pragmatism is intrinsically wicked: it represents a major concession by conservative scholars that enables authorities ranging from the staunchly conservative F. F. Bruce to the moderately liberal C. K. Barrett to discuss Acts from a similar perspective. This concurrence therefore embraces both those who view Acts as Deutero-Pauline and those who prefer to associate it with a companion of Paul. ("Deutero-Pauline" refers primarily to the "disputed" letters of Paul—i. e., letters written in his name by successors—and secondarily to post-Pauline constructions of Paul's life and thought.) The dominant consensus certainly has its values. The question is whether these values are worth the price.

THE SOURCES OF ACTS

Those who write works of non-fiction today are expected to identify their sources through annotation with bibliography and, in particular, to label clearly and carefully identify material taken from other writers. Ancient writers were under no obligation. As a general rule, even historians neglected to name their sources—except, of course, unless they wished to criticize them. At times one is tempted to believe that Greco-Roman historians regularly failed to name the sources that they did use, but freely mentioned the names of authorities that they did *not* use. Their goal has endured in the practice that teachers urge upon students assigned a research paper: to summarize the content of a source in their own words and style. An important difference is that current values frown upon paraphrases that alter facts, change meanings, and expect readers to recognize the unacknowledged authorities whose views are being expounded.

One may therefore summarize the ancient "rules" about sources thus: literary sources may be used with or without acknowledgment, so long as they are presented in one's own genre-appropriate vocabulary and style. Authors are free to alter facts and to bend authorities to conform to their own interpretation.[21] Many clear and relevant examples are available in the Jewish historian Flavius Josephus' paraphrases of the Greek Bible. (See Tables 1.1 and 1.2.)

Not even the words for "Pharaoh," "rod," and "snake" remain unchanged in the account of Josephus. Further adjustments include the elimination of God and Aaron from the story, as well as the introduction of an edifying contrast between "magic" and "religion." A full investigation would inquire about possible contamination from another Jewish historian, Artapanus, and other matters,[22] but the foregoing data will suffice to show that Josephus did all that an ancient author was supposed to do with his sources.[23] No one could reconstruct

Table 1.1: Moses and Pharaoh

Exodus 7:8–12	Josephus, *Ant.* 2.284–287
8 Καὶ εἶπεν κύριος πρὸς Μωυσῆν καὶ Ααρων λέγων 9 Καὶ ἐὰν λαλήσῃ πρὸς ὑμᾶς **Φαραω** λέγων Δότε ἡμῖν σημεῖον ἢ τέρας, καὶ ἐρεῖς Ααρων τῷ ἀδελφῷ σου Λαβὲ τὴν ῥάβδον καὶ ῥῖψον αὐτὴν ἐπὶ τὴν γῆν ἐναντίον Φαραω καὶ ἐναντίον τῶν θεραπόντων αὐτοῦ, καὶ ἔσται δράκων. 10 εἰσῆλθεν δὲ Μωϋσῆς καὶ Ααρων ἐναντίον Φαραω καὶ τῶν θεραπόντων αὐτοῦ καὶ ἐποίησαν οὕτως, καθάπερ ἐνετείλατο αὐτοῖς κύριος· καὶ ἔρριψεν Ααρων τὴν ῥάβδον ἐναντίον Φαραω καὶ ἐναντίον τῶν θεραπόντων αὐτοῦ, καὶ ἐγένετο δράκων. 11 συνεκάλεσεν δὲ Φαραω τοὺς σοφιστὰς Αἰγύπτου καὶ τοὺς φαρμακούς, καὶ ἐποίησαν καὶ οἱ ἐπαοιδοὶ τῶν Αἰγυπτίων ταῖς φαρμακείαις αὐτῶν ὡσαύτως. 12 καὶ ἔρριψαν ἕκαστος τὴν **ῥάβδον** αὐτοῦ, καὶ ἐγένοντο **δράκοντες**· καὶ κατέπιεν ἡ ῥάβδος ἡ Ααρων τὰς ἐκείνων ῥάβδους.	Χλευάσαντος δὲ τοῦ **βασιλέως** Μωυσῆς ἔργῳ παρεῖχεν αὐτῷ βλέπειν τὰ σημεῖα τὰ κατὰ τὸ Σιναῖον ὄρος γενόμενα· ὁ δ᾽ ἀγανακτήσας πονηρὸν μὲν αὐτὸν ἀπεκάλει καὶ πρότερον φυγόντα τὴν παρ᾽ Αἰγυπτίοις δουλείαν καὶ νῦν ἐξ ἀπάτης αὐτοῦ τὴν ἄφιξιν πεποιημένον καὶ τερατουργίαις καὶ μαγείαις καταπλήξειν ἐπικεχειρηκότα. [285] καὶ ταῦθ᾽ ἅμα λέγων κελεύει τοὺς ἱερεῖς τὰς αὐτὰς ὄψεις αὐτῷ παρασχεῖν ὁρᾶν, ὡς Αἰγυπτίων σοφῶν ὄντων καὶ περὶ τὴν τούτων ἐπιστήμην, καὶ ὅτι μὴ μόνος αὐτὸς ἔμπειρος ὢν εἰς θεὸν δύναται τὸ ἐν αὐτῇ παράδοξον ἀναφέρων πιθανὸς ὥσπερ ἀπαιδεύτοις ὑπάρχειν. καὶ μεθεμένων ἐκείνων τὰς βακτηρίας δράκοντες ἦσαν. [286] Μωυσῆς δ᾽ οὐ καταπλαγείς, "οὐδ᾽ αὐτὸς μέν, εἶπεν, ὦ βασιλεῦ, τῆς Αἰγυπτίων σοφίας καταφρονῶ, τοσῷδε μέντοι κρείττονα τὰ ὑπ᾽ ἐμοῦ πραττόμενα τῆς τούτων μαγείας καὶ τέχνης φημί, ὅσῳ τὰ θεῖα τῶν ἀνθρωπίνων διαφέρει. δείξω δὲ οὐ κατὰ γοητείαν καὶ πλάνην τῆς ἀληθοῦς δόξης τἀμά, κατὰ δὲ θεοῦ πρόνοιαν καὶ [287] δύναμιν φαινόμενα." καὶ ταῦτ᾽ εἰπὼν μεθίησιν ἐπὶ τῆς γῆς τὴν βακτηρίαν κελεύσας αὐτὴν εἰς **ὄφιν** μεταβαλεῖν· ἡ δ᾽ ἐπείθετο καὶ τὰς τῶν Αἰγυπτίων **βακτηρίας**, οἳ δράκοντες ἐδόκουν, περιοῦσα κατήσθιε μέχρι πάσας ἀνήλωσεν· εἶτ᾽ εἰς τὸ αὐτῆς σχῆμα μεταπεσοῦσαν κομίζεται Μωυσῆς.

the text of Exodus 7:8–12 if *Antiquities* 2.284–87 were the only extant account. Scholars could reconstruct the outline of a story about an Egyptian king who challenged Moses to a contest with his own magicians, whose trick of transforming rods into serpents was trumped by Moses. Additions like the little speech contrasting divine reality to deceiving appearances are often readily detectable, but not even a source critic learned in all the wisdom of the Egyptians could, from this passage alone, detect the absence of Aaron.

"Source criticism" is an academic discipline devoted to ferreting out the sources of a particular author or writing. "Intertextuality," a more recent concept, embraces traditional source criticism, but is much more sophisticated in conception and broader in application. "Intertextuality" recognizes that ". . . the production and reception of texts is always conditioned by a larger web of 'texts,' both written and unwritten."[24] Scholars have always known, for

Table 1.2 Moses and Pharaoh, with Subtitles

8 The Lord said to Moses and Aaron, *9* "When Pharaoh says to you, 'Give us a sign or a prodigy,' then you shall say to Aaron, 'Take your staff and throw it down before Pharaoh and his retinue, and it will become a snake.'" *10* So Moses and Aaron went to Pharaoh and his retinue and did as the Lord had commanded; Aaron threw down his staff before Pharaoh and his officials, and it became a snake. *11* Then Pharaoh summoned the wise men and the sorcerers; and they also, the magicians of Egypt, did the same by their secret arts. *12* Each one threw down his staff, and they became snakes; but Aaron's staff swallowed up theirs.[25]	But when the king derided Moses, he made him in earnest see the signs that were done at Mount Sinai. Yet was the king very angry with him, and called him an ill man, who had formerly run away from his Egyptian slavery, and came now back with deceitful tricks, and wonders and magical arts, to astonish him. And when he had said this, he commanded the priests to let him see the same wonderful sights; as knowing that the Egyptians were skilful in this kind of learning, and that he was not the only person who knew them, and pretended them to be divine; as also he told him, that when he brought such wonderful sights before him, he would only be believed by the unlearned. Now when the priests threw down their rods, they became serpents. But Moses was not daunted at it; and said, "O king, I do not myself despise the wisdom of the Egyptians, but I say that what I do is so much superior to what these do by magic arts and tricks, as divine power exceeds the power of man: but I will demonstrate that what I do is not done by craft, or counterfeiting what is not really true, but that they appear by the providence and power of God" And when he had said this, he cast his rod down upon the ground, and commanded it to turn itself into a serpent. It obeyed him, and went all round, and devoured the rods of the Egyptians, which seemed to be dragons, until it had consumed them all. It then returned to its own form, and Moses took it into his hand again.[26]

example, that authors and readers may associate one verse from the Psalter with another. Intertextuality seeks to bring this appreciation to the surface, investigate its workings, and develop some theoretical models.

Discussion of the sources of Acts has, with one important exception, followed a path similar to the controversies about date. Once hotly contested, the issue has become relatively quiescent.[27] The reasons for this are valid and apparent. The search for the sources of the Synoptic Gospels (Matthew, Mark, and Luke) was a major enterprise of the nineteenth century. The force that first impelled this search was historical: to identify the earliest and thus the best sources for the life of Jesus. The general results of that quest were, and are, widely accepted. The leading sources of the Synoptic Tradition are Mark and the hypothetical sayings gospel, Q.[28] Few, however, would now claim that Mark is the "best" source for the life of Jesus. Scholars now use this theory to study how Matthew and Luke received and modified their sources ("redaction criticism"). In the case of Acts no such motive applied: there was no competing canonical source for the story of Christian origins. Therefore the object of this quest remained essentially *historical*: where (and how and in what form) did Luke (as the author of Acts is conveniently named) get his material? The result has been frustrating, for Luke has so recast his unknown sources into his own language and style that material can be separated only by delicate and debatable operations. In so doing he was, as has been shown, fulfilling the obligations of an ancient author. Jacques Dupont, a prolific and insightful investigator of Acts, published in 1960 a study of its sources, subsequently revised and expanded in an English translation.[29] His oft-quoted conclusion is quite indicative:

> The predominant impression is certainly very negative . . . no theory has managed to impose itself by its probability and in virtue of the indications given by the texts . . . This can be explained by the literary work of the author: he is not satisfied with transcribing his sources, he rewrites the text by putting the imprint of his vocabulary and his style everywhere . . . Everything is done as if Luke were at the origin not only of the edited version, but even of the sources on which this version is based.[30]

The effect of this skepticism is most apparent in the *Anchor Bible* commentary of Joseph Fitzmyer. After an incisive review and critique of earlier theories, Fitzmyer closes with the comment that ". . . [I]n the end, Acts is a thoroughly Lucan composition."[31]

The other reason for a general lack of present interest in source questions goes back to the work of Martin Dibelius (1883–1947), published in essays from 1923 onwards and posthumously collected. Dibelius focused upon Luke as an *author*, rather than as a gatherer of traditions or a collector of sources. In his famous commentary, first published in 1956, Ernst Haenchen (1896–1975) proclaimed that the only certain contribution of source criticism had been to distract people from attempting to discern what Luke had to say. Twenty-five years later, when the vast influence he had cast upon the study of Acts was on the wane, Haenchen's viewpoint was one cause of the revitalized study of Matthew, Mark, Luke, John, and Acts. Just as the scrutiny of individual evangelists as editors (redaction criticism) returned primary attention to the text of the gospels (rather than to their sources or constituent forms) and led in due course to considering the gospels as books and evangelists as authors, so the work embodied by Haenchen effectively opened the way to consideration of (Luke and) Acts as literature.[32] His allergy to source-questions was in part heuristic, i.e., a device intended to expose blind alleys, and in part a response to the scholarly tradition of earlier times.[33]

As with much early Christian literature, investigating the origins of Acts involves sources of several different types that should be carefully distinguished. From the viewpoint of ancient history, the best sources were immediate and personal, based upon the eyewitness experiences of the author. The use of "we" in the narrative, as well as the traditional ascription of Acts to a companion of Paul have led many to postulate that some of Acts comes from an eyewitness. There are obvious differences between written and oral sources, although modern notions can be misleading here. It would, for example, be erroneous to assume that oral sources are ever subject to error and distortion, while written materials are relatively stable. Oral traditions *could*, when deemed necessary, be preserved with considerable fixity, while copyists of written texts routinely made not only the inevitable accidental but also deliberate changes to their sources.[34] This distinction clearly bears upon the nature, scope, and genre of possible sources. At 20:35 the author of Acts quotes a saying of Jesus in a formula suggestive of oral tradition: ". . . remembering the words of the Lord Jesus, for he himself said, 'It is more blessed to give than to receive.'"[35] One presumes that this was not a part of the written text of Q that Luke used, for it is not found in the gospel, apt as it would have been in "The Sermon on the Plain" (Luke 6:20–49).[36] If, as is likely, Luke knew stories about Peter and Paul, it would be useful to know whether one or more of them belonged to a written document or whether some or all were oral anecdotes picked up from here and there. A subsequent question will address the nature of these hypothetical sources. Were they stories about the origins of *communities* like Jerusalem or Antioch, or legends about *leaders* like Peter or Paul?[37] Moreover, how can one isolate and define such stories and genres?

On such questions the major investigations of Acts' sources have foundered. For not only are all oral sources hypothetical, but among written sources one may distinguish the following types:

1. *Explicit, extant sources.* An example of such a source in Acts is the Greek Bible, the Septuagint (LXX). The source is extant, and its use in Acts is overt and manifest.[38]
2. *Hypothetical extant sources.* The letters of Paul are extant. The questions include whether Luke knew of these letters, and, if so, in what form, and whether he made use of them.

3. *Hypothetical reconstructed sources*

    A. Written. Many have proposed that the author of Acts used an "Antiochene Source" that narrated the foundation and mission of the (or a) Christian community in Syrian Antioch, and/or a travel-diary, a record of Paul's independent missionary work. Various means have been adduced for identifying sources that have no independent attestation, including the nature and form of certain materials and, in particular, passages (or parts thereof) that conflict with the style or ideas of the author. This is a legitimate, albeit always debatable, enterprise.

    B. *Oral.* To this category would belong information transmitted to the author by word of mouth. Such sources range from eyewitness accounts to gossip at the Nth remove. A "weasel word" in almost universal use is "traditions." The great value of this concept is that it is true. Traditions grow up around every human entity and enterprise that has ever existed, from individuals and families to nations and empires. Some traditions are general, such as the placement of silverware (a traditional term that now includes implements made of stainless steel or even plastic). Others are particular: "George Washington slept here."

Many of the "historical traditions" of Acts belong to the "Washington slept here" category, expanded: "George Washington stayed here for two days on the way to Yorktown and helped to rescue a child whose horse had gone out of control." Two pertinent questions for such traditions deal with their origin and their veracity. How do you know that Washington slept there? (a) The story appeared in a February 1832 edition of the county newspaper, as related by Mrs. Pettigrew, who learned it from her aunt, who was five years old at the time of the visit. (b) The boy, now kindly old Captain Adams, is not reluctant to share his experiences and have them recorded in the local paper. (c) A manuscript letter written in 1781 describes the visit and incident in detail. (d) "Everybody" in Cabbageville knows about the incident. As historical evidence, (c) would be the strongest and (d) the weakest, but any of the sources could be untrustworthy or correct. Ideally, the investigator would know something about the characters, whether the letter-writer was scrupulous and unimaginative, whether Captain Adams could supply any corroboration, and so forth. Critical historians ask the same question as detectives, "*cui bono?*," that is, "Who would have gained something by committing the crime?"[39] This is one aspect of determining the *function* of a particular tradition.

    Investigators of the traditions in Acts must answer several questions. First, they must attempt to determine whether a textual unit or fragment represents data from an immediate source, a tradition, or authorial composition. This is a task of form criticism, the study of literary types and their transformation. Next come efforts to discover the origin and function of the alleged tradition. The final judgment deals with historical probability, but such decisions do not always depend upon the initial steps, at least not transparently. In many cases the deciding factor is an element of historical improbability that leads to a choice between authorial "invention" or the presence of a tradition. Most analyses of "traditions" in Acts operate from an *a priori* basis that assumes either general "accuracy," as does F. F. Bruce, or pervasive skepticism, of which Ernst Haenchen is the leading example. More purely "inductive" approaches can be seen in the often non-committal analyses of Cadbury and Lake (*The Beginnings of Christianity*, Volume 4) and, more recently, in the work of Gerd Lüdemann (*Early Christianity according to the Traditions in Acts*), who is not hesitant to make judgments. Lüdemann does not, however, offer a fully developed source theory for Acts. In some ways his detailed work is a preliminary to such a theory, but without a detailed source theory his labors are in danger of fragmentation.[40]

The difficulty is that conclusions about sources depend upon the critic's understanding of the historical reliability of Acts, while source theories should serve as one means for helping to establish that reliability.[41] Without doubting that Luke made use of oral traditions and other hypothetical sources, I, who fall far short of mastery of all the wisdom of the Egyptians and a great deal else, shall not here make a general attempt to reconstruct them.[42] The primary focus of the following chapters is the discussion of sources that have a bearing upon the date of Acts, and/or upon questions of literary genre and historicity. The composition of insightful and accurate history long after the events under consideration is quite possible, and while much more so now than in the first and second centuries, yet still possible then.[43] The goal of historiography proper is, however, the present. Historians write about the past with a view to its effect upon the events of their own day.[44] Date is one means for grasping the author's perspective and for determining the issues that author sought to address. Acts may have been written c. 60 and be wildly inaccurate or have been composed c. 100 and be quite accurate, but the items selected for emphasis and the interpretive thrust laid upon them would greatly differ if the work were written before the deaths of James and Paul rather than after the emergence of communities with a substantial history behind them facing challenges quite different from those of the previous generation. In other words, this project relates to date and sources primarily in so far as they *do* make a difference to interpretation. To put it yet another way, one attraction of a date c. 80—one that has contributed to its standing as the scholarly consensus—is that it is late enough for important changes to have occurred but not so late that the author could not have had access to first-hand information.

THE UNITIES OF LUKE AND ACTS
AND THE QUESTION OF DATE

The prevailing and most productive approach to Luke and Acts speaks of Luke-Acts and is even willing to reopen the old question of whether the division between the two books is a secondary development contrary to the author's intentions and composition.[45] Unfortunately, the only viable alternative view is that Acts is a sequel to the Gospel. Most contemporary scholars study the works as a literary and theological unity,[46] and a "natural" though sometimes unstated corollary to this way of studying the Lucan writings is the assumption of a single date. If Acts followed the gospel by a decade or so, the arguments for fundamental unity lose some — but not all — of their cogency.

Still, such a delay in date of issuance would account for some of the differences between the two books. And even more relevant to the argument of this book is that the consideration of Luke and Acts as a single literary production has had a dual effect upon calculations of the date of Acts. For one thing, recognition that the edition of Mark known to Luke is post-70 CE makes it difficult to ascribe to the Third Gospel a date before 80. And since almost all agree that Acts follows Luke in date — the use of Mark in Acts makes that all but certain — then this second volume can be no earlier than 80.[47] At the same time, emphasis upon unity calls for a single publication. Most current students of Luke and Acts would wince at S.G. Wilson's claim that one should not demand the same teaching from both volumes, on the grounds that the author wrote Acts a ". . . considerable time after the Gospel, and that in the interim period his view developed and changed."[48] Proposals like this appear to ignore the literary unity of the two books and the single definite plan thereby implied. In short, the most vital contemporary scholarship understands the date of Acts to depend upon that of Luke, as the two reflect a single conception. If c. 85 looks good for Luke, then the date of Acts should be pegged at c. 85.

The various unities that Luke and Acts exhibit in structure and plan could be accommodated to a range of hypotheses, ranging from a sequel originally planned or unplanned and written at a later date to a single work in two volumes carefully planned and promptly executed. The truth is that no one has any defensible notions regarding how rapidly Luke wrote, or how long he had planned his two books, or what plan was in his mind when he began to write.[49] I have not hesitated to include data from Luke where appropriate, largely on the grounds that Luke is prior to Acts. My goal is to examine evidence for the date of Acts and let Luke catch up or fall behind as may be.[50]

Dating early Christian writings is a bit like artillery fire control. After establishing a "bracket" by salvoes that successively straddle the target, the battery commander seeks to refine the range until the projectiles begin to strike the target. In scholarship the brackets are the *terminus a quo* (limit from which, earliest possible date) and the *terminus ante quem* (limit before which, latest possible date). With regard to Acts there is essentially universal agreement that the absolute *terminus a quo* is c. 60 (c. 58–62, to be more precise); estimates of the *terminus ante quem* range from c. 135 to c. 180.

In determining the date of texts, scholars use a number of techniques: some are relatively concrete or "direct," others are inferences from direct evidence, while yet others are almost purely inferential. As in the case of sources, it is important to distinguish various types of evidence.

1. *Direct evidence*
   A. *Paleographical evidence,* i.e., datable manuscripts. For our period,
      the chief means for dating mss. is by type of handwriting. Although
      the evolution of different styles can be fixed within certain limits,
      estimates do vary, so that one must be content with a range of
      twenty-five years or more when applying this criterion.[51]
   B. *External citation*
       i. Verifiable or explicit quotations of the work under investigation
          by another author or work of determined date (or date range).
      ii. Intertextual usage that does not refer to its host or source but
          does establish its availability. For example, if a book printed in
          London in 1595 contained such expressions as "the time is out of
          joint," "the glass of fashion and the mold of form," and "to be or
          not to be," one could argue that *Hamlet* was written prior to that
          date.[52]
   C. Specific *internal data.* A work can be (in its final form) no earlier than
      the latest datable person or event mentioned within it. Any U.S.
      writing that says "since 9/11 . . ." was composed following the events
      of 11 September 2001. Of course, not all such references are crystal
      clear, and thus allow room for argument and debate.
2. *Indirect evidence*
   A. Sources. If unnamed but identifiable sources can be dated, the result
      will be a relatively firm *terminus a quo.* This is the mirror image of
      1.B.2, above. For example, if the manuscript of an unknown essay
      were to include the phrase, "when we have shuffled off this mortal
      coil," one would be justified in dating it subsequent to the first
      known production of *Hamlet.*
   B. Reference to institutions, matters of ideology, or other datable trends
      or movements. Should a character in a novel contemplate joining the
      Sierra Club, one could locate a *terminus a quo* for the dramatic date
      of the novel by learning when the Sierra Club was founded.[53] If, on
      the other hand, a novel set in the 1780s spoke of the Sierra Club, that
      reference would be an anachronism. Anachronisms can be useful
      tools for determining the actual date of composition. Oft-asserted
      if rarely argued is the principle that historical works set even a few
      decades after the persons and events they treat will contain at least
      some anachronisms, and that the number tends to grow rapidly with
      each passing decade. Furthermore, data are susceptible to different
      interpretations. It seems likely that the use of the term "Christians"
      by the Roman historian Tacitus (early second century) in his Annals
      15.44 is an anachronism, but the same reference can be held to show
      that the word was known (and familiar) in 64.[54]
   C. Comparative analysis of vocabulary and style. As movements
      gain maturity and stability and acquire the characteristics of an

institution, their language will reflect these changes. In the case
of early Christianity, at least, language tends to show increasing
affinities with that of the general culture. (C) is therefore related to
(B), but is even more tenuous. The two are usefully employed in
tandem, for changes in structure and doctrine will almost certainly
bring linguistic changes.[55]

With these issues in mind, then, and these tools in hand, I am about to
descend into the warrens and tunnels of the site selected for excavation. The
object, to pursue this metaphor, is to see whether any untapped veins or, in
particular, old veins worthy of fresh investigation will shed light upon the date
of (Luke and) Acts and the sources of the latter. It just may be that some "arguments aiming at greater precision" in the matters of source and date are more
compelling and revealing than Talbert asserts.

The first task will be to establish the broadest possible range for the date of
Acts by examination of relatively "hard" data. Chapter two will do little to close
the range that Talbert proposes (c. 60–c. 150). Its purpose is to build a firm basis
for what will become a gradually shrinking span and at last a more precisely
definable target.

2 Establishing the Range

The Earliest and Latest Possible Dates for Acts

THE END IS A GOOD PLACE TO BEGIN

The previous chapter attempted to enumerate various types of sources and their uses, then to clarify and distinguish the several criteria and various instruments relevant to establishing the date of an ancient writing. In this chapter I shall first review data and proposals that seek to establish the latest possible date of Acts (*terminus ante quem*) and then see what can be said about the other pole. The preliminary results confirm established views: 60–150 as the maximum range and 70–115 as a probable range.

Paleographical evidence is not relevant to this inquiry, as no one proposes to date Acts later than 175 CE, and there are no manuscripts of Acts that are indisputably earlier than 200–250. The oldest parchment manuscript with data from the New Testament, 0189, contains Acts 5:3–21 and is dated c. 200. $\mathfrak{P}^{38}$ is sometimes dated in the third century, sometimes in the fifth.[1] $\mathfrak{P}^{45}$, a very important manuscript, once contained the four gospels and Acts. This is no earlier than 200; c. 250 would be a reasonable estimate.[2] $\mathfrak{P}^{91}$, containing parts of Acts 2, also dates to the third century. The criterion of manuscript evidence, which is not very precise, does not provide certain evidence for the existence of Acts in the second century. Other criteria will have to be invoked. The next is the criterion of external citation.[3]

Scholars have devoted more than a century to careful scrutiny of possible allusions to Acts in early Christian writings.[4] I shall seek to accomplish no more than to subject some of the familiar cases to a more detailed public examination than is found in the standard commentaries.[5] The earliest datable authors who clearly identify Acts and quote or summarize it are Irenaeus, Clement, and Tertullian. All of these writers were educated Christian theologians. Irenaeus, bishop of Lyons in France c. 180, knew and quoted Acts, for which he uses different titles.[6] Clement, an early Christian theologian in Alexandria, who wrote c. 180–200,[7] cites and quotes from Acts, which he identifies by the title known to us.[8] Tertullian was a feisty Christian layperson in early third century North Africa, where the language of culture was Latin.[9] This evidence is indisputable and requires no fresh examination. 175–180 therefore constitutes a solid *terminus ad quem*. As an independent book with those contents (but not precise wording) known to us, Acts cannot be later than the end of the third quarter of the second century.

Scholars are both naturally and for good reason prejudiced in favor of works by other scholars. A danger of this bias is that it tends to overlook the possibility that something may have been a subject of interest in less scholarly circles. That is the case with Acts. Well before Irenaeus realized how useful Luke and Acts could be as tools to oppose various heresies, its influence can be seen in a number of less learned works that appeared from around 150 onwards, including the *Acts of Peter*, the *Acts of Paul*, and the (sources of the) Pseudo-Clementines, in each of which the use of Acts is beyond doubt. Another text that very probably made use of Acts is the *Epistle of the Apostles*.[10] Each of these texts (or components thereof) belongs to the second half of the second century. This relatively wide dissemination suggests that Acts could not have appeared much later than c. 160, and probably a bit earlier. How much further can one push back the clock of reasonable certainty?

Dibelius/Conzelmann observe: "Further, it is difficult to deny the impression that the Pastorals know the book of the Acts of the Apostles."[11] They do not offer 2 Timothy 3:11 as evidence for this view. One early commentator, the source of the bracketed gloss ([ ]) refers the reader to the *Acts of Paul*.[12] That work portrays Paul as working successively in Antioch, Iconium, Lystra (3.1–3), but this sequence may derive from Acts. Acts, the Pastorals, and the *Acts of Paul* participate in a complex *ménage à trois*. From the perspective of the Pastorals, the most active binary relationship is with the *Acts of Paul*, but the leading exponent of this relationship, Dennis R. MacDonald, does not argue for direct dependence, nor does he view the Pastorals as dependent upon Acts.[13] Richard Bauckham, however, does argue for dependence of the *Acts of Paul* upon the Pastorals.[14] See Table 2.1.

One difficulty in viewing 2 Timothy 3:11 as dependent upon Acts is the beginning of the sentence (v. 10): "Now you have observed . . ." In a choice irony this word "observed" is the very verb παρακολουθέω that is so troublesome to interpreters of Luke 1:3.[15] Here it means "you have paid careful attention to" and does not require participation in or observation of the events[16]. The verb

Table 2.1: The Pastoral Epistles

Acts 13–14	2 Timothy 3 (10–)11
13:50: Persecution in Pisidian *Antioch* 14:5–6: Threatened violence in *Iconium* 14:19–20: Suffering in *Lystra* No mention of suffering in *Derbe*	(Now you have observed my teaching, my conduct, my aim in life, my faith, my patience, my love, my steadfastness,) my persecutions, and my suffering the things that happened to me in *Antioch*, [that is, sufferings believers in Christ *he (sic)* underwent because of Thecla],[17] **Iconium**, and **Lystra**. What persecutions I endured! Yet the Lord rescued me from all of them. (2 Timothy does not include **Derbe** in this list.)

does not, therefore, necessarily contradict Acts—nor does contradiction rule out dependence. On the whole, however, this catalogue of sites is a very thin thread upon which to pin literary dependence. Given the number of legends about Paul's work in this area not recorded in Acts, the case for "independent tradition" is not merely conjectural;[18] rather, I conclude, there is insufficient evidence to establish dependence.[19] The Pastorals may know Acts, but too few data exist to warrant making this knowledge an assumption.

POLYCARP OF SMYRNA

In the second edition of his magisterial *Introduction*, Helmut Koester allows that "... [I]n the fourth decade of the 2d century, Polycarp of Smyrna apparently knew Luke-Acts (cf. *Phil.* 1.2 with Acts 2:24) . . ."[20] Polycarp, doughty bishop of the important city of Smyrna in Asia Minor and the subject of a famous story of martyrdom, wrote a letter, more probably letters, to Christians at Philippi.

The leading editors of Polycarp's correspondence consider this passage to be a citation of Acts,[21] but most commentators on Acts are, at best, hesitant.[22] Polycarp's (later) letter is replete with elements from early Christian texts, among which are more reminiscences from 1 Peter than from any other writing.[23] One doubts that Polycarp desires or expects readers to recognize many of these allusions.[24] He is not citing the "New Testament," after all, for it does not yet exist.[25] (See Table 2.2.)

Lightfoot calls Polycarp *Philippians* 1:2 "an inexact quotation."[26] The differences are not major. The finite clause, "whom God raised," is a common creedal expression.[27] Luke often uses the verb ἐγείρω ("raise," as in Acts 3:15 and 4:10), while Polycarp does not employ ἀνίστημι ("rise," "cause to rise" in some cases). The variation in word order is equally negligible. The only variance in the participial phrase is between "death" and the metonymy "Hades"("Death"). This contrast gains no strength from the D-text variant "Hades," read or rendered in D, it[d.e.gig], Peshitta, Coptic G067 and Bohairic, Irenaeus (Latin), Ephraem, and Augustine, since one could argue that Polycarp knew Acts with "Hades" at this point.[28] This is the only occurrence of that word in Polycarp.[29] Moreover, Lightfoot cites a Latin ms. (p) of Polycarp, which reads "death," although this may be the result of assimilation to Acts—i.e., a copyist or translator may have altered his text of Polycarp to agree with his knowledge of Acts. This phrase in Acts 2:24 is quite unusual.

Excursus: The Pangs of Death

Although the background of λύσας τὰς ὠδῖνας τοῦ θανάτου ("having eased the pangs of death") is clear, its meaning is not. The phrase derives from the LXX, as the citations in Table 2.2 demonstrate. Contemporary scholars refer to alternate vocalizations of *chvl*, which can yield the equivalents of "pang" or "cord."[30] One could make a good case for a Semitic language background here, as "bonds of death" is well complemented by the second half of the verse: καθότι οὐκ ἦν δυνατὸν κρατεῖσθαι αὐτὸν ὑπ' αὐτοῦ ("because it was impossible for

Table 2.2: Pangs of Death

Polycarp Phil 1.2 and Some Parallels	Acts 2:24 and Some Parallels
ὃν ἤγειρεν ὁ Θεὸς λύσας τὰς ὠδῖνας τοῦ ᾅδου, [Jesus] whom God raised, having eased the pangs of Death 2 Samuel 22:6; ὠδῖνες θανάτου ἐκύκλωσάν με, προέφθασάν με σκληρότητες θανάτου. the **cords of Sheol** entangled me, the snares of death confronted me. Psalm 17:5–6 5 περιέσχον με ὠδῖνες θανάτου, καὶ χείμαρροι ἀνομίας ἐξετάραξάν με ὠδῖνες ᾅδου περιεκύκλωσάν με, προέφθασάν με παγίδες θανάτου. the cords of Sheol entangled me; the snares of death confronted me. Psalm 114:3 περιέσχον με ὠδῖνες θανάτου, κίνδυνοι ᾅδου εὕροσάν με· θλῖψιν καὶ ὀδύνην εὗρον. The snares of death encompassed me; the pangs of Sheol laid hold on me; I suffered distress and anguish.	ὃν ὁ Θεὸς ἀνέστησεν λύσας τὰς ὠδῖνας τοῦ θανάτου, καθότι οὐκ ἦν δυνατὸν κρατεῖσθαι αὐτὸν ὑπ' αὐτοῦ [Jesus] whom **God** made rise, **having eased the pangs of death.** Note also Job 39:1–3. εἰ ἔγνως καιρὸν τοκετοῦ τραγελάφων πέτρας, ἐφύλαξας δὲ ὠδῖνας ἐλάφων; 2 ἠρίθμησας δὲ αὐτῶν μῆνας πλήρεις τοκετοῦ, ὠδῖνας δὲ αὐτῶν ἔλυσας; 3 ἐξέθρεψας δὲ αὐτῶν τὰ παιδία ἔξω φόβου; ὠδῖνας αὐτῶν ἐξαποστελεῖς; "Do you know when the mountain goats give birth? Do you observe the **calving** of the deer? Can you number the months that they fulfill, and do you know the time when they give birth, when they crouch to give birth to their offspring, and are delivered of their young?[31] Note also 1QH XI, 8–10: For the children have come to the throes of death, and she labours in her pains who bears a man for amid the throes of Death (*twm yrbv*) she shall bring forth a man-child, and amid the pains of Hell (*lwv ylbhb*) there shall spring from her child-bearing crucible a Marvellous Mighty Counsellor; and a man shall be delivered from out of the throes.[32]

him to be held in its power"). The parallel expressions in 1QH XI also show how the images of birth pains and pangs of hell could be associated. This linguistic approach would yield "But God raised him up, shattering the fetters of death, because death could not keep him in its restraints."[33] Nonetheless, research has to deal with the Greek text rather than with the hypothetical source of an allegedly incompetent translator.[34] Examples are extant of λύειν ὠδῖνας for the relief of labor pains.[35] Patristic preachers, who had good ears for Greek, seem to have loved this phrase. One question is whether ὠδίνες bears some resemblance to the primary connotation or has the generalized sense of "terrible pain," and, if the latter, whether this is itself metaphorical, like English "this is a real headache" If the former, it is possible to introduce eschatological meaning (as in "messianic birth pangs"). Thus Georg Bertram.

> . . . [T]he ref. is to the birth of the Messiah or rather to new birth through the resurrection . . . God Himself has relieved the pangs of birth out of death. The abyss can no more hold the Redeemer than a pregnant woman can hold the child in her body. Under severe labour pains the womb of the underworld must release the Redeemer. God Himself helps it to end the pains.[36]

Barrett considers another proposal, advanced by Field and supported by Stählin and Wilcox, that the resurrection of Jesus terminated the messianic woes.[37] This reading views Death as the personified bearer of children (the dead).[38] In this exegetical thicket, one can see why many find it preferable to apply the principle that, if the LXX provides sufficient grounds for a locution, it is the least question-begging and most secure explanation.[39] However the origin and interpretation is understood, the subsequent question will be whether Luke was responsible for the phrase. The probability is that he was not its creator.

"Pangs of death" is an unusual trope for Luke, a bit of a unexpected elegance. The numerous parallels from Acts to this passage contain nothing like it[40]. In discussing the death of Jesus Acts emphasizes the absence of bodily decay (2:26 *cit*; 13:35[41]). Lucan theology steers away from "cosmic" or "mystical" concepts, including "Messianic birth pangs."[42] Jervell says that, if the translation ὠδῖνες θανάτου is valid,

> . . . The Septuagint understands 'the pangs of death' as a mysterious expression for the power of death. We have no notion of Christ as born from the dead, for God is always the actor; God has broken the power of death through the resurrection. Accordingly, death is understood in a mythological sense, as a power.[43]

Paul (and his followers) would not shrink from a "mythological" personification of death;[44] Luke avoids such concepts, but he does speak of the defeat of the Devil (e.g., Acts 10:38). The resurrection of Jesus is more a sign of this defeat than the means of effecting it.[45] If, then, as seems quite probable, Luke did not "invent" this imagery, it is likely that he took it up from tradition.

This proposal gains support from the formal context and the "poetic" quality of the phrase. The antithesis "You/they killed him, but God raised him . . ." is a rhetorical manifestation of an early creedal formula.[46] λύσας τὰς ὠδῖνας τοῦ θανάτου may well derive from a hymnic or liturgical context, as Haenchen and Plümacher propose.[47] Later liturgical texts do not use this specific phrase, but the frequency with which it appears in patristic rhetoric indicates its mellifluous appeal.[48] Why would Luke have taken up the phrase in this place? Verse 24b, provides one explanation: "because it was impossible for him to be held in its power." This lays the ground for (and interprets) the citation from Psalm 15:10 (LXX) in v.27: ὅτι οὐκ ἐγκαταλείψεις τὴν ψυχήν μου εἰς ᾅδην ("For you will not abandon my soul to Hades"). The circumstantial participial phrase ("Easing the pangs of death") serves both to introduce the subject of death, which 24b requires, and to evoke the language of Hebrew poetry, a helping of which will constitute the next course. In conclusion, the strong probability that the participial expression is not a Lucan composition and the good probability that it stems from liturgical language make this parallel an unlikely case for *demonstrating* that Polycarp made use of Acts.[49] However, the absence of any other direct use of the phrase, and the unlikelihood that Luke concocted the formula do not preclude the possibility that Polycarp took it up from Acts. In view of the strong verbal coincidence the matter cannot be certain.

There are three options to explain the shared phrase, "having eased the pangs of death/Hades": (1) Both writers draw upon liturgical tradition. This is attractive and not unlikely, but lacks support from other data. (2) Luke took the phrase from Polycarp. This is the least likely solution. Therefore, (3) that Polycarp had heard or read the phrase in Acts has the strongest probability. The evidence and argumentation are far from overwhelming, but it would be unwise to set this datum aside.[50] Polycarp may have known Acts.[51]

PAPIAS OF HIERAPOLIS

Papias was a Christian writer active in the first third of the second century, c. 130 according to most, although some advocate a date as early as 110. His work survives only in a few pages of fragments, many from the Church Historian Eusebius, who claims that Papias had been the Bishop of Hierapolis in Asia Minor (*Ecclesiastical History* 3.36.2), which is not certain, and that he was intellectually challenged (3.39.2), which is Eusebius's way of disparaging Papias's theology. Eusebius transmits comments of Papias about the nature and origins of the Gospels of Matthew and Mark, but not about Luke and John. This silence has three possible explanations: (1) that Papias had no knowledge of Luke, (2) that he knew of Luke and did not approve of it, or (3) that his statements about the third gospel were not acceptable to Eusebius, who consequently omitted them. If Papias knew of Acts, he deemed it either unauthoritative or unreliable, for he twice contradicts it.[52] The importance of Papias here is that he is *not* a witness to the existence of Luke or of Acts.[53]

HEGESIPPUS

Hegesippus (c. 110–180) produced five volumes of *Hypomnemata* ("notebooks," "memoirs"). Eusebius has preserved a number of fragments from these works, especially those dealing with the lists of bishops in major sees. Despite his interest in tracing origins and his presence in Rome c. 160–170, Hegesippus displays no knowledge of Acts. Like Papias, he is of interest because he is silent about Luke's second volume.[54]

JUSTIN MARTYR

Justin, called "the martyr," was executed c.165. At Rome he wrote both a defense of the Christian faith against its polytheist opponents, which is known as *(1–2) Apology*,[55] and a defense of Christian beliefs in response to Judaism, known as the *Dialogue with Trypho*. These are the only surviving authentic works. Justin was certainly familiar with Matthew and Luke, but there is no persuasive evidence that he makes use of John, while he does not so much as mention Paul. Another dispute revolves around his use of Acts.[56] *1 Apology* 50.12, reasonably dated c. 160, is advanced as proof that Justin knew and used Acts.[57] Haenchen states that this "quotes the substance of Luke 23:49a . . . makes clear use of Luke 24:25, 44f., as the account continues, and finally narrates the Ascension and the conferring of the Holy Spirit with a verbal echo of Acts 1:8. . . ." (See Table 2.3.)

Table 2.3: Acts and Justin Martyr

Justin *I Apology* 50.12	Luke 23–24
1.) μετὰ οὖν τὸ σταυρωθῆναι αὐτὸν καὶ οἱ γνώριμοι αὐτοῦ **πάντες** ἀπέστησαν, ἀρνησάμενοι αὐτόν.	1.) 23:49 εἱστήκεισαν δὲ **πάντες** οἱ γνωστοὶ αὐτῷ ἀπὸ μακρόθεν
2.) ὕστερον δέ, ἐκ νεκρῶν ἀναστάντος καὶ ὀφθεντος αὐτοῖς καὶ ταῖς **προφητ**είαις ἐντυχεῖν, ἐν αἷς πάντα ταῦτα προείρητο γενεσόμενα διδάξαντος,	2.) 24:25 καὶ αὐτὸς εἶπεν πρὸς αὐτούς, Ὢ ἀνόητοι καὶ βραδεῖς τῇ καρδίᾳ τοῦ πιστεύειν ἐπὶ πᾶσιν οἷς ἐλάλησαν οἱ **προφῆται** 44 Εἶπεν δὲ πρὸς αὐτούς, Οὗτοι οἱ λόγοι μου οὓς ἐλάλησα πρὸς ὑμᾶς ἔτι ὢν σὺν ὑμῖν, ὅτι δεῖ πληρωθῆναι πάντα τὰ γεγραμμένα ἐν τῷ νόμῳ Μωϋσέως καὶ τοῖς προφήταις καὶ ψαλμοῖς περὶ ἐμοῦ 45 τότε διήνοιξεν αὐτῶν τὸν νοῦν τοῦ συνιέναι τὰς γραφάς.
3.) καὶ **εἰς οὐρανὸν** ἀνερχόμενον ἰδοντες καὶ πιστεύσαντες	3.) Luke 24:51 . . . καὶ ἀνεφέρετο **εἰς τὸν οὐρανόν**[59] Acts 1:9–10 καὶ ταῦτα εἰπὼν βλεπόντων αὐτῶν ἐπήρθη, καὶ νεφέλη ὑπέλαβεν αὐτὸν ἀπὸ τῶν ὀφθαλμῶν αὐτῶν. 10 καὶ ὡς ἀτενίζοντες ἦσαν **εἰς τὸν οὐρανὸν** πορευομένου αὐτοῦ . . .
4.) καὶ **δύναμιν ἐκεῖθεν** αὐτοῖς πεμφθεῖσαν παρ ' αὐτοῦ **λαβόντες** καὶ εἰς πᾶν γένος ἀνθρωπῶν ἐλθόντες, ταῦτα ἐδίδαξαν καὶ ἀπόστολοι προσηγορεύθησαν. For after he was crucified even **all** his **acquaintances** deserted him, denying him. But later, when he rose from the dead and appeared to them, and taught them to consult the **prophecies**, in which it was predicted that all these things would happen; and when they had seen him **ascending into heaven,** and believed on him, and received the power which he sent them from there, and went into every race of men, they taught these things and were known as apostles.[58]	4.) Luke 24:49 . . . ὑμεῖς δὲ καθίσατε ἐν τῇ πόλει ἕως οὗ ἐνδύσησθε ἐξ **ὕψους δύναμιν** . . . Acts 1:8 ἀλλὰ **λήμψεσθε δύναμιν** ἐπελθόντος τοῦ ἁγίου πνεύματος ἐφ' ὑμᾶς . . . But **all** his **acquaintances** stood at a distance . . . watching these things. Then he said to them, Oh, how foolish you are, and how slow of heart to believe all that the **prophets** have declared. Then he said to them, "These are my words that I spoke to you while I was still with you—that everything written about me in the law of Moses, **the prophets,** and the psalms must be fulfilled." Then he opened their minds to understand the scriptures, While he was blessing them, he withdrew from them and was carried up **into heaven**. When he had said this, as they were watching, he was lifted up, and a cloud took him out of their sight. While he was going and they were gazing up toward heaven, suddenly two men in white robes stood by them. And see, I am sending upon you what my Father promised; so stay here in the city until you have been clothed with **power from on high.**"

Haenchen's claim is surprising. Rather than "The substance of Luke 23:49a," Justin reports the withdrawal of *all* the disciples, which is a Markan theme (Mark 14:50) omitted by Luke. Justin likewise generalizes the denial of Peter so that it characterizes all of the followers of Jesus. If this passage does depend upon Luke 24, it makes substantial changes, the most important of which is a shift from viewing the prophetic writings as texts requiring interpretation to the claim that they are transparent forecasts of the passion and resurrection. According to Justin, the disciples require no more than an exhortation to consult those scriptures to which they have been referred. In Luke and Acts Jesus and others must interpret these texts to demonstrate that they prove that "the messiah must suffer."[60]

The word δύναμις ("power") occurs in Luke 24:49, which is the presumed context. One can make an equally good case for reading ἐκεῖθεν ("from there," *viz.* heaven) as equivalent to ἐξ ὕψους ("from on high"). The phrase δύναμιν . . . λαβόντες ("receiving power"), upon which Haenchen bases his "verbal echo" (with λήμψεσθε δύναμιν, "you will receive power") is not unique. It can be found (without reference to this passage or to the gift of the Spirit) in *Hermas Similitude* 9.13.7, and in Origen, *Commentary on Matthew* 11.13.3. Finally, the notion of the apostles as universal missionaries *might* be derived from the closing scene of Luke, but not from Acts.[61] If Justin knew Acts, he disregarded or rejected much of its content. Consider his famous portrayal of Simon "the magician."[62]

> . . . [A]fter Christ's ascent into heaven the demons put forward various persons who said that they were gods, and you [Romans] not only did not persecute them, but thought them worthy of honors. One was a certain Simon, a Samaritan from the village of Gitta, who in the time of Claudius Caesar, through the arts of the demons who worked in him, did mighty works of magic in your imperial city of Rome and was thought to be a god. He has been honored among you as a god by a statue, which was set up on the River Tiber, between the two bridges, with this inscription in Latin, SIMONI DEO SANCTO [to Simon the holy god].[63] Almost all the Samaritans, and a few in other nations, confess this man as their first god and worship him as such, and a woman named Helena, who traveled around with him in those days—and had formerly been a public prostitute[64]—they say that she was the first Thought produced from him.[65]

From this citation one might contend that Justin had read a book of Acts—the *Acts of Peter*, that is—for much of the extant text of those Acts describes Simon's "mighty works of magic in . . . Rome." The portrait of Simon in the canonical Acts is quite different. There he is no god, but a local wonder-worker whose nascent Christian faith could not overcome his desire to remain competitive in his chosen trade.

A certain Dionysius was bishop of Corinth around 170. He collected a number of the letters written to other communities.[66] Eusebius knew these letters and summarized them in his *Ecclesiastical History* 4.23. His account of the letter to Athens says that Dionysius (of Corinth) says: "Dionysius the Areopagite was converted by the Apostle Paul to the faith, according to the narrative in the Acts, and was the first to be appointed to the bishopric of the diocese of Athens."[67] 3.4.10 is slightly different:

> . . . Dionysius, one of the ancients, the pastor of the diocese of the Corinthians, relates that the first bishop of the Church at Athens was that member of the Areopagus, the other Dionysius, whose original conversion after Paul's speech to the Athenians in the Areopagus Luke described in the Acts.

The question is whether Dionysius of Corinth referred to Acts in his letter. The passage from book 3 does not appear to make Dionysius of Corinth responsible for the reference to Acts. This view gains strength from the context, in which Eusebius identifies the Linus and Clement of the Pauline letters (2 Timothy 4:21; Philippians 4:3) as the second and third bishops of Rome. It is therefore not certain that Dionysius of Corinth referred to Acts, but he may have known it.[68]

Rather close to the above-mentioned Irenaeus in time and place (France, c. 177) is the possible citation of Acts 7:60 in the letter of the churches in Vienne and Lyons to believers in Asia and Phrygia, preserved in the *Ecclesiastical History* of Eusebius: "Indeed, they prayed for those who had used them so cruelly, much as Stephen, the perfect martyr, did: *Lord, do not blame them for this sin.*"[69] This is a clear citation of 7:60.[70] However, Musurillo, the editor, admits that the presumed original of this document was probably re-edited in the early third century, so that one cannot make an absolute claim for dependence.[71]

In conclusion: Irenaeus (c. 180) remains as the earliest certain witness to the existence of Acts. Polycarp (c. 130) is a tenuous possibility, while Justin (c. 160) remains problematic. If Justin did know of Acts, he did not accept it as authoritative or accurate.[72] One may put it rather more strongly: if Justin knew Acts, he did not approve of it, preferring to view the apostles as a collective group of teachers rather than as rabble-rousing, miracle-working purveyors of vulgar religion. A work that singled out Paul as the leading Christian missionary would scarcely have been to Justin's taste, for he does not so much as mention the name of Paul. Acts cannot be later than c. 175 CE; it is highly probable that the work was in use not long after 150. To reiterate, the foregoing arguments do not establish when Acts was written. They do establish that it could not have been later than the third quarter of the second century. That means the time has come to follow the pendulum to the other end of its period. What is the earliest possible date for Acts?

The latest datable event in Acts is the accession of (Porcius) Festus as Procurator of Judea (24:27, etc.). An exact date is unavailable; 57–59 seems to set a probable range.[73] By addition of two and one-half years for the voyage to Rome and the announced stay of Paul there, one reaches the year 60 CE. Acts 20:17–38 makes it apparent that the work is written after the death of Paul. The formal reason for this is that the speech belongs to the category of farewell addresses made by one who is approaching death.[74] The immediate structural parallel in Luke is the final speech of (the earthly) Jesus, 22:14–38. Contextual parallelism derives from the elaborate series of similarities to the passion of Jesus.[75] The material basis is in Acts 20:22 and 38, Paul's statement that the audience will not see him again, and their strong emotional reaction to this prediction. The exact date of Paul's death is not known. The apostle perished between 60 and 65, more probably earlier in that period than later.[76] Convincing as this evidence is to many, one may consider it as an inference from the text and thus indirect. In any case, even conceding this point does little to narrow the range.

Some may ask why the attestation of the gospel according to Luke has not been introduced into this discussion. Although I subscribe to the general view that the same person composed both Luke and Acts, other theories are possible, such as the proposal that a later editor revised Luke and composed Acts. An especial concern is that enthusiasm for the unity/unities of Luke and Acts not lead to the assumption that the two books were written in one continuous period. One or the other may have been later.[77] I hope to establish that Acts was written after the gospel, but some years could have separated the two volumes. Moreover, Luke and Acts did not need to circulate everywhere together, nor did they. It is invalid to assume that where Luke is, there Acts must also be.[78] Nonetheless, it is reasonable to examine the data about Luke, especially in view of the evidence that Acts is later than the Gospel. Once more, Irenaeus is the first to cite the gospel by name and to quote from it. Justin Martyr does know and use material from the Gospel according to Luke in its present form, but he does not name it, and his own practice suggests the use of a "harmony" of Gospels and traditions.[79]

Excursus: Marcion of Sinope

Proponents of the recurrent suggestion that religious bodies would benefit from management by successful businesspersons usually overlook their prospective patron saint: Marcion, the scion of a wealthy ship-owning family of Sinope, a city on the Black Sea coast of present-day Turkey, in the Roman province of Pontus. Marcion exhibited a number of characteristics common to those who have been successful in the world of commerce: considerable energy and excellent organizational skills, a "no nonsense, cut to the bottom line" approach to data, superb marketing ability, and unswerving devotion to a single basic concept. Marcion the businessman was quite aware of the dangers of product dilution and corruption. He had no patience for the likes of hyper-educated academics who could turn black into white and make accounts say the opposite of their plain intent.

According to tradition Marcion was the son of the local Christian "bishop." After some time in Asia Minor (where he encountered Polycarp), he followed the roads (or shipping lanes) to Rome in c. 137, where he expounded and possibly developed his own understanding of the Christian message. Marcion was a reformer, who, like more or less all reformers, believed that the original message had been corrupted by subsequent alterations. One of his dislikes was the notion of religious development or evolution. Divine revelation can contain no "contradictions," and the best interpretation of the Bible is literal interpretation. Marcion solved the problem of "contradictions" by underlining them in a work called *Antitheses*. Marcion held that the god of the Jewish scriptures was not the same god revealed in Jesus Christ. The former was responsible for creation and all of its woes, exercised strict justice and demanded retribution. The god revealed in Christ was a loving and merciful savior revealed out of God's care for the human race. Paul had got it right, Marcion believed, but others had distorted his understanding of salvation.

Dispensing with Hebrew sacred writings left a vacuum that he filled by a scripture of two parts, "Gospel" and "Apostle," corresponding to Law and Prophets. Marcion made several contributions to emerging catholic Christianity. One seems to have been the title "Gospel" for the story/stories of Jesus (Matthew, Mark, and others). Another was at least a strong impulse toward the establishment of a Christian scripture that would contain an "Old" and a "New" Testament. Finally, he forced Christians either to accept his point of view or to work out a theology that coordinated both creation and redemption, Israel and the Church, Moses and Jesus.

It may seem surprising that the basis of Marcion's "Gospel" was an edition of what we call Luke, since, together with Acts, that book constitutes the preeminent description of continuity between Israel and the Church. Marcion's "Apostle" consisted of ten letters of Paul. According to tradition the Christian community at Rome excommunicated Marcion in 144 and returned his large financial contribution. Marcion thereupon established his own church, which spread widely and lasted for centuries. In sum, Marcion severed the knot between "Christianity" and "Judaism" by finding the latter utterly irrelevant for the new revelation of the previously unknown god proclaimed by Paul.[80]

Marcion is the first certain witness to the gospel of Luke. Among the unknowns are the date at which Marcion encountered Luke and the form in which he found it. If one accepts the reasonable hypothesis that the gospel which we call Luke was known to Marcion before he revised it (i.e., that it was "the gospel" in use in his community at Sinope), the date of his initial activity could shift back to a hypothetical 110–120. Closely related to this is the question of whether Marcion simply "never heard of Acts" or whether he knew of the book and rejected it. Adolph v. Harnack claimed that Marcion rejected Acts. His evidence is based upon the statement of Marutha, Bishop of Maipherkat in Mesopotamia c. 400, that the Marcionites had rejected the book of Acts and replaced it with another—a text that Harnack argues was the *Antitheses*[81] This interpretation may well be correct, but it is not definite evidence for Marcion's own views. In their on-going "dialogue" with Catholic Christians the followers of Marcion altered their views about various books. Marutha may be evidence for the placement of the *Antitheses* between the "Gospel" and the "Apostle" in his own time, and the idea that it served in place of Acts may correspond to Marcionite thought in later eras, but it does not firmly establish that Marcion himself knew Acts.[82]

In light of the contemporary lack of enthusiasm for Luke's "Paulinism," the second century exhibits a certain irony: in those circles that would later be regarded as orthodox, Paul and Acts appear to go hand in hand. No writer who makes explicit use of Acts does not also make explicit use of Paul, and *vice-versa*. Justin and Irenaeus are pivotal examples. Justin evidently used Luke, but he does not seem to have used Acts.[83] Justin does not mention Paul. Irenaeus identifies and cites both. Polycarp, the earliest possible—but far from certain—witness to the existence of Acts, was an admirer of Paul. One could almost speak of an *altum silentium* (profound silence)[84] about Acts in the period before c. 180—so long as one imagines that the only people who count are the pastors and theologians eventually approved by emerging orthodoxy. That approach is, I have claimed, erroneous. Acts was not in the hands of the heretics before Irenaeus; it was in the hands of those inspired by popular narrative.[85]

This preliminary survey and probe has led to a position very much like that set forth in 1922 by Henry J. Cadbury, who established the limits of 60 and 150, regarding 70–115 as "probable."[86] The difficulties enumerated in this chapter help to clarify why so few have devoted much time and effort to dating Acts. I nonetheless believe that a good deal more precision can be established, and shall proceed to make that attempt in what follows. Identification of sources will play a major role in that effort. The *terminus ad quem* remains firmly established. Acts cannot be later than c. 150; c. 130 is not improbable. No further efforts will be made at the high end of the scale. The rest of this book will be devoted to refinement of the *terminus a quo*. The first step in that process will be to demonstrate that Acts uses the Gospel of Mark. Mark, I shall argue, cannot be earlier than 75.

Excursus: Criteria for Intertextuality

Over the course of more than a decade of research and reflection Dennis R. MacDonald has developed and honed a set of criteria for the determination of intertextual relationships.[87] These criteria are accessibility, analogy, density, order, distinctiveness, and interpretability. In the jargon of the discipline "hypertext" refers to the receptor text, the proposed user of a source, and "hypotext" to the undoubted or hypothetical source.[88] Accessibility deals with the fundamental question of whether one might reasonably suspect that the author had access to the hypotext. Analogy looks for a tradition of imitation or use. The third criterion, density, takes into account the quantity and quality of proposed parallels. Order asks whether the items in the hypertext occur in similar sequence to those of the putative hypotext. Distinctiveness looks for the appearance of a rare or atypical word, theme, or expression that may betray the use of a source. Interpretability raises the question of whether the hypothesis that "X used or imitated Y" clarifies difficulties, enhances interpretation, and solves more problems than it creates. This is, in effect, the payoff, for if the claim that a source has been imitated or utilized does not make a real contribution to understanding the hypertext, that claim rarely merits more than a sentence in an introduction or a footnote thereto.

Because of the sheer volume of parallels adduced in this book I have not attempted to apply these criteria to each case, but, with two exceptions, they are implicit throughout and often brought to the surface, especially in the closing summaries of each section or chapter. The exception is accessibility. The general line of argumentation in what follows is, in effect, "Because Luke used this particular source, it *must* have been accessible, and therefore Acts must be dated after the appearance of said writing."[89] Other matters relating to the criterion of accessibility are primarily cultural and boil down to the question of whether the author of the hypertext would have been likely to encounter the hypotext in her or his particular culture, in this case the worlds of early gentile Christianity and Hellenistic Judaism. On those grounds the sources proposed are eminently suitable.

The second exception is that of order, which is peculiar to mimesis proper, especially the use of a single model, such as the *Aeneid* of Virgil as a leading model for Luke and Acts. This criterion applies scarcely at all to the source proposals that follow.

3 Acts among the Prophets, Apostles and Evangelists

Information about sources can help to clarify a number of issues important to the interpretation of a work.[1] One of these, the *terminus a quo*, may be substantiated if the use of a particular source can be securely established and if that source can itself be dated. As it happens, the least disputable written source of Acts can be dated, but it is of no use for determining the date of Acts. That source is, of course, the Greek Bible, called the Septuagint (hereafter, LXX).[2]

THE SEPTUAGINT AS A SOURCE OF ACTS

The chief importance of the LXX in the investigation of Acts' sources is the light it sheds upon *how* Luke made (or could make) use of them. Biblical references and citations are abundant, and, since the source is, within certain limits, controllable, form relatively sound judgments. The LXX appears in Acts in two different ways, each of which has two subdivisions. Explicit quotations may appear with or without acknowledgment. Examples of citations marked by formulae are in 2:16, "This is what was spoken through the prophet" and 2:25, "David says." Yet Stephen's speech (7:2–53) contains many indirect quotations—like 7:5–6—that are not acknowledged as such. Such citations can show considerable variation from the "original."[3] Still other passages that contain such "informal" or non-explicit quotations, as in verses 19–21 of that same speech, are essentially paraphrases.

Such informal quotations shade toward the second category, which includes a "micro level" and a "macro level" of passages shaped to correspond with biblical narratives or to evoke characters from those narratives. The former can be summarized by saying that Luke writes like the Bible.[4] A very good analogy for English-speakers would be the phrasing and diction of the 1611 A.V. ("King James") Bible, which has long been imitated to emphasize the ridiculous or to express the sublime. (One may envision the range by taking note of the different contemporary uses of "thou shalt not.") This practice belongs to a widespread literary phenomenon called *mimesis*, a Greek word meaning "imitation."[5] Writers and speakers use mimesis for any number of reasons, including the learning, evocation, and conveyance of some feeling or effect. Mimesis exhibits an especially powerful attraction in cultures and eras devoted to the exaltation of past achievements and/or any context in which there is a pervasive sense of what is "right" or "correct."[6] The cultivation of mimesis governed Greco-

Roman education from the fifth century BCE to the end of that cultural era and beyond.[7] One learned by imitating the masters, and people demonstrated their education by making (and recognizing) apt allusions in the course of their writing and reading. Luke's use of the LXX therefore places him in the suburbs of the realm of literature.[8]

Moving from quotation or general allusion to the actual casting of stories in biblical form by inventing or conforming details to the heroic tradition may be a short step for authors, but it is a great leap for historiography. The creation of episodes through appropriation of biblical prototypes is, in the minds of most, more a plunge than a pace. W. K. L. Clarke, for example, accepts the composition of speeches as "a recognized practice among the historians of antiquity" and declares the practice to be "without prejudice to the literary honesty of our author . . . But such a latitude cannot be transferred without question to the narrative. If we find descriptions of events moulded to any serious extent on the LXX, the character of a conscientious historian claimed in the prologue to the Gospel is considerably impaired."[9] Clarke then goes on to find just such potential impairment in the famous episode of the Ethiopian Eunuch (Acts 8:26–39). Others have subsequently reaped where Clarke sowed.[10]

The literarily effective and theologically important use of allusions by Luke is the bane of source critics—and one reason why source critics now earn scant respect. Matthew is admired, or, failing that, recognized for his capacity to make things clear. When that evangelist wishes to make an important scriptural connection, he interrupts the narrative to announce, "This took place in order to fulfill what is written in the Prophet . . ."[11] Luke is different. His gospel opens with an aging, childless couple who have come to the end of the road. It soon transpires that they will have a son. The informed and reflective reader will be reminded of stories from the Hebrew Bible about childless couples and will shortly recall Abraham and Sarah and the promise of *universal* beatitude. In a few deft strokes, with words and phrases that positively reek of the LXX, Luke links the new to the "old" and foreshadows the gentile mission (Luke 1:5–23). Such brilliant use of evocation and allusion shows why Luke is popular in an era devoted to literary criticism of the Gospels—and why sources may seem simply irrelevant and/or utterly irrecoverable. Another example, Acts 20:7–12, possesses warm humor and considerable charm:[12]

> On the first day of the week, when we met to break bread, Paul was holding a discussion with them; since he intended to leave the next day, he continued speaking until midnight. There were many lamps in the room upstairs where we were meeting. A young man named Eutychus, who was sitting in the window, began to sink off into a deep sleep while Paul talked still longer. Overcome by sleep, he fell to the ground three floors below and was picked up dead. But Paul went down, *threw himself upon him, and embraced him,*[13] then said, "Do not be alarmed, for his life is in him (ἡ γὰρ ψυχὴ αὐτοῦ ἐν αὐτῷ ἐστιν.)." Then Paul went upstairs, and after he had broken bread and eaten, he continued to converse with them until dawn; then he left. Meanwhile they had taken the boy away alive and were not a little comforted. (NRSV, *alt.,* with emphasis added)

—

There seems no compelling motive to engage in source-criticism here, for this story is ostensibly the report of an eyewitness ("we").[14] Martin Dibelius none-theless found this story as "secular" as can be. He thought that Luke would not adapt a story of this quality to the person of Paul and therefore suggested that Luke took it over from tradition.[15] Gerd Lüdemann affirms its secular character, but assigns to Luke responsibility for "Christianizing" the legend, which he found in the course of his "secular" reading. Dennis MacDonald has nomi-nated as a candidate for this secular exercise: Homer's *Odyssey*, which has the great advantage of being a text that every literate person would know, as it was the first material read in school.[16] Some may wonder why a story of a miracle located in a Christian "liturgy" of word and sacrament is "secular." Dibelius did agree that the author ". . . has introduced a certain Christian interest into the framing of the story . . ."[17] His judgment of its non-Christian origin rests upon what he views as its original ambiguity (good diagnosis or miracle?) and the lack of edification, as well as the narrative focus in general, not to mention the element of humor. (To this one might add, as Dibelius did not, the comic irony of the name Eutychus, which means "Lucky.")[18]

The thinness of the Christian veneer becomes more evident in the light of the heavy patina of "Septuagintalism." Two similar stories from the Elijah/Elisha tradition recount resurrections. In 1 Kings 17:17–24 Elijah revives the son of the widow of Zarephath.[19] Elisha revives a Shunammite woman's son in the finely crafted narrative of 2 Kings 4:18–37. The Elijah story speaks of an *upper room* (and contains the verb *sitting*, rendered in NRSV as "lodging"), describes the prophet as *lying upon* the child (NRSV: "he stretched himself upon," and includes the expression "Let [his] *life* (ἡ ψυχή) return to him" (v. 21). The story ends with an announcement that the child is alive. In 2 Kings 4 the boy *sleeps*, then *dies*. The prophet eventually comes in person, *lies prone upon him*,[20] and can ultimately restore the child to his mother (verses 20, 34, and 36).[21] Some of the details are minor and differently employed, but it is very difficult to get around the word "life" (ψυχή), which is not used in conventional resurrection stories, and, most particularly, the rather embarrassing action of "embracing" the patient.[22]

Corresponding to this in the system of internal Lucan parallels, in which the actions and experiences of Jesus are repeated in the career of Peter, whose deeds correspond to incidents in the life of Paul, are two other cases: the raising of Tabitha (Acts 9:38–41) by Peter,[23] an event that also takes place in an upper room and has several reminiscences of the Elijah/Elisha stories,[24] and the story of how Jesus raised the son of the Widow of Nain, Luke 7:11–17, which amounts to a near re-telling of Elijah's miracle in 1 Kings 17.[25] These parallels between Luke and Acts, wherein a story in one book is matched by another in the sequel have important bearings upon both historical and source questions. If a tradition has been so transformed by imitation of another work that an underlying basis is no longer detectable, that source is of no historical value, even if it depends upon an historical event. Further, if Luke takes great pains to establish parallels between the Gospel and Acts, responsible critics must seriously consider the possibility of invention. One who doubts that all of these pleasing coincidences happened in order to accommodate the narrative theology of Luke is likely to conclude that he created some episodes. The presence in Luke and Acts of parallel episodes *both* of which evince imitation of the LXX raises this possibility to the level of probability.

The story of the finally fortunate Eutychus is no "potted" transplant from Homer or the books of the Kings. Rather, it contains numerous allusions, most of which escape all but the most biblically (and otherwise) literate of readers; and after these intertextual allusions and internal parallels in 20:7–12 have been set to one side, very little "original source" remains. This is not to say that Luke concocted the episode, although he may have, possibly inspired by Homer. What it does mean, to reiterate the principle, is that the isolation and identification of an underlying source is a risky undertaking.[26] The passage is also a major stumbling block for analysis of a "we-source," as Acts 20:7–12 is anything but an eyewitness reminiscence. Nor is the little tale quite so devoid of edification as Dibelius claimed. Sunday, lamps, eucharist, and (new) life for the dead are potential symbols. This is no allegory, but the story is redolent with symbolic suggestions. Those who demand something on the didactic side may turn to Luke 21:34–36 and other exhortations to stay awake.[27] Meanwhile, back in the desert . . .

Questions about the source(s) of the Conversion of the Ethiopian official (Acts 8:26–39) engaged the attention of W. K. L. Clarke and remain pressing. One hypothesis is that there wasa cycle of stories about Philip or the Seven, a "Hellenist" source. Ernst Haenchen regards this passage as ". . . the Hellenistic parallel to Luke's account of the first Gentile-conversion by Peter: its parallel — and rival."[28] He also notes that the two stories about Philip are "extraordinarily different," and proceeds to show how different they are.[29] Samaria is for Luke the place of "the other" who is unreceptive (Luke 9:53), but useful for embarrassing examples intended to shock the faithful into new ways of seeing (Luke 10:25–37; 17:11–19). The mission of Philip to an unspecified Samaritan city (Acts 8:4–25) is marked by specified competition and considerable success. The story of the Ethiopian official (Acts 8:26–39) takes place in another kind of "Bible country" — "the desert," a place of wandering and miracle, temptation and failure, a genuine "never-never land," populated in this case by a most exalted and exotic creature, a minister of the Queen of Ethiopia. Ethiopians were another kind of "other," ideal inhabitants of a dwelling place that served as one illustration of "the ends of the earth."[30] In his last words to the disciples in Acts 1:8 Jesus stated, "You will be my witnesses in Jerusalem, in all Judea and Samaria, and to the ends of the earth." The inference is difficult to resist.[31]

The structure of 8:26–39 closely parallels that of Luke 24:13–35.[32] (See Table 3.1.)

This pattern is a bit more than a random collection of items arranged into a good plot. Here one comes to grips with a basic expression of Lucan theology and of Lucan method: faith coming to life amidst dialogue nourished and

Table 3.1: Emmaus and the Road to Gaza

Incident	Luke 24	Acts 8
1. Traveler meets traveler(s)	24:15	8:29
2. Question answered with question	24:17–18	8:30–31
3. Subject of conversation is the death and the resurrection of Jesus, demonstrated by scriptural interpretation	24:26–27	8:32–35
4. Invitation/request	24:29	8:36
5. Sacramental action	24:30–31	8:38[33]
6. Disappearance of teacher	24:31	8:39
7. Emotional Reaction of guests	24:32	8:39

invigorated by "word and sacrament" in the course of a journey. If Luke and Acts contain *any* examples of authorial composition, Luke 24:13–35 would have to stand very close to the head of the queue.[34] This thoroughly Lucan program leads to the conclusion that the shape of both stories derives from the author. In the tale of the Ethiopian, Luke is also responsible for the relatively elegant Greek that marks the opening of the conversation between the evangelist and the official.[35] The quotation from Isaiah 53:7–8 is not likely to have been transmitted in a narrative legend. The passage matches Luke's theological orientation,[36] and the splendid coincidence that has the official reading just this passage at that moment fits Lucan narrative theology like a glove, as does the fortuitous appearance of water in the desert. Popular narrative requires and revels in useful coincidences. For Luke such moments are not only delightful, they also manifest the providence of God. Equally Lucan is the absence of "The Spirit"/"spiritual gifts" from baptisms administered by Philip.[37] The Spirit is not on sabbatical, however, for there is but one other passage in the New Testament that is so marked by explicit supernatural guidance as this: the conversion of Cornelius, Acts 10:1–11:18.[38] Luke invokes sustained "micro-management" from on high in that narrative to eliminate the slightest doubt that God endorses the conversion of (uncircumcised male) gentiles. At this point very little of the story remains to assign to a source, and the situation will not improve when references to the LXX come into view.

Allusions to the Elijah/Elisha tradition are quite dense and also indicate the very probable hand of Luke. Thomas Brodie argues that 2 Kings 5 is a major source.[39] Like Elijah, Philip is guided by an angel of the Lord (1 Kings 19:5–7; 2 Kings 1:3, 15); runs to complete his mission (1 Kings 18:46); and is swept up by the Spirit (1 Kings 18:12; 2 Kings 2:11, 16). 2 Kings 2 features a chariot and mentions, in addition to the "rapture" of the prophet, a statement that the other no longer saw Elijah. And not only does Ethiopia stand for "the ends of the earth"—note that a triumphant psalm summons God to conquer the nations: "Let bronze be brought from Egypt; let Ethiopia hasten to stretch out its hands to God" (Psalm 68:31)—but the eunuch carries symbolic weight. He is a great catch, both as a marginal figure (inasmuch as actual eunuchs were theoretically excluded from the people of God) and as a member of the ruling class. And his acceptance would fulfill the promise of Isaiah 56:3–7. To top all this off, Philip has converted a person of high social status. This is the kind of acquisition about which people will brag.[40]

W. K. L. Clarke has been left sitting out in the midday heat. In his view, ". . . [I]t may be plausibly maintained that the narrative has been built up out of hints contained in Zephaniah and other parts of the Old Testament." What is one to make of his data, displayed in Table 3.2[41] At first there seems to be little more than a collection of names—Gaza, Ashdod/Azotus, and Ethiopia—as well as a few concepts: noon, desert, and foreigners bowing down before the God of Israel. Yet one will search in vain to find all of these items elsewhere in such close proximity. Zephaniah proclaims the joy of Zion at God's universal reign of justice, and that passage is well suited to the universalistic message of Acts 8:26–39. More concretely, there is the Greek pun upon γάζα, meaning both a

Table 3.2: Acts 8 and Zephaniah

Acts 8	Zephaniah
26. Ἄγγελος δὲ κυρίου ἐλάλησεν πρὸς Φίλιππον λέγων, Ἀνάστηθι καὶ πορεύου κατὰ **μεσημβρίαν** ἐπὶ τὴν ὁδὸν τὴν καταβαίνουσαν ἀπὸ Ἰερουσαλὴμ **εἰς Γάζαν·** . . . "Get up and go toward the **south** to the road that goes down from Jerusalem to **Gaza**	2:4 Διότι **Γάζα** διηρπασμένη ἔσται . . . καὶ **Ἄζωτος μεσημβρίας** ἐκριφήσεται For Gaza shall be deserted . . . Ashdod's people shall be driven out at noon,
27. καὶ ἀναστὰς ἐπορεύθη· So he got up and went. καὶ ἰδοὺ ἀνὴρ **Αἰθίοψ** εὐνοῦχος δυνάστης Κανδάκης βασιλίσσης Αἰθιόπων, ὃς ἦν ἐπὶ πάσης τῆς **γάζης** αὐτῆς, ὃς ἐληλύθει **προσκυνήσων** εἰς Ἰερουσαλήμ Now there was an **Ethiopian** eunuch, a court official of the Candace, queen of the Ethiopians, in charge of her entire **treasury**. He had come to Jerusalem to worship.	2:11–12 . . . καὶ **προσκυνήσουσιν** αὐτῷ ἕκαστος ἐκ τοῦ τόπου αὐτοῦ, πᾶσαι αἱ νῆσοι τῶν ἐθνῶν. and to him shall bow down, each in its place, all the coasts and islands of the nations. 12 Καὶ ὑμεῖς, **Αἰθίοπες**, τραυματίαι ῥομφαίας μού ἐστε. You also, O Ethiopians, shall be killed by my sword.
40. Φίλιππος δὲ εὑρέθη εἰς **Ἄζωτον** But Philip found himself at Azotus	3:10 ἐκ περάτων ποταμῶν **Αἰθιοπίας** οἴσουσιν θυσίας μοι. From beyond the rivers of Ethiopia my suppliants, my scattered ones, shall bring my offering.

place, Gaza, and "treasure," a word play exploited, evidently, in both LXX and Acts. To many it will remain improbable that Luke picked up these bits from Zephaniah, laced them thoroughly with chariots, officials, divine guidance and other motifs from the story of Elijah, then poured the mixture into the mold provided by Emmaus. Still, there is no getting around the "facts": Philip is in an unusual place, at an unusual time, heading in a strange direction, and happens to meet a most unusual person who has been engaged in a highly atypical pilgrimage. This is a very odd "conversion story," for it trails off into the happy and almost literally wild blue yonder. The story of the Ethiopian official would be a highly unusual "foundation legend" for the first conversion of a gentile.[42] In all the rest of Acts no one ever recalls it, and with good reason; for it would seem strange, even to the credulous. When Peter converted Cornelius and his household, he had a good half-dozen witnesses to see his sermon interrupted by the descent of the Spirit. Had Philip been challenged as was Peter in Acts 11, he could have said no more than that he had been directed by the Spirit to this eminent individual, that at the man's urgent request Philip baptized him, and that nobody has seen him since.[43]

The foregoing has not intended to overwhelm the reader with data, nor do I wish to cloud the matter with a thick fog of irresolution. In my own view it is not improbable that Luke has composed this episode to such a degree that a hypothetical source would reveal little more than that Philip was said to have converted someone (perhaps a person of importance?) somewhere at some time.[44] The purpose of the exercise has been to show once again how Luke can use the LXX in such a manner and to such a degree that other underlying sources are fully obscured. Nonetheless, even if all these allusions are accepted, the result is not simply a meaningless pastiche to those who do not recognize the allusions. It is a mark of Lucan talent that this *is* a good story, altogether compelling and so seductive that only subsequent reflection leads one to find it somewhat strange, while no amount of critical dissection and analysis can dispel its charm or dull its force.[45] Josephus could also tell a story like that of the Eunuch, a bit less charming, perhaps, but no less interesting. That story, however, must await another occasion.[46]

THE GOSPEL ACCORDING TO MARK AS A SOURCE OF ACTS

After some of the vexatious questions raised by even a brief review of the LXX, it may come as a relief to learn that the dependence of Acts upon Mark is indisputable. This was, to be sure, no more than a minor source, but from the "odds and ends" of Mark utilized in Acts it will be possible to derive some interesting insights. By way of preparation I shall now attempt to demonstrate—largely through the observations of established scholars of varying perspectives—some evidence for the use of Mark in Acts.

Table 3.3: Knowing Which End Is up

Mark 13:31–32	Luke 21:33–34
31 ὁ οὐρανὸς καὶ ἡ γῆ παρελεύσονται, οἱ δὲ λόγοι μου οὐ μὴ παρελεύσονται. 32 Περὶ δὲ τῆς ἡμέρας ἐκείνης ἢ τῆς ὥρας οὐδεὶς **οἶδεν**, οὐδὲ οἱ ἄγγελοι ἐν οὐρανῷ οὐδὲ ὁ υἱός, εἰ μὴ ὁ **πατήρ**. **Heaven and earth will pass away, but my words will not pass away.**	ὁ οὐρανὸς καὶ ἡ γῆ παρελεύσονται, οἱ δὲ λόγοι μου οὐ μὴ παρελεύσονται. 34 Προσέχετε δὲ ἑαυτοῖς μήποτε βαρηθῶσιν ὑμῶν αἱ καρδίαι ἐν κραιπάλῃ καὶ μέθῃ καὶ μερίμναις βιωτικαῖς, καὶ ἐπιστῇ ἐφ' ὑμᾶς αἰφνίδιος ἡ ἡμέρα ἐκείνη· **Heaven and earth will pass away, but my words will not pass away.** Be on guard so that your hearts are not weighed down with dissipation and drunkenness and the worries of this life, and that day does not catch you unexpectedly,
	Acts 1:7 εἶπεν δὲ πρὸς αὐτούς, Οὐχ ὑμῶν ἐστιν γνῶναι χρόνους ἢ καιροὺς οὓς ὁ **πατὴρ** ἔθετο ἐν τῇ ἰδίᾳ ἐξουσίᾳ·
32 "But about that day or hour no one **knows**, neither the angels in heaven, nor the Son, but only **the Father**.	*Jesus* replied, "It is not for you to **know** the times or periods that **the Father** has set by his own authority.

There are no grounds for doubting that Luke intentionally omitted Mark 13:32, which appears, with minor variations, in Matthew 24:36 (Table 3.3). The verse, which answers the question raised in Mark 13:4, is awkward in its place, although it does serve to introduce the following section (Mark 13:33–37). Since Luke does not utilize that section of Mark at this point in chapter 21, the verse would have been even more awkward. Literary explanations for the omission may be more convincing than proposals grounded in Lucan theology.[47] Commentators on Acts, like those on Luke, generally view Mark 13:32 as the source of Acts 1:7.[48] The judgment appears reasonable. Though only the words for "the Father" and "know" are in common, Luke paraphrases "that day or the hour" with the more conventional "times and seasons" of early Christian edification.[49] The relative clause elegantly avoids attributing ignorance to the Son.[50] Luke would scarcely have reproduced so crude a phrase as οὐδεὶς οἶδεν, οὐδὲ . . . (No one knows, neither . . .)[51] In conclusion: there is general agreement, with good reason, that Acts 1:7 is a Lucan transposition of Mark 13:32.

The Markan summary in Table 3.4 comes from the section known as Luke's "great omission" (Mark 6:45–8:26, which has no parallel in Luke's gospel). Summaries very rarely, if ever, derive from tradition.[52] They normally represent the work of an (editor or) author.[53] One effect of such units is to transform each reported incident into a synecdoche, as it were, filling in the narrative by suggesting that there were many such instances of healing, sharing, and the like.[54] Henry Cadbury makes the strongest claim for the dependence of this summary upon Mark 6:55–56: " [these passages] . . . are influenced by the gospels—by Mark more than by Luke's version of it (cf. Mark i.26; vi.56 *et al.*)."[55] He notes

Table 3.4: Beyond a Shadow of a Doubt?

Mark 6:55–56	Acts 5:12–16; 19:11–12
περιέδραμον ὅλην τὴν χώραν ἐκείνην καὶ ἤρξαντο ἐπὶ τοῖς **κραβάττοις** τοὺς κακῶς ἔχοντας **περιφέρειν** ὅπου ἤκουον ὅτι ἐστίν. 56 καὶ ὅπου ἂν εἰσεπορεύετο εἰς κώμας ἢ εἰς **πόλεις** ἢ εἰς ἀγροὺς ἐν ταῖς ἀγοραῖς **ἐτίθεσαν** τοὺς **ἀσθενοῦντας**, καὶ παρεκάλουν αὐτὸν **ἵνα κἂν** τοῦ κρασπέδου τοῦ ἱματίου αὐτοῦ ἅψωνται· καὶ ὅσοι ἂν ἥψαντο αὐτοῦ ἐσῴζοντο. [People] rushed about that whole region and began to bring the sick on **mats** to wherever they heard he was. And wherever he went, into villages or **cities** or farms, they **laid the sick** in the marketplaces, and begged him **that they might** touch even the fringe of his cloak; and *all* who touched it were healed.	12 Διὰ δὲ τῶν χειρῶν τῶν ἀποστόλων ἐγίνετο σημεῖα καὶ τέρατα πολλὰ ἐν τῷ λαῷ· καὶ ἦσαν ὁμοθυμαδὸν ἅπαντες ἐν τῇ Στοᾷ Σολομῶντος. 13 τῶν δὲ λοιπῶν οὐδεὶς ἐτόλμα κολλᾶσθαι αὐτοῖς, ἀλλ᾽ ἐμεγάλυνεν αὐτοὺς ὁ λαός· 14 μᾶλλον δὲ προσετίθεντο πιστεύοντες τῷ κυρίῳ πλήθη ἀνδρῶν τε καὶ γυναικῶν, 15 ὥστε καὶ εἰς τὰς πλατείας ἐκφέρειν τοὺς ἀσθενεῖς καὶ **τιθέναι** ἐπὶ κλιναρίων καὶ **κραβάττων**, ἵνα ἐρχομένου Πέτρου **κἂν** ἡ σκιὰ ἐπισκιάσῃ τινὶ αὐτῶν. 16 συνήρχετο δὲ καὶ τὸ πλῆθος τῶν πέριξ **πόλεων** Ἰερουσαλήμ, **φέροντες ἀσθενεῖς** καὶ ὀχλουμένους ὑπὸ πνευμάτων ἀκαθάρτων, οἵτινες ἐθεραπεύοντο ἅπαντες. Now many signs and wonders were done among the people *through the apostles*. And they were all together in Solomon's Portico. None of the rest dared to join them, but the people held them in high esteem. Yet more than ever believers were added to the Lord, great numbers of both men and women, so that they even **carried out the sick** into the streets, and laid them on cots and **mats**, **in order that** Peter's shadow might fall on some of them as he came by. A great number of people would also gather from the towns around Jerusalem, **bringing the sick** and those tormented by unclean spirits, and they were *all* cured.
	Acts 19:11–12
	11 Δυνάμεις τε οὐ τὰς τυχούσας ὁ θεὸς ἐποίει διὰ τῶν χειρῶν Παύλου, 12 ὥστε καὶ ἐπὶ τοὺς **ἀσθενοῦντας** ἀποφέρεσθαι ἀπὸ τοῦ χρωτὸς αὐτοῦ σουδάρια ἢ σιμικίνθια καὶ ἀπαλλάσσεσθαι ἀπ᾽ αὐτῶν τὰς νόσους, τά τε πνεύματα τὰ πονηρὰ ἐκπορεύεσθαι. God did extraordinary miracles through Paul, so that when the handkerchiefs or aprons that had touched his skin were **brought** to the **sick**, their diseases left them, and the evil spirits came out of them.

that the "vulgar" word κράβαττος ("mat"), eschewed by Matthew and Luke, appears twice in Acts.[56]

Mark's summary in 6:56 is itself a generalization of the story of the woman with the continuous flow (5:25–34), as this novelistic detail is specific to that passage.[57] Luke makes use of the healing power of cloth in Acts 19:11–12. In that case the apostle is scarcely inferior to his master, as the cloth is effective even when removed from its charismatically endowed owner.[58] It is far from impossible that the ultimate source of these potent fabrics is Mark, rather than an independent tradition; and since these verses belong to a summary, the possibility begins to approach the realm of probability.

With regard to the summary in Acts 5: (12–14) 15–16, the resemblance to its alleged source is more thematic than verbal, although there is the telltale κἄν.[59] Both summaries report a healing ministry that embraced a general territory.[60] Rather than imitate the therapeutic fringe of Jesus' garment, Luke elects to depict healing through the mere "touch" of Peter's shadow, enabling the apostle to conduct missions of mercy without even the need to pause and wave a beneficent hand.[61] "No more astounding piece of miracle-working is described in the NT; Peter does not need to speak, to touch, or, it seems, to give any attention to the sick person."[62] (In the background is the notion of the shadow as an extension of one's person or personality.[63]) The report leads Haenchen to cast the full force of his critical shadow upon Luke's theology.[64] For the author of Acts, the shadow of Peter and the used clothing of Paul were clearly intended to be parallel demonstrations of divine empowerment.[65] The inspiration for the form and wording of these two summaries comes from Mark, especially Mark 6:55–56.[66]

Table 3.5 presents data that do not seem to demand detailed argumentation. Dependence is rather clear. The themes of "false witness(es)," destruction of the Temple, and blasphemy were omitted by Luke from the Passion of Jesus and utilized for the agitation against and "trial" of Stephen.[67] Luke's purposes for this "transfer" included more than assimilation of the passion of Stephen to that of Jesus—although that is no doubt one object. This rearrangement shows a growing intensity of opposition to the mission, with particular reference to Hellenophone (Greek-speaking) activity, which will presently lead to a gentile mission. Previous encounters with the Sanhedrin exposed judicial arrogance and brutality. Now the opponents must dig deeper into their store of lethal recipes in order to bring up a packet of instant slander spiced with a potent dash of perjury. With this intensification comes foreshadowing of animosity toward the Temple and its leadership, a theme that will be prominent in Stephen's address.

Table 3.6 indicates that Luke 8:51 appears to be a combination of Mark 5:37 and 5:40. The expulsion of all "outsiders" is restricted to these two passages in Mark 5 and Acts 9.[68] Mark is quite probably the source, for the theme of privacy is congruent with the "Messianic Secret."[69] Barrett views the interesting similarity between Mark's "Talitha" and the "Tabitha" of Acts as most probably "pure coincidence."[70] One of the theses of this book is that purity is a rather much less common virtue of coincidences than is often assumed. The case for coincidence here is possibly weakened by the variants at Mark 5:41, where some manuscripts read the equivalent to "Tabitha" rather than "Talitha.[71] One could doubtless argue that the contamination has worked backwards from Acts, but even that claim would indicate that early Christian editors and scribes saw a

Table 3.5: Framing Stephen

Mark 14:55-60, 63-64	Luke 22:66-71	Acts 6:11-14; 7:1
55 οἱ δὲ ἀρχιερεῖς καὶ ὅλον τὸ συνέδριον ἐζήτουν κατὰ τοῦ Ἰησοῦ μαρτυρίαν εἰς τὸ θανατῶσαι αὐτόν, καὶ οὐχ ηὕρισκον· 56 πολλοὶ γὰρ ἐψευδομαρτύρουν κατ' αὐτοῦ, καὶ ἴσαι αἱ μαρτυρίαι οὐκ ἦσαν. 57 καὶ τινες ἀναστάντες ἐψευδομαρτύρουν κατ' αὐτοῦ λέγοντες 58 ὅτι Ἡμεῖς **ἠκούσαμεν αὐτοῦ λέγοντος ὅτι** Ἐγὼ **καταλύσω τὸν ναὸν τοῦτον τὸν** χειροποίητον καὶ διὰ τριῶν ἡμερῶν ἄλλον ἀχειροποίητον οἰκοδομήσω· 59 καὶ οὐδὲ οὕτως ἴση ἦν ἡ μαρτυρία αὐτῶν. 60 καὶ ἀναστὰς ὁ **ἀρχιερεὺς** εἰς μέσον ἐπηρώτησεν τὸν Ἰησοῦν λέγων, Οὐκ ἀποκρίνῃ οὐδέν; τί οὗτοί σου καταμαρτυροῦσιν. 63 ὁ δὲ ἀρχιερεὺς διαρρήξας τοὺς χιτῶνας αὐτοῦ λέγει, **Τί ἔτι χρείαν ἔχομεν μαρτύρων;** 64 ἠκούσατε τῆς **βλασφημίας·** τί ὑμῖν φαίνεται; οἱ δὲ πάντες κατέκριναν αὐτὸν ἔνοχον εἶναι θανάτου.	66 Καὶ ὡς ἐγένετο ἡμέρα, συνήχθη τὸ πρεσβυτέριον τοῦ λαοῦ, ἀρχιερεῖς τε καὶ γραμματεῖς, καὶ ἀπήγαγον αὐτὸν εἰς τὸ συνέδριον αὐτῶν, 67 λέγοντες, Εἰ σὺ εἶ ὁ Χριστός, εἰπὸν ἡμῖν. εἶπεν δὲ αὐτοῖς, Ἐὰν ὑμῖν εἴπω οὐ μὴ πιστεύσητε· 68 ἐὰν δὲ ἐρωτήσω οὐ μὴ ἀποκριθῆτε. 69 ἀπὸ τοῦ νῦν δὲ ἔσται ὁ υἱὸς τοῦ ἀνθρώπου καθήμενος ἐκ δεξιῶν τῆς δυνάμεως τοῦ θεοῦ. 70 εἶπαν δὲ πάντες, Σὺ οὖν εἶ ὁ υἱὸς τοῦ θεοῦ; ὁ δὲ πρὸς αὐτοὺς ἔφη, Ὑμεῖς λέγετε ὅτι ἐγώ εἰμι. 71 οἱ δὲ εἶπαν, **Τί ἔτι ἔχομεν μαρτυρίας χρείαν;** αὐτοὶ γὰρ ἠκούσαμεν ἀπὸ τοῦ στόματος αὐτοῦ.	11 τότε ὑπέβαλον ἄνδρας λέγοντας ὅτι Ἀκηκόαμεν αὐτοῦ λαλοῦντος ῥήματα **βλάσφημα** εἰς Μωϋσῆν καὶ τὸν θεόν· 12 συνεκίνησάν τε τὸν λαὸν καὶ τοὺς πρεσβυτέρους καὶ τοὺς γραμματεῖς, καὶ ἐπιστάντες συνήρπασαν αὐτὸν καὶ ἤγαγον εἰς τὸ συνέδριον, 13 ἔστησάν τε **μάρτυρας ψευδεῖς** λέγοντας, Ὁ ἄνθρωπος οὗτος οὐ παύεται λαλῶν ῥήματα κατὰ τοῦ τόπου τοῦ ἁγίου [τούτου] καὶ τοῦ νόμου· 14 **ἀκηκόαμεν** γὰρ **αὐτοῦ λέγοντος ὅτι** Ἰησοῦς ὁ Ναζωραῖος οὗτος **καταλύσει τὸν τόπον τοῦτον** καὶ ἀλλάξει τὰ ἔθη ἃ παρέδωκεν ἡμῖν Μωϋσῆς. Εἶπεν δὲ **ὁ ἀρχιερεύς**, Εἰ ταῦτα οὕτως ἔχει;

Table 3.5: Framing Stephen *Continued*

Now the chief priests and the whole council were looking for testimony against Jesus to put him to death; but they found none. For many gave **false testimony** against him, and their testimony did not agree Some stood up and gave false testimony against him, saying, **"We heard him say, 'I will destroy this temple** that is made with hands, and in three days I will build another, not made with hands.'" But even on this point their testimony did not agree. Then **the high priest** stood up before them and asked Jesus, "Have you no answer? What is it that they testify against you?" Then the high priest tore his clothes and said, "Why do we still need witnesses? You have heard his blasphemy! What is your decision?" All of them condemned him as deserving death.	When day came, the assembly of the elders of the people, both chief priests and scribes, gathered together, and they brought him to their council. They said, "If you are the Messiah, tell us." He replied, "If I tell you, you will not believe; and if I question you, you will not answer. But from now on the Son of Man will be seated at the right hand of the power of God." All of them asked, "Are you, then, the Son of God?" He said to them, "You say that I am." Then they said, "What further testimony do we need? We have heard it ourselves From his own lips!"	11 Then they secretly instigated some men to say, "We have heard him speak blasphemous words against Moses and God." 12 They stirred up the people as well as the elders and the scribes; then they suddenly confronted him, seized him, and brought him before the council.13 They set up **false witnesses** who said, "This man never stops saying things against this holy place and the law; 14 for **we have heard him say that** this Jesus of Nazareth **will destroy this place** and will change the customs that Moses handed on to us." 1 Then **the high priest** asked him, "Are these things so?"

Table 3.6: A Minor Example

Mark 5:37, 40–41 (Luke 8:51, 54)	Acts 9:40
37 καὶ οὐκ ἀφῆκεν οὐδένα μετ' αὐτοῦ συνακολουθῆσαι εἰ μὴ τὸν Πέτρον καὶ Ἰάκωβον καὶ Ἰωάννην τὸν ἀδελφὸν Ἰακώβου. 40 καὶ κατεγέλων αὐτοῦ. αὐτὸς δὲ **ἐκβαλὼν πάντας** παραλαμβάνει τὸν πατέρα τοῦ παιδίου καὶ τὴν μητέρα καὶ τοὺς μετ' αὐτοῦ, καὶ εἰσπορεύεται ὅπου ἦν τὸ παιδίον· 41 καὶ κρατήσας τῆς χειρὸς τοῦ παιδίου λέγει αὐτῇ, Ταλιθα κουμ, ὅ ἐστιν μεθερμηνευόμενον Τὸ κοράσιον, σοὶ λέγω, ἔγειρε.	**ἐκβαλὼν** δὲ ἔξω **πάντας** ὁ Πέτρος καὶ θεὶς τὰ γόνατα προσηύξατο, καὶ ἐπιστρέψας πρὸς τὸ σῶμα εἶπεν, Ταβιθά, ἀνάστηθι. ἡ δὲ ἤνοιξεν τοὺς ὀφθαλμοὺς αὐτῆς, καὶ ἰδοῦσα τὸν Πέτρον ἀνεκάθισεν.
He allowed no one to follow him except Peter, James, and John, the brother of James. And they laughed at him. Then he **put them all outside**, and took the child's father and mother and those who were with him, and went in where the child was. 41 He took her by the hand and said to her, "*Talitha* cum," which means, "Little girl, get up!"	Peter **put all of them outside**, and then he knelt down and prayed. He turned to the body and said, "*Tabitha*, get up." Then she opened her eyes, and seeing Peter, she sat up.
Luke 8:51, 54 ἐλθὼν δὲ εἰς τὴν οἰκίαν οὐκ ἀφῆκεν εἰσελθεῖν τινα σὺν αὐτῷ εἰ μὴ Πέτρον καὶ Ἰωάννην καὶ Ἰάκωβον καὶ τὸν πατέρα τῆς παιδὸς καὶ τὴν μητέρα. 54 αὐτὸς δὲ κρατήσας τῆς χειρὸς αὐτῆς ἐφώνησεν λέγων, Ἡ παῖς, ἔγειρε. When he came to the house, he did not allow anyone to enter with him, except Peter, John, and James, and the child's father and mother. 54 But he took her by the hand and called out, "Child, get up!"	

link between the two passages. Luke wishes to show that the power of Jesus continues in his followers.

"Aha," the crafty skeptic might interject upon glancing at Table 3.7, "Here we have a bit common to Matthew, Mark, *and* Luke. In this case one cannot prove dependence on Mark." One can, nonetheless, observe that Matthew utilizes this phrase to describe the conclusion of the Sermon on the Mount, whereas Luke closely follows Mark, and will continue to do so, since Luke 4:33–37 is nearly identical with Mark 1:23–28, an episode not found in Matthew. I think it quite apparent that Luke intends that the opening incident in Paul's gentile mission will recall the initial deed of Jesus.[72] The synoptic allusion is quite intentional and informative. In these circumstances it would be unnecessarily laborious to argue that Luke excavated the reference from Matthew 7:28 rather than from its clear parallel in Mark 1:22, and then re-utilized the phrase in Acts in a distinctly

Table 3.7: A Point on Marcan Priority—and . . .

Matthew 7:28–29	Mark 1:21–22	Luke 4:31–32	Acts 13:12
28 Καὶ ἐγένετο ὅτε ἐτέλεσεν ὁ Ἰησοῦς τοὺς λόγους τούτους ἐξεπλήσσοντο οἱ ὄχλοι ἐπὶ τῇ διδαχῇ αὐτοῦ· 29 ἦν γὰρ διδάσκων αὐτοὺς ὡς ἐξουσίαν ἔχων καὶ οὐχ ὡς οἱ γραμματεῖς αὐτῶν.	21 Καὶ εἰσπορεύονται εἰς Καφαρναούμ. καὶ εὐθὺς τοῖς σάββασιν [εἰσελθὼν] εἰς τὴν συναγωγὴν ἐδίδασκεν. 22 καὶ ἐξεπλήσσοντο ἐπὶ τῇ διδαχῇ αὐτοῦ, ἦν γὰρ διδάσκων αὐτοὺς ὡς ἐξουσίαν ἔχων καὶ οὐχ ὡς οἱ γραμματεῖς.	31 Καὶ κατῆλθεν εἰς Καφαρναοὺμ πόλιν τῆς Γαλιλαίας. καὶ ἦν διδάσκων αὐτοὺς ἐν τοῖς σάββασιν· 32 καὶ ἐξεπλήσσοντο ἐπὶ τῇ διδαχῇ αὐτοῦ, ὅτι ἐν ἐξουσίᾳ ἦν ὁ λόγος αὐτοῦ.	τότε ἰδὼν ὁ ἀνθύπατος τὸ γεγονὸς ἐπίστευσεν ἐκπλησσόμενος ἐπὶ τῇ διδαχῇ τοῦ κυρίου.
Now when Jesus had finished saying these things, the crowds **were astounded at his teaching**, for he taught them as one having authority, and not as their scribes.	They went to Capernaum; and when the sabbath came, he entered the synagogue and taught. They were astounded at his teaching, for he taught them as one having authority, and not as the scribes.	He went down to Capernaum, a city in Galilee, and was teaching them on the sabbath. They were astounded at his teaching, because he spoke with authority.	When the pro-consul saw what had happened, he believed, for he was **astonished at the teaching** about the Lord.

different situation. Such phrases as this illuminate Lucan compositional technique.[73] One could almost imagine the evangelist carefully preserving excerpts cut from his text of Mark and finding a home for these in Acts.

Luke omits the famous story of the Baptizer's death (Mark 6:14–29); but out of sight was not out of mind, for he quite evidently utilized this material to describe how Paul passed some of his time in confinement. Instead of the Markan triangle of prophet, ruler, and wife, there is a trio: missionary, ruler, and wife. (See Table 3.8.) The part of Mark's narrative that most appealed to Luke was the summary of repeated consultations, marked by the use of the frequentative imperfects in both books.[74] The analytic eyes of modern scholars were not the first to light upon this relationship, for the italicized D-text variations in verses 24 and 27a of the translation show that some ancient editor(s) recognized the link and sought to develop it by fashioning Drusilla into a wannabe Herodias, by whose machinations Paul was fated to languish in durance vile contrary to the better knowledge and judgment of her husband.[75] In this instance it is difficult to contend that Luke merely used the story from Mark to "color" the account, for this is not color: it is the very substance of the account.[76]

Table 3.8: Cherchez la Femme (Italics = D-Text.)

Mark 6:18–20	Acts 24:24–27
18 ἔλεγεν γὰρ ὁ Ἰωάννης τῷ Ἡρῴδῃ ὅτι Οὐκ ἔξεστίν σοι ἔχειν τὴν γυναῖκα τοῦ ἀδελφοῦ σου. 19 ἡ δὲ Ἡρῳδιὰς ἐνεῖχεν αὐτῷ καὶ ἤθελεν αὐτὸν ἀποκτεῖναι, καὶ οὐκ ἠδύνατο· 20 ὁ γὰρ Ἡρῴδης ἐφοβεῖτο τὸν Ἰωάννην, εἰδὼς αὐτὸν ἄνδρα **δίκαιον** καὶ ἅγιον, καὶ συνετ**ή**ρ**ε**ι αὐτόν, καὶ ἀκούσας αὐτοῦ πολλὰ ἐποίει, καὶ ἡδέως **αὐτοῦ ἤκουεν**.	Μετὰ δὲ ἡμέρας τινὰς παραγενόμενος ὁ Φῆλιξ σὺν Δρουσίλλῃ τῇ ἰδίᾳ γυναικὶ οὔσῃ Ἰουδαίᾳ μετεπέμψατο τὸν Παῦλον καὶ **ἤκουσεν αὐτοῦ** περὶ τῆς εἰς Χριστὸν Ἰησοῦν πίστεως. 25 διαλεγομένου δὲ αὐτοῦ περὶ **δικαιο**σύνης καὶ ἐγκρατείας καὶ τοῦ κρίματος τοῦ μέλλοντος ἔμφοβος γενόμενος ὁ Φῆλιξ ἀπεκρίθη, Τὸ νῦν ἔχον πορεύου, καιρὸν δὲ μεταλαβὼν μετακαλέσομαί σε· 26 ἅμα καὶ ἐλπίζων ὅτι χρήματα δοθήσεται αὐτῷ ὑπὸ τοῦ Παύλου· διὸ καὶ πυκνότερον αὐτὸν μεταπεμπόμενος ὡμίλει αὐτῷ. 27 Διετίας δὲ πληρωθείσης ἔλαβεν διάδοχον ὁ Φῆλιξ Πόρκιον Φῆστον· θέλων τε χάριτα καταθέσθαι τοῖς Ἰουδαίοις ὁ Φῆλιξ κατέλιπε τὸν Παῦλον δεδεμένον.
For John had been telling Herod, "It is not lawful for you to have your brother's wife." And Herodias had a grudge against him, and wanted to kill him. But she could not, for Herod feared John, knowing that he was a righteous and holy man, and he protected him. When he heard him, he was greatly perplexed; and yet he liked to listen to him.	**24:24–27** Some days later when Felix came with his wife Drusilla, who was Jewish, *who asked to see Paul and **hear** the word. Wishing therefore to satisfy her,* he sent for Paul and heard him speak concerning faith in Christ Jesus. And as he discussed **justice**, self-control, and the coming judgment, Felix became frightened and said, "Go away for the present; when I have an opportunity, I will send for you." At the same time he hoped that money would be given him by Paul, and for that reason he used to send for him very often and converse with him. 27 After two years had passed, Felix was succeeded by Porcius Festus, *but* Felix *let* Paul *stay* in prison *because of Drusilla*.

The argument that Luke concocted this vignette is rather more probable than any claim that the resemblance was coincidental or that Luke took advantage of an historical coincidence to exploit a parallel. Luke had no wish to portray Paul as the victim of court sexual intrigue, but rather as the unfortunate captive of a corrupt official intent upon either appeasing influential subjects or lining his own pockets—and if he achieved both, so much the better.[77]

The author could also use Mark in both his Gospel *and* Acts. The first deed of Jesus' "public ministry" in Mark (1:21–28) is an exorcism, symbolizing and achieving the irruption of divine rule.[78] The first mighty act of Paul's mission after the "apostolic council" of Acts 15 is also an exorcism (16:16–18). To effect a parallel between the ministries of Jesus and Paul Luke borrows from Mark 1 *and* from the story of the Gerasene demoniac (Mark 5:1–20), both of which appear also in Luke (4:31–37; 8:26–39). Accordingly, just as that exorcism is Jesus' first deed in gentile territory, so Paul's first mighty act in "Europe" after full endorsement of the gentile mission contains echoes of the first public wonder of Jesus as well as an allusion to his initial deed in a gentile region. Luke is thus aware of the significance of Jesus' actions on the east side of the lake of Galilee in Mark, although he omits much of this material and does not allow any direct contact between Jesus and a gentile.

Furthermore, demons (Table 3.9) recognize Paul just as they recognize Jesus, and Paul, like his Lord, forbids evil spirits to "propagate the gospel." In both Mark/Luke and Acts the "gentile-friendly" phrase "most high god" appears in the context of polytheism.[79] The incidents at Gerasa and Philippi also share such features as the problem of economic loss and an eventual request for the missionary to leave town. The most frequent approach to these similarities has been a literary examination of Jesus-Paul parallelism. One can, of course, engage in such analysis without reflecting upon the matters of historicity and of source, but the latter is an integral part of literary study, for it addresses the grounds of the author's inspiration. And from the perspective of the investigation of so-called "historicity," reflection upon these parallels renders some questions quite pressing. The direct verbal correspondence in this case is slight, but the thematic repetitions are sufficient to establish the similarities and thereby indicate dependence. If one expunges these details as circumstantial adumbration, what remains? A "source" reporting that Paul performed an exorcism in Philippi, which Luke then shaped into a form evocative of Jesus? The "kernel" of an exorcism is quite soft, for that is, itself, a circumstantial detail.[80]

Table 3.10 presents a passage from the "little apocalypse" of Mark 13 that has no parallel in Luke 21, although the opening words seem to have been utilized in Luke 17:23. Once again precise verbal correspondence is limited, but the themes are similar. Luke does not speak of "false messiahs," as these were not a part of his environment. "False prophets" are those who "twist things" (διαστρέφειν). An excellent specimen of the breed is Elymas, who seeks to divert Sergius Paulus from the true path (Acts 13:8, 10).[81] Luke writes of apostasy from an established faith, but does not speak of miracle-working prophets, for he regards "signs and wonders" as authentication of legitimate prophecy. False teachers may utilize magic or attempt exorcisms, but the inferiority of these contrivances is patent.[82] Since the community is a flock, its opponents are wolves, whose object is to devour the sheep and lay heavy burdens upon them, as it were.[83] Luke has transformed these words into an ecclesial context and stripped them of their apocalyptic flavor. False teachers will not be signs of the approaching end, but a challenge to be met through proper leadership.[84]

There is no particular need to include the original text in Table 3.11, for the argument depends upon Luke's using but one Greek word ("Passover," τὸ πάσχα) of Mark. By omitting the rationale of Mark 14:2, "not during the festival," Luke creates a *non sequitur*. One may, of course, argue that Luke omitted that clause because Jesus *was* killed during the festival. That may be so, but the author does "recycle" the idea of Mark 14:2 at Acts 12:4: executions should not

Table 3.9: The First Exorcism

Mark 1	Luke 4:8	Acts 16:16–18
1:23–24 ἀνέκραξεν, λέγων, Τί ἡμῖν καὶ σοί, Ἰησοῦ Ναζαρηνέ; ἦλθες ἀπολέσαι ἡμᾶς; οἶδά σε τίς εἶ, ὁ ἅγιος τοῦ θεοῦ. *The demon* cried out, "What have you to do with us, Jesus of Nazareth? Have you come to destroy us? I know who you are, the Holy One of God."	4:34 Ἔα, τί ἡμῖν καὶ σοί, Ἰησοῦ Ναζαρηνέ; ἦλθες ἀπολέσαι ἡμᾶς; οἶδά σε τίς εἶ, ὁ ἅγιος τοῦ θεοῦ "Let us alone! What have you to do with us, Jesus of Nazareth? Have you come to destroy us? I know who you are, the Holy One of God."	Ἐγένετο δὲ πορευομένων ἡμῶν εἰς τὴν προσευχὴν παιδίσκην τινὰ ἔχουσαν πνεῦμα πύθωνα ὑπαντῆσαι ἡμῖν, ἥτις ἐργασίαν πολλὴν παρεῖχεν τοῖς κυρίοις αὐτῆς μαντευομένη. 17 αὕτη κατακολουθοῦσα τῷ Παύλῳ καὶ ἡμῖν ἔκραζεν λέγουσα, Οὗτοι οἱ ἄνθρωποι δοῦλοι **τοῦ θεοῦ τοῦ ὑψίστου** εἰσίν, οἵτινες καταγγέλλουσιν ὑμῖν ὁδὸν σωτηρίας. 18 τοῦτο δὲ ἐποίει ἐπὶ πολλὰς ἡμέρας. διαπονηθεὶς δὲ Παῦλος καὶ ἐπιστρέψας τῷ πνεύματι εἶπεν, Παραγγέλλω σοι ἐν ὀνόματι Ἰησοῦ Χριστοῦ ἐξελθεῖν ἀπ' αὐτῆς· καὶ ἐξῆλθεν αὐτῇ τῇ ὥρᾳ.
1:34b καὶ οὐκ ἤφιεν λαλεῖν τὰ δαιμόνια, ὅτι ᾔδεισαν αὐτόν.	4:41 ἐξήρχετο δὲ καὶ δαιμόνια ἀπὸ πολλῶν, **κραυγάζοντα** καὶ λέγοντα ὅτι Σὺ εἶ ὁ υἱὸς τοῦ θεοῦ. καὶ ἐπιτιμῶν οὐκ εἴα αὐτὰ λαλεῖν, ὅτι ᾔδεισαν τὸν Χριστὸν αὐτὸν εἶναι.	One day, as we were going to the place of prayer, we met a slave-girl who had a spirit of divination and brought her owners a great deal of money by fortune-telling.*17* While she followed Paul and us, she would cry out, "These men are slaves of **the Most High God**, who proclaim to you a way of salvation."*18* She kept doing this for many days. But Paul, very much annoyed, turned and said to the spirit, "I order you in the name of Jesus Christ to come out of her." And it came out that very hour.
he would not permit the demons to speak, because they knew him	Demons also came out of many, shouting, "You are the Son of God!" But he rebuked them and would not allow them to speak, because they knew that he was the Messiah.	
5:7 καὶ κράξας φωνῇ μεγάλῃ λέγει, Τί ἐμοὶ καὶ σοί, Ἰησοῦ **υἱὲ τοῦ θεοῦ τοῦ ὑψίστου**; ὁρκίζω σε τὸν θεόν, μή με βασανίσῃς he shouted at the top of his voice, "What have you to do with me, Jesus, Son of the Most High God? I adjure you by God, do not torment me."	8:28 ἰδὼν δὲ τὸν Ἰησοῦν ἀνακράξας προσέπεσεν αὐτῷ καὶ φωνῇ μεγάλῃ εἶπεν, Τί ἐμοὶ καὶ σοί, Ἰησοῦ υἱὲ **τοῦ θεοῦ τοῦ ὑψίστου**; δέομαί σου, μή με βασανίσῃς. When he saw Jesus, he fell down before him and shouted at the top of his voice, "What have you to do with me, Jesus, Son of the Most High God? I beg you, do not torment me"	

Table 3.10: False Prophets

Mark 13:21–23	Luke 17:23a; Acts 20:29–31a
καὶ τότε ἐάν τις ὑμῖν εἴπῃ, Ἴδε ὧδε ὁ Χριστός, Ἴδε ἐκεῖ, μὴ πιστεύετε· 22 ἐγερθήσονται γὰρ ψευδόχριστοι καὶ ψευδοπροφῆται καὶ δώσουσιν σημεῖα καὶ τέρατα πρὸς τὸ ἀποπλανᾶν, εἰ δυνατόν, τοὺς ἐκλεκτούς. 23 ὑμεῖς δὲ βλέπετε· προείρηκα ὑμῖν πάντα.	καὶ ἐροῦσιν ὑμῖν, Ἰδοὺ ἐκεῖ [ἤ,] Ἰδοὺ ὧδε· They will **say** to you, '**Look there!**' or '**Look here!** Acts 20:29–30 ἐγὼ οἶδα ὅτι εἰσελεύσονται μετὰ τὴν ἄφιξίν μου λύκοι βαρεῖς εἰς ὑμᾶς μὴ φειδόμενοι τοῦ ποιμνίου, 30 καὶ ἐξ ὑμῶν αὐτῶν ἀναστήσονται ἄνδρες λαλοῦντες διεστραμμένα τοῦ ἀποσπᾶν τοὺς μαθητὰς ὀπίσω αὐτῶν. 31 διὸ γρηγορεῖτε,[85]
21 And if anyone **says** to you at that time, '**Look! Here** is the Messiah!' or '**Look! There he is!**' — do not believe it. 22 False messiahs and false prophets will appear and produce signs and omens, to lead astray, if possible, the elect.	I know that after I have gone, savage wolves will come in among you, not sparing the flock. 30 Some even from your own group will come distorting the truth in order to entice the disciples to follow them. Therefore, *be alert.*
23 But *be alert*; I have already told you everything.	

Table 3.11: Paschal Schedule

Mark 14:1–2	Luke 22:1–2	Acts 12:1–4
		About that time King Herod laid violent hands upon some who belonged to the church. 2 He had James, the brother of John, killed with the sword. 3 After he saw that it pleased the Jews, he proceeded to arrest Peter also. (This was during the festival of Unleavened Bread. [ἦσαν δὲ ἡμέραι τῶν ἀζύμων]) 4 When he had
It was two days before the Passover and the festival of Unleavened Bread (τὸ πάσχα καὶ τὰ ἄζυμα μετὰ δύο ἡμέρας). The chief priests and the scribes were looking for a way to arrest Jesus by stealth and kill him; 2 for they said, "Not during the festival, or there may be a riot among the people."	Now the festival of Unleavened Bread, which is called the Passover, was near (ἡ ἑορτὴ τῶν ἀζύμων ἡ λεγομένη πάσχα). 2 The chief priests and the scribes were looking for a way to put Jesus to death, for they were afraid of the people.	seized him, he put him in prison and handed him over to four squads of soldiers to guard him, intending to bring him out to the people after the Passover (μετὰ τὸ πάσχα).

be carried out during holidays.[86] Two observations emerge from this indication of intertextual activity. In Luke the general public shifted from support of Jesus to opposition; in Acts his followers experience the same reversal of public opinion. Luke 22:2 and Acts 5:36 assign identical words to the high priestly leadership: "for they were afraid of the people" (ἐφοβοῦντο γὰρ τὸν λαόν).[87] The former applies to Jesus, the latter to the apostles. In Luke 23:17 (the Barabbas incident) the people call for the death of Jesus, while Acts attributes the shift to the mission of Stephen, and a general persecution follows his execution (8:1). "King Herod" can therefore presume that he will gain popular favor by "bringing Peter out to the people" after Passover. A more important consequence of this transfer of a passage from Mark to Acts is its reinforcement of the interpretation of Acts 12 as a passion (and resurrection) of Peter, a matter that will receive attention in Chapter Seven.[88]

CONCLUSION

The conclusion is that there can be no defensible doubt that the gospel of Mark is a source, however minor, of Acts.[89] As more than intimated above, this conclusion lends weight to the supposition that some of the material in Acts is Lucan composition imitative of Mark. As indicated above, the leading candidates are the miracle stories of 3:1–9; 9:33–35; 9:36–42; 14:8–10; and 28:8–9.[90] Justification for this hypothesis arises from Luke's evident proclivity for turning such Markan accounts and summaries as 5:21–43 and 6:56 into entirely new *incidents*. The means by which he assimilates the passions of Stephen and Paul to that of Jesus have long been observed;[91] Further reflection upon the use of Mark in Acts strengthens the hypothesis that much of this parallelism results not from the mere "tweaking" of sources, but from outright composition.[92]

This hypothesis receives additional nourishment from the use of Mark as a source, i.e., inspiration, for Luke's gospel. Two leading examples of this activity are the healing of the crippled woman, Luke 13:10–17, and the cleansing of the ten lepers, Luke 17:11–19. The former conforms to the contents of Mark 3:1–6// Luke 6:6–11, a Sabbath exorcism in the synagogue that leads to a controversy. The longer story in Luke 13 contains many features proper to miracle stories, as well as those pertinent to a pronouncement story. Mixed types are more likely to be secondary, i.e., editorial. That does not establish Lucan composition, but literary features are suggestive. These include the number "eighteen," which links to the previous passage (Luke 13:4), and the puns upon λύω ("loose," verses 12, 15, 17) and δεῖ ("must," verses 14 and 16 [twice]), all of which suggest literary reflection. Note also that the final acclamation in verse 17 applies not to the healing, which is formally "proper," but to the alteration or supersession of Torah, and that the dual effect of shaming of the leaders and rejoicing by the people is typically Lucan.[93] The latter case (17:11–19) is based upon Mark 1:40–45: cleansed lepers are to show themselves to the priests. Yet Lukan invention is evident. Luke is the only evangelist who features Samaritans in positive roles, most famously in 10:29–37.[94] Further, the situation is highly unrealistic, since Samaritans would hardly resort to Jewish priests affiliated with Jerusalem. Finally, the story is fashioned with 2 Kings 5:10–19 in view, much of which it imitates.[95] All in all, it is very likely that Luke 17:11–19 is a Lucan composition based upon Mark and quite likely that 13:10–17 is also an authorial creation inspired by Mark. From the identification of Mark as an occasional source for the author of Luke and Acts emerge some rather important collateral benefits:

1. Utilization of Mark as a source of Acts constitutes a minor—but rather firm—buttress in the argument for Markan priority, for that gospel is independently attested in the book of Acts. Any hypothesis that accepted the nearly undeniable presence of Mark in the book of Acts but withheld that presence from Luke would require a contraption of baroque detail and dimension.

2. The use of Mark as a source of Acts supports the generally accepted hypothesis that the gospel of Luke is prior to Acts, as it would be positively byzantine to construct an author who would peruse Mark, extract some stray bits for use in Acts, then hit upon the notion of composing a gospel using some edition of Mark[96]) as a major source, and finally proceed to write that gospel while carefully omitting the previously used scraps.

3. The direct evidence reviewed above gives sufficient, if not overwhelming, encouragement to hypotheses that other material in Acts may have been inspired by Marcan scenes or incidents.

4. As promised, Luke's use of Mark in Acts reveals an author who could handle his sources with considerable freedom and aplomb.

Item (2) may be of some assistance in the discussion of Luke's methods of composition. Conclusion (3) could be quite fruitful for "historical" and other purposes, as it affords some weight to conjectures that this or that passage is an original composition based upon gospel material. With regard to some of the traditional source theories, these compositions bridge a wide range, including material assigned by some to "Jerusalem" or "Palestinian" Sources (Acts 1; 5; 6; 9); "Hellenist" material (Acts 6); "Petrine" stories (Acts 9:36–43); "Antiochene" sources (Acts 13); "Pauline" (or direct) material (Acts 24); and even the alleged "We" source (Acts 16:16–18).[97] If the use of the LXX indicated that Luke could do more than supply a passage with allusions, consideration of the use of Mark in Acts adds strong weight to the probability of that "more."[98] For the historian these findings mean that the recovery of Luke's source material in Acts is perilously difficult. An even graver challenge to historicity is the possibility that Luke actually *created* episodes upon the basis of Mark and the LXX. Possibility is not certainty, but the question demands consideration in every applicable case. The historical Paul *may*, for example, have performed an exorcism in Philippi (cf. Acts 16:16–18), but the state of the evidence permits no more than the assertion of a general possibility. Finally, item (4) is of considerable importance for the subsequent chapters, which will argue that our author has used other sources in high-handed and not always easily detectable ways.[99]

Since this discussion of sources is closely related to the question of date, the obvious next step is to address the date of Mark. Here the boundaries are a bit narrower. Few would date Mark before the late 60s or later than 85. R. Brown finds the consensus in the late 60s or very early 70s.[100] Debate persists about the relation of Mark to the First Jewish Revolt (66–73/4). In my view the evidence that Mark is post-70 is quite clear, not simply from the prophecy in 13:1–2,[101] or from the balance of that chapter (such as the warning in v. 23), or even in the evidently decisive Parable of the Tenants in 12:1–12. *The "Jerusalem Ministry" of Jesus in Mark is predicated upon the destruction of the Temple as an accomplished fact.* Mark 11:1–24 frames the symbolic closing of the Temple with the cursing of the fig tree. The Temple has been cursed and will "die."[102] Shortly thereafter (12:1–12), Jesus, teaching in the Temple, tells the story of the "Wicked" Tenants. In its present form this is an allegory of salvation history, ending with two questions asked and answered by Jesus (9–11), both of which are secondary to the hypothetical earlier parable.[103] The first question reads: "What then will the owner of the vineyard do?" The answer: "He will come and *destroy* the tenants and *give* the vineyard to others." (τί [οὖν] ποιήσει ὁ κύριος τοῦ ἀμπελῶνος; ἐλεύσεται καὶ ἀπολέσει τοὺς γεωργούς, καὶ δωσει τὸν ἀμπελῶνα ἄλλοις, Mark 12:9) This verse refers to the *destruction* of Israel (a recurrent theme in Mark 11–13) and to subsequent operation under new management. The latter is less a claim of religious supersession than a description of the political fate of Judea. According to Josephus *Jewish War* 7.216 Vespasian directed the Procurator [L.] Liberius Maximus to sell (ἀποδόσθαι, a compound of the verb "give" used in Mark 12:9) all the land of the Judeans.[104] This action, however extensive it eventually became, was scarcely launched before 72.[105] Mark 12 was written in the light of this proposed redistribution.

I think that the burden of proof lies upon those who wish to date Mark *prior* to 75 rather than after 70. Since Mark is a source of Acts, as it had been for Luke, the *terminus a quo* of Acts is therefore c. 75 CE. One may now move up by fifteen years the *terminus a quo* of 60 that was established by the dramatic date of Acts 26–28. The earliest possible date for Acts is 75–80, [106] and the range is 75/80–130. Attempts to narrow this range through the identification of sources as chronological benchmarks will continue in the next two sections. Chapters Four and Five will revisit the hypotheses that Luke used letters of Paul and had access to at least some of the writings of the Jewish historian Flavius Josephus. Both of these investigations will build upon the far from novel insights of this chapter about Luke's creative approach to his sources. In addition to the contribution they may make to the question of date, these studies will further illuminate the character of Luke as historian and theologian.

4 Acts among the Apostles
The Letters of Paul[1]

INTRODUCTION

Sir William Mitchell Ramsay, late nineteenth century explorer of Turkey and pioneer scholar of the immediate geographical and historical background of much of Acts, ardent opponent of the "Tübingen School," and a convert from the views of F. C. Baur who became a tireless missionary against critical skepticism, shared one conclusion with Baur and his heirs.[2] After discussing a number of the personal authorities for and oral sources of Acts, including Paul and John Mark, he continues:

> Luke added to these authorities an obvious acquaintance with Paul's own letters. He rarely states anything that is recorded in them; he assumes them as known; and he makes it one of his objects to set them in a clearer light.[3]   78

The "obvious acquaintance with Paul's own letters" that Ramsay could treat in two sentences is one of the great man's confident assertions that his ideological successors have allowed to languish. Colin Hemer, whose assumption of Ramsay's mantle is widely acknowledged, begins his effort to refute any claims of disparity between Acts and Paul's letters on what he holds to be safe ground:

> We start from the widely accepted point that Luke shows no knowledge of the Pauline Epistles. There are diverse explanations of that phenomenon. It has been used to argue a very early or a very late for Acts. It could mean that the Epistles were not seen as a matter of special note during Paul's life. But our present point is a simple one, that Acts is agreed to be essentially independent of the Epistles, whatever the explanation for the fact.[4]

The silence of Acts on the subject of Paul's letter-writing looms like a dense and impenetrable fog over the traditional "introductory questions." Efforts to cope with this miasma have been ingenious and numerous. If there is any consensus on this matter, it is well stated by Hemer. One may seek to skirt the edges of the fog or barge through it; the least acceptable solution is to turn on a fog light. Those who skirt the edges invoke this silence to claim that Acts was written before the letters of Paul became well known or after they had become too well-known to be discussed in "polite" (proto-orthodox) society.[5] A substantial majority of scholars simply barge through, oblivious to the academic wreckage in which they have become entangled. I side with those who are imprudent

51

enough to turn on a fog light. Such a beacon reveals the utter risibility of any contention that the author of Acts was unaware of Paul's epistolary creations; indeed, it renders that claim unworthy of serious scholarly consideration.[6] Scarcely more credible is the claim that Luke would have found these letters of little if any use, even if he had known of them. These assertions would scarcely see the light of day were it not for the established consensus that Luke did not use Paul's letters.

Because of that consensus this chapter is both lengthy and detailed. My openly avowed strategy is to provide arguments so numerous, varied, and supported in depth that only the most brazen critics will pretend that they can dismiss them by saying, "I find the claims that Luke used Pauline correspondence unconvincing." Arguments of the following sort are of necessity quantitative and cumulative, for their intended aim is not simply to build the case that Luke used a few Pauline letters that enjoyed early and independent circulation—specifically, Romans and 1 Corinthians—but to demonstrate that Luke and Acts establish their author's knowledge and use of a published collection of letters. Since the existence of such an edition cannot safely be dated prior to c. 100 CE, this source would establish a *terminus a quo* of that date. Moreover, here and in Chapters Six and Seven I seek to demonstrate that Luke operated from a Deutero-Pauline perspective: i.e., his views of Paul belong to the reception and reinterpretation of Paul's thought that emerged in the final decade of the first century and the opening two decades of the second. A further suggestion is that the sources of Acts may have included correspondence that is no longer extant.

The significance of these arguments extends beyond their relevance for the date and theology of Acts. This further relevance touches upon the core of the reluctance to acknowledge that Luke knew Paul's letters, a disinclination arising from the fact that if he did know them, his standing as an historian lies open to censure. As in the cases of Mark and the Septuagint already presented, and in the matter of Josephus, use of which will occupy the following chapter, Luke's appropriation of Paul demonstrates that he did not employ primary sources to discover "what actually happened," but as aids in imposing his own construction of the past. This proposal contains nothing novel; indeed, appreciation of Luke's overall use of sources has led to the deterioration of the old consensus that he could not have used the letters of Paul. In short, a grasp of Luke's attitude toward his sources has prepared the way for a fresh appreciation of the question of whether he knew and used the letters.

Paul the Letter-Writer and Letters in Early Christianity

Luke and Paul differ greatly in method. Paul wrote letters, and did so when he could not visit a particular community.[7] As modern scholarship has emphasized, a letters substitutes for a visit between two parties who are separated by physical, social, legal, or emotional distance. One writes absent friends, remote superiors, and/or when careful wording or concrete proof is needed. In Acts, however, Paul does not write; he visits. And the absence of reported conflicts or problems removes the sense of urgency often evident in the letters. But two anomalous situations are worth noting. First, upon failing to stop at Ephesus in Acts 20, Paul does not write a letter but summons its leaders to visit with (i.e., to listen to) him. This was not an option that the historical Paul could have utilized with great frequency. Second, after Paul's arrest is reported in 21:33, Acts reports not a single word about any of the churches he has founded. With the farewell at Ephesus Paul had finished his task in the East and did not resume his missionary burden until he had come to Rome. That perspective is exactly the view taken in Romans 15. This document, written from Ephesus, should prove inter- *v. 23* esting to those who wonder where Luke acquired this notion. Others may wish to assert, with perfect certitude, that one item Luke did *not* take from the letters of Paul was his "daily pressure because of my anxiety for all the churches" (2 Corinthians 11:28).

It should also be noted that those who wanted to correct or criticize Paul did so, in part, by writing letters (James, 2 Thessalonians, 2 Timothy, 2 Peter). When the Christian community at Rome took exception to an action of its fellow believers at Corinth around 100, it wrote them a letter (*1 Clement*). The Roman Christians were evidently familiar with stories about Paul:

> Because of jealousy and strife, Paul showed how to win the prize of patient endurance: seven times he was in bonds, he was banished, he was stoned, he became a messenger (of the gospel) in both east and west, and earned well-merited fame for his faith; for he taught righteousness to the whole world, having traveled to the limits of the west; and when he had borne his witness before the rulers, he departed from the world an outstanding example of patient endurance.[8]

They were also familiar with letters. At the beginning of chapter 47 the Corinthians are exhorted to "take up the letter of blessed Paul the apostle." The letter alluded to is 1 Corinthians, which *1 Clement* could cite in full assurance that its contents were familiar to those at Corinth.[9] Paul's letter-writing technique made such an impact that it became the normal means of communication among believers, even when the document more closely resembles a sermon or treatise than an actual letter (cf. James, Hebrews). Imitations included not only the "deutero-Pauline" (i. e., non-authentic) Colossians, Ephesians, 2 Thessalonians, 1–2 Timothy, and Titus, and the work of the above mentioned critics of Paul, but also that of such ardent admirers as Ignatius of Antioch and Polycarp of Smyrna, as well as the "non-aligned" 1 Peter and 2–3 John. To these one may add Jude and the seven letters in the book of Revelation. Although no one claims that Paul invented the epistle or that no early Christian would have written a letter had the apostle not initiated the practice, the prominence of letters in early Christian literature is heavily indebted to the example and impact of Paul. The continuous production of Deutero-Pauline letters from c. 75 to c. 125 (and beyond[10]) decisively refutes the theory that the epistles were long neglected.[11]

Paul's letters were already controversial in his own lifetime. "I do not want to seem as though I am trying to frighten you with my letters. For they say, 'His letters are weighty and strong, but his bodily presence is weak, and his speech contemptible.'" (2 Corinthians 10:9–10.) In 2 Corinthians 3:1–6 Paul has to contend with a painful deficit in his résumé: letters of recommendation. Luke is familiar with the genre, for Acts 18:27 mentions a letter of recommendation dispatched to, of all places, Corinth. The subject of that epistle was Apollos.[12] Nor is the author of Acts unfamiliar with the use of letters as instruments for the communication of church policy. John Knox says,

> It is striking that, although Paul does not write letters in the Acts narrative, the Twelve *do* write a letter . . . It is given to Paul and Barnabas to deliver. Paul's only connection with church letters in the Acts of the Apostles is as *the bearer of a letter written by the Twelve.*[13]

I fear that Knox is guilty of exaggeration when he says that Paul is no more than a mailman in Acts, for in fact that important task was entrusted to the Jerusalem representatives Judas Barsabbas and Silas. Far from being elevated to an active role in the postal service, Paul and Barnabas did no more than to *accompany* the letter carriers.[14] The Paul of Acts not only fails to write letters, he is scarcely allowed to touch one. At this point one looks for someone to propose that, like the well-known lady, the author "doth protest too much."

Morton Enslin is thus following the proper, if unladylike, scent when he says that "the real question" is not, "Why did Luke not make use of the letters?" but "Why does Luke never hint that Paul wrote letters?"[15] For a half century Enslin was a rather lonely voice in repeatedly raising the question,[16] but the dialectical tide now appears to be flowing, albeit slowly, once more in the direction of acknowledging some use of Paul's letters by Luke.[17] This chapter is an attempt to go with that flow. Enslin states that rejection of Paul's letters as a source for Acts was a result of the reaction against the Tübingen school and claims that this reaction became, like its polar opposite, *"une sorte de these qui n'a pas besoin de démonstration,"* the "assured results of higher criticism."[18]

The major reasons for the deterioration of the long-held claim of non-usage are the contemporary view of Luke as a creative writer who made free use of some of his sources and scholarly acceptance of the view that Luke's purposes differed from those of present-day historians. This is to say that the question can no longer be dismissed by resorting to the shoulds and woulds that posit what Luke *would* have done and how he *should* have used Paul. Statements of this nature reveal what their proponents would do, but shed no light upon ancient practices in general or upon Lucan practice in particular. They are egocentric and anachronistic. Especially painful for some has been the inevitable conclusion that, if Luke knew Pauline letters, he ignored them at some points and contradicted them at others. Why this experience should be more painful than it is with regard to the gospel of Mark—which Luke also ignored at some points and contradicted more than once—is not perfectly clear, but there can be no doubt that it has been a burden.[19] As Enslin says, "The common denial . . . that Luke knew or used the Pauline letters needs fresh consideration instead of automatic repetition."[20] As the followers of the Artemis of Ephesus allegedly learned (Acts 19:21–40), constant reiteration of a claim does not make it valid or effective.

Revising Paul

Those who like analogies might wish to compare Luke to a public relations director who has most happily taken up the task of refurbishing the image of Paul. The problem is not that Paul has been *forgotten*. Dear me, no. Everyone in the Greek-speaking Jesus movements knows of him. People tend either to revere Paul or revile him. The truly neutral are few in number, while the merely indifferent could meet on a park bench with room to spare. While some may revere Paul just a shade too much or possibly for some of the wrong reasons, the Paul-haters are often misinformed and frequently misguided. Were those creatures to win, the fruits of the gentile mission would be driven to find solace with the radicals, whose victory would cut nearly all ties with the Israelite past and thus sever links with more observant believers.[21] Luke believes that he knows what is needed to keep the ship afloat, and he is keenly aware of what most people want, of "what sells" in his day and age. But he is not without principles. If Luke knew of any Pauline letters, Romans and 1 Corinthians would be leading candidates, for these enjoyed the widest early currency.[22] 1 Corinthians provided dire warnings of the dangers of divisions, particularly those associated with factions that appealed to different leaders, including Peter, Paul, and Apollos.[23] For its part, Romans offered a picture of a Paul in pursuit of peace and eager to place himself in a good light with believers who were more observant of Torah. And the Paul of Ephesians 6:10–17 campaigns upon a rather militant platform of peace.

Grounded in this view of a Paul who sought peace among different groups of Christians and abhorred divisiveness, Luke could set out to show that figure in action. Not unlike those who now contend that Luke would have used this or said that had he known the letters, the author of Acts knew what Paul would or should have said and done given the present circumstances and proceeded to show him saying and doing it. If Peter, Paul, and James were ardent seekers after unity, later Christians who appealed to individual authorities in support of partisan views could be exposed as betrayers of apostolic ideals. Luke's Paul is, as all seem at least in part to agree, a "revisionist" Paul, a figure shaped to meet the needs of a later era. The most likely grounds for Luke's refusal to mention Paul as a writer of letters was the potentially divisive quality of these documents in certain circles. Others "revised" Paul by issuing new letters under his name. Letters like Colossians and Ephesians stressed (and/or sought to manage) certain speculative thrusts within the Pauline legacy; another, 2 Thessalonians, spouted the fire and brimstone of apocalyptic vigor, while yet others (the

Pastoral Epistles—1–2 Timothy and Titus) placed Paul firmly in the camp of doctrinal orthodoxy and conservative social values.[24] Luke shares some of these goals, including much of the social orientation of the pastorals and the peace program of Ephesians, but his narrative left the matter of letter writing to one side. Any for whom such a revision seems highly improbable are referred to the revisions of Israelite history in Deuteronomy and in 1–2 Chronicles.

Excursus: An Analogy from American History

To those who may desire a more pertinent analogy there is the revisionist history of the American Civil War and the figure of Robert Edward Lee. In the period between c. 1900 and c. 1950 the United States achieved some unity through accepting a number of compromises. Among these were legal segregation, followed by the eventual disenfranchisement of southern Blacks, and a re-writing of history. In this history the anti-slavery advocates of "radical reconstruction" were the "bad guys." Abraham Lincoln was a moderate. As for the war, its towering figure was R. E. Lee, the finest general of the conflict, if not of history, who could be defeated only by brute force. Lee was himself a moderate, opposed to slavery. He was thus equipped to become a national hero, revered, like Lincoln, by all. On the other hand, the victorious generals, especially Grant and Sherman, were dreadful villains. The former was a drunken butcher who had no better strategy than crude attrition, while the latter was a barbarian who left a host of slaughtered civilians in his wake as he ravaged innocent Georgia and poor South Carolina. To epitomize the callous incompetence of Grant one need only point to the gruesome slaughter at Cold Harbor, 3 June 1864. The gallantry of Lee and company was incarnated in Pickett's heroic charge at Gettysburg, 3 July 1863. In fact, both attacks were bad ideas, and each resulted in similar casualties.[25] Yet Cold Harbor was a mistake that became no more than a grim incident, while Gettysburg was a major defeat with vast consequences.

For the purposes of this analogy, it is important to note that the revisionist view did not make a silk purse out of a sow's ear. Robert Lee *was* a general of considerable ability and great moral strength, a beloved leader and an often compassionate and considerate man, proud but never arrogant, always courteous and intent upon conforming his life to Christian principles as he saw them. The revisionist picture magnified virtues of "the historical Lee" and ignored some unpleasant facts.[26] In this picture his opponent, Grant, shone only when he offered Lee's army generous terms.[27]

The revisers certainly never emphasized that Lee fought with great persistence and brilliant audacity on the side of disunion and slavery, or that he had taken an oath to defend the United States against all enemies, foreign and domestic. This is the great silence that has ruled Civil War history up to the present. Like the protagonist of *The Man without a Country*, one must never hear the words "United States."[28] We have, of course, Confederate armies representing the would-be C.S.A., but their opponents are always "Union" or "Federal" forces, not the U. S. Army that all acknowledged them to be. It would appear that the United States of America disappeared between December 1860 and June 1865, and in the interval groups of states engaged in a lamentable armed conflict, "the War between the States." In short, Lee and other Confederates never fought against the U.S. Recent years have brought much pointed and welcome criticism to the revision, not least to its racism.[29] This needed "counter-revision" should not obscure what the earlier revision achieved: a strong sense of national unity.[30]

If Luke's project involved a number of disturbing silences and adjustments of the truth, it accomplished much in the service of early and subsequent Christian unity. Crafting this story with its various facets and particular nuances was vastly more important to Luke than "accuracy" in reporting stages on journeys and the nicer points of particular theologies. It was more expedient that Paul should lose the corpus of his letters than that his whole body go into hell.

Several important but rarely stated objections to the possible dependence of Acts upon Pauline letters derive neither from thorough investigation nor the difficulty of explaining why Luke had not heard of these letters, but from the assumed "historicity" of Acts. The proposal that Luke utilized letters of Paul infringes upon the standing of Luke the historian not only because of its implications for Luke as a reliable reporter of data from his sources,[31] but also because if Luke did have access to Paul, all of the arguments based upon factual overlap between Acts and the epistles would evaporate. Gone would be the "undesigned coincidences" between Paul and Luke.[32] A a vast amount of paper filled with elaborate lucubrations intended to show agreements and harmonize alleged conflicts between Luke and Paul would go up in smoke. In terms of ethical warrants, there long prevailed the anachronistic assumption that such activity on Luke's part would have been immoral, and that conviction of tampering with Paul's letters would have disqualified his testimony to the Christian faith. The nineteenth century dogma of the "inerrancy of the Bible" walked hand in hand with the notion that what Luke is now known to have done with his sources (including Mark and Scripture) is "wrong." Many who have abandoned the concept of biblical inerrancy have, consciously or otherwise, retained its anachronistic Victorian moral correlative.[33]

The Issue and a Touchstone

Another problem is, to put it succinctly, that if the narrative of Acts "deconstructs," little more than sand remains upon which to erect a narrative of Christian history between c. 30 and c. 60 CE. Many critical scholars would subscribe in theory to the proposition that the Paul of Acts is no more and no less the historical Paul than the Jesus of Luke is the historical Jesus.[34] Critical scholarly writing reveals that a majority of the guild endorses this proposition with silent reservations, most of which boil down to a desperate plea: "But, without Acts, we should have nothing." It would be unseemly for the emperor to be without clothing. One goal of the Westar Institute's Acts Seminar has been to expose these reservations and demand that they be subjected to scrutiny. The object of this enterprise is not to acquire notoriety or to bask in the pleasure of bashing absent "Fundamentalists." It is the same object that resulted in one of the most honored accomplishments of American biblical scholarship: *The*

Beginnings of Christianity: Part One, whose leaders, F. J. Foakes Jackson (1855–1941) and Kirsopp Lake (1872–1946), presumed that the first step toward writing the history of primitive Christianity was a painstaking, objective scrutiny of the book of Acts.[35] In a decidedly post-Constantinian age it is imperative to determine whether the emperor has any clothes.[36]

But if despite considerable reluctance the use of Pauline correspondence in Acts is established, two major problems relative to the value of this hypothesis for dating the book remain: whether Luke knew a *collection* of Pauline letters, and if so, the extent and date of that collection.[37] If Luke did have access to a seven or ten-letter collection, a date before 100 would be unlikely.[38] A smaller anthology, including Romans and 1 Corinthians, each of which seems to have enjoyed individual circulation, may have existed twenty or even thirty years earlier.[39] A sort of "Carbon-14" benchmark is provided by 2 Corinthians, a composite text not attested before Marcion (c. 140) and not circulated before 100 CE.[40] If Acts made use of 2 Corinthians as we know it, its *terminus a quo* can reasonably be set at c. 100.

The foregoing leads to some preliminary investigative presuppositions. Luke *was* aware that Paul wrote letters. Even if the letters lacked so much as an occasional reading in the assemblies of Christians who valued a Pauline heritage, it is highly unlikely that he had never heard or read at least some of them.[41] The actual question, then, is not *whether,* but *how* and *how much* Paul's thought and letters influenced Luke. To the best of my knowledge, not simply consensus but *unanimity* obtains on the question of Pauline influence upon Acts. This includes the full range of scholarly opinion, from those who date it near 60 and view that influence as personal, to those who date the work c. 150 and think that Luke has retained faint traces of Pauline thought and made some careless (mis)use of the epistles. As with examples from Josephus (which will receive attention in the following chapter), this endeavor will not resemble the type of source criticism common in the investigation of the Synoptic Gospels, in which the verbal evidence for dependence of one sort or another is overwhelming. With the possible exception of Luke 22:17–20, the examples will be relatively subtle and often tentative—more typical of the customary ancient use of sources than what one finds in the relations among Matthew, Mark, and Luke. The journey will begin with a short but important step: consideration of the general influence of Pauline thought upon Luke and Acts.

Justification by Faith

Acts 13:38–39 is a sound starting point: At the climax of his sermon in the synagogue at Antioch in Pisidia, Paul proclaims,

> Let it be known to you therefore, my brothers, that through this man forgiveness of sins is proclaimed to you; by this Jesus everyone who believes is set free (δικαιοῦται) from all those sins from which you could not be freed (δικαιωθῆναι) by the law of Moses.

In this dramatic setting the claim that the Torah was defective would have angered—or at least confused—the faithful. Luke is providing the speech with a proper splash of Pauline color and presenting a mild form of the Pauline doctrine of justification by faith. William O. Walker puts it sharply: "it is far from clear, from this passage, that Luke really understands the doctrine, and it is evident that the doctrine holds little real interest for him." Luke's own understanding of that doctrine emerges in a speech of Peter (Acts 15:7–11).[42] This is an essentially gentile view of the Torah as an impossible burden that could not be fulfilled.[43] Luke was therefore aware of distinct Pauline theological views, which, he is pleased to record, were shared by Peter and by . . . Jesus.

> Jesus also told this parable to some who trusted in themselves that they were righteous (δίκαιοι) and regarded others with contempt: "Two men went up to the temple to pray, one a Pharisee and the other a tax collector. The Pharisee, standing by himself, was praying thus, 'God, I thank you that I am not like other people: thieves, rogues, adulterers, or even like this tax collector. I fast twice a week; I give a tenth of all my income.' But the tax collector, standing far off, would not even look up to heaven, but was beating his breast and saying, 'God, be merciful to me, a sinner!' I tell you, this man went down to his home justified (δεδικαιωμένος) rather than the other; for all who exalt themselves will be humbled, but all who humble themselves will be exalted." (Luke 18:9–14)[44]

This "Parable of the Pharisee and the Publican" is unique to Luke and marked by several Lucan features, such as the Temple as a place for prayer, sympathy for the "marginal," interest in appealing to the rich, and a sentimental outlook.[45] The view of "justification" on display here is very much like the Pauline "justification of the ungodly," justification based upon faith, not determined by "works." God "forgave" the toll-collector because he repented.[46] Luke thus anchors firmly in the teaching of Jesus his own understanding (or limitation) of the Pauline doctrine of justification by faith.[47] This both acquits Paul of the charge of innovation and establishes him as a faithful witness to Jesus, attested by one more "parallel."[48] But the parable in Luke 18 is very general, and the doctrine expressed in Acts 13 seems quite the same. Can one relate the latter to any particular passage? Andreas Lindemann thinks not.[49] While this is doubtless a prudent conclusion, I should like to note that the expression "by law" (Acts 13:39: ἐν τούτῳ/ἐν νόμῳ, where the preposition has an instrumental thrust) is found in association with the verb "justify" (δικαιόω) elsewhere *only* in Galatians (3:11; 5:4).[50]

Further evidence comes from the crucial and pivotal chapter 15 of Acts. As will be shown below, Peter's speech in Acts 15:7–11 recasts the story of the Conversion of Cornelius that was narrated in Acts 10 and summarized by Peter in a speech in 11:1–18. In Acts 15 Peter appeals to the acceptance of Cornelius, an event that was ratified by the spirit, as proof of what Paul taught—that is, as Luke chose to understand the Pauline doctrine of justification by faith. Although Cornelius had been characterized as pious and moral and therefore amenable to religious instruction, 10:1–11:18 does not appeal to or even mention the power of faith. This new slant, "... in cleansing their hearts by faith *God* has made no distinction between them [gentiles] and us (15:9)," implies that the first gentile convert, won by Peter at divine behest, had entered the body of the faithful on the same grounds as had all those converted by Paul. This reinterpretation is no minor matter. With the other examples, it demonstrates that Luke not only found in Paul's letters an important source of particular facts, but also that he subscribed to a Pauline theology: deutero-Pauline, to be sure, but none the less Pauline.

Those who enjoy collecting interesting "coincidences" will need a large basket to get through this chapter. It will soon be supplied. In this and the cases to follow, relevant data will be presented in convenient tables, as in earlier chapters. In these tables, unless otherwise indicated:

> *Italics* call attention to a word or words indicating a relationship to another passage.[51]
> **Bold face** calls attention to identical words.

A Definitive Example: 2 Corinthians

The two passages presented in Table 4.1a refer to the same "event," Paul's flight from Damascus.[52] They share a setting (Damascus), attempted apprehension (by "Jews"/governor guarding the city), a threat (to kill/seize Paul), and an escape by the picturesque device of being lowered to the ground from an aperture high in the wall. Of the two, Luke's account is clearly secondary, for it

Table 4.1a: 2 Corinthians 1: The Basket Case

Acts 9:23–25	2 Corinthians 11:32–33
(In *Damascus*)	ἐν *Δαμασκῷ* ὁ ἐθνάρχης Ἁρέτα
Ὡς δὲ ἐπληροῦντο ἡμέραι ἱκαναί,	τοῦ βασιλέως ἐφρούρει τὴν πόλιν
συνεβουλεύσαντο οἱ Ἰουδαῖοι	Δαμασκηνῶν πιάσαι με, 33 καὶ διὰ
ἀνελεῖν αὐτόν· 24 ἐγνώσθη δὲ	θυρίδος **ἐν σαργάνῃ ἐχαλάσθην**
τῷ Σαύλῳ ἡ ἐπιβουλὴ αὐτῶν.	**διὰ τοῦ τείχους** καὶ ἐξέφυγον τὰς
παρετηροῦντο δὲ καὶ τὰς πύλας	χεῖρας αὐτοῦ.
ἡμέρας τε καὶ νυκτὸς ὅπως	
αὐτὸν ἀνέλωσιν· 25 λαβόντες	
δὲ οἱ μαθηταὶ αὐτοῦ νυκτὸς **διὰ**	
τοῦ τείχους καθῆκαν αὐτὸν	
χαλάσαντες ἐν σπυρίδι.	
After some time had passed, the Jews plotted to kill him, but their plot became known to Saul. They were watching the gates day and night so that they might kill him; but his disciples took him by night and *let him down through an opening in the wall, lowering him in a basket.*	In Damascus, the governor under King Aretas guarded the city of Damascus in order to seize me, but I *was let down in a basket through a window in the wall,* and escaped from his hands.

is difficult to believe that no sooner was Paul converted and preaching his new faith than a murder plot boiled up in the synagogues of Damascus. Given the view of Acts that Jerusalem authorities could have dispatched a letter ordering his detention and extradition this seems strange; after all, Paul had originally come to Damascus on just such a mission. Rather than, say, whack him in his bed or chop him down on the street, "the Jews" elect, with apparent conniv- ance from the authorities, to guard the city gates in order to slay the nefarious missionary as he leaves town. By one means or another Saul uncovers this vile scheme. Rather than wait his adversaries out (and add numerous converts to the band of Jesus' followers at Damascus), the resourceful vessel of election (9:15), aided by intrepid disciples, engineers a daring nocturnal escape.

Outside of the logical and political anomaly—one wonders who would authorize "the Jews" to mount a watch at the city gates to apprehend a reli- gious deviant whose undesirable behavior within the city would therefore continue as long as he desired—is the improbability of flight to Jerusalem in order to evade a Jewish plot. Paul flits from frying pan to fire. The little tale in 2 Corinthians *does* make sense. Evidently his adversary, the ethnarch (governor) of King Aretas, lacked jurisdiction within the limits of Damascus and posted guards to arrest Paul the moment he left the city. Alternatively, the danger was from within, and Paul eluded the sentinels posted to arrest him.[53]

Luke has written a nice little adventure complete with base villains thwarted by boldness and ingenuity. Paul, for his part, was telling a story on himself as part of a mock-heroic catalogue of exploits boasting of his "weakness" and "folly" (2 Cor. 11:1–12:10).[54] This particular "credential" is the inverse of the decoration given to the first soldier to scale a wall during an assault.[55] At one time I speculated that the source might have been "a rumor circulated to dis- credit Paul by describing his cowardice."[56] Perhaps this was a good guess, but I herewith retract and recant it. Yet in favor of that conjecture was the implicit recognition that Luke had no "heroic legend" upon which to improve. The lack of any grounds for positing an independent source for the story of Paul's depar- ture from Damascus means that the only feasible candidate for Luke's source is 2 Corinthians 10–13.[57] This conclusion gains support from the relatively rare words that link the two accounts, but the stronger reason is the improbability that either a "Pauline tradition" glorifying the apostle or a hostile (oral) source would preserve the distinctive language.[58] Luke has taken up and transformed an item from Paul's correspondence. The camel's nose, to use a metaphor con- genial to the environs of Damascus, is under the tent. While one clear case does not validate every contention; it does resolve the basic question and provide authorization for further investigation and other proposals. The inversion of fact represented in the appropriation of 2 Corinthians to Acts 9 is quite in character with Luke's uses of sources and highly characteristic of his "portrait of Paul" with its related political agenda, which is to place the blame for Paul's problems on "the Jews" whenever possible—and sometimes, as in this case, when not possible. In brief, this is what one would expect Luke to do with a story of this sort, when the source of that story is a letter of Paul.[59]

Therefore the likely conclusion is that Luke made use of canonical 2 Corinthians, which is not attested before c. 120–130 (Marcion, possibly Polycarp)[60] and was not available before 100. A rather compelling argument for 100 as the *terminus a quo* of 2 Corinthians is a negative one: *1 Clement*, which makes some use of Romans and much of 1 Corinthians, does not know 2 Corinthians. The latter would have been manna from heaven for the composer(s) of *1 Clement*, because it presents the founding apostle, Paul, vigorously chastising the Corinthian believers for rebelling against lawful ("apostolic") authority—and that is the very subject of *1 Clement* itself.[61] Since a community as important and diverse as Rome would in all probability, have been among the first to obtain a full collection of Pauline letters, *1 Clement*'s ignorance of 2 Corinthians is a robust argument from silence. A secondary argument, exploration of which transcends the limits of this study, is the composite nature of 2 Corinthians—an assemblage of varied pieces predicated upon an idealized picture of Paul not unlike that of Acts. The character and content of canonical 2 Corinthians suggest that it was compiled toward the end of the first century, if not later.[62]

As so often happens, an insect has infiltrated the unction. It is possible though not highly probable that the author of Acts could have consulted—presumably at Ephesus—the original of the fragment found in 2 Corinthians 10–13 from which the Damascus incident derives.[63] That possibility remains. If, however, further investigation reveals that Luke shows knowledge of other parts of 2 Corinthians and that he made use of not only Romans and the Corinthian correspondence, but also Galatians, 1 Thessalonians, and possibly Philippians, the probability that Luke made use of a published edition of Pauline letters will be too strong to be dislodged. I believe that further investigation will reveal just that.[64] (See Table 4.1b.)

If Luke had access to canonical 2 Corinthians or to the fragment that now comprises 2 Corinthians 10–13, the question of the "catalogue of hardships" in 11:21b-29 arises. Table 4.1b cites the relevant portion from that passage, together with data from Acts. For comparative purposes the table includes some items from the summary of *1 Clement* 5:5–7 and data from the *Acts of Paul*. The last is quite incomplete, however, and it would be unwise to make inferences from negative evidence. I assume that the data from *1 Clement* are not derived from the epistles.[65] Further assumptions are that Acts may have known *1 Clement*, but that the *Acts of Paul* perhaps did not; that both of the Acts were familiar with at least of some Pauline letters; and that the *Acts of Paul* knew the canonical Acts.

2 Corinthians 11:23–26 could be introduced on both sides of the dependency question, but with less than overwhelming force in either case, for both must explain what is absent in Acts. To be sure, any who would argue against knowledge of 2 Corinthians by Luke on the grounds that Luke "should" have narrated three additional shipwrecks and three beatings with rods—not to mention bandits, river, and wilderness—have a poor case. Ten "shoulds" add up to zero.[66] These data also constitute a problem for those who hold that the

Table 4.1b: 2 Corinthians 2: Catalogues and Data

2 Cor 11:23–26	1 Clem 5:6	Acts	Acts of Paul
23. "far more imprisonments"[67]	Seven times in bonds	16:23; 21:33–end[68]	3:17–18[69]; 7, p.3; 8.3.35; 11.3
24 Five times I have received from the Jews the forty lashes minus one.	–	–	–
25 Three times I was beaten with rods.	–	16:23 (once)	–
Once I received a stoning.	Stoned	14:19	–
Three times I was shipwrecked . . .	–	27:39–44 (once)	–
26 on frequent journeys, in danger from rivers,	"Herald in East & West"	X	X
	–	–	
danger from bandits, danger from	–		–
my own people,		X	
danger from		X	X
Gentiles, danger in		X	X
the city, danger in			1[70]
the wilderness,		–	
danger at sea,		27	–
danger from false			3.4; 8.3
brothers and sisters;	Exiled	13:50 (cf. 16:37)	3.21

Note: In **Table 4.1b** "X" represents a theme that is found a number of times in the Acts.

author of Acts was a companion of Paul and/or that he had access to first-hand sources, for in that case also it becomes necessary to explain Luke's selectivity.[71] This is precisely the line most likely to be adopted by those who would argue that Luke *had* seen this material. Excepting matters of great importance, such as the conversions of Paul and Cornelius, Luke prefers variety and tends to provide a single example of each specific kind of incident. Prior to the climactic events of chapter 27, Mother Nature prefers to smooth the missionary path; travel is never dangerous or arduous for Paul until his final voyage. And so forth. All in all, arguments based upon Lucan theology and technique provide better arguments for omission than does the evocation of the "shoulds," but neither rationale may be labeled "decisive." The sole exception is the stoning of verse 25, not because of the adverb "once," but because Acts 14:19–20 is part of a section where tradition seems thin and the episode itself quite tenuous. At its basis is the scenario of hostile Jews pursuing Paul from place to place. In 14:5 Iconian Jews and gentiles threatened to stone Paul and Barnabas. In verse

19 Jews from Antioch and Iconium arrive in Lystra hot on the heels of the missionaries, and persuade those who had just attempted to worship the missionaries to stone them. Although stoning was a typical form of communal punishment, the episode is improbable. It could have been inspired by 2 Corinthians 11, but the likelihood is slight. From the historical perspective, the "omissions" of Acts are rather more interesting.

Only two items appear in all four columns: that Paul was arrested on a number of occasions, and that he engaged in extensive travel. Neither of these is unusual or particularly specific. Equally unsurprising, from the perspective of Acts, is omission of the threat of "danger from false brothers and sisters." Luke holds the view that "heresy" did not appear until after the first teachers of the Way had gone to their reward.[72] Errant believers usually repented or dropped dead. And 2 Corinthians 11:24 is quite intriguing. Luke has but one example of a whipping ordered by Jewish authorities (5:40). "The Jews" do not discipline Paul; they attempt to kill him. Whether he read this passage or was present on the scene or received the account from knowing informants, it is not difficult to understand why Luke would have omitted these punishments. The Paul of Acts does not submit to judgment by the synagogue. When rejected, he withdraws from it, taking his adherents with him (13:46; 18:6; 28:28).[73] In sum, 2 Corinthians 11:23–26 is a fascinating passage for discussions of Acts and history, but it does not demonstrate dependence upon the epistles.

Gospel Traditions

The next example relates to the theme of justification by showing the coherence of ethics in Luke and Paul. Table 4.2 examines lists of sinful types. The catalogue of Luke 18:11, "Thieves, rogues, adulterers . . ." also has similarities to the Pauline tradition. "Thieves" occurs here, in Matthew 7:15; and in 1 Corinthians

Table 4.2: Listing Sinners

Luke 18:11	1 Corinthians 6:9–10
ὁ Φαρισαῖος σταθεὶς πρὸς ἑαυτὸν ταῦτα προσηύχετο, Ὁ θεός, εὐχαριστῶ σοι ὅτι οὐκ εἰμὶ ὥσπερ οἱ λοιποὶ τῶν ἀνθρώπων, **ἅρπαγες**, **ἄδικοι, μοιχοί**, ἢ καὶ ὡς οὗτος ὁ τελώνης·	9 ἢ οὐκ οἴδατε ὅτι **ἄδικοι** θεοῦ βασιλείαν οὐ κληρονομήσουσιν; μὴ πλανᾶσθε· οὔτε πόρνοι οὔτε εἰδωλολάτραι οὔτε **μοιχοὶ** οὔτε μαλακοὶ οὔτε ἀρσενοκοῖται 10 οὔτε κλέπται οὔτε πλεονέκται, οὐ μέθυσοι, οὐ λοίδοροι, οὐχ **ἅρπαγες** βασιλείαν θεοῦ κληρονομήσουσιν.
The Pharisee, standing by himself, was praying thus, 'God, I thank you that I am not like other people: **thieves,**[74] **rogues, adulterers**, or even like this tax collector	Do you not know that **wrongdoers** will not inherit the kingdom of God? Do not be deceived! Fornicators, idolaters, **adulterers**, male prostitutes, sodomites, 10 thieves, the greedy, drunkards, revilers, **robbers**—none of these will inherit the kingdom of God

5:10–11 and 6:10. "Rogues" is also found in 1 Corinthians 6:9 (and ten times elsewhere, three and Luke/Acts, two in Paul), "Adulterers" once in Hebrews and in 1 Corinthians 6:9. The Pharisee's list of the theologically objectionable has more in common with the catalogue in 1 Corinthians 6:9–10 than with any other passage or list in the New Testament. One may claim that Luke has simply utilized a "Hellenistic Jewish catalogue of vices" here, but given the number of such catalogues in the New Testament, it is more difficult to explain the overlap as coincidence than dependence.

The next example treats one of the most important formulas in early Christianity, the citation of Jesus' words and actions called the "Institution Narrative." (See Table 4.3.) If Luke's form of this material includes the "longer text," with verses 19b–20, the case for its Pauline character (and ultimate dependence upon 1 Corinthians 11) is overwhelming.[75] The most striking items are the "anamnesis" ("memorial") formula ("Do this in remembrance of me") and the "cup-formula" ("In the same way after supper. . . ."). Schenk puts the case in a nutshell: "All the noteworthy deviations of Luke from Mark are in accordance with 1 Corinthians 11.23–25."[76] The difficulty resides with the textual evidence for the Gospels. Until the last third of the twentieth century there was a general preference for the shorter text, as can be seen from the Nestle text through its twenty-fifth edition and such translations as the RSV and the NEB. Thereafter a reaction set in. The current Nestle-Aland[27], the fourth edition of the United Bible Societies' Greek text, and versions such as the NRSV and the NIV print the longer form.

On the grounds of manuscript evidence, the longer text has by far the best support. The essential principle of text criticism at the micro-level is to prefer the reading that best explains the origin of the others. This is often the "more difficult" reading. It is easier to understand why a scribe would change "Antioch in Judea" to "Antioch in Syria" than the reverse. On these grounds, it is rather more difficult to explain the origin of the shorter text as an abbreviation than *vice-versa*. In the end supporters of the longer text must fall back upon its strong manuscript support.[77] Although the longer text is now in the ascendant, I am reluctant to use it as firm evidence in this instance. Its chief interest in the present context is to raise a question: Why, if the shorter text is "original," did a reviser choose to "correct" it by a mixture of 1 Corinthians 11 and Mark 14 rather than by supplying the missing material from Matthew or Mark alone, as is the more customary practice?[78] Verse 19a of Luke shares but one feature with Paul against Mark: the verb "give thanks" (εὐχαριστῶ) rather than "bless" (εὐλογῶ). The order cup-bread (cf. Luke 22:17–18) is found in 1 Corinthians 10:16–17 (and *Didache* 9:1–5).[79]

Michael Goulder proposes another connection between 1 Corinthians 11 and Luke 22.[80] (See Table 4.4.) This is the occurrence of the word "strife" in a similar context. In favor of his argument is the rarity of the stem φιλονεικ-, (contend), which is found only in these two places in the New Testament.[81] Goulder's proposal is certainly interesting, and it adds weight to the argument It is, of

Table 4.3: The Institution Narrative

1 Corinthians 11: 23–25	Luke 22:19–20	Mark 14:22–24
23 ὅτι ὁ κύριος Ἰησοῦς ἐν τῇ νυκτὶ ᾗ παρεδίδετο	17 Then he took a cup, and after giving thanks he said, "Take this and divide it among yourselves; 18 for I tell you that from now on I will not drink of the fruit of the vine until the kingdom of God comes.	Καὶ ἐσθιόντων αὐτῶν
ἔλαβεν ἄρτον 24 καὶ εὐχαριστήσας ἔκλασεν καὶ εἶπεν, Τοῦτό μού ἐστιν τὸ σῶμα τὸ ὑπὲρ ὑμῶν· τοῦτο ποιεῖτε εἰς τὴν ἐμὴν ἀνάμνησιν. 25 ὡσαύτως καὶ τὸ ποτήριον μετὰ τὸ δειπνῆσαι, λέγων, Τοῦτο τὸ ποτήριον ἡ καινὴ διαθήκη ἐστὶν ἐν τῷ ἐμῷ αἵματι· τοῦτο ποιεῖτε, ὁσάκις ἐὰν πίνητε, εἰς τὴν ἐμὴν ἀνάμνησιν.	¹⁹καὶ λαβὼν ἄρτον εὐχαριστήσας ἔκλασεν καὶ ἔδωκεν αὐτοῖς λέγων, Τοῦτό ἐστιν τὸ σῶμά μου [τὸ ὑπὲρ ὑμῶν διδόμενον· τοῦτο ποιεῖτε εἰς τὴν ἐμὴν ἀνάμνησιν. 20 καὶ τὸ ποτήριον ὡσαύτως μετὰ τὸ δειπνῆσαι, λέγων, Τοῦτο τὸ ποτήριον ἡ καινὴ διαθήκη ἐν τῷ αἵματί μου, τὸ ὑπὲρ ὑμῶν ἐκχυννόμενον].	λαβὼν ἄρτον εὐλογήσας ἔκλασεν καὶ ἔδωκεν αὐτοῖς καὶ εἶπεν, Λάβετε, τοῦτό ἐστιν τὸ σῶμά μου. 23 καὶ λαβὼν ποτήριον εὐχαριστήσας ἔδωκεν αὐτοῖς, καὶ ἔπιον ἐξ αὐτοῦ πάντες. 24 καὶ εἶπεν αὐτοῖς, Τοῦτό ἐστιν τὸ αἷμά μου τῆς διαθήκης τὸ ἐκχυννόμενον ὑπὲρ πολλῶν·
23 that the Lord Jesus on the night when he was betrayed *took a loaf of bread,* 24 and *when he had given thanks,* he *broke it* and said, *"This is my body* that is *for you. Do this in remembrance of me."* 25 *In the same way he took the cup also, after supper, saying, "This cup is the new covenant in my blood.* Do this, as often as you drink it, in remembrance of me."	19 Then he took a loaf of bread, and when he had given thanks, he broke it and gave it to them, saying, "This is my body, [which is given for you. Do this in remembrance of me." 20 *And he did the same with the cup after supper, saying, "This cup* that is poured out for you is *the new covenant in my blood.*]	22 While they were eating, he *took a loaf of bread,* and after blessing it he *broke it, gave it to them, and said, "Take; this is my body."* 23 Then he took a cup, and after giving thanks he gave it to them, and all of them drank from it. 24 He said to them, "This is my blood of the covenant, which is poured out for many.

Italics = Paul, Luke, Mark
Underlined = Luke + Mark
Italics and Underlined = Paul + Luke
[ ] mark that part of Luke 22:19–20 which is textually uncertain.

Table 4.4: Contention

1 Corinthians 11:16	Luke 22:24
Εἰ δέ τις **δοκεῖ φιλόνεικος** εἶναι But if anyone is disposed to be con- tentious	Ἐγένετο δὲ καὶ **φιλονεικία** ἐν αὐτοῖς, τὸ τίς αὐτῶν **δοκεῖ** εἶναι μείζων. A **dispute** also arose among them as to which one of them **was to be regarded** as the greatest

Table 4.5: High Anxiety[82]

1 Corinthians 7: 32–35	Luke 10 (38) 40–42
32 ... ὁ ἄγαμος **μεριμνᾷ** τὰ τοῦ κυρίου, πῶς ἀρέσῃ τῷ κυρίῳ· 33 ὁ δὲ γαμήσας μεριμνᾷ τὰ τοῦ κόσμου, πῶς ἀρέσῃ τῇ γυναικί, 34 καὶ μεμέρισται ... 35 τοῦτο δὲ πρὸς τὸ ὑμῶν αὐτῶν σύμφορον λέγω, οὐχ ἵνα βρόχον ὑμῖν ἐπιβάλω, ἀλλὰ πρὸς τὸ εὔσχημον καὶ εὐπάρεδρον τῷ κυρίῳ **ἀπερισπάστως.** The unmarried man is **anxious** about the affairs of the Lord, how to please the Lord; but the married man is anxious about the affairs of the world, how to please his wife, and his interests are divided. And the unmarried woman and the virgin are anxious about the affairs of the Lord, so that they may be holy in body and spirit; but the married woman is anxious about the affairs of the world, how to please her husband. I say this for your own benefit, not to put any restraint upon you, but to promote good order and **unhindered** devotion to the Lord. Cf. Philippians 4:6: μηδὲν μεριμνᾶτε ... Do not worry about anything ...	40 ἡ δὲ Μάρθα **περιεσπᾶτο** περὶ πολλὴν διακονίαν· ἐπιστᾶσα δὲ εἶπεν, Κύριε, οὐ μέλει σοι ὅτι ἡ ἀδελφή μου μόνην με κατέλιπεν διακονεῖν; εἰπὲ οὖν αὐτῇ ἵνα μοι συναντιλάβηται. 41 ἀποκριθεὶς δὲ εἶπεν αὐτῇ ὁ κύριος, Μάρθα Μάρθα, **μεριμνᾷς** καὶ θορυβάζῃ περὶ πολλά, 42 ἑνὸς δέ ἐστιν χρεία· Μαριὰμ γὰρ τὴν ἀγαθὴν μερίδα ἐξελέξατο ἥτις οὐκ ἀφαιρεθήσεται αὐτῆς. *Now as they went on their way, he entered a certain village, where a woman named Martha welcomed him into her home. She had a sister named Mary, who sat at the Lord's feet and listened to what he was saying.* But Martha **was distracted** by her many tasks; so she came to him and asked, "Lord, do you not care that my sister has left me to do all the work by myself? Tell her then to help me." But the Lord answered her, "Martha, Martha, you are **worried** and distracted by many things; there is need of only one thing. Mary has chosen the better part, which will not be taken away from her."

course, possible that Luke 22:24 derives from 1 Corinthians even if the shorter text of Luke's institution narrative is the more original, but the importance of this parallel is its contiguity, for that presents the strong suggestion that Luke was consulting a written text of 1 Corinthians 11 while composing chapter 22 of his Gospel.

At first glance the passages in Table 4.5 seem to share no more than a pair of verbal stems (μεριμν-, περισπατ-); nevertheless, so far as I have determined,

Table 4.6: Those Who Curse

Matthew 5:44	Luke 6:27–28	Romans 12:14
... *ἀγαπᾶτε τοὺς ἐχθροὺς ὑμῶν καὶ προσεύχεσθε ὑπὲρ τῶν διωκόντων ὑμᾶς.* **Love your enemies** and **pray** for those who persecute you	... *ἀγαπᾶτε τοὺς ἐχθροὺς ὑμῶν*, καλῶς ποιεῖτε τοῖς μισοῦσιν ὑμᾶς, 28 <u>εὐλογεῖτε τοὺς καταρωμένους ὑμᾶς</u>, προσεύχεσθε περὶ τῶν ἐπηρεαζόντων ὑμᾶς. *Love your enemies,* do good to those who hate you, <u>bless</u> those who <u>curse</u> you, pray for those who abuse you.	<u>εὐλογεῖτε τοὺς</u> **διώκοντας**, εὐλογεῖτε καὶ μὴ <u>καταρᾶσθε</u>. εὐλογεῖτε τοὺς **διώκοντας** [ὑμᾶς] Bless those who **persecute** you; <u>bless</u> and do not <u>curse</u> them

Italics = Matthew + Luke (Q)
Bold = Matthew + Paul
<u>Underline</u> = Luke + Paul.

the two are found in relation to one another only in this passage.[83] Another item worthy of note is the application of the title "Lord" to Jesus three times in five verses of Luke. The lexical data might bear limited weight were the two passages not variants upon the same theme: possible tension between the distractions of daily life (Luke 21:34: μέριμναι βιωτικαί) and the demands of "The Lord." For Paul this tension, which has distant roots in the philosophical and wisdom traditions,[84] is an argument for celibacy—or, more precisely, an argument against marriage.[85] Luke has presented the issue in the form of a memorable story susceptible to numerous interpretations and applications.[86] In this case many would agree that Luke has chosen the better part. It is also far from unlikely that 1 Corinthians provided his point of departure.[87] This incident, like the parable of the Pharisee and the Publican (Luke 18:9–14), is characteristically Lucan in that it presents an ethical or religious concept in narrative form. Luke makes his point by telling stories.[88] Since Luke prefers to illustrate morals through narrative, this story could represent an appropriate transformation and application of a Pauline principle.

The next example, found in Table 4.6, comes from the "Sermon on the Plain." William Walker says, "It is surely at least possible that Luke's third clause [in Luke 6:27–28] was suggested by Rom 12:14."[89] The possibility exists, but a glance at a Gospel Synopsis (Greek Gospel Parallels) will reveal how widely these exhortations are attested in similar forms. Although commentators upon Luke, Q, and the Sermon(s) on the Mount/Plain would do well to consider Romans as a possible source of this passage in Luke 6, it is not an outstanding case when seen in the light of James 3:9–10, *P. Oxy.* 1224, Polycarp *Philippians* 12:3, *Didache* 1:2–5, and Justin *I Apology* 15.[90] Since the editors of the critical edi-

Table 4.7: A Saying of John the Baptizer

Luke 3:14	1 Corinthians 9:7a
ἐπηρώτων δὲ αὐτὸν καὶ **στρατευόμενοι** λέγοντες, Τί ποιήσωμεν καὶ ἡμεῖς; καὶ εἶπεν αὐτοῖς, Μηδένα διασείσητε μηδὲ συκοφαντήσητε, καὶ ἀρκεῖσθε τοῖς **ὀψωνίοις** ὑμῶν. Soldiers also asked *John*, "And we, what should we do?" He said to them, "Do not extort money from anyone by threats or false accusation, and be satisfied with your **wages**."	τίς **στρατεύεται** ἰδίοις **ὀψωνίοις** ; Who at any time pays the **expenses for doing military service** **Ignatius,** *Polycarp* **6:2** Ἀρέσκετε ᾧ **στρατεύεσθε**, ἀφ᾽ οὗ καὶ τὰ **ὀψώνια** κομίζεσθε Please the one for whom you **soldier**, from whom you also receive your **wages**.

tion of Q do not include the third and fourth of Luke's commands, however, there remains room for doubt.[91] To be sure, Luke 10:8b ("Eat what is set before you") is missing from the parallel in Matthew 10:11, but since it is found in the *Gospel of Thomas* 14, 1 Corinthians 10:27b is probably not the source.[92] Walker's proposal that comparison of dominical sayings in Luke with the Pauline letters will be "extremely fruitful" may require some nuance.[93] I should prefer to say that the so-called "L-sayings" deserve scrutiny in this regard, since the L-material—items peculiar to Luke—may be compositions of the author and therefore possibly of Pauline derivation.[94] In any case, I shall more or less abandon the subject after sampling one small morsel that has nothing to do with a saying of Jesus.

This example in Table 4.7, which treats a saying of John the Baptizer, has been appropriated from Michael D. Goulder.[95] It possesses the distinct advantage of nearly absolute sterility. The phrase is utterly innocuous, and the contexts could not be more different. Goulder points to the present middle participle in Luke. Why not use the ordinary noun στρατιῶται, ("soldiers"), found fifteen times in Luke and Acts (and eleven other times in the New Testament)? A TLG search revealed no other combinations of στρατεύομαι ("engage in military service") with ὀψωνίοις (provisions, "wages" by metonymy), except citations from one of these passages.[96] And although the quotation from Ignatius has yet a third and quite different meaning, 1 Corinthians may well be the source of this quotation from John, for which few claim authenticity.[97] John's views about the practice of "liberating" property serve to introduce one of Goulder's most telling observations. He notes at several points in the course of his study that nearly all of the extensive research into the relationship between Paul and the Synoptic Tradition has investigated whether Paul used sayings from that tradition. The opposite possibility receives almost no consideration. This is a good example of how scholarly prejudice can influence the work of those who operate with the best of intentions. From the perspective of words and ideas, the possibility that Luke used Paul is often at least as strong as the conventional approach.[98] Insofar as various elements of L are arguably Pauline (for example, 18:9–14, discussed above), the view that much of L may be Lukan composition gains strength.

The Appearances of the Risen Jesus

Although they offer *reports about* the exclusive appearance of the Risen Lord to Peter, the canonical Easter stories do not *narrate* this appearance. in the canonical Easter stories.[99] This is quite remarkable, given Peter's standing among the followers of Jesus and such passages as Matthew 16:16–18 and John 21. (See Table 4.8.) Two passages identify Peter as the recipient of the first Easter appearance. The earliest list of appearances is in 1 Corinthians 15:

> [3]I handed on to you as of first importance what I in turn had received: that Christ died for our sins in accordance with the scriptures, [4]and that he was buried, and that *he was raised* (ἐγήγερται) on the third day in accordance with the scriptures, [5]and that *he appeared to Cephas, then to the twelve.* (ὤφθη Κηφᾷ, εἶτα τοῖς δώδεκα) [6]Then he appeared to *more than five hundred brothers and sisters at one time*, most of whom are still alive, though some have died. [7]Then he *appeared to James*, then *to all the apostles.*

Luke 24 follows the order of 1 Corinthians 15:4–5, with the same words, mentioning an appearance to "Simon" followed by an appearance to the entire group. "The Lord has been raised and has appeared to Simon" (ἠγέρθη ὁ κύριος καὶ ὤφθη Σίμωνι, v. 34). The combination of "raise" and "appear" in the passive voice may seem unremarkable, but it is found only in these two places. Wolfgang Schenk has developed a detailed argument based upon the similarities among Luke 24, 1 Corinthians 15, and Galatians 1.[100] Although the relation may seem tenuous at first sight, the question deserves serious attention. Luke 24:34 may well be a reflection of 1 Corinthians 15:4–5.[101]

Ananias and Sapphira

1 Corinthians 5:3–5 (13) is often adduced in discussions of Acts 5:1–11, the story of the downfall of Ananias and Sapphira.[102] (See Table 4.9.) The two passages have a similar context: the removal from the community of one who has done something that cannot be forgiven. The sanction may involve the demise of the individual.[103] Although there is general agreement that Acts 5:1–11 has some basis in tradition, the specific nature and limits of that tradition are not easy to recover. Luke is probably responsible for "doubling" the story, i.e., adding the punishment of Sapphira. The main verbs in 5:1–2 are singular and refer to the husband. Sapphira enters the story in two adverbial phrases at verse 7. The function of this repeated result is very much like the "double dreams" of Acts 9 and 10, wherein two persons have complimentary or identical revelations. "Doubling" effectively excludes explanations based upon coincidence or accident.[104] God was at work in these sudden deaths.

Table 4.8: Narratives of the Appearance of the Risen One

Matthew	Luke	John	"Canonical Apocrypha"[105]	Other
1.) To women at Tomb on Sunday. (28:9–10) 2.) To *the Eleven* on mountain in Galilee on unspecified day. (28:16–20).	1.) To two travelers at Emmaus on Sunday evening. (24:13–35). 2.) To *the Eleven and others* in Jerusalem on Sunday evening (24:36–43)	1.) To *Mary of Magdala* at Tomb on Sunday (20:11–18) 2.) To *a number of followers* (excluding Thomas) 3.) To *a number of followers* (including Thomas, "one of the twelve") on Sunday a week later (20:24–29)	Pseudo-Mark 16 1.) Ineffective appearance to *Mary of Magdala* (9–11). 2.) Jesus then appeared in a different form to *two* of the followers as they were on their way to a field, (12–13) 3.) third appearance at meal (eucharistic theme) to (rest of?) the *disciples*, (14–18). *John 21:* 1.) Miracle of catch: commission to fish. Galilee. Post resurrection. Risen Lord revealed in the eucharist. (1–14) 2). Commission of Peter. (15–17)	*IgnSm*, 3.1–2, attributed to *Gospel of the Hebrews]*: I know and believe that after his resurrection he lived in the flesh. For when the Lord came to Peter and his followers, he said to them, "Lay hold, handle me, and see that I am not an incorporeal spirit." And immediately they touched him and believed, being convinced by his flesh and spirit. *Gospel of Hebrews*[106] Risen Christ appears to *James*

Table 4.9: Excommunication with a Vengeance

Acts 5:1–6 (-11)	1 Corinthians 5:3–5, 13
Ἀνὴρ δέ τις Ἀνανίας ὀνόματι σὺν Σαπφείρῃ τῇ γυναικὶ αὐτοῦ ἐπώλησεν κτῆμα 2 καὶ **ἐνοσφίσατο** ἀπὸ τῆς τιμῆς, συνειδυίης καὶ τῆς γυναικός, καὶ ἐνέγκας μέρος τι παρὰ τοὺς πόδας τῶν ἀποστόλων ἔθηκεν. 3 εἶπεν δὲ ὁ Πέτρος, Ἀνανία, διὰ τί ἐπλήρωσεν **ὁ Σατανᾶς** τὴν καρδίαν σου ψεύσασθαί σε τὸ πνεῦμα τὸ ἅγιον καὶ νοσφίσασθαι ἀπὸ τῆς τιμῆς τοῦ χωρίου; 4 οὐχὶ μένον σοὶ ἔμενεν καὶ πραθὲν ἐν τῇ σῇ ἐξουσίᾳ ὑπῆρχεν; τί ὅτι ἔθου ἐν τῇ καρδίᾳ σου τὸ πρᾶγμα τοῦτο; οὐκ ἐψεύσω ἀνθρώποις ἀλλὰ τῷ θεῷ. 5 ἀκούων δὲ ὁ Ἀνανίας τοὺς λόγους τούτους πεσὼν ἐξέψυξεν· καὶ ἐγένετο φόβος μέγας ἐπὶ πάντας τοὺς ἀκούοντας. 6 ἀναστάντες δὲ οἱ νεώτεροι συνέστειλαν αὐτὸν καὶ ἐξενέγκαντες ἔθαψαν.	3 ἐγὼ μὲν γάρ, ἀπὼν τῷ σώματι παρὼν δὲ τῷ πνεύματι, ἤδη κέκρικα ὡς παρὼν τὸν οὕτως τοῦτο κατεργασάμενον 4 ἐν τῷ ὀνόματι τοῦ κυρίου [ἡμῶν] Ἰησοῦ, συναχθέντων ὑμῶν καὶ τοῦ ἐμοῦ πνεύματος σὺν τῇ δυνάμει τοῦ κυρίου ἡμῶν Ἰησοῦ, 5 *παραδοῦναι τὸν τοιοῦτον* **τῷ Σατανᾷ** *εἰς ὄλεθρον τῆς σαρκός, ἵνα τὸ πνεῦμα σωθῇ ἐν τῇ ἡμέρᾳ τοῦ κυρίου.* 13 τοὺς δὲ ἔξω ὁ θεὸς κρινεῖ. ἐξάρατε τὸν πονηρὸν ἐξ ὑμῶν αὐτῶν.
1 But a man named Ananias, with the consent of his wife Sapphira, sold a piece of property; *2* . . . **he kept back** some of the proceeds, and brought only a part and laid it at the apostles' feet. *3* "Ananias," Peter asked, "why has **Satan** filled your heart to lie to the Holy Spirit and to keep back part of the proceeds of the land? *4* While it remained unsold, did it not remain your own? And after it was sold, were not the proceeds at your disposal? How is it that you have contrived this deed in your heart? You did not lie to us but to God!" *5* Now when Ananias heard these words, he fell down and died. And great fear seized all who heard of it. *6* The young men came and wrapped up his body, then carried him out and buried him.	3 For though absent in body, I am present in spirit; and as if present I have already pronounced judgment 4 in the name of the Lord Jesus on the man who has done such a thing. When you are assembled, and my spirit is present with the power of our Lord Jesus, 5 you are to *hand this man over to* **Satan** for the destruction of the flesh, so that his spirit may be saved in the day of the Lord. 13 God will judge those outside. "Drive out the wicked person from among you."
	Joshua 7:1 Καὶ ἐπλημμέλησαν οἱ υἱοὶ Ισραηλ πλημμέλειαν μεγάλην καὶ **ἐνοσφίσαντο** ἀπὸ τοῦ ἀναθέματος· καὶ ἔλαβεν Αχαρ υἱὸς Χαρμι υἱοῦ Ζαμβρι υἱοῦ Ζαρα ἐκ τῆς φυλῆς Ιουδα ἀπὸ τοῦ ἀναθέματος· καὶ ἐθυμώθη ὀργῇ κύριος τοῖς υἱοῖς Ισραηλ.
	But the Israelites broke faith in regard to the devoted things: Achan son of Carmi son of Zabdi son of Zerah, of the tribe of Judah, **took some** of the devoted things; and the anger of the LORD burned against the Israelites.
	1 Timothy 1:20 ὧν ἐστιν Ὑμέναιος καὶ Ἀλέξανδρος, οὓς *παρέδωκα* **τῷ Σατανᾷ** *ἵνα παιδευθῶσιν μὴ βλασφημεῖν* among them are Hymenaeus and Alexander, whom I *have turned over to* **Satan**, so that they may learn not to blaspheme.

The shape of the story shows the influence of the tale of Achan, Joshua 7:1, 6–26. The verb ἐνοσφίσατο ("kept back") is a signal flag for the reader. In biblical literature this term appears only in Joshua 7:1, 2 Maccabees 4:32 (which depends upon Joshua), and Titus 2:10.[107] The questions put by Peter to each partner in turn resemble Joshua 7:25: "Why did you bring trouble on us? The LORD is bringing trouble on you today."[108] Death is the immediate sequel in all three instances.[109] Luke is most likely responsible for conforming this story to the LXX.[110] That view poses a difficulty, however, because the reference to Sapphira in verse 1 looks like an editorial addition. Lüdemann is among the majority who therefore see a punitive "rule miracle" behind Acts 5:1–11.[111] The procedure described in the penultimate sentence is not unthinkable, however, and, as in the case of all the Jerusalem traditions in Acts that have no links to the gentile mission, the matter of Luke's source must remain vague. Except for the "Cursing of the Fig Tree" (Mark 11:12–14, 20–21), punitive miracles in the New Testament are restricted to Acts. Luke does recount a parable about an unproductive representative of the species (Luke 13:6–9) but he tells no story about a chastised fig tree.[112]

[handwritten margin note: 2 Cor, 10–13]

An alternative hypothesis is to regard Acts 5:1–11 as a narrative inspired by 1 Corinthians 5:3–5. Both represent "magical" means for maintaining discipline.[113] Paul requires a formal community assembly at which he is present in "spirit." The curse will arguably lead to the malefactor's death. Acts 5 also presupposes an assembly (5:5–6). The difference is that the community in Acts serves only as onlookers (and, in part, as burial party). The apostle has the active role. Such a transformation is typical of a later period in which the status, authority, and potency of apostles receives much greater emphasis. Those conditions are, of course, represented in Acts and enhanced in the developing tradition.[114] 1 Timothy 1:20, a passage that is very likely to have been inspired by 1 Corinthians 5:3–5, shows the tendency: "Among them are Hymenaeus and Alexander, whom I have turned over to Satan (παρέδωκα τῷ σατανᾷ), so that they may learn not to blaspheme." The technical use of παραδίδωμι there corresponds to that of 1 Corinthians 5:5: παραδοῦναι τὸν τοιοῦτον τῷ σατανᾷ ("turn over X to Satan"). Like the author of Acts, the Pastor speaks not of a curse pronounced by the community but of a judgment rendered by the apostle. The proposal that the leading sources of Acts 5:1–11 are Joshua 7 and 1 Corinthians 5:3–5 alleviates the need to account for a piece of "floating tradition" and corresponds to Lucan ideology and compositional techniques. This is not the only explanation for this passage, but it is the most economical.

Acts and Galatians

The question of Luke's use of Galatians is quite interesting; it is both the most controversial of possibilities and the best attested. This section will consider twenty-five possible uses of this short epistle in Acts, with the result that dependence will become almost incontestable. That Luke knew Galatians seems beyond doubt; yet of all the epistles, this one exhibits more conflicts with Acts than any other. Of course, those who wish to defend the historicity of Acts seek to minimize these disagreements, but they will find highly distressing the demonstration that Luke must have had access to Galatians. I shall argue that the author of Acts quite intentionally revised what Paul said in that letter in order to create a construction more conducive to Christian unity. The curtain rises to show Paul engaged in persecuting followers of Jesus.

Table 4.10 showcases a ravishing little example in the character of the simple verb πορθεῖν. The concrete and customary use of this term is military, with reference to the pillage (Philo, *Against Flaccus* 54) and rape (Euripides, *The Phoenician Women* 565) associated with the capture of cities, as well as to the devastation of agricultural resources.[115] This sense of utter ruin tends to appear in translations; see, for example, Acts 9:21: "All who heard him were amazed and said, 'Is not this the man who *made havoc* (ὁ πορθήσας), in Jerusalem among those who invoked this name?'" and Galatians 1:13: ". . . I was violently persecuting the church of God and *was trying to destroy it* (NRSV).[116] Paul uses

Table 4.10: Paul the Persecuting Zealot

Acts 9:21; 22:3	Galatians 1:13–14, 23
ἐξίσταντο δὲ πάντες οἱ ἀκούοντες καὶ ἔλεγον, Οὐχ οὗτός ἐστιν ὁ **πορθήσας** ἐν Ἰερουσαλὴμ τοὺς ἐπικαλουμένους τὸ ὄνομα τοῦτο, καὶ ὧδε εἰς τοῦτο ἐληλύθει ἵνα δεδεμένους αὐτοὺς ἀγάγῃ ἐπὶ τοὺς ἀρχιερεῖς; 21 All who *heard* him were amazed and said, "Is not this the man who **made havoc** in Jerusalem among those who invoked this name? And has he not come here for the purpose of bringing them bound before the chief priests?"	Ἠκούσατε γὰρ τὴν ἐμὴν ἀναστροφήν ποτε ἐν τῷ Ἰουδαϊσμῷ, ὅτι καθ' ὑπερβολὴν ἐδίωκον τὴν ἐκκλησίαν τοῦ θεοῦ καὶ **ἐπόρθουν** αὐτήν, 14 καὶ προέκοπτον ἐν τῷ Ἰουδαϊσμῷ ὑπὲρ πολλοὺς συνηλικιώτας ἐν τῷ γένει μου, περισσοτέρως **ζηλωτὴς ὑπάρχων** τῶν πατρικῶν μου παραδόσεων. 23 μόνον δὲ ἀκούοντες ἦσαν ὅτι Ὁ διώκων ἡμᾶς ποτε νῦν εὐαγγελίζεται τὴν πίστιν ἥν ποτε **ἐπόρθει**, 24 καὶ ἐδόξαζον ἐν ἐμοὶ τὸν θεόν
Acts 22:3 Ἐγώ εἰμι ἀνὴρ Ἰουδαῖος, γεγεννημένος ἐν Ταρσῷ τῆς Κιλικίας, ἀνατεθραμμένος δὲ ἐν τῇ πόλει ταύτῃ, παρὰ τοὺς πόδας Γαμαλιὴλ πεπαιδευμένος κατὰ ἀκρίβειαν τοῦ πατρῴου νόμου, **ζηλωτὴς ὑπάρχων** τοῦ θεοῦ καθὼς πάντες ὑμεῖς ἐστε σήμερον· "I am a Jew, born in Tarsus in Cilicia, but brought up in this city at the feet of Gamaliel, educated strictly according to our *ancestral law*, being zealous for God, just as all of you are today."	13 You have heard, no doubt, of my earlier life in Judaism. I was **violently persecuting** the church of God and was trying to destroy it. 14 I advanced in Judaism beyond many among my people of the same age, for I **was** far more **zealous** for the *traditions of my ancestors* 23 they only heard it said, "The one who formerly was persecuting us is now proclaiming the faith he once **tried to destroy.**"

the verb in the imperfect tense (ἐπόρθουν, ἐπόρθει), with conative meaning: *"trying* to destroy." In Galatians this word is a vivid metaphor, intended to highlight the differences between Paul before and after Damascus.[117] The verb is relatively uncommon. In the range of material covered by the standard lexicon of the New Testament and other early Christian literature (BDAG) it appears three times: Acts 9:21 and Galatians 1:13, 23. One may therefore narrow the range and say that in the New Testament πορθεῖν is used to describe a *single event*: Paul's "persecution" of the Jesus movement. This uniqueness increases the probability that Luke took the verb from Galatians.[118] On this narrow base one may erect two working hypotheses. One will call for an examination of the relations between Galatians 2 and Acts 15 to test an assumption of dependence rather than by pursuing a general, "open question" approach. To that matter I shall later turn

The other is suggestive, if not revelatory. Luke evidently took Paul's usage in a concrete sense, as is apparent in his descriptions of Saul's savage activity (8:3; 9:1; 26:9–11). One explanation of this "literalism" is to presume that Luke's sources highlighted the atrocities of the "pre-conversion" Paul. Another is that Galatians inspired, or helped to inspire, the Lucan depiction. (These are not exclusive alternatives.) Armed with this word—to use an appropriate trope—the author of Acts could provide illustrative detail with a few of his patented evocative phrases: "Saul was ravaging[119] the church by entering house after house; dragging off both men and women, he committed them to prison" (Acts 8:3). "Meanwhile Saul, still breathing threats and murder against the disciples of the Lord, went to the high priest and asked him for letters to the synagogues at Damascus, so that if he found any who belonged to the Way, men or women, he might bring them bound to Jerusalem." (9:1–2) "Indeed, I myself was convinced that I ought to do many things against the name of Jesus of Nazareth. And that is what I did in Jerusalem; with authority received from the chief priests, I not only locked up many of the saints in prison, but I also cast my vote against them when they were being condemned to death." (26:9–10) These verses are excellent glosses upon Paul's ἐπόρθουν, taken in a concrete sense ("I was engaged in the destruction of").[120] This hypothesis suggests how Luke might construct a summary upon the basis of a single word.[121]

Galatians offers some other minor parallels that might elude those whose notions of source criticism have been forged exclusively in the workshop of the Synoptic Gospels. In a verse following one of those just discussed, Paul writes, "I advanced in Judaism beyond many among my people of the same age, for I was far more zealous for the traditions of my ancestors" (ζηλωτὴς ὑπάρχων τῶν πατρικῶν μου παραδόσεων) (Galatians 1:14). A more famous autobiographical statement—one that Paul did not make—appears in Acts 22:3: "I am a Jew, born in Tarsus in Cilicia, but brought up in this city at the feet of Gamaliel, educated strictly according to our ancestral law, being zealous for God, (πεπαιδευμένος κατὰ ἀκρίβειαν τοῦ πατρῴου νόμου, ζηλωτὴς ὑπάρχων τοῦ θεοῦ), just as all of you are today." The context is, of course, the same. Each has two identical words, ζηλωτὴς ὑπάρχων ("being a zealot"), and a reference to ancestral law or tradition. The three points of convergence make a strong case for intertextual connection.[122] This case gains further momentum from a TLG search that indicates these to be the only two occurrences of ζηλωτὴς ὑπάρχων in Greek literature from 3 BCE through 2 CE. Galatians 1:13 and 14 thus contain one verb and a participial phrase that occur only there and in the book of Acts, and in both cases with reference to Paul's "pre-Christian" viewpoint and activity. I do not know how to calculate the statistical odds that all this is mere coincidence, or whether they can be calculated; but certainly they are too small to give either mathematicians or historians even momentary pause. The data strongly support the hypothesis that Luke has made use of Galatians 1. Charles Masson introduces some other possible borrowings from the same chapter.[123]

The parallel in Table 4.11 illustrates the shifts in thinking that transpire when Lukan dependence upon Paul enters the picture. In Paul's famous account of his "conversion" (Galatians 1:15–17), the revelation of Jesus as God's son and his commission to preach Christ to gentiles represent two components of a single event. In Acts the first report of Paul's evangelistic activity following the conversion is summarized in creedal form: "He is the Son of God." This is the sole occurrence in Acts of the phrase "Son of God."[124] It is tempting to agree with Masson. Gerd Lüdemann also suggests that this may be "a remote echo of Gal. 1:16."[125] Here is a case in which Luke employs the same expression ("Son of God") with reference to the same situation. If so—"remote echoes" being far from decisive—this allusion would indicate not so much an overt use of sources as a subtle alignment of the stories. Luke's Paul is doing what the Paul of Galatians claimed, but not without a slight adjustment, since, although the Paul of Acts does proclaim that Jesus is the Son of God, his audience is Jewish rather than gentile. By such means Luke does not simply allude to the letters of Paul.[126] He interprets them. There will be other "fortuitous" agreements of this sort, the cumulative effect of which will make them seem anything but fortuitous.[127]

Paul's defense of gentile Christianity (See Table 4.12.) rests to a substantial degree upon the promises to Abraham, delivered and confirmed by the gift

Table 4.11: A Creedal Formula

Acts 9:20	**Galatians 1:16**
καὶ **εὐθέως** ἐν ταῖς συναγωγαῖς ἐκήρυσσεν τὸν Ἰησοῦν ὅτι οὗτός ἐστιν **ὁ υἱὸς τοῦ θεοῦ**. and **immediately** he began to *proclaim* Jesus in the synagogues, saying, "He is the **Son of** God."	ἀποκαλύψαι **τὸν υἱὸν αὐτοῦ** ἐν ἐμοὶ ἵνα εὐαγγελίζωμαι αὐτὸν ἐν τοῖς ἔθνεσιν, **εὐθέως** οὐ προσανεθέμην σαρκὶ καὶ αἵματι, to reveal **his Son** to me, so that I might *proclaim* him among the Gentiles, I did not confer with any human being

of the Spirit. He developed this argument in Galatians in an *ad hoc* situation, against opponents who demanded that all who wished to share in the blessings of Abraham had to participate in the Covenant via obedience to at least some of the Torah, most notably male circumcision. Romans shows further refinement of this line of thought. Except in Hebrews, where it has a particular meaning, the theme belongs to the Pauline sphere.[128] The word "promise" (verb and noun) is also important to Luke. It appears at the end of the Gospel (24:49) and eight times in Acts. The little phrase "promise of the (Holy) Spirit" looks like another precarious foundation for invoking intertextuality, but a TLG search uncovered only the instances from Acts and Galatians. Despite its inversion of the genitive and its referent, Ephesians belongs to the same tradition, as the NRSV translation indicates.[129]

The Pauline understanding of promise and fulfillment has evidently influenced Lucan thought, as can be seen in Paul's first missionary address, Acts 13:16–41. Although this sermon seems to begin with a review of salvation history that conveniently resumes where Stephen's summary had broken off (Acts 7), the speech makes no reference to the giving of the law,[130] or to the covenant, but focuses upon the promises of God. The content of this review of "Old Testament Salvation History" in 13:17–23 is therefore determined by Christian priorities. Stephen also spoke of the promise to Abraham before noting the "covenant of circumcision" (Acts 7:5–8).[131] The most likely source of those priorities is the letters of Paul, specifically Galatians and Romans.

In Galatians 3:19–20 (See Table 4.13.) Paul speaks of the Torah as "ordained by angels," as does Stephen at the close of his speech to the Sanhedrin. This is not stated in the Hebrew of Exodus, but it represents the tendency of post-Exilic Israelite religion (after c. 536 BCE) to avoid anthropomorphism, i.e., not to rep-

Table 4.12: Promised Spirit

Acts 2:33	Galatians 3:14	Ephesians 1:13
... τήν τε **ἐπαγγελίαν τοῦ πνεύματος τοῦ ἁγίου λαβὼν** παρὰ τοῦ πατρὸς ἐξέχεεν τοῦτο ὃ ὑμεῖς [καὶ] βλέπετε καὶ ἀκούετε having **received** from the Father **the promise of the Holy Spirit**, he has poured out this that you both see and hear	14 ἵνα εἰς τὰ ἔθνη ἡ εὐλογία τοῦ Ἀβραὰμ γένηται ἐν Χριστῷ Ἰησοῦ, **ἵνα τὴν ἐπαγγελίαν τοῦ πνεύματος λάβωμεν** διὰ τῆς πίστεως in order that in Christ Jesus the blessing of Abraham might come to the Gentiles, so that we might **receive the promise of the Spirit** through faith.	13 ... τὸ εὐαγγέλιον τῆς σωτηρίας ὑμῶν, ἐν ᾧ καὶ πιστεύσαντες ἐσφραγίσθητε **τῷ πνεύματι τῆς ἐπαγγελίας τῷ ἁγίῳ** the gospel of your salvation, and had believed in him, were marked with the seal of the **promised Holy Spirit**

Table 4.13: Laying down the Law

Acts 7:53	Galatians 3:19	Hebrews 2:2
οἵτινες ἐλάβετε τὸν νόμον εἰς **διαταγὰς ἀγγέλων**, καὶ οὐκ ἐφυλάξατε.	Τί οὖν ὁ νόμος; τῶν παραβάσεων χάριν προσετέθη, ἄχρις οὗ ἔλθῃ τὸ σπέρμα ᾧ ἐπήγγελται, **διαταγεὶς δι' ἀγγέλων** ἐν χειρὶ μεσίτου.	2 εἰ γὰρ ὁ **δι' ἀγγέλων** λαληθεὶς λόγος ἐγένετο βέβαιος, καὶ πᾶσα παράβασις καὶ παρακοὴ ἔλαβεν ἔνδικον μισθαποδοσίαν
You are the ones that received the law as **ordained by angels**, and yet you have not kept it. cf. also 7:38	Why then the law? It was added because of transgressions, until the offspring would come to whom the promise had been made; and it was **ordained through angels** by a mediator.	For if the message declared **through angels** was valid, and every transgression or disobedience received a just penalty

resent God as rushing about to perform various chores, but rather as assigning such tasks to intermediary beings ("angels"). What Paul and Luke's Stephen allude to is thus Jewish tradition, at least as old as the LXX.[132] Dependence upon a common notion is generally assumed; commentators sense no obligation to discuss possible literary dependence. Yet the phrase in Acts ". . . is strange and difficult to translate."[133] Paul uses the participle to stress that the Law was "delivered by messenger boys," so to speak, rather than the subject of a proper epiphany. Stephen stresses that although the Law arrived at the hands of messengers, these were perfectly subordinate and fully instructed agents. The three-point convergence and the awkwardness of Acts are potent evidence for literary dependence.[134] Why, one might ask, should Luke choose to use Galatians here? After all, like much of Galatians this passage certainly appears hostile to the Torah. Yet through a close paraphrase that makes a different, rather more positive, point about the Law, Luke is suggesting how Paul should be understood by providing an interpretation of Galatians that is less offensive to admirers of the Torah.[135] It is quite arguable, as William Ramsay said in the words that opened this chapter, that one intention of Acts was to provide a hermeneutical key to the letters of Paul, a means for understanding the apostle and his thought.[136] The letters of Paul could provide Luke with a good deal more than bits and pieces of useful data about people and places. Ideas also counted. One advantage of an intertextual model is that it permits, even urges, investigators to ask not only about the possible influence of Paul's letters upon Acts, but also about the possibility of Lukan influence upon understandings of Paul. That influence is ubiquitous and indisputable.[137] Galatians also contains a brief reference to Paul's Collection for Jerusalem.

THE COLLECTION

In speaking of his agreement with leaders at Jerusalem Paul takes note of a single "request," "that we remember the poor, which was actually what I was eager to do" (ὃ καὶ . . . ποιῆσαι, Galatians 2:10). The relationship between this offering and the "famine relief" undertaking of Acts 11:27–30 has inspired so much discussion that in their less energetic moments researchers are tempted to write a footnote saying, "See the commentaries."[138] This is the text:

> [27]At that time prophets came down from Jerusalem to Antioch. [28]One of them named Agabus stood up and predicted by the Spirit that there would be a severe famine over all the world; and this took place during the reign of Claudius. [29] The disciples determined that according to their ability, each would send relief to the believers living in Judea; [30]this they did (ὃ καὶ ἐποίησαν), sending it to the elders by Barnabas and Saul.

The basic question for debate has been whether there was more than one "collection," and, if not, whether Luke invented the "famine relief" offering to diffuse allegations about the Pauline "collection for Jerusalem."[139] Acts 11:30 shares a phrase with Galatians 2:10: "This they did, (ὃ καὶ ἐποίησαν) sending it to the elders by Barnabas and Saul." Once more there is a close linguistic parallel: a relative pronoun serving as direct object, adverbial καί, and aorist active indicative of a verb meaning "do." One might expect that such a combination is common enough, but facts dispute this presumption. The one other New Testament instance of ὃ καί ("which also") with the verb ποιεῖν ("do") does not strengthen the case against dependence, for it occurs in Acts 26:10: "And that is what I did (ὃ καὶ ἐποίησα) in Jerusalem." Four of the six New Testament uses of ὃ [=direct object] καί are in the undisputed letters of Paul.[140] More important, the context of Galatians 2:10 and Acts 11:30 is the same: a collection for Jerusalem. Dependence is probable here.[141]

GALATIANS 2 AND ACTS 15

The extensive bibliography on the relations between Galatians 1–2 and Acts 15 should be enough to satiate the most voracious scholarly appetite.[142] Leading questions include whether these accounts (especially Galatians 2:1–10 and Acts 15:1–29) represent the same meeting, and if so, which of the two accounts is the more accurate. With most scholars I hold that they refer to the same meeting and that Galatians is generally the more "accurate" of the two. One can scarcely improve upon the clarity of J. B. Lightfoot:

86

> The *geography* is the same. In both narratives the communications take place between Jerusalem and Antioch: in both the headquarters of the false brethren are at the former place, their machinations are carried on in the latter: in both the Gentile apostles go up to Jerusalem apparently from Antioch, and return thence

to Antioch again. The *time* is the same, or at least not inconsistent . . . [T]he *persons* are the same: Paul and Barnabas appear as the representatives of the Gentile churches, Cephas [=Peter[143]] and James as the leaders of the circumcision. The agitators are similarly described in the two accounts: in the Acts, as converted Pharisees, who had imported their dogmas into the Christian Church; in the Epistle, as false brethren who attempt to impose the bondage of the Law on the Gentile converts. The two apostles of the Gentiles are represented in both accounts as attended: "Certain other Gentiles" (ἐξ αὐτῶν) are mentioned by St Luke; Titus, a Gentile is named by St. Paul. The *subject of dispute* is the same: the circumcision of the Gentile converts. The *character of the Conference* is in general the same: a prolonged and hard-fought contest. The *result* is the same: the exemption of the Gentiles from the enactments of the Law, and the recognition of the apostolic commission of Paul and Barnabas by the leaders of the Jewish Church.[144]

That the two accounts speak of the same events is well beyond reasonable doubt. In most situations the proposal of an intertextual relationship would be an open and shut case. But little or nothing that involves Acts and Galatians, and least of all this matter, is likely to be settled without "a prolonged and hard-fought contest," to apply the phrase of the late Bishop of Durham to a different situation. The reasons for this extend well beyond the possible textual relations between two early Christian writings. What Luke has so ably fashioned into an event worthy of the label "Apostolic Council"[145] has become a watershed of Christian history and a major event of world history. From the mundane perspective, credit for this distinction belongs to those who brought opponents of Paul into Galatia; for had that controversy not erupted, we should not have Paul's account of his relations with Peter and others in Jerusalem, and in all probability we should not have had Acts 15.

That meeting in Jerusalem has the importance it does because Paul made it the centerpiece of his argument in Galatians. Various constructions and ingenious rumors about what went on in that consultation were not lacking then or later. Acts resolves whatever doubts about the matter that Galatians might happen to leave. It is easy to presume that this meeting was generally viewed as foundational when it took place, but that is far from certain. Much more certain is that the agreements allowed for divergent interpretations, of which at least three are known: those of Paul, Peter, and James. From Galatians 2 it transpires that Paul's conviction was that believers of Jewish origin should forego the demands of observance on occasions when Jewish and gentile believers interacted in more or less public settings, notably worship. Peter evidently believed that observance was not required, but that it was desirable for Jews? to be observant if (some) Jews were likely to take offense. James seems to have held to the view that the requirements of Torah remained compulsory for those of Jewish origin. On an ideological spectrum Paul would here stand on the left and James on the right, while Peter would occupy a classical liberal position that promoted, as we should say, diversity through tolerance.[146] One accomplishment of Acts 15 was to preserve a protocol to which all the "players" in Jerusalem seem to have subscribed: an agreement that male gentile converts to the Jesus movement need not be circumcised, and a resolution through skillful compromise of the issue of *kashrut* (dietary rules), the major cause of the subsequent disintegration. Acts 15 gives a solution to the problems described in Paul's epistle to the Galatians, not to the question as James saw it, nor from Peter's perspective (although the historical Peter may have found the compromise a reasonable solution) and certainly not as Paul would have found acceptable,[147] for Acts 15 deals only with the conduct of gentiles and says nothing about how "Jewish-Christians" should deport themselves. In one way or another Galatians 2 *is* the chief source of Acts 15. The outstanding question is whether the influence is directly textual or only through intermediary sources. The structure and content of Acts 15 rule out the thesis that Luke knew nothing about what Galatians 2 discussed, for Galatians 2 provides his framework. Since Galatians 2 is the only extant account that claims any credibility, it is also "our" framework and thus obscures the rather obvious connection. Acceptance of this conclusion resolves the historical question and opens the way for an "objective" examination of the data. One penultimate point: discussion of this matter must rest upon how Luke *might* reasonably have read Galatians, rather than upon assumptions of "what Paul meant to say." It simply will not do to operate with the ingenuous viewpoint that "This is what Galatians says (to me) and therefore what it would have said to the author of Acts." Finally, Acts 15 exists in at least two editions. Although I agree that in general the D- text is demonstrably secondary, some of the D-text variants in Acts 15 could reflect a very early text and, in any case, these diverse readings provide important data about the early interpretation of Acts.

The chief reason for providing the data in Table 4.14[148] is to establish the propensity for revising such provisions as the requirements of the "Apostolic Decree." A survey of early Christian "Church Orders"—including the *Didache*, the *Apostolic Tradition*, and the *Apostolic Constitutions*, as well as the decisions of various local and general Church Councils—will reveal that texts dealing with Christian life and practice are frequently revised to suit contemporary understandings. Rather than publish a fresh edition of Canon Law or a Book of Discipline, Ancient and early Medieval Christians revised *ancient* rules and disciplines while leaving their claims to apostolic origin intact.[149] There are not two accounts of the "Apostolic Council," but a good half-dozen: one in Galatians and others in different editions of Acts. The D-text is both less "Pauline" and more influenced by Pauline and Deutero-Pauline notions. It is less Pauline in that it even more fully and firmly reposes judgment in the hands of the Jerusalem leadership, to whom Paul gladly yields in subjection (cf. Galatians 2:5); it is more so both in evoking 1 Corinthians ("Paul resolutely maintained that believers ought to remain as they were when they came to believe."),[150] and in its transposition of the four prohibitions of Acts 15:20 into what can be read as a "moral" code that condemns idolatry, sexual immorality, and murder, while summarizing relations among believers under the rubric of the "Golden Rule."[151]

Table 4.14: Some Textual variants in Acts 15

"standard text"	"standard text"	"D-text"	"D-text"
1 Καί τινες κατελθόντες ἀπὸ τῆς Ἰουδαίας ἐδίδασκον τοὺς ἀδελφοὺς ὅτι Ἐὰν μὴ περιτμηθῆτε τῷ ἔθει τῷ Μωϋσέως, οὐ δύνασθε σωθῆναι. 2 γενομένης δὲ στάσεως καὶ ζητήσεως οὐκ ὀλίγης τῷ Παύλῳ καὶ τῷ Βαρναβᾷ πρὸς αὐτοὺς ἔταξαν Παῦλον καὶ Βαρναβᾶν καί τινας ἄλλους ἐξ αὐτῶν πρὸς τοὺς ἀποστόλους καὶ πρεσβυτέρους εἰς Ἰερουσαλὴμ περὶ τοῦ ζητήματος τούτου.	Then certain individuals came down from Judea and were teaching the brothers, "Unless you are circumcised according to the custom of Moses, you cannot be saved." 2 And after Paul and Barnabas had no small dissension and debate with them,	καί τινες κατελθόντες ἀπὸ τῆς Ἰουδαίας τῶν πεπιστευκότων ἀπὸ τῆς αἱρέσεως τῶν Φαρισαίων ἐδίδασκον τοὺς ἀδελφοὺς ὅτι ἐὰν μὴ περιτμηθῆτε καὶ τῷ ἔθει Μωϋσέως περιπατῆτε, οὐ δύνασθε σωθῆναι. 2 γενομένης δὲ στάσεως καὶ ζητήσεως οὐκ ὀλίγης τῷ Παύλῳ καὶ τῷ Βαρναβᾷ σὺν αὐτοῖς, ἔλεγεν γὰρ ὁ Παῦλος μένειν οὕτως καθὼς ἐπίστευσαν διαϊσχυριζόμενος, οἱ δὲ ἐληλυθότες ἀπὸ Ἰερουσαλὴμ παρήγγειλαν αὐτοῖς ἀναβαίνειν πρὸς τοὺς ἀποστόλους καὶ πρεσβυτέρους εἰς Ἰερουσαλὴμ ὅπως κριθῶσιν ἐπ' αὐτοῖς περὶ τοῦ ζητήματος τούτου.	*Some believers who belonged to the party of the Pharisees came down . . .*
4 παραγενόμενοι δὲ εἰς Ἰερουσαλὴμ παρεδέχθησαν ἀπὸ τῆς ἐκκλησίας . . . 7 πολλῆς δὲ ζητήσεως γενομένης ἀναστὰς Πέτρος εἶπεν . . . 12 Ἐσίγησεν δὲ πᾶν τὸ πλῆθος	Paul and Barnabas and some of the others were appointed to go up to Jerusalem to discuss this question with the apostles and the elders.		*"Unless you are circumcised and 'walk' in the custom of Moses, you cannot be saved."*
20 . . . τοῦ ἀπέχεσθαι τῶν ἀλισγημάτων τῶν εἰδώλων καὶ τῆς πορνείας καὶ τοῦ πνικτοῦ καὶ τοῦ αἵματος . . .	4 When they came to Jerusalem, they were welcomed by the church . . .	παρεδέχθησαν μεγάλως ἀπὸ τῆς ἐκκλησίας. 7 πολλῆς δὲ ζητήσεως γενομένης ἀνέστησεν ἐν πνεύματι Πέτρος καὶ εἶπεν. συγκατατεθειμένων τοῖς ὑπὸ τοῦ πρεσβυτέρων Πέτρου.	*For Paul resolutely maintained that believers ought to remain as they were when they came to believe. Those, then, who had come from Jerusalem ordered them—Paul, Barnabas, and some others—to go up to Jerusalem to the apostles and elders to be judged about this matter under them.* *. . . they received a splendid welcome . . .*

7 After there had been much debate, Peter stood up and said to them	Ἐσίγησεν δὲ πᾶν τὸ πλῆθος.	After there had been much debate, Peter, *moved by the* Spirit, stood up and said to them
12 The whole assembly kept silence,	20 . . . τοῦ ἀπέχεσθαι τῶν ἀλισγημάτων τῶν εἰδώλων καὶ τῆς πορνείας καὶ τοῦ πνικτοῦ καὶ τοῦ αἵματος. <u>καὶ ὅσα μὴ θέλουσιν ἑαυτοῖς γένεσθαι ἑτέροις μὴ ποιεῖτε</u>	*After the elders had concurred with what Peter said,* the entire assembly fell silent.
20 . . . to abstain only from things polluted by idols and from fornication and from whatever has been strangled and from blood.		20 To abstain
		From things polluted by idols And from fornication And from blood[shed] And whatever they do not wish to happen to themselves, "Don't do to others."

This "D" textual tradition also identifies the visitors to Antioch as "Christian" Pharisees who possess sufficient authority to order Paul, Barnabas and company to Jerusalem. This variant is certainly a revision that has transferred the information from verse 5.[152] The effect is quite different: whereas Luke does not identify the two groups of objectors, leaves open the question of whether those in Jerusalem were followers of Jesus, and apparently differentiates between their demands, the D-text tradition effectively transfers both the personnel and the issue to Jerusalem.[153] "The show went on the road" to Jerusalem, where the entire debate is repeated, evidently word for word. The difference is that Jerusalem comes equipped with the venerable Peter and also with James, who can promulgate decisive rulings. It is apparent that the "D" reviser sought to alleviate problems raised by the earlier text. "One leading motive for rewriting was to obviate the strange lack of sequence by which . . . the controversy at Jerusalem is introduced in vs. 5 quite as if no previous controversy at Antioch had just been described."[154] What is the origin of this controversy?

One possible explanation comes by hypothesizing that Galatians was the principal source. (See Table 4.15.) Paul does not say why he and Barnabas went to Jerusalem, accompanied by Titus, other than that the visit was in consequence of a "revelation."[155] From the immediate (Galatians 2:3) and general[156] context, it is manifest that demands for circumcision and (some) observance

Table 4.15: Conflict in Antioch

Acts 15:1–2	Galatians 2:11–13
Καί **τινες** κατελ**θόντες** ἀπὸ τῆς Ἰουδαίας ἐδίδασκον τοὺς ἀδελφοὺς ὅτι Ἐὰν μὴ **περιτμηθῆτε** τῷ ἔθει τῷ Μωϋσέως, οὐ δύνασθε σωθῆναι. 2 γενομένης δὲ στάσεως καὶ ζητήσεως οὐκ ὀλίγης τῷ **Παύλῳ** καὶ τῷ **Βαρναβᾷ** πρὸς αὐτοὺς ἔταξαν ἀναβαίνειν Παῦλον καὶ Βαρναβᾶν καί τινας ἄλλους ἐξ αὐτῶν πρὸς τοὺς ἀποστόλους καὶ πρεσβυτέρους εἰς Ἰερουσαλὴμ περὶ τοῦ ζητήματος τούτου.	Ὅτε δὲ ἦλθεν Κηφᾶς εἰς Ἀντιόχειαν, κατὰ πρόσωπον αὐτῷ ἀντέστην, ὅτι κατεγνωσμένος ἦν. 12 πρὸ τοῦ γὰρ **ἐλθεῖν τινας ἀπὸ** Ἰακώβου μετὰ τῶν ἐθνῶν συνήσθιεν· ὅτε δὲ ἦλθον, ὑπέστελλεν καὶ ἀφώριζεν ἑαυτόν, φοβούμενος τοὺς ἐκ **περιτομῆς**. 13 καὶ συνυπεκρίθησαν αὐτῷ [καὶ] οἱ λοιποὶ Ἰουδαῖοι, ὥστε καὶ **Βαρναβᾶς** συναπήχθη αὐτῶν τῇ ὑποκρίσει.
Then **certain individuals came down from** Judea and were teaching the brothers, "Unless you are **circumcised** according to the custom of Moses, you cannot be saved." 2 And after **Paul and Barnabas** had no small dissension and debate with them, Paul and Barnabas and some of the others were appointed to go up to Jerusalem to discuss this question with the apostles and the elders	But when Cephas came to Antioch, I opposed him to his face, because he stood self-condemned; 12 for until **certain people came from** James, he used to eat with the Gentiles. But after they came, he drew back and kept himself separate for fear of **the circumcision faction.** 13 And the other Jews joined him in this hypocrisy, so that even **Barnabas** was led astray by their hypocrisy.

propelled the issue. Paul further states that he made a private presentation to the leaders ("would-be leaders"). Circumcision raises its head in verse 3, the probable meaning of which is "They didn't even require that Titus, who was with me (a Greek, by the way), be circumcised." One could also join William O. Walker in construing the verse to mean: "Titus was not *forced* to be circumcised (but he accepted the rite voluntarily)."[157] This interpretation gains power from the next verse: "But because of false believers secretly brought in, who slipped in to spy on the freedom we have in Christ Jesus, so that they might enslave us—" (Galatians 2:4). Verse 4, which is not a sentence, could be taken as the conclusion to verse 3, with the ellipsis (—) to be filled with the above parenthesis (but . . . voluntarily).[158] Another move is to assume (or pretend) that the surreptitiously introduced false believers came to *Antioch* and had done so prior to Paul's visit to Jerusalem.[159] In any case, those persons, and the "certain people from James" (Galatians 2:12) take the role(s) of the observant believers of Acts 15:1 and 5. Acts 15:2 states rather coyly that " 'they' arranged for/ordered Paul and Barnabas" (NSRV, "were appointed"): ἔταξαν. This verb has two possible subjects: the "certain persons from Judea" (which is grammatically "correct") and "the believers." The D-text clarifies the situation by having the visitors command this visit: (οἱ δὲ ἐληλυθότες ἀπὸ Ιερουσαλημ παρήγγειλαν. . . .) One may reasonably ask why Luke is so ambivalent at this point. If Galatians were the source, the reason would be that Luke did not know the answer, but concluded from Galatians 2:1 that some direction had been issued. Whatever one thinks of that, it seems certain that Luke had no better source than Galatians for what took place at Antioch *before* the meeting in Jerusalem. Where Galatians is foggy, Acts is bland.

The reverse side of this obscurity is the well-known and highly transparent use of anonymity in Acts 15. Verse 1 speaks of "some persons from Judea" who came to Antioch. Galatians 2:12 takes note of "certain persons from James." This construction, τινες ἀπό, in which there is some overlap between origin ("*from* Jerusalem") and affiliation ("*of* James and/or his viewpoint"), is relatively uncommon.[160] Where Paul speaks of his visit to Jerusalem with Barnabas and their companion Titus (Galatians 2:1), Acts 15:2 mentions "Paul, Barnabas, and some others." Needless to say, in Acts neither Peter nor James has anything further do with Antioch in person. Their views are incorporated in the letter of "the apostles and the elders," which is delivered by delegates (Acts 15:23, 27) and which explicitly repudiates the notion that the Judean believers who had started the controversy were acting under orders (Acts 15:24). The highly charged verb used in 15:24 to describe their activity (ταράσσω, "instigate," "stir up") is applied to intra-Christian disputes only two other times in early Christian writings: Galatians 1:7 and 5:10.[161] It is a surprisingly strong term for Luke in the circumstances he outlines. Although Jerusalem saw nothing but vigorous, friendly debate, the events at Antioch can be described as agitation and harassment. Paul would not hesitate to apply these nouns to what happened at Antioch *after* the meeting in Jerusalem, but Luke assures his readers that

Table 4.16: Sequence of Events in Galatians 2 and Acts 15

Galatians 2	Acts 15
1, *Paul, Barnabas, and* Titus go from *Antioch* to *Jerusalem* (2:10)	1. *Paul, Barnabas, and* some others go from *Antioch* to *Jerusalem* (15:1–3)
2, To deal with question of whether gentile believers must observe Torah, especially *circumcision* (2:3)	2. To deal with question of whether gentile believers must observe Torah, especially *circumcision* (15:1, 3)
3. Opposition based in *Jerusalem*, active in *Antioch* (cf. 2:12)	3. Opposition based in *Jerusalem*, active in *Antioch* (15:1)
4. Leaders at Jerusalem are *James, Peter,* and John (2:6–9, of whom Peter was most important to Paul).	4. Leaders at Jerusalem are *James* and *Peter* (15:6–21; cf. 12:17).
5. Agreement to impose no burden upon gentile converts (2:6). Other than "Collection" (2:10).	5. Agreement to impose no burden upon gentile converts (15:19). Other than some basic rules for social and sacramental life (15: 20).
6. *Jerusalem leaders accept mission of Paul and Barnabas* (2:9).	6. *Jerusalem leaders accept mission of Paul and Barnabas* (15:25).
7. *Paul and Barnabas* return from *Jerusalem* to *Antioch* (implicit).	7. *Paul and Barnabas* return from *Jerusalem* to *Antioch* with others (15:30).
8. *Paul and Barnabas subsequently quarrel* (2:13) *and separate* (no longer partners in letters).	8. *Paul and Barnabas subsequently quarrel and separate* (15:36–39).

all such unpleasantness came to an end once the question had been promptly decided by the proper authorities in the preferred setting.

The strongest argument in favor of literary dependence is that advanced by Lightfoot, although he had no desire to make the case. He sought only to show that Acts 15 and Galatians 2 refer to the same meeting, and his grounds were the similarities of narrative incidents and sequence.

The several Lukan additions, described above, are reasonable inferences for filling in the gaps of Galatians. (See Table 4.16.) The opponents at Jerusalem are Pharisees, noted for their strict adherence to Torah.[162] The difficulties their presence and posture raise, in the light of claims later made by Paul, is just the sort of thing Luke does not worry about.[163] One omission is Titus, here and elsewhere. Acts appears to "replace" Galatians 2:3 (the non-circumcision of Titus) with an account of the circumcision of Timothy. William O. Walker has ably presented that case.[164]

Here follow some brief observations and comments upon the parallels in Table 4.17:[165]

1. Both passages deal with the issue of the circumcision of a colleague of Paul, a subject not elsewhere treated.
2. The relation between Paul and his colleague is expressed with the same preposition for accompaniment, "with" (σύν).

Table 4.17: Circumcision of Timothy

Galatians 2:3–5	Acts 16:1–3
ἀλλ' οὐδὲ Τίτος ὁ σὺν ἐμοί, Ἕλλην ὤν, ἠναγκάσθη **περιτμηθῆναι·** 4 **διὰ** δὲ **τοὺς** παρεισάκτους ψευδαδέλφους, οἵτινες παρεισῆλθον κατασκοπῆσαι τὴν ἐλευθερίαν ἡμῶν ἣν ἔχομεν ἐν Χριστῷ Ἰησοῦ, ἵνα ἡμᾶς καταδουλώσουσιν· *85* 5 οἷς οὐδὲ πρὸς ὥραν εἴξαμεν τῇ ὑποταγῇ, ἵνα ἡ ἀλήθεια τοῦ εὐαγγελίου διαμείνῃ πρὸς ὑμᾶς. 3 But even Titus, who was **with me,** was not compelled to be **circumcised,** though he was a **Greek.** 4 But **because of** false believers secretly brought in, *who slipped in* to spy on the freedom we have in Christ Jesus, so that they might enslave us—5 we did not submit to them even for a moment, so that the truth of the gospel might always remain with you.	Κατήντησεν δὲ εἰς Δέρβην καὶ εἰς Λύστραν. καὶ ἰδοὺ μαθητής τις ἦν ἐκεῖ ὀνόματι Τιμόθεος, υἱὸς γυναικὸς Ἰουδαίας πιστῆς πατρὸς δὲ Ἕλληνος, 2 ὃς ἐμαρτυρεῖτο ὑπὸ τῶν ἐν Λύστροις καὶ Ἰκονίῳ ἀδελφῶν. 3 τοῦτον ἠθέλησεν ὁ Παῦλος **σὺν αὐτῷ** ἐξελθεῖν, καὶ λαβὼν **περιέτεμεν** αὐτὸν **διὰ τοὺς** Ἰουδαίους τοὺς ὄντας ἐν τοῖς τόποις ἐκείνοις, ᾔδεισαν γὰρ ἅπαντες τὸν πατέρα αὐτοῦ ὅτι Ἕλλην ὑπῆρχεν. Paul went on also to Derbe and to Lystra, where there was a disciple named Timothy, the son of a Jewish woman who was a believer; but his father was a **Greek** 2 He was well spoken of by the believers in Lystra and Iconium. 3 Paul wanted Timothy to **accompany him;** and he took him and had him **circumcised because of** the Jews *who were in those places,* for they all knew that his father was a Greek

3. The individual is characterized as "a Greek." This word appears ten times in Acts, but only here in the singular. Paul uses it about a dozen times, in this passage alone of a specific person. Titus and Timothy are the only individuals characterized in the New Testament by this ethnic label

4. The motive (διά) is the presence (Galatians: "slipped in;" Acts "in those places") of others (Galatians: "false believers," almost certainly of Israelite background; Acts: "the Jews") for whom the non-circumcised missionary would be a scandal.

Picking up upon a remark of Cadbury and Lake that Acts 16:1–3 "is a confused and perhaps erroneous memory" of Galatians 2:3–5,[166] Walker proceeds to demonstrate with clarity and concision that the memory was anything but erroneous and confused. The absence of Titus has nothing to with the alleged obscurity of that individual. Luke omits references to him because of his involvement in controversial events: the meeting in Jerusalem and its aftermath (Galatians 2, above), the Collection, and Paul's difficult conflict with Corinth (2 Corinthians). Luke transformed the dross of Galatians 2 into the gold of Acts 15 and omitted both the activity of the Collection and its evident later rejection in Jerusalem. None of Paul's controversies with his converts is permitted to soil Luke's portrait of the nascent church.

These two discussions about circumcision take place in close proximity to the respective reports of the Jerusalem conference at which the matter was debated. This suggests that Luke casts 16:1–3 to play the role in Acts that Galatians 2:3–5 plays in Paul. As I noted earlier, Walker proposes that Luke could have understood Galatians 2:3, "even Titus, who was with me, was not compelled to be circumcised," to mean "Titus was not *compelled* to be circumcised (but accepted circumcision voluntarily)."[167] The issue is not whether that reflects Paul's meaning but whether it is a *possible* interpretation, forced and unlikely as it is.[168] (The context of Galatians makes this reading all but impossible, since Paul would not have introduced into an argument against the [voluntary or otherwise] circumcision of male converts evidence against his case, but interpreters do not always take context into account.) If anyone could read Galatians 2:3 in that unlikely sense, Luke could have done so, for the idea that Paul voluntarily had Titus circumcised conforms to his desire to reflect harmony based upon compromise. Acts 16:1–3 removes any doubt that Luke could have so interpreted Galatians. Walker then proceeds to note and discuss the verbal similarities highlighted in Table 4.17. He caps that discussion by appeal to "certain general 'tendencies' of the author of Acts."[169] These include the desire to show Paul and other missionaries avoiding provocation of Jewish believers or sensibilities. The circumcision of a gentile would have violated the agreement of Acts 15, but the circumcision of one who was of partial Jewish heritage would not.[170] The reasoning may seem muddled, but is no more improbable than other attempts to understand Luke's views. Walker concludes his argument by noting that this Lukan revision is perfectly consistent with the general program of Luke and other early Christian writers to attribute problems to external sources, not least "the Jews."[171] This is a model study of proposed intertextuality. Walker identifies substantial verbal and other circumstantial parallels, but he does not stop there. He also relates the proposed borrowing to the general scheme of Acts and to the known views and proclivities of its author. His solution to the "mystery" of Acts 16:1–3 supplies all the requisites: means, motive, and opportunity.

Another person from Galatians 2 who has dropped out of Luke's narrative about the dispute is John.[172] He has but a "silent part" in Galatians, a role he also plays in Acts 3 and 8. And a further important difference is that in Galatians the visits to Antioch—first by Peter, then by some representatives of James— *follow* the meeting. As noted above, Luke omitted these events because he wished to show that all decisions were final and terminated any controversy. This alteration does not, of course, exclude the use of Galatians. As I have argued above, Luke uses Galatians 2:10 in Acts 11:27–30, but he is also silent about the collection here. In the place of the agreement to raise a collection comes the "Apostolic Decree." That is the most remarkable difference in content.[173]

On those grounds some may seek to postulate an alternative source for Acts 15, presumably an "Antiochene Source." This sounds like a good idea, to say the least, but even its more ardent proponents do not achieve a persuasive reconstruction of that source, apart from the decree.[174] Acts 15:1–3 would be from this source, if anything were, but both Lüdemann and Barrett view the language of those verses as Lucan, and anyone can see the contrast with 13:1–3.[175] For an Antiochene source to give so little credit and attention to its authorized representatives takes modesty beyond the limits of propriety. Paul and Barnabas appear in two very brief and stereotyped summaries that say nothing about Torah observance (15:6, 12), receive a favorable reference in the letter (15:25–26), and return with Judas and Silas. All of the argumentation is left in the hands of Peter and James. That Luke would so dispose matters is no cause for comment, but it is difficult to reconcile his presentation with the local pride and perspective of Antioch. *maybe Antioch was no longer proud of its initial support of Paul.* *OK, see below*

One question worthy of being posed is what an "Antiochene source" would have said about Paul's role in this dispute. It seems likely that his name would have been omitted. In the light of subsequent events, the important actors from the perspective of Antioch would have been Peter and Barnabas. The decree addresses the problem described in Galatians 2:11–13. Acceptance of it permitted social and sacramental fellowship among believers of both Jewish and polytheist origins. Traditions preserved at Antioch would have been unlikely to speak in any detail, if at all, about the meeting in Jerusalem, for the consequences of that meeting were nearly disastrous. The decision that counted was that contained in the "decree," which was doubtless given apostolic (Peter) warrant and may have been endorsed by Jerusalem (James). In due course it would become an "Apostolic Decree," but so would the catechisms and church orders of the *Didache*, the *Apostolic Constitutions*, and, for that matter, "The Apostles' Creed."[176] By Luke's time these commandments were evidently viewed as generally binding upon gentiles (cf. Acts 21:25).[177] Acts 15 endorses the Pauline mission to the gentiles and does so in a thoroughly Lucan fashion, by letting Peter (and James) take Paul's part and by coming to a conclusion that Paul would not have accepted.[178] If there is an Antiochene source behind Acts 15, Luke has very probably grafted Paul into it. For the rest, once one has eliminated the speeches, summaries, and other clearly Lucan expressions, there is a skeleton that corresponds to the details of Galatians. Since the evidence for use of Galatians is otherwise strong, it is preferable to see Galatians 2 as the major source of Acts 15 rather than to postulate vague "traditions" whose setting and function lack convincing delineation. As Dibelius argued, Acts 15 is intelligible without engaging in source criticism.[179] To that I should add that the author of Acts wished to correct some (mis)understandings of Galatians 2.[180]

Table 4.18 raises the question of whether one can posit intertextuality on the basis of a single word. Heikki Leppä makes a good case that in this instance one may do just that.[181] συμπαραλαμβάνω ("take with") is a rare word, used only in these passages in the New Testament, and but once in the LXX in this sense (3 *Maccabees* 1:1). The key factor is the context. Galatians 2:1 and Acts 12:25 refer to individuals who accompany (Barnabas and) Paul to Jerusalem.

Table 4.18:Companions in the Way

Galatians 2:1	Acts 12:25; 15:37–38
Ἔπειτα διὰ δεκατεσσάρων ἐτῶν πάλιν ἀνέβην εἰς Ἱεροσόλυμα μετὰ Βαρναβᾶ, **συμπαραλαβὼν** καὶ Τίτον· Then after fourteen years I went up again to Jerusalem with Barnabas, **taking** Titus **along** with me	25. Βαρναβᾶς δὲ καὶ Σαῦλος ὑπέστρεψαν εἰς Ἱερουσαλὴμ πληρώσαντες τὴν διακονίαν, **συμπαραλαβόντες** Ἰωάννην τὸν ἐπικληθέντα Μᾶρκον. Then after completing their mission Barnabas and Saul returned to Jerusalem and **brought with** them John, whose other name was Mark. 37. Βαρναβᾶς δὲ ἐβούλετο **συμπαραλαβεῖν** καὶ τὸν Ἰωάννην τὸν καλούμενον Μᾶρκον· 38 Παῦλος δὲ ἠξίου τὸν ἀποστάντα ἀπ' αὐτῶν ἀπὸ Παμφυλίας καὶ μὴ συνελθόντα αὐτοῖς εἰς τὸ ἔργον μὴ **συμπαραλαμβάνειν** τοῦτον. 37 Barnabas wanted to **take with** them John called Mark. 38 But Paul decided not to **take with** them one who had deserted them in Pamphylia and had not accompanied them in the work.

Acts 15:37–38 relates to the rupture between Paul and Barnabas. In place of John Mark Paul will presently acquire a new colleague, Timothy (Acts 16:1–3, noted above). Whereas Luke erases the uncircumcised Titus from the story while narrating the circumcision of Timothy, here he uses a verb associated with Titus in relation to another person. This unusual verb appears in Galatians and Acts in association with a cluster of ideas and motifs: Paul's associates, the Jerusalem Conference and its consequences, a collection, circumcision, and Paul's break with Barnabas. συμπαραλαμβάνω in Acts 12:25; 15:37–38 very probably derives from Gal 2:1. These are the only uses in the New Testament, and the contexts are similar.

"Circumcision" and "foreskin" are metonymies that identify male Jews and gentiles by a characteristic.[182] (See Table 4.19.) Greek, like English, can make any grammatical construction, including prepositional phrases, into a noun by placing the article before it. οἱ ἐκ περιτομῆς ("those of/from circumcision," the preposition indicating origin) is just such a construction. The expression is otherwise quite rare.[183] In so far as the New Testament is concerned this language belongs to the Pauline world. The context makes it apparent that Luke derived the phrase from Galatians.

ἀκροβυστία (literally "foreskin," "prepuce") appears only here in Acts.[184] As Leppä notes, it refers to Peter, thus evoking Galatians 2:7.[185] Rather more important is the verb συνεσθίω ("dine with"). This verb appears but five times in the New Testament, only in Luke/Acts and Paul.[186] The contrast between Galatians 2 and Acts 10–11 deserves attention. Paul criticizes Peter for eating with gentile believers but drawing back under pressure from Jerusalem believers represent-

Table 4.19: Galatians 2:12

Galatians 2:12	Acts	Other
12 πρὸ τοῦ γὰρ ἐλθεῖν τινας ἀπὸ Ἰακώβου μετὰ τῶν ἐθνῶν **συνήσθιεν·** ὅτε δὲ ἦλθον, ὑπέστελλεν καὶ ἀφώριζεν ἑαυτόν, φοβούμενος **τοὺς ἐκ περιτομῆς.** for until certain people came from James, **he used to eat** with the Gentiles. But after they came, he drew back and kept himself separate for fear of **the circumcision faction** Cf. 2:7 ἀλλὰ τοὐναντίον ἰδόντες ὅτι πεπίστευμαι τὸ εὐαγγέλιον τῆς **ἀκροβυστίας** καθὼς Πέτρος τῆς περιτομῆς On the contrary, when they saw that I had been entrusted with the gospel for the **uncircumcised,** just as Peter had been entrusted with the gospel for the circumcised	10:45 καὶ ἐξέστησαν **οἱ ἐκ περιτομῆς** πιστοὶ ὅσοι συνῆλθαν τῷ Πέτρῳ, ὅτι καὶ ἐπὶ τὰ ἔθνη ἡ δωρεὰ τοῦ πνεύματος τοῦ ἁγίου ἐκκέχυται **The circumcised** believers who had come with Peter were astounded that the gift of the Holy Spirit had been poured out even on the Gentiles 11: 2–3 ὅτε δὲ ἀνέβη Πέτρος εἰς Ἰερουσαλήμ, διεκρίνοντο πρὸς αὐτὸν **οἱ ἐκ περιτομῆς** 3 λέγοντες ὅτι Εἰσῆλθες πρὸς ἄνδρας **ἀκροβυστίαν** ἔχοντας καὶ **συνέφαγες** αὐτοῖς. So when Peter went up to Jerusalem, **the circumcised** believers criticized him, 3 saying, "Why did you go to uncircumcised men and **eat with** them?"	**Romans 4:12** καὶ πατέρα περιτομῆς **τοῖς οὐκ ἐκ** περιτομῆς μόνον ἀλλὰ καὶ τοῖς στοιχοῦσιν τοῖς ἴχνεσιν τῆς <u>ἐν ἀκροβυστίᾳ</u> πίστεως τοῦ πατρὸς ἡμῶν Ἀβραάμ. and likewise the ancestor of the circumcised **who are** not only **circumcised** but who also follow the example of the faith that our ancestor Abraham had before he was circumcised. **Colossians 4:11** . . . καὶ Ἰησοῦς ὁ λεγόμενος Ἰοῦστος, **οἱ ὄντες ἐκ περιτομῆς** οὗτοι μόνοι συνεργοὶ εἰς τὴν βασιλείαν τοῦ θεοῦ, οἵτινες ἐγενήθησάν μοι παρηγορία. . . . And Jesus who is called Justus greets you. These are the only **ones of the circumcision** among my co-workers for the kingdom of God, and they have been a comfort to me. **Titus 1:10** Εἰσὶν γὰρ πολλοὶ [καὶ] ἀνυπότακτοι, ματαιολόγοι καὶ φρεναπάται, μάλιστα **οἱ ἐκ τῆς**[187] **περιτομῆς** There are also many rebellious people, idle talkers and deceivers, especially **those of the circumcision.**

ing James (Galatians 2:11–12). In Acts observant believers in Jerusalem criticize Peter for the same practice. He gives a vigorous, indeed spirited defense, appealing to his vision and the manifest outpouring of the Spirit upon "the uncircumcised."

This action is a "Jesus-Peter parallel." When criticized for eating with (συνεσθίω) sinners in Luke 15:2, Jesus replies with three parables that speak of celebrating with and because of those who repent. The theme of repentance likewise climaxes Acts 11:1–18. The association of three words or phrases, two of them quite rare, in a similar circumstance makes it quite probable that Luke has utilized Galatians 2 in his account of the first conversion of a gentile. The dependence is not trivial or incidental. Luke is revising the story of Peter. To put it rather sharply, in the matters of the dispute at Antioch Luke has turned Galatians 2 upside down. Galatians appears to be his major source, but what he claims is quite opposed to what Paul says in Galatians. In other words, Luke can sometimes transform Galatians as he sometimes rewrites Mark.

More than a century ago Carl Weizsäcker stated that the speech of Peter in Acts 15:7–11 is based upon Pauline thought in general and Galatians in particular.[188] This proposal has been revived by M.-E. Boismard, E. Refoulé, W. O. Walker, Jr., and H. Leppä[189] The speech comes at a dramatic moment: the impasse of 15:2 remains unbroken, [190] and Peter rises to deliver his views. (See Table 4.20.)

Verses 7–9 are a brief summary of the Conversion of Cornelius (Acts 10:1–11:18). That reminder would justify a speech to the effect of "Why are we talking about this subject? The matter was settled some time ago, in a similar meeting when I was taken to task by 'the circumcised.'[191] Have you people *forgotten* all of this?" Peter does not take this approach, however, because his words are addressed to the readers of the book, the author of which subscribes to the principle that *repetitio mater studiorum* (repetition nurtures learning). The speech has a rather "Pauline" ring, emphasized by the last verse, which is even more "Pauline" than Acts 13:38–39 (discussed above). A hallowed (and valid) approach to Acts notes that the author "petrinizes" Paul and "paulinizes" Peter, but concludes that he " Lucanizes" both. Walker does not stop with this observation, nor is he content to state that the speech is primarily a summary of the Cornelius episode.

After noting that the closing verse states the Pauline view that both Jews and gentiles are saved by the grace of God,[192] Walker proceeds to argue for connections between *"Peter's speech as a whole . . .* and *Paul's report regarding the Jerusalem Conference."*[193] The chief of these is a kind of "role reversal." Whereas Paul describes Peter as a missionary to Jews and himself as a missionary to gentiles (Galatians 2:6–9), Acts 15 assigns to Peter the gentile mission. With the role reversal come a number of terms and concepts. The first example is (the message of the) *Gospel* (Acts 15:7; Galatians 2:7). εὐαγγέλιον ("good news," "gospel") is very much a Pauline expression, in all of Luke and Acts found only here and in the Pauline address of 20:24.[194] Walker then turns to the obscure division of spheres of responsibility or accountability marked out in Galatians 2:7: "I [Paul] had been entrusted with the gospel for the uncircumcised, just as Peter had been entrusted with the gospel for the circumcised," to which he compares the equally cloudy "God made a choice among you . . ." of Acts 15:7. Peter holds the primacy, in so far as the gentile mission is concerned. The first-time reader of Acts might expect the following chapters to describe Peter's continued endeavors in this sphere, but after four verses [8–11] he will utterly disappear from the narrative, which thereafter focuses exclusively upon the actions of Paul

i.e. Acts as a whole

Table 4.20: Peter's Speech in Acts 15

Acts 15:7–11	Galatians 2:15–16; 5:1–5
πολλῆς δὲ ζητήσεως γενομένης ἀναστὰς Πέτρος εἶπεν πρὸς αὐτούς, Ἄνδρες ἀδελφοί, ὑμεῖς ἐπίστασθε ὅτι ἀφ' ἡμερῶν ἀρχαίων ἐν ὑμῖν ἐξελέξατο ὁ θεὸς διὰ τοῦ στόματός μου ἀκοῦσαι τὰ ἔθνη τὸν λόγον τοῦ εὐαγγελίου καὶ πιστεῦσαι· 8 καὶ ὁ καρδιογνώστης θεὸς ἐμαρτύρησεν αὐτοῖς δοὺς τὸ πνεῦμα τὸ ἅγιον καθὼς καὶ ἡμῖν, 9 καὶ οὐθὲν διέκρινεν μεταξὺ ἡμῶν τε καὶ αὐτῶν, **τῇ πίστει** καθαρίσας τὰς καρδίας αὐτῶν. 10 νῦν οὖν τί πειράζετε τὸν θεόν, ἐπιθεῖναι **ζυγὸν** ἐπὶ τὸν τράχηλον τῶν μαθητῶν ὃν οὔτε οἱ πατέρες ἡμῶν οὔτε ἡμεῖς ἰσχύσαμεν βαστάσαι; 11 ἀλλὰ διὰ **τῆς χάριτος** τοῦ κυρίου Ἰησοῦ **πιστεύομεν σωθῆναι** καθ' ὃν τρόπον κἀκεῖνοι. Peter stood up and said to them, "My brothers, you know that in the early days God made a choice among you, that I should be the one through whom the Gentiles would hear the message of the good news and become believers. 8 And God, who knows the human heart, testified to them by giving them the Holy Spirit, just as he did to us; 9 and in cleansing their hearts **by faith** he has made no distinction between them and us. 10 Now therefore why are you putting God to the test by placing on the neck of the disciples a **yoke** that neither our ancestors nor we have been able to bear? 11 On the contrary, **we believe that we will be saved through the grace of the Lord Jesus**, just as they will."	2:15–16 Ἡμεῖς φύσει Ἰουδαῖοι καὶ οὐκ ἐξ ἐθνῶν ἁμαρτωλοί, 16 εἰδότες [δὲ] ὅτι οὐ δικαιοῦται ἄνθρωπος ἐξ ἔργων νόμου ἐὰν μὴ διὰ **πίστεως** Ἰησοῦ Χριστοῦ, καὶ ἡμεῖς εἰς Χριστὸν Ἰησοῦν **ἐπιστεύσαμεν**, ἵνα δικαιωθῶμεν ἐκ πίστεως Χριστοῦ καὶ οὐκ ἐξ ἔργων νόμου, ὅτι ἐξ ἔργων νόμου οὐ δικαιωθήσεται πᾶσα σάρξ. We ourselves are Jews by birth and not Gentile sinners; yet we know that a person is justified not by the works of the law but through faith in Jesus Christ. And we have come to believe in Christ Jesus, so that we might be justified by faith in Christ, and not by doing the works of the law, because no one will be justified by the works of the law 5:1–5 τῇ ἐλευθερίᾳ ἡμᾶς Χριστὸς ἠλευθέρωσεν· στήκετε οὖν καὶ μὴ πάλιν **ζυγῷ** δουλείας ἐνέχεσθε. 2 Ἴδε ἐγὼ Παῦλος λέγω ὑμῖν ὅτι ἐὰν περιτέμνησθε Χριστὸς ὑμᾶς οὐδὲν ὠφελήσει. 3 μαρτύρομαι δὲ πάλιν παντὶ ἀνθρώπῳ περιτεμνομένῳ ὅτι ὀφειλέτης ἐστὶν ὅλον τὸν νόμον ποιῆσαι. 4 κατηργήθητε ἀπὸ Χριστοῦ οἵτινες ἐν νόμῳ δικαιοῦσθε, **τῆς χάριτος** ἐξεπέσατε. 5 ἡμεῖς γὰρ πνεύματι ἐκ πίστεως ἐλπίδα δικαιοσύνης ἀπεκδεχόμεθα. 1 For freedom Christ has set us free. Stand firm, therefore, and do not submit again to a *yoke* of slavery. 2 Listen! I, Paul, am telling you that if you let yourselves be circumcised, Christ will be of no benefit to you. 3 Once again I testify to every man who lets himself be circumcised that he is obliged to obey the entire law.4 You who want to be justified by the law have cut yourselves off from Christ; you have fallen away from *grace*. 5 For through the Spirit, by faith, we eagerly wait for the hope of *righteousness* **Ephesians 2:8** τῇ γὰρ **χάριτί ἐστε σεσῳσμένοι** διὰ **πίστεως**· καὶ τοῦτο οὐκ ἐξ ὑμῶν, θεοῦ τὸ δῶρον· For **by grace you have been saved through faith**, and this is not your own doing; it is the gift of God

as a missionary to Jews and gentiles. Walker next notes the theme of "divine impartiality" that appears in Galatians 2:6 and Acts 15:9, admittedly in different contexts. Both Paul and Luke argue from the gift of the Spirit to the validity of gentile conversions: Acts 15:8 (cf. 10:44–47) and Galatians 3:2–5—to which I should add Galatians 4:6.[195] In Acts 15:10 the image of "yoke" is used in a pejorative sense, as it is in Galatians 5:1 ("yoke of slavery"), with the suggestion that the hearers ("you") are seeking to impose the Torah upon others.[196] This, as Walker states, sounds very much like the complaints of Paul in Galatians. Peter's allegation that Torah is an impossible burden in fact represents a gentile view and reveals how Paul's soteriology was misunderstood.[197] The "superficially Pauline" verse 11[198] reiterates the theme of soteriology first raised at Antioch (15:1); it is close to a paraphrase of Galatians 2:15–16. In short, Peter alludes to the Cornelius incident, but the heart of his brief speech is a Pauline argument derived from Galatians.

Walker concludes that the similarity of words and ideas supports the view that Galatians served Luke as "... [A] source in constructing Peter's speech at the Jerusalem Conference."[199] He then observes that Galatians 2:12 refers to "persons from James."[200] James is so far from provoking schism in Acts that he decrees the imposition of no burdens upon gentile believers, except for ...[201] The result is the first "harmonization" of Galatians 2 and Acts 15! By this I mean that Luke provided a hermeneutical key and narrative model for reducing the tensions between Paul and the leaders at Jerusalem. He did so by putting the "Pauline position," as he chose to understand it, into the mouth of Peter and by having James initiate a compromise of the "Petrine" sort.[202] Paul's jagged edges—his animosity toward Jerusalem together with his sarcastic remarks about its leaders and such radical departures as talk about "works of the law" and a willingness to discuss eating food offered to idols that make him sound like a libertine willing to compromise with idolatry and an abrasive promoter of painful divisions—all disappear.

In the light of the numerous and varied indicators for the use of Galatians, Walker's argument cannot easily be dismisssed. F. Refoulé has made a similar proposal.[203] He had earlier introduced the relevance of the term "yoke" in connection with circumcision in Galatians 5:1–6. Refoulé also points to Ephesians 2:8, an observation that in my view is apposite. In the Deutero-Pauline environment, "justification" was no longer a crucial word; it came from Paul's conflicts in a Jewish environment and was readily construed as an ethical term.[204] The explicit language of "salvation" or "deliverance" spoke more clearly and with greater appeal. The Peter of Acts 15 conveys the ideas of Paul in Galatians, but he does so with the accents of Ephesians. In short, the speech of Peter in Acts 15:7–11 is a paraphrase of Galatians as Galatians could be understood in a later period.[205] The speaker is a "Deutero-Pauline Peter."[206]

As Refoulé shows, Acts 15:7–11 is more than a matter of "Paulinizing" and "Lucanizing" Peter. Luke's target is the famous conflict between Peter and Paul at Antioch (Galatians 2:15–18). The author of Acts wishes to show that whatever that quarrel meant or involved, it was absolutely ephemeral, for—and here Luke could draw, as have many since, upon Galatians 2:1–10—the two leaders were in full and complete agreement about the essentials, which were that circumcision had no soteriological significance whatsoever, and that Jews and gentiles alike are saved by faith.[207] The quarrel was a hot subject at the time, for Paul labored with great care to put his side of the story on the record, but Luke appears to be responding less to rumors and legends than to the specifics of Galatians 2. In so doing he stands at the head of a lengthy chain, the last link of which has not yet been forged.[208]

Not until the account of Paul's final trip to Jerusalem does Acts reveal the persistence of the conflict seemingly resolved in chapter 15. (See Table 4.21.) The smoldering issue is whether the presence of gentile believers required *good way* Jews to compromise their observance. In this passage Luke introduces matters *to describe it*

Table 4.21: Paul's Last Visit to Jerusalem

Acts 21:18–28	Galatians 2:1–14
1.) Paul arrives in Jerusalem with a delegation including believers of gentile origin.	2:1. Paul arrives in Jerusalem with a group, including the uncircumcised Titus
2.) The delegation meets with James, who is the leader of a body of observant believers.	2:12. James is the leader of the most observant believers.
3.) There thus are two distinct missions: to Jews and to gentiles.	2:7. There are evidently two distinct missions: to Jews and to gentiles.
4.) James says that there are rumors to the effect that Paul seeks to compel Jewish believers to abandon the Torah.	2:4. Paul complains of "false believers," whose views are not unlike those of the "Christian Pharisees" of Acts 15:5 (cf. 15:1). 2:11–14. There was a conflict between Paul and others of Jewish origin about the behavior of Jewish believers in their association with gentile believers.
7.) James reiterates the "Apostolic Decree" of Acts 15, regulating the conduct of gentile believers.	2:10. The sole obligation upon gentile believers is that they "remember the poor," i.e., the Collection.
6.) Paul agrees to compromise and link himself to observant believers. He "submits to them for a moment."	2:5. Paul refuses to submit to the "false believers" "even for a moment."
7.) Trouble breaks out over Paul's alleged conduct with some gentile believers.	2:3–5. The uncircumcised Titus was the source of conflict.

discussed in Galatians 2 that he omitted from Acts 15. They appear in Acts 21 because of the necessity to explain why Paul is in danger in Jerusalem. He will, like Jesus, be arrested on false charges. Acts neglects the actual reason for this visit: to deliver the Collection. Since it is very likely that James' rejection of this offering resulted in some incident that brought about the arrest of Paul, Luke had to devise another explanation. In so doing he utilized some apparent facts: the acceptability of a certain type of believers and the payment of money. The former he inverted: the question is now whether observant believers are acceptable to Paul rather than whether Jerusalem will recognize the validity of the gentile mission. Galatians 2 shows that the question of observance was valid, for there Paul takes the position that the unity of the community takes priority over the requirements of Torah. Although Luke almost certainly had other source material relating to the delivery of the Collection, I think it likely that he also used Galatians 2 (and Acts 15) in constructing his story of Paul's reception in Jerusalem.[209] His aim was, after all, to refute Galatians 2, or at least some implications of it.[210]

Acceptance of the hypothesis that Acts makes use of Galatians does not greatly challenge the views of the more critical scholars. To name but a few, what Dibelius, Haenchen, and even Barrett have written could remain with scarcely any modification. The difference is that researchers would now have one specific basis for comparison and could cease to write about some traditions that must have been available but cannot be securely located, and thus hover about the material like harmless but disconcerting insects. From the traditional perspective, nonetheless, Galatians would be the *least* likely letter for Luke to have used, since his account is so often in tension with that epistle. Galatians is by quantitative criteria the *most* likely example of a Pauline letter used in Luke and Acts. The implications of this usage emerge in the dissertation of Heikki Leppä. Not for nothing does he describe Luke's use of Galatians as "critical." In an effort that would prove to be one of Luke's greatest successes, Acts seeks in various subtle and blunt ways to submerge Galatians. It also constitutes an effective arrow in the quiver of those who contend that Acts is an attempt to refute Marcion (or other radical interpretations of Paulinism). Not every proposal that Luke used Paul's letters involves the assumption of a strong contrast.

A Quantitative Approach

Anthony J. Blassi operates from the perspective that wide knowledge of Paul as a writer of letters and familiarity with said letters places the burden of proof upon those who argue that Luke did not know the epistles.[211] He distinguishes his method from that used in Synoptic criticism, which strives to discover who copied from whom. Blassi is seeking "to find compatibilities."[212] These compatibilities are like the signs of general Pauline influence, discussed above with regard to Luke 18:9–14 and Acts 13:38–39. Blassi assumes that, "If the narrative in Acts is inconsistent with Paul at some point, we can assume that Luke, who was careful to put things in order (Luke 1.3), did not have the Pauline letter in question."[213] Critical scholarship does not agree with him on this, but his proposal does provide a hard criterion.[214] On that basis Blassi eliminates Galatians from consideration.[215] The last sentence should be sufficient to demonstrate that his methods are quite different from those of the scholars hitherto cited and that they will provide confirmation—or disproof—from a distinct, essentially quantitative, orientation.[216]

The itinerary of Paul's missionary travels is Blassi's point of departure. One division of Paul's career is the point at which he broke with Antioch and Barnabas and thereafter worked as an independent missionary. His letters all date from this latter period. In them Paul says very little about his earlier work, which was extensive and lasted for at least a decade—longer, in fact, than did his independent mission.[217] In Galatians 1:17 Paul states that, after his "conversion," he went to Arabia and returned to Damascus. Some two or three years later he visited Jerusalem and then set off for "the environs of Syria and Cilicia." Then, "after fourteen years," he returned to Jerusalem (Galatians 1:18–2:1).[218] Paul's object was not to provide an autobiographical sketch but to recount his contacts with Jerusalem, Peter in particular.

Acts, which either does not know of or does not recognize this division in Paul's missionary career, itself an inference from Paul's letters, does recount some of Paul's missionary activity before the Jerusalem meeting. His labors in Damascus—to which he did not "return" but rather entered into after his vision, and which lasted no more than "many days" (Acts 9:23)—are the subject of a brief, stereotyped summary lacking any concrete data. After escaping from Damascus, Paul went to Jerusalem, whence, after trouble arose, he departed for Tarsus, which is in the province of Cilicia (Acts 9:26–30). There he evidently remained until Barnabas went to Tarsus and later summoned him to Antioch, where they worked together for an entire year (Acts 11:25–26). Antioch was in the province of *Syria*. Acts 13:1–3—a passage that has as good a claim as any to represent Antiochene tradition—reports the beginning of their itinerant career. This so-called "first journey" may well include some actual missionary sites, but it is deficient in specific data—the only convert named is the Roman governor of Cyprus—and unusual in plan.[219] Citing P. H. Menoud, Conzelmann says that Luke "... understands this as a 'model journey'," then notes that, "In actual fact it replaces the thirteen years of missionary work mentioned in Galatians 1:21 and 2:1."[220] The purpose of the foregoing observations is to affirm once more that, where Galatians is terse, Acts is vague.[221] The only other datum about Paul's work in Arabia (then outside of the Roman empire) is found in 2 Corinthians 11:32. Nothing is said about what Paul did in Cilicia and no more than a few words recount his work in Syria.[222] Paul mentions Athens but once, where he was willing to be "alone." Alone he also finds himself at Athens in Acts. This silence and solitude allows Luke to write a brilliant story that makes no claims for success and appears to owe little to tradition (17:16–34).[223]

He made what historically could only have been the meagerest and most casual of contacts into a moment frozen in time, the exemplary meeting between Jerusalem and Athens . . . As in other such set-pieces, we discover here not what happened but Luke's idealized version of what ought to have happened, so marvelously wrought that for its readers it provided the emblem of what possibly could happen."[224]

Paul does not mention Berea, which lies on the way from Thessalonica to Greece (Achaea) proper. Luke offers a brief and utterly stereotyped episode of the mission there (17:10–14). As previously indicated, Acts 13–14 offer very slender data about places.[225] Salamis and Paphos are scarcely more than names (13:6–12).[226] About Antioch in Pisidia (which was a Roman colony), the reader learns no more than that there was a synagogue in a city populated with the normal complement of "jealous Jews," as well as "leading citizens," a commodity one might safely infer to be present in any city (13:14, 45, 50).[227] Iconium also comes equipped with a synagogue, hostile Jews, and (presumably civic) "leaders" (14:1–5). At Lystra is a cripple whose origin can be found in Acts 3:1–9, and a splendid story that has all the marks of Lucan composition (14:8–18).[228] Derbe was the site of a tersely noted evangelization (14:21).[229] It seems that Luke had—or wished to utilize—only very sketchy data about these places.

Romans 15:19 (". . . from Jerusalem and as far around as Illyricum I have fully proclaimed the good news of Christ") comes as a bit of a shock both to those whose concept of Paul's missionary journeys depends upon Acts and to those who know the other letters.[230] Illyricum was a Roman province on the east coast of the Balkan Peninsula. Whatever the verse means, it suggests that the tentacles of the mission reached more places than Acts or the epistles specifically note.[231] There is a strong correlation between places either addressed or spoken about in surviving Pauline letters and the sites that receive detailed and specific discussion in Acts. (See Table 4.22.)

Except for the epistle addressed to its inhabitants, the undisputed letters contain no reference to Rome. The same silence applies to Colossae (or Laodicea) and even to Corinth. Galatia appears in 1 Corinthians 16:1, Ephesus in 1 Corinthians 15:32, 16:8; Philippi in 1 Thessalonians 2:2; and Thessalonica at Phil 4:16. Paul also refers to provinces, sometimes by metonymy or synecdoche:

Table 4.22: Itinerary Correlations[232]

Letters	Acts
Rome	28:16–31
Corinth	18:1–18
Galatia	16:6; 18:23; (13:13–14:23?)[233]
Ephesus	18:19–21; 19:1–40
Philippi	16:12–40
Colossae	—[234]
Thessalonica	17:1–9

Asia (including Ephesus) three times,[235] Achaea (Corinth) three times,[236], and Macedonia (including Philippi and Thessalonica) is mentioned eight times.[237] Acts mentions Rome five times, Corinth once, "Galatia" twice, Ephesus eight times, Philippi twice, and Thessalonica four times, as well as making three references to Achaea, fourteen to Asia, and eight to Macedonia. To be sure, these data will fit more than one explanation and offer no proof of Luke's use of Paul's letters.[238] They do, however, contribute to the overlap between Acts and epistles in regard to missionary sites. Luke shows more interest in (and knowledge about) the places to which Paul addressed (extant) letters than does the Apostle himself.

I return to the conclusions of Anthony Blassi. He worked patiently through the material and summarized his findings in three convenient tables.[239] His methods differ from those of other investigators; they are not philological but social-scientific, based upon the accumulation and tabulation of concrete data. One weakness of his approach is that he does not seek to determine how and in what form Luke would have gained access to Pauline correspondence. Many of the conventional historical objections and questions appear not to have crossed his mind. But that historical-critical observation is probably immaterial. Blassi's model is very economical, grounded in quantitative research, seeking a specific answer to a particular question rather than laying out all of the ramifications and then electing to jump in at some point. He cannot be dismissed as a maverick. He excludes Galatians, as stated above, on the grounds of conflict with Acts. He accepts other sources, including personal contact. The letters are but one possible source. In pursuit of his goal Blassi subsumes the data under four categories:

1. "Itinerary," references to Paul's travels.
2. "Redaction Themes," largely matters of faith and morals.[240]
3. "Named Christians."
4. "Paul's Background."

Listed below are his totals for all four categories in the several letters. (Items in parentheses indicate how many of these are "Redaction themes," the most subjective of his categories)

1 Thessalonians	5 (2)
1 Corinthians	29 (13)
2 Corinthians	11 (4)
Romans	11 (10)[241]
Philippians	8 (5)
Philemon	2

Adnittedly, many of Blassi's data can be objected to on the grounds that the possibility of Luke's having obtained this or that fact from an epistle does not prove that he *did* thus obtain it. In response to this valid caution I note once again, as Enslin would say, that sixty-six items are a considerable body of data.

What kinds of sources and how many of them would be required to supply this material? The letters provide here, as elsewhere, the most parsimonious solution. This does not mean that it is automatically the correct solution; it does mean that alternatives need to be spelled out in as much detail and with all the rigor used in generating the hypothesis that Luke used letters of Paul.

TENTATIVE CONCLUSION

In the face of the data thus far presented, the two strongest hypotheses are:

1. Luke used the letters of Paul.
2. Luke had direct contact with Paul and/or his some of his associates.

Each of these proposals must presume that Luke used his information quite selectively, repressing some items, making substantial alterations to Paul's theology, papering over his conflicts with other followers of Jesus, establishing him as a subordinate of Jerusalem, and so on. Proponents of (2) make Luke a thorn in Paul's flesh, better, a viper in his bosom. All of the efforts to transform this viper into a harmless garden snake gliding along in the apostle's path end up slighting both Luke and Paul, neither of whom is allowed to speak his own piece. For advocates of (1) the Paul of Acts is a Lucan construction designed to deal with issues of a later period.

An Example: The "Pre-Christian" Paul

Most of the extant data about Paul's "pre-Christian" background comes from Acts.[242] His name was Saul (7:58); he was a citizen of Tarsus (21:39) and a Roman citizen by birth (22:25–29). He was also a Pharisee in the family tradition (23:6), reared and long resident in Jerusalem, where a sibling also (evidently) lived (23:16), and was educated by Gamaliel (22:3). By trade he was a "tentmaker" (18:3). Two of these items are also found in the epistles: Paul was a Pharisee (Philippians 3:5), who engaged in manual labor (1 Corinthians 4:12; cf. 1 Thessalonians 2:9). From the letters no one would know that Paul had a (Grecized) Hebrew name, or that he came from Tarsus and was a citizen of that place, or that had long lived in Jerusalem, or that he held Roman citizenship. In the letters Paul appears as a diaspora Jew for whom the Bible was a Greek book. He is sufficiently familiar with Greek culture to engage in successful missionary work among gentiles.[243] Galatians would lead one to think that Paul lived in *Damascus* at the time of his "conversion" (Galatians 1:17); indeed, Galatians excludes the possibility that he persecuted believers in Jerusalem (1:23).[?] Nearly life-long residence in Jerusalem might not readily equip one to become a diaspora missionary, but Acts claims that there was a substantial body of Greek-speaking Jews in the holy city, and that claim is probably correct. Since Jews inhabited places from at least as far west as Italy to the Parthian empire in the east, Jerusalem was a cosmopolitan city—even exclusive of pilgrims and visitors. Education by Gamaliel is, however, unlikely—and not consonant with Acts itself.[244] Luke knew of Paul's "Hebrew roots," whether from the letters (Romans 11:1; 2 Corinthians 11:32; Philippians 3:5) or from some other source. He is almost certainly responsible for magnifying this into education at Jerusalem and eventual membership in the Sanhedrin (Acts 26:10).

Granted that the name "Saul" would not be unusual (Jews and members of other "ethnic" groups often had two names) and is thus possible, Luke's use of the designation serves his own ends. The name Saul appears exclusively until the missionary converts a specific gentile—a Roman proconsul at that—and becomes the prominent member of the team. Thereafter he is only "Paul." Those who suspect that Luke concocted this additional name look to Romans 11:1 and Philippians 3:5, where Paul identifies his tribe as that of Benjamin. From that tribe came the first Israelite monarch, Saul, as Luke well knew (Acts 13:21). Further, one may note that this "double name" establishes another parallel with Simon, whom Jesus called "Peter" (Luke 6:14).

Similar observations apply to Tarsus. Paul may have come from Tarsus, as Acts 9:11 suggests.[245] Tarsian citizenship is much less likely. It would require residence and education, including participation in the ephebate (and, normally, in polytheistic worship).[246] Paul could not have possessed both the Greek/Tarsian résumé and the Jewish/Jerusalem background that Luke awards him. In fact, it is not very likely that he had either. Luke does not care that his most important character could be called "Paul of Tarsus." What Luke relishes is the learned credentials that Paul whips out of his pocket at the very moment when he is being despised as a "barbarian" (21:39).[247] Readers of the letters would not for a moment imagine that the author held Roman citizenship. Since the letter to believers at Rome is an attempt to win their support, it would not have been out of place for Paul to note that he held Roman citizenship, but this says no more than that Paul missed an opportunity to clarify a historical problem. 2 Corinthians 11:25, "Three times I was beaten with rods" speaks against citizenship, since Roman citizens, as Acts is quite aware (chapters 16 and 21), were exempt from such penalties. These objections do not get to the core of the matter, which is ideological and literary. Luke does not portray Paul as a Roman citizen by accident of birth from freed slaves, for example, but as a citizen of high status. This serves his "apologetic" ends. Paul's citizenship is a (literal and figurative) "get out of jail free" card played at dramatic points in the narrative (Acts 16:37; 22:25—but not when Paul appeals to the emperor: 25:11!). Whatever basis in fact they may have had, Paul's citizenship at Tarsus and his possession of the Roman franchise function in Acts as literary devices with apologetic ends. Although Paul could have been a Roman citizen, it is most unlikely that he was a person of the resources and prominence depicted in Acts.[248]

Readers who come upon the information that Paul plied a trade in Acts 18:3 would be surprised at this—surprised, that is, if the word "tentmaker" had not entered the English language as a trope for non-stipendiary clergy.[249] Nothing in Acts has hinted that Paul needed to earn his daily bread by the sweat of his brow, nor, it should be observed, did this burden last longer than two verses—although it is generalized at 20:34. This is one item of the "tradition" that Luke has given the soft pedal, possibly introducing it in chapter 18 so that it would not be too improbable in chapter 20. Luke takes simple data: Paul was a Pharisee of proper pedigree, he worked for a living, perhaps he also bore the name Saul and came from Tarsus, and he had a Latin name (most of which he could glean from the epistles), and transforms them into wonderful and comprehensive credentials, while enrolling all of this impressive material in the service of his plot.

Corinth

The case of Corinth is interesting, for in that setting Acts first speaks of Paul's physical labor—also mentioned explicitly in 1 Corinthians 4:12—and it introduces this subject in conjunction with Prisca and Aquila. Their subsequent career in Acts is also relevant to 1 Corinthians, for they reappear in 18:18 as fellow passengers of Paul to Ephesus, where he deposits them before engaging in a "hit and run" mission to the synagogue. 1 Corinthians 16:19 relays the couple's greetings to *Corinth* from *Ephesus*, where they head up a house church. Luke might well have determined the couple's movements from 1 Corinthians.[250] Into that same environment Luke introduces Apollos. Given the controversial nature of Apollos in 1 Corinthians (1:11–4:6), it is noteworthy that Luke employs his narrative hand to extricate Paul from the stage while Apollos is present in Ephesus.[251] The statement in Acts states that Apollos came from Alexandria, information not derived from the epistles, although inferable, for he was an eloquent and learned man (Acts 18:24). His wisdom and rhetoric gave him more luster than Paul in the eyes of some Corinthians who were also enamored of spiritual gifts, a quality in which Apollos was not deficient. The language used to characterize his spiritual endowments, "burning with spiritual ardor," (ζέων τῷ πνεύματι, Acts 18: 25), appears to derive from the almost identical wording of Romans 12:11, τῷ πνεύματι ζέοντες. The expression is quite rare, occurring elsewhere only in writings that appear to cite Acts or Romans.

Despite these manifold talents, Apollos "knew only the baptism of John" (Acts 18:25). For Luke this level of awareness appears to stand for unsound or defective theology (cf. Acts 19:1–7). Prisca and Aquila discreetly corrected this deficit, whereupon Apollos came up with the idea of moving on to Greece, where, properly recommended, he carried on a successful mission among the Jews (Acts 18:26–28). Of course, no blame for his doctrinal shortcomings attaches to Paul, who had yet to encounter Apollos before the latter's trip to Greece. All of these movements and events could have been developed on the basis of 1 Corinthians. The entire matter is handled with great delicacy. To say that 1 Corinthians *could* have been the source is not to say that it *was* the source, nor that it was the only source.[252] It does indicate how much Luke could have done with scanty data.

If the preceding survey has led the reader to conclude that Luke could and did make creative use of sources, including the letters of Paul, the example in

Table 4.23: Corinthian Converts

Acts 18:8	1 Corinthians 1:14
Κρίσπος δὲ ὁ ἀρχισυνάγωγος ἐπίστευσεν τῷ κυρίῳ σὺν ὅλῳ τῷ οἴκῳ αὐτοῦ, καὶ πολλοὶ τῶν Κορινθίων ἀκούοντες ἐπίστευον καὶ ἐβαπτίζοντο. Crispus, the official of the synagogue, became a believer in the Lord, together with all his household; and many of the Corinthians who heard Paul became believers and were baptized	εὐχαριστῶ ὅτι οὐδένα ὑμῶν ἐβάπτισα εἰ μὴ Κρίσπον καὶ Γάϊον, I thank God that I baptized none of you except Crispus and Gaius Cf. 1:16: ἐβάπτισα δὲ καὶ τὸν Στεφανᾶ οἶκον· λοιπὸν οὐκ οἶδα εἴ τινα ἄλλον ἐβάπτισα. (I did baptize also the *household* of Stephanas; beyond that, I do not know whether I baptized anyone else.)

Table 4.23 will be attractive. In both 1 Corinthians and Acts, the first person whom Paul is said to have baptized bears the name "Crispus." Identification of the two is common. Commentators on 1 Corinthians may choose to flesh out the details from Acts 18.[253] If Luke took this information from Paul, he made two important changes and inferred another. First, he made Crispus a Jew. 1 Corinthians does not specify this, and most readers would suppose that he was a gentile. Second, Luke promoted Crispus to a prominent place in the synagogue. Both of these changes, as well as the generalization to include the entire household, are quite characteristic of Luke, who likes to emphasize Paul's Jewish missionary activity and the social status of his converts.[254] Yet the account is confused and seems to demand some explanation. Acts 18:6–7 reports that Paul withdrew from the synagogue in response to opposition from "the Jews" and took up residence in a house adjacent to the synagogue. The subsequent verse reports the conversion of the head of that synagogue, *en famille*. This order is not very logical, since one would expect a report of the synagogue leader's conversion to precede that of Paul's abandonment of the synagogue

Acts 18:17 introduces one Sosthenes, identified as *the* head of the synagogue. Readers are likely to fill in blanks and conclude that, after Paul withdrew from the synagogue, Crispus left to affiliate with the new community, following which a new synagogue chief was chosen. This interpretation is reasonable enough, for it presumes that baptism incorporated Crispus into a different religious community, the formation of which did not occur until Paul ceased his work in the synagogue; but the text does not make these simple connections. Luke may well have based his statement about Crispus upon 1 Corinthians. An alternative would require the preservation of his name in some "tradition," together with details. Lüdemann inclines toward such a tradition and says that the data about Crispus's office "may be historically credible," but he does not explain the transmission and function of this tradition.[255] The leading obstacle to attributing this report to a foundation legend is that all of the details conform, as noted, to Lucan redactional interests. The mission follows his standard pattern: initial success, followed by conflict with unbelieving Jews that leads to separation from the synagogue, followed by greater success that climaxes in a legal action in which Paul is victorious, but after which he nonetheless leaves town. Putative traditions preserving just such data as suit Luke's agenda are the sort of felicitous coincidences that ought to arouse critical suspicion.[256] The statement that Paul was a "tentmaker" by trade has a strong claim to be independent tradition, for it does not conform to Luke's view of Paul's status. Luke does appear to have some traditions about Paul's mission to Corinth. He has blended these into an account that includes data from 1 Corinthians.

Jews First

Ben Witherington considers the influence of Paul's epistles upon Acts to be minimal, but he regards Romans 1:16//Acts 3:26 as an instance of that influence.[257] (See Table 4.24.) His example touches upon an important point: Where did Luke acquire the idea, which is more accurately called a conviction, that Paul always began his missionary work among people of his own religious heritage? Paul's self-understanding is that of a missionary to gentiles. The letters

Table 4.24: Jews First

Acts	Romans 1:16; 2:9–10
3:26 *Peter says to the people of Jerusalem:* "When God raised up his servant, he sent him **first** to you, to bless you by turning each of you from your wicked ways." 13:46 (Pisidian Antioch): Then both Paul and Barnabas spoke out boldly, saying, "It was necessary that the word of God should be spoken **first to you**. Since you reject it and judge yourselves to be unworthy of eternal life, we are now turning to the Gentiles 18:6 (Corinth): When **the Jews** opposed and reviled him, in protest he shook the dust from his clothes and said to them, "Your blood be on your own heads! I am innocent. From now on I will go to the Gentiles." 19:8–9 9 (Ephesus): He entered the synagogue and for three months spoke out boldly, and argued persuasively about the kingdom of God. When some stubbornly refused to believe and spoke evil of the Way before the congregation, he left them, taking the disciples with him, and argued daily in the lecture hall of Tyrannus 28:28 (Rome): "Let it be known to you then that this salvation of God has been sent to the Gentiles; they will listen."	16 For I am not ashamed of the gospel; it is the power of God for salvation to everyone who has faith, to **the Jew first** and also to the Greek. 9 There will be anguish and distress for everyone who does evil, **the Jew first** and also the Greek, 10 but glory and honor and peace for everyone who does good, **the Jew first** and also the Greek

to his converts seem to assume that the recipients are of polytheist background. The controversies known from the undisputed letters do not relate to his acquisition of Jewish adherents. In Acts, however, Paul is primarily a missionary to Jews, who turns to gentiles only in the face of rejection (9:20, 29; 13:5, 16, 46; 14:1; cf. 16:3; 16:13; 17:1, 10, 16–17; 18:4, 19). Luke here expresses what most regard as a salvation-historical principle. The Jews are first and are therefore the first to receive the good news. He "historicized" the claims of Romans 1:16, etc. (especially Romans 9–11) by making Paul the executor of this principle. This tactic served any number of ends, including the defense of Paul against various theological charges. It is difficult to imagine that various local traditions portrayed the apostle to the gentiles as an apostle to the Jews who did not take up his vocation (Galatians 1:16) until other doors were shut—that believers at Thessalonica and Corinth, for example, maintained foundation stories to the effect of "Paul established our community only after he failed to persuade any substantial number of Jews." With the deconstruction of this unlikely proposition, much of the potential for Pauline traditions behind Acts effervesces. What is left is a theological axiom that has become a narrative cliché. The self-described "Apostle to the gentiles" (Romans 11:13!; cf. Galatians 1:16) has become a missionary to Jews who converts gentiles as a second choice. If one asks where Luke got his idea, Romans becomes the one extant source. This does not establish certainty, but it is more probable than the speculative alternatives, certainly more probable than the hypothesis of local tradition.[258]

A Gentile Era

Anthony Blassi proposes that Luke may have acquired his notion of an era of gentile domination from Romans 11:25. See Table 4.25. This is interesting, and it does have the merit of seeking to provide some explanation for an obscure verse, but the link is far from clear.[259] If there is one, Luke 21:24 would be a transformation of a Pauline notion.

Table 4.25: Time for Gentiles

Luke 21:24	Romans 11:25
καὶ πεσοῦνται στόματι μαχαίρης καὶ αἰχμαλωτισθήσονται εἰς τὰ ἔθνη πάντα, καὶ Ἰερουσαλὴμ ἔσται πατουμένη ὑπὸ ἐθνῶν, **ἄχρι οὗ πληρωθῶσιν καιροὶ ἐθνῶν.** they will fall by the edge of the sword and be taken away as captives among all nations; and Jerusalem will be trampled on by the Gentiles, **until** the times of the **Gentiles** are **ful**filled	Οὐ γὰρ θέλω ὑμᾶς ἀγνοεῖν, ἀδελφοί, τὸ μυστήριον τοῦτο, ἵνα μὴ ἦτε [ἐν] ἑαυτοῖς φρόνιμοι, ὅτι πώρωσις ἀπὸ μέρους τῷ Ἰσραὴλ γέγονεν **ἄχρις οὗ** τὸ **πλήρωμα** τῶν **ἐθνῶν** εἰσέλθη. So that you may not claim to be wiser than you are, brothers and sisters, I want you to understand this mystery: a hardening has come upon part of Israel, **until the full** number of the **Gentiles** has come in.

The passages cited in Table 4.26 receive further consideration elsewhere for their place in the transformation of Paul's dialectical approach to ritual purity.[260] The issue here is whether Luke is dependent upon Romans for his account of Peter's vision. The subject is the same. Luke 11:41 reveals that its author is familiar with the slogan "all things are pure," which he spiritualizes. Acts 10:10–20 and Romans 14:14–23, from which I have printed excerpts, share three words or stems: κοιν- in the sense of "impure," καθαρ- "clean/cleanse," and διακρίνομαι, "distinguish," "decide," "dispute," "doubt." The last is certainly the most important, for Luke uses the verb only four times, always with regard to the vision of Peter and the conversion of Cornelius (10:20; 11:2, 12; 15:9). That he uses it in the same sense as does Paul in Romans 14:23 hardly argues against dependence; no doubt Luke wished to use Paul's term to establish his own understanding.[261] This is another intriguing example of how Luke used Pauline terminology to invest it with new meaning. Luke did not merely abolish the relative, dialectical, situation-based orientation that could make decisions so difficult for Paul. He removed the issue from the realm of human decision by attributing the principle to God. Furthermore, Luke holds that Paul was neither the source of the principle nor the recipient of the vision. Jesus had taught

Table 4.26: Pure Coincidence?

Acts 10: 10–20 (14–15, 20)	**Romans 14:14–23 (14, 20, 23)**
14 ὁ δὲ Πέτρος εἶπεν, Μηδαμῶς, κύριε, ὅτι οὐδέποτε ἔφαγον πᾶν **κοινὸν** καὶ **ἀκάθαρτον**. 15 καὶ φωνὴ πάλιν ἐκ δευτέρου πρὸς αὐτόν, Ἃ ὁ θεὸς **ἐκαθάρισεν** σὺ μὴ **κοίνου**. 20 ἀλλὰ ἀναστὰς κατάβηθι καὶ πορεύου σὺν αὐτοῖς μηδὲν **διακρινόμενος**, ὅτι ἐγὼ ἀπέσταλκα αὐτούς.	14 οἶδα καὶ πέπεισμαι ἐν κυρίῳ Ἰησοῦ ὅτι οὐδὲν **κοινὸν** δι' ἑαυτοῦ· εἰ μὴ τῷ λογιζομένῳ τι **κοινὸν** εἶναι, ἐκείνῳ **κοινόν**. 20 μὴ ἕνεκεν βρώματος κατάλυε τὸ ἔργον τοῦ θεοῦ. **πάντα** μὲν **καθαρά**, ἀλλὰ κακὸν τῷ ἀνθρώπῳ τῷ διὰ προσκόμματος ἐσθίοντι. 23 ὁ δὲ **διακρινόμενος** ἐὰν φάγῃ κατακέκριται, ὅτι οὐκ ἐκ πίστεως· πᾶν δὲ ὃ οὐκ ἐκ πίστεως ἁμαρτία ἐστίν.
14 But Peter said, "By no means, Lord; for I have never eaten anything that is **profane** or **unclean**."15 The voice said to him again, a second time, "What God has *made clean*, you must not *call profane*."20 Now get up, go down, and go with them **without hesitation**; for I have sent them."	14 I know and am persuaded in the Lord Jesus that nothing is **unclean** in itself; but it is **unclean** for anyone who thinks it **unclean**. 20 Do not, for the sake of food, destroy the work of God. **Everything is indeed clean**, but it is wrong for you to make others fall by what you eat; 23 But those who **have doubts** are condemned if they eat, because they do not act from faith; for whatever does not proceed from faith is sin
Luke 11:41	
πλὴν τὰ ἐνόντα δότε ἐλεημοσύνην, καὶ ἰδοὺ **πάντα καθαρὰ** ὑμῖν ἐστιν. So give for alms those things that are within; and see, **everything will be clean** for you.	

that all things are pure and Peter received a revelation to the same effect. Luke rescues an idea associated with the Pauline mission by keeping Paul out of the picture.[262]

The Power of Darkness

The important parallel set out in Table 4.27 certainly belongs among the Deutero-Pauline expressions shared by Acts. The question is whether it deserves consideration from the perspective of intertextuality. In favor of such a finding is that before Clement and Origen, i.e. from the late second century onward, this phrase occurs only in these two passages. Also in support of literary dependence is the close relation between Acts 26:18 and Colossians 1:12–14.[263] The phrase is evocative of the language and thought of the Dead Sea Scrolls.[264] The writer of Colossians employs spatial imagery to argue that believers have been translated into a new realm. By joining "power of darkness" with "hour" Luke resists a purely spatial application. The "power of darkness" may refer to the limited period of Satanic dominance that brought about the death of Jesus (cf. Luke 22:3). This could be instanced as an example of Luke's resistance to the speculative theology of Colossians in general. If this is a reminiscence, it may well come from memory rather than from consultation of the text. Again, the phrase may derive from otherwise unattested liturgical language. While literary dependence of Acts upon Colossians is unsure, what is certain is that Luke participates in a Deutero-Pauline thought world.

Table 4.27: Power of Darkness

Luke 22:53	Colossians 1:13
καθ' ἡμέραν ὄντος μου μεθ' ὑμῶν ἐν τῷ ἱερῷ οὐκ ἐξετείνατε τὰς χεῖρας ἐπ' ἐμέ· ἀλλ' αὕτη ἐστὶν ὑμῶν ἡ ὥρα καὶ **ἡ ἐξουσία τοῦ σκότους**.	ὃς ἐρρύσατο ἡμᾶς ἐκ **τῆς ἐξουσίας τοῦ σκότους** καὶ μετέστησεν εἰς τὴν βασιλείαν τοῦ υἱοῦ τῆς ἀγάπης αὐτοῦ
When I was with you day after day in the temple, you did not lay hands on me. But this is your hour, and the **power of darkness**!" cf. **Acts 26:18** ἀνοῖξαι ὀφθαλμοὺς αὐτῶν, τοῦ ἐπιστρέψαι ἀπὸ **σκότους** εἰς φῶς καὶ τῆς **ἐξουσίας** τοῦ Σατανᾶ ἐπὶ τὸν θεόν, τοῦ λαβεῖν αὐτοὺς ἄφεσιν ἁμαρτιῶν καὶ κλῆρον ἐν τοῖς ἡγιασμένοις πίστει τῇ εἰς ἐμέ. to open their eyes so that they may turn from **darkness** to light and from the **power** of Satan to God, so that they may receive forgiveness of sins and a place among those who are sanctified by faith in me.'[265]	He has rescued us from **the power of darkness** and transferred us into the kingdom of his beloved Son

Divine Impartiality and Heavenly Peace

Behind the idiom rendered "(God shows) no partiality" is a Hebrew phrase translated rather literally in the LXX.[266] (See Table 4.28a.) Those unfamiliar with its meaning will not make sense of the Greek. Paul uses the LXX idiom in Galatians 2:6. The other texts employ nouns formed from this noun + verb combination, in a phrase οὐκ ἔστιν (there is not) combined with a noun. Those nouns appear only in Christian texts, although it is very likely that they were found in the literature of Hellenistic Judaism. Colossians, followed by Ephesians, applies this principle to the treatment of slaves. Ephesians 6:9 may show the influence of Romans, but this is not certain for Colossians.[267] Acts 10:34 probably depends upon Romans 2, for it uses the same relatively rare vocabulary in the same context: the relation of Jew to Greek in missionary perspective. (See Table 4.24.) Jouette Bassler says:

> Paul's vision of divine impartiality as an acceptance that transcends ethnic boundaries does not immediately fade from view in early Christian writings. A similar understanding of this theologumenon is presented in a more narrative fashion in the book of Acts, but there associated with the Apostle Peter."[268]

Bassler does not consider the possibility of literary dependence, for that is not her subject, but she lends support to the proposal by indicating the congruity of the respective arguments. The same theme is echoed in different wording in Peter's speech, Acts 15:9, on which see Table 4.20. Apart from Paul and Acts the concept tends to apply to the insignificance of social distinctions, as may be seen in Colossians and its parallels.[269]

The specific parallels exhibited in Table 4.28b do not, *per se*, constitute a strong argument for dependence, because this is a matter of a two-word construction and because Isa 52:7 is a popular text for citation. The interest arises not only because each modifies Isa 52:7 in the same way (in contrast to Paul's abbreviation in Romans 10:15), but also because of the overlapping contexts: Acts seems to use Ephesians 2:15–18 elsewhere.[270] Ephesians appears to have been one of Luke's "favorite" epistles, and the beginning of Peter's speech in Acts 10:34–43 has numerous Pauline allusions. An intertextual relation is therefore quite likely.

Converting Saul

Luke evidently subscribed to the view that if anything is worth saying, it is worth saying three times. Table 4.29 compares the elements of such a triad. This famous example from Acts is the Conversion of Paul, first narrated in 9:1–19a, then described by Paul in two important autobiographical addresses, 22:3–21 and 26:2:23.[271] Equally well known are the differences among the several accounts in Acts and the tensions between Acts 9 and Paul's own account in Galatians 1:15–17. Whatever the source of Acts 9, it treats the event as the "conversion" of a notorious enemy of the people of God,[272] while Galatians describes it in language evocative of a prophetic call.[273] In addition, whereas Paul states most emphatically that this call was unmediated, Acts 9 and 22

Table 4.28a: Respect for Persons

Acts 10:34–35	Romans 2:11	to me
Ἀνοίξας δὲ Πέτρος τὸ στόμα εἶπεν, Ἐπ᾽ ἀληθείας καταλαμβάνομαι ὅτι **οὐκ ἔστιν προσωπολήμπτης ὁ θεός**, 35 ἀλλ᾽ ἐν παντὶ ἔθνει ὁ φοβούμενος αὐτὸν καὶ **ἐργαζόμενος δικαιοσύνην** δεκτὸς αὐτῷ ἐστιν. Then Peter began to speak to them: "I truly understand that **God shows no partiality,** 35 but in every nation anyone who fears him **and does** what is right is acceptable to him	10 δόξα δὲ καὶ τιμὴ καὶ εἰρήνη παντὶ τῷ **ἐργαζομένῳ** τὸ ἀγαθόν, Ἰουδαίῳ τε πρῶτον καὶ Ἕλληνι. οὐ γάρ ἐστιν **προσωπολημψία** παρὰ τῷ θεῷ. but glory and honor and peace for everyone who does good, the Jew first and also the Greek; for God **shows no partiality**. Cf. **Gal 2:6c** πρόσωπον [ὁ] θεὸς ἀνθρώπου οὐ λαμβάνει And from those who were supposed to be acknowledged leaders (what they actually were makes no difference to me; **God shows no partiality**)—those leaders contributed nothing	**Deutero-Pauline Col 3:25** (with reference to slaves) ὁ γὰρ ἀδικῶν κομίσεται ὃ ἠδίκησεν, καὶ **οὐκ ἔστιν προσωπολημψία**. For the wrongdoer will be paid back for whatever wrong has been done, and there is no partiality. Cf. **Eph 6:9d** (with reference to slaves) **προσωπολημψία οὐκ ἔστιν** παρ᾽ αὐτῷ. And, masters, do the same to them. Stop threatening them, for you know that both of you have the same Master in heaven, and **with him there is no partiality**

Table 4.28b: Proclaiming Peace

Acts 10:36a	Ephesians 2:17
τὸν λόγον [ὃν] ἀπέστειλεν τοῖς υἱοῖς Ἰσραὴλ **εὐαγγελιζόμενος εἰρήνην** διὰ Ἰησοῦ Χριστοῦ You know the message he sent to the people of Israel, **preaching peace** by Jesus Christ Cf. Isa 52:7a ὡς ὥρα ἐπὶ τῶν ὀρέων, ὡς πόδες **εὐαγγελιζομένου** ἀκοὴν **εἰρήνης**, How beautiful upon the mountains are the feet of the messenger who **announces peace,**	καὶ ἐλθὼν **εὐηγγελίσατο εἰρήνην** ὑμῖν τοῖς μακρὰν καὶ εἰρήνην τοῖς ἐγγύς So he came and **proclaimed peace** to you who were far off and peace to those who were near Cf. **Rom 10:15**: πῶς δὲ κηρύξωσιν ἐὰν μὴ ἀποσταλῶσιν; καθὼς γέγραπται, Ὡς ὡραῖοι οἱ πόδες τῶν **εὐαγγελιζομένων** ἀγαθά. And how are they to proclaim him unless they are sent? As it is written, "How beautiful are the feet of those who bring good news!" **Eph 6:15**: καὶ ὑποδησάμενοι τοὺς πόδας ἐν ἑτοιμασίᾳ **τοῦ εὐαγγελίου τῆς εἰρήνης** As shoes for your feet put on whatever will make you ready **to proclaim the gospel of peace.**

Table 4.29: Converting Saul

Items	Galatians 1–2	Acts 9	Acts 22	Acts 26
Prelude	Paul persecutes	Paul persecutes	Paul persecutes	Paul persecutes
Location	Not stated (cf. 1:17)	On road to Damascus	On road to Damascus	On road to Damascus
Form	Like prophetic call	Punishment and "Conversion" of enemy of God	Punishment and "Conversion" of enemy of God	Mixture of Punishment story and prophetic call
Intermediary and Role	None	Ananias Has vision instructing him to heal Saul Learns of Saul's mission Heals Baptizes (?)	Ananias Comes to Paul Heals Announces that Paul will have universal mission Invites Paul to be baptized	None
Commission	In vision To gentiles	Told to Ananias To gentiles, monarchs, Jews	Intimated by Ananias; received in Temple Entire world Gentiles	In vision To gentiles

describe his subsequent contact with a certain Ananias, who baptized and healed the former persecutor. The third account in Acts 26 introduces two important changes. The missionary commission comes directly from the heavenly Jesus, rather than from the prophetic announcement of a human intermediary. With Ananias eliminated, the conversion of Paul has become a prophetic call.[274] Although literary considerations may help explain these alterations, they do not exclude the view that Luke has, through his retellings, manipulated the story in Acts 9 until it better conforms to that of Galatians 1.[275] Evidence for viewing Luke as the first harmonizer of Acts and Galatians continues to accumulate. In the end he preferred Paul's understanding of his "conversion." Circumstances evidently required that he accept the rival and evidently "normative" story of the conversion and only gradually and with some delicacy did he adjust it until he achieved his goal, which is to leave the reader with the picture painted in Acts 26.[276] This is the most memorable of the commissioning statements, it appears in the final and most decisive place, and it is the closest of the three to Galatians 1. For whatever reasons, Acts 9 agrees with the view of Paul's opponents in Galatians that his commission was mediated by human agency (cf. Galatians 1:1, 11–12, 16).[277] By the time that Luke has finished repeating the story, that difference between the Paul of Acts and the Paul of the letters has been eliminated.

Table 4.29 indicates the extent to which Acts 26 conforms to Galatians. The table summarizes the gradual shifts that take place within the sequence. Acts 26 is the climactic account of Paul's "conversion." It is also the climax of Luke's attempts to reshape this story into conformity with Paul's own. There is, it would seem, more than one way to skin a cat. That Acts 26 is rather closer to Galatians 1 than are the accounts in chapters 9 and 22 is not disputed. The most economical and least problematic solution is to posit that for the account in Acts 9:1–19a, Luke probably had a source that he reshaped by bringing the story of the conversion into closer conformity with that of Paul in Galatians.

The Farewell Address at Miletus (Acts 20:17–35)

"... [T]he speech of Paul to the elders of the Ephesian Church in xx. 18–35 contains so many echoes of the language of Pauline epistles that we must suppose, either that the writer had access to these epistles (which is on other grounds improbable), or that he worked upon actual reminiscence of Paul's speech upon this or some similar occasion."[278]

That fine word "consensus" characterizes the view that Paul's address to the presbyters (elders) of the Church of Ephesus (Acts 20:17–35) has a Pauline character.[279] Yet little agreement exists on the specific nature of this character, although—or because—the address has been subjected to repeated examinations and microscopic scrutiny. For some researchers this speech "proves" that Luke knew and heard Paul.[280] Dibelius and others speak of, or imply, a "Pauline tradition."[281] Another hypothesis, argued in great detail by Lars Aejmelaeus, is that the speech reveals general and/or particular knowledge of various letters. Finally, this speech—hereafter "Miletus"—serves still others as evidence that some of the Deutero-Pauline writers used Acts.[282] The intertextual table is full.

Miletus is unusual in several ways. The most important of these is that since this is Paul's only speech in Acts to a group of fellow believers, the content is pastoral rather than evangelistic. Information about Paul's "missionary techniques" is not prominent in the letters because they were pastoral instruments, in most cases written to communities that Paul had founded. Acts, however, focuses upon Paul as the founder of communities rather than as a pastor.[283] The speech at Miletus reveals the pastoral side of the missionary, and more. It is as if "the Paul of Acts" has slipped into a telephone booth from which he presently emerges, wearing eyeglasses and a business suit. Were Acts the only source of our knowledge about Paul, 20:17–35 would be shocking. Those familiar with the letters are less surprised. This speech presents a known Paul, brimming with useful, if not universally welcome, advice, issuing dire warnings, and freely willing to share examples of his selfless sacrifice and suffering.

Acts 20 contains other important differences, for Miletus is an address to Christian *leaders*, a setting not found in the undisputed epistles, which address the entire community.[284] The audience at Miletus invites comparison with the world of the Pastoral Epistles (1–2 Timothy and Titus), 1 Peter, and the "Apostolic Fathers," the era of the emergence of Christian officers.[285] Comparison with the Pastorals is particularly apt, for both speech and letters seem to address community leaders and communicate with the faithful by telling leaders what they should teach. The technique provides three for the price of one: a paradigm for leadership, reinforcement of leaders' authority, and guidance for believers.[286] The speech belongs, I shall argue, to the post-Pauline era and makes use of a suitable genre, the Testament, a formalized medium for setting out the final wishes and predictions of a dying man.[287] In early Judaism and Christianity this genre was often blended with the Farewell Address, to which Acts 20:17–35 also conforms.[288] Another factor to be taken into account is the place of this address in the structure of Acts and its parallel, if any, with the gospel. The latter is obvious: Jesus' final speech to his disciples prior to his arrest (Luke 22:14–38).[289] Luke's parallelism emphasizes the readily apparent fact that this is the last speech of Paul to his followers and successors.[290] Within the plot structure of Acts this passage initiates a shift toward apologetic. All of the subsequent speeches of Paul in Acts (except the brief discourses in chapter 27) defend his views and conduct.

The above "modern liberal" view begins with the relatively conservative Martin Dibelius, who claimed that "[T]his is how Luke wishes him [Paul] to be regarded, and in this retrospect we are told many things which have not been said in the story . . ."[291] Dibelius went on to observe that reminders and claims that would seem inappropriate—what popular American culture would label "paranoid"—to the dramatic audience are directed toward a wider circle. This is the right speech in the right place, quite in accord with the "classical historiographical tradition."[292] Such analysis makes Colin Hemer's blood boil. His point of departure is that this address is

> ". . . [T]he only speech embedded in a 'we-passage' account of a public occasion, with the implication that Luke was present, and also beginning to make an explicit and immediate record of his renewed companionship with Paul.[293]

Hemer regards matters of genre as structure are misplaced and question-begging. He prefers the "simplest explanation," which lies in ". . . [T]he emotional farewell, the introspective retrospect, and the admonitions for the future . . ." as ". . . the natural reflection of a real situation."[294] For Hemer, any attempts to identify the genre of this speech or to analyze its structure are threats to its historical integrity—as if Paul wrote and spoke without structure or never resorted to the use of rhetorical patterns or literary forms![295] That different scholars propose different structural plans is sufficient, Hemer holds, to show the want of structure.[296] Returning to the realm of the psychological, he mentions the proximity of "the prolonged Corinthian controversy" to explain his subject's emotional state.[297] One item he neglects to bring into consideration is that as far as readers of Acts are concerned, the "prolonged controversy" never took place. If for no other reason, the argument that the "Paulinism" of the Miletus speech reflects the actual words of the apostle on that occasion will gain few adherents, but that argument has an intrinsic probability that Hemer did not emphasize.[298] Dibelius noted similarities to 1 Thessalonians and rebuffed an earlier attempt to attribute to Luke knowledge of that letter, but he did not take the matter further.[299]

The "Paulinism" of this speech is an issue that Dibelius and others address all too vaguely. I think that the only theories that adequately account for the "parallels" to the epistles in this text are the appeal to intertextuality (Luke knew some letters), or the claim that the author of Acts was on the scene and/or knew Paul and his thought rather well, or that Acts makes use of some direct source other than the epistles.[300] Two questions that come to the inquisitive mind are:

1. Why does Paul address Ephesian believers at *Miletus*, which lies a good eighty kilometers from Ephesus and would require a journey of several days?[301] For Paul to require that these (dignified and elderly?) persons come to him does not strike one as very "pastoral."
2. What were presbyters/elders at that time (c. 55) and how many of them were there in one community or another?[302]

A broad consensus holds that the data of the itinerary of Paul's journey to Jerusalem rests upon tradition. Ephesus was evidently not one of the stopping places. This has a number of possible explanations. Perhaps the group could not find a ship that was scheduled to stop there. If the purpose of this voyage was to deliver the Collection, as it almost certainly was, there was no reason to stop at Ephesus, as the believers there had not taken part in the Collection (Romans 15:26). Critics prefer less mundane motives. In 1914 the renowned Old Testament scholar Julius Wellhausen, in a brief but provocative study of Acts, suggested that Paul did not visit Ephesus because it was not safe for him to go there.[303] This idea derives from the difficulties Paul experienced in Ephesus, including a possible imprisonment.[304] Whatever the explanation, Luke imports officers from Ephesus because that place was central to him (Acts may have been written at Ephesus), and because Ephesus was to become the site of considerable controversy in the post-Pauline period.[305] These conflicts are pertinent to the date of Acts and will receive attention in a subsequent chapter.

Elders, better called "presbyters,"[306] begin to make their appearance in Christian literature by the close of the first century. As a recent monograph devoted to the subject concludes,

> 'The elders', we have argued, was a collective way of referring to a group of leaders acting representatively, and did not appear in the churches (because it was not appropriate) until the household congregations began to multiply and consolidate their position in a town.[307]

The author of Acts seems to presume that the implied readers will know what presbyters are. They appear in a group in Jerusalem in Acts 11:30 as the recipients of "famine relief" from Antioch. Thereafter they are found at Jerusalem with "the apostles" (Acts 15:2, 4, 6, 22, 23; 16:4), except in 21:18, when they accompany James (with no reference to apostles). This expression "Apostles and Presbyters" corresponds with references to Jewish leadership: "leaders, presbyters, and scribes," "leaders of the people and presbyters," "high priests and presbyters," "presbyters and scribes," "high priests and presbyters," "the high priest with some presbyters," "the high priests and the presbyters of the Jews."[308] The closest parallel is between "apostles and presbyters" and "high priests and presbyters." Luke is at least willing to let readers imagine that the nascent Jerusalem church has a structure not unlike that of its Jewish parents and rival.[309] One must, however, distinguish between "presbyter" as a member of a council such as a *Gerousia* (a term that derives from another Greek word for "old"[310] and corresponds to "Senator" and "Senate," which, in turn, derive from Latin terms for "old") and "presbyter" as a community official. The Jewish presbyters whom Acts associates with high priests etc. are the former: members of a council.[311] Apparently of a different type are the presbyters whom Paul and Barnabas appoint in Lystra, Iconium, and Pisidian Antioch in 14:23,[312] and probably those of Ephesus in chapter 20. The Ephesian presbyters seem to have been formally designated community leaders, for the speech addresses them in their capacity as those who have pastoral charge over others.

If one takes Acts 20:17–38 as a realistic account of a meeting that took place c. 55 CE, how many presbyters would have been present? On the basis of Campbell's model—one presbyter per house church—a half-dozen would be a generous estimate.[313] Yet Luke does not give the impression that the audience was of a compact size suitable for a conference or an informal chat. Paul delivers a major address on a major occasion.[314] Even before any consideration of the content of the speech—in which Paul never uses the term "brothers," freely used to Jewish audiences—the "realistic" approach collapses.[315] The Pauline churches at Ephesus c. 55 CE probably had no presbyters, and it is highly unlikely that Paul would have summoned leaders from only that community to meet with him at Miletus.[316] Luke has, as indicated above, strategic reasons for directing the speech to Ephesus.

The farewell address has some features of the aforementioned "testament" form. Among these are presenting the speaker as an example for moral imitation and making predictions about future events.[317] The apostle knows that troubles will break out after his "departure." His example provides the model and methods by which the "wolves" may be subdued. The two interests meld quite successfully to form a brief treatise on leadership. The difference between this speech and the epistles is that in the letters Paul is *being* a pastor. Here he shows others how to embrace that charge and to fulfill the pastoral task. With regard to both the task of handing down the Pauline tradition and the content of the tradition itself, the speech belongs to a milieu that is a good half-century later than its dramatic date. Miletus also demonstrates that the author of Acts was quite conversant with "authentic" Pauline tradition viewed through Deutero-Pauline lenses, a fact that further helps to establish the date.

The present purpose is to attempt to determine the source of that "authentic" tradition. The letters of Paul speak only indirectly or generally about the foundation of communities, but they are not lacking in pastoral matter. The various parallels between Miletus and the letters are well known.[318] They include several types of real or alleged affinities: such verbal parallels as identical words or synonymous expressions involving similar words; conceptual, ideological, or thematic comparisons; and formal, rhetorical, or structural resemblances. Particularly important are clusters of parallels of more than one kind. The issue is how to account for them. What follows is a far from exhaustive "intertextual commentary" on the Miletus speech, largely based upon comparisons between Acts 20:18–35 and ten Pauline epistles[319] that have previously been adduced by others.[320]

ACTS 20:18

Ancient pedagogy was quite fond of three techniques that are amenable to the blandishments of the mnemonic: "memory, maxims, and morals."[321] Paul uses the expression "you know" about twenty-five times in his undisputed epistles.[322] Since this practice was peculiar neither to Paul nor to any passage in his writings, specific dependence is out of the question, but the verb shows at least that Luke knew Paul's style and could borrow a stylistic feature (albeit with a different verb).[323] This expression recurs in verse 34. The phrase "from the first

Table 4.30: Acts 20:18

ὡς δὲ παρεγένοντο πρὸς αὐτὸν εἶπεν αὐτοῖς, Ὑμεῖς ἐπίστασθε **ἀπὸ πρώτης ἡμέρας** ἀφ' ἧς ἐπέβην εἰς τὴν Ἀσίαν πῶς μεθ' ὑμῶν τὸν πάντα χρόνον **ἐγενόμην**	E.g., **1 Thessalonians 1:5; 2:1** 1:5 καθὼς οἴδατε οἷοι ἐγενήθημεν [ἐν] ὑμῖν δι' ὑμᾶς 2:1 Αὐτοὶ γὰρ οἴδατε, ἀδελφοί, τὴν εἴσοδον ἡμῶν τὴν πρὸς ὑμᾶς ὅτι οὐ κενὴ γέγονεν ... just as *you know* what kind of persons we proved to be among you for your sake. 2:1 *You yourselves know*, brothers and sisters, that our coming to you was not in vain, **Philippians 1:5** ... **ἀπὸ τῆς πρώτης ἡμέρας** ἄχρι τοῦ νῦν **from the first day** until now
When they came to him, he said to them: "*You yourselves know* how I lived among you the entire time	
From the first day that I set foot in Asia,	

day" looks utterly unremarkable, yet a TLG search[324] uncovered few matches.[325] As in Philippians, the expression here serves to bind together speaker/writer and recipients/hearers. See Table 4.30.

ACTS 20:19

"Serving the Lord" evokes Paul's description of himself (and all believers) as "slaves" of the "master" (lord) Jesus Christ.[326] (See Table 4.31.) Here, as in some epistles, the concept comes near the opening of the piece in question. The same participial phrase occurs at Romans 12:11, of interest because that verse was also cited above in reference to Apollos (Acts 18:25). Two such "hits" increase the probability of usage for each case. The only other Lukan usage of the expression is in the Q saying of Luke 16:13 ("serving two masters"). "Service of the Lord" is a typically Pauline expression, used in a typical Pauline position and manner.[327]

"With all humility" has a *prima facie* claim to be a borrowing from Ephesians. The noun is rare in the NT, found only six times elsewhere, all but one (1 Peter 5:5) in the Pauline corpus.[328] The style is typical of Ephesians, where some form of "all" is nearly ubiquitous.[329] A TLG search indicates that these two passages represent the only occurrences of this exact phrase. Since the affinities between Acts and Ephesians extend well beyond the narrowly linguistic, it is unlikely that this is merely a fortuitous coincidence.[330]

Real men *did* cry in the ancient world—at least in its literature. Odysseus bursts into tears whenever anything untoward happens—as it often does.[331] The use of "tears" in Acts 20:19 and 31 fits the same rhetorical goal of *pathos* (gaining the sympathy of an audience) as does that in 2 Corinthians, but is here

Table 4.31: Acts 20:19

δουλεύων τῷ κυρίῳ μετὰ πάσης ταπεινοφροσύνης καὶ δακρύων καὶ πειρασμῶν τῶν συμβάντων μοι ἐν ταῖς ἐπιβουλαῖς τῶν Ἰουδαίων **serving the Lord with all humility** and with **tears**, enduring the trials that came to me through the plots of the Jews. Cf. **Acts 20:31** διὸ γρηγορεῖτε, μνημονεύοντες ὅτι τριετίαν νύκτα καὶ ἡμέραν οὐκ ἐπαυσάμην μετὰ **δακρύων** νουθετῶν ἕνα ἕκαστον. Therefore be alert, remembering that for three years I did not cease night or day to warn everyone with **tears**.	**Eph 6:7** μετ' εὐνοίας **δουλεύοντες**, ὡς τῷ **κυρίῳ** καὶ οὐκ ἀνθρώποις [slaves:] Render service with enthusiasm, as to the Lord and not to men and women. **Romans 12:11** τῇ σπουδῇ μὴ ὀκνηροί, τῷ πνεύματι ζέοντες, τῷ **κυρίῳ** **δουλεύοντες** Do not lag in zeal, be ardent in spirit, **serve the Lord**. **Eph 4:1–2** Παρακαλῶ οὖν ὑμᾶς . . . περιπατῆσαι . . . 2 **μετὰ πάσης ταπεινοφροσύνης** καὶ πραΰτητος, μετὰ μακροθυμίας, . . . I . . . beg you to lead a life . . . **with all humility** and gentleness, with patience, **2 Corinthians 2:4** ἐκ γὰρ πολλῆς θλίψεως καὶ συνοχῆς καρδίας ἔγραψα ὑμῖν διὰ πολλῶν **δακρύων** . . . For I wrote you out of much distress and anguish of heart and with many **tears**,

generalized. Such generalization could suggest a common use of sources, but dependence is far from demonstrable in this case. In its support is the relative rarity of tears, which are applied to Paul only in 2 Corinthians 2:4 and Acts 20. Had Luke used the preposition διά, which is rare with "tears," the case would be much stronger.

ACTS 20:20–21, 27

τὸ σύμφερον, "that which is preferable, expedient," ("helpful," NRSV), belongs to the realm of deliberative rhetoric, which seeks to lead the audience to make the correct choice. (See Table 4.32.) This is another "Pauline" term, appearing five times in the Corinthian correspondence, but not in this sense elsewhere in Acts.[332] Luke once more shows that he is familiar with Paul's thought-world. The question is not just *whence* did he derive this familiarity, but, more importantly, *why* does he utilize it? The answer to the latter is clear enough: Luke wants to make Paul speak in the manner Paul employed when in his pastoral mode. It is not likely that this was merely in conformity to the historian's obligation to compose a suitable speech for a particular character. I think it just as probable that Luke expected his audience to appreciate this similarity, to be familiar, in short, with the letters of Paul—perhaps through having heard them read in Christian assemblies.[333]

"Both Jews and Greeks," (using τε καί in Greek), is a Pauline phrase that is especially prominent in Romans (1:16; 2:9–10; 3:9; 10:12; also 1 Corinthians 12:13), and a Lucan phrase (Acts 14:1; 19:10, 17; 20:21).[334] Otherwise it is quite rare.[335] For both Paul and Luke the term expresses salvation-historical priority ("to the Jew first"). Luke develops the idea quite concretely, even mechanically: It is tempting to think that Luke uses the expression here to conform to Paul's "doctrine," elsewhere to show how it should be understood: that Paul was a missionary to both Jews and gentiles, with priority to the former, and that in this he was following the steps of Peter (Acts 3:26).[336] For Luke, as for Ephesians, this priority is not opportunistic or fortuitous. The conversion of gentiles is part of God's providential care for the human race, an element of the divine "plan" for universal salvation. Although he did not use this terminology, Paul would not disagree. Acts and Ephesians come from an era when the gentile mission had become the object of intellectual reflection. For Paul (Romans 9–11) the success of his gospel among gentiles and the lack of enthusiasm from Jews was a surprise. For Luke gentile acceptance was no longer a surprise, except to those who reject the plan of God (Luke 7:30).[337]

"Faith toward our Lord Jesus" (πίστιν εἰς τὸν κύριον ἡμῶν Ἰησοῦν), although coupled with "repentance" almost as a hendiadys, has a Pauline ring.[338] See, for example, Galatians 2:16, 3:26, and Ephesians 1:15//Colossians 1:4.

Table 4.32: Acts 20:20–21, 27[339]

20 ὡς οὐδὲν ὑπεστειλάμην τῶν συμφερόντων τοῦ μὴ ἀναγγεῖλαι ὑμῖν καὶ διδάξαι ὑμᾶς δημοσίᾳ καὶ κατ' οἴκους, 21 διαμαρτυρόμενος **Ἰουδαίοις τε καὶ Ἕλλησιν** τὴν εἰς θεὸν μετάνοιαν καὶ πίστιν εἰς τὸν κύριον ἡμῶν Ἰησοῦν. 20 I did not shrink from doing anything **helpful**, proclaiming the message to you and teaching you publicly and from house to house 21 as I testified to both **Jews and Greeks** about repentance toward God and faith toward our Lord Jesus. 27 οὐ γὰρ ὑπεστειλάμην τοῦ μὴ ἀναγγεῖλαι πᾶσαν **τὴν βουλὴν** τοῦ θεοῦ ὑμῖν. for I did not shrink from declaring to you the whole **purpose** *of God*	**1 Corinthians 1:24** αὐτοῖς δὲ τοῖς κλητοῖς, **Ἰουδαίοις τε καὶ Ἕλλησιν**, Χριστὸν θεοῦ δύναμιν καὶ θεοῦ σοφίαν·[340] **Ephesians 1:11** ἐν ᾧ καὶ ἐκληρώθημεν προορισθέντες κατὰ πρόθεσιν τοῦ τὰ πάντα ἐνεργοῦντος κατὰ **τὴν βουλὴν** τοῦ θελήματος αὐτοῦ In *Christ* we have also obtained an inheritance, having been destined according to the purpose of him who accomplishes all things according to his **counsel** and will

ACTS 20:22–23

Luke and Paul use the same phrase, "I am going toward Jerusalem" with reference to the same (final) journey.[341] (See Table 4.33.) A TLG search indicates that these are the only two uses of this phrase. The combination of unique wording and identical setting make a strong case for dependence upon Romans. The atmosphere of suspense raised in verse 22, "not knowing what will happen to me there," equally breathes the atmosphere of Romans 15, in which Paul expresses fears about what might happen to him in Judea.[342] Luke is fond of suspense, even when, as in this case, he cancels the grounds for it in the next clause.[343] In my view it is indubitable that Romans 15 has left its mark upon these verses.[344]

Paul and Luke employ θλῖψις ("suffering") in a kindred matter. In general early Jewish and Christian usage this word applies to eschatological events ("tribulations," "persecutions"[345]), while these two authors apply them to the harassments and struggles of daily life.[346] An examination of the Pauline pas-

Table 4.33: Acts 20:22–23

καὶ νῦν ἰδοὺ δεδεμένος ἐγὼ τῷ πνεύματι **πορεύομαι εἰς Ἰερουσαλήμ**, τὰ ἐν αὐτῇ συναντήσοντά μοι μὴ εἰδώς, 23 **πλὴν ὅτι** τὸ πνεῦμα τὸ ἅγιον κατὰ πόλιν διαμαρτύρεταί μοι λέγον ὅτι **δεσμὰ** καὶ **θλίψεις** με μένουσιν. And now, as a captive to the Spirit, **I am on my way to Jerusalem**, not knowing what will happen to me there, 23 **except that** the Holy Spirit testifies to me in every city that **imprisonment and persecutions** are waiting for me.	**Rom 15:25** νυνὶ δὲ **πορεύομαι εἰς Ἰερουσαλήμ** At present, however, I am going to Jerusalem **1 Thessalonians 3:3–4** τὸ μηδένα σαίνεσθαι ἐν ταῖς **θλίψεσιν** ταύταις. αὐτοὶ γὰρ οἴδατε ὅτι εἰς τοῦτο κείμεθα· 4 καὶ γὰρ ὅτε πρὸς ὑμᾶς ἦμεν, προελέγομεν ὑμῖν ὅτι μέλλομεν **θλίβεσθαι**, καθὼς καὶ ἐγένετο καὶ οἴδατε. so that no one would be shaken by these **persecutions**. Indeed, you yourselves know that this is what we are destined for.
Cf. Acts 14:22 . . . ὅτι διὰ πολλῶν **θλίψεων** δεῖ ἡμᾶς εἰσελθεῖν εἰς τὴν βασιλείαν τοῦ θεοῦ "It is through many **persecutions** that we must enter the kingdom of God."	**Phil 1:17–18** οἱ δὲ ἐξ ἐριθείας τὸν Χριστὸν καταγγέλλουσιν, οὐχ ἁγνῶς, οἰόμενοι **θλῖψιν** ἐγείρειν τοῖς **δεσμοῖς** μου. 18 τί γάρ; **πλὴν ὅτι** παντὶ τρόπῳ, εἴτε προφάσει εἴτε ἀληθείᾳ, Χριστὸς καταγγέλλεται, καὶ ἐν τούτῳ χαίρω· ἀλλὰ καὶ χαρήσομαι The others proclaim Christ out of selfish ambition, not sincerely but intending to increase my **suffering in my imprisonment**.18 What does it matter? **Just this**, that Christ is proclaimed in every way, whether out of false motives or true; and in that I rejoice. Yes, and I will continue to rejoice

sages indicates how Luke might well view Paul as foretelling frequent "suffering" for himself. Philippians 1:17–18 is quite intriguing, for it links "suffering," "chains" (a metonymy for "imprisonment"), and the phrase πλὴν ὅτι, "except that."[347] That expression occurs only in these two places in the NT.[348] In the rest of Acts, "chains" and kindred words will be an important symbol, and the portrait of "Paul the Prisoner" will become a leading theme. These images are a part of the Deutero-Pauline portrait. The evidence continues to mount.

ACTS 20:24

Acts 20:24 is a complex and somewhat awkward verse that is quite revelatory of what might be termed "Lucanizing Paulinism." (See Table 4.34.) The leading theme is the heart of Paul's own understanding of his vocation: the free surrender of himself as ministry to his Lord, Jesus, who also freely surrendered himself.[349] This is at best implicit in Acts, which inclines rather more to presenting Paul's imitation of Jesus in working miracles. Here, however, Luke and Paul "agree," as it were.[350] Central Pauline terms in this verse are διακονία ("ministry"), χάρις ("grace"), and εὐαγγέλιον ("gospel"). Steve Walton calls attention to Paul's tendency to associate the term "gospel" with self-giving (e.g., 1 Thessalonians 2:2, 8, 9). "This cluster shows Luke's Paul speaking in similar manner and phraseology to the Paul of 1 Thessalonians."[351] Mitton, however, observes "common elements" between Acts and Ephesians: 1) Paul fulfills a ministry 2) that is ordained from above rather than self-initiated; 3) ministry is associated with "the gospel" and also 4) with the grace of God. The parallel from Colossians shows that Acts is much closer to Ephesians in wording.

"Ministry" is an important concept for Luke, also,[352] but only here does his understanding of the word coincide with Paul's general usage.[353] The term also dovetails with the alleged reference in the previous verse of Acts to Rom 15:25, where Paul says, "I am going to Jerusalem in a ministry (διακονῶν) to the saints." There Paul says that he received his commission "from the Lord Jesus." This statement does not conform to Acts 9, where his commission is mediated, but it does conform to Galatians 1.[354] Nor is "grace" foreign to Luke, for whom it often refers to a particular gift or to the general sense of "blessing." The major exception is Peter's "Pauline" speech in Acts 15:11: ". . . we believe that we will be saved through the grace of the Lord Jesus."[355] For Paul grace is the basis of salvation and not one of its products or symptoms.

Luke does avoid the noun "gospel," however; the only two exceptions are here and in the above-mentioned speech of Peter (Acts 15:7).[356] Both are intentional "Paulinisms." A description of Paul's ministry that combines both "grace" and "gospel" is ultra Pauline. This stacking up of genitives sounds like something one would find in Ephesians. Indeed, Ephesians is quite possibly where Luke did find the expression. Ephesians 3:2, 6, and 7 contain the terms "minister" and "gospel," as well as two examples of "of the grace of God." This relatively rare genitive phrase belongs to the Deutero-Pauline and later world.

Table 4.34: Acts 20:24

ἀλλ' οὐδενὸς λόγου ποιοῦμαι τὴν **ψυχὴν** τιμίαν ἐμαυτῷ ὡς τελειώσω τὸν δρόμον μου καὶ **τὴν διακονίαν** ἣν **ἔλαβον παρὰ** τοῦ **κυρίου Ἰησοῦ,** διαμαρτύρασθαι τὸ εὐαγγέλιον **τῆς χάριτος τοῦ θεοῦ.** But I do not count my **life** of any value to myself, if only I may finish my course and **the ministry** that **I received from** the Lord Jesus, to testify to the **good news of God's grace.**	**1 Thessalonians 2:8** οὕτως ὁμειρόμενοι ὑμῶν εὐδοκοῦμεν μεταδοῦναι ὑμῖν οὐ μόνον τὸ **εὐαγγέλιον** τοῦ θεοῦ ἀλλὰ καὶ τὰς ἑαυτῶν **ψυχάς,** διότι ἀγαπητοὶ ἡμῖν ἐγενήθητε. So deeply do we care for you that we are determined to share with you not only the **gospel** of God but also our own **selves**, because you have become very dear to us. **Galatians 1:12** οὐδὲ γὰρ ἐγὼ παρὰ ἀνθρώπου **παρέλαβον** αὐτό, οὔτε ἐδιδάχθην, ἀλλὰ δι' ἀποκαλύψεως **Ἰησοῦ** Χριστοῦ for I did not **receive** it [*the gospel*] from a human source, nor was I taught it, but [I received it] through a revelation of **Jesus** Christ. **Colossians 4:17** καὶ εἴπατε Ἀρχίππῳ, Βλέπε **τὴν διακονίαν ἣν παρέλαβες** ἐν κυρίῳ, ἵνα αὐτὴν πληροῖς. And say to Archippus, "See that you complete **the task** that you have **received** in the Lord." **Ephesians 3:2, 6, 7** εἴ γε ἠκούσατε τὴν οἰκονομίαν **τῆς χάριτος τοῦ θεοῦ** τῆς δοθείσης μοι εἰς ὑμᾶς. 6 εἶναι τὰ ἔθνη συγκληρονόμα καὶ σύσσωμα καὶ συμμέτοχα τῆς ἐπαγγελίας ἐν Χριστῷ Ἰησοῦ διὰ **τοῦ εὐαγγελίου,** 7 οὗ ἐγενήθην **διάκονος** κατὰ τὴν δωρεὰν **τῆς χάριτος τοῦ θεοῦ** τῆς δοθείσης μοι κατὰ τὴν ἐνέργειαν τῆς δυνάμεως αὐτοῦ. for surely you have already heard of the commission **of God's grace** that was given me for you Of this **gospel** I have become a **servant** according to the gift of **God's grace** that was given me by the working of his power cf. **Colossians 1:23, 25** . . . τοῦ **εὐαγγελίου** . . . οὗ ἐγενόμην ἐγὼ Παῦλος **διάκονος.** 25 ἧς ἐγενόμην ἐγὼ διάκονος κατὰ τὴν οἰκονομίαν τοῦ θεοῦ τὴν δοθεῖσάν μοι εἰς ὑμᾶς πληρῶσαι τὸν λόγον τοῦ θεοῦ . . . the **gospel** . . . I, Paul, became a **servant** of this gospel . . . *25* I became its servant according to God's commission that was given to me for you, to make the word of God fully known

It is found in the three places under consideration as well as Hebrews 12:15; *1 Clement* 8:1, 55:3, and the *Martyrdom of Polycarp* 7.3.[357] "The Gospel of the grace of God" probably derives from Ephesians 3.[358] Evidence of dependency upon Ephesians elsewhere strengthens this probability. Since Acts 20:25–26 present no likely cases of borrowing from the epistles, it is omitted.[359] For verse 27 see above, under verse 20, where the two were treated in tandem.

ACTS 20:28

Other than grammatical function words, nearly every term found here is unusual for Luke. (See Table 4.35.) The ecclesiological language, which speaks of "bishops"/overseers instituted by the Holy Spirit to shepherd the flock, belongs to a time well after the dramatic date.[360] Ephesians 4:11 shows the emergence of this language in the Pauline sphere.[361] The expression "Church of God" is not later in date, but it is common in Paul, while found only here in

Table 4.35: Acts 20:28

προσέχετε ἑαυτοῖς καὶ παντὶ τῷ **ποιμνίῳ**, ἐν ᾧ ὑμᾶς τὸ πνεῦμα τὸ ἅγιον ἔθετο ἐπισκόπους, ποιμαίνειν **τὴν ἐκκλησίαν τοῦ θεοῦ**, ἣν **περιεποιήσατο διὰ τοῦ αἵματος τοῦ ἰδίου.** Keep watch over yourselves and over all the **flock,** of which the Holy Spirit has made you overseers, to shepherd the church of God that he **obtained with the blood of his own Son**	**1 Thessalonians 5:9–10** ὅτι οὐκ ἔθετο ἡμᾶς ὁ θεὸς εἰς ὀργὴν ἀλλὰ εἰς **περιποίησιν** σωτηρίας **διὰ** τοῦ κυρίου ἡμῶν Ἰησοῦ Χριστοῦ, 10 τοῦ ἀποθανόντος ὑπὲρ ἡμῶν ἵνα εἴτε γρηγορῶμεν εἴτε καθεύδωμεν ἅμα σὺν αὐτῷ ζήσωμεν. For God has destined us not for wrath but for **obtaining** salvation **through** our Lord Jesus Christ, 10 who died for us, so that whether we are awake or asleep we may live with him. **Ephesians 1:7, 13–14; 4:11–12** ἐν ᾧ ἔχομεν τὴν ἀπολύτρωσιν **διὰ τοῦ αἵματος αὐτοῦ,** τὴν ἄφεσιν τῶν παραπτωμάτων, κατὰ τὸ πλοῦτος τῆς χάριτος αὐτοῦ 13 ἐν ᾧ καὶ ὑμεῖς ἀκούσαντες τὸν λόγον τῆς ἀληθείας, τὸ εὐαγγέλιον τῆς σωτηρίας ὑμῶν, ἐν ᾧ καὶ πιστεύσαντες ἐσφραγίσθητε τῷ πνεύματι τῆς ἐπαγγελίας τῷ ἁγίῳ, 14 ὅς ἐστιν ἀρραβὼν τῆς κληρονομίας ἡμῶν, εἰς ἀπολύτρωσιν τῆς **περιποιήσεως,** εἰς ἔπαινον τῆς δόξης αὐτοῦ. In him we have redemption **through his blood,** the forgiveness of our trespasses, according to the riches of his grace 13 In him you also, when you had heard the word of truth, the gospel of your salvation, and had believed in him, were marked with the seal of the promised Holy Spirit; 14 this is the pledge of our inheritance toward redemption **as God's own people,** to the praise of his glory. 4:11 καὶ αὐτὸς ἔδωκεν τοὺς μὲν ἀποστόλους, τοὺς δὲ προφήτας, τοὺς δὲ εὐαγγελιστάς, τοὺς δὲ **ποιμένας** καὶ διδασκάλους, 12 πρὸς τὸν καταρτισμὸν τῶν ἁγίων εἰς ἔργον διακονίας, εἰς οἰκοδομὴν τοῦ σώματος τοῦ Χριστοῦ 4:11 The gifts he gave were that some would be apostles, some prophets, some evangelists, some **pastors** and teachers, 12 to equip the saints for the work of *ministry,* for building up the body of Christ

Acts.[362] The soteriology (system of salvation) is also quite unusual, but recognizably within the Pauline realm. "Blood," a synecdoche for "life," is not found elsewhere in a soteriological sense in (Luke and) Acts, but is not alien to Paul (Rom 3:35; 5:9). This is another reference to Jesus's death as a "saving event," an approach that is not characteristic of Lukan theology but does appear when Luke wishes to be "Pauline."[363]

The relatively rare terms περιποιέω, περιποίησις (obtain, gain possession of, possession), which occur only five times in the New Testament outside of those passages under consideration, appear to clinch the case. To be sure the sense of "obtaining" differs,[364] but this is no argument against intertextuality. Quite the contrary, since one of the better grounds for arguing that a letter is Deutero-Pauline is the number of Pauline words used in non-Pauline ways.[365] The crucial factor is the ". . . similar use of a rare NT word-group in a common sense followed by a similar grammatical construction which states the same ground for the obtaining of the church/salvation."[366] The word group in view is περιποιη- followed by the preposition διά with the genitive. The TLG reveals no actual parallels to this language. The construction appears to have enjoyed a brief post-Pauline vogue. In this instance it is possible to observe the intertextual process from 1 Thessalonians to Ephesians to Acts.[367] The preceding chapter included an exploration of the possible dependence of Acts 20:29–30 upon Mark.[368] These two verses are also further indications of the "post-apostolic" date of the speech and will receive further consideration in Chapter Six.

ACTS 20:31

Acts 20:31 is, from the intertextual perspective, complicated and difficult to consider in isolation. (See Table 4.36.) The relationship between Luke 21:34–36 (which is independent of Mark) and 1 Thessalonians 5 is debatable, because much of the material is traditional parenesis (advice), but it is arguable. The frequency of parallels between 1 Thessalonians and Acts 20:18–35 demands some accounting, as Aejmelaeus and Walton, with their different proposals, acknowledge and demonstrate.[369] Luke avoids two Marcan uses of the "eschatological" imperative "keep alert" (γρηγορεῖτε, Mark 13:35; 14:38), but he uses it here in the Pauline manner.[370] νουθετέω ("admonish") is another word that is otherwise restricted to the Pauline corpus.[371] "Remember" (μνημονεύω) belongs to that trinity of "memory, maxims, and morals" earlier identified. This verb is often found in the Pauline and Deutero-Pauline sphere.[372] εἷς ἕκαστος ("each," "every one") is not rare in Luke and Acts and relatively frequent in Ephesians (4:7, 16; 5:33). The interest here is its presence in a cluster. Similarly, "night and day" gains attention because of other words and phrases.[373]

Whether one is going to investigate this material on an intertextual basis (as does Aejmelaeus) or on the grounds of an author steeped in Paul's language and thought (the path taken by Walton) it is obligatory to present some working

Table 4.36: Acts 20:31

διὸ γρηγορεῖτε, μνημονεύοντες ὅτι τριετίαν νύκτα καὶ ἡμέραν οὐκ ἐπαυσάμην μετὰ δακρύων νουθετῶν ἕνα ἕκαστον. Therefore **be alert, remembering** that for three years I did not cease **night or day** to **warn** everyone with tears	**1 Thessalonians 2:9, 11–12** μνημονεύετε γάρ, ἀδελφοί, τὸν κόπον ἡμῶν καὶ τὸν μόχθον· **νυκτὸς καὶ ἡμέρας** ἐργαζόμενοι πρὸς τὸ μὴ ἐπιβαρῆσαί τινα ὑμῶν ἐκηρύξαμεν εἰς ὑμᾶς τὸ εὐαγγέλιον τοῦ θεοῦ. 11 καθάπερ οἴδατε ὡς ἕνα ἕκαστον ὑμῶν ὡς πατὴρ τέκνα ἑαυτοῦ 12 παρακαλοῦντες ὑμᾶς καὶ παραμυθούμενοι καὶ μαρτυρόμενοι εἰς τὸ περιπατεῖν ὑμᾶς ἀξίως τοῦ θεοῦ τοῦ καλοῦντος ὑμᾶς εἰς τὴν ἑαυτοῦ βασιλείαν καὶ δόξαν. You remember our labor and toil, brothers and sisters; we worked night and day, so that we might not burden any of you while we proclaimed to you the gospel of God. 11 As you know, we dealt with each one of you like a father with his children, 12 urging and encouraging you and pleading that you lead a life worthy of God, who calls you into his own kingdom and glory.
Luke 21:34–36 Προσέχετε δὲ ἑαυτοῖς[374]μήποτε **βαρηθῶσιν** ὑμῶν αἱ καρδίαι ἐν κραιπάλῃ καὶ **μέθῃ** καὶ μερίμναις βιωτικαῖς, καὶ ἐπιστῇ ἐφ' ὑμᾶς αἰφνίδιος ἡ **ἡμέρα** ἐκείνη· 35 ὡς παγὶς γὰρ ἐπελεύσεται ἐπὶ πάντας τοὺς καθημένους ἐπὶ πρόσωπον πάσης τῆς γῆς. 36 ἀγρυπνεῖτε δὲ ἐν παντὶ καιρῷ δεόμενοι ἵνα κατισχύσητε ἐκφυγεῖν ταῦτα πάντα τὰ μέλλοντα γίνεσθαι, καὶ σταθῆναι ἔμπροσθεν τοῦ υἱοῦ τοῦ ἀνθρώπου. **Be on guard** so that your hearts are not weighed down with dissipation and **drunkenness** and the worries of this life, and that **day** does not catch you unexpectedly, 35 **like** a trap. For it will come upon all who live on the face of the whole earth. 36 Be alert at all times, praying that you may have the strength to escape all these things that will take place, and to stand before the Son of Man."	**1 Corinthians 16:13** Γρηγορεῖτε, στήκετε ἐν τῇ πίστει, ἀνδρίζεσθε, κραταιοῦσθε Keep alert, stand firm in your faith, be courageous, be strong. **1 Thessalonians 5:2, 6–7, 12, 14** αὐτοὶ γὰρ ἀκριβῶς οἴδατε ὅτι **ἡμέρα** κυρίου **ὡς** κλέπτης ἐν νυκτὶ οὕτως ἔρχεται 6 ἄρα οὖν μὴ καθεύδωμεν ὡς οἱ λοιποί, ἀλλὰ **γρηγορῶμεν** καὶ νήφωμεν. 7 οἱ γὰρ καθεύδοντες νυκτὸς καθεύδουσιν, καὶ οἱ **μεθυσκόμενοι** νυκτὸς μεθύουσιν· For you yourselves know very well that the **day** of the Lord will come like **a thief** in the night. So then let us not fall asleep as others do, but let us **keep awake** and be sober for those who sleep sleep at night, and those who are **drunk** get drunk at night. 12 Ἐρωτῶμεν δὲ ὑμᾶς, ἀδελφοί, εἰδέναι τοὺς κοπιῶντας ἐν ὑμῖν καὶ προϊσταμένους ὑμῶν ἐν κυρίῳ καὶ **νουθετοῦντας** ὑμᾶς. But we appeal to you, brothers and sisters, to respect those who labor among you, and have charge of you in the Lord and **admonish** you 5:14 παρακαλοῦμεν δὲ ὑμᾶς, ἀδελφοί, **νουθετεῖτε** τοὺς ἀτάκτους, παραμυθεῖσθε τοὺς ὀλιγοψύχους, ἀντέχεσθε τῶν ἀσθενῶν, μακροθυμεῖτε πρὸς πάντας. And we urge you, beloved, to **admonish** the idlers, encourage the fainthearted, help the weak, be patient with all of them.

model or situation that goes beyond a catalogue of resemblances.[375] I propose the following model and scenario: Luke, who has access to a collection of Paul's letters, faces some challenges. He must

1. Transform material directed to all believers into advice for leaders.
2. Adapt Paul's advice to the circumstances and requirements of a later era.
3. Demonstrate that Paul serves as a model in varied circumstances, a model that conforms to Jesus, who is also a model for all.
4. Compress all of this into a short address.
5. Make the address convincingly Pauline.

This last is important for the task of "making Paul relevant (and acceptable)" to those of a later generation, including many who have reservations about Paul's teaching as well as those who believe that his heritage is being compromised. The number of subjects addressed leads to a sense that the speech is longer than it is.[376] Given the restraints, there is no room for rhetorical development beyond bare example (item 4). Item 3 conforms to Luke's tendency toward an "exemplarist" Christology and his desire to show Paul as a true follower of his Lord.[377] The first two subjects also apply to the need for "contemporization," adapting Paul's ideas to the needs of a later time. These qualities are shared with the Deutero-Pauline letters and invite comparison with the Pastoral Epistles.

Romans, Ephesians, and 1 Thessalonians were, for Luke, the most amenable documents from the collection. None of them involve strong attacks against false teaching, a notion that would embarrass Luke, who holds that heresy will not emerge until after the death of Paul. Romans and Ephesians promote Paul as the ambassador of unity, not least between Jewish and gentile believers. 1 Thessalonians is a friendly, pastoral communication with a splendid portrait of the apostolic lifestyle (2:3–12). The pressure of items 4 and 5 produces a confluence of themes and the occasional association of phrases suitable to different subjects.[378] How well Luke might have known Paul's letters—or his mode of speech, for that matter—cannot be known. Aejmelaeus can be reproached for treating Luke as a "walking concordance,"[379] but his method and models are clear. Walton cannot be subjected to similar criticism because his conclusions are vague: Luke may have known Paul, or he may have been using "independent Pauline tradition."[380] Walton leaves the nature of the latter to the reader's imagination or prejudice—but then, one can "solve" almost anything by appeals to the unknown. What *is* known is a lengthy procession of words and themes which, taken together, are more conducive to the hypothesis of an intertextual model than to "explanations" that rely largely upon the implicit assumption that the author garnered this material from an intimate familiarity with a speaker who had the rare habit of using the stem περιποι- with the preposition διά and the genitive. We do not know how Paul spoke. We do know how he *wrote*. This Paul speaks in the way he writes.

Intertextual solutions to the resemblances between letters and the Miletus speech can also readily account for its later, "Deutero-Pauline" flavor and ambience.[381] Proponents of a "first-hand acquaintance" solution can do little more than brush this off (unless they accept Pauline authorship of all the epistles).[382] The speech presents one or more persons with formal titles exercising pastoral jurisdiction over a Church that will experience an outbreak of heresy after Paul has gone. This is not a case of whether "presbyter" is a harmless anachronism. The situation speaks to and about the post-Pauline world. This strikes me as an undeniable fact. Two hard facts—a Paul who speaks as he writes and a Deutero-Pauline perspective—tip the scales against personal reminiscence and towards literary dependence. In the face of those same two facts, those who argue for independent traditions will do well to retreat.

ACTS 20:32

The commendation, which teeters upon the edge of being a "succession formula,"[383] also reads, in its fulsome language, like a verse from Ephesians. (See Table 4.37.) The view of God's word as empowering is Pauline, as in the example from 1 Thessalonians 2—which is not to imply that it is alien to Luke.[384] "Build up" (οἰκοδομέω) in the metaphorical sense of "edify" also appears at Acts 9:31, but all other occurrences in this sense are found in the Pauline correspondence.[385] The noun οἰκοδομή appears eleven times in the undisputed letters and three times in Ephesians. Ephesians 4:12 (cf. also 16) serves a useful example, for it is akin to Acts, which nonetheless avoids describing the Church as the Body of Christ, indicating ways in which Luke is and is not "Pauline."[386] "Saints" (ἅγιοι) appears four times in Acts, quite often in Paul.[387] "Inheritance" (κληρονομία) is an eschatological metaphor, derived ultimately from the biblical notion of inheriting the (promised) land and of the heirs to the promises made to Abraham. Other than Galatians 3:18 this term belongs to the later Pauline and contingent realms: Ephesians 1:14, 18 (above); 5:5, and Colossians 3:24.[388] The close parallel in Acts 26:18 also invites comparison with Colossians and Ephesians. These two passages from Acts show familiarity with the Deutero-Pauline world of "realized eschatology" (believers *now* live in the realm of light), with a potentially dualistic language (light vs. darkness), that is quite at variance with Lukan theology in general.[389] Luke knows how to make his hero talk like the Pauline Corpus. Some general themes are here, to be sure, as well as the use of other material,[390] but explanations that reject intertextuality place a strain upon credulity.[391] Ephesians stands behind Acts 20:32 and 26:18. Leslie Mitton notes that the themes of Acts 26:16–18 occur in one sentence of Colossians (1:12–14), whereas they are scattered about in Ephesians.[392] Since Ephesians is based upon Colossians, the situation is difficult. It is more correct to say that the wording of Acts is closer to Ephesians than to Colossians, but that the thematic cluster is more like that of Colossians. The influence of both Deutero-Pauline epistles is possible. I think it safer to posit Ephesians as the source.

After noting a half-dozen parallels between Miletus and Ephesians, Mitton concluded:

> When each [of these parallels] is considered individually, in isolation from the others, the correspondences with Ephesians may appear as little more than curiosities. But when six passages, all of which contain 'curious' coincidences with Ephesians, stand so near together, one wonders whether 'coincidence' is the correct description of them, especially when it is noted that this passage of twenty verses is the record of Paul's farewell address at Miletus to the elders *from the church at Ephesus.*[393]

Wonder one does. Mitton's general orientation came from Edgar Goodspeed, who resolved the problem of Acts' failure to mention the letters of Paul by proposing that the publication of Acts stimulated interest in Paul, and thus his letters. An intertextual solution to these "coincidences" was not especially attractive to Mitton, particularly the possibility that Acts used Ephesians. He was, nonetheless, an honest researcher.

ACTS 20:33–35

Acts 20:33 introduces the issue of financial exploitation. (See Table 4.38.) To the reader of Acts it is altogether perplexing that Paul should raise this topic, for there has not been the slightest hint that he has been accused of greed or indicted for taking money from his charges. Greed certainly motivates such religious hustlers and quacks as Simon (8:4–25), the owners of a slave in Philippi (16:16–19), the manufacturers of devotional souvenirs at Ephesus (19:25–27), and no doubt others.[394] In the letters, on the other hand, this is a common subject.[395] Paul's failure to accept money from his converts as a common procedure indicated to some that he lacked legitimacy. Furthermore—although this may be difficult for many in our enlightened day and progressive times to accept— some evidently charged that Paul garnered personal funds on the pretext of raising charitable donations, i.e., that he treated the collection for Jerusalem as a personal resource.[396] Here, if anywhere, one could appeal to rumors and stories, for the collection was still too hot a topic for Luke to touch.[397]

Those who seek links between this speech and the epistles find 1 Thessalonians especially rewarding. Steve Walton, who rejects the possibility that Luke used Pauline letters, draws deeply upon the contents of 1 Thessalonians for his discussion of these verses.[398] 1 Thessalonians 2:3–12 contrasts Paul's nurturing and self-supporting style to the conduct of greedy and rapacious "professionals" whose services, such as they are, come with heavy demands and at a high price tag.[399] The antithesis to charging fees for one's services is to provide them without charge and to earn one's own keep.[400] Hans Conzelmann hits the nail on the head: "Passages such as 1 Thessalonians 2:9 and 4:11 are now formed into a timeless prototype."[401] Such "timelessness" is precisely the object and quality

Table 4.37: Acts 20:32

καὶ τὰ νῦν παρατίθεμαι ὑμᾶς τῷ θεῷ καὶ τῷ λόγῳ τῆς χάριτος αὐτοῦ τῷ **δυναμένῳ** **οἰκοδομῆσαι** καὶ δοῦναι	αὐτῶν, **Ephesians 3:20** Τῷ δὲ **δυναμένῳ** ὑπὲρ πάντα ποιῆσαι ὑπερεκπερισσοῦ ὧν αἰτούμεθα ἢ νοοῦμεν κατὰ τὴν δύναμιν τὴν ἐνεργουμένην ἐν ἡμῖν, 21 αὐτῷ ἡ δόξα ἐν τῇ ἐκκλησίᾳ καὶ ἐν Χριστῷ Ἰησοῦ εἰς πάσας τὰς γενεὰς τοῦ αἰῶνος τῶν αἰώνων· ἀμήν. Now to him who by the power at work within us **is able** to accomplish abundantly far more than all we can ask or imagine
And now I commend you to God and to the message of his grace, a message that is *able* to build you up and to give you the **inheritance among all who are** sanctified	**1 Thessalonians 2:13** Καὶ διὰ τοῦτο καὶ ἡμεῖς εὐχαριστοῦμεν τῷ θεῷ ἀδιαλείπτως, ὅτι παραλαβόντες λόγον ἀκοῆς παρ' ἡμῶν τοῦ θεοῦ ἐδέξασθε οὐ λόγον ἀνθρώπων ἀλλὰ καθώς ἐστιν ἀληθῶς λόγον θεοῦ, ὃς καὶ ἐνεργεῖται ἐν ὑμῖν τοῖς πιστεύουσιν. We also constantly give thanks to God for this, that when you received the word of God that you heard from us, you accepted it not as a human word but as what it really is, God's word, which is also at work in you believers
τὴν **κληρονομίαν** ἐν τοῖς **ἡγιασμένοις** πᾶσιν	**Colossians 1:12–14** εὐχαριστοῦντες τῷ πατρὶ τῷ ἱκανώσαντι ὑμᾶς εἰς τὴν μερίδα τοῦ **κλῆρου τῶν ἁγίων** ἐν τῷ φωτί· 13 ὃς ἐρρύσατο ἡμᾶς ἐκ τῆς **ἐξουσίας** τοῦ **σκότους** καὶ μετέστησεν εἰς τὴν βασιλείαν τοῦ υἱοῦ τῆς ἀγάπης αὐτοῦ, 14 ἐν ᾧ ἔχομεν τὴν ἀπολύτρωσιν, **τὴν ἄφεσιν τῶν ἁμαρτιῶν** giving thanks to the Father, who has *enabled* you to share in the **inheritance of the saints** in the light He has rescued us from the power of darkness and transferred us into the kingdom of his beloved Son in whom we have redemption, the forgiveness of sins. **Ephesians 1:7** ἐν ᾧ ἔχομεν τὴν ἀπολύτρωσιν διὰ τοῦ αἵματος αὐτοῦ, **τὴν ἄφεσιν** τῶν παραπτωμάτων, κατὰ τὸ πλοῦτος τῆς χάριτος αὐτοῦ In him we have redemption through his blood, the **forgiveness** of our trespasses

Cf. **Acts 26:18** ἀνοῖξαι ὀφθαλμοὺς

τοῦ ἐπιστρέψαι ἀπὸ **σκότους** εἰς φῶς καὶ τῆς **ἐξουσίας** τοῦ Σατανᾶ ἐπὶ τὸν θεόν, τοῦ λαβεῖν αὐτοὺς **ἄφεσιν ἁμαρτιῶν** καὶ **κλῆρον ἐν τοῖς ἡγιασμένοις** πίστει τῇ εἰς ἐμέ.

to open their eyes so that they may turn from darkness to light and from the power of Satan to God, so that they may receive forgiveness of sins and **a place among those who are sanctified** by faith in me.'

Ephesians 1:14 ὅς ἐστιν ἀρραβὼν τῆς **κληρονομίας** ἡμῶν, εἰς ἀπολύτρωσιν τῆς περιποιήσεως, εἰς ἔπαινον τῆς δόξης αὐτοῦ
this is the pledge of our inheritance toward redemption as God's own people, to the praise of his glory

Ephesians 1:18 πεφωτισμένους τοὺς ὀφθαλμοὺς τῆς καρδίας [ὑμῶν] εἰς τὸ εἰδέναι ὑμᾶς τίς ἐστιν ἡ ἐλπὶς τῆς κλήσεως αὐτοῦ, τίς ὁ πλοῦτος τῆς δόξης τῆς **κληρονομίας** αὐτοῦ ἐν τοῖς ἁγίοις so that, with the eyes of your heart enlightened, you may know what is the hope to which he has called you, what are the riches of his glorious **inheritance among the saints**

Ephesians 4:12 πρὸς τὸν καταρτισμὸν τῶν ἁγίων εἰς ἔργον διακονίας, εἰς **οἰκοδομὴν** τοῦ σώματος τοῦ Χριστοῦ
to equip the saints for the work of ministry, for **building up** the body of Christ

Cf. **Ephesians 2:2** ... περιεπατήσατε ... κατὰ τὸν ἄρχοντα τῆς ἐξουσίας τοῦ ἀέρος,
in which you once lived ... following the ruler of the power of the air

1 Thessalonians 5:11 Διὸ παρακαλεῖτε ἀλλήλους καὶ οἰκοδομεῖτε εἰς τὸν ἕνα, καθὼς καὶ ποιεῖτε
Therefore encourage one another and build up each other, as indeed you are doing

Table 4.38: Acts 20:33–35

ἀργυρίου ἢ χρυσίου ἢ ἱματισμοῦ οὐδενὸς ἐπεθύμησα· 34 αὐτοὶ γινώσκετε ὅτι ταῖς **χρείαις** μου καὶ τοῖς οὖσιν μετ' ἐμοῦ ὑπηρέτησαν αἱ **χεῖρες** αὗται. I coveted no one's silver or gold or clothing. 34 You know for yourselves that I worked with my own **hands** to **support** myself and my companions 35 πάντα ὑπέδειξα ὑμῖν ὅτι οὕτως **κοπιῶντας** δεῖ ἀντιλαμβάνεσθαι τῶν ἀσθενούντων, μνημονεύειν τε τῶν λόγων τοῦ κυρίου Ἰησοῦ ὅτι αὐτὸς εἶπεν, Μακάριόν ἐστιν μᾶλλον διδόναι ἢ λαμβάνειν. 35 In all this I have given you an example that by such **work** we must support the weak, remembering the words of the Lord Jesus, for he himself said, 'It is more blessed to give than to receive.' "	**1 Thessalonians 4:11–12; 5:12** καὶ φιλοτιμεῖσθαι ἡσυχάζειν καὶ πράσσειν τὰ ἴδια καὶ ἐργάζεσθαι ταῖς **χερσὶν** ὑμῶν, καθὼς ὑμῖν παρηγγείλαμεν, 12 ἵνα περιπατῆτε εὐσχημόνως πρὸς τοὺς ἔξω καὶ μηδενὸς **χρείαν** ἔχητε. to aspire to live quietly, to mind your own affairs, and to work with your **hands**, as we directed you, 12 so that you may behave properly toward outsiders and be **dependent on no one**. 5:12. Ἐρωτῶμεν δὲ ὑμᾶς, ἀδελφοί, εἰδέναι τοὺς **κοπιῶντας** ἐν ὑμῖν καὶ προϊσταμένους ὑμῶν ἐν κυρίῳ καὶ *νουθετοῦντας* ὑμᾶς 12 But we appeal to you, brothers and sisters, to respect those who **labor** among you, and have charge of you in the Lord and admonish you; **1 Thessalonians 2:3, 5, 7–9, 11** 3 ἡ γὰρ παράκλησις ἡμῶν οὐκ ἐκ πλάνης οὐδὲ ἐξ ἀκαθαρσίας οὐδὲ ἐν δόλῳ, 5 οὔτε γάρ ποτε ἐν λόγῳ κολακείας ἐγενήθημεν, καθὼς οἴδατε, οὔτε ἐν προφάσει πλεονεξίας, θεὸς μάρτυς, 7 δυνάμενοι ἐν βάρει εἶναι ὡς Χριστοῦ ἀπόστολοι. ἀλλὰ ἐγενήθημεν ἤπιοι ἐν μέσῳ ὑμῶν, ὡς ἐὰν τροφὸς θάλπῃ τὰ ἑαυτῆς τέκνα· 9 μνημονεύετε γάρ, ἀδελφοί, τὸν **κόπον** ἡμῶν καὶ τὸν μόχθον· νυκτὸς καὶ ἡμέρας ἐργαζόμενοι πρὸς τὸ μὴ ἐπιβαρῆσαί τινα ὑμῶν ἐκηρύξαμεν εἰς ὑμᾶς τὸ εὐαγγέλιον τοῦ θεοῦ. 10 ὑμεῖς μάρτυρες καὶ ὁ θεός, ὡς ὁσίως καὶ δικαίως καὶ ἀμέμπτως ὑμῖν τοῖς πιστεύουσιν ἐγενήθημεν, 11 καθάπερ οἴδατε ὡς ἕνα ἕκαστον ὑμῶν ὡς πατὴρ τέκνα ἑαυτοῦ 3 For our appeal does not spring from deceit or impure motives or trickery, 5 As you know and as God is our witness, we never came with words of flattery or with a pretext for greed; 7 though we might have made demands as apostles of Christ. But we were gentle among you, like a nurse tenderly caring for her own children. 8 So deeply do we care for you that we are determined to share with you not only the gospel of God but also our own selves, because you have become very dear to us. 9 You remember our **labor** and toil, brothers and sisters; we worked night and day, so that we might not burden any of you while we proclaimed to you the gospel of God 11 As you know, we dealt with each one of you like a father with his children **Ephesians 4:28** ὁ κλέπτων μηκέτι κλεπτέτω, μᾶλλον δὲ **κοπιάτω** ἐργαζόμενος ταῖς ἰδίαις **χερσὶν** τὸ ἀγαθόν, ἵνα ἔχῃ μεταδιδόναι τῷ **χρείαν** ἔχοντι. Thieves must give up stealing; rather let them **labor** and work honestly with their own **hands**, so as to have something to share with the **need**y.

of Deutero-Paulinism, which seeks to make the contingent—local and temporal—advice of Paul applicable to all believers at all times and in all places.

ACTS 20:34

Lars Aejmelaeus illustrates how the echo of an earlier exhortation in 1 Thessalonians is applied—with a different "memory" formula—in Acts to community leaders:[402] (See Table 4.39.) In the philosophical/educational tradition, self-support and self-sufficiency went hand in hand with the avoidance of sponging, abject dependence upon patrons, or collecting fees. Acts blends this abjuration of dependency with an exhortation to "labor" on behalf of "the weak." This is an example of the compression of several components of Pauline exhortation into the confines of a brief address.[403] For seasoning Luke offers hyperbole: Paul has supported not only himself but his companions as well. The final words are "these hands." Of this phrase F. F. Bruce observes: "This is the language not of a full-time manual worker but of a professional man who by policy or by necessity engages in manual work to support himself."[404] That comment would please Luke, but it is Jacques Dupont who grasps the pathos: "These hands which perform miracles (Acts 14:3; 19:11; 28:8) and convey the Holy Spirit (19:6) are also the coarse hands of a worker, gnarled by hard labor."[405] The text deals with rhetorical motifs that were quite flexible, witness Ephesians 4:28, which applies them not to the faithful in general or to leaders in particular, but to thieves.

For "apologetic" and other reasons—probably including the problem of early "rice Christians," who rightly or wrongly were suspected of converting to take advantage of charity—the Deutero-Pauline and other later traditions take a strong line on the obligation to work, most notably in 2 Thessalonians 3:7–12.[406] Acts 20 may be viewed as moving in that direction. Work is now a necessity (δεῖ), even if the motive is the assistance of others.[407] Two other terms favored by Paul make an appearance here: the stem κοπ- κόπος, κοπιάω "work" (both verb and noun) and the stem ἀσθεν- (ἀσθενέω, ἀσθενῆς), "(be) weak," used in several senses, most of which apply to those of limited resources, privileges, and education, as well as to the "sick" in general. Poverty contributed to illness, and in large measure vice-versa. The substantive participle, "being weak/ill" is common in Paul (1 Thessalonians 5:14; Galatians 6:2; Rom 15:1), but found elsewhere in Acts only at 19:12, where it means "the sick."[408] Here the term is probably inclusive of the sick and those afflicted with other adversities. Paul uses

Table 4.39: Acts 20:34

1 Thessalonians 4:11–12	Acts 20:34
We commanded	You know
(to work with one's) *hands*	(I labored with) these *hands*
(to eliminate) *need*	(to meet my) *needs*

"work" in both with reference to "church work" (Romans 16:6, 12; 1 Corinthians 15:10; 16:16; Galatians 4:11; Philippians 2:16) and in a general sense.[409] The substantive participle κοπιῶντας ("those who labor"), which in 1 Thessalonians 5:12 refers to the "work" of church leaders, has here the primary sense of "earning money to help the poor," but incorporates this into the general idea of "religious work." Clearly Luke has larded this passage with words evocative of Paul. The outstanding question is his source. Traditions would certainly preserve ideas like "justification" and "grace." Apologetic would encourage clichés like "I coveted no one's silver or gold or clothing" (v. 34), which are not Pauline,[410] but the presence of technical or semi-technical language urges an intertextual solution.

The speech climaxes, surprisingly, with a suitable saying from the Jesus tradition. The conclusion is surprising because only one other speech in Acts otherwise appeals to the words of Jesus. That example comes at 11:16, in the penultimate verse of Peter's defense of his conversion of gentiles. The two citations constitute a "Peter-Paul parallel" both in form (a saying of Jesus) and position (at the point that represents the close of their respective missionary careers). Paul speaks of a revelation of the heavenly Lord in 1 Corinthians 7:10, but the more relevant example is 1 Thessalonians 5:15–17, in which the saying (λόγος, cf. Acts 20:35) concludes the argument. In both these cases the saying of Jesus is the warrant for exhortation.[411] This is a purely formal parallel, lacking the least verbal resemblance. In addition to the other similarities of words, themes, and forms, it caps a rather formidable body of evidence that adduces use of the epistles in the Miletus address.

The argument that these connections derive from the presence of the narrator at the speech fails because it ignores both the improbability of the scene—an address to officials of Ephesus at Miletus—and the "Deutero-Pauline" character of the content, indicated by the titles—presbyters, and bishops/overseers (ἐπίσκοποι)—and content. Steve Walton's conclusion that either memory of Paul or knowledge of traditions about him explains the speech must also brush aside the later milieu. "Tradition" is, quite obviously, a rather vague word. At this point it is unfortunate that Walton has little if any use for form criticism, since the purpose of the formal studies of Gunkel, Bultmann, and other pioneers of that discipline intended to establish some criteria for the discovery and analysis of "traditions." These include seeking to determine both why and how the alleged tradition was preserved. Central to the former question is the task of *Sitz im Leben*, an appropriate social setting and function. For example, early Christians neglected to transmit information about Jesus's preferences in food and hair-styles because they had no reason to do so, but his views on Sabbath observance were a different matter.[412] The crux of the latter issue is the identification of the various literary types in which traditions are encapsulated to make them memorable and intelligible. By proposing answers to these two questions it becomes possible (with invaluable assistance from such disciplines as philology, the history of religions, and theology) to construct hypotheses about the history of various traditions.[413] It is now incumbent upon those who postulate various "traditions" as explanations of the similarities between Acts and the epistles to propose models that will be no less compelling and subject to discussion than are the intertextual models. Bare and unsupported appeal to "tradition/s" alone does not suffice because it is not discussable. The leading exponent of this model has been Gerd Lüdemann. He is not rigorous in his grounds for establishing the nature, setting, and form of "tradition." Moreover, Lüdemann is at times willing to consider dependence upon Paul's letters. At present I am content to leave the task of identifying and isolating putative traditions to others.[414]

Throughout the discussion of Acts 20:17–35 I have not concealed my conviction that the milieu of the speech is post-Pauline, that it belongs to the era of "Pauline schools," to a Deutero-Pauline world. More evidence for this conviction will appear in Chapters Six and Seven.[415] Since the foregoing has made much use of the data adduced by Steve Walton in his *Leadership and Lifestyle*, it would be unfair to ignore his conclusions. Walton, as observed, does not argue for literary dependence upon 1 Thessalonians. He would place this speech in the world of the historical Paul and thus rejects Deutero-Pauline associations.[416] His argument is that the parallels from Ephesians and 2 Timothy are not close to those of the Miletus speech in "both words and ideas," whereas those from 1 Thessalonians are.[417] In my view, this is not a strong argument. I see more proximity in both words and ideas than he does, and I think that the latter proximity is more important. The crucial issue, however, is the framework of the entire speech, which looks to the situation after Paul's death. Verses 24 and 29 allude to it, and conclusion in 20:36–38 underlines the point. Since the approaching absence of Paul is the dominating theme, the perspective of Miletus is clearly Deutero-Pauline, whatever sources may have been used. In this speech one sees the post-Pauline workshop in action. This would be true even if the speech were a *verbatim* report, for the editor would have to select which of a number of addresses to retain for posterity. Two questions dominated the post-Pauline environment: What would Paul say to *us, now*? How would Paul respond to *our* problems? To obtain answers his disciples selected from (and modified) things that Paul had written. Acts 20:17–38 has many of the features of a Deutero-Pauline letter. It is, to say the least, none the worse for that. The Pauline schools and their letters are indicators of the apostle's success in stimulating the growth of various intellectual flowers without sacrificing his essential orientation toward the vitality and growth of particular communities.

Matters about Which Luke Is Silent but Not Ignorant

Certain matters about which Acts shows a rather nice discretion have generally served as (often unstated) arguments *against* his knowledge of Paul's letters. Chief among these is conflict with other followers of Jesus, conflict that is implicit (e.g. Romans[418]) or explicit (e.g. Galatians) in every letter but 1 Thessalonians, and found even there by some.[419] In general, Paul's opponents in Acts are Jews or polytheists. Luke's view is that which became enshrined in Eusebius: false teachers from within and without the community emerge only after the death of the apostles and other early leaders (Acts 20:29–30).[420] Critical scholarship tends to regard the omission of intra-Christian conflict in Acts as grounded in dogma. The near-exception that establishes knowledge of the letters is Acts 15. Earlier I argued that Acts 15 depends upon Galatians. There it was noted that the report of 15:1 does not identify the proponents of circumcision as believers, although those who hold that position in Jerusalem (15:5) are characterized as believing Pharisees who demand both circumcision and general observance of the Torah. And arguments for dependence upon Galatians apart, Acts 15 establishes that Luke *was* aware of at least one controversy. Therefore his silence about others can hardly be offered in evidence that Luke did not know the letters.

A second issue that Luke glosses over is Paul's Collection for Jerusalem, which has also been fully canvassed above and elsewhere.[421] Luke's knowledge of this project is nearly indisputable: "Now after some years I came to bring alms to my nation and to offer sacrifices" (Acts 24:17). About this F. F. Bruce says ". . . [T]he majority of exegetes are certainly right in seeing here a reference to the collection . . ."[422] The majority of exegetes also agree that the journey described in Acts 20–21, whatever Luke's source may have been, had as its object the delivery of the collection. The conclusion is not that Luke was unaware of this offering, but that he chose to deflect it as "alms for my nation." Once more I invoke the late Professor Bruce: "Luke plainly knew about the collection, but, equally plainly, he is very reticent about it. This may have been because it failed so disastrously to achieve its purpose (the most probable explanation) . . ."[423]

A third matter is Luke's failure throughout most of Acts to mention that Paul was a controversial figure among *believers*. This status is related to intra-Christian conflicts and is manifest—to cite but one example—throughout Romans. Acts 21:18–25 explodes this appearance of ignorance:

> *James and the elders* said to *Paul*, "You see, brother, how many thousands of believers there are among the Jews, and they are all zealous for the law. They have been told about you that you teach all the Jews living among the Gentiles to forsake Moses, and that you tell them not to circumcise their children or observe the customs." (Acts 21:20–21)

Insofar as the readers of Acts are aware, this is a calumny.[424] 16:1–3 reports the circumcision of Timothy. Although the text has not hesitated to take note of rumors and slander, it has avoided any mention of Paul's advice to believers of Jewish background. One solution might have been for James and other leaders to repudiate this allegation in the strongest manner possible. They undoubtedly had some influence in the community. Another would be for Paul to address a representative community meeting at which he could personally deny the charges.[425] James's solution, which is couched in the form of an order, does not address the subject of Paul's teaching. He demands that the missionary to Jews and gentiles demonstrate his personal piety, that Paul "become a Jew to Jews" (cf. 1 Corinthians 9:20). From the letters one could imagine that Paul *might* engage in an act of Jewish piety, but not that he fostered Torah-observance, for the requirements of strict observance made mixed communities, like that in Antioch, all but impossible (Galatians 2). Acts 21 certainly shows that Luke appreciated Paul's controversial standing among believers. The solution it offers *might* be based upon the epistles. Sidestepping the issue of Paul's teaching by requesting an act of private piety introduces a nuance that reflects the complicated facts in a more suitable fashion than would result from gossip, stories, or legends, in which nuance is rarely present.[426] James's stated concern about the *teaching* of Paul is a solid indication that post-Pauline issues are the primary subject: what is the implication of Pauline though for those of Jewish background? Luke wishes to emphasize that Paul not only did not act against Torah (cf. Acts 16:1–3) but also that he did not condemn its practice out of hand.

Luke famously eliminates Titus from the company of Paul's colleagues. He will suppress persons and events when the circumstances require, but he is aware that the superior tactic is to revise or redirect. Apollos is a good example of this method. Other than his Alexandrian origin, everything credible said about Apollos in Acts could have come from 1 Corinthians:[427] Apollos was an eloquent exponent of wisdom who came to Corinth after Paul had founded the community.[428] Luke declines to report on any activity in Corinth other than disputes with Jews about scriptural interpretation, and he separates him from contact with Paul. It is possible that Apollos later fell into disrepute and that Luke knows it, but the generally favorable review suggests instead that Luke wishes him to stand beneath Paul at one full remove, and he strongly implies that Apollos had nothing to do with Paul's Corinthian converts. The evident source of Luke's information about the Christian career of Apollos is 1 Corinthians. While he does not explicitly deny any of the facts in that letter—Apollos was brimming with wisdom and he did follow Paul in Corinth—Luke gives them a particular interpretive spin. All of the potentially controversial issues about Apollos—baptism, wisdom, eloquence, unsolicited cultivation of Paul's garden—have been anticipated in Acts. Luke may have known some independent traditions about Apollos, but his sketch just happens to touch upon matters addressed or hinted at in the epistle. The similarities are not limited to matters of fact; they touch upon specific issues. How many kilograms of coincidence can that camel which emerged in Damascus bear? The burden of coincidence has become, to paraphrase the Apostle Peter, unbearable (Acts 15:10). Just as the case of Apollos may well stand as one example of how Luke works with Paul's letters, it also illustrates how he adjusts the facts they present.

CONCLUSION

Enterprises like this are caught on the horns of a dilemma, the opposing points of which are proverbially labeled "Where there's smoke, there's fire" and "Don't miss the woods for the trees." The scholarly form of the latter is the warning to be suspicious of arguments based upon an accumulation of small points. One cannot create a forest by accumulating twigs, no matter how many. Moreover, scholars are no less inept at blowing smoke than other people. For as long as the period surveyed in Acts (three decades), I refused to be tempted by suggestions that Luke had used Paul's letters. This was not because I believed that Luke did not know that Paul wrote letters or that they would have been unavailable, but because I regarded the non-use of the letters as a deliberate choice. My view was essentially that of John Knox at the conclusion of his work as a creative scholar.[429] But the hypothesis that failure to use the letters was the result of choice does not distinguish between *ignoring* the existence of Paul's letters as a matter of policy and *using* such information from them as one might choose to appropriate. Once it is conceded that Luke knew about Paul's letters and that he chose to remain silent about them, the possibility of use takes on a different color. The use of unacknowledged sources was an accepted practice in the Greco-Roman world.[430] Luke was no less free to fail to mention his use of Paul than he was to fail to mention his use of Mark. The position that remains difficult to explain is that of those who place Luke at the end of the first century or later and agree that he was aware that Paul wrote letters, but then exclude those letters from consideration as sources. Having ignored the composition of the letters, they seem to argue, it would have been "unfair" for Luke to "take a peek at" them. Knox was reduced to his position because he found limited merit in Morton Enslin's arguments for Lukan dependence upon Paul. "They can all be explained by independent traditions."[431] That claim, I have sought to demonstrate, requires a much more copious substantiation than it has received. Lüdemann's effort to demonstrate these traditions by discovering their traces has not been entirely successful. In the end he raises more questions than he answers. The second contention of Knox is important. He asserts "the absence of adequate evidence of *verbal* dependence . . ." and goes on to ask, "Can it be supposed that Luke used the letters of Paul as sources for *facts* or *data* but succeeded in avoiding (or would even have tried to avoid!) any trace of their actual language?"[432]

As was established earlier, from the perspective of Greco-Roman literature the answer to his rhetorical question would be "Yes."[433] Ancient authors were expected to recast sources in their own language and style, of which Luke's and Matthew's use of Mark are apposite examples, however imperfect in execution. Moreover, this assertion seems to posit the absence of Paul's "actual language" from the hypothetical traditions in question. Is it logical to presume that, although Luke could not have avoided traces of Paul's actual language, these "traditions" would consistently have done so? I do not see why this should be the case, and am certain that it is not a valid *a priori* assumption. Finally, it is no longer possible to repeat Knox's confident claims about the absence of any trace of Pauline language. However one is to account for them, traces abound.

Four factors explain why the claim of non-use can no longer simply be stipulated:

1. The study and methods of intertextuality have grown vastly more sophisticated.
2. Powerful research tools like the TLG can now show whether particular phrases are significant indicators of literary relationships.
3. Patient, exhaustive studies of relations between Acts and epistles have provided substantial bases for examination of a question that was often resolved in the past by informed intuition and educated conjecture.[434]
4. The most important factor has been the shift in the understanding of Luke as a writer. For decades—indeed for over a millennium—Luke was an "historian." Redaction criticism (c. 1945–) replaced this figure with "Luke the Theologian." Literary criticism has brought "Luke the Author" to the forefront.[435] In the eyes of many, Luke the historian could not have used the letters because they would have helped him clarify some issues and correct some errors. The theological Luke didn't use the letters because they presented a different theology.[436] Luke the author, however, is free to use or not use what he will as he will.

Another objection to Luke's possible knowledge (and thus use) of Pauline letters is that he did not belong to the Pauline "sphere."[437] I rather think that more than one "Pauline sphere" or "school" existed, that such groups might overlap, and that Luke *did* belong to a Pauline sphere. Some followers of Paul who knew and used his letters likewise had ideas that differed from those of Paul. Ignatius and Polycarp are examples. Still more cogent is *1 Clement*, which certainly knows of Paul and at least two letters, but is theologically quite distinct.[438] The decisive example is the Epistle of James, which, in 2:14–26 engages in a clear debate with what is perceived to be Pauline theology, taking up the theme of faith and works with reference to the same scriptural passages invoked by Paul.[439] As James and *1 Clement* attest, knowledge of Pauline letters was not restricted to a closed circle, not even in the last decades of the first century.[440]

The conclusion of this chapter is that the evidence for Lucan knowledge and use of the epistles is quite compelling. As the accompanying summary tables indicate, the author of Luke and Acts apparently had access to a collection of Pauline letters, indeed to a corpus rather than to two or three individual letters. The particular shape of this collection (seven letters to seven churches or ten letters) is unknown. The most interesting indication is that this collection evidently included Romans 15 and may well have contained 2 Corinthians.[441] The possibility remains that Luke knew some letters in more than one copy or form, and I regard it as quite possible that Luke had access to "uncollected" letters no longer extant.[442]

One suggestion that has arisen in the course of this investigation is that Luke's data for the "itinerary" of Paul's final trip to Jerusalem arises from a lost letter of Paul (and/or his colleague[s]) describing the fate of the collection. If that offering had been rejected, there would have been little interest in retaining this testament to Christian disunity, quite possibly betrayal.[443] The primary destination of such a letter would have been the churches of Galatia and Achaea (Greece), which had contributed to the collection (Romans 15:26), but Ephesus may have been an intermediate or additional destination.[444] This source is, of course, purely hypothetical, but so is the "itinerary source," and this hypothesis has the benefits of both a well-known form, the letter, and a function, accounting to contributors about what came of their gift.[445]

Ephesus is the most probable—but by no means the sole—candidate for the origin of the first major collection of Paul's letters. That city is also a likely provenance for Luke and Acts.[446] Luke's apparent familiarity with Ephesians, which probably stems *from* Ephesus, provides more support for this hypothesis.[447] The likelihood that the full collection of Paul's letters appeared before 90 CE is quite low. Soon after 100 the corpus begins to leave its mark. Luke's use of a Pauline letter collection thus establishes a *terminus a quo* of c. 95–100. It is arguable that Luke knew the letters quite well. At the end of his painstaking study Lars Aejmelaeus reaches back to Morton Enslin's observation in 1938, supported by William Walker nearly fifty years later, that Luke had often heard or read the letters.[448] In that same note Aejmelaeus compares Luke's ability to write in "Pauline style" to his well-known "Septuagintal style." This is an apt comparison. Luke had thoroughly imbibed the style of Paul. This familiarity enables a double thrust. For one part of his intended audience Luke wishes to present a Paul shorn of intra-Christian controversy and his notoriously provocative epistles; for others there is the reassurance of the familiar pastoral leader, using words very close to Paul's own.

In the eventual canonical arrangement, the book of Acts serves as both a transition from Jesus to Paul and as a kind of introduction to the epistles. Not only does this arrangement distract scholars generally, but it is also the bane of many students of "Luke-Acts," for whom it destroys the unity of the Lukan contribution. They have a point.[449] Still and all, the description of Acts as an "introduction to the letters of Paul" does capture one of its functions, for although Luke is quite ready to accept the possibility that his work will be a substitute for the letters, he would have those who must use the letters understand them in the light of the background and perspective that he has provided. In this effort he was not the first,[450] but he has proved far from the least successful. Without this introduction (and other efforts) those epistles would have had a difficult time establishing themselves among the foundational documents of the Christian religion.[451] To return to the proverbs: the woods are filled with smoke. One need but turn over a leaf to see flame burst forth. Examination of the Pauline trees does not lead to neglect of the forest, since the purpose of looking for this variety of tree has never had any other justification than improving one's understanding of the forest.

STATISTICAL SUMMARY OF SPECIFIC PASSAGES

Comments: In a few cases I have used a lower-case *x* to suggest that the parallel is of limited scope. "Verbal" means just that, not paraphrase. "Themes" is quite general. A negative (–) indicates that the texts being compared are speaking about quite different matters. "Setting" is usually an event, such as the Jerusalem conference. "Context" relates to the text. A positive (X) mark indicates either that other material from the same Pauline context is found in Luke or Acts or that the section of Luke/Acts in view has affinities with other Pauline letters. In most cases (as in the first entry, Rom 12:11) it points to another alleged similarity from the same Pauline source. Since, for example, there are a number of entries from 1 Thessalonians 2, every "hit" from that chapter will have a positive (X) mark in "context." (See Tables 4.40–49.)

Tables 4.40-47 summarize the qualitative research of the preceding chapter. Charts reflect no subtleties and do not distinguish between more and less compelling examples. They do permit some quantitative generalizations.

Table 4.40: Romans

Reference	Luke/Acts	Verbal	Themes	Setting	Context
1:16 (etc.)	Acts 3:26 (etc.)	X	X	X	–
2:10	Acts 10:34	X	X	–	X
12:11	Acts 18:25	X	X	–	X
12:11	Acts 20:19	X	X	–	X
12:14	Luke 6:28	X	X	X	–
14:14–23	Acts 10:10–20	X	X	X	X
14:20	Luke 11:41	X	X	X	X
15:29–31	Acts 20:22	X	X	–	–

Sub-total 8

Table 4.41: 1 Corinthians

Reference	Luke/Acts	Verbal	Themes	Setting	Context
1:11–4:6	Acts 18:24–28	–	X	–	X
1:14	Acts 18:8	X	X	–	X
1:24	Acts 20:20	X	X	–	–
4:1–2	Luke 12:41–48[452]	–	X	X	X
5:3–5	Acts 5:1–11	–	X	X	–
6:9–10	Luke 18:11	X	X	–	–
7:32–35	Luke 10:38–42	X	X	–	–
9:7	Luke 3:14	X	–	–	–
10:16–17	Luke 22:17–18	X	X	X	X
11:16	Luke 22:24	X	X	X	X
11:23–25	Luke 22:19–20[453]	X	X	X	X
15:4–5	Luke 24:34	X	X	X	X
16:13	Acts 20:31	X	X	X	–
16:19	Acts 18:24–28	X	X	X	–

Sub-total 14

Table 4.42: 2 Corinthians

Reference	Luke/Acts	Verbal	Themes	Setting	Context
2:4	Acts 20:19, 31	X	–	–	–
11:25	Acts 14:19–20	X	X	–	–
11:32–33	Acts 9:23–25	X	X	X	–

Sub-total 3

Table 4.43: Galatians

Reference	Luke/Acts	Verbal	Themes	Setting	Context
1:7/5:10	Acts 15:24	X	X	X	X
1:12	Acts 20:24	X	X	–	–
1:13, 23	Acts 9:21	X	X	X	X
1:14	Acts 22:3	X	X	X	X
1:15–17	Acts 26:16–18	–	X	X	X
1:16	Acts 9:20	X	X	X	X
chap. 2	Acts 15	X	X	X	X
eight items of narrative sequence					
2:1	Acts 15:2				
2:1	12:25; 15:37–38	X	X	X	X
2:6	Acts 15:9	X	X	?	–
2:7	Acts 11:30	–	X	X	–
2:7	Acts 15:7	x	X	X	X
2:10	Acts 15:1, 5	X	X	X	X
2:10	Acts 11:30	X	X	X	X
2:12	Acts 15:1	X	X	X	X
2:12	Acts 11:2–3	X	X	X	
2:15–16	Acts 15:9–11	X	X	X	X
2:1–14	Acts 21:18–28	x	X	X	X
3:2–5/4:6	Acts 15:8	X	X	X	X
3:11	Acts 13:39	X	X	–	X
3:14	Acts 2:33	X	X	–	–
3:19–20	Acts 7:53	X	X	–	X
4:6; cf. 3:2–5					–
5:1	Acts 15:10	X	X	X	X
5:4	Acts 13:39	X	X	X	X

Sub-total 25

Table 4.44: Ephesians

Reference	Luke/Acts	Verbal	Themes	Setting	Context
1:7	Acts 20:28	X	X	–	X
1:7	Acts 26:18	X	X	–	X
1:11	Acts 20:27	X	X	–	X
1:13	Acts 2:33	X	X	X	X
1:13–14	Acts 20:28	X	–	–	X
1:14	Acts 20:32	X	X	–	–
2:3–5	Acts 16:1–3	X	X	–	X
1:18	Acts 20:32	X	X	–	–
2:8	Acts 15:11	X	X	X	X
2:15–18	Acts 15:7–11	–	X	X	X
2:17	Acts 10:36	X	X	X	X
3:2;	Acts 20:24	X	X	–	–
3:6–7	Acts 20:24	X	X	–	X
3:20	Acts 20:32	X	X	–	X
4:1–2	Acts 20:19	X	–	–	X
4:11–12	Acts 20:28	X	X	–	X
4:12	Acts 20:32	X	X	–	X
4:28	Acts 20:33–35	X	X	–	X
6:7	Acts 20:19	X	X	–	X

Sub-total 19

Table 4.45: Philippians

Reference	Luke/Acts	Verbal	Themes	Setting	Context
1:5	Acts 20:18	X	X	–	–
1:17–18	Acts 20:22–23	X	–	–	X
3:5	Acts 22:3	X	X	X	X
3:5	Acts 23:6	X	X	X	X

Sub-total 4

Table 4.46: Colossians

Reference	Luke/Acts	Verbal	Themes	Setting	Context
1:12–13	Acts 20:32	X	X	–	–
1:13	Luke 22:53	X	X	–	–
1:12–14	Acts 26:18	X	X	–	–
4:17	Acts 20:24	X	X	–	–

Sub-total 3/4

Table 4.47: 1 Thessalonians

Reference	Luke/Acts	Verbal	Themes	Setting	Context
1:4–5	Acts 20:18	X	X	X	X
2:1	Acts 20:18	X	X	X	_
2:3–12	Acts 20:31	_	X	_	X
2:3, 5, 7, 9, 11	Acts 20:33–35	X	X	X	X
2:8	Acts 20:24	X	X	_	X
2:9, 11–12	Acts 20:31	X	X	X	X
2:13	Acts 20:32	X	_	_	X
3:3–4	Acts 20:22–23	X	X	X	X
4:11–12	Acts 20:33–35	X	X	_	X
5:2, 6–7, 12, 14	Luke 21:34–36	X	X	X	_
					_
5:9–10	Acts 20:28	X	X	_	_
5:11	Acts 20:32	X	X	_	X
5:12	Acts 20:33–35	X	X	_	X

Sub-total 13

Table 4.48: Itinerary Parallels

Event or Destination	Correspondence	Acts
Persecution	Gal 1:13–14	Acts 8:3; 9:1–2
Conversion	Gal 1:15–17a	Acts 9:1–22, etc.
Arabia	Gal 1:17b	—
Damascus	Gal 1:17c	Acts 9
Flight from Damascus	2 Cor 11:32–33	Acts 9:23–25
Jerusalem	Gal 1:18–20	Acts 9:26–29
Syria, Cilicia	Gal 1:21	Cf. Acts 9:30; 11:25
Jerusalem (14 years later)	Gal 2:1–10	?Acts 11; Acts 15
("North") Galatia	1 Cor 16:1; Gal 4:13	Acts 16:6 (!!!)
Philippi	1 Thess 2:1–2; Phil 4:15–16	Acts 16:11–40
Thessalonica	1 Thess 2:1–2; Phil 4:15–16	Acts 17:1–9
Athens	1 Thess 3:1–3	Acts 17; 15–34
Corinth	2 Cor 1:9; 11:7–9	Acts 18:1–18a
Ephesus	1 Cor 16:8–9	Acts 19
Galatia again	Gal 4:13	Cf. Acts 18:3
Troas	2 Cor 2:12	—(cf. 19:21)
Macedonia	2 Cor 8–9	Acts 20
Corinth	2 Cor 12	Acts 20:2b-3
Plans for		
a) Jerusalem	Rom 15:22–25	Acts 19:21: Acts 21
b) Rome	Rom 15:22–25	Acts 28

Table 4.49: Acts and Galatians[454]

Event	Galatians	Acts
Paul Persecutes	1:13–14	8:1–3; 9:1–2
"Conversion" of Paul	1:15–17a	9:3–19a
Proclamation in Arabia/	1:17b	9:19b-20, 22
Damascus	*1:22–24*	*9:21*
Rumor/Gossip regarding	(*cf. 2 Corinthians 11:32–33*	*9:23–25*
Paul	1:18–20	9:26–29
Escape from Damascus	1:21	9:30
Visit to Jerusalem	*cf. 2:1a*	*9:31–11:24*
To Tarsus/Syria & Cilicia		
INTERLUDE: Acts inter-		
rupts the story of Paul to		
report a mission of Peter,		
including the conversion		
of a gentile, the acceptance		
of that act in Jerusalem,		
and the beginnings of a		
mission in Antioch that		
included gentiles		
Saul/Paul with Barnabas		11:25–29
Saul/Paul and Barnabas in	2:1b	11:30; 12:25
Jerusalem	2:1b-10	*Acts 12:1–24 is another*
		departure, dealing with
		the tyranny and death
		of Herod, including the
		martyrdom of James and
Gentile Mission		*the escape of Peter*
Authorized	*2:7–9*	*10:1–11:18*
Missionary Journey		*13:3–14:23*
Argument in Antioch	2:11–14	15:1–2a

These are the totals:

Romans	8
1 Corinthians	14
2 Corinthians	3
Galatians	25
Ephesians	19
Philippians	4
Colossians	3/4
1 Thessalonians	13
Grand Total	89/90

Many students of Christian origins are suspicious of quantitative data: there are lies, yes, even damnable lies, and then there are statistics. And to be sure, objections can be made to a number of these proposals. They do not have equal value. Grant the skeptics their point. Throw out half of these proposed affinities. If the negotiator is a veritable descendant of Abraham, the researcher may, like God, sigh and say, "O.K. Remove two thirds of them" (cf. Genesis 18:22-33). There would still be sufficient evidence that Luke used the letters of Paul. What might change is the extent of Luke's collection. Once the hypothesis that Luke used Pauline letters has been accepted, however, the impetus is to look for more data, not fewer. In the next decades there will be continued refinement of this question. Work is still in a very early stage.

At present I believe that the data lead to the conclusion that Luke had access to a collection of Pauline epistles rather than to a few independent items.[455] Quantities reveal his interests: historical (Galatians), ecclesiological (Ephesians) and pastoral (1 Thessalonians). Luke's far from superficial knowledge of "Paul the pastor" was no obstacle to his representation of the missionary, nor did he hesitate to make adjustments to Pauline statements that he did not find in the better interests of either that apostle or his own historical/theological program. Not for the first time do I observe that such a statement would scarcely stimulate the elevation of an eyebrow if applied to Mark, but that it will be unacceptable to many when applied to Paul.

Anthony Blassi (Table 4.48) argued from data about Paul's travels in Acts toward use of the letters.[456] This has not been the customary thrust of such arguments. These agreements have rather constituted a pillar of the claims for Acts' independent knowledge of Paul's movements and thus of its historical reliability.[457] There are more gaps than Table 4.48 indicates, most notably Galatia, while Acts mentions stations not mentioned in the correspondence and apparently varies in order at points.[458] However, such differences have not overthrown the contention that these data from Acts show that Luke had excellent, perhaps first-hand, information and that his reports should therefore be accepted even when they are not independently confirmed by the epistles—or, from a more critical perspective, open to suspicion when they conform to stereotypes or authorial interests.[459]

Table 4.48 indicates some of the damage done by the hypothesis that Luke used Pauline letters. At first sight this may seem strange. Does not this table showcase our Luke engaged in doing just what historians should do: employing primary sources as the grounds for a plausible reconstruction? This the table may well do, but it also exposes the tendentious quality of Luke's reconstruction, for it reveals nearly as much of what is likely to be called misuse of the letters as it does their use. Luke, unlike the general public of Jerusalem and gentiles (Acts 3:17; 17:23), cannot be excused on the grounds of ignorance. He took from the letters such data as suited his purpose, overlooked what did not, and shaped other material to conform to his intentions. It should also be noted that he was neither the first nor the last researcher ever to have done such things, and that the possibility of deriving information about Paul's travels from the letters does not exclude the use of other sources.[460] These important qualifications do not change the essential finding, which is that Acts is, to a large degree, a secondary source for data about the life of Paul. If, as the evidence indicates, Luke used Paul's letters, the canonical Acts will stand much closer to the Pastoral Epistles and to Acts of Paul as a historical source than to the undisputed letters. For many, this will be a very bitter pill to swallow, but in due course all will be better for the treatment.

Heikki Leppä shows (Table 4.49) what occurs when some of these parallels are examined from the perspective of literary dependence. Underlined items are in different sequence or lacking in one of the sources. The intention of this table is to show that although Luke interweaves or interpolates other material, his outline is very close to that of Galatians. As Leppä notes, it has been customary for about a century to attribute this material in Acts to an "Antiochene Source."[461] Overlap with Galatians—and this table ignores the notorious problems of Paul's visits to Jerusalem—was deemed reasonable, for Galatians 1-2 present the simple facts of the case. That view is no longer tenable. Paul's selection and arrangement of the data are part of his arguments designed to support his case in a highly controversial situation.[462] Both "prosecution" and "defense" have to contend with the same "facts," challenging some, downplaying others, and stressing those most favorable to their strategies and constructions. The "Antiochene" account of these events would most likely have told a rather different story, quite likely one that featured as its "hero" the moderate Peter rather than Paul, who had left the community in disappointment and anger. Although Luke makes some important changes, such as adding a trip to Jerusalem to defuse the Collection controversy, his departures from the outline of Galatians fit his own particular interests. Finally, as Leppä, following Enslin, notes, where Paul is silent, Acts is also silent.[463] The "three years" of Galatians 1:18 and the "fourteen years" of 2:1 vanish. This is a very telling point and not just another questionable "argument from silence." It is highly improbable that these corresponding gaps are due to coincidence.

The cumulative evidence that Luke made use of Pauline letters is rather persuasive. That Luke possessed a goodly amount of information about Paul cannot be doubted. The customary explanation for this information is that Luke had access to oral or written traditions about what Paul did or said, or that he acquired this material from his personal experience. What Acts so often reveals is that Luke was acquainted with the very words and phrases and ideas found in the letters. The Paul he knows is, in good part, the Paul of the letters. Had Luke been a companion of Paul, one would expect that he would report Paul's thought in his own words. Instead, he communicates his own ideas in the words of Paul. Intertextuality is not simply the most economical or most probable explanation of this phenomenon; it is the only feasible explanation.

The intertextual solution often shows not only the how (words) but also the why of Luke's narrative. Nevertheless, appeal to the letters resolves far more problems than it creates. The objections to this hypothesis are not based upon detailed examination of numerous parallels. They are essentially a priori objections grounded in the view that Luke would not have made the "mistakes" he made or asserted some of his claims if he had access to this crucial source. These objections are anachronistic, for they apply contemporary criteria to an ancient text. Even if Luke viewed himself as an historian (a claim that is far from established), by the standards of ancient historiography his use of Paul's letters was not inappropriate. Ancient authors neglect to mention many of their sources, and Luke had good reason to avoid reference to Paul's letters.

I should like to close with a disclaimer, a preview, and an excursus. The disclaimer is to emphasize that the thesis that Luke used Pauline letters should not be taken to imply that Acts had no other substantive sources, that it is entirely an amalgam of data from the extant epistles and Lucan invention. My views are not those of Barbara Thiering.[464] In the next chapter the pot (fired with smoking wood culled from fallen trees) will reach the boiling point, for it will raise questions about "Luke the Historian's" use of actual historical writing. The subject, as advertised previously, is the Jewish historian Flavius Josephus, the major source for the history of Palestine and of Jews in the first century.

Excursus: Some Reflections on Method

Consideration of unpopular arguments, such as claims that Luke used letters of Paul or rejection of Luke's contention that Paul was a Roman citizen, not to mention deviations from convention in dating Acts, has revealed a practice that seems to have acquired legitimacy through frequent use. The practice in question is the pretense that identification of an alternative explanation is tantamount to refutation. Professor 1 has come up with hypothesis y to explain phenomena a, b, and c. In defense of hypothesis x, Professor 2 announces that there are other possible explanations for a, b, and c and proceeds to list the same, announcing at the end that hypothesis x continues to rule.

It should not have to be said that there are always different explanations. Refutation requires, among other things, demonstration that hypothesis x is in some way or ways preferable because it better accounts for the data. Furthermore, lists of point-by-point alternatives need to cohere in a logical structure, since the goal is refutation of an entire hypothesis rather than just inflicting damage upon individual claims. Finally, even a coherent refutation of hypothesis y does not establish hypothesis x. Tearing down one building does not erect another. This methodological sloppiness is, as noted above, more likely to go unchallenged when it serves to support traditional views. Behind this stands the dictum that the burden of proof always lies upon those who challenge the traditional explanation. The dictum possesses sociological and psychological validity. "If it ain't broke, don't fix it" is the creed of those who are doing well enough with things as they are. That which some view as not broken may look quite different to those who are, for example, broke. Scientifically, however, the dictum is meaningless, for science demands a level playing field.

A related issue in the analysis of Acts as a work of history is the apparent assumption that demonstrating possibility establishes probability. This has a corollary: what is improbable is impossible. Although historiography cannot operate on the basis that all things are possible, historians are well advised to keep their lists of the impossible as short as . . . well, possible. The assumption that refutation of impossibility establishes probability is quite prevalent in writers of an "apologetic" orientation, in this case those who seek to establish and defend the historical reliability of Acts. This perspective is not illegitimate, but it behooves those who take it up to be explicit, for a false pose of "neutrality" is not legitimate. The defenders of Luke should also concede that establishment of impossibility is quite rare, and that failure to do so is very slender evidence. The text-book case of this methodological failure is the matter of Paul's alleged citizenship at Tarsus and Rome. In support of the claims of Acts, Brian Rapske and Rainer Riesner, to cite two more recent examples, go to great lengths to establish the possibility that a Jew could have been a citizen at Tarsus or Sardis and that Roman citizenship could be acquired in several ways.[465] Neither seems to feel obliged to do more than refute impossibility. The result is, in my estimate, that both overlook the key issues.[466] They have not refuted the counter-arguments.[467]

An example of "refutation" though the postulation of an alternative explanation is Ben Witherington's critique of the possibility that Luke made use of Josephus. This argument will receive detailed consideration in the following chapter.[468] A more general example is the routine rejection of the hypothesis explored in this chapter, a widespread disavowal of Luke's use of Pauline letters based on an appeal to "traditions"—of which, as observed, there seems to be no need for delineation and specification.

The preceding observations emerge from the reexamination of rejected hypotheses. What they reveal has more general application. These observations warn against the tendency toward methodological laxity when there is a consensus about the subject under consideration. J. A. T. Robinson saw this problem clearly. His *Redating the New Testament* subjects that laxity to repeated exposure and continual laceration. His recompense was neglect, much of it for the wrong reasons.[469]

5 Acts among the Historians
Luke and Josephus

This chapter will revisit another apparently outdated hypothesis: the possibility that Luke made use of some of the writings of Josephus. The grounds for resistance to this idea, often unstated, are very much the same as those involved in questions about Luke's knowledge of Paul's letters. If Luke did employ Josephus, his standing as an historian will be diminished in the eyes of some. This question also bears upon the date of Acts. If Luke derived material from the last books of Josephus' major work, the *Antiquities*, Acts cannot be earlier than c. 100. That an edition of Paul's collected letters did not appear before the close of the first century is quite probable, but not certain. The date when Josephus completed the *Antiquities* is known.[1]

Flavius Josephus lived in the first century. Taken at his word, he was of aristocratic and priestly Jewish background Although he initially opposed the first Jewish revolt against Rome (66–74), he subsequently joined it.[2] After capture by the Romans, Josephus reverted to his earlier position and received patronage from the ruling family. His works include a history of the revolt (*Bellum/Jewish War*), the *Antiquities*, a history of the Jewish people from creation to the Revolt, an autobiography (*Vita/Life*), and an apology (*Contra Apionem/Against Apion*) A mere eight decades ago one could calmly discuss the possibility that Luke made use of Josephus' *Antiquities*:

> The material for a discussion of the relation of Josephus to the Lucan writings was given in the eighteenth century by J. B. Ott, *Spicilegium sive excerpta ex Flavio Josepho ad Novi Testamenti illustrationem*, 1741, and by J. P. Kreb's *Observationes in Novum Testamentum e Flavio Josepho*, 1755. This material was worked over in the nineteenth century, and the theory evolved that Luke was dependent on Josephus.[3]

Francis Crawford Burkitt (1864–1935), who was no more hasty in his conclusions nor less orthodox on matters of substance than an Edwardian Professor of Divinity at Cambridge should have been, believed that Acts was written by a companion of St. Paul and that the book appeared c. 95–105. The basis for that date is ". . . evidence which convicts the Third Evangelist of having used the *Antiquities*, not always with complete accuracy . . ."[4]

One reason for the decline of support for this hypothesis, it is now claimed, has been its most exhaustive statement. Max Krenkel's 1894 monograph contending that Luke used Josephus as a source is one of those works that have produced "assured results," albeit of a negative character.[5] Written in an era dominated by rather mechanical models of source criticism, employing sloppy methods and indulging in the indiscriminate listing of evidence, Krenkel unintentionally placed the entire question under a cloud.[6] Cadbury *et al.* comment that the view ". . . was most fully stated by Krenkel . . . In some ways, indeed, it was even too fully stated . . ."[7] Colin Hemer was a touch more blunt: "The best refutation of this position may actually be to look at Krenkel's classic defence of it."[8] Krenkel did for Luke the reader of Josephus what Hobart did for Luke the practitioner of medicine.[9] By the late 1980s Hemer could refer, without a trace of nostalgia, to ". . . the theory of Lucan dependence on Josephus . . ." which ". . . had in its day a certain vogue . . ."[10] Krenkel was no less dated than the bustle. Hemer did not exaggerate. For at least half a century students of Luke and Acts have encountered the name of Krenkel only in association with a discredited theory. Very few could have been motivated to pay the study more than a passing glance.[11] The hour has come for some brave soul to point out that Max Krenkel's methodological shortcomings do not in and of themselves prove that Luke did not use Josephus.[12] Identification of methodological defects in an argument does not automatically disprove its hypothesis.[13] An hypothesis that is not sustained is quite different from one that is demonstrably erroneous.

The actual reason for the long reign of this fallacy is very much like that regarding Paul's letters: it was long assumed that, if Luke had access to Josephus, he would have made more substantial and careful use of his work.[14] This methodological flaw is far more insidious than all of Krenkel's wearisome lists because it is often left unstated. When stated, it is unsupported—largely because, as with the denial of Paul's letters as a possible source of Acts, it is insupportable. If Dr. Smith shows that Luke did not use the Pauline themes and texts that Smith would have used, the good doctor has established no more than that Winston Smith did not write Acts and that he would have written it differently. Scholarship does not move forward by such discoveries. The purpose of this chapter is to make a case that Luke *did* use at least some of Josephus's writings, and that the manner in which he used them is quite consistent with the practice of ancient writers. This hypothesis is equally consistent with evidence for Luke's use of other sources, including the LXX, Mark, and Paul. Adoption of this hypothesis will serve to elucidate a number of other problems relative to the interpretation of (Luke and) Acts. This investigation intends to accomplish more than the clarification of some pieces of information found here and there in Acts. Finally, it will provide a very secure *terminus a quo*, for the final book of Josephus's *Antiquities* can be dated to 93/94 CE.

From the ebb of Tübingen's radical nineteenth-century skepticism emerged the portrait of "Luke the Historian." A part of that job description, shared with many biblical writers, included the commitment to a rather mechanical use of sources. One obligation of biblical historians was to insert their sources into their texts with as little adjustment as possible. They were to follow this practice for the convenience of modern scholars, who were thereby enabled to identify and isolate those sources with relative confidence and ease. Among the leading motives for reopening the source question are 1) a more informed view of ancient historiography; 2) an appreciation of how ancient writers utilized their sources; and, most important, 3) a change in the understanding of Luke's own particular methods and goals. The bath water used by Krenkel has long since evaporated. Perhaps it contained a baby.

Steve Mason has been willing to reopen the matter, somewhat hesitantly and, as he concedes, without an in-depth investigation.[15] His modest proposals reflect the application of methods unfamiliar to Krenkel's era, in particular, redaction criticism. At the outset it should be stipulated that no case for dependence can be made on such close verbal similarities as those found in the previous chapter and often, for example, in discussions of the "Synoptic Problem." Luke did not imitate the style of Josephus, nor did he take over passages with but slight adaptations.[16] One must further note that Josephus would have served Luke as a source quite differently from Mark, Q, Paul, or even the LXX. In the light of redaction criticism, the study of sources must now include attention to such matters as why a writer might have utilized a particular source and how that writer might be expected to exploit it—and not in accordance with the canons and criteria of modern historiography or the views of the investigator, but from discovery of the writer's methods, style, ideas, interests, and so forth.

The writings of Josephus have long served as a kind of comparison and "corrective" for the New Testament in general and Luke/Acts in particular. Comparison includes genre, as, for example, in the comprehensive work of Gregory Sterling.[17] "Correction" refers to the tradition of dating, verifying, and criticizing historical and chronological material on the basis of Josephus's presumably more "accurate" writings. The assumption that Josephus presents "history" with which the possibly tendentious and erroneous writings of Luke may be compared is, as Mason states in another context, erroneous.[18] That assumption may be an even greater obstacle than dating to the consideration of Josephus as a source of Acts. The illustrations and arguments to follow are not, please note, predicated upon the assumption that Josephus is "superior" to or more "accurate" than Luke in any one particular.[19] Each of these authors had his own biases and agenda, traits they have in common with every other author.

Mason's *Josephus and the New Testament* engages not only specific incidents for comparison but also broader questions of viewpoint and affinity. This orientation sharply distinguishes his work from the purely (and sometimes mechanically) source-critical approach. He finds that both Luke and Josephus exhibit the conventions and techniques of Hellenistic historiography.[20] Mason then succinctly summarizes their common "apologetic" goal of establishing the legitimacy of a movement or institution through demonstration of its "antiquity" and virtue. Both ancient authors faced the formidable task of showing that their respective subjects were not hotbeds of "unroman activities." The two authors have similar strategies, pursuit of which may sometimes require the assumption of diametrically opposed positions.[21] The first example to be considered is the cornerstone of the argument, a cornerstone that has long been the stumbling block for those who insist Luke had no knowledge of Josephus.

JUDAS AND THEUDAS

The following discussion examines a passage in which Luke's use of Josephus is extremely probable and alternative explanations quite tenuous. That demonstration will open the door to further exploration of the topic, since establishing knowledge of Josephus in one instance will both justify the search for other instances and reinforce the possibility that Josephus was a source for Luke. The case in question is not obscure; scholars have discussed it for more than a century. The subject is the speech of Gamaliel in Acts 5:34–39. Please consult Table 5.1.

Antiquities 20 narrates the deterioration of Judea during the twenty-two years between the death of Agrippa I and the outbreak of the First Revolt (44–66). Josephus does not shy away from accounts of Roman misrule, unsympathetic as he is to those who pursue violent solutions. The procurator Fadus has received no attention since 20.14.[22] The intervening "excursus" deals with the conversion of the royal family of Adiabene.[23] At 20.100 the narrative will move on to the next Procurator, Tiberius Alexander, whose regime was peaceful, despite a grievous famine, because, as a Jew, he did not provoke his subjects by interfering with their religious practices. That he was no pushover is apparent from his execution of James and Simon, sons of Judas the Galilean, who was, according to Josephus, the founder of a rebellious dynasty.[24] Those who read between the lines might conclude that Alexander nipped some revolts in the bud and avoided provocations that might enkindle others. Had there been more governors like him, Josephus seems to imply, the entire mess might have been avoided.

Luke's agenda is no less different from Josephus's than is his form. The references to the personalities in question come at a moment of great tension. Official animosity to the nascent Jesus-movement has been building for three chapters. At 5:33 the apostles faced imminent death. Deliverance came at the unlikely hands of a prominent member of the Sanhedrin, Gamaliel, who delivers a pretty little speech to an executive session. Historical *exempla* (examples) being highly appropriate to deliberative rhetoric,[25] Gamaliel supplies two useful precedents to establish his thesis that authorities should leave the fate of new religious movements to the judgment of God.[26] As telling as these precedents may be, it should be noted that they appear in the wrong chronological order.

Those who maintain that Luke here reproduces an actual speech have taken on a formidable challenge, not only because of its extreme brevity, but also because Acts represents the action as taking place behind closed doors.[27] Exponents of the idea that Luke simply reports what others said are, however, fortuitously relieved of any embarrassment deriving from alleged errors,[28] for any gaffe here must be laid at the feet, as it were, of Gamaliel. It is quite revelatory that nothing of the sort seems to have maintained a foothold on the critical horizon. The very tradition that harshly rejects the notion of Luke as an outright composer of speeches has labored long and hard to deal with the historical difficulties raised in this speech, difficulties all but brushed off or relegated to footnotes by proponents of Lucan composition.[29] At the conclusion of his brief consideration of whether Acts 5:34–39 shows the use of Josephus, Dibelius concludes: "On the contrary, Luke has obviously recorded these incidents as freely as he composed the whole speech."[30]

"Some time ago" (cf. Acts 5:36) the argument for Lucan composition could be invoked to support the use of Josephus: "Here, if anywhere in the Acts, the details of the speech must be due to the author, for all the Christians had been put outside." The author of this proposal, the above-mentioned F. C. Burkitt, went on to list "strong reasons for believing" that Josephus was the source. *Antiquities* 20.97–102, he argues,

> "... is consistent, and his information about these agitators, for aught we know to the contrary, is accurate. The passage in Acts, on the other hand, occurs in a speech where it is probable that the narrator is freely setting down such details as seemed appropriate; it is chronologically faulty ... That the author of the book of Acts should have been careless in his choice of suitable historical instances to put into the mouth of Gamaliel is not very surprising, and surely quite excusable ..."[31]

Dibelius, for his part, continues the thought cited above by observing, "we can ascribe to the author both the desire of the educated man to employ such elements, and also the error of one who was not fully informed on the subject ..." One matter that Dibelius *et al.* do not explain is where Luke obtained his faulty or misapplied information. It is extremely unlikely that these provincial incidents were at the fingertips of every educated person in 60 or 80 or 100 CE. Even less probable is the idea that Luke garnered these tidbits from Peter or Philip or Paul. Only an historian seeking to establish the background of the First Revolt would extend his horizon to include Judas of Galilee, and even then not every historian would do so.

The reason why no one seems willing to leave any errors resting securely at the master's feet is that the first of Gamaliel's persuasive historical examples will not take the stage for a good decade after the dramatic date of his speech, while its chronological successor took place nearly three decades *earlier* than said dramatic date. A contemporary analogue might read thus:

> Winston Churchill sagely said, in the course of an acrimonious debate in the House of Commons during 1932 about cutting back expenses for Imperial Defense, "Do you not recall the costly and desperate haste with which we had to attempt to re-arm ourselves in order to stave off the hideous Nazi menace, and what a close-run thing it was. After that there confronted us the continental and colonial ambitions of the brutish Kaiser Wilhelm, resulting in yet another most sanguinary and white-knuckled struggle."

Table 5.1: Rebels in Order

Josephus Ant. 20.97–102	Acts 5:36–37
Φάδου δὲ τῆς Ἰουδαίας ἐπιτροπεύοντος γόης τις ἀνὴρ Θευδᾶς ὀνόματι πείθει τὸν πλεῖστον ὄχλον ἀναλαβόντα τὰς κτήσεις ἕπεσθαι πρὸς τὸν Ἰορδάνην ποταμὸν αὐτῷ· προφήτης γὰρ ἔλεγεν εἶναι, καὶ προστάγματι τὸν ποταμὸν σχίσας δίοδον ἔχειν ἔφη παρέξειν αὐτοῖς ῥᾳδίαν. [98] καὶ ταῦτα λέγων πολλοὺς ἠπάτησεν ... πολλοὺς μὲν ἀνεῖλεν, πολλοὺς δὲ ζῶντας ἔλαβεν, αὐτὸν δὲ τὸν Θευδᾶν ζωγρήσαντες ἀποτέμνουσι τὴν κεφαλὴν καὶ κομίζουσιν εἰς Ἱεροσόλυμα. [99] τὰ μὲν οὖν συμβάντα τοῖς Ἰουδαίοις κατὰ τοὺς Κουσπίου Φάδου τῆς ἐπιτροπῆς χρόνους ταῦτ' ἐγένετο. [100] Ἦλθε δὲ Φάδῳ διάδοχος Τιβέριος Ἀλέξανδρος Ἀλεξάνδρου παῖς τοῦ καὶ ἀλαβαρχήσαντος ἐν Ἀλεξανδρείᾳ γένει τε καὶ πλούτῳ προὔτευσάντος τῶν ἐκεῖ καθ' αὑτόν. διήνεγκε καὶ τῇ πρὸς τὸν θεὸν εὐσεβείᾳ τοῦ παιδὸς Ἀλεξάνδρου· τοῖς γὰρ πατρίοις οὐκ ἐνέμεινεν οὗτος ἔθεσιν. [101] ἐπὶ τούτου δὲ καὶ τὸν μέγαν λιμὸν κατὰ τὴν Ἰουδαίαν συνέβη γενέσθαι, καθ' ὃν καὶ ἡ βασίλισσα Ἑλένη πολλῶν χρημάτων ὠνησαμένη σῖτον ἀπὸ τῆς Αἰγύπτου διένειμεν τοῖς ἀπορουμένοις, ὡς προεῖπον. [102] πρὸς τούτοις δὲ καὶ οἱ παῖδες Ἰούδα τοῦ Γαλιλαίου ἀνῃχθησαν τοῦ τὸν λαὸν ἀπὸ Ῥωμαίων ἀποστήσαντος Κυρινίου τῆς Ἰουδαίας τιμητεύοντος, ὡς ἐν τοῖς πρὸ τούτου δεδηλώκαμεν, Ἰάκωβος καὶ Σίμων, οὓς ἀνασταυρῶσαι προσέταξεν Ἀλέξανδρος.	προ γὰρ τούτων τῶν ἡμερῶν ἀνέστη Θευδᾶς, λέγων εἶναί τινα ἑαυτόν, ᾧ προσεκλίθη ἀνδρῶν ἀριθμὸς ὡς τετρακοσίων· ὃς ἀνῃρέθη, καὶ πάντες ὅσοι ἐπείθοντο αὐτῷ διελύθησαν καὶ ἐγένοντο εἰς οὐδέν.
Now it came to pass, while Fadus was procurator of Judea, that a certain magician, whose name was Theudas, persuaded a great part of the people to take their effects with them, and follow him to the river Jordan; for he told them he was a prophet, and that he would, by his own command, divide the river, and afford them an easy passage over it; and many were deluded by his words. However, Fadus did not permit them to make any advantage of his wild attempt, but sent a troop of horsemen out against them; who, falling upon them unexpectedly, slew many of them, and took many of them alive. They also took Theudas alive, and cut off his head, and carried it to Jerusalem. This was what befell the Jews in the time of Cuspius Fadus's government. Then came Tiberius Alexander as successor to Fadus; he was the son of Alexander the alabarch of	For some time ago Theudas rose up, claiming to be somebody, and a number of men, about four hundred, joined him; but he was killed, and all who followed him were dispersed and disappeared
	37 μετὰ τοῦτον ἀνέστη Ἰούδας ὁ Γαλιλαῖος ἐν ταῖς ἡμέραις τῆς ἀπογραφῆς καὶ ἀπέστησεν λαὸν ὀπίσω αὐτοῦ· κἀκεῖνος ἀπώλετο, καὶ πάντες ὅσοι ἐπείθοντο αὐτῷ ἐσκορπίσθησαν
	After him Judas the Galilean rose up at the time of the census and got people to follow him; he also perished, and all who followed him were scattered

Alexandria, who was a leading person among all his contemporaries, both for his family and wealth: he was also more eminent for his piety than this his son Alexander, for he did not continue in the religion of his country. Under these procurators that great famine happened in Judea, in which queen Helena bought wheat in Egypt at a great expense, and distributed it to those that were in want, as I have related already. And besides this, [the sons of] Judas of Galilee were now slain [or brought to trial], I mean of that Judas who caused the people to revolt, when Cyrenius came to take a census of the estates of the Jews, as we have related. The names of those sons were James and Simon, whom Alexander commanded to be crucified.[32]

It is essentially impossible to believe that Gamaliel actually used the specific examples attributed to him. Insofar as one might judge from Acts alone, the threat of a massacre of the apostolic college quashed by Gamaliel took place only a few weeks after Pentecost, i.e. in the year 30.[33] The sole historical account about an insurrectionist known as Theudas is Josephus, who locates him under Fadus, i.e., 44–46, following the death of Agrippa I. And the excellent Gamaliel's second instance of what happens to those who rebel without divine backing is the case of Judas of Galilee, whose movement was ignited by the introduction of direct Roman rule in 6 CE. Extrication of Gamaliel (or Luke) from this quandary requires the ingenuity of . . . well, a Gamaliel. The most common recourse is quite prosaic: to posit a second Theudas, rather a former Theudas. Bruce says,

> "While it is usually precarious to cut this kind of Gordian knot by assuming
> that the person in question is someone else of the same name, the assumption
> is acceptable here (1) because Luke is as credit-worthy a historian as Josephus,
> (2) because Theudas is a common name . . . and (3) because there were many such
> risings under similar leaders . . ."[34]

The first argument does no more than beg the question; the second is only partially relevant and not entirely correct. With reference to Palestine the name Theudas *is* rather rare, and "by no means common".[35] Indeed, someone wishing to be naughty might, with similar justification, posit two characters named Paul, early Christian missionaries who worked in the Eastern Mediterranean. One, A.K.A. Saul, a life-long Pharisee who labored to convert Jews and gentiles, a great orator and potent miracle-worker, who worked in close harmony with James, imposed the "apostolic decree," did not need to write letters because his communities experienced no serious problems, etc. The other, who worked in much of the same territory . . .

Rather than take this course, I shall instead turn to Bruce's third ground for positing another Theudas. "According to Jos. *Ant.* 17.269 there were innumerable tumults and disorders in Judaea after Herod's death (4 B.C.), and this rising may have been one of those."[36] So it might, but Josephus does not enumerate it among the innumerable. Given so many possibilities, it remains unclear why Gamaliel (or Luke) would elect a relatively obscure example. More pointedly, the leaders of those major uprisings assigned by Josephus to the later years of Herod and the era of Archelaus were messianic, i.e., royal, claimants and pretenders, whereas leaders of movements during and after the time of Jesus are usually characterized in prophetic terms.[37] Many of the latter promised to reiterate the great wonders of the Exodus. Theudas, for example, claimed to be a Joshua *redivivus*. Josephus labels him as a γόης, an impostor or, in more specifically Jewish terminology, a false prophet. Acts 5 says nothing about Theudas's proposed mission. It does, however, report that his claim: λέγων εἶναί τινα ἑαυτόν "Saying that he was somebody"). The claim to be "someone" does not appear unduly grandiose. Everyone can boast of at least that much status. A similar expression appears in Acts 8:9: Ἀνὴρ δέ τις ὀνόματι Σίμων προϋπῆρχεν ἐν τῇ πόλει μαγεύων καὶ ἐξιστάνων τὸ ἔθνος τῆς Σαμαρείας, λέγων εἶναί τινα ἑαυτὸν μέγαν[38] ("Now a certain man named Simon had previously practiced magic in the city and amazed the people of Samaria, saying that he was someone great"). The characterizations of Theudas and Simon "Magus" are nearly identical. What label would Josephus apply to a person like Simon? γόης ("charlatan," a word that Luke does not use) would do quite well. Luke/Gamaliel thus characterizes Theudas in terms very much like those of Josephus. If this were an item of comparison between Acts and the epistles, it would be celebrated as an "undesigned coincidence." One early collector of such coincidences found it to be just that. Eusebius appeals to Josephus *Antiquities* 20.97–98, in support of the historical reliability of Acts. After summarizing Acts 5:34–36, he throws down the gauntlet, "Come, let us also set out the text of Josephus about him [Theudas]," followed by a full citation of 97–98.[39] Eusebius saw no need for a second Theudas

There are, of course, differences between the two accounts. Josephus states that Theudas persuaded τὸν πλεῖστον ὄχλον, which one might render as "the biggest mob imaginable," rather than "the majority" of the unwashed multitude. Gamaliel/Luke is more modest and specific: Theudas rounded up four hundred. Yet even historians can be quite casual about statistics. With reference to "The Egyptian" (on whom see below) Josephus says in *War* 2.263 that most of his followers were captured or killed, while in *Antiquities* 20.171 he is more specific: four hundred killed, two hundred captured. Regarding the size of his army, the current text of Josephus reads "c. thirty thousand," while the same individual (evidently) could muster but four thousand in Acts 21:38. For those who do not believe that Luke was aiming at anything like "historical accuracy" here, this divergence is inconsequential. For those who would preserve the accuracy of Acts at nearly any cost, this is a gate for the two-Theudas bandwagon to pass through. But given the difficulties numbers caused to ancient copyists, the casual approach of ancient historians to statistics, and the challenges Josephus may have had in determining numbers, the gate seems little larger than the eye of a needle.[40]

Reflection upon another difference may be of value. *Antiquities* 20.98 relates that many of Theudas's followers were either captured or slain, while the leader was taken and then beheaded (in the manner of defeated leaders, such as Darius, Crassus, and Pompey).[41] Luke/Gamaliel states that Theudas was killed and his band broken up and reduced to nothing. There is a good explanation for this variation: Gamaliel's comparison requires a movement that suffered a general collapse when, like Jesus, its leader was killed. To mention the execution of others would be implicit support for imposing the death penalty upon the apostles. Four hundred is a common enough round number and provides a good comparison with the Jesus movement. Theudas began with four hundred and ended with zero followers. The post-resurrection Jesus movement began with one hundred twenty (Acts 1:15) and had quickly grown into the thousands. A word to the wise is sufficient. Both of Gamaliel's examples emphasize, in the rhetorically parallel conclusion to each instance, that the organizations in question collapsed: καὶ πάντες ὅσοι ἐπείθοντο αὐτῷ διελύθησαν/διεσκορπίσθησαν ("all who followed him [*lit.* "were persuaded by him"] were dispersed/scattered," Acts 5:36–37). In each case the leaders die and the movement disintegrates. The examples move from the lesser (Theudas) to the greater (Judas).[42]

On chronological, rather than rhetorical, grounds, this is intolerable, for Judas revolted, as Gamaliel says, "in the days of the Census." Luke has already been there and done that, resulting in considerable censure. In Luke 2:1–7 a worldwide census provides an ecumenical venue for the birth of the universal savior. Probably the least important aspect of this justly famous passage is its historical difficulties, which include the absence of any attempt by Augustus to tax the entire world, let alone the Roman Empire; the administrative nightmare and dislocation that return to ancestral domiciles would create; and the date—for Rome could not undertake a registration of persons and property in Judea while Herod ruled. To be sure, a census of Judea took place in 6/7 CE after the deposition of Archelaus, and most discussions presume that Luke has this census in mind.[43] As with Theudas, so with the census: William Ramsay and others have suggested that there was more than one census.[44] However, Acts 5:37 appears to be fatal to this proposal, for it relates "the registration/census" to the revolt of Judas, and that rebellion is so closely associated with the imposition of direct Roman rule that no one has, to my knowledge, proposed another Judas (although that name was so common as to verge upon vulgarity[45]).

This census is important for both Luke and Josephus (Luke 2:1–7; Acts 5:37; Josephus *War* 2.117–18; *Antiquities* 18.1–5). Both writers associate it with the Proconsul of Syria, Quirinius, and with the rebel leader Judas the Galilean. Mason holds that the importance of the census is due to Josephus, who assigns this event "its crucial function."[46] This shared perspective leads Steve Mason to consider the possibility that Luke knew (some parts of) Josephus's writings, for alternative explanations would constitute a difficult coincidence. "Yet if Luke had known Josephus, it is difficult to understand why he placed Quirinius' census at the end of Herod's reign, flatly contradicting Josephus." Mason is then obliged either to question Luke's concern for the details or to ask whether he knew only "highlights" of Josephus's story.[47] One item that may help to alleviate Mason's difficulty is the "firm" datum, one of the few "infancy" traditions common to Matthew and Luke: that Jesus was born in the reign of Herod the Great.[48] A second is that he was born at Bethlehem. The depiction of the census in Luke 2 explains why a Nazarene was from Bethlehem, affirming Davidic lineage and messianic domicile, a well-crafted fiction destined to become "fact," a legend made more solemn and vivid by its reference to Quirinius.

As for that chronological detail in Acts 5, wherein Gamaliel embarrasses Luke by placing the historically prior revolt of Judas after the disturbance of Theudas, it is quite interesting that Josephus also discusses Theudas and (the sons of) Judas in proximity (*Antiquities* 20.97–102)[49] Since the order Theudas-Judas in the *Antiquities* stems from Josephus's own narrative purpose and arrangement, the most economical solution to the error of Acts 5 is to attribute it to Luke's use of Josephus.[50] The error can thus be explained by presuming that the author of Acts overlooked "the sons of" and wrote, or remembered, only "Judas." Obstacles to acceptance of this thesis are traditional and two in number.

One is the view of Luke as an error-free historian, even if the error was committed by another (as in Acts 5:34–39). The other is the implication for dating, since the *Antiquities* did not appear until 93/4 CE. I propose to test the hypothesis that Luke used Josephus elsewhere, and thus to determine whether the possibility of dependence will shed light upon other problems. The case of Acts 5:34–38 achieves both, for it not only elucidates a famous *crux*, but also suggests one way in which Luke could make use of circumstantial data. If Luke had access to part or all of the *Antiquities*, this hypothesis could explain how he came upon the theme of the "census," and, more specifically, it would explain his association of this event with the name of the Roman legate Quirinius.[51] In two cases, the prominence given to the Roman census of 6 CE and the order Theudas-Judas, Luke happens to share with Josephus not simply historical *data* but the results of historical *interpretation*. In this case two is not a company; it is a crowd, too much of a good thing to refuse.

In summary form, this argument, which is basic to my proposals, proceeds as follows. In their narratives Luke and Josephus share certain viewpoints and convictions:

1. The Roman Census of Palestine was a watershed event.
2. The Revolt of Judas took place at the time of this census.
3. The names of Judas and of Theudas, a later rebel, occur in the non-chronological narrative order Theudas . . . Judas.

Each of these items belongs to the realms of historical interpretation, "adjustment," and presentation. Josephus is the only known historical authority who attempts to construct a history of the First Revolt that begins with the Roman Census. This view expresses Josephus' own particular thesis. It is not a "natural" consequence of reflection upon the events.[52] The revolt of Judas can also be associated with the death of Herod (4 BCE), possibly followed by another under the same leader at the time of the census.[53] The activity of Theudas was subsequent to that of Judas. All of these interpretations and arrangements are peculiar to Josephus but not in the least peculiar in the context of his own literary structure and historical thesis. They also appear in Luke and Acts, where they have quite different functions in writings that have no interest in the particular ideas of Josephus. This is especially noteworthy in the matter of "the census," a rather and routine bureaucratic event. Luke agrees with Josephus that the Roman census of its newly-acquired Palestinian territories was of great

significance, although the respective estimates differ. For Luke the census sig-
naled the beginning of universal salvation; to Josephus it was the beginning of
the destruction of the homeland.[54]

The conclusion is not that Luke can be accused of "misreading" Josephus,
nor that he is likely to have had an alternative source with quite identical viewpoints and some different data, a thesis that requires a frosting of special pleading applied to a cake of great improbability. Rather, Luke has plainly made
use of arrangements and inferences derived from the writings of Josephus.
The "footprints" that can be found in Luke and Acts are not so much verbal as
editorial, and can be assigned with a high degree of certitude to a single pair
of sandals, owned by one Flavius Josephus. These sandals fit and, as popular
wisdom has it, should be worn.[55]

THE SYNCHRONISM OF LUKE 3

The most thoroughly (but not exclusively[56]) historiographic device in Luke and
Acts is found not in Acts but the Gospel, which in Luke 3:1–2 announces the
"beginning" of the saving events with an elaborate synchronism :[57]

> In the fifteenth year of the reign of Tiberius Caesar,
> Pontius Pilate being governor of Judea,
> and Herod being tetrarch of Galilee,
> and his brother Philip tetrarch of the region of Ituraea and Trachonitis,
> and Lysanias tetrarch of Abilene,
> in the high-priesthood of Annas and Caiaphas, (RSV)

The ostensible purpose of this mechanism is to establish a precise chrono-
logical reference in the absence of generally recognized system of reckoning.
A prominent literary function is to signal the advent of the central theme, as in
Thucydides 2:2.[58] Luke's synchronism is a literary success.

> The sixfold synchronism serves the historical perspective of Lucan theology . . . It
> cannot be understood as an exact dating of the appearance of John on the
> Palestinian scene—nor, consequently, of the beginning of Jesus' ministry. It is,
> rather, intended to provide a Roman and Palestinian ambience . . .[59]

The synchronism presents a number of challenges, not all of which are the
result of actual or putative Lukan error. This passage leads one to think that if
Luke had had access to Josephus, he could have learned that Annas was not
the high priest at this time and gotten it right.[60] Once more, this presumes that
Luke wanted to "get" matters like this "right"[61] Stifling such distractions for the
moment, it should be noted that Lysanias is generally accepted as something of
an enigma. Luke's synchronism begins with the reigning emperor and ends with
the current high priest. The first intermediate authority, Pontius Pilate, requires
neither introduction nor justification, nor does the Tetrarch "Herod," whom
we know as Antipas, an important figure in the stories of Jesus and John. This

is Philip's sole appearance, but he was another Herodian, ruling some Jewish territories. Lysanias generates two questions: Who was he, and why include him on this list? Abilene is a district north and west of Damascus, named for the town of Abila, which will play no part in the story. The better known local Lysanias lost his head over Cleopatra in 36 BCE or shortly thereafter.[62] To resolve this difficulty scholars have conceived . . . yes, another Lysanias. Observe that Josephus is less than crystal clear, that at least one known inscription will most easily be understood as referring to a later Lysanias the Tetrarch, and so forth.[63] Granting this hypothetical figure, the mystery remains: Why include Lysanias in the synchronism? Why is this information helpful? What purpose does it serve? Schürmann thinks that it reflects Luke's reconstruction of earlier divisions of Palestine from a map belonging to his own period.[64]

One may also turn to Josephus. In *Antiquities* 18.237, while describing the aftermath of the death of *Tiberius*, the historian relates that Gaius sent for Agrippa ". . . and appointed him king of the *tetrarchy of Philip*, presenting him also with the *tetrarchy of Lysanias*."[65] Moreover, 20.138, with reference to the arrival of Felix, relates that Nero presented Agrippa (II) with the tetrarchy of Philip and what had been the tetrarchy of Lysanias.[66] Once again, those who will permit Luke to be somewhat casual if not simply careless with regard to sources of this type, will find in such references good grounds for suspecting Luke to have deduced from Josephus that prior to the death of Tiberius, Lysanias was tetrarch of Abilene, and will then proceed to propose that Lysanias had been dragged into the synchronism by association with Philip. Competing explanations will be no less complicated. Luke did, after all, have to resort to some kind of a source for his synchronism, and such candidates as oral tradition, Mary the Mother of Jesus, and Peter will not do just here. Many ancient historians were wont to prefer to employ one source at a time. This practice is manifest in Luke, who in contrast to Matthew generally alternates use of Mark and Q. One may hypothesize a source no longer extant, but, since the extant source, Josephus, has features that appear also in Luke, that source must be a strong contender. Known sources are widely agreed to be stronger than unknown sources.

THE EGYPTIAN AND FRIENDS

Just as Paul was about to be brought into the barracks, he said to the tribune, "May I say something to you?" The tribune replied, "Do you know Greek? Then you are not the Egyptian who recently stirred up a revolt and led the four thousand assassins out into the wilderness?" (Acts 21:37–38)

One assumes that Paul has had easier days. (See Table 5.2a.) Having eluded death at the hands of a mistaken mob, he learns that his "rescuer," a Roman officer, takes him for a guerilla bandit who is eligible for the most hideous death that Roman law has to offer. That tribune, who will turn out to be one Claudius Lysias, has jumped to a rather startling conclusion that he is prepared to share

Table 5.2a: The Egyptian Liberator

Josephus *War* 2.261-63	Josephus *Ant.* 20.169-171	Acts 21:38
Μείζονι δὲ τούτου πληγῇ Ἰουδαίους ἐκάκωσεν **ὁ Αἰγύπτιος** ψευδοπροφήτης· παραγενόμενος γὰρ εἰς τὴν χώραν ἄνθρωπος γόης καὶ προφήτου πίστιν ἐπιθεὶς ἑαυτῷ περὶ τρισμυρίους μὲν ἀθροίζει τῶν ἠπατημένων, [262] περιαγαγὼν δὲ αὐτοὺς **ἐκ τῆς ἐρημίας** εἰς τὸ ἐλαιῶν καλούμενον ὄρος ἐκεῖθεν οἷός τε ἦν εἰς Ἱεροσόλυμα παρελθεῖν βιάζεσθαι καὶ κρατήσας τῆς τε Ῥωμαϊκῆς φρουρᾶς καὶ τοῦ δήμου τυραννεῖν χρώμενος τοῖς συνεισπεσοῦσιν δορυφόροις. [263] φθάνει δ' αὐτοῦ τὴν ὁρμὴν Φῆλιξ ὑπαντήσας μετὰ τῶν Ῥωμαϊκῶν ὁπλιτῶν, καὶ πᾶς ὁ δῆμος συνεφήψατο τῆς ἀμύνης, ὥστε συμβολῆς γενομένης τὸν μὲν Αἰγύπτιον φυγεῖν μετ' ὀλίγων, διαφθαρῆναι δὲ καὶ ζωγρηθῆναι πλείστους τῶν σὺν αὐτῷ, τὸ δὲ λοιπὸν πλῆθος σκεδασθὲν ἐπὶ τὴν ἑαυτῶν ἕκαστον διαλαθεῖν. But there was an Egyptian false prophet that did the Jews more mischief than the former; for he was a cheat, and pretended to be a prophet also, and got together thirty thousand men that were deluded by him; (262) these he led round about from the wilderness to the mount which	[169] ἀφικνεῖται δέ **τις ἐξ Αἰγύπτου** κατὰ τοῦτον τὸν καιρὸν εἰς Ἱεροσόλυμα προφήτης εἶναι λέγων καὶ συμβουλεύων τῷ δημοτικῷ πλήθει σὺν αὐτῷ πρὸς ὄρος τὸ προσαγορευόμενον ἐλαιῶν, ὃ τῆς πόλεως ἄντικρυς κείμενον ἀπέχει στάδια πέντε· [170] θέλειν γὰρ ἔφασκεν αὐτοῖς ἐκεῖθεν ἐπιδεῖξαι, ὡς κελεύσαντος αὐτοῦ πίπτοι τὰ τῶν Ἱεροσολυμιτῶν τείχη, δι' ὧν καὶ τὴν εἴσοδον αὐτοῖς παρέξειν ἐπηγγέλλετο. [171] Φῆλιξ δ' ὡς ἐπύθετο ταῦτα, κελεύει τοὺς στρατιώτας ἀναλαβεῖν τὰ ὅπλα καὶ μετὰ πολλῶν ἱππέων τε καὶ πεζῶν ὁρμήσας ἀπὸ τῶν Ἱεροσολύμων προσβάλλει τοῖς περὶ τὸν Αἰγύπτιον, καὶ τετρακοσίους μὲν αὐτῶν ἀνεῖλεν, διακοσίους δὲ ζῶντας ἔλαβεν. Moreover, there came out of Egypt about this time to Jerusalem, one that said he was a prophet, and advised the multitude of the common people to go along with him to the Mount of Olives, as it was called, which lay over against the city, and at the distance of five furlongs. (170) He said farther, that	οὐκ ἄρα σὺ εἶ **ὁ Αἰγύπτιος ὁ πρὸ τούτων τῶν ἡμερῶν ἀναστατώσας καὶ ἐξαγαγὼν εἰς τὴν ἔρημον** τοὺς τετρακισχιλίους ἄνδρας τῶν σικαρίων; Then you are not the Egyptian who recently stirred up a revolt and led the four thousand assassins out into the wilderness?"

was called the Mount of Olives, and was ready to break into Jerusalem by force from that place; and if he could but once conquer the Roman garrison and the people, he intended to domineer over them by the assistance of those guards of his that were to break into the city with him, (263) but [Felix] prevented his attempt, and met him with his Roman soldiers, while all the people assisted him in his attack upon them, insomuch that, when it came to a battle, the Egyptian ran away, with a few others, while the greatest part of those that were with him were either destroyed or taken alive; but the rest of the multitude were dispersed every one to their own homes and there concealed themselves.

he would show them them from hence, how, at his command, the walls of Jerusalem would fall down; and he promised that he would procure them an entrance into the city through those walls, when they were fallen down. (171) Now when [Felix] was informed of these things, he ordered his soldiers to take their weapons, and came against them with a great number of horsemen and footmen, from Jerusalem, and attacked the Egyptian and the people that were with him. He also slew four hundred of them, and took two hundred alive.[67]

in full with his captive. What has led him to infer that his prisoner is a revolt-
ing Egyptian with particular appeal to urban guerillas? After all, the only other
information about that individual comes from Josephus.

The account in the (earlier) *War* describes a military rebellion of thirty thousand. Despite the vast disparity in training and arms, Felix would have had a
difficult time defeating this movement with only his own troops. The claim
that the entire citizen body joined his forces achieves something of a balance.
In any case the *War* presents an urban-rural conflict, in which the "Egyptian"
leads a new exodus from the wilderness into the promised land. Both accounts
include the eschatologically effervescent Mount of Olives. The story related in
the *Antiquities* features quite another "new Joshua," who will take the Holy
City with divine aid. Were this the sole account, one might well suspect that
the Egyptian led a mass demonstration of unarmed people dependent upon
help from on high. With its prophetic symbolism, an affair of that nature would
have affinities with the similarly non-violent "triumphal" entry of Jesus into
Jerusalem (Mark 11:1–10 and parallels). Which account may be the more accurate is not relevant to the issue at hand.

Following this leap into the midst of things, it may be helpful to step back
for a moment. The narrator of Acts has taken the reader of 21:27–22:29 on a
literary roller coaster ride. While topping off his Jewish charity and piety, Paul
has been mistakenly accused of bringing gentiles into the sacred precinct. The
faithful take the law into their own hands and attempt to administer summary
capital punishment.[68] In due course word of the turbulence reaches the commander of the Roman garrison, whose arrival with troops quiets the mob. Once
he has properly subdued and secured the victim, the officer asks who he is and
what he has done. Unable to learn anything useful from the crowd, the tribune
decides to have Paul removed for interrogation. It soon appears that the tribune
did know—or thought he knew—who Paul was: "the Egyptian who recently
stirred up a revolt . . ."[69]

This is "where we came in." The tribune's identification should strike the
reader of Acts as an utterly bizarre shot in the dark. Its narrative purpose is to
provide Paul with an opportunity to demonstrate his Hellenic culture. Granted
that it is no more than an authorial lob, why did Luke choose this particular
example? If one hypothesizes that the "sub-text" is the conflict between the
rural "Egyptian" prophet and the urban population of Jerusalem, often swollen
by holiday crowds, the question seems a bit less unintelligible. If Luke did have
such a conception, it was a bridge to be burned after crossing, for the rest of the
verse confounds the program of the rural prophet with the mission of urban
guerillas: "and led the four thousand assassins out into the wilderness." The
"assassins," *sicarii*,[70] carried out a terrorist campaign that became prominent
in the 50s. Their initial strategy involved the destabilization of society through
removing "collaborators," i.e., members of the Jewish ruling class.[71] The *Sicarii*
were distinct in every way from prophetic leaders. Their tactics were realistic.
These activists were not desperate peasants swept away on a bold venture by

Table 5.2b: The Sicarii

Josephus *War* 2.254	Josephus *Ant.* 20.164–65	Acts 21:38
But while the country was thus cleared of these pests, a new species of banditti (λη
σταί) was springing up in Jerusalem, the so-called **sicarii** . . .[72]	Certain of these brigands (λῃσταί) went up to the city as if they intended to worship God. With daggers concealed under their clothes, they mingled with the people about Jonathan and assassinated him. As the murder remained unpunished, from that time forth the brigands with perfect impunity used to go to the city during the festivals . . .[73]	οὐκ ἄρα σὺ εἶ ὁ Αἰγύπτιος ὁ πρὸ τούτων τῶν ἡμερῶν ἀναστατώσας καὶ ἐξαγαγὼν εἰς τὴν ἔρημον τοὺς τετρακισχιλίους ἄνδρας τῶν **σικαρίων**; Then you are not the Egyptian who recently stirred up a revolt and led the four thousand **assassins** out into the wilderness?"

a charismatic herald. They were urban fanatics committed to the discipline of a conspiratorial organization. What source could have led to placement of this oxymoron in the dictionary of colonial rebellion upon the lips of the Tribune Lysias? Not Josephus, one might say, for he is the basis for the foregoing distinction between charismatic prophets and urban guerilla warriors. Note, however,

The passages from Josephus cited in Table 5.2b come just prior to his report about "the Egyptian," cited in Table 5.2a. Mason, who notes this proximity, says that it appears to be Josephus's "own narrative arrangement."[74] Two pages later he is even more confident:

> Notice first that, although Josephus does not make the Egyptian's followers *sicarii*, he mentions both groups in the same breath. As we have seen, he discusses the Egyptian immediately after describing the dagger-men (*War* 2.261; *Ant.* 20.167–169). But this is clearly part of his literary artistry. How did Luke, then, come to associate the Egyptian, incorrectly, with the *sicarii*? If he did so independently of Josephus, the coincidence is remarkable. It is even more remarkable because *sicarii* is a Latin term for assassins. Josephus seems to have been the first to borrow this word and make it a technical term for the Jewish rebels in his Greek narrative.[75]

Mason had earlier invited readers to "Notice Josephus' repeated assertion that there were *numerous* impostors, false prophets, and wizards around in the period before the revolt. These unnamed popular leaders typically led the masses out into the desert . . ."[76] Of those "many," however, Josephus gives but a single, identical example in each work. That example is none other than "The Egyptian." It further transpires that these revolutionaries receive attention in close proximity to the prophet from Egypt. By any standards, Luke has evidently confounded the Egyptian prophet with those who led their followers

Table 5.3: Brigands and Friends

Josephus *War* 2.258–61	Josephus *Ant.* 20. 160–72
Besides these there arose another body of villains . . . 259 Deceivers and imposters (πλάνοι καὶ ἀπατεῶνες) . . . persuaded the multitude to act like madmen, and led them out into the desert . . . 261 A still worse blow was dealt at the Jews by the Egyptian false prophet.[77]	In Judaea matters were constantly going from bad to worse. For the country was again infested with bands of brigands and imposters (ληστηρίων, γοήτων) who deceived the mob . . . 167 . . . Moreover, impostors and deceivers called upon the mob to follow them into the *desert* . . . 169 At this time there came to Jerusalem from Egypt a man who declared that he was a prophet . . .[78]

into the wilderness and certainly confused such rebels with the quite different *sicarii*. The best explanation for this confusion is that he has culled these names from Josephus and dropped them in a compressed batch into his narrative, the purpose of which, after all, was not to supply detailed and accurate information about dissident activists in Judea prior to the Revolt.

The coincidence presented in Table 5.3 is quite striking: *Sicarii*, prophetic pretenders seeking a fresh beginning in the wilderness, and "the Egyptian." Moreover, Josephus speaks of three leading rebels prior to the great rebellion: Judas the Galilean, Theudas, and "The Egyptian." This is the same trinity known to Luke, who gives each of them features that also mark the accounts of Josephus: Mason concludes that "the hypothesis that Luke had some knowledge of Josephus [is] more likely than not."[79] The material in Acts about the three rebels constitutes a small but very powerful body of evidence, for Luke's references to each of these involve anomalies or difficulties that exegetes must labor to resolve, while they occur in contiguous passages in the narratives of Josephus in an arrangement and with features that correspond to that writer's known interests and tendencies. To describe such evidence as "irrefutable" would be an exaggeration, but no overstatement is involved in proposing that this evidence is of sufficient weight to make dependence of Acts upon Josephus more probable than any alternative. This evidence also justifies examination of other cases.

URBAN DISORDER

The passage from Acts under scrutiny in Table 5.4 precedes the officer's contention that Paul is "The Egyptian." The elements of the parallel are clear: in response to a *disturbance in the Temple*, a *tribune of the cohort* is sent to *arrest the trouble-maker(s)*. Of the many incidents of uproar in the temple noted by Josephus, this is the sole occasion in which this tactic appears.[80] Although the parallel is narrow in scope, it is sufficiently precise to qualify for inclusion

Table 5.4: Riot in the Temple

Acts 21:30–33	Josephus *War* 2.11 (4 BCE)	3 Maccabees 1:18–19, 23, 28–29
ἐκινήθη τε ἡ πόλις ὅλη καὶ ἐγένετο **συνδρομὴ** τοῦ λαοῦ, καὶ ἐπιλαβόμενοι τοῦ Παύλου εἷλκον αὐτὸν ἔξω τοῦ ἱεροῦ, καὶ εὐθέως ἐκλείσθησαν αἱ θύραι. 31 ζητούντων τε αὐτὸν ἀποκτεῖναι ἀνέβη φάσις τῷ **χιλιάρχῳ τῆς σπείρης** ὅτι ὅλη συγχύννεται Ἰερουσαλήμ, 32 ὃς ἐξαυτῆς παραλαβὼν στρατιώτας καὶ ἑκατοντάρχας κατέδραμεν ἐπ' αὐτούς· οἱ δὲ ἰδόντες τὸν χιλίαρχον καὶ τοὺς στρατιώτας ἐπαύσαντο τύπτοντες τὸν Παῦλον. 33 τότε ἐγγίσας ὁ χιλίαρχος **ἐπελάβετο αὐτοῦ** . . . Then all the city was aroused, and the people rushed together. They seized Paul and dragged him out of the temple, and immediately the doors were shut. 31 While they were trying to kill him, word came to the **tribune of the cohort** that all Jerusalem was in an uproar. 32 Immediately he took soldiers and centurions and ran down to them. When they saw the tribune and the soldiers, they stopped beating Paul. 33 Then the tribune came, **arrested him** . . .	πρὸς ὃ δείσας Ἀρχέλαος πρὶν δι' ὅλου τοῦ πλήθους διαδραμεῖν τὴν νόσον ὑποπέμπει μετὰ **σπείρας χιλίαρχον** προστάξας βίᾳ τοὺς ἐξάρχοντας τῆς στάσεως κατασχεῖν. *The presence of agitators in the Temple* alarmed Archelaus, who, wishing to prevent the contagion from spreading to the whole crowd, sent in a **tribune in command of a cohort**, with orders to restrain by force the ringleaders of the sedition[81] Cf. **Judith 10:18** καὶ ἐγένετο **συνδρομὴ** ἐν πάσῃ τῇ παρεμβολῇ, διεβοήθη γὰρ εἰς τὰ σκηνώματα ἡ παρουσία αὐτῆς· καὶ ἐλθόντες ἐκύκλουν αὐτήν . . . There was great excitement in the whole camp, for her arrival was reported from tent to tent . . .	Ptolemy Philopator plans to enter and thus profane the sanctuary. αἵ τε κατάκλειστοι παρθένοι . . . καὶ στεναγμῶν ἐνεπίμπλων τὰς πλατείας. 19 αἱ δὲ καὶ προσαρτίως ἐσταλμέναι τοὺς πρὸς ἀπάντησιν διατεταγμένους παστοὺς καὶ τὴν ἁρμόζουσαν αἰδὼ παραλείπουσαι δρόμον ἄτακτον ἐν τῇ πόλει συνίσταντο. 23 φωνήσαντες δὲ τὴν ὁρμὴν ἐπὶ τὰ ὅπλα ποιήσασθαι καὶ θαρραλέως ὑπὲρ τοῦ πατρῴου νόμου τελευτᾶν ἱκανὴν ἐποίησαν ἐν τῷ τόπῳ . . . 28 ἐκ δὲ τῆς πυκνοτάτης τε καὶ ἐμπόνου τῶν ὄχλων συναγομένης κραυγῆς ἀνείκαστός τις ἦν βοή· 29 δοκεῖν γὰρ ἦν μὴ μόνον τοὺς ἀνθρώπους, ἀλλὰ καὶ τὰ τείχη καὶ τὸ πᾶν ἔδαφος ἠχεῖν ἅτε δὴ τῶν πάντων τότε θάνατον ἀλλασσομένων ἀντὶ τῆς τοῦ τόπου βεβηλώσεως Young women who had been secluded in their chambers rushed out . . . and filled the streets with groans and lamentations. 19 Those women who had recently been arrayed for marriage abandoned the bridal chambers prepared for wedded union, and, neglecting proper modesty, in a disorderly rush flocked together in the city. 23 They shouted to their compatriots to take arms and die courageously for the ancestral law, and created a considerable disturbance in the holy place . . . 28 The continuous, vehement, and concerted cry of the crowds resulted in an immense uproar; 29 for it seemed that not only the people but also the walls and the whole earth around echoed, because indeed all at that time preferred death to the profanation of the place.

among possible borrowings. To indicate that Josephus was not the only, or even the principal, source, a linguistic parallel from Judith and a more thematic incident from *3 Maccabees* are also included.[82] Material like this strongly suggests the Lukan *modus operandi*: certainly not a meticulous copier of sources, he seems rather to have drawn upon his general fund of reading and recollection. "Memory" can be a "weasel word" in source criticism, but memory was much in use.[83] In addition to popular themes and motifs, Luke appears to have drawn upon a specific incident described by Josephus.[84] The leading objection to this hypothesis is that unlike the material about the various insurrectionary leaders, this incident comes from a different context, and one having only a thematic connection to the narrative of Acts.

Mason did not take up the kind of possibility illustrated above in his general study. He turned instead to broader issues, matters apart from arguments about particular persons and specific incidents.[85] He reflects upon the practice, common to Luke and Josephus, of describing their respective religions as "philosophies," and designating religious factions or parties as philosophical "sects."[86] At the outset one is inclined to question this proposal, for the practice of viewing Judaism and, later, Christianity, as "philosophies" became a standard apologetic ploy and intellectual tool.[87] But Mason does not seek to demonstrate that Luke follows Josephus in the depiction of Christianity as a philosophy.[88] Instead, he focuses upon the use of the term αἵρεσις, "school" or "party," claiming that it is "truly remarkable" for Acts to employ the term *hairesis* for Jewish parties "as if this terminology were self-evidently appropriate." No other author characterizes either the Pharisees or Sadducees as a *hairesis*, he contends, noting that the term is congruent with Josephus's "carefully developed defense of Judaism."[89] The second part of the statement is certainly true, although one might note that Philo uses the term in writing about the "Therapeutae."[90]

One may argue that for Luke, *hairesis* applies only to Jewish parties: Sadducees in 5:17, Pharisees in 15:5 and 26:5, and three times to the "party of the Nazoreans" or "Christians," 24:5, 14; 28:22. *Hairesis* is not a positive term for Luke. Only non-believers apply the term to all members of what Luke calls "the movement," or "way." Luke may well have taken over this concept from Josephus, since he uses it to mean religio-political parties, but the value he places upon the term approximates that of Paul (especially in 1 Corinthians 11:19, cf. Galatians 5:20). Indeed, not unlike Paul and rather like *1 Clement*, Luke regards Christianity as inimical to the very idea of parties.[91] This is to say that he seems to view the use of the term (as found, for example, in 1 Corinthians) in the sense of "factions" rather than as "parties." Where there is *hairesis* there is conflict.[92] Believing Pharisees energize the conflict in Acts 15; party feuding rends the Sanhedrin (and very nearly Paul) in 23:6–10; and non-believers apply the term as something like an epithet in the closing chapters of Acts. Luke thus opposes the theory that the Jesus movement is a Jewish sect.[93] This view is a factor in the dating of Acts, since it posits a clear distinction between two religions (which Luke would label something like "authentic" and "unauthentic" manifestations of the religion of Israel). Whereas modern scholars describe early Christianity as a Jewish sect, or a mélange of several sects, Luke sees only true Israel and apostate Israel.[94]

In sufficient time the language of Paul would appear on the alleged lips of Jesus to characterize one of the eschatological afflictions: ἔσονται σχίσματα καὶ αἱρέσεις ("There will be divisions and factional conflicts." Justin, *Dialogue* 35.3, explaining that some so-called Christians ate meat offered to idols.)[95] *Haireseis* are but one of the many wiles of the evil one. Luke would not disagree. He uses the term as a label precisely as does Josephus, but provides it with a "negative spin" that arises from the Pauline world.[96] The most economical explanation is that Luke learned from Josephus to call Jewish parties "sects" and to use the label after the manner of Paul and his followers to criticize ecclesiastical divisions.[97]

Luke's portrait of the Pharisees shares several elements with that of Josephus. One of these is firm adherence to the doctrine of the resurrection, to which the Sadducees do not adhere (Acts 23:7–12; *Antiquities* 18.14, 16). This could, of course, be viewed as general knowledge; for even Mark, whose knowledge of Jewish practice is limited, includes a tradition that Sadducees opposed the doctrine of the resurrection (12:18–27). Nevertheless, Josephus's account of the execution of James is of interest here:

> [The] younger Ananus, who . . . took the high priesthood, was a bold man in his temper, and very insolent; he was also of the sect (αἵρεσιν) of the Sadducees, who are very rigid in judging offenders, above all the rest of the Jews, as we have already observed; when, therefore, Ananus . . . thought he had now a proper opportunity . . . he assembled the sanhedrin of judges, and brought before them the brother of Jesus, who was called Christ, whose name was James, and some others; and when he had formed an accusation against them as breakers of the law, he delivered them to be stoned; but those who seemed the most equitable of the citizens, and who (or those who) were severely strict in the matter of the commandments (περὶ τοὺς νόμους ἀκριβεῖς βαρέως) disliked what was done; (*Ant.* 20.199–201, Trans. Whiston, *alt.*)

Acts features a high priest with the same name who belongs to the sect of the Sadducees and who, along with his colleagues, harbors rage against the followers of Jesus (4:6; 5:17). Elsewhere, too, in Acts the Sadducees support the death penalty as the appropriate remedy for the followers of Jesus. They go so far as to participate in arrests of the apostles (4:1; 5:17) and ardently desire their execution (5:33). More important in the present context is that Ananus' opponents in the above quote were very likely Pharisees, because Josephus characterizes them as "strict" (ἀκριβεῖς).

This adjective and its derivatives constitute for Josephus the essential characteristic of the Pharisees, who are the most precise in interpretation and scrupulous in observance of the ancestral commandments. "They are distinguished from the others by their precise knowledge (or precision, *akribeia*) regarding the ancestral regulations."[98] In Acts the stem *akrib-* occurs seven times, with the connotations of strictly correct or precise learning, knowledge, or life-style. In general usage the stem often conveys the sense of the formal English "nice," (discriminating) readily shading into "punctilious," or "overly nice." For Luke the term seems always positive. In two instances he has Paul apply it to the Pharisees: ". . . educated strictly according to our ancestral law (κατὰ ἀκρίβειαν τοῦ πατρῴου νόμου[99]), being zealous for God . . ." (22:3), and ". . . I have belonged to the strictest sect (κατὰ τὴν ἀκριβεστάτην αἵρεσιν) of our religion and lived as a Pharisee . . ." (26:5). Günther Stemberger views this coincidence as confirmation of the validity of the definition of the Pharisees.[100] An alternative is to understand Luke as dependent upon Josephus for this characterization. No other writers so characterize the Pharisees. When the Gospels speak of the Pharisees' punctilious observance, it is to denounce them for carefully cultivating a single bush while neglecting the forest (cf. Luke 11:39–42, etc.) If anything, the Pharisees are precisely blind. Except for Paul, however, Pharisees in Acts are likely to be less hasty in seeking the death penalty (5:34–39; cf. 23:1–10). The view is consistent with the respective attitudes implied in Josephus's account of the execution of James.

THE DEATH OF A RULER

Hardly anyone interested in reopening the question of Lukan dependence upon Josephus would be likely to cite the incident featured in Table 5.5, for it seems reasonable to suppose that in this case each author presents a variation of a popular legend. The published dissertation of O. W. Allen examines the two accounts as variant examples of the typical renditions of the Death of a Tyrant.[101] It would require a stiff uphill fight to argue that Josephus invented this story or that he conformed the death of Agrippa I to a common type, for he did not regard Agrippa as anything like a tyrant deserving a gruesome end in order to satisfy public demands for divine justice. A rather more likely hypothesis is that interpretations of Agrippa I's death were so widespread and/or well-entrenched that Josephus had to adopt the role of what is now known as a "spin doctor."

The story of Agrippa's death is a "cautionary tale" about the susceptibility of rulers to flattery, in particular to the phenomenon of the ruler cult. Anecdotes of this ilk could find a place in the philosophical opposition to the principate, in particular during the rule of Domitian.[102] One form of opposition, not unfamiliar to writers (and readers) of apocalypses, was the use of code. Although forthright attacks upon an emperor guaranteed one a ticket out of Rome, if not out of this world, denunciations of *ancient* tyrants were safe exercises for boys learning rhetoric.[103] The Herodian family in general and Agrippa in particular incurred their full share of enmity from representatives of widely disparate groups. Stories about his untimely death might well have acquired currency

Table 5.5: The Death of a Ruler

Josephus Antiquities 19.343–50	Acts 12:20–23
Agrippa . . . came to the city **Caesarea** . . . and there he exhibited shows in honor of Caesar, upon his being informed that there was a certain festival celebrated to make vows for his safety. At which festival, a great multitude was gotten together of the principal persons, and such as were of dignity through his province. On the second day . . . he put on a **garment** made wholly of silver, and of a contexture truly wonderful, and came into the theatre early in the morning; at which time the silver of his garment being illuminated by the fresh reflection of the sun's rays upon it, shone out after a surprising manner, and was so resplendent that it produced awe among those who looked intently at it. and presently his flatterers cried out, one from one place, and another from another (though not for his good), that he was a god; and they added, "Be gracious to us; for *although we have hitherto honored you only as a man, yet shall we henceforth acknowledge you as superior to mortal nature.*" The king did neither rebuke them, nor reject their impious flattery. But, as he presently afterwards looked up, he saw an owl sitting on a rope over his head, and immediately understood that this bird was the **messenger** (ἄγγελος) of ill tidings, as it had once been the messenger of good tidings to him; and fell into the deepest sorrow. A severe pain also arose in his belly . . . He therefore looked upon his friends, and said, "I whom you call a god, am commanded presently to depart this life; for fate [or Providence] thus reproves the lying words you just now said to me" . . . and the rumor went abroad everywhere, that he would certainly die in a little time. But the multitude presently sat in sackcloth, with their wives and children . . . and besought God for the king's recovery . . . And when he had been quite worn out by the pain in his belly for five days, he *departed this life* . . .[104]	Herod . . . went down from Judea to **Caesarea** and stayed there. Now Herod was angry with the people of Tyre and Sidon. So they came to him in a body; and after winning over Blastus, the king's chamberlain, they asked for a reconciliation, because their country depended on the king's country for food. On an appointed **day** Herod **put on his royal robes**, took his seat on the platform, and delivered a public address to them. The people kept shouting, "*The voice of a god, and not of a mortal!*" And immediately, because he had not given the glory to God, an **angel** of the Lord struck him down, and he was eaten by worms *and died.*

in non-Jewish circles. In short, any number of people could have enjoyed, for a variety of reasons, the story of how a provincial kinglet who got "too big for his britches" received his just dues and due reward.

Luke includes the theme of deification, but this is not his major "explanation"; readers of Acts are to understand this incident as the death of a *persecutor*. For Josephus Agrippa was a fine, if extravagant, ruler, loved by his people. Had he lived longer, the Revolt might not have occurred. In the eyes of Luke, however, the ruler was a "King Herod," a callous avatar of Pharaoh bent upon slaughtering the people of God but summarily struck down by the hand of God. Both forms of this legend may have existed. The path to such clarification as may emerge requires reflection upon its shape and form.[105]

To establish his typology, Wesley Allen has assembled and evaluated a great deal of information for comparative purposes.[106] Useful examples for the present purpose are Josephus's presentations of the death of Herod the Great, *War* 1.647–56 and *Antiquities* 17.146–99. Although the account in *Antiquities* is a good deal longer and spares few rhetorical punches, the two do not reveal a changed point of view.[107] Both begin with an intimation of mortality: the aged Herod is quite ill. His debility leads some strict teachers to harangue some young students to remove a golden eagle from the Temple, which object they view as a violation of Torah. This action leads to numerous executions, after which his symptoms increase in type and virulence. His gangrenous penis, for instance, could produce only worms.[108] As his end draws near, the good king hits upon a plan to guarantee general mourning: a slaughter of the (not necessarily innocent) prominent men of every Judean town.[109] Shortly thereafter, King Herod exited this life.

Now *these* are accounts of the death of a tyrant. That was a task Josephus knew how to handle.[110] He spares no details, and those details do not spare Herod. He was a king whom only those fond of mass murder garnished with the serial execution of one's own children could admire. Nearly all readers of Josephus would agree that Herod got just what he deserved at the hands of God. This is particularly true of the later rendition, which includes no fewer than three "passion explanations."

1. (151) It was indeed because of his audacity in making these things [i.e., the image] in disregard of the Torah's provisions . . . [the legal interpreters] said, that all those misfortunes, with which he had become familiar to a degree uncommon among humankind, had happened to him, in particular his illness.[111]

2. (168) But Herod's illness became more and more acute, for God was inflicting just punishment (δίκην) upon him for his lawless deeds.[112]

3. (170) Accordingly it was said by the men of God and by those whose special wisdom led them to proclaim their opinions on such matters that all this was the penalty that God was exacting of the king for his great impiety.[113]

Each item of this ABA arrangement receives rhetorical enhancement. To the first is decoratively added an elaborate *dulce et decorum est* (how pleasant and proper is a patriotic death) speech adapted from the rhetoric of resistance to tyranny (152–154).[114] Between the second and third stands a catalogue of hideous symptoms in the fashion of *grand guignol*, and following the third, in the midst of various therapies and apparent death, comes the hatching of his plot for the slaughter of leading citizens.

Frederick F. Bruce entitles Acts 12:20–23, "Death of Herod Agrippa I."[115] One piece of Colin Hemer's "Evidence from Historical Details in Acts" is "12:1 The Herod mentioned here is Herod Agrippa I."[116] This seems utterly unremarkable, until one asks the source of the name. Luke knows of no character named Agrippa other than the one whom we designate Agrippa II (Acts 26). His name for the king in Acts 12 is "Herod." There is but one textual basis for identifying this particular "Herod" with King Agrippa I, and that is the story of the death of Agrippa I in Josephus. Even sharply critical scholars, such as Ernst Haenchen, accept this identification. The New Testament in general might seem to suggest that "Herod" was, like "Caesar," a nickname for any member of the family.[117] But one person to whom that epithet was evidently not applied was Agrippa.[118] This is a case in which Josephus *is* a source for Acts, in the sense that every venture at constructing a chronology of Acts identifies the two deaths and derives the date from Josephus.[119] This presumption stems from the similarity of the stories, "type-scenes" as they may be. In general these two accounts include a king at a public appearance in Caesarea wearing royal garb. In response to acclamations of divinity, the king does not demur, whereupon he presently comes to an unpleasant death.[120] If the two accounts share a common background, it would not be an "historical kernel," but a (Jewish) legend, for, since such explanations are interpretations of an event, attribution of causation (divine judgment in this case) cannot be part of any historical kernel. Dibelius thus seeks to evaluate the two accounts and finds that of Acts formally "older," i.e., more purely legendary.[121]

The closest analogy in New Testament narrative is the story of the death of John the Baptizer (Mark 6:14[17]–29, omitted by Luke). That is a court-novella which retails gossip about Antipas and Herodias from a viewpoint inimical to the desires of Herodian men and women to conduct themselves like Hellenistic royalty.[122] Agrippa's efforts to conduct himself as a pious Jew in Israelite circles and a pro-Roman philhellene elsewhere were likely to stir up resentment from both polytheist and Jewish subjects, as they certainly did in the case of the former.[123] One possible setting for the legend about Agrippa's death would be among those Jews who regarded him as a hypocrite.[124] From there the tale could have been picked up and disseminated by enemies of Agrippa, of the Herodian family, or of the Jews in general. All three categories were amply represented.[125] Josephus appears to have been under some compulsion to make the best possible use of this story. He did not, or could not, attempt to deny or suppress it. The contrast between his tale of the demise of Agrippa and his narration of the death of Herod the Great (and others) shows that this is a sad ending to a rather encomiastic account. In addition there is the possibility that Josephus discovered the story in a source favorable to his subject, possibly an "official biography."[126] The most promising alternatives are either that Josephus took up the story from an oral or written tradition or that he found it in a continuous source. In favor of the latter is the nicely crafted inclusion that ends his royal career. According to *Antiquities* 18.195–202, the recently manacled and imperiled Agrippa leaned against a tree upon which a horned owl landed. A German fellow-prisoner, borrowing a leaf from the story of Joseph, interpreted this an omen foretelling a great reversal of fortune, adding that, when Agrippa next saw this bird, he would have no more than five days to live. Things turned out just so. At the apparent apex of glory, acclaimed at Caesarea, the same species of owl appeared on a rope over his head (346). My tentative conclusion is that Josephus found this story in an extensive source.

One may now ask about Luke's source for the story. Haenchen was untroubled: "[Agrippa] died in Caesarea after a few days' painful sickness. This sudden end led the Jews to wonder why God so swiftly snatched away the king."[127] Such reasoning is one of the lurking fallacies of the "historical kernel," which begins with the "facts" and then asks why they took legendary form. So Haenchen presumes that the story arose as an etiological explanation of why Agrippa suddenly died. I rather think that its function was to provide evidence that Agrippa was unrighteous, not that he suffered for one momentary slip.[128] Behind Haenchen stands the study of Dibelius, who states that in Acts the account ". . . arises out of an historical episode . . . But this motivation is abbreviated by Luke and becomes obscured."[129] Witherington, for his part, appears to attribute 12:20–23 to Luke's "Herodian source," whatever that is.[130] Witherington requires and Dibelius suggests such a source because of the circumstantial "historical" detail. Legends are unlikely to begin with the sort of information found in Acts 12:20:

> Now he was angry with the people of Tyre and Sidon. So they came to him in
> a body; and after winning over Blastus, the king's chamberlain, they asked for
> a reconciliation, because their country depended on the king's country for food.
> (NRSV, *alt.*)

These detailed circumstances and their awkward obscurity lead to the redaction-critical solution widely held.[131] I should like to ask why Luke chose to take up at this point a (different) source, and one so seemingly abrupt, disruptive, and irrelevant. Things would be vastly improved had he said less and certainly better had he said more. Eusebius, who provides the following summary, did a bit of each:

> As to the king's attempt on the Apostles there was no more delay, but the aveng-
> ing minister of the sentence of God overtook him at once, immediately after his
> plot against the apostles, as the Scripture relates in the Acts. He had gone to

Caesarea, and there on the set day of the feast, adorned with splendid and royal robes, he addressed the people, standing on high before his judgement-seat. The whole people applauded his address, as though at the voice of a god and not of a man, and the story relates that an angel of the Lord smote him at once, and he was eaten of worms and expired.[132]

Eusebius firmly establishes the connection between the two episodes. Nothing is said about problems with Tyre and Sidon, and the story is much improved for it. A more expansive option appealed to the editor of the D-text. In the following translation additions to or differences from the conventional text are italicized.

For he was furious with the people of Tyre and Sidon. So *representatives from both cities* came to him in a body; and after winning over Blastus, the king's chamberlain, they requested peace, because their *region/s* city depended on the king's country for food. On an appointed day Herod put on his royal robes, took his seat on the bench, and delivered a public address to them. *After he had been reconciled with the Tyrians*, the people began to exclaim, "The voice/*sounds* of a god, and not of a mortal/*mortals*!" And immediately, because he had not given the glory to God, an angel of the Lord struck him down, and, *after he had descended from the bench*, he was eaten by worms *while still alive* and thus died.[133]

As is often the case, these variants address difficulties in the text.[134] The replacement of "and" (δέ) with "for" (γάϱ) in verse 20 introduces a causal connection between verses 19 and 20. Herod went to Caesarea to address another problem. The addition in verse 20 eases the (typically Lukan) hyperbole by explaining that delegations presented a petition. The interpolation at the opening of verse 22 makes a unit of 19–23. Eloquent acceptance of reconciliation has replaced virulent anger.

These able attempts to rescue the story make one wonder even more why Luke, who could begin it with the most economical narration, devotes many more words to a political quarrel of no apparent import to his leading theme. Surely the author of Acts 12:1–3 could have written a more compact account: "Herod left Jerusalem for a sojourn in Caesarea. On a certain day he addressed his subjects while solemnly enthroned in his most splendid regalia. Awed by all this, the mob began to acclaim him as a god in their midst." One can summarize the source question thus: Josephus may well have found the story of Agrippa's death in a substantial source; in any case he adapted it to both his larger narrative context and to his judgment of Agrippa. At all events, Acts 12:20–23 did not come to Luke as a "naïve" oral legend; his source was to some degree literary. Yet one is again driven to ask *why* Luke included this material—disregarding for now the vexatious source issue, which is more useful for the questions it raises than for the problems it resolves.[135]

Difficult as these verses seem when seen through a microscope, they do resonate with the general context. 11:27–30 and 12:20–23 describe two "famines" and their relief. Neither is without historical difficulties. In chapter 11 a prophet from Jerusalem predicted a world-wide famine. In response to this forecast the believers at Antioch raised funds for their colleagues in Judea.[136] At the other pole is an utterly contrived threat of famine, the result of Herod's enmity with Tyre and Sidon. Their backs against the wall, these cities sue for peace. Then, as now, such actions depended upon "networking." Chamberlains were no doubt quite concerned with the merits of issues and fond of petitioners' eloquence, but they were also exceedingly busy men of the world whom circumstances often compelled to heed the voice of the largest bidder. Suppliers of food (including those who do no more than let it be sold) are benefactors. Benefactors expect and demand adulation. Poor Herod died from an overdose of it. As for benefaction, he qualifies as the antitype of the true benefactor. In Lukan theology, that aligns our Herod with the antichrist.[137] His campaign against the biblically notorious Tyre and Sidon may, at first sight, appear to be messianic retribution, but, in the end, it is no more than a shakedown.[138] Acts 12:20 therefore supplies a second example of tyrannical rage, showing that Herod's issues with anger management were not restricted to his transactions with followers of Jesus.[139]

The most important internal parallels are between Herod and Peter, with intertextual enhancement from the Exodus story. The shackled apostle gains liberation through an angelic epiphany. The good news of Herod's public *Parousia* (advent, arrival) is hailed as a veritable epiphany. Both protagonists put on their proper clothes. Most notably, each experiences the buffet of an angel, by which ministration Peter was awakened to a "new life" (ἄγγελος κυρίου . . . πατάξας, 12:6–7), and Herod struck down to death (ἐπάταξεν αὐτὸν ἄγγελος κυρίου). Acts 12:20–23 completes a balanced antithesis.

Through the evocation of Exodus themes, Luke both provides generalization of the experience of Peter and achieves his characterization of Herod as a contemporary Pharaoh and enemy of the People of God.[140] For this purpose only a "Herod" would do,[141] and a Herod is what Luke gives us. The result is a typical Lukan hodgepodge. Acts 12:1–23 is well-crafted literary unity marked on each side by references to the mission of Paul and Barnabas (11:30; 12:25). The stories of Peter's deliverance and Herod's death are mirror twins. For the death of Herod Luke may have used a legendary source more "popular" than the account (or source) of Josephus, but which begins with detailed historical information that trails off into vagueness. It is barely possible that the same source might have contained both a gaffe like Mark 6:14's "King Herod" and the circumstantial information of Acts 12:20.[142] Nor could the reader of Acts, even of Luke *and* Acts, be faulted for presuming that this Herod is the same person mentioned in 4:27 and previously in Luke 23:7–15.[143] The narrator does not inform us that Judea once more has a client king with capital jurisdiction, that this "Herod" is a new player in the game. Readers of today, equipped with historical references, complete the hiatus by concluding that the date is c. 44 and that Agrippa I is the head of a once more independent client kingdom.[144]

An alternative hypothesis is that Luke developed his portrayal of "Herod" through a combination of Josephus's accounts of the deaths of Herod the Great and Agrippa I. The former contributes the extortionate and murderous tyrant, not to mention the worms (*Antiquities* 17.169), which are epidemic among tyrants anyway. In support of dependence upon Josephus's account of the death of Agrippa I are one general observation and several important details. A critical consensus holds that Luke has abbreviated *something*; commentators are likely to supply details from Josephus that serve, often silently, to fill in the gaps.[145] Haenchen observes that "only in Josephus does the mention of the robes make real sense, and the flattery of courtiers is more probable than the unmotivated shout of the (pagan) populace."[146] The robes serve Luke as an ironic correspondent to the dressing of Peter (Acts 12:8/21). That would have been a detail worth preserving, even if its effect were suppressed. Luke had no interest in explaining the action of the crowd. The blasphemy could speak for itself, and better if unmotivated. His interest is in viewing the death as punishment for persecution. Verse 23 appears to report an instantaneous death, like that of Ananias and Sapphira (5:5, 10),[147] but the adjective "eaten by worms" or "worm-devoured" requires some time to be effective (and suitably gruesome). The most interesting correspondence is the double use of a messenger in each account. Martin Dibelius discussed a proposal of Theodor Zahn that Josephus was dependent upon Acts. Zahn thought that Josephus had transformed the "Angel of the Lord" of tradition (ἄγγελος κυρίου) into the bird of ill omen (ἄγγελος κακῶν). Dibelius was dubious.[148] Or possibly Luke transformed the harbinger of misfortune into the angel of the Lord[149] In the history of traditions it is more common that "supernatural" or irrational explanations are rationalized, especially when the account emerges in a more elevated literary context. The hypothesis that Luke used an historical source must explain the gaps as well as the "cruder" form of the legend. A less difficult, and more concrete, explanation is that Luke took up, abbreviated, and modified the story in Josephus, with some assistance from the latter's account of Herod the Great's demise, and inspiration from the story of Agrippa's two-fold messenger. Such modification is less radical than his transposition of stories from the LXX.[150] Other solutions are certainly possible, but none is less complex or intrinsically more probable. The principal objection will be that this hypothesis all but requires that Luke invented the quarrel with Tyre and Sidon and, perhaps, the Chamberlain Blastus.[151]

In the view of Steve Mason, with reference to the death of Agrippa and the accounts about ". . . Felix and Drusilla, Agrippa II and Berenice . . . Luke's narrative seems to depend squarely on such information as Josephus presents."[152] The importance of this observation is that an alternative explanation will need to postulate a source or sources equally consistent with what Josephus has chosen to say. To explain evident matters of difference or disagreement, Mason states, one can readily posit conflation, misunderstanding, ". . . imperfect memory or deliberate schematization." The net result is that ". . . Luke's product is much more difficult to explain if he had no knowledge of Josephus." Mason lays even greater weight upon their common presentation of movements as "philosophical schools," of which the Pharisees are the "most precise." He concludes that, although a jury might not find these arguments to be proof beyond reasonable doubt, either Luke did know Josephus or one must explain "a nearly incredible series of coincidences." The ball, in short, is in the other court.

THE PARABLE OF THE POUNDS

Application of the hypothesis that Luke knew and used Josephus will ease a number of vexatious questions raised by various passages in Luke and Acts.[153] One example is the oft-discussed relation of the "throne-claimant" section of Luke's edition of the "Parable of the Pounds/Talents" (Matthew 25: 14–30; Luke 19:11–27). Comparison with Matthew's "Parable of the Talents" and discussion of sources tend to work against analysis of Luke's narrative in its own right. Luke 19:12–27 is a *novella*, like the so-called "example stories," such as the Good Samaritan (10:25–37) and the Prodigal Son (15:11–32). Like the latter, albeit with considerably less success, the "Pounds" contains two stories, one about faithful servants and the other about enemies, in A B A_2 B_2 arrangement. The drama is not like that of Matthew's comparable parable, where the slaves have a free hand, for in Luke they are charged to put the royal resources to work. Suspense develops during the retardation of the lengthy A_2 section, which takes up almost the entire story. Throughout the extended account of reward and punishment, readers will wonder about the hostile citizens, who were left dangling. When in the final verse their end comes, it is brief and brutal.[154] I shall now turn to the source question.

There are sufficient, if less than overwhelming, grounds for positing that Q contained an edition of this parable.[155] Luke's edition thus represents Q + X. At one time it was fashionable to understand the Pounds as a blend of two parables, one from Q or the like, the other a story of "The Throne Claimant." A classic representative of this viewpoint is Joachim Jeremias, who saw the parable as admonishing against false security. (He also regarded it as based upon the story of Archelaus).[156] Few now support this analysis, in part because the excerpts do not look like a true parable, in part because the individuals involved were not seduced by a false sense of security. They gambled on winning and could expect little mercy otherwise.[157] Brandon Scott agrees that this material does not stem from a parable, but is satisfied to find here a common motif of popular literature, in which stories about throne claimants are plentiful enough.[158]

So they may be, but it is quite unusual for such claimants to go to *another* country to *receive* their crown and title.[159] The situation is not about a fairy-tale king or a figure from the pages of Herodotus, individuals who must spend some time in exile, but about an imperial regime that makes and unmakes various satellite rulers, "client kings." C. F. Evans is far from alone in his comment that "It has long been observed that all this corresponds with events . . ."[160] The "events" in view are those surrounding the attempt of Archelaus to secure the provisions of his father Herod's will. Like the well-born gentleman of Luke 19:12, Archelaus set out for a distant place to receive his crown, leaving subordinates in charge of his estates (Josephus *Antiquities* 17.222–23). Archelaus, too, met opposition in the form of an embassy from his own people (Luke 19:14; *Antiquities* 17.300). After returning, he was less than charitable to his subjects in general, not to mention his political opponents (Luke 19:27; *Antiquities* 17.342; cf. *War* 2.111[161]).

The details fit the story of Archelaus closely enough to make other proposals unlikely, at best.[162] The pertinent question is the proximate source. Was this general and still "hot" news in the time of Jesus? Possibly. Was this common knowledge both for Luke, writing outside of Judea some time well after 70, and for his readers? Jeremias, who views Josephus as the source, speaks as if this were so, but he is certainly wrong.[163] As in the case of Judas the Galilean, it is unlikely that Luke's implied audience would have even heard of Archelaus. Since Luke is responsible for the additional material, which corresponds to Josephus's rendition of Archelaus' adventures, Josephus is the most probable source of the record of those adventures. Here, in a context quite different from that of Gamaliel's speech in Acts 5, one can see another instance of Luke transforming history into *exemplum*, specific in one case, as the situation required, suitably and properly general in the other.[164]

PRIVILEGES FOR VICTIMS

Robert Stoops has examined the account of a riot in Ephesus, Acts 19:23–40 in the light of a Jewish apologetic approach to the much and long disputed issue of the social standing of Jewish communities within the cities of the Empire. This issue, in turn, had become embroiled in the wider question of the rights and privileges of the cities themselves.[165] Stoops summarizes the core of the argument in these words: "Because our opponents riot our rights ought to be confirmed."[166] Behind this thesis stands the snobbery of an aristocratic elite: whomever and whatever the urban rabble seeks to eradicate by terror should be held in high-esteem by all right-thinking persons. Luke just happens to share this ingenious (and disingenuous) argument.[167] In their attempt to understand his writings, scholars must ask whether he came up with this idea on his own or developed it from others. The probability is that he took over the theme from Jewish apologetic, where the argument seems to have met with some success.[168] Although Philo composed two treatises dealing with violence in Alexandria in the period from 37–41, Josephus is the leading source. Granting the lack of a "form" for riot stories, Stoops finds that ". . . a number of motifs recur with regularity in reports of rioting connected with Jewish rights, and many of those motifs appear in Acts 19:23–41."[169] Although he does not require that Luke had read Josephus,[170] Stoops believes that "Luke's account of the riot in Ephesus may be modeled on a single report of an anti-Jewish riot. Josephus's description of the violence directed against the Jews of Antioch . . . contains parallels to almost every element of Luke's story."[171] Stoops does not enumerate these parallels with *War* 7.46–62; 100–11, many of which appear in Table 5.6.

Table 5.6: Urban Disorder

Josephus *War* 7.46–62	Acts 19:23–38
But about this time (κατ᾽ ὃν δὲ καιρὸν) when the present war began, and Vespasian was newly sailed to Syria, (47) and all men had taken up a great hatred against the Jews, then it was that a certain person, whose name was Antiochus, being one of the Jewish nation, and greatly respected . . . came upon the theater at a time when the people of Antioch were assembled together, and became in informer against his father; and accused both him and others, that they had resolved to burn the whole city in one night;; he also delivered up to them some Jews that were foreigners, as partners in their resolutions. (48) When the people heard this, they could not refrain their passion, but commanded that those who were delivered up to them should have fire brought to burn them; who were accordingly all burnt in the theater immediately. (49) They did also fall violently upon the multitude of the Jews, as supposing, that by punishing them suddenly, they should save their own city. (50) As for Antiochus, he aggravated the rage they were in, and thought to give them a demonstration of his own conversion, and of his hatred of the Jewish customs, by sacrificing after the manner of the Greeks: (51) he persuaded the rest also to compel them to do the same, . . . (54) Now, after these misfortunes had happened to the Jews at Antioch, a second calamity befell them. . . . (55) for upon this accident, whereby the foursquare marketplace was burnt down, as well as the archives, and the place where the public records were preserved, and the royal palaces . . . Antiochus accused the Jews as the occasion of all the mischief that was done. (56) Now this induced the	23 About that time (κατὰ τὸν καιρὸν ἐκεῖνον) no little disturbance broke out concerning the Way. 24 A man named **Demetrius**, a silver-smith who made silver shrines of Artemis, brought no little business to the artisans. 25 These he gathered together, with the workers of the same trade, and said, "Men, you know that we get our wealth from this business. 26 You also see and hear that not only in Ephesus but in almost the whole of Asia this Paul has persuaded and drawn away a considerable number of people by saying that gods made with hands are not gods.27 And there is **danger** not only that this trade of ours may come into disrepute but also that the temple of the great goddess **Artemis will be scorned**, and she will be deprived of her majesty that brought all Asia and the world to worship her." 28 When they heard this, they were enraged and shouted, "Great is Artemis of the Ephesians!" 29 The city was filled with the confusion; and people rushed together to the **theater**, dragging with them Gaius and Aristarchus, Macedonians who were Paul's travel companions. . . . 32 Meanwhile, some were shouting one thing, some another; for the assembly was in **confusion**, and most of them did not know why they had come together. 33 Some of the crowd gave instructions to **Alexander, whom the Jews had pushed forward. And Alexander motioned for silence and tried to make a defense before the people.** 34 But when they recognized that he was a Jew, for about two hours all of them shouted in unison, "Great is Artemis of the Ephesians!"

people of Antioch—who were now under the immediate persuasion, by reason of the disorder they were in, that this calumny was true . . . they all fell violently upon those that were accused; (57) and this, like madmen, in a very furious rage also, even as if they had seen the Jews in a manner setting fire themselves to the city; (58) nor was it without difficulty that one Cneius Collegas, the legate, could prevail with them to permit the affairs to be laid before Caesar[172]

35 **But when the town clerk had quieted the crowd**, he said, "Citizens of Ephesus, who is there that does not know that the city of the Ephesians is the temple keeper of the great Artemis and of the statue that fell from heaven? 36 Since these things cannot be denied, you ought to be quiet and do nothing rash. 37 You have brought these men here who are neither temple robbers nor blasphemers of our goddess. 38 If therefore Demetrius and the artisans with him have a complaint against anyone, the courts are open, and there are proconsuls; let them bring charges there against one another.

Luke has certainly not copied Josephus's account of the disturbances at Antioch, for it was much more extensive, led to vast destruction, and had enduring consequences. The accounts are so different that a superficial examination unearths few similarities beyond the place of the theater. Yet behind the two stories are a number of structural devices and shared motifs. Among these are 1) an *agitator*, who, acting in his own interest, proclaims 2) a *threat* to the community that is associated with lack of observance of the 3) *local cult(s)*. The agitator whips the crowd into 4) a *frenzy* in the 5) *theater*, leading to general 6) *confusion*, and widespread 7) *disorder* based upon 8) *false charges*. Both accounts deal with the place of 9) *Jews* in social life—Acts most darkly, but urban antipathy toward Jews *in the light of the Revolt* is definitely a Lukan theme in the passage. Both affairs end with the intervention of 10) an *official*. In Josephus it is the legate (Roman senatorial governor). The "Clerk" at Ephesus notes that such persons are close at hand. This is not a general event, such as an exorcism, nor even an example of urban unrest, but a disturbance related to specifics.

The cautious suggestion of Stoops may well be correct. I think it likely that Luke drew from Josephus the idea of using the theme of a riot to place the Jesus movement in a good light. This passage from the *War* may well have provided substantial inspiration for the details of his description. But the differences are at least equally important. Josephus maintains an apologetic posture throughout, whereas Luke's none too subtle ridicule of polytheism indicates that his account is not oriented toward approval from the "pagan" establishment. If part of the problem is that "Jesus-people" were caught up in an outbreak of hostility against Jews, the entire matter cannot be charged against the account of the Christians. Urban mobs can be quite inclusive when identifying scapegoats. Luke takes no one off the hook other than Paul and the believers in Christ.

Stoops's portrayal of Acts 19:23–40 as apologetic is an important but incomplete explanation of the manifold problems raised by this exciting interlude.[173] As he affirms, the narrative would proceed quite adequately—indeed, more smoothly—if the riot were omitted. Loisy was correct, in my judgment, in his claim that the riot is a cloak beneath which the author gathers all of the difficulties faced by Paul in Asia. Luke here provides his equivalent for the problems noted in 1 Corinthians 15:32 and 2 Corinthians 1:8.[174] An anti-Christian riot stirred up by the basest of people for the vilest of motives in which Paul played not the smallest direct part (he would, to be sure, have tried to intervene, but the Asiarchs persuaded him to exercise the better part of valor) served Luke's purposes quite well. Acts 19:23–40 is a smokescreen that has all the attraction of a fireworks display. For the readers there are lots of thrills and considerable edification. As for Paul, doing lunch with the Asiarchs was far preferable to doing time in the local pokey.[175] In light of the difficulties of attempting to extricate an "authentic" source used by Luke and of providing a coherent explanation for this passage, the solution of Lukan composition is cogent. If Josephus served Luke as a source for "particulars" elsewhere, he could surely have provided here the outline of an event as well as numerous motifs. The riot in Ephesus does not constitute compelling primary evidence for Luke's use of Josephus. It does offer quite appealing material for illustrating how Luke may have used Josephus and of how acceptance of Josephus as a source for Acts can enhance our understanding of its purpose and offer resolutions for some of its enigmas.

BAPTIZING JOHN AS A HELLENISTIC MORALIST

The crowds asked *John*, "What then should we do?" [11]In reply he said to them, "Whoever has two coats must share with anyone who has none; and whoever has food must do likewise." [12]Even tax collectors came to be baptized, and they asked him, "Teacher, what should we do?" [13]He said to them, "Collect no more than the amount prescribed for you." [14]Soldiers also asked him, "And we, what should we do?" He said to them, "Do not extort money from anyone by threats or false accusation, and be satisfied with your wages."

Luke 3:10–14 has no parallels in the canonical gospels.[176] In this unit Luke provides his readers with a sample of the ethical ideas promulgated by the preacher of the imminent end (v. 9) and coming judgment (v. 17). John does not urge soldiers to turn their swords upon their officers, nor does he cajole toll-collectors into giving their receipts to the poor. John's ideals are those of Jesus, and, oddly enough, the ideals of Luke (and others). Persons endowed with more than the minimum should share with those who have little or nothing, while bureaucrats and soldiers are not to use their positions as means for exploitation. From the viewpoint of the popular moralists, this is standard stuff.[177] John is like a Cynic street-preacher, a bit uncouth and annoying, perhaps, but no danger to society. If such preachers can abstain from criticizing the ruler, they will usually be able to go about their business. Gadflies that wish to survive will be careful about whom they sting. The framework of this segment is Lukan, as the form of the initial question indicates.[178] Fitzmyer's views are far from atypical:

> . . . [H]is words here lack any eschatological motivation. Nor are they related to the coming of a messiah. Instead, John advocates a selfless concern for others — good advice for Jews, Christians, or pagans . . . The radical character of John's eschatological preaching here yields to a different emphasis: assistance, honesty, and equity.[179]

Luke has not been able to convince many that John the Baptizer was generally perceived as a Hellenistic moralist, but he was not the only historian who ever ran the idea up a flag pole to see if any would salute.[180] Josephus did the same: John ". . . was a good man, and had exhorted the Jews to lead righteous lives, to practise justice towards their fellows and piety towards God . . ."[181]The wording and ideas of Luke 3:10–14 certainly belong to the author, but they fully conform to the summary of Josephus. If Luke wished to fill in some of the blanks that might describe righteous living, he would be expected to say what is here attributed to John. Luke would have had reasons for his portrayal of John as a preacher of popular ethics, reasons not greatly different from those of Josephus. The idea that the world is about to end can act as a solvent to the social fabric—not to mention the ever-present danger that those who believe in an imminent fiery end might reach for a convenient torch.[182]

It is quite possible that both Josephus and Luke came up with the idea of giving John an ideological make-over and that each produced a similar product, since the number of options was limited. Those whose appetite for coincidences is less than insatiable may be tempted to ask whether this portrait also depends upon Josephus. In my view the latter explanation has stronger probability than the former. Josephus's portrait of John might have offended Mark, while Matthew had other fish to fry, but to Luke this was just what he was looking for. John lectured the rank and file, Jesus came to the aid of an officer, and Peter will convert one.[183]

THE PRIOR MR. HERODIAS

Luke also declines to give a detailed report of the execution of John. Although he repeats, in summary form, John's reproach about Herodias (which, he claims, is but one of Antipas's numerous iniquities, 3:19–20), his account does not include the story found in Mark 6:17–29. (See Table 5.7.) Not only does his version show considerable divergence from the account in Josephus, but this

Table 5.7: The Former Husband of Herodias

Mark 6:17//Matthew 14:3	Luke 3:19–20	Josephus Ant. 18.109–110
17 For **Herod** himself had sent men who arrested John, bound him, and put him in prison on account of **Herodias**, his brother *Philip's* wife, because Herod had married her 3 For Herod had arrested John, bound him, and put him in prison on account of Herodias, his brother *Philip's* wife,	But **Herod the tetrarch**, who had been rebuked by him because of **Herodias**, his brother's wife, *and because of all the evil things that Herod had done* (NRSV, *alt.*) 20 added to them all by shutting up John in prison.	. . . The **tetrarch Herod** had taken the daughter of Aretas as his wife . . . When starting out for Rome, he lodged with his half-brother *Herod*, who was born of a different mother . . . Falling in love with **Herodias**, the wife of this half-brother . . . he brazenly broached to her the subject of marriage.[184] **116–119**. Herod has John killed because of the fear that his popular movement would lead to rebellion.

omission raises a number of questions. Luke may have believed that Mark had not gotten the story quite right or may have found it otherwise unsuitable. For example, he reserves contact with royalty for Jesus (Luke 23:7–12) and especially for Paul (Acts 26). Not only could Josephus have served to justify this omission,[185] but he could also be the reason for failing to follow Mark (as does Matthew) in saying that Philip was the former husband of Herodias. Those inclined toward Luke's occasional use of Josephus will see in Luke 3:19 an example of that influence.

MEANWHILE, BACK IN GAZA . . .

Suspense takes various forms. Chapter Three suggested that the tale of the Ethiopian official was not complete, but left the question hanging. The time has come to look at the story in a different intertextual garment. In *Antiquities* 20.17– 96 Josephus relates the fortunes of the royal house of Adiabene, a small kingdom in northern Mesopotamia that was generally subordinate to the Parthian empire. Larry Wills characterizes this as a Jewish historical novel. "One of the closest parallels, in fact, may be found in the *Acts of the Apostles*, a Christian historical novel that is roughly contemporary."[186] The hero of Josephus's tale, Izates, is not only graced with divinely arranged origins like Moses in Jewish tradition, but like Joseph he experiences the jealous ire of his siblings. Sent away for his own safety, like many throne claimants, Izates becomes convinced of the validity of Jewish belief. When he returns home he brings his Jewish teacher, one Ananias.[187] Izates wished to be circumcised, but his mother opposed this desire as politically ruinous, and Ananias agreed, since he held that the will to worship God was more important than circumcision.[188] For a while Izates accepted this missionary strategy based upon cultural accommodation and political sensitivity.

> Afterwards, however, since he had not completely given up his desire, another Jew, named Eleazar, who came from Galilee and who had a reputation for being extremely strict when it came to the ancestral laws (περὶ τὰ πάτρια δοκῶν ἀκριβής[189]), urged him to carry out the rite. For when he came to him to pay him his respects and found him reading the law of Moses, he said: "In your ignorance, O King, you are guilty of the offence against the law and thereby against God. For you ought no merely to read the law but also, and even more, to do what is commanded in it. How long will you continue to be uncircumcised?[190]

And immediately he was circumcised (and ruled successfully, through many and great dangers, thereafter). The question here is whether the parallel to Acts 8:26–39 is purely phenomenological. It could be intertextual. Both stories deal with persons of high status from realms outside of the Roman Empire who are profound admirers of Jewish belief but not properly initiated. Both are experiencing a quandary. In each case the "missionary" comes upon the subject engaged in reading scripture and takes advantage of the opportunity to teach the faith in full. The initiatory rite (circumcision/baptism) takes place without further ado.[191] In favor of intertextual inspiration is the relative rarity of conversion stories that take their departure from bible reading. Unlike most of the other examples, there is no historical question at stake here.

BERNICE AND DRUSILLA

In that same twentieth book of the *Antiquities* Josephus takes up the marriages of Drusilla and Ber(e)nice (20.141–147). This is what he reports about the marriage of Felix to Drusilla:

> Not long afterwards Drusilla's marriage to Azizus was dissolved under the impact of the following circumstances. At the time when Felix was procurator of Judaea, he beheld her; and, inasmuch as she surpassed all other women in beauty, he conceived a passion for the woman. He sent to her one of his friends, a Cyprian Jew named Atomus, who pretended to be a magician, in an effort to persuade her to leave her husband and to marry Felix. Felix promised to make her supremely happy if she did not disdain him. She, being unhappy and wishing to escape the malice of her sister Berenice—for Drusilla was exceedingly abused by her because of her beauty[192]—was persuaded to transgress the ancestral laws and to marry Felix. (20.141–143)[193]

Much of what Josephus says here would be quite at home in ancient fiction: captivating beauty, love at first sight, envy aroused by that attraction, and resort to intrigue to gain possession of the object of one's desire. As far as Acts is concerned, Drusilla appears only as the object of a preposition: "Some days later when Felix came with his wife Drusilla, who was Jewish, he sent for Paul and heard him speak concerning faith in Christ Jesus." (Acts 24:24). What is the source of Luke's information about the spouse of Felix? Why does Acts mention her name? Is her Jewish background the basis for Felix's knowledge about the way?[194] Acts does not identify the wives of "King Herod," Sergius Paulus, Gallio, or Festus. Luke may have taken the information from Josephus, who is the only known source of it, as Tacitus seems to supply Drusilla with a different pedigree.[195]

For those who ask whether Luke made use of Josephus, the leading interest here is whether the story of Drusilla may have been a source for Elymas, domestic chaplain and spiritual director to the Roman governor of Cyprus, Sergius Paulus (Acts 13:6–12). "It has been suggested that Atomos and Etoimas (a strong variant here) are one and the same man: this is possible, but no more."[196] The similar features are summarized in Table 5.8.

The differences are obvious: In Josephus the "magician" is a member of Felix's entourage who is sent on a mission at the governor's request. Luke's "magician" intervenes in his own self-interest. Further, the account in Acts is defective: "The story has no exposition and no conclusion."[197] Nock (writing in less egalitarian times) observed: "The proconsul's conversion, which would have been an event of the first importance, is just stated as though it were that of a washer-woman.

Table 5.8 : The Tale of the Magi

Motif	Josephus	Acts
Roman Governor	Felix	Sergius Paulus
A Jewish magician from Cyprus who is agent of governor	Atomos/Simon	Bar-Jesus=Elymas/ Etoimas
Task:	Dissuade Drusilla from Azizus to Felix	Dissuade Governor from Barnabas and Saul
(Governor seeks to hear the Word)	—	(Acts 13:7; 24:24)

And it has no consequences."[198] Rather than remain in Paphos and found a community based upon the large household of the governor, with its spacious amenities and capacious resources, the two missionaries depart for Pamphylia, on the coast of Asia Minor. Conversions based upon miracle are common, but conversions motivated by punitive miracles are the sort of base material one should expect to find in the later and less edifying Apocryphal Acts.

The jumble of names—each religious leader has two—has led to the most ingenious (and desperate) proposals.[199] Joseph's magician is identified as "Simon" in major manuscripts,[200] while "Etoimas" (etc.) has D-text support in Acts.[201] Intertextuality may provide the best solution to the text-critical issues. Christian editors of Josephus altered the unusual "Atomos" to "Simon" in honor of the villain of early Christianity, Simon the Magician (Acts 8). Correspondingly, a later editor of Acts may have adopted "Etoimas" because of the account of Josephus, but the original reading of Acts 13:8 is much less secure.[202]

A key contribution of Acts 13:6–12 to the work as a whole is to establish a parallel between Peter and Paul.[203] Just as the former cursed a magus (8:20–24), so does the latter—both, it might be noted, without a conclusion. Moreover, the blinding not only has its parallel in Paul's own experience (Acts 9:1–19a), but also endows him with another Petrine credential: the performance of a punitive miracle. (In Acts 5:1–11 Ananias and Sapphira die when Peter exposes their deceit). Earlier scholarship, as represented by Wikenhauser, Nock, and their contemporaries, asked whether the same historical character, a Cypriote Jewish magician, might be involved in both Josephus and Acts. Interest in such identifications has faded.[204] The question today is more likely to be whether the kinship is intertextual. Those who concede that Luke has evidently made use of Josephus elsewhere can maintain that intertextuality provides for the source-question of Acts 13:6–12 a solution that is at least as strong as any other.

The central issue concerning Luke's interest in Bernice (or Berenice) is Luke's interest in Bernice. (See Table 5.9.) The narrative mentions her on three

Table 5.9: Pomp and Circumstances

Acts 25:23; 26:30	Josephus *Ant.* 16.29–30 (–57)	Josephus *Ant.* 17.93
Τῇ οὖν ἐπαύριον ἐλθόντος τοῦ Ἀγρίππα καὶ τῆς Βερνίκης μετὰ πολλῆς φαντασίας καὶ εἰσελθόντων εἰς τὸ ἀκροατήριον σύν τε χιλιάρχοις καὶ ἀνδράσιν τοῖς κατ' ἐξοχὴν τῆς πόλεως, καὶ κελεύσαντος τοῦ Φήστου ἤχθη ὁ Παῦλος.	τοιαῦτα καταβοώντων παρεστήσατο μὲν ὁ βασιλεὺς ἀκοῦσαι τὸν Ἀγρίππαν αὐτῶν δικαιολογουμένων, Νικόλαον δέ τινα τῶν αὐτοῦ φίλων ἔδωκεν εἰπεῖν ὑπὲρ αὐτῶν τὰ δίκαια. [30] τοῦ δὲ Ἀγρίππου Ῥωμαίων τε τοὺς ἐν τέλει καὶ βασιλέων καὶ δυναστῶν τοὺς παρόντας αὐτῷ συνέδρους ποιησαμένου καταστὰς ὁ Νικόλαος ὑπὲρ τῶν Ἰουδαίων ἔλεξεν:	Τῇ δ' ἑξῆς συνήδρευεν μὲν Οὔαρός τε καὶ ὁ βασιλεύς, εἰσεκλήθησαν δὲ καὶ οἱ ἀμφοῖν φίλοι καὶ οἱ συγγενεῖς βασιλέως Σαλώμη τε ἡ ἀδελφή . . .
So on the next day Agrippa and Bernice came with great pomp, and they entered the audience hall with the military tribunes and the prominent men of the city. Then Festus gave the order and Paul was brought in. 26:30 Ἀνέστη τε ὁ βασιλεὺς καὶ ὁ ἡγεμὼν ἥ τε Βερνίκη καὶ οἱ συγκαθήμενοι αὐτοῖς Then the king got up, and with him the governor and Bernice and those who had been seated with them	While *the Jews of Ionia* were protesting in this fashion, the king induced Agrippa to listen to them as they pleaded their cause, and he assigned Nicolas, one of his friends, to speak in behalf of their rights. And when Agrippa had taken as councilors the Roman officials and those kings and princes who were present, Nicolas arose and spoke in behalf of the Jews.[205]	On the following day Varus and the king held a council, to which were invited the friends of both sides and the relatives of the king, including his sister Salome . . .[206]

occasions, 25:13, 23; 26:30, always in the phrase "Agrippa and Bernice." She is otherwise ignored.[207] Were the three instances of "and Bernice" to be omitted, no one would notice. The first question, therefore, is like that raised by the reference to Drusilla: why does Acts mention her name? What is the purpose of these bagatelles? The second question deals with her identity. Was the implied reader expected to know who Bernice was? The answer to the latter may be yes. Bernice was a mid-range Cleopatra who was still the subject of interest in the opening decades of the second century.[208] The sad duty of informing his dear readers that the depraved denizens of the Roman Empire appear to have been fascinated with gossip about royalty has already fallen upon this poor author.

To this depraved and archaic proclivity Bernice made substantial, albeit almost certainly quite involuntary, contributions.

One obvious reason for including Bernice in the narrative is that she was present when Paul addressed her brother, King Agrippa II. Alas, the historicity of this episode is highly dubious. It seems to have been developed by Luke to fill out the promise made about Paul in Acts 9:15: "[H]e is an instrument whom I have chosen to bring my name before Gentiles and kings[209] and before the people of Israel," a theme that in turn derives from Mark 13:9 (cf. Luke 21:12).[210] When the passage is examined from a literary viewpoint, the presence of Bernice raises the possibility that she will constitute one corner of another prophet/king/(wicked) queen triangle.[211] This does not materialize, but it could generate suspense for the first-time hearer or reader.

Josephus provides another explanation, one that does not exclude the first. He discusses Bernice and her long association with her brother immediately after his description of Drusilla's marriage to Felix (*Antiquities* 20.145–146, discussed above). Mason's statement that Luke could have obtained what he says about Bernice from Josephus is quite true, but it is equally true that what he says about Bernice amounts to almost nothing except for the hardly electrifying news that she could occasionally be found in the company of her brother. What Josephus contributes is *proximity*. This is less persuasive than in the case of Theudas and Judas, discussed above, but it is quite possible. If Luke learned about Drusilla from Josephus, he might well have noted the place of Bernice in that narrative and thus hit upon the idea of dropping another name into the list of the rich and famous who had heard Paul speak. At a minimum this explanation is no worse than any other, while it also helps to resolve a minor mystery.[212]

POMP AND CIRCUMSTANCES

Gazing upon the splendid setting for Paul's great speech of Acts 26, Luke T. Johnson says:

> The panoply surrounding the hearing may at first seem excessive and a sign of fictional coloring: Paul is to be heard by a governor, by a king and his influential wife, by the military officials, and the leading citizens of Caesarea (25:23). But the procedure Luke describes does not in any way conflict with what we know of Palestinian politics in the first century. Josephus, for example, relates at least two such incidents which in their basic structure and in many of their details resemble the Lukan account . . . Luke's portrayal of the scene, as so often in his narrative, conforms impressively to the customs of the place.[213]

Johnson's argument is open to criticism. He implies, without committing the error, that verisimilitude (accuracy in details)=historical accuracy. That is a fallacy.[214] Neither of his examples from Josephus (*Antiquities* 17.93//*War* 1.620 and *Antiquities* 16.30) derives from the first century CE, and the second is not situated in Palestine. Even so, I find these parallels interesting. The first treats the trial of Herod's son Antipater. In the *Antiquities* the account of this action runs from 17.93–145, more than twelve pages of Greek in the Loeb edition, much of which is in summary form.[215] By contrast Luke deals with the trial of Paul in thirty-seven *verses*; this amounts to about one fourth of the length of Josephus' account, and Luke does not summarize. Here, as always, the reports of trials in Acts are much briefer than a full account would require.[216]

Johnson's observations do, however, indicate the prominence Luke would assign to the "trial" of Paul in Acts 26: this is an event comparable to the extravagant setting orchestrated for the arraignment and trial of Herod's son and heir. By providing a comparable setting Luke displays the high esteem that he accorded to Paul and his case. I fear that this setting is indeed "excessive and a sign of fictional coloring." The remaining issue, in the context of this investigation, is whether these passages from Josephus *inspired* Luke's portrait of the personnel assembled to hear Paul's self-defense.

Table 5.9 indicates that the differences are more noticeable than are the similarities. Although royalty, governors, and other notables are present in all three cases, the circumstances vary. *Antiquities* 16.29–30 is more like Acts in that there is no formal trial, whereas all of the personalities assembled in *Antiquities* 17.93 are to have a role in the proceedings.[217] Both passages from Josephus use the stem *synhedr*- (from which "Sanhedrin" derives) to indicate the presence of a formally constituted body. The passage from *Antiquities* 16 shares two other features with Acts 25–26: the hearing took place as the result of a conversation between a client king and a Roman official, and the object of the speech was a defense of certain rights and privileges. Further, the respective speeches of Nicolas of Damascus and Paul of Tarsus display common features. Both take note of Jewish customs (ἔθη) Acts 26:3; *Ant.* 16.35) and the public nature of the religious views (Acts 26:26; *Ant.* 16.43). Even "madness" comes up in both (Acts 26:25–26; *Ant.* 16.39). These parallels establish no more than that both Luke and Josephus were familiar with the conventions of the rhetoric of philosophical defense. If either of these passages helped Luke to create or illustrate the speech of Acts 26, it was 16.29. This is a possibility, but not a strong possibility.

HAIR OF THE HEAD

Discussions of the proposal that Paul engage in a rite of purification (Acts 21:23–24) customarily introduce the example of Agrippa I to indicate that such benefactions were acceptable.[218] Another way to look at the matter is from the perspective of a possible intertextual connection. Table 5.10 displays the data. Several factors support such an examination: 1) The recommendation of James is probably fictional, since the actual subject was the money raised by Paul for the poor in Jerusalem. 2) The act of paying for the vows of others is far from typical, as the gesture of Agrippa indicates. Such gestures were the prerogative of wealthy people, but this befits the status of Paul in Acts.[219] 3) Both writers

Table 5.10: Hair of the Head

Acts 21:23b-24	Josephus *Antiquities* 19.294
εἰσὶν ἡμῖν ἄνδρες τέσσαρες εὐχὴν ἔχοντες ἐφ' ἑαυτῶν. 24 τούτους παραλαβὼν ἁγνίσθητι σὺν αὐτοῖς καὶ δαπάνησον ἐπ' αὐτοῖς ἵνα **ξυρήσονται** τὴν κεφαλήν . . . We have four men who are under a **vow**. Join these men, go through the rite of purification with them, and pay for the **shaving** of their heads Cf. 18:18d . . . κειράμενος ἐν Κεγχρεαῖς τὴν κεφαλήν, εἶχεν γὰρ εὐχήν. At Cenchreae *Paul* had his hair cut, for he was under a **vow**.	διὸ καὶ ναζιραίων **ξυρᾶσθαι** διέταξε μάλα συχνούς Accordingly, *Agrippa (I)* also arranged for a very considerable number of Nazirites to be **shorn**.[220] Cf. *War* 2.313–14: Now Bernice dwelt then at Jerusalem, in order to perform a **vow** which she had made to God; for it is usual with those that had been either afflicted with a distemper, or with any other distresses to make vows; and for thirty days before they are to offer their sacrifices, to abstain from wine, and to shave the hair of their head. (314) Which things Bernice was now performing, and stood barefoot before Florus's tribunal, and besought him[221]

use the same verb (ξυράομαι, "shear") in the same sense,[222] involving a far from common synecdoche for "completion of the vow."[223] 4) In Acts 18 Luke uses different language for shaving one's head in conjunction with the discharge of a vow. The source(s) of his information about religious vows is uncertain. Josephus is one possible authority. This intertextual solution is attractive for those who do not believe that Luke had a source that depicted James as suggesting that payment for the discharge of Nazirite vows was what we should describe as a means for "laundering" the collection money.[224] In brief: if you think that this passage is a Lucan invention, you are likely to be receptive to the proposal that Josephus provided inspiration for it.

ROOTS OF A CONSPIRACY

The following specimen (see Table 5.11) is even more adventurous, for it likewise depends upon the assumption of Lucan creation, specifically of the dire plot against Paul and its subsequent detection in 23:12–22, which led to an elaborate rescue operation in verses 13–33.[225] From the time of Paul's arrival at Jerusalem (21:17) to the conclusion of the book there is not a great deal that can persuasively be attributed to a primary written source, with the possible exception of 27:1–28:16. The dull facts are simply that Paul was evidently arrested in Jerusalem, transported thence to the capital, Caesarea, and eventually sent to Rome for (judgment and) execution. Luke may have known, and certainly could have told, other stories. If all the manuscripts of Acts ended at 21:16, no important fact of early Christian history would be lost.[226] From Luke's view-

Table 5.11: Roots of a Conspiracy

Josephus, *Antiquities* 15.282–91	Acts 23:12–35 (*et al.*)
1. Herod the Great is accused of departing from Israelite traditions. (280)	1. Paul is accused of violating Jewish law and traditions (21:21, 28)
2. *Ten* men conspire to kill Herod at any risk. They **swear an oath** (συνομοσάμενοι 282 [cf. 288 συνωμοσία]).	2. More than *forty* men conspire to kill Paul or die. They **swear an oath** (συνωμοσία, 23:12–13)
3. Plan is to **ambush** Herod in *theater* (284)	3. Plan is to **ambush** Paul en route to Sanhedrin (23:15)
4. **Plot exposed** by a spy (286)	4. **Plot exposed** by an informer (23:16)
5. **Plot thwarted**; conspirators executed. (286–289)	5. **Plot thwarted** by removing Paul under cover of night with a large protecting force (23:23–33) cf. 23:10. Danger that Paul will be **dismembered**.
cf. 289. Informer **dismembered**.	

point, however, much of great importance would have been lost, for in these chapters he is very much a biographer of Paul and an apologist for him and for the movement Paul represents. The latter object is at least as important as the former.

The passage from Josephus could have provided no more than general inspiration. Conspiracies to assassinate are elsewhere attested, as is their failure due to discovery of the plot. Conjuration is far from ubiquitous, however, and the two accounts share five motifs. Inspiration from Josephus is a possibility. If nothing else, the parallel shows how prominent and important Paul was. His removal merited the lives of more than forty presumably devoted and loyal Jews, whereas ten seemed a sufficient number for dealing with Herod. Comparison with Josephus reveals some awkward features of Luke's episode. In order to introduce the element of desperation—risk of life—Luke contrives the rather desperate strategy of having his plotters abstain from all nourishment, including water. Such deprivation is not the approved procedure for those about to launch a violent undertaking. The notion of another examination of Paul by the Sanhedrin is quite feeble. The tribune could hardly be expected to consent to a repeat performance of the shambles described in 23:1–11. Finally, the narrator simply abandons the conspirators, just as he abandoned James and Paul's four fellow devotees. The fate of these desperadoes remains unknown to this day. Rather than increase protection for Paul and authorize mass arrests followed by torture and confession, the narrator has the Roman officer remove the target from the board. The account of Acts is no less leaky than was the conspiracy it thwarted. This comparison shows that investigation of Josephus as a possible source can yield other fruit than the mere identification of Luke's resources.

Table 5.12: The Famine under Claudius

Josephus Antiquities 20.101	Acts 11:27–29
ἐπὶ τούτου δὲ καὶ **τὸν μέγαν** **λιμὸν** κατὰ τὴν **Ἰουδαίαν** συνέβη γενέσθαι, καθ' ὃν καὶ ἡ βασίλισσα Ἑλένη πολλῶν χρημάτων ὠνησαμένη σῖτον ἀπὸ τῆς Αἰγύπτου διένειμεν τοῖς ἀπορουμένοις, ὡς προεῖπον. Under these procurators that **great famine** happened in **Judea**, in which queen Helena bought wheat in Egypt at a great expense, and distributed it to those that were in want, as I have related already[227]	Ἐν ταύταις δὲ ταῖς ἡμέραις κατῆλθον ἀπὸ Ἱεροσολύμων προφῆται εἰς Ἀντιόχειαν· 28 ἀναστὰς δὲ εἷς ἐξ αὐτῶν ὀνόματι Ἅγαβος ἐσήμανεν διὰ τοῦ πνεύματος **λιμὸν μεγάλην** μέλλειν ἔσεσθαι ἐφ' ὅλην τὴν οἰκουμένην· ἥτις ἐγένετο ἐπὶ Κλαυδίου. 29 τῶν δὲ μαθητῶν καθὼς εὐπορεῖτό τις ὥρισαν ἕκαστος αὐτῶν εἰς διακονίαν πέμψαι τοῖς κατοικοῦσιν ἐν τῇ **Ἰουδαίᾳ** ἀδελφοῖς· *While Barnabas and Saul were active in Antioch*, prophets came down from Jerusalem to Antioch. One of them named Agabus stood up and predicted by the Spirit that there would be a **severe famine** over all the world; and this took place **during** the reign of Claudius. The disciples determined that according to their ability, each would send relief to the believers living in **Judea**

THE FAMINE UNDER CLAUDIUS

Luke does not directly quote the oracle allegedly delivered by Agabus. (See Table 5.12.) The final words ("this took place . . .") are authorial comment. In the subsequent verses, discussed elsewhere, Antiochene believers send the funds they have gathered to Judea by the hands of Barnabas and Saul.[228] The obvious difficulty in this passage is that Agabus predicts universal famine while the response appears to address a *local* famine in Palestine. Prophecies of widespread famine are typical items in lists of the afflictions that will signal the end.[229] There is ample evidence for local famines in the eastern Mediterranean in the late 40s (during the reign of Claudius).[230] Aune concludes that the prophecy spoke of an end-time famine, but that Luke ". . . removed the eschatological features of the prediction of Agabus."[231] This is a reasonable solution. Since, however, this "famine visit" is derived from Galatians 2 and is related to Luke's desire to defuse tensions about the collection,[232] Luke may have taken the forecast of a famine from Mark 13:8 rather than from a source.[233] Whichever solution is correct, the question of why this famine is dated "under Claudius" remains. In a well-known study of the subject, K. S. Gapp turned for verification of Acts to Josephus *Antiquities* 3.320–21, which speaks of a famine during the reign of Claudius. He may have been on the right track. The information in *Antiquities* 20.51–53 is also summarized in 20.101, cited above (Table 5.1) in conjunction with Theudas. Those who read these two passages in book 20 of the *Antiquities* will find Queen Helena of Adiabene praised for her efforts to provide *famine relief*. This activity took place while Tiberius Alexander was procurator, that is, in 46–48, during the reign of *Claudius*. As Table 5.12 indicates, the two accounts share the terms "great famine" and also the preposition translated "during the reign of"/"under" (ἐπί).[234] Moreover, Acts 11:29 reads "Judea," the same geographical term that occurs in Josephus, although one would expect "Jerusalem," as in 12:25.

For the long-troublesome vagueness of Luke's chronology[235] Josephus provides a possible solution: Luke, wishing to present an alternative understanding of the Collection, learned from Josephus of the famine in Judea during the time of Claudius and, motivated by the benefaction of Queen Helena, described a similar gesture by believers in Antioch. This stone eliminated several birds. The author of Acts was simultaneously able to divert some controversy from Paul, depict solidarity among followers of Jesus from both the Diaspora and the homeland, and provide an outstanding example of "Christian charity" in action. Those who regard this "famine visit" as a fiction, or at least as an error, will find the proposal that Luke used Josephus to date, if not to concoct, the incident attractive. Those who regard Acts 11:27–30 as the narrative of a separate visit may find the parallel a bit troublesome, even if they continue to cite it as proof of the historicity of the event.

OBJECTIONS TO THE PROPOSAL
THAT LUKE USED JOSEPHUS

The best arguments for Luke's use of Josephus came at the beginning. The later examples support the case, but their more important function is to show how the hypothesis that Luke had access to Josephus facilitates understanding of Acts. Although arguments based upon an accumulation of small items can be suspect, however large the list, the number of cases examined hitherto does begin to tell. If one may say of each case in isolation, "not at all improbable but not fully demonstrative," the refrain begins to wear thin. The number of Mason's "coincidences" has begun to look less and less coincidental. If dependence upon Josephus once seemed unlikely because of its implications for Luke's use of sources and his standing as an historian, these objections have lost much of their force. On the issue of sources, evidence from Mark and the LXX alone is sufficient to satisfy doubt. Data for that judgment have been available since the early 1920s.[236] The contemporary view of Luke as a theologian and evangelist who proclaims his message by telling stories has eroded confidence in Luke the historian who would utilize sources as we should like to see them handled. Could Luke read his sources carelessly and err in details? By all means. Most ancient and more than a few subsequent historians have done the same. Did he care more about his particular points than particular accuracy? So one might expect of an early Christian evangelist, though some would not have it so. The ultimate question is not which scholar most ingeniously "defends" or "debunks" Luke, but which approaches shed new and/or genuine light upon the text.

One who would not have it so is Ben Witherington III, who devotes an excursus in his book on Acts to a critique of Mason.[237] His explicit concern is the matter of "historical reliability."[238] He states that Mason views Josephus as "a measuring rod" of accuracy. This is both somewhat irrelevant and highly incorrect[239] After cataloguing the various tendencies and nefarious proclivities to which the tribe of rhetorically trained historians were congenitally prone, Witherington puts away his bottle of poison and gets down to specifics.[240] His opening contention is that the individuals studied by Mason—Judas, Theudas, and the Egyptian prophet—were "... *major* political figures whose lives and exploits were widely known among Jews, especially among Jews in the Holy Land."[241] The sole basis for this fulsome assertion is that ignominious creature Flavius Josephus, who, as Mason had noted, claimed that these persons were but a sample of many rebels. Witherington further contends that Luke could easily have uncovered this information during his researches while in Caesarea and Jerusalem. Outside of the debatable assumptions that the implied readers of Acts were as interested in or as well informed as, "Jews in the Holy Land," and that author of Acts engaged in on-the-spot research about Jewish history, Witherington seems to have forgotten that these characters appear in specific contexts linked to Christian leaders in Acts, rather than to general historical reviews.[242]

In any case, Witherington finds that the Egyptian makes a "perfectly plausible" appearance in Acts 21—when measured by "*some*" of Josephus's data. Be that as it may—the assassin has his instrument poised for the kill—he charges the incompetent Mason with stupidly failing to see that "... Luke is reporting here the off-the-cuff remarks of a Roman tribune under duress ..." The rest of this refutation could scarcely be other than anti-climactic.[243] Following this, our critic turns to what Luke *ought* to have done were he cribbing from Josephus: portray Theudas as an anti-Moses and thus "a perfect foil" to Jesus.[244] Outside of space limits (there is scarcely room in the small speech of Acts 5:34–39 for the development of such characteristics,), the contention that an hypothesis is invalid because the author in question "should" have included this or omitted that is utterly fallacious and ought to have no place in proposals of this type.[245] In short, Witherington has not presented a coherent critique of Mason's hypothesis. His refutation consists of little more than a concatenation of declamatory tricks and scholarly dodges that demonstrate no more than his distaste for Mason's impropriety. One can scarcely imagine what form this critique might have taken had Witherington elected to imitate those nasty rhetorical historians.

Heinz Schreckenberg offered a rather more sober and thoughtful critique of the theory of Lukan dependence upon Josephus in his contribution honoring K. H. Rengstorf.[246] Schreckenberg's major interest was in the general comparison of

Luke with Josephus, with particular attention to alleged differences between the two. Many of the cases are treated as historical problems rather than as issues of authorial interest or literary arrangement. In Schreckenberg's opinion, the two authors often had independent and, for the most part, equally valid, information. On the question of the parable of the throne claimant (Luke 19:12–27, above), for instance, he agrees that the story of Archelaus is in view, but holds that this was very well known and derivable from many sources.[247] He thus glibly disposes of this matter, but against that assertion I have contended above that these matters were not widely known and that unknown sources cannot without further ado be preferred to known sources.[248]

The question of Judas and Theudas receives serious and detailed attention.[249] Schreckenberg does not avoid the difficulties or recommend the creation of a second Theudas. He rather focuses upon the differences in details and the lack of verbal agreement to bolster his conclusion that the speech of Gamaliel was taken from an unreliable historical source.[250] He concludes that Luke and Acts do not know Josephus and are therefore to be dated before 93/94. (One suspects that the question of date was one of Schreckenberg's leading concerns.) For those who do not think that Luke made use of Josephus his objections may seem weighty. Others will observe that he does not address the central question of how Luke came to share so many of Josephus's personal points of view and arrangements. Schreckenberg does show that these two writers cannot be compared to one another in a vacuum, with a preference for the account of Josephus, but such arguments are no longer required. His concomitant warning that it is dangerous to assume that these are the only two accounts dealing with the (relatively small number of) incidents they have in common is equally valid, but not pertinent to the case developed above.[251] This is a useful article, but it will no longer be possible to resolve the issue with a footnote to Schreckenberg.

ANOTHER ANGLE

Evidence of cracks in the dam emerge in Barbara Shellard's *New Light on Luke*.[252] This dissertation takes an unconventional approach to source-questions in general. Although Shellard can at times be rather superficial, she does erect her argument upon conclusions about genre, date, and provenance.[253] Since she dates Acts c. 100 and locates it in Rome, she is quite open to possible use of Josephus.[254] Shellard has no axe to grind in this matter. She is not aware of Mason's work, and the hypothesis of Lucan dependence upon Josephus is not material to her thesis. She simply looks at the question with an open mind. As far as one can tell, Shellard's conclusions are the result of independent study and reflection.[255] Luke's "errors" may derive from careless reading or "over-hasty note-taking."[256] Some of her suggestions—she presents no detailed evidence beyond links between the prefaces of Luke and *Against Apion*—differ from Mason's.[257] In conclusion she decides that use of the *War* is "more than likely," that of the *Antiquities* "quite likely," and use of *Against Apion* "possible."[258] Shellard has clearly followed a different path from that pursued in this chapter. If this light is not entirely new, it is certainly refreshing.[259]

SUMMARY OF THE EVIDENCE

The results of all of the foregoing inquiries are summarized in Table 5.13, which deals with specific passages and does not embrace themes, such as the views of the various parties. The distribution shows a high concentration of parallels in the closing books of the *Antiquities*. In part this may be attributed to chronology: Luke/Acts covers the same period of time as these books. When this observation has been duly noted, the concentration still strengthens the argument for dependence. Were these parallels scattered rather evenly over the thirty rolls produced by Josephus, the argument would have to take a different course and would lose some of its cogency. For the purpose of dating Acts, *Antiquities* 20 is of great importance, for at its conclusion Josephus supplies the date of 93/4 .[260]

CONCLUSION

My conclusion is that the hypothesis that Luke made some use of Josephus—in particular, the closing rolls (books) of the *Antiquities*—is deeply compelling and inherently attractive, for it is both the most economical hypothesis and one that

Table 5.13: Summary

Item	Luke or Acts	Josephus (W.=*War*; A.=*Antiquities*)	Rank
1.	2:1–7 (cf. Acts 5:37)	W. 2.117–118; A. 18.1–5	A
2.	Luke 3:1–2	A. 18.237; 20.138	A-
3.	Luke 3:10–14	A. 18.117	B+
4	Luke 3:19	A. 18.109–119	A-
5.	Luke 19:11–27	A. 17.222–342	A
6.	Acts 5:36–37	A. 20.97–102	A
7.	Acts 8:26–39	A. 20.44–46	B-
8.	Acts 13:7	A. 20.141–143	B
9.	Acts 11:27–29	A. 20.101	B+
10.	Acts 12:20–23	A. 19.343–350	B
11.	Acts 19:23–38	W. 7.42–62	B-
12.	Acts 21:23b-24	A. 19.294	B
13.	Acts 21:30–33	W.2.11	B-
14.	Acts 21:37–38	W. 2.261–263; A. 20.162–172	A
15.	Acts 23:12–35	A. 15.282–291	B (-)
16.	Acts 24:24	A. 20.241–243	B+
17.	Acts 25:13, 23; 26:30	A. 20.145–146	A-
18.	Acts 25:23–26:32	A. 16.29–57	B-

Ranking System. A/A-=high/strong probability of dependence. B+/B/B-=rather good/good/fairly good probability of dependence. I have omitted parallels that I regard as C (less probability) and lower.

helps to resolve a number of outstanding issues and particular questions. One must either agree that Luke made such use of Josephus as seemed sufficient in his eyes to acquire particular information for diverse purposes, or one must hypothesize the use of another narrative history that made the same associations from a similar viewpoint. To be sure, the viewpoint of Josephus contains many elements that are typical of histories written by members of the elite in the Roman Imperial era, but his work is also driven by motives peculiar to his own situation and era, and is the product of his own literary plan and authorial decisions. Luke made use either of Josephus or someone who could qualify as a clone of Josephus. *Tertium non datur* (There is no other option). On the one hand is an elegant Copernican model, simple and satisfactory. The alternative is a Ptolemaic contraption complete with epicycles and sundry paraphernalia.

Luke is the only evangelist who attempts to relate Christian origins to the broader society, including the histories of Israel and of Rome. Matthew and Mark, let alone John, represent small worlds in comparison. In order to fulfill this project, Luke needed data. The bible (LXX) was one indisputable source, but nearly every item of "modern" history to which Luke refers can be found in Josephus. That may not be remarkable. Yet, when Luke calls Jewish parties philosophical "sects," when he views the census of 6 CE as a watershed event; when he introduces such characters as Judas, Theudas, "the Egyptian," and sicarii; it is appropriate to introduce the adjective "remarkable." Luke places the nascent Christian movement on a world stage that is very much like that designed by Flavius Josephus. In other cases (e.g., items 6, 7, and 10 in Table 5.13) Luke may well have used Josephus as inspiration very much as he used the LXX.[261]

In the light of this evidence and the concomitant arguments, the time has come to re-examine Krenkel in order to determine whether additional wheat can be sifted from the putative chaff. More sharply, I propose that it is now incumbent upon those who reject the idea that Luke made some use of Josephus to make arguments of a merit at least equal to those above. Absolute proof is impossible, but there is nothing unusual about that. After all, even the case for Lucan dependence upon Mark has had its opponents.

194 f.

IMPLICATIONS

The most obvious implication of Luke's use of Josephus for this study applies to the question of date. Dependence upon the last books of the *Antiquities* would establish a *terminus a quo* of 93–94. A second, the subject of several allusions above, is the light it sheds upon Luke as researcher and author. This light should not be globalized or used to discredit by association every possible historical reference in Acts. Only those who view Luke as a "great" historian of the caliber of Thucydides or Polybius (neither of whom were inerrant or devoid of bias) will hasten to extinguish it. Yet, as in the case of Paul's letters, references to Josephus often employed to support the trustworthiness of Acts will lose much of their potency if a number of these references refer simply to the *use* of Josephus rather than to concurrence with his histories. Third comes the question of genre. If Luke made use of Josephus, is he thus to be regarded as an imitator of one or more of Josephus's forms?

The question seems to have particular import for the thesis of Gregory Sterling, who sees generic similarities between Luke-Acts and Josephus, in particular the *Antiquities*.[262] The answers to questions about the relationships between the prefaces, long since canvassed,[263] may look different, but I should underscore the observation that the proposal of dependence as herein presented does not in the least suggest that Luke was a careful, diligent, and reflective student of Josephus's entire *oeuvre*, or even that he had access to all of it, let alone that he possessed the time and interest for the pursuit of minutiae. Luke *may* have drawn direct generic inspiration from Josephus, but evidence for use of the Jewish historian does not, by itself, establish generic imitation.[264]

Areas that warrant further investigation include the possible influence of Josephus upon the theology of Luke. Josephus's translation of the Hellenistic doctrine of divine providence into Jewish history has served as a reasonable basis for comparison with Luke and Acts.[265] Although these philosophical ideas were not limited to Josephus, recognition of dependence upon him opens the possibility that the Jewish historian was a major channel through which Luke received and imbibed (and transformed) such ideas.[266] Related concepts include Luke's "natural theology" and his anthropology.[267] And even a tentative acceptance of the hypothesis that Luke had access to Josephus could allow scholars to specify more sharply how Luke adapted these learned doctrines into his writings.[268] At the very least, those who investigate Lukan theology in the context of Hellenistic Judaism may argue that Luke *could* have found this or that notion in Josephus.

The first two chapters established c. 130 CE as the earliest possible *terminus ad quem* for Acts. Chapters three through five have identified sources that set a *terminus a quo* at c. 100. Having established these brackets, the instrument of source criticism has made its major contribution to this study and will move to the back burner. The subsequent chapters will both confirm and reinforce this proposed range by showing that the vocabulary, ideas, and ecclesial outlook of (Luke and) Acts belong to the first third of the second century.

6

Acts among
the Apostolic Fathers

INTRODUCTION

A basic and fundamental principle of historical scholarship is that a work is to be dated by reference to the *latest* identifiable ideas, material, and events found in its final text.[1] "Events" present few challenges. The other categories are less precise.[2] Dating by material (sources) is not difficult when, for instance, a text explicitly quotes from the 6 August 1945 edition of the *New York Times*. That reference is both specific and subject to independent verification: one can still consult the *Times* of that day. I have had both to argue for the use of unspecified sources and then, with one exception, to postulate a date for those sources. The exception, Josephus's *Antiquities*, is important. If Luke had access to that work, he did not write earlier than the middle 90s. That date in turn supports the probability that he was aware of Paul's letters, and evidence for the use of a collection of those epistles yields a similar *terminus a quo*. On the basis of these sources I maintain that Acts was written no earlier than c. 100 CE. The object of the present chapter is to show that these hypotheses gain support from data internal to Acts.

The opening sentence of the previous paragraph is vital, for one argument about the date of Acts appeals to the "primitive" character of its theology. That adjective can be a snare for the unwary. In the first place, "primitive" is a typological, not a chronological, concept. I confess to maintaining a primitive filing system (although "primeval," in the sense of a "formless void" [Genesis 1:1] might often be a more honest label). The general and ubiquitous temptation to assume and apply a developmental model to nearly every field of human endeavor produces such models to allow one to see that and how organisms, societies, machines, and so forth develop from simple and primitive to complex and sophisticated. The process takes time, which it is convenient to imagine as a series of equal periods, i.e., regular developmental stages: five years/decades/centuries for each step with development at a constant pace.[3] A popular "history" of Christology begins with the "simple" teaching of Jesus about loving God and neighbor while deprecating oppression and greed. With the help of messianic ideas, apocalyptic structure, Jewish wisdom and, ultimately, Greek philosophy, this pristine belief culminates in the Christ of the Council of Chalcedon (451), who is both human and divine in nature. Attractive as this model of gradual development may seem, it is erroneous. Christology did not develop like the automobile. Within a few years of the first Easter, Paul embraced (he did not "invent" it) the belief that Jesus was the heavenly Lord, whom he would later identify with Divine Wisdom (1 Corinthians 1:24). And all this took place a half century before the famous prologue to the Fourth Gospel (John 1:1–14).[4]

"Primitive" is not merely a typological marker. In cultures like ours it is often a pejorative word, used to castigate something that is disapproved. "Primitive theology" did not disappear the moment someone came up with a more elaborate model. Except for the letters of Ignatius of Antioch, the "Apostolic Fathers" (*Barnabas*, Polycarp, *Didache*, *Hermas*, and *1–2 Clement*)[5] are theologically "primitive," as is much of the material included in the collections of Christian Apocrypha. Were relative theological complexity the criterion for date, the *Acts of Paul* would be placed earlier than the canonical book of Acts.[6] Nonetheless, some very capable scholars have sought to date Acts by reference to its earliest theological features.

Adolph v. Harnack listed a number of "positive observations in favor of an early date."[7] These include christological titles ("Jesus," "Lord," "the Messiah," "Servant of God," *et al.*); Christology in general; such terms as "disciples" and "the church"; and occasions of worship. Harnack argued that all of these usages supported an early date. The same arguments still recur, with or without attribution.[8] For Ben Witherington, Acts could not be so late as c. 100 because of its primitive Christology and lack of a "developed theology of the cross" (!), its primitive ecclesiology, and its ". . . failure to address even indirectly some of the major third- and fourth generation problems, such as Gnosticism, Montanism, and the like." To this one might puckishly add "apparent ignorance of many of the elements of Pauline theology." This argument, which reads like a mediocre undergraduate's unintentional caricature of Harnack,[9] is subject to the same criticism as that applied to Harnack.

An analogy from archaeology may be of use. During times of peril and for other reasons, residents of the Roman Empire sometimes buried their metallic wealth in sealed clay jars. Treasures consigned to this early equivalent of "offshore banking" were sometimes discovered in antiquity (witness Matthew 13:44) and subsequently. If one were to unearth and investigate such a jar and find that it contained two hundred silver denarii minted under the Emperor Antoninus Pius (138–161) and *one* from the reign of Septimius Severus (193–211), a necessary conclusion would be that the hoard had been hidden no earlier than the date of the Severus coin—presuming that the jar had been carefully sealed and that it was being opened for the first time. So it is with the date of Acts, which cannot be determined by any list of its early features, but only from its latest integral elements. One can scarcely prove that Luke was a companion of Paul (who wrote c. 60 or earlier) by claiming that he was not aware of what Paul thought and said. Furthermore, Luke was trying to characterize and describe the "primitive church," and he was in possession of such material as Q to assist him in this task. Finally, "primitive" was not a disparaging term in ancient culture.

INSTITUTIONS AND
ORGANIZATION

Margaret MacDonald applies the following useful typology to her study of the development of the Pauline tradition: "community building" (as in the genuine letters), "community stabilizing" (Colossians, Ephesians), and "community protecting" (Pastorals).[10] The function of her model is to permit research to focus upon the differences in *emphasis* of the several stages, each of which represents roughly one generation. All churches were (and are) engaged in all three activities much or all of the time. As with all models, MacDonald's categories involve a high level of generalization, and therefore should not be taken as absolutes; nevertheless, this framework will help organize the subsequent examination of Acts

The setting of a large part of the story told in Acts, and thus its dramatic date, is prior even to that of the letters, for Luke highlights the foundation of communities and dispenses with the rest in summary treatment.[11] Two major exceptions are Acts 15 and 20. Comparison of the former to Galatians indicates the difference in perspective. Whereas Paul was engaged in a full-fledged debate about the legitimacy of his message and vocation, a battle in which no quarter was sought and none offered, the Jerusalem leaders of Acts 15 were *Antioch?* concerned with stability—not at any price, to be sure, but with the presumption of the need for give and take. This conflict burst into flames with the arrival of "outside agitators" demanding that male followers of Jesus be circumcised and resulted in "no small dissension" (στάσις, Acts 15:2).

A *leitmotif* in Greek political oratory of the first and second centuries was the avoidance of dissent/disorder/unrest (στάσις) and the promotion of civic unity (ὁμόνοια).[12] The extant material constitutes, according to C. P. Jones, but a drop in what must have been a very full bucket.[13] The themes of community unity and harmony constitute a nexus incorporating 1 (-2) Corinthians, Acts, and *1 Clement*, as well as the epistles of Ignatius.[14] While the epistolary texts appeal for unity through deliberative rhetoric, Acts formulates its exhortation by describing the achievement of concord in the life of the early Christian churches.[15] The need for harmony and good order, which is close to the surface in all the accounts of meetings in Acts, was an important part of the "political" program of Pauline Christianity both during and after the apostle's lifetime.[16] Acts 15 displays the church's leaders as protectors of the community's unity and promoters of stability. This observation, which is little more than a truism, illuminates the perspective of Acts: leaders are to nurture the communities in their charge through prompt resolution of controversy in a manner that is sensitive to various points of view. Paul displays a similar sensitivity in his discussion of different approaches to food in 1 Corinthians 8 and Romans 14, but his solution was found untenable. What was needed was a few clear and simple rules.

LEADERSHIP

Prior to Acts 20, Luke has *shown* leaders how to lead. In the speech of 20:18–35, Paul *tells* leaders how to lead, largely through following the example he has given, which is, of course, also the example of Jesus. The theme of community protection looms large here. (See Table 6.1.)

The leaders are shepherds charged with protection of their flock from wolves. The image of god or ruler as shepherd was already ancient and venerable in the first century.[17] In the Synoptic tradition the wolves are there: Matthew 7:15 (wolves in sheep's clothing); Luke 10:3//Matthew 10:16 (lambs in the midst of wolves), while the sheep must do without a shepherd. John portrays Jesus as the ideal shepherd who protects the flock from wolves (John 10:1–16). An appendix to John endorses the role of earthly shepherds (John 21:15–17). The concept of Acts 20:28 also appears in 1 Peter 5:1–4 and Ephesians 4:11.[18] Paul, like Jesus, predicts the coming of false prophets and teachers, "wolves."[19] The metaphor of the community as a "(little) flock" (ποίμνιον) emerges in similar contexts: 1 Peter 5:2–3; *1 Clement* 16:1; 44:3; 54:2; 57:2. With that image is associated, even in Acts, the picture of the shepherd who has laid down his life for the sheep. The flock will have to confront two types of "wolf": external (verse 29) and internal (verse 30). This two-front outlook is like that envisaged by the Pastoral Epistles, in which the opponents may come from within (1 Timothy) or without (Titus). This "one size fits all" prediction of heresy will accommodate many situations. To be sure, the metaphorical picture of shepherd and sheep assumes paternalism, but although Paul could be an authoritarian parent who threatened to use the stick (1 Corinthians 4:21), he preferred to help his "children" grow, to equip them to deal with false teaching. His successors did not attempt to teach sheep how to fight wolves. That task belonged to the shepherds.

The Pastorals know of divisions over the Pauline heritage in Ephesus and environs: 2 Timothy 1:15 states: "You are aware that *all who are in Asia have turned away from me*, including Phygelus and Hermogenes." These letters are not isolated witnesses.[20] The seven letters to the seven Asian churches embedded in Revelation 1–3 speak of false apostles and "the Nicolaitans" at Ephesus (2:2, 6), slanderous "Jews" at Smyrna (2:9), "the teaching of Balaam" and other "Nicolaitans" at Pergamum (2:14–15), while Thyatira is plagued with those who "tolerate that woman Jezebel, who calls herself a prophet and is teaching and beguiling my servants" (2:20–23), and Philadelphia has to endure "the synagogue of Satan" (3:9). Ignatius of Antioch, who, like Paul, was taken to Rome and eventually executed, wrote to Christian groups in the Asian cities of Ephesus, Magnesia, Tralles, Philadelphia and Smyrna. False teaching is his leading concern.[21] In short, the Paul of Acts 20:28–30 was not taking a wild shot in the dark. There *were* prophets and teachers with differing messages in Asia Minor after his "departure." How does this information assist with determining the date of Acts? None of the texts introduced has a firm date. Revelation is usually dated c. 95,[22] Ignatius c. 115 (although this date is probably too early),[23] and the Pastoral Epistles from the 90s to 120 or later.[24] Acts 20:28–30 is closest to the Pastorals in style, but this may have little bearing upon the date. All three of these sources speak of "heresy" in Asia Minor in the period 90–120. They provide additional support for a *terminus a quo* of c. 95 CE for Acts, or, at the very least, no impediment to that benchmark.

Since the farewell speech of Paul (Acts 20:17–35) is quite aware of post-Pauline conflicts, while similar language and issues appear in Revelation, Ignatius, Polycarp,[25] and the Pastorals, little imagination and minimal specula-tion is required to locate Acts in the turbulent milieu of theological conflict in Asia c. 100–130 CE. I thus take strong exception to Barrett's description of Acts as a "history of the church in a time of conflict written in a time of consensus."[26] Luke was urging and proposing a consensus in a later era of conflict. Two ways of managing these conflicts were appealing to the methods of earlier times and stating the message in clear and concrete terms.[27] The historian's problem is not that Luke depicted a fictitious consensus; it is that his description became so successful that it eventually passed for simple fact.

One basis for placing Acts earlier than Revelation is that its ". . . perspective of the Roman government and of Christians within the empire is so different."[28] This is not a potent argument. Apocalyptic hatred of the evil empire may be more popular in periods of widespread persecution (the first of which came in the middle of the third century), but this attitude is not a simply a response to contemporary events. Jewish allegiances and opinions during the decades leading up to the revolt that began in 66 ranged from the strongly pro-Roman (e.g., the Sadducees) to the bitterly anti-Roman (the Qumran sect and various rebel groups). Even in the face of persecution, Paul and the writers of 1 Peter and *1 Clement* urge obedience to authority.[29] One means of attacking injustice is to burn down the city (Rev 18:1–19:3); another is to protest that the victims are loyal subjects. "Attitude toward the imperial government" may help locate the social milieu of a text, but it is an insecure criterion for establishing date.[30] By this criterion the vigorously apocalyptic and militantly anti-Roman *Acts of Paul* would be earlier than the canonical book.

Warnings about eschatological false prophets continue into the second cen-tury and beyond (e.g., *Didache* 16). One characteristic of some later writings is to associate these admonitions with followers of the Lord. The author of 1 John, an anonymous community leader, (2:18), came in due course to be seen as the "Beloved Disciple." Others appealed to "the apostles" in general, as in Jude 17–18: "But you, beloved, must remember the predictions of the apostles of our Lord Jesus Christ; for they said to you, 'In the last time there will be scoffers, indulging their own ungodly lusts.'" Jude is followed by 2 Peter 3:2–4; both are rather clumsy fictions that simultaneously look back to the apostolic age and pretend to be products of that age. Acts belongs among works that assign the task of thwarting false teachers to the successors of Paul (and others), earthly "shepherds" with responsibility for the flock. The closest "fit" to the picture in Acts is that of the Pastoral Epistles, although 1–2 Timothy and Titus do not use

Table 6.1: Shepherds and Teachers

Acts 20:28 προσέχετε ἑαυτοῖς καὶ παντὶ τῷ **ποιμνίῳ**, ἐν ᾧ ὑμᾶς τὸ πνεῦμα τὸ ἅγιον ἔθετο **ἐπισκόπους, ποιμαίνειν** τὴν ἐκκλησίαν τοῦ θεοῦ, ἣν περιεποιήσατο διὰ τοῦ αἵματος τοῦ ἰδίου. Keep watch over yourselves and over all the **flock**, of which the Holy Spirit has made you **overseers**, to **shepherd** the church of God that he obtained with the blood of his own Son. **2 Clem 5:2–4** For the Lord said, "You will be like lambs among **wolves**." But Peter replied, "What if the wolves tear the lambs to pieces?" Jesus answered: "After their death the lambs should not fear the wolves . . ." **Ignatius Phil 2:1b–2** Where the **Shepherd** is, there follow like sheep. For there are many specious **wolves** who, by means of wicked pleasures, capture those who run God's race. **Didache 16:3** For in the final days multitudes of false prophets and seducers will appear. Sheep will turn into **wolves**, and love into hatred.[31]	**Ephesians 4:11** καὶ αὐτὸς ἔδωκεν τοὺς μὲν ἀποστόλους, τοὺς δὲ προφήτας, τοὺς δὲ εὐαγγελιστάς, τοὺς δὲ **ποιμένας** καὶ διδασκάλους The gifts he gave were that some would be apostles, some prophets, some evangelists, some **pastors** and teachers **1 Timothy 4:1** Τὸ δὲ πνεῦμα ῥητῶς λέγει ὅτι ἐν ὑστέροις καιροῖς ἀποστήσονταί τινες τῆς πίστεως, προσέχοντες πνεύμασιν πλάνοις καὶ διδασκαλίαις δαιμονίων Now the Spirit expressly says that *in later times* some will renounce the faith by paying attention to deceitful spirits and teachings of demons. **2 Timothy 3:1** Τοῦτο δὲ γίνωσκε, ὅτι ἐν ἐσχάταις ἡμέραις ἐνστήσονται καιροὶ χαλεποί You must understand this, that *in the last days distressing times* will come. **2 Timothy 4:3–4** ἔσται γὰρ καιρὸς ὅτε τῆς ὑγιαινούσης διδασκαλίας οὐκ ἀνέξονται, ἀλλὰ κατὰ τὰς ἰδίας ἐπιθυμίας ἑαυτοῖς	**1 Peter 5:1–4** Πρεσβυτέρους οὖν ἐν ὑμῖν παρακαλῶ ὁ συμπρεσβύτερος καὶ μάρτυς τῶν τοῦ Χριστοῦ παθημάτων . . . 2 **ποιμάνατε** τὸ ἐν ὑμῖν **ποίμνιον** τοῦ θεοῦ, **ἐπισκοποῦντες** μὴ ἀναγκαστῶς ἀλλὰ ἑκουσίως κατὰ θεόν, μηδὲ αἰσχροκερδῶς ἀλλὰ προθύμως, 3 μηδ' ὡς κατακυριεύοντες τῶν κλήρων ἀλλὰ τύποι γινόμενοι τοῦ **ποιμνίου·** 4 καὶ φανερωθέντος τοῦ ἀρχιποιμένος κομιεῖσθε τὸν ἀμαράντινον τῆς δόξης στέφανον. Now as an elder myself and a witness of the sufferings of Christ . . . I exhort the elders among you to tend the **flock** of God that is in your charge, **exercising the oversight**, not under compulsion but willingly, as God would have you do it—not for sordid gain but eagerly. Do not lord it over those in your charge, but be examples to the **flock**. And when the chief shepherd appears, you will win the crown of glory that never fades away. **Jude 17–18** Ὑμεῖς δέ, ἀγαπητοί, μνήσθητε τῶν ῥημάτων τῶν προειρημένων ὑπὸ τῶν ἀποστόλων τοῦ κυρίου ἡμῶν Ἰησοῦ Χριστοῦ· 18 ὅτι ἔλεγον ὑμῖν, Ἐπ' ἐσχάτου [τοῦ] χρόνου ἔσονται

Acts 20:29–30

29. ἐγὼ οἶδα ὅτι εἰσελεύσονται μετὰ τὴν ἄφιξίν μου λύκοι βαρεῖς εἰς ὑμᾶς μὴ φειδόμενοι τοῦ ποιμνίου, 30 καὶ ἐξ ὑμῶν αὐτῶν ἀναστήσονται ἄνδρες λαλοῦντες διεστραμμένα τοῦ ἀποσπᾶν τοὺς μαθητὰς ὀπίσω αὐτῶν

I know that after I have gone, savage wolves will come in among you, not sparing the flock. Some even from your own group will come distorting the truth in order to entice the disciples to follow them."

ἐπισωρεύσουσιν διδασκάλους κνηθόμενοι τὴν ἀκοήν, 4 καὶ ἀπὸ μὲν τῆς ἀληθείας τὴν ἀκοὴν ἀποστρέψουσιν, ἐπὶ δὲ τοὺς μύθους ἐκτραπήσονται.

For the time is coming when people will not put up with sound doctrine, but having itching ears, they will accumulate for themselves teachers to suit their own desires, 4 and will turn away from listening to the truth and wander away to myths.

ἐμπαῖκται κατὰ τὰς ἑαυτῶν ἐπιθυμίας πορευόμενοι τῶν ἀσεβειῶν.

But you, beloved, must remember the predictions of the apostles of our Lord Jesus Christ; for they said to you, "In the last time there will be scoffers, indulging their own ungodly lusts."

the metaphor of shepherding. John 21, which belongs to the period c. 100–120, does use this imagery (verses 15–17).[32]

SUCCESSION

Chapter Four claimed and asserted that Luke's picture of "presbyters" as local church officers is anachronistic. In general Acts views apostles and "others" (James and Paul) as persons who "govern" presbyters. Paul explicitly "hands over" authority to the presbyters of Ephesus in Acts 20:17–38. Acts 21:18–25 presents James with "the presbyters." This picture resembles the ideal of an Ignatian bishop, surrounded by a circle of silent presbyters, except that Luke has the group deliver their message in unison.[33] I believe that the author of Acts is aware of desires and efforts to have one "bishop" in each community, assisted by deacons and supported by presbyters, but that he has some reservations about this development. The era of "one-man rule" should have been buried with Peter and James—who themselves were not practitioners of strict "monarchy."

The subject is made difficult by anachronism. On the one hand there is continuity. In the course of the second century, the Christian bodies of most cities came to accept an organization headed by one bishop, who was assisted by "deacons," (διάκονοι) and associated with presbyters. This government has continued to the present day among catholic bodies, including Roman Catholics, the Orthodox, the Anglican, and some Lutheran churches. On the other hand, when the system developed, there was as yet no "laity," for the distinction between "clergy" and "people" did not yet exist and would not be clearly drawn before the third century. Not until the last part of the second century would this mode of government by bishops, presbyters, and deacons be related to the formal doctrine of succession.

Irenaeus, Bishop of Lyons c. 180, presents the first developed statement of the apostolic succession of bishops.[34] 1 *Clement* (see below) advances rather tentative notions of succession but does not exhibit a notion of episcopal government. At times the terms *episkopos* and *presbyteros* are interchangeable, and the Corinthian community addressed in 1 *Clement* is led by a group of presbyters. Ignatius of Antioch advocated the idea of one bishop per community as a source and symbol of unity, but he does not speak of succession. Irenaeus is the first surviving author to emphasize the idea of succession together with that of episcopal government.[35] The origin of the concept of succession is in the philosophical tradition. The concept also appears in the writings of the Rabbis.[36] "Apostolic Succession" was a means to guarantee the orthodoxy of the incumbent bishop. In many places and for a long time, succession did not involve "tactile" ordination by a bishop so much as it portrayed the sequence of accredited leaders.[37]

On the question of "succession" Acts stands rather close in practice to the theory expressed in 1 *Clement* 42:1–4; 44:2–3:

The apostles received the gospel for us from the Lord Jesus Christ; Jesus, the Christ, was sent from God. Thus Christ is from God and the apostles from Christ. In both instances the orderly procedure depends on God's will. And so the apostles, after receiving their orders and being fully convinced by the resurrection of our Lord Jesus Christ and assured by God's word, went out in the confidence of the Holy Spirit to preach the good news that God's Kingdom was about to come. They preached in country and city (κατὰ . . . πόλεις),[38] and appointed their first converts, after testing them by the Spirit, to be the bishops and deacons (ἐπισκόπους καὶ διακόνους) of future believers. 44.2 Now our apostles, thanks to our Lord Jesus Christ, knew that there was going to be strife over the title of bishop (ἐπισκοπῆς). It was for this reason and because they had been given an accurate knowledge of the future, that they appointed the officers we have mentioned. Furthermore, they later added a codicil to the effect that, should these die, other approved (δεδοκιμασμένοι) men should succeed to their ministry.[39] In the light of this, we view it as a breach of justice to remove from their ministry those who were appointed either by them [i.e., the apostles] or later on and with the whole church's consent, by others of the proper standing, and who, long enjoying the everybody's approval, have ministered to Christ's flock faultlessly, humbly, and unassumingly.[40]

This narrative is a logical development of the idea that those who receive the emissaries of Christ receive the one who sent Christ (Matthew 10:40; John 13:20). *1 Clement*, in a passage often reminiscent of Luke and Acts,[41] presents the essence of the notion of succession without the formality of a list or a "doctrine." God sends Christ who sends apostles who approve "bishops and deacons,"[42] and, it will transpire, the last are to approve of *their* successors.[43] All of this is related to an appeal to the church at Corinth to reinstate deposed *presbyters*. At 54:2 the author proposes a solution. The individual responsible for the problem should say: "If it is my fault that revolt, strife, and schism have arisen, I will leave, I will go away wherever you wish, and do what the congregation orders. Only let Christ's flock live in peace with their appointed presbyters."[44] Luke is evidently aware of the theory that presbyters have succeeded the apostles, but because he does not articulate the idea, he cannot be said to promote a doctrine of succession.[45] Yet he is willing to describe the Jerusalem presbyters as taking over responsibilities earlier performed by the apostles. In Acts 11:30 the believers in Antioch send the money they have collected to Jerusalem, "sending it to the elders by Barnabas and Saul." Earlier (4:35, 36; 5:2) such funds had been presented to the *apostles*.

The Pastor has a similar viewpoint: "You then, my child, be strong in the grace that is in Christ Jesus; and what you have heard from me through many witnesses entrust to faithful people who will be able to teach others as well." (2 Timothy 2:1–2) The temporal perspective of the text is as follows:

1. Paul, first generation and source of the tradition, which is public ("many witnesses"),[46] was followed by

2. Timothy, second generation, who was equipped with grace to say the right things to the right persons, that is, the
3. Faithful people, those of the third generation (in the present time), who will hand on the tradition to
4. Others, who will emerge in the future.

The Pastor is less interested in accredited tradents, a line of succession, than in the *content* of the tradition.[47] The name of Paul alone will not suffice, since rival traditions also appeal to his authority. The key word is "entrust" (παράθου), with its related noun, παραθήκη "deposit," which Timothy is to "protect" (φυλάσσειν).[48] "Protection" is the essence of the job-description for a shepherd. The Lucan approach to this matter emerges in his use of that verb παρατίθημι: "And now I commend (παρατίθεμαι) you to God and to the message of his grace . . ." (Acts 20:32).[49] Luke prefers to speak of ministry in dynamic and *conceptual* terms rather than in terms of offices. Consider the "parable" in Luke 17:7–10:

> "Who among you would say to your slave who has just come in from plowing or tending sheep (ἀροτριῶντα ἢ ποιμαίνοντα) in the field, 'Come here at once and take your place at the table' Would you not rather say to him, 'Prepare supper for me, put on your apron and serve me (διακόνει) while I eat and drink; later you may eat and drink'? Do you thank the slave for doing what was commanded? So you also, when you have done all that you were ordered to do, say, 'We are worthless slaves; we have done only what we ought to have done!' "

Cultivation and planting are standard metaphors for evangelization (Mark 4:1–8 and its parallels, especially the parables of Matthew 13; cf. 1 Corinthians 3:6, "I planted, Apollos watered . . ." and 9:7). Tending sheep becomes the standard trope for "pastoral care,"[50] and the verb "serve" derives from the noun "servant," (διάκονος), adopted into English as "deacon." The Lucan parable comes in response to a demand posed by "the Apostles" (Luke 17:5) in the context of pastoral care: protection of the weak and forgiveness of sins. Neither type of "ministry" is superior, nor should leaders focus upon their status and emoluments.[51] Interpreters have proposed readings of the anecdote about Mary and Martha (Luke 10:38–42) in relation to the ministry of service and possible debates about its relation to the ministry of the word.[52] Luke's definitive statement on the subject comes during the "Last Supper," into which he inserts some of the material from Mark 10:35–45:[53]

GENUINE BENEFACTORS

Table 6.2 reveals that Luke retains the formal parallelism of Mark but alters the language. His clauses are shorter, sharper, and more specific. He notes that Gentile monarchs rejoice in the title "benefactor." They certainly did.[54] The plural is valid but even more discreet: the one gentile king who really mattered

Table 6.2: True Benefactors

Mark 10:42–44	Luke 22:25–27
... ὁ Ἰησοῦς λέγει αὐτοῖς, Οἴδατε ὅτι οἱ δοκοῦντες ἄρχειν τῶν ἐθνῶν κατακυριεύουσιν αὐτῶν καὶ οἱ μεγάλοι αὐτῶν κατεξουσιάζουσιν αὐτῶν.	ὁ δὲ εἶπεν αὐτοῖς, Οἱ βασιλεῖς τῶν ἐθνῶν κυριεύουσιν αὐτῶν
	καὶ οἱ ἐξουσιάζοντες αὐτῶν εὐεργέται καλοῦνται.
43 οὐχ οὕτως δέ ἐστιν ἐν ὑμῖν·ἀλλ' ὃς ἂν θέλῃ μέγας γενέσθαι ἐν ὑμῖν, ἔσται ὑμῶν διάκονος, 44 καὶ ὃς ἂν θέλῃ ἐν ὑμῖν εἶναι πρῶτος, ἔσται πάντων δοῦλος·	26 ὑμεῖς δὲ οὐχ οὕτως, ἀλλ' ὁ μείζων ἐν ὑμῖν γινέσθω ὡς ὁ νεώτερος, καὶ ὁ ἡγούμενος ὡς ὁ διακονῶν. 27 τίς γὰρ μείζων, ὁ ἀνακείμενος ἢ ὁ διακονῶν; οὐχὶ ὁ ἀνακείμενος; ἐγὼ δὲ ἐν μέσῳ ὑμῶν εἰμι ὡς ὁ διακονῶν.
Jesus said to *the disciples,* "You know that among the Gentiles those whom they recognize as their rulers lord it over them, and their great ones are tyrants over them. But it is not so among you; but,, whoever wishes to become great among you must be your servant, and whoever wishes to be first among you must be slave of all	*Jesus* said to *the disciples,* "The kings of the Gentiles lord it over them; and those in authority over them are called benefactors. But not so with you; rather the greatest among you must become like the youngest, and the leader like one who serves. For who is greater, the one who is at the table or the one who serves? Is it not the one at the table? But I am among you as one who serves.

had his headquarters in Rome. Luke has no objection to benefaction. He can summarize the ministry of Jesus with two participles, one of which is "doing benefaction" (Acts 10:38); the other is "healing." What Luke does object to is the practice of benefaction as a means of self-glorification and as a warrant for the manipulation of others. Examples of pseudo-benefaction include the wicked "King Herod" of Acts 12[55] and the rich man of Luke 12:16–20 (21), who, rather than distribute his abundance to the poor, will erect larger barns to hoard his surplus (and thereby make a killing by selling at exorbitant prices in a time of scarcity).[56] Leaders of Christian communities need expect no credit. They do what they ought to do. Luke replaces the "servant" (διάκονος) of Mark with, literally, "the younger," (ὁ νεώτερος), a term that can refer to "junior" (its Latin equivalent) functionaries. Its antonym is presbyter. Acts 5:6 represents one duty of the "younger": the disposal of dead bodies.[57] Little prestige attached to that task. In place of Mark's more general "first," i.e., a leading person, Luke uses the term "the leader," used generally in Greek as in English and specifically for leaders of Christian communities.[58] The role model for the leader is that of the "servant." Jesus is the example of the kind of service and benefaction to which leaders should aspire and which they should emulate.[59] One emerging candidate for this role of "the leader" was "the bishop."

Ignatius, an early second century Bishop of Antioch, had no qualms about following Christ on the path to martyrdom.[60] In his images for what we call "ministers," however, Ignatius is more apt to compare the bishop to God the Father, the deacons to Jesus Christ, and the presbyters to the apostles.[61] Behind this "three-fold ministry" evidently stand two different "systems," one of presbyters, the other of Bishops and Deacons. These have merged/are merging in the time (and very much in the hope) of Ignatius. Where Luke would (and did?) disagree with the conception of Ignatius is in attributing to "the leader" the *image* of authority (God the father) rather than the ministry of christly service. Luke, as stated, prefers to speak of "ministerial functions" in conceptual terms. In the narrative of the selection of a replacement for Judas (Acts 1:15–26), the words ἐπισκοπή, διακονία, and ἀποστολή ("oversight," related to "bishop;" "ministry," related to "deacon," and "apostleship") appear as designations for the office (1: 17, 20, 25). "Ministry" (διακονία) appears eight times in Acts, never in Luke.[62] The verb "to minister" occurs twice in Acts and eight times in Luke, but their author does not use the noun "minister," i.e., "deacon."

At the beginning of Acts 6 Luke seems to discard the ideal of a single type or order of ministry:

> Now during those days, when the disciples were increasing in number, the Hellenists complained against the Hebrews because their widows were being neglected in the daily distribution (διακονία) of food. And the twelve called together the whole community of the disciples and said, "It is not right that we should neglect the word of God in order to wait on tables (διακονεῖν τραπέζαις). Therefore, friends, select from among yourselves seven men of good standing, full of the Spirit and of wisdom, whom we may appoint to this task, while we, for our part, will devote ourselves to prayer and to serving (διακονία) the word." (6:1–4)[63]

Henceforth separate groups will engage in the "ministry of service" and the "ministry of the word." This is not a theological change. Like the dramatic reversal of Luke 22:35–38, which effectively annuls the instructions of Luke 9:1–6; 10:1–12, this change reflects different circumstances: growth and attendant diversity. Luke does not call the seven "deacons." (Nor does he narrate details about their ministry of service; Stephen and Philip engage in a full-fledged "ministry of the word.") Nonetheless, Christians have used Acts 6: (1) 2–7 as the Epistle for the Ordination of Deacons. One reason for this practice is Acts 6:6, wherein the seven stand before the apostle, followed by prayer and the imposition of hands. From the late second century onward this ceremony impressed its readers as an ordination.[64]

Luke's notion(s) of presbyters came under review in Chapter Four, in connection with the farewell speech of Paul. That address contains the single use in Luke/Acts of the noun *episkopos*, ("supervisor" or "overseer"), the source of the English word "bishop." Luke and Acts are thus familiar with the concepts of oversight, seniority, and service that underlie the three orders of Ignatius. Luke prefers to describe these functions dynamically with verbs (such as "serving") or with abstract nouns (such as "service"). "Presbyter" has two apparent senses. Always in the plural, the noun refers to a body of unknown origin at Jerusalem that functions as a kind of council associated first with the apostles and later with James (Acts 15 and 21).[65] The other usage refers to community officers appointed by Paul and Barnabas in (Derbe?) Lystra, Iconium, and Pisidian Antioch 14:23,[66] with the suggestion that more than one presbyter was named in each church.[67] So at Ephesus in 20:17, there are "presbyters of the church." They have, as described in chapter four, pastoral jurisdiction and "shepherd the flock." In that capacity these officers are characterized as "supervisors" (*episkopoi*). They are to serve the "weak," in response to the Lord's command (20:33–35). Luke may not care whether church leaders are called "presbyters" or "bishops," but he does insist that all "ministers"—not only subordinate "deacons"—adhere to a "servant" model; and he displays no support for the model of Ignatius that calls for a single pastor in charge of each church.[68] I reiterate the hypothesis that Luke was aware of the discussions and developments that stand behind the ideal model of church organization expounded and propounded by Ignatius of Antioch—one Christian leader in each city with deacons as his agents and a council of presbyters for support—and that he has some reservations about this model.[69] At this point the subject of Luke and "Early Catholicism" enters (from stage left).

EARLY CATHOLICISM

"Early Catholicism" is, for good reasons, a somewhat moribund subject nowadays. In its heyday—the 1960s and 1970s—the term became a rallying cry for the renewal of an early Lutheran principle. The reforming slogan *sola scriptura* held that scripture was the single criterion for doctrine and set the Bible against ecclesiastical tradition. Martin Luther himself established a criterion for scripture: "that which puts forth Christ." On this basis his first edition of the German NT relegated Hebrews, James, Jude, and Revelation to an appendix. Although this proposal did not gain acceptance, most of the bodies that separated from Rome removed from the OT those books not found in the Hebrew Bible[70] Adjustments were required before scripture could serve as the criterion.[71] With the rise of historical criticism it transpired that the New Testament contained some post-apostolic writings, and this weakened the (by now traditional) foundation of Protestantism. While some rejected the findings of critical scholars and maintained the "traditional" dates and authors, the more radical looked for new grounds.[72] Among these was Ernst Käsemann, who advocated a "canon within the canon." For that courageous scholar and others, mainly liberal German Protestants, the pursuit of "authentic Christianity" required the ferreting out of every taint of post-apostolic dilution and contamination.[73] Luke and Acts became a "storm center" of their inquisition.[74]

The essence of "Early Catholicism" is what Americans call "moving into the mainstream." Time and growth require adjustments, one of which involves becoming an institution. At the heart of the issue is the task of maintaining what seems to be an oxymoron: an "otherworldly institution." The author of Acts is no torch-brandishing counter-cultural fanatic. He is open to Roman Imperial Society, but mindless flag-waving is no more his style than is that brandished torch. Luke attacks the greed of the newly well-to-do (a group from which many leaders would be drawn) and does not wish them to put on the airs of the real aristocracy, to revel in honor due to "benefactors." Ironically, it was the development of the episcopal system that staved off the encroachment of benefactors for at least several centuries.[75] The irony is that Luke evidently suspected that powerful bishops would soon "lord it over" their subjects and rejoice in the status of benefactor (cf. Luke 22:25, above). His fears would not be fulfilled for something like a millennium.

As Haenchen came to recognize in the later editions of his commentary on Acts, "Early Catholic" is not the appropriate label for Luke.[76] One explanation that he provides for this unsuitability is that Acts was written prior to the emergence of Early Catholicism. A better explanation, in my view, is that Luke to some degree opposes certain aspects of the development. If the spirit is a bit of an opportunist, it still blows where it wills, as any will discover who try to find in Acts a fixed pattern in the relation between spiritual gifts and Baptism.[77] This ambiguity (if that is the proper term for it) is manifest in Acts 13:1–3.

"ORDINATIONS"

In Acts 13:1–3 the five named "prophets and teachers" receive an oracle in the context of worship.[78] (See Table 6.3.) The ceremony that follows appears to be a sort of "commissioning," but it has essential features of an ordination, as, for that matter, did the "appointment" of the Seven (6:6), discussed above. The "charismatic phenomenon," if you would, precedes the "institutional rite." Barnabas and Saul are not instituted into an office, but dispatched upon a task. Any who wish to imagine a clear transition from the charismatic to the institutional church will find the continuing association of a prophetic element in 1 Timothy 1:18 and 4:14 (as well as 2 Timothy 1:6) a bit disappointing.[79] A survey of Church Orders from antiquity through the present will reveal that Christians have never taken a purely formal, institutional view of Church offices. The difference in Acts is not that it is earlier, for it employs the language of developed rites; it is that Luke resists any efforts to "hem the Spirit in." While Acts 14:23 describes the appointment of presbyters in a manner that closely corresponds to Titus 1:5–6 and exhibits features that will characterize subsequent ordinations, notably the verb χειροτονέω. Luke has no compunctions about referring to prophets and oracles; and this is true even in chapters 20–21, where problems caused by false teachers and prophets are frankly acknowledged.[80] Although he transforms glossolalia into a miracle of multiple languages and will not for an instant suggest that Christian assemblies are uncontrolled frenzies of

Table 6.3: "Ordinations"

Acts 13:1–3

Ἦσαν δὲ ἐν Ἀντιοχείᾳ κατὰ τὴν οὖσαν ἐκκλησίαν **προφῆται** καὶ διδάσκαλοι ὅ τε Βαρναβᾶς καὶ Συμεὼν ὁ καλούμενος Νίγερ, καὶ Λούκιος ὁ Κυρηναῖος, Μαναήν τε Ἡρῴδου τοῦ τετραάρχου σύντροφος καὶ Σαῦλος. 2 λειτουργούντων δὲ αὐτῶν τῷ κυρίῳ καὶ νηστευόντων εἶπεν τὸ πνεῦμα τὸ ἅγιον, Ἀφορίσατε δή μοι τὸν Βαρναβᾶν καὶ Σαῦλον εἰς τὸ ἔργον ὃ προσκέκλημαι αὐτούς. 3 **τότε νηστεύσαντες καὶ προσευξάμενοι καὶ ἐπιθέντες τὰς χεῖρας** αὐτοῖς ἀπέλυσαν.

Now in the church at Antioch there were prophets and teachers: Barnabas, Simeon who was called Niger, Lucius of Cyrene, Manaen a member of the court of Herod the ruler, and Saul. While they were worshiping the Lord and **fasting**, the Holy Spirit said, "Set apart for me Barnabas and Saul for the work to which I have called them." Then after **fasting and praying they laid their hands on them** and sent them off.

Acts 6:6

οὓς ἔστησαν ἐνώπιον τῶν ἀποστόλων, καὶ **προσευξάμενοι ἐπέθηκαν αὐτοῖς τὰς χεῖρας**
They had these men stand before the apostles, who **prayed and laid their hands on them.**

Acts 14:23

χειροτονήσαντες δὲ αὐτοῖς κατ᾽ ἐκκλησίαν πρεσβυτέρους **προσευξάμενοι μετὰ νηστειῶν** παρέθεντο αὐτοὺς τῷ κυρίῳ εἰς ὃν πεπιστεύκεισαν.
And after they had *appointed* elders for them in each church, with **prayer and fasting** they entrusted them to the Lord in whom they had come to believe

1 Timothy 4:14

μὴ ἀμέλει τοῦ ἐν σοὶ χαρίσματος, ὃ ἐδόθη σοι **διὰ προφητείας μετὰ ἐπιθέσεως τῶν χειρῶν** τοῦ πρεσβυτερίου.
Do not neglect the gift that is in you, which was given to you through **prophecy with the laying on of hands** by the council of elders.

1 Timothy 1:18

Ταύτην τὴν παραγγελίαν παρατίθεμαί σοι, τέκνον Τιμόθεε, κατὰ τὰς προαγούσας ἐπὶ σὲ **προφητείας,** ἵνα στρατεύῃ ἐν αὐταῖς τὴν καλὴν στρατείαν
I am giving you these instructions, Timothy, my child, in accordance with the **prophecies** made earlier about you, so that by following them you may fight the good fight,

2 Timothy 1:6

δι᾽ ἣν αἰτίαν ἀναμιμνῄσκω σε ἀναζωπυρεῖν τὸ χάρισμα τοῦ θεοῦ, ὅ ἐστιν ἐν σοὶ **διὰ τῆς ἐπιθέσεως τῶν χειρῶν μου**
For this reason I remind you to rekindle the gift of God that is within **you through the laying on of my hands.**

1 Timothy 5:22

Χεῖρας ταχέως μηδενὶ **ἐπιτίθει,** μηδὲ κοινώνει ἁμαρτίαις ἀλλοτρίαις· σεαυτὸν ἁγνὸν τήρει.
Do not **ordain** anyone hastily

Titus 1:5–6

Τούτου χάριν ἀπέλιπόν σε ἐν Κρήτῃ, ἵνα τὰ λείποντα ἐπιδιορθώσῃ καὶ **καταστήσῃς κατὰ πόλιν πρεσβυτέρους,** ὡς ἐγώ σοι διεταξάμην, 6 εἴ τίς ἐστιν ἀνέγκλητος, μιᾶς γυναικὸς ἀνήρ, τέκνα ἔχων πιστά, μὴ ἐν κατηγορίᾳ ἀσωτίας ἢ ἀνυπότακτα
I left you behind in Crete for this reason, so that you should put in order what remained to be done, and should **appoint elders in every town**, as I directed you: someone who is blameless, married only once, whose children are believers, not accused of debauchery and not rebellious

rabid fanatics, Luke does not advocate full-scale "law-and-order" solutions to the problems of growth or social aberration. Still, he does show a preference for describing the gift of the Spirit as—or even restricting it to—the ceremonial imposition of hands by apostles (8:14–17) or Paul (19:1–7). Nevertheless, it should be noted that Paul himself received this gift at the hands of the otherwise unknown Ananias (9:17). The texts in Acts 8 and 19 appear to imply an incomplete or defective initiation and have long posed exegetical problems. Like the "ordination" ceremonies, they testify to an author who wishes to regulate but not to institutionalize the Spirit. Luke's view is not that of an author who is seeking to accommodate the "new idea" of imposition of hands by officials. He accepts it and will attribute the practice to the apostles, but he rejects any intimation that the Church has God within its control.[81]

"Bourgeois Morality"

Luke may well have had no strong objections to the conventional notions of the "Household Codes," in which the duties and responsibilities of husbands and wives, parents and children, owners and slaves are set forth in clear and simple terms. The impact of this standard for contemporary "family values" is ubiquitous in Christian texts of Asia Minor from c. 80–140 CE (Colossians, Ephesians, 1 Peter, 1 Clement, the Pastoral Epistles, Ignatius of Antioch, and Polycarp of Smyrna),[82] but one would have some difficulty reconstructing the Code from Luke and Acts. This is not simply because of Q passages like Luke 14:26 that seem a bit dissonant with the ideals of the Codes: "Whoever comes to me and does not hate father and mother, wife and children, brothers and sisters . . ." or 12:51–53.[83] Even more basic is Luke's lack of enthusiasm for marriage, in the absence of which exhortations to obey husband and parents lose much of their impetus.[84] Critics of Early Catholicism have not often included in their indictments its assumption that believers will marry and rear families, but this attitude is general and is as vulnerable to the charge of betraying the Pauline heritage (1 Corinthians 7!) as is any other allegation. Had Luke written the Pastoral Epistles, he would not have required that a bishop or deacon be "married only once" and be able to manage a household, which includes keeping his children in line (1 Timothy 3:1–4, 12). On the question of marriage and family life as *the* Christian ideal Luke sharply dissents from the post-Pauline world of Early Catholicism.[85]

Women

Although Luke is not the foremost promoter of women in leadership roles, he happily describes Tabitha/Dorcas as the head of a group of widows (Acts 9:36–42),[86] and since Tabitha and company were all women, more notably identifies Lydia as the head of the first community founded in the great missionary effort that followed the "Apostolic Council" (Acts 16:13–15, 40). The Pastor would not suffer women to teach (1 Timothy 2:12), but Luke permits Priscilla and Aquila to instruct no less (or more) a figure than Apollos (Acts 18:26).[87] The flame of emancipation may be dimming, but Luke has not plunged its torch into the icy water of circumscribed social structures.

I am unaware of any who posit antagonism toward marriage as an indication of early date, but arguments that any of these factors suggest a date earlier than that of *1 Clement* or the Pastoral Epistles have difficulty explaining Luke's familiarity with emerging church offices.[88] As shown above, Luke is quite aware of the concepts of "supervision," "seniority," and "ministry," the first and third of which are present as abstract nouns. He uses the terms "presbyters" and "bishops," but not "deacon(s)." The sole use of *episkopoi* in Acts (20:28) applies to those also called "presbyters" (20:17). The lack of a clear distinction between these two "titles" is also found, as noted previously, in *1 Clement* and in the Pastoral Epistles.[89] The matter is quite complex, but it may be said that these texts propose, in effect, "It makes no great difference whether these leaders are known as "presbyters" or "*episkopoi*."[90] In both Acts and the Pastoral Epistles, these leaders are to stave off false teaching and to lead by moral example.[91] *1 Clement* shares with Acts use of the term ἐπισκοπή, "oversight." In 44:1 and 3 it refers to a title and function that, in this case, relate to the Corinthian *presbyters*.[92] To sum up: In (Luke and) Acts one can see both emerging church order and debates about it. This is the world of *1 Clement*, Ignatius, Polycarp, and the Pastoral Epistles, the milieu of the "Apostolic Fathers." The texts relate to debates over the nature and function of church offices (cf. Luke 10:38–42; 17:7–10; 22:24–27; Acts 6:1–7). The author is sufficiently aware of "bishops" of the Ignatian type to have reservations about them. Like the Pastor, he anachronistically presents Paul as ordaining presbyters. These issues of the proper titles and functions of church leaders are at home in the opening decades of the Second Century.

Ecclesial Structure

Whatever his doctrine of the church, Luke's view of the *structure* of the Jerusalem community (which was not, after all, some primeval St. Swithun's in the Swamp, but the premier community of the movement) lacks anything that smacks, however faintly, of primitivism.[93] Τότε ἔδοξε τοῖς ἀποστόλοις καὶ τοῖς πρεσβυτέροις σὺν ὅλῃ τῇ ἐκκλησίᾳ . . ."Then the apostles and the elders, with the consent of the whole church, decided . . ." (Acts 15:22). This introductory phrase is redolent with the verbiage of official decrees, a style seen most clearly in 15:24–26.[94] If this sounds a bit pretentious today, it was far from unusual at its time. Throughout the Imperial period "lesser folk" unabashedly imitated the turgid gravity of official pronouncements: "Where two neighbors at a corner pub today will raise their glasses and at most exchange a friendly 'Cheers!' the two in antiquity seem to have said, 'Be it resolved, to call ourselves the society of . . .'"[95] Yet, Luke's object was not simply to demonstrate that this fresh sect could employ bureaucratic jargon in all its sonorous plenitude. Even more important was the tableau of a duly constituted corporation executing its task with that crisp efficiency which proper hierarchy alone can provide—and to which "sects" would never dream of aspiring.

Acts 15 offers its audience a memorable picture of a civic body, with officers ("apostles" and "presbyters") and a "citizen" body. The former debate, orate, and propose; the latter listen, applaud, and vote the resolution up or down. A scene from Hellenistic Jewish history illustrates the "political" character of this scene. 1 Maccabees 14:25–45 was probably familiar to the author of Acts and may have provided some inspiration:

> [28]In Asaramel, *in the great assembly of the priests and the people and the rulers of the nation and the elders of the country*, (ἐπὶ συναγωγῆς μεγάλης ἱερέων καὶ λαοῦ καὶ ἀρχόντων ἔθνους καὶ τῶν πρεσβυτέρων τῆς χώρας) the following was proclaimed to us: [29] "*Since* wars often occurred in the country, Simon son of Mattathias, a priest of the sons of Joarib, and his brothers . . . [41]The Jews and their priests *have resolved* (εὐδόκησαν) that Simon should be their leader and high priest forever . . ." [46]*All the people agreed* (εὐδόκησεν πᾶς ὁ λαὸς) to grant Simon the right to act in accordance with these decisions.

Such "imitation" was not an isolated phenomenon, for it could not have escaped the attention of Luke that various craft and cultic guilds executed just such decrees. Ramsay MacMullen, just cited on the convivial habits of the ancients, says that the "internal organization" of such organizations mimicked "the high-sounding terminology of larger, municipal bodies, the nomenclature of officialdom . . . At least the larger craft associations constituted in every detail miniature cities."[96] Be it therefore known to all persons by these presents that the Church at Jerusalem was no congeries of contentious and competitive "house-churches." It was a properly organized body that conducted its business in proper accordance with conventional procedures, a "miniature city." The contrast between the Jerusalem Church and the Sanhedrin lay not in their respective structures, but in their contrasting ways of conducting business.[97] Christian assemblies ran like Swiss watches; meetings of the Sanhedrin looked little different from mob-scenes on their worst days and from kangaroo courts on their best.[98]

GREED IN ITS INSTITUTIONAL PERSPECTIVE

Some may take it upon themselves to contend that the questions of money and the use of individual and community resources are the most ecumenical and suprahistorical of issues, providing no basis for dating—or nearly anything else. Nonetheless, clusters of issues can be important. Widows and resources walk hand in hand. John Chrysostom said that managing the demands of widows required considerable φιλοσοφία ("philosophy").[99] One doubts that he had reference to the nicer facets of ontology. The widows of Acts 6:1–7 and 9:36–43 have needs and a willingness to articulate them.

Widows

Acts 6:1 juxtaposes two groups of widows. The importance of this description is that Luke visualizes "widows" as a group—or perhaps "groups," since one segment is complaining about the treatment accorded another. So also in 9:36–43: when Peter arrives from Lydda, he is welcomed by a chorus of weeping widows ("all the widows," 9:39), whose clothing, it transpires, was made by their now deceased patron, Tabitha.[100] Although Luke does not speak of a formal organization and represents widows as a pressure group, his perspective implies that widows constituted a body. Such a body is also present in the Pastoral Epistles. The Pastor devotes more space to discussing the qualities of widows—and with a good deal more immediate relevance and specificity—than he does to the qualifications of the "clergy": (1 Tim 5:3–16 vs. 3:1–7 [bishop] and 3:8–13 [deacons].[101] The passage opens and closes with the expression "the *genuine* (ὄντως) widows."[102] Real widows must be at least sixty, no mean feat in an era when life expectancy was around thirty and teenage girls—or younger—might often marry men a good decade older. To be eligible these widows can never have remarried and must be without any relatives capable of providing support. Naturally, they will be of good character; financial concerns are real, but money is not the only issue.[103] Actually or potentially organized widows and their financial dependence upon the community are also part of the Lucan horizon. Luke can describe the sort of "real widow" whom the Pastor would honor.

Anna has the requisite three score years, plus an enviable forty percent margin of safety. (See Table 6.4.) She was married but once and occupies herself

Table 6.4: Widows

Luke 2:36–37	1 Timothy 5:5, 9
Καὶ ἦν Ἄννα προφῆτις, θυγάτηρ Φανουήλ, ἐκ φυλῆς Ἀσήρ· αὕτη προβεβηκυῖα ἐν ἡμέραις πολλαῖς, ζήσασα μετὰ ἀνδρὸς ἔτη ἑπτὰ ἀπὸ τῆς παρθενίας αὐτῆς, 37 καὶ αὐτὴ **χήρα** ἕως ἐτῶν ὀγδοήκοντα τεσσάρων, ἣ οὐκ ἀφίστατο τοῦ ἱεροῦ νηστείαις καὶ **δεήσεσιν** λατρεύουσα **νύκτα καὶ ἡμέραν**.	5 ἡ δὲ ὄντως **χήρα** καὶ μεμονωμένη ἤλπικεν ἐπὶ θεὸν καὶ προσμένει ταῖς **δεήσεσιν** καὶ ταῖς προσευχαῖς **νυκτὸς καὶ ἡμέρας**. 9 Χήρα καταλεγέσθω μὴ ἔλαττον ἐτῶν ἑξήκοντα γεγονυῖα, ἑνὸς ἀνδρὸς γυνή
There was also a prophet, Anna the daughter of Phanuel, of the tribe of Asher. *She was of a great age, having lived with her husband seven years after her marriage,* then as a widow to the age of eighty-four. She never left the temple but worshiped there with fasting and prayer night and day	The real **widow**, left alone, has set her hope on God and continues in supplications and **prayers night and day**; Let a widow be put on the list if she is *not less than sixty years old* and has been *married only once*

with ceaseless devotion. This means that she will lack both the desire and the opportunity for becoming one of those roaming viragos that haunt the Pastor's dreams (1 Timothy 5:13). The important difference is that Anna is a prophet. That would not please the author of 1–2 Timothy and Titus, although he could draw consolation from the general and indirect character of her prophecy. Luke acknowledges the presence of women prophets, but he does not record what they said in mixed company. This is a classic example of a "mixed message." Luke prefers his female prophets to be widows or, even better, virgins. Other than Mary and the elderly matron Elizabeth, these women bequeath no inspired utterances to the future.[104] Luke understands the Pastor's concerns; those in search of issues regarding the prophetic activity of women need look no further and no later than 1 Corinthians 11:2–16 (cf. 1 Timothy 5:3–6). Luke might say, "Honor women prophets so long as they belong to the sacred past, or remain silent." Whereas the Pastor would rather speak of strict eligibility requirements, firmly administered, Luke believes that the Church possesses the "philosophy" needed to care for widows; such is wisdom enough for him.[105] The character of Anna ". . . focuses Luke's concerns about ascetic widowhood in the service of God." She is the patron of and model for widows and therefore another indicator of the presence of a "Widow's Order."[106] The perspective of Acts derives from an era in which widows were an organized, quasi-official group.[107]

Youth Groups

A more tenuous indicator of community size and date is the reference to "youth" or "young persons," (νεώτεροι, νεανίσκοι, Acts 5:6 and 10, respectively). Terminological variation does not enhance the argument that there was an organized body of "young people," and the data for such groups in early Christianity is scanty. "In the grouping of citizens in Hellenistic cities or in relation to societies it becomes a technical term for younger men over 20 as a group or body."[108] It is possible to consider references to "youth" in 1 Peter 5:5 and the Pastorals (Titus 2:4–8; 1 Timothy 5:1) as indicators of an organized body, but this is rather far from certain.[109] Polycarp can be read in support of the "order"/organized body position in that his *Philippians* 5:2 treats "deacons," while the subject of 5:3 is the νεώτεροι, but Polycarp (like the Pastor) commingles the "Church Order" with the "Household Code."[110] The term "youth" does appear in "Household Codes," so at the very least one can say that Luke's references to them cohere with that world. The community was large enough to have a body of young men who could function as a group for the performance of specific tasks. The implied audience of Acts understood the allusions in chapter 5, just as would the readers of 1 Peter and the Pastoral Epistles. Sex (or gender) is not everything. There is also money.

Money

This commodity pervades the book of Acts. As Luke T. Johnson ably demonstrates, possessions are both an important symbol and a vital reality to Luke.[111] The present task is not to review all of the relevant data, but to see whether the relationship between leadership and money has close affinities to literature c. 100 and later. Money was a recurrent issue for Paul the missionary, and the command that missionaries not carry cash was already a part of the pre-Synoptic tradition (Mark 6:8; Q [Luke] 10:4). One might be tempted to view Peter's words to the crippled beggar in Acts 3:8 ("Silver and gold have I none") in this light, but Peter (and John) are not itinerant missionaries, and the narrative has just mentioned the liquidation and distribution of assets in accordance with need (2:45). Peter does not keep community funds in his pocket. The one specific and positive example of an individual who sold property and placed the revenue at the feet of the apostles is Barnabas (4:37). He will later emerge as a leader.

It would be difficult to make a case from Acts for paid religious leaders. The next occurrence of the words "silver" and "gold" will be on the lips of Paul, whose "tentmaking" brought in enough to put his entire "ministry team" under canvas (20:33). Peter may have left everything to follow Jesus (Luke 5:11; 18:22), but Paul seems to have remained a wealthy man.[112] On the question of making money from the provision of religious services, however, Luke reveals himself to be lamentably unsound with regard to the doctrine of free enterprise. Polytheists attack Paul at Philippi (16:16–21), and Ephesus (19:21–27) because he has wounded them in their pocketbooks.[113] Luke has provided history with the eponym for the purchase of religious authority: Simony. "Peter said to Simon: 'The hell with you and your silver! Did you think that you could buy what God gives away?'" (Acts 8:20, my translation) Peter has no silver to give, nor, when grace is at stake, will he accept a dime. What we now call "clerical greed" is the single item of moral exhortation in Paul's farewell address.

Table 6.5 exhibits the intersection and coalescence of a number of themes examined in this study. "Greed" (πλεονεξία) is generally condemned as a vice, especially, but not exclusively, in the Pauline tradition.[114] Associations of greed with sexual misconduct, and idolatry (Colossians 3:5) were common in Judaism.[115] "Pursuit of wealth" (φιλαργυρία, etc.) and being "avaricious" (αἰσχροκερδής) are, for the present purpose, synonyms.[116] These words belong to the world of 1 Peter, the Pastoral Epistles, the Apostolic Fathers, and the Lukan writings.[117]

In exhorting leaders to spurn greed, these writers were not breaking new moral ground. Teachers who charged fees for their services had been targets of criticism since the days of the Sophists (fifth century BCE),[118] and all civilized cultures of the ancient world held that greed was a very bad thing. In the days of Plato (fourth century BCE) the claim that the pursuit of wealth lay behind many types of wrongdoing (cf. 1 Timothy 6:10) was already familiar.[119] Indeed, none of the qualities required for officers in the texts surveyed seem unduly rigorous. Did these people really need be told that potential bishops should not have problems with drinking or anger management? These are general virtues, also demanded, as the parallels show, of generals (and midwives).[120]

Difficult as this may be to believe, ancient people were willing to indulge in gossip about religious scandals, despite the fact that most of these passages appear to have treated sex or greed, and preferably both. That the subjects

Table 6.5 Greed

Luke and Acts; Paul	Qualifications	Heretics and General
Acts 20:33–35	**1 Tim 3:3**	**2 Peter 2: 3, 15**
ἀργυρίου ἢ χρυσίου ἢ ἱματισμοῦ οὐδενὸς ἐπεθύμησα· 34 αὐτοὶ γινώσκετε ὅτι ταῖς χρείαις μου καὶ τοῖς οὖσιν μετ' ἐμοῦ ὑπηρέτησαν αἱ χεῖρες αὗται. 35 πάντα ὑπέδειξα ὑμῖν ὅτι οὕτως κοπιῶντας δεῖ ἀντιλαμβάνεσθαι τῶν ἀσθενούντων . . .	μὴ πάροινον, μὴ πλήκτην, ἀλλὰ ἐπιεικῆ, ἄμαχον, **ἀφιλάργυρον**, [qualities of bishops] not a drunkard, not violent but gentle, not quarrelsome, and not a **lover of money**	3 καὶ ἐν **πλεονεξίᾳ** πλαστοῖς λόγοις ὑμᾶς ἐμπορεύσονται· οἷς τὸ κρίμα ἔκπαλαι οὐκ ἀργεῖ, καὶ ἡ ἀπώλεια αὐτῶν οὐ νυστάζει 15 καταλείποντες εὐθεῖαν ὁδὸν ἐπλανήθησαν, ἐξακολουθήσαντες τῇ ὁδῷ τοῦ Βαλαὰμ τοῦ Βοσόρ, ὃς μισθὸν ἀδικίας ἠγάπησεν
I coveted no one's silver or **gold** or clothing. You know for yourselves that I worked with my own hands to support myself and my companions. In all this I have given you an example that by such work we must support the weak . . .	**Didache 15.1** χειροτονήσατε οὖν ἑαυτοῖς ἐπισκόπους καὶ διακόνους ἀξίους τοῦ κυρίου, ἄνδρας πραεῖς καὶ **ἀφιλαργύρους**[122] καὶ δεδοκιμασμένους. Ordain for yourselves, therefore, bishops and deacons worthy of the Lord, men who are meek and **no lovers of money**, both tested and true.	And in their **greed** they will exploit you with deceptive words. Their condemnation, pronounced against them long ago, has not been idle, and their destruction is not asleep. 15 They have left the straight road and have gone astray, following the road of Balaam son of Bosor, who loved the wages of doing wrong,
Luke 16:14 Ἤκουον δὲ ταῦτα πάντα οἱ Φαρισαῖοι **φιλάργυροι** ὑπάρχοντες, καὶ ἐξεμυκτήριζον αὐτόν The Pharisees, who were	**Titus 1:7** δεῖ γὰρ τὸν ἐπίσκοπον ἀνέγκλητον εἶναι ὡς θεοῦ οἰκονόμον, μὴ αὐθάδη, μὴ ὀργίλον, μὴ πάροινον, μὴ πλήκτην, μὴ **αἰσχροκερδῆ** For a bishop, as God's steward, must be blameless; he must not be arrogant or quick-tempered or addicted to wine or violent or **greedy for gain**	**2 Tim 3:2**[126] ἔσονται γὰρ οἱ ἄνθρωποι φίλαυτοι, **φιλάργυροι,** ἀλαζόνες, ὑπερήφανοι, βλάσφημοι, γονεῦσιν ἀπειθεῖς, ἀχάριστοι, ἀνόσιοι For people will be lovers of themselves, **lovers of money**, boasters, arrogant, abusive, disobedient to their parents, ungrateful, unholy
	1 Timothy 3:8 Διακόνους ὡσαύτως σεμνούς, μὴ διλόγους, μὴ **αἰσχροκερδεῖς** Deacons likewise must be serious, not double-tongued, not indulging in much wine, **not greedy for money**	**1 Tim 6:10** ῥίζα γὰρ πάντων τῶν κακῶν ἐστιν ἡ **φιλαργυρία** For **the love of money** is a root of all kinds of evil.
	Polycarp 5:2 ὁμοίως διάκονοι ἄμεμπτοι κατενώπιον αὐτοῦ τῆς δικαιοσύνης ὡς θεοῦ καὶ Χριστοῦ διάκονοοι καὶ οὐκ ἀνθρώπων. μὴ διάβολοι, μὴ	**Titus 1:11** οὓς δεῖ ἐπιστομίζειν, οἵτινες ὅλους οἴκους ἀνατρέπουσιν διδάσκοντες ἃ μὴ δεῖ **αἰσχροῦ κέρδους χάριν.** They must be silenced, since they are upsetting whole families by teaching **for sor**

lovers of money, heard all this, and they ridiculed him

1 Thess 2:5[121]

οὔτε γάρ ποτε ἐν λόγῳ κολακείας ἐγενήθημεν, καθὼς οἴδατε, οὔτε ἐν προφάσει **πλεονεξίας,** θεὸς μάρτυς. As you know and as God is our witness, we never came with words of flattery or with a pretext for **greed**

δίλογοι, **ἀφιλάργυροι,** ἐγκρατεῖς περὶ πάντα εὐσπλάγχνοι, ἐπιμελεῖς.[123] Likewise the deacons should be blameless before his righteousness, as servants of God and Christ and not of mortals, not slanderers or double-tongued, **nor lovers of money,** temperate in all matters, compassionate, careful . . .[124]

1 Peter 5:2[125]

ποιμάνατε τὸ ἐν ὑμῖν ποίμνιον τοῦ θεοῦ, ἐπισκοποῦντες μὴ ἀναγκαστῶς ἀλλὰ ἑκουσίως κατὰ θεόν, μηδὲ **αἰσχροκερδῶς** ἀλλὰ προθύμως, to tend the flock of God that is in your charge, [exercising the oversight], not under compulsion but willingly, as God would have you do it—**not for sordid gain** but eagerly . . .

did gain what it is not right to teach.

Polycarp Phil 4:1

ἀρχὴ δὲ πάντων χαλεπῶν **φιλαργυρία. Love of money** is a source of all unpleasantnesses.

Col 3:5

Νεκρώσατε οὖν τὰ μέλη τὰ ἐπὶ τῆς γῆς, πορνείαν, ἀκαθαρσίαν, πάθος, ἐπιθυμίαν κακήν, καὶ τὴν **πλεονεξίαν** ἥτις ἐστὶν εἰδωλολατρία Put to death, therefore, whatever in you is earthly: fornication, impurity, passion, evil desire, and **greed** (which is idolatry)

Eph 5:3, 5

πορνεία δὲ καὶ ἀκαθαρσία πᾶσα ἢ **πλεονεξία** μηδὲ ὀνομαζέσθω ἐν ὑμῖν, καθὼς πρέπει ἁγίοις . . . πᾶς πόρνος ἢ ἀκάθαρτος ἢ **πλεονέκτης,** ὅ ἐστιν εἰδωλολάτρης, οὐκ ἔχει κληρονομίαν ἐν τῇ βασιλείᾳ τοῦ Χριστοῦ καὶ θεοῦ

But fornication and impurity of any kind, or greed, must not even be mentioned among you, as is proper among saints. 5 . . . no fornicator or impure person, or one who is **greedy** (that is, an idolater), has any inheritance in the kingdom of Christ and of God.

might be adherents of a rival religion seemed to have had no deterrent effect. Even the Jewish historian Josephus found space to write about a noble and virtuous woman of Rome, Paulina, with whom a knight, Decius Mundus, had fallen in love.[127] Nothing availed, not even the promise of 200,000 drachmas for a single night of bliss. He determined upon suicide. A freedwoman, Ida, came to his rescue, promising satisfaction for a mere 50,000. Knowing Paulina's devotion to Isis, the pious Ida engaged some priests, for whose assistance she was prepared to make a donation of 25,000 to the goddess. One of these devout clergymen visited our matron to announce that the god Anubis had become enamored of her and desired that she dine with him, followed by services of a more intimate nature. Thrilled by this signal honor, Paulina told her friends and husband. She visited the temple and slept, in a darkened room, with the god, represented in this instance by Mundus. Afterward she boasted about her experience. Mundus could not restrain himself from sharing the truth with her. Mortified, Paulina advised her husband, who informed Emperor Tiberius. Justice followed: authorities crucified the priests, razed the temple of Isis, and consigned her statue to the Tiber. Mundus had to go into exile. For those who cherish tales showing that crime does not pay, Josephus just happens to have another. A certain unnamed Jewish charlatan, together with some confederates, fleeced a highly placed Roman convert named Fulvia of some gold and purple, on the pretense of accepting contributions for the temple in Jerusalem. In fact, they found more personal and immediate uses for these valuables. Exposure of this fraud led Tiberius to expel the Jewish community from Rome.[128] Christian writers were able to dig up some material about polytheists—indeed they scarcely needed to go beyond the stories related in the mythical tradition—and could often point to the moral failings of heretics. Justin supposes that no one could believe in a god like Zeus, who, "... moved by desire ... descended on Ganymede." In addition there were "... [T]he many women whom he seduced ..."[129] Irenaeus claims that one Marcus was able by means of magic to deceive women, not least those of wealth and rank, inducing them to offer their money and their bodies.[130] Opponents of Paul allegedly claimed that, disappointed in his suit for the hand of the high priest's daughter, he became an implacable enemy of Torah.[131] Of more immediate applicability are charges raised against Paul for such conduct in connection with his collection for Jerusalem.[132] For sheer malice (and luridness), however, the best story of this ilk is the account of the missionary priests of the Syrian goddess (Atargatis) in the *Metamorphoses* of Apuleius.[133] To complete the circle, Lucius, hero of that same novel, becomes a convert to the worship of Isis.

No one among the texts and authors under consideration condemns greed so ardently as does Polycarp (2:2; 4:1, 3; 11:1–2). *Philippians* 11 mentions the case of the presbyter Valens, who, together with his wife, was evidently found guilty of misappropriating community funds. The Bishop of Smyrna urges rather better treatment for them than that accorded to Ananias and Sapphira (Acts 5:11).[134] This is, to my knowledge, the first documented case of financial mismanagement by Christian leaders.[135] It was, regrettably, probably not the first instance.

Table 6.6 offers grounds for suspecting that Luke has modified the parable of the Reliable Manager in a Pauline direction through borrowings from 1 Corinthians.[136] Luke despises greed on the part of the relatively well to do.[137] By attributing the pursuit of riches to the Pharisees (Luke 16:14, above), he dispatches two birds with a single missile. Many of the criticisms of Jewish leaders found in the Gospels are relevant because of their applicability to Christian leaders. I believe that Luke was familiar with Paul's image of leaders as "managers" or "stewards" of the mysteries of God" (1 Corinthians 4:1)[138] *and agrees that the primary quality of a manager is fidelity* (1 Corinthians 4:2). This Pauline phrase appears in both the Pastorals and in Luke. Titus 1:7 removes the mystery: "Bishops" are to be "managers of God['s household]." One criterion for suitability is that the candidates be able to manage their own households (1 Tim 3:4, 5, 12, 15; 5:4). Others used the term "manager(s)" without application to leadership, as the examples from 1 Peter and Ignatius indicate.[139]

Luke's presentation of the Q parable is a brief discourse on the nature and qualities of leadership. Leaders are *managers*, not owners, slaves serving as deputies in the master's absence.[140] Luke 12:37 should be seen in the light of 17:7–10, and, in particular, of 22:24–27, both discussed earlier.[141] If the master (Jesus) takes the role of a servant, what are the slaves to do? Peters' question in verse 41 establishes the application: "to us," that is, to community leaders.[142] Leaders are to see that "rations" are doled out equitably, to keep from abusing those placed in their care, and to abstain from treating the master's property as their own. The addition of verses 47–48 underlines the importance of accountability.[143] Titus 1:7 and Luke 12:45 take account, in their own ways, of drunken and abusive behavior.[144]

This example from Luke's use of the tradition of Jesus' sayings indicates how he has transformed more general exhortations of an eschatological nature into paradigms of leadership. Paul's essentially theological metaphor of the missionary/teacher as "manager" or "steward" has been expanded to include, indeed to emphasize, the pastoral side. To be sure, this does not prove that Acts is later than 100. Nonetheless, it is of more than passing interest that the most cogent parallels come from the late Deutero-Pauline world, from the Pastoral Epistles and Polycarp, while the more general denunciations of greed emerge in Colossians, 2 Thessalonians, and Ephesians, the latter two of which are close to the turn of the century. The need for managers and administrators loudly hints at a later stage of development. What was needed at the time of Acts was not so much church founders and builders as those who can keep an established community shipshape and on course. In the footsteps of successful visionaries will come the accountants. As Paul well knew, the ability to manage accounts is a spiritual gift.

One final observation is derived from Acts 6:1–7. Luke was aware of communities that were too large to be managed by one leader, or even by several. The institution of "the Seven" is authorization for leaders to surrender the notion that they must both bring home the bacon and fry it in the pan. The appointment of assistants to handle "charitable work" was not a betrayal of

Table 6.6: Managers

1 Cor 4:1–2	Luke 12:37, 41–48	Tit 1:7
Οὕτως ἡμᾶς λογιζέσθω ἄνθρωπος ὡς ὑπηρέτας Χριστοῦ καὶ **οἰκονόμους μυστηρίων θεοῦ**. 2 ὧδε λοιπὸν ζητεῖται ἐν τοῖς οἰκονόμοις ἵνα **πιστός** τις εὑρεθῇ. Think of us in this way, as servants of Christ and **stewards of God's mysteries**. Moreover, it is required of stewards that they be found **trustworthy**. Cf. 4:5 ὥστε μὴ πρὸ καιροῦ τι κρίνετε, ἕως ἂν ἔλθῃ ὁ κύριος Therefore do not pronounce judgment before the time, before the Lord comes	μακάριοι οἱ δοῦλοι ἐκεῖνοι, οὓς ἐλθὼν ὁ κύριος εὑρήσει γρηγοροῦντας· ἀμὴν λέγω ὑμῖν ὅτι περιζώσεται καὶ ἀνακλινεῖ αὐτοὺς καὶ παρελθὼν διακονήσει αὐτοῖς. *Blessed are those slaves whom the master finds alert when he comes; truly I tell you, he will fasten his belt and have them sit down to eat, and he will come and serve them.* 41 Εἶπεν δὲ ὁ Πέτρος, Κύριε, πρὸς ἡμᾶς τὴν παραβολὴν ταύτην λέγεις ἢ καὶ πρὸς πάντας; 42 καὶ εἶπεν ὁ κύριος, Τίς ἄρα ἐστὶν **ὁ πιστὸς οἰκονόμος** ὁ φρόνιμος, ὃν καταστήσει ὁ κύριος ἐπὶ τῆς θεραπείας αὐτοῦ τοῦ διδόναι ἐν καιρῷ [τὸ] σιτομέτριον; 43 μακάριος ὁ δοῦλος ἐκεῖνος, ὃν ἐλθὼν ὁ κύριος αὐτοῦ εὑρήσει ποιοῦντα οὕτως· 44 ἀληθῶς λέγω ὑμῖν ὅτι ἐπὶ πᾶσιν τοῖς ὑπάρχουσιν αὐτοῦ καταστήσει αὐτόν. 45 ἐὰν δὲ εἴπῃ ὁ δοῦλος ἐκεῖνος ἐν τῇ καρδίᾳ αὐτοῦ, Χρονίζει ὁ κύριός μου ἔρχεσθαι, καὶ ἄρξηται τύπτειν τοὺς παῖδας καὶ τὰς παιδίσκας, ἐσθίειν τε καὶ πίνειν καὶ μεθύσκεσθαι, 46 ἥξει ὁ κύριος τοῦ δούλου ἐκείνου ἐν ἡμέρᾳ ᾗ οὐ προσδοκᾷ καὶ ἐν ὥρᾳ ᾗ οὐ γινώσκει, καὶ διχοτομήσει αὐτὸν καὶ τὸ μέρος αὐτοῦ μετὰ τῶν ἀπίστων θήσει. 47 ἐκεῖνος δὲ ὁ δοῦλος ὁ γνοὺς τὸ θέλημα τοῦ κυρίου αὐτοῦ καὶ μὴ ἑτοιμάσας ἢ ποιήσας πρὸς τὸ θέλημα αὐτοῦ δαρήσεται πολλάς· 48 ὁ δὲ μὴ γνούς, ποιήσας δὲ ἄξια πληγῶν, δαρήσεται ὀλίγας. παντὶ δὲ ᾧ ἐδόθη πολύ, πολὺ ζητηθήσεται παρ᾽ αὐτοῦ, καὶ ᾧ παρέθεντο πολύ, περισσότερον αἰτήσουσιν αὐτόν. *Peter said, "Lord, are you telling this parable for us or for everyone?" And the Lord said, "Who then is the* **faithful** *and prudent* **manager** *whom his master will put in charge of his slaves, to give them their allowance of food at the proper time? Blessed is that slave whom his master will find at work when he arrives. Truly I*	δεῖ γὰρ τὸν ἐπίσκοπον ἀνέγκλητον εἶναι **ὡς θεοῦ οἰκονόμον**, μὴ αὐθάδη, μὴ ὀργίλον, μὴ πάροινον, μὴ πλήκτην, μὴ αἰσχροκερδῆ *For a bishop, as* **God's steward**, *must be blameless; he must not be arrogant or quick-tempered or addicted to wine or violent or greedy for gain* 1 Peter 4:10 ἕκαστος καθὼς ἔλαβεν χάρισμα, εἰς ἑαυτοὺς αὐτὸ διακονοῦντες ὡς καλοὶ **οἰκονόμοι** ποικίλης χάριτος **θεοῦ**. *Like good* **stewards** *of the manifold grace* **of God**, *serve one another with whatever gift each of you has received.* Ignatius, *Polycarp* 6.1 συγκοπιᾶτε ἀλλήλοις, συναθλεῖτε, συντρέχετε, συμπάσχετε, συγκοιμᾶσθε, συνεγείρεσθε **ὡς θεοῦ οἰκονόμοι** καὶ πάρεδροι καὶ ὑπηρέται. *…Share your hard training*

tell you, he will put that one in charge of all his possessions. But if that slave says to himself, 'My master is delayed in coming,' and if he begins to beat the other slaves, men and women, and to eat and drink and get drunk, the master of that slave will come on a day when he does not expect him and at an hour that he does not know, and will cut him in pieces, and put him with the *unfaithful*. *That slave who knew what his master wanted, but did not prepare himself or do what was wanted, will receive a severe beating. But the one who did not know and did what deserved a beating will receive a light beating. From everyone to whom much has been given, much will be required; and from the one to whom much has been entrusted, even more will be demanded.*	together—wrestle together, run together, suffer together, go to bed together, get up together, as **God's stewards**, assessors, and assistants.[145]

Bold—important common words
Italics—significant Lucan differences from Matthew (24:42–51), i.e., Lukan alterations of Q.[146]

the Lord's command—so long as leaders remembered the model. Relief from charitable work would also remove from top leaders the interminable management of petty conflicts, freeing them, as Luke says, for the "broader mission" while providing for concrete services of superior quality. Although Luke does not acknowledge "deacons," he does describe what they are to do, and this description is not vitiated by his failure to show them engaged in this task. If the readers of Acts were unaware of subordinate "ministers," Acts 6:1–8:39 would be even more incomprehensible.

Alms

Emphasis upon giving is pervasive in Luke. A good example is in passages of the "Sermon on the Plain" such as Luke 6:34–35 and 38a-d that lack parallels in Matthew. Giving is also the subject of the single quotation from the Jesus tradition in Acts:[147]

In Acts 20 Paul introduces the saying with a formula used for citing oral tradition.[148] (See Table 6.7.) The formula first appears in Christian literature in 1 Clement (13:1–2; 46:7), and thereafter in the fragments of Papias and in Polycarp.[149] Koester is linguistically correct in saying that this is "a Greek Aphorism,"[150] but the earliest Greek source (Thucydides) attributes it to the Persians.[151] While the subject of national origin is jejune and hardly grounds for discrimination here,[152] a case can be made for considering whether in this instance Luke is dependent upon 1 Clement. Lars Aejmelaeus has pursued the claim.[153] The impetus comes from the context in 1 Clement, a context that must tease or intrigue everyone who reflects upon the situation, for there the passage continues, "Content with Christ's rations and mindful of them, you stored his sayings (τοὺς λόγους αὐτοῦ) carefully up in your hearts and held his sufferings before your eyes."[154] The "logic" is patent: Luke (or anyone else) could understand that this reference to the teachings of Christ embraced the foregoing references to humility and giving. The gospel tradition includes many examples of both.[155] The "oral quotation formula" could also have been derived from 1 Clement, as the verbal parallels indicate.

The intertextual solution has its appeal. 1 Clement enjoyed considerable popularity in early Christianity and has explicit external attestation that is about as early as any for Acts.[156] In this case the attempt to argue from 1 Clement to Acts is quite useful, for most believe that 1 Clement is later than Acts, and dependence of 1 Clement upon Acts is frequently postulated.[157] If "Clement"[158] borrowed from Acts, he would thus first have stripped the saying of dominical authority (removed its attribution to Jesus), then replaced the conventional introduction to a macarism ("blessed are they . . .") with "more pleasant," in order to give the phrase a dash of good Greek flavor. This is rather unlikely, for the tendency at that time (c. 100) was to attribute additional sayings to Jesus,[159] and 1 Clement does not cringe at the language of the LXX, from which it can cite lengthy extracts without apology.[160] In my view, the chief obstacle to the proposal that Acts 20:35 uses 1 Clement is that both components, the proverb and the

Table 6.7: The Superior Blessing

Acts 20:35	1 Clement 2:1; 13:1; 46:7–8
πάντα ὑπέδειξα ὑμῖν ὅτι οὕτως κοπιῶντας δεῖ ἀντιλαμβάνεσθαι τῶν ἀσθενούντων, **μνημονεύειν τε τῶν λόγων τοῦ κυρίου Ἰησοῦ** ὅτι αὐτὸς εἶπεν, Μακάριόν ἐστιν **μᾶλλον διδόναι ἢ λαμβάνειν** In all this I have given you an example that by such work we must support the weak, remembering the words of the Lord Jesus, for he himself said, 'It is **more** blessed **to give than to receive.'"** Luke 22:61 . . . καὶ **ὑπεμνήσθη** ὁ Πέτρος **τοῦ ῥήματος τοῦ κυρίου ὡς εἶπεν** αὐτῷ ὅτι Πρὶν ἀλέκτορα φωνῆσαι σήμερον ἀπαρνήσῃ με τρίς The Lord turned and looked at Peter. Then Peter **remembered the word of the Lord, how he had said** to him, "Before the cock crows today, you will deny me three times."	πάντες τε ταπεινοφρονεῖτε μηδὲν ἀλαζονευόμενοι, ὑποτασσόμενοι **μᾶλλον** ἢ ὑποτάσσοντες, **ἥδιον διδόντες ἢ λαμβάνοντες.** You were humble and without any pretensions, obeying orders rather than issuing them, **more gladly giving than receiving**[161] 13.1 μεμνημένοι τῶν **λόγων τοῦ κυρίου Ἰησοῦ**, ὃς ἐλάλησεν Remembering the sayings of the lord Jesus, which he spoke . . . 46.7–8 **μνήσθητε** τῶν **λόγων Ἰησοῦ τοῦ κυρίου** ἡμῶν. **εἶπεν** γάρ Remember the sayings of Jesus our lord, for he said . . . **Thucydides 2.97.4** κατεστήσαντο γὰρ τοὐαντίον τῆς Περσῶν βασιλείας τὸν νόμον . . . **λαμβάνειν μᾶλλον ἢ διδόναι** For there was established [in Thrace] a custom opposite to that prevailing in the Persian kingdom, of **receiving rather than giving**. **Didache 1:5**[162] **μακάριος** ὁ **διδοὺς** κατὰ τὴν ἐντολήν· ἀθῷος γάρ ἐστιν. οὐαὶ τῷ **λαμβάνοντι** εἰ μὲν γὰρ χρείαν ἔχων λαμβάνει τις, ἀθῷος ἔσται· ὁ δὲ μὴ χρείαν ἔχων δώσει δίκην **Blessed are they who give** as the commandment urges, for they are guiltless. Woe to those who **receive**. If they receive because they are in need, they will be guiltless. But, if they are not in need, they will have to give account . . .

quotation formula, are traditional. Intertextual studies cannot exist in a vacuum that ignores such disciplines as form criticism and the history of traditions. On the other hand, it must be conceded that the case for intertextuality gains force from both the relative rarity of the Christian use of the proverb at this time and the close similarity of the quotation formula, which is subject to variation. If the relationship is to be resolved by postulating literary dependence, Acts uses *1 Clement*.[163]

CHURCH AND STATE

One obstacle to the analysis of "church and state" in the ancient world is that no such dichotomy existed. The "secular state"—by which is meant not antagonism towards faith but a government not based upon religious sanctions—did not emerge until the American and French Revolutions, in the late eighteenth century. The idea that every person has a right to at least voice, if not vote, in government is so fixed in Western consciousness that it is difficult to imagine a world in which people did not participate in decisions that affected their lives, a world in which few would take issue with the principle that their opinions should not be sought, while the ruling class could not have cared less whether the vast bottom of the steep social pyramid supported their policies or not. Statements like "If anyone forces you to go one mile, go also the second mile" (Matthew 5:41) strike us as invitations to utter passivity. For the ancient masses taxes and impressments were little different from natural misfortunes like droughts or floods.[164] Christians and others fervently prayed to be spared from merciless government just as they prayed to be spared from fire, famine, war, plague, and pestilence. The absence of restraining legislation, or of the effectiveness of such legislation, places a high premium upon official clemency and compassion.

Ancient peoples lived in societies that included both gods and mortals arranged in hierarchical structures that were mutually reinforcing. "Church" and "state" were inseparable because religion was an integral component of daily, civic, domestic, and political life. To speak of separating religion from "politics" in an ancient society would have made no more sense to a resident of Jerusalem or Ephesus or Rome than would the idea of separating government from public finance to us. Finally—and not to be ignored—the ancient view of society was, in terms of its fundamental institutions, essentially static. Both the poor and slaves will always be there (cf. Mark 14:7). The social roles of men, women, and children were no more likely to undergo major alteration than would summer be followed by spring.

This context illuminates why Paul, who knew that imperial and other officials might be less helpful than he could hope for (cf. 2 Corinthians 11:22–33), wrote positively of the ruling powers (Romans 13:1–7), and 1 Peter, which is quite aware of persecution (e.g. 4:12–19), urges respect for authority, culminating with an exhortation to "honor the emperor" (2:13–17), while 1 Clement, which knows that things have been bad and that worse may come, climaxes with a fulsome intercession for rulers (61:1–3).[165] This is not to deny that deviants and resisters often protest that they are good citizens, who, unlike the slack and complacent, have the best interests of the community at heart. Nor was antiquity ignorant of the rhetorical tactic of seeking to ingratiate oneself with those in authority by praising them for possessing qualities that the speaker fondly wishes they would embrace.[166]

Good Citizens

To contend that believers should be good citizens is to take a stance quite different from that apocalyptic posture which denounces the state root and branch and thinks that there are some priorities ever so much higher than better housing and drainage.[167] Luke typifies one approach of a later generation to this subject. His attitude about the "Christian citizen" is a major pillar of the largely discredited attempt to portray him as an apologist defending the Christian movement against the Roman government. Such advocates certainly do insist that Christians are not deserving of persecution and that they are obedient subjects. "We are in fact of all people your best helpers and allies in securing good order (εἰρήνη)," says Justin; and after quoting "render unto Caesar," he continues: "So we worship God only, but in other matters we gladly serve you, recognizing you as emperors and rulers . . . and praying that along with your imperial power you may also be found to have a sound mind."[168] An admirable sentiment that last, we may agree, and quite untarnished despite the passage of a good eighteen centuries; but few rulers will be swept away by subjects who, having deigned to recognize them, express a preference that their sovereigns not be imbeciles or lunatics. With due reservations, the term in question, "good citizen," is quite suitable here, for it applies to those who "do their part," i.e., contribute appropriately to the life of a group. One form that such contribution takes is conformity to community standards. In our parlance a "good citizen" is one who volunteers to contribute or help and who conforms to general social standards. Both of these senses, ethical conformity and "doing one's bit," apply to the early Christian understanding of this subject.

In 1 Timothy 2:1 the Pastor exhorts his hearers to offer prayers of various types for all people. Of these "all" the Pastor identifies but one social group, those in authority. One means for indicating the difference between this and other views is a comparison with the invitation of Jesus to discipleship.

AUTHENTIC EXISTENCE

Two different understandings of "life" are attested in the passages set out in Table 6.8. Even more striking is that each relates its view of life to soteriology. True life and genuine existence has salvation as its object. Whereas Mark's definition is harshly antithetical, paradox is far from the mind of the Pastor both here and elsewhere.[169] What has quite obviously changed is the meaning of "life." More is at stake here than the use of different words, although that is important. Mark's term is that often translated as "soul" ("real self"), life as defined by factors other than those of a physical or "worldly" nature. The Pastor's word connotes the course and order of existence, as in "I don't want to spend my life in a library."

The difference comes from competing valuations of time. What shall I do if I am saved and tomorrow is the next day of the rest of my life? For the Pastor as for Luke—as well as for *1 Clement* and Polycarp—the most threatening solution was to leave time behind, to view salvation as complete and time no more than part of the deceiving structure of an evil universe. The Pastor knows of "Hymenaeus and Philetus," who "are upsetting the faith of some" "by claiming that the resurrection has already taken place."[170] He did not welcome other-worldliness of this sort, as it found its most amenable home in religious trends that resembled Gnosticism. The alternative was set forth by Luke with a theol-

Table 6.8:Disciples and Citizens

Mark 8:34b-36	1 Timothy 2:2–4
. . . "If any want to become my followers, let them deny themselves and take up their cross and follow me. 35 For those who want to save their life (**τὴν ψυχὴν αὐτοῦ σῶσαι**) will lose it, and those who lose their life for my sake, and for the sake of the gospel, will save it (σώσει αὐτήν). For what will it profit them to gain the whole world and forfeit their life?" Cf. **Luke 9:23** "If any want to become my followers, let them deny themselves and take up their cross daily (καθ' ἡμέραν) and follow me.	. . . [F]or kings and all who are in high positions, so that we may lead a quiet and peaceable life in all godliness and dignity (ἵνα ἤρεμον καὶ **ἡσύχιον** βίον διάγωμεν ἐν πάσῃ εὐσεβείᾳ καὶ σεμνότητι). This is right and is acceptable in the sight of God our Savior, who desires everyone to be saved (σωθῆναι) and to come to the knowledge of the truth. **1 Clement 63:1** θεμιτὸν οὖν ἐστὶν τοῖς τοιούτοις καὶ τοσούτοις ὑποδείγμασιν προσελθόντας ὑποθεῖναι τὸν τράχηλον καὶ τὸν τῆς ὑπακοῆς τόπον ἀναπληρῶσαι ὅπως **ἡσυχάσαντες** τῆς ματαίας στάσεως ἐπὶ τὸν προκείμενον ἡμῖν ἐν ἀληθείᾳ σκοπὸν δίχα παντὸς μώμου καταντήσωμεν. Hence it is only right that, confronted with such examples and so many of them, we should bow the neck and adopt the attitude of obedience. Thus by **giving up** this futile revolt, we may be free from all reproach and gain the true goal ahead of us.[171] **1 Thessalonians 4:11–12** καὶ φιλοτιμεῖσθαι **ἡσυχάζειν** καὶ πράσσειν τὰ ἴδια καὶ ἐργάζεσθαι ταῖς χερσὶν ὑμῶν, καθὼς ὑμῖν παρηγγείλαμεν, 12 ἵνα περιπατῆτε εὐσχημόνως πρὸς τοὺς ἔξω καὶ μηδενὸς χρείαν ἔχητε. to aspire to **live quietly**, to mind your own affairs, and to work with your hands, as we directed you, so that you may behave properly toward outsiders and be dependent on no one.

ogy of history, and by the Pastor and others generally through ethics for daily living. It reflected no desire to "betray Paul" or to "sell out the Gospel"; rather, they wished to counter a devaluation of the world that made ethics largely irrelevant, concern for the needy immaterial, and continuity with the past either unimportant or undesirable.

The different view of time stands out in Luke's rendition of the summons to take up one's cross (Luke 9:23, above); cross-bearing is a daily activity.[172] It is thus incontestably a metaphor, possibly quite potent, but nonetheless oriented to the kind of life that "goes on" rather than to a sense of imminence.[173] Further insight comes from Luke's form of the Our Father. (See Table 6.9.)

An ultra-literal translation of Luke would be "Keep on giving us day by day the food we need," while a similar rendering of Matthew would read "Give us

Table 6.9

Matthew 6:11	Luke 11:3
Τὸν ἄρτον ἡμῶν τὸν ἐπιούσιον δὸς ἡμῖν *σήμερον*	τὸν ἄρτον ἡμῶν τὸν ἐπιούσιον δίδου ἡμῖν *τὸ καθ᾽ ἡμέραν*
Give us *this day* our daily bread.	Give us *each day* our daily bread.

today the food we need for today." Luke has turned away from an eschatological understanding of this petition.[174]

This need for a relatively clear and workable ethic of daily life ". . . based on common sense, pragmatism, and the natural order of things" characterizes the "mainstream" Christian literature of the era around 100 CE and after.[175] The object of the "ethics of good citizenship" is to "serve to regulate the time until the Parousia, which is no longer felt to be imminent."[176] In Acts this "good citizenship" involves rather more of the carrot than the stick—the tribulations of Ananias and Sapphira (5:1–11) notwithstanding. The fruits of this adherence to civic virtues and life are narrated in Acts. Followers of Jesus include many of wealth and status, including Cornelius, a Roman centurion (roughly equivalent to a "colonel" in nineteenth century U. S. society); Sergius Paulus, governor of Cyprus, and therefore a representative of the highest levels of Roman society; Dionysius, a member of the elite council of the Areopagus; and numerous "lesser lights."

> How thrilling it was for Luke's audience to hear of the grace and charm of Paul, of the reception accorded their foundational heroes by their social superiors! The achievements of Paul coincide with the fondest social aspirations of the "petite bourgeoisie" of that time, of the very people to whom Luke was making his primary pitch. Success like this was a pleasant subject for meditation. Implicit within the story of Paul is the message that worldly recognition and success are possible and desirable for Christians. They are an incentive to good Christian citizenship . . .[177]

A previous section of this chapter looked at the common stance of Luke, the Pastorals, and other early Christian texts against greed. Recall also the "social ethics" of John the Baptizer (Luke 3:10–14).[178] Sharing with the very needy and restraining official rapacity are very good things, indeed, but it would be difficult to find anything in these instructions designed to exacerbate the powers that be.[179] Luke's John does not sound like a hell-fire and damnation prophet of imminent disaster just here. His advice is just as good when the end is not at hand as when it is.

"A quiet and peaceable life" is the goal of Christian life in this world (1 Timothy 2:2, Table 6.8). The word group that includes "Peaceable" (ἡσύχιος) is essentially negative, "the absence of turmoil." Comparison with 1 Thessalonians 4:11, where the verb appears,[180] reveals both the grounding in and the distance from Paul.[181] The apostle may seem to be giving similar advice and for similar (missionary) reasons, but he does not view work as a good in itself, simply as one means for staying out of trouble. If this life-style looks proper to outsiders, well and good. If it helps open doors to conversions, so much the better. Staying out of trouble, Paul proclaims, is a worthy object of Christian ambition. For the Pastor the Church *must* look seemly to outsiders. Luke shows the Church looking as pretty as a picture. Followers of Jesus help the poor and root out socially dangerous and exploitative magic.[182] Believers have nothing to do with questionable religious practices and represent the antithesis of those who provoke civic disorder. For specific references on these items, one need only consult Acts 19. It's all there (but not only there). The two leading factors that affirm this seemliness are the quality of converts, as stated above, and the character of community meetings, also a subject of previous discussion. Cicero shows how difficult it was for members of the Roman elite to distinguish between anarchy and democracy:

> Remember, then, that when you hear Greek resolutions, you are not hearing evidence; you are hearing the wild decisions of a mob, the voice of every nonentity, the din of ignoramuses, an inflamed meeting of the most unstable of nations (19). I go further; I say that what you call Greek resolutions are not evidence at all, but the clamour of the impoverished and some reckless impulse of a meeting of Greeklings (23). And I here repeatedly urge you to remember the irresponsibility of the crowd, the instability characteristic of Greeks and the force that a seditious speech has in a public meeting. (57)[183]

Those who wonder what Luke might have had to say about "Greek democracy" can satisfy their curiosity by turning to the multi-purpose Acts 19. The views of *1 Clement* are even less mysterious, since the purpose of the letter is to protest against a community decision to oust their leadership.[184]

The sharp contrast between Luke and the Pastor on the topic of marriage has already been noted. The ethical corollary to the Pastor's preference for married life is what might be called an ethic of family life. Luke may not recommend marriage, but he knows of and implicitly commends multi-generational families of believers, such as the family of Mary in Jerusalem, which produced John Mark (Acts 12:12), and that of Timothy, whose mother was a "believing Jew" (Acts 16:1) His paradigm, of course, is the family of Jesus, whose mother is an archetype of faith (Luke 1, especially verses 26–56; cf. Acts 1:14), and whose brother James became the leader of the Jerusalem faithful. Of such families the Pastor has an outstanding example: that of Timothy, who belongs to the third generation of believers nurtured on the scriptures that proclaim salvation in Jesus Christ (2 Timothy 1:5; 3:14–15). If this strikes us as a bit unlikely for the historical Timothy, it does show the perspective of the Pastoral Epistles, a perspective that I shall argue below is also that of Acts. In that state of un/wedded bliss the matter will have to rest, as the subject is moving from the general to the particular.

THE DIFFUSION OF CHURCH LETTERS

Although Acts betrays no explicit awareness of Paul's correspondence, Acts 15 indicates, as noted, familiarity with the function of letters in early Christianity.[185] The fate of the "Apostolic Letter" of 15:23–29 suggests awareness of how letters were handled in the post-Pauline period. The letter of Acts 15 resolves a conflict that arose in Antioch and is thus addressed to gentile believers in "Antioch and Syria and Cilicia" (15:23). In 15:30, after the emissaries arrived at Antioch, ". . . [T]hey gathered the congregation together . . . [and] delivered the letter. When its members read it, they rejoiced at the exhortation" (15:30–31). Such a public reading is just what Paul directed in 1 Thessalonians 5:27: "I solemnly command you by the Lord that this letter be read to all of them."

When Paul, Silas and Timothy return to the cities of southern Asia Minor, which had been evangelized in Acts 13–14, "they delivered to them for observance the decisions that had been reached by the apostles and elders who were in Jerusalem" (16:4). Acts presumes that the provisions of the letter apply to all gentile believers and not only to its original addressees. This idea of reading (and complying with) other people's mail can be seen in an early Deutero-Pauline parallel to 1 Thessalonians 5:27: "And when this letter has been read among you, have it read also in the church of the Laodiceans; and see that you read also the letter from Laodicea" (Colossians 4:16). Already with the appearance of what is quite probably the earliest Deutero-Pauline epistle, a strong impetus toward collecting letters is evident.

This was part of the effort at overcoming what is called the "problem of the particularity of Paul's letters" Simply stated the problem is this: " How are things that Paul may have had to say to people in Corinth then relevant for us here and now?" Through various techniques editors of the Pauline corpus sought to make these epistles applicable to and relevant for all believers everywhere.[186] Acts, which is no less interested in presenting Paul as a universal missionary, shares the same outlook seen in Colossians, Ephesians, and editions of the Pauline corpus.[187] However particular their addresses, "apostolic" letters are addressed to all believers. James confirms this in Acts 21:25, where he says that the "Apostolic Decree" applies to all gentile believers. Acts therefore shares the early second century understanding of Paul's teaching as a message to all Christians.

SOME CENTRAL THEOLOGICAL
AND ETHICAL CONCEPTS

Vocabulary and style can help to resolve the question of date. Various words come into fashion and fall out of use. Changed circumstances can demand the introduction of new terms and attention to different concepts. Styles also come into popularity and pass out of favor. In the New Testament "better" style and more "secular" Greek can serve to determine that the text in question is not among the earliest. Still and all, there are many nice questions and few hard and fast rules in these matters.

1 Timothy 2:2 is a convenient place of reentry (see Table 6.8, above). Christians are to pray for rulers "so that we may lead a quiet and peaceable life in all godliness and dignity." The last two nouns, εὐσεβεία and σεμνότης are no less interesting than the preceding adjectives. The meaning of the first is elusive enough to illustrate by itself the difficulty of positing "religion" as a separate category in antiquity.[188] The noun denotes "respect" or "reverence" towards the established order and conventional values. The adjective may mean no more than "respectful." The group (noun, verb, adjective, and adverb) is represented twenty-two times in the New Testament. Thirteen of these are in the Pastorals, five in 2 Peter, and four in Acts.[189] In the Apostolic Fathers *1 Clement* has eight uses and *2 Clement* three.[190] The LXX includes fifty-eight/nine entries for the noun, only four of which appear in books found in the Hebrew Bible.[191] Forty-seven of the remainder are from *IV Maccabees*. εὐσεβεία has deep roots in Hellenistic culture, where it is one virtue among others.[192] When the word is rendered as "godliness," it has exactly the meaning "godliness" enjoys when it is ranked just above "cleanliness," i.e., as a moral quality. This is a good example of a term that belongs to the later strata of the New Testament, but one swallow does not make a spring.[193]

With "piety" (εὐσεβεία) the Greeks often associated "righteousness" (δικαιοσύνη), which is part of a family that includes verb, adjective, and adverb. This term is especially familiar in the Pauline world, where it has a particular meaning, often rendered as "justification": God's action to right wrongs[194]. This word is very important to Paul and is one of the terms most open to misunderstanding when read by those lacking a "Jewish background," for in the realm of Greek culture this is one of the four "cardinal virtues" and characterizes the condition of one who *is* righteous, fair, correct, etc., and of those marked by their propensity for "doing the right thing." An English analogy can be seen in "tuition," which in Great Britain and the Commonwealth nations still means "instruction," while an American metonymy has made it a term for the fees paid to receive instruction. Many from Africa or the Indian sub-continent, for example, would understand the grim announcement "tuition will increase next year" to be a good thing, since it implies more teaching. On the matter of "justification" Paul is an American at Oxford.

Chapter four recounted generally accepted arguments that Luke was aware of the Pauline use of the verb δικαιόω ("justify," Luke 18:14; Acts 13:38–39). In general, however, he uses the word group to mean "being righteous" rather than "being in a right relationship with God." So, for example, when Paul spoke with Felix about "justice (δικαιοσύνη), self-control, and the coming judgment," the procurator did not take fright because he believed that God had declared him righteous (Acts 24:25). Peter's characterization of the suitability of gentile converts in Acts 10:35, "but in every nation anyone who fears *God* and does

Table 6.10

1 Timothy 6:11	2 Timothy 2:22
Σὺ δέ, ὦ ἄνθρωπε θεοῦ, ταῦτα φεῦγε· δίωκε δὲ δικαιοσύνην, εὐσέβειαν, πίστιν, ἀγάπην, ὑπομονήν, πραϋπαθίαν But as for you, man of God, **shun** all this; **pursue righteousness, godliness, faith, love**, endurance, gentleness	τὰς δὲ νεωτερικὰς ἐπιθυμίας φεῦγε, δίωκε δὲ δικαιοσύνην, πίστιν, ἀγάπην, εἰρήνην μετὰ τῶν ἐπικαλουμένων τὸν κύριον ἐκ καθαρᾶς καρδίας **Shun** youthful passions and **pursue righteousness, faith, love**, and peace

what is right (ἐργαζόμενος δικαιοσύνην) is acceptable to *God*" could not be less Pauline. A very similar situation obtains in the Pastorals, where "righteousness," can be one virtue in a catalogue of moral qualities.

The two catalogues in Table 6.10 follow the same form: "Stay away from *a, b, c*; but strive for *x, y, z*." "Righteousness" comes first in each list of precepts.[195] Other items vary, although homage to Pauline tradition is clear in the common presence of "faith" and "love." On the other side of the ledger stands Titus 3:5–7:

> God saved us, not because of any works of righteousness that we had done, but according to his mercy, through the water of rebirth and renewal by the Holy Spirit. This Spirit he poured out on us richly through Jesus Christ our Savior, so that, having been justified by his grace, we might become heirs according to the hope of eternal life.[196]

This, like the passages in Luke 18, Acts 13, and Acts 15 elsewhere discussed, clearly intends to uphold the Pauline view, but Paul would not have written "works of righteousness," and he would have spoken of "faith" as the agency. Nor is the view of Baptism presented here antithetical to Paul's own (cf. Romans 6:3–11), but the passage is more strongly sacramental in character than are Paul's typical summaries of salvation by grace.[197] "Tit 3:5ff. shows that the Pastorals did not forget Paul's concept of 'righteousness'... But in the understanding of 'righteousness,' which means 'the right behavior,' 'upright conduct'... the Pastoral Epistles agree with Acts."[198]

1 Clement uses "righteousness" fourteen times. Five of these are citations, one of which (10:6) is Genesis 15:6 ("*Abraham* believed the LORD; and the LORD reckoned it to him as righteousness"), a passage used by Paul at Galatians 3:6 and Romans 4:3, 9 as the scriptural "proof" for his view of "justification." James 2:23 cites it as scriptural warrant for "*his*" view of "justification." Although *1 Clement* knows Romans,[199] the author could cheerfully follow this citation by saying that Abraham was awarded a son "because of his faith and hospitality" (10:7),[200] a phrase that sends shivers of horror into the hearts of those who prefer to take their Paulinism without dilution or adulteration. 31:2 indicates that *he* could take this posture without flinching: "For what reason was our forebear Abraham blessed? Was it not because he acted righteously and truthfully, through faith?"(Τίνος χάριν ηὐλογήθη ὁ πατὴρ ἡμῶν Ἀβραάμ, οὐχὶ δικαιοσύνην καὶ ἀλήθειαν διὰ πίστεως ποίησας;) Once more Genesis 15 stands in the background; "righteousness" is something one *does*, motivated "by faith." What of Paul? He is a model of patient endurance (ὑπομονή), who "taught righteousness to the whole world" (δικαιοσύνην διδάξας ὅλον τὸν κόσμον). It is difficult to imagine that Paul would have approved of this statement, which views him as teaching "righteousness" by his example of "hanging tough."[201] The description fits quite neatly into the Deutero-Pauline world, however; and like Acts and the Pastorals, *1 Clement* can also affirm the Pauline view, or something very much like it:

> And we, therefore, who by his will have been called in Jesus Christ, are not justified of ourselves or by our wisdom or insight or religious devotion or the holy deeds we have done from the heart, but by that faith by which almighty God has justified all people from the very beginning. (32:4)[202]

In this passage *1 Clement* aptly updates the teaching of Paul. Rather than oppose "faith" to "deeds of the law," as Paul did in his conflicts with "Judaizers," *1 Clement* states that justification is not a result of personal holiness or devotion. Martin Luther, who made a similar updating, could only have approved.

The last clause is less certain. Is the faith in question the "faithfulness" of God? Does the author contend that "all people" have been justified, whether they believe or not? On the grounds of the examples of Abraham, Isaac, and Jacob (chapter 31), it is arguable that the text means that faith is the basis for the justification of whomsoever God has justified.[203] Differences from Paul come to the surface in the subsequent chapter, but Romans has inspired the course and nature of the argument.[204] In any case, *1 Clement*, like Acts, shows followers of Paul engaged in applying his thought to different circumstances. This is the essence of Deutero-Paulinism, best seen not as the "betrayal" of Paul's central doctrine of justification, but its application to situations where conflicts over Torah no longer applied and in which the ethical values and norms of Jewish Scripture were regarded as utterly positive.

When "righteousness" is paired with "holiness" (see Table 6.11), it seems to be a liturgical-sounding phrase resonant of Septuagintal style (cf. Joshua 24:14), but "the combination is an indication of a high degree of ἀρετή (virtue), the mark of an exceptional citizen."[205] The introduction of words beginning in ὁσ- ("devout," "pious"") reflects the tendency to express "religious" values in the language of contemporary ethics. That tendency is marked in the Pastorals, but is also characteristic of Luke, Ephesians, and *1 Clement*.[206] In the New Testament only Luke and Ephesians use the noun "holiness."

Table 6.11: Holiness and Righteousness

Joshua 24:14[207]	Wisdom 9:3	Luke 1:74–75	Ephesians 4:24	1 Clement 48.4
καὶ νῦν φοβήθητε κύριον καὶ **λατρεύσατε αὐτῷ ἐν εὐθύτητι καὶ ἐν δικαιοσύνη** Now therefore revere the Lord, and serve him in uprightness and in righteousness	καὶ διέπη τὸν κόσμον ἐν **ὁσιότητι καὶ δικαιοσύνη** καὶ ἐν εὐθύτητι ψυχῆς κρίσιν κρίνη and rule the world **in holiness and righteousness,** and pronounce judgment in uprightness of soul.	**Λατρεύειν αὐτῷ** 75 **ἐν ὁσιότητι καὶ δικαιοσύνη** ἐνώπιον αὐτοῦ πάσαις ταῖς ἡμέραις ἡμῶν To serve God in holiness and righteousness before him all our days.	καὶ ἐνδύσασθαι τὸν καινὸν ἄνθρωπον τὸν κατὰ θεὸν κτισθέντα ἐν **δικαιοσύνη καὶ ὁσιότητι** and to clothe yourselves with the new self, created according to the likeness of God in true **righteousness and holiness.** Cf. **1 Thess 2:10** ὑμεῖς μάρτυρες καὶ ὁ θεός, ὡς **ὁσίως καὶ δικαίως καὶ** ἀμέμπτως ὑμῖν τοῖς πιστεύουσιν ἐγενήθημεν You are witnesses, and God also, how **pure, upright,** and blameless our conduct was toward you believers	ἐν ᾗ μακάριοι πάντες οἱ εἰσελθόντες καὶ κατευθύνοντες τὴν πορείαν **αὐτῶν ἐν ὁσιότητι καὶ δικαιοσύνη ἀταράχως πάντα ἐπιτελοῦντες** Blessed are all who enter by [the gate of righteousness] and direct their way **in holiness and righteousness,** by doing everything without disorder.[208]

GOOD CONSCIENCE

When Paul speaks of "conscience" in relation to meat (possibly) utilized in poly-theist ceremonies,[209] he means something very much like the modern notion of a "consciousness" that can be "raised," a freedom arising from the recognition that these "gods" do not exist. The antonym is a "weak conscience," which is not "bad," but hesitant and/or uninformed, "unliberated" in more recent jargon. His usage is quite different from the formulaic "good conscience," which can be expressed with a number of essentially synonymous adjectives: "pure," "clear," "noble," etc. The antonym to this construct is a "bad conscience." The latter usage conforms to popular ethics and is not surprising in the vocabulary of Christians who are adjusting themselves to life in the world. It indicates the rise of "individualism" and treats individual believers as moral agents. Such "democratization" would have astonished philosophers like Seneca, a first century Roman Stoic, who spoke often of a "good conscience," but would not have imagined that cobblers or merchants could possess this quality, nor thought it desirable that they might attempt to do so. For the Pastor and others the motivation is patent: those without a "good conscience" cannot hope to enjoy a tranquil life.[210] Acts—indeed, the "Paul of Acts"—belongs to this sphere. One cannot, in good conscience, overlook this usage in attempting to find a suitable date for Acts. (See Table 6.12.)

IGNORANCE

Nor do I wish you to be ignorant, dear reader, of the implications of "ignorance" in Acts. Paul rejected the possibility of "ignorance of the law" and thus denied that it could be an excuse (Romans 1:18–32). For Luke and others, however, ignorance often *is* an excuse, the means by which the playing field is made level. For the knowledgeable, ignorance is a multi-purpose tool, a basis for attack, as in Acts 13:27—where it serves to denounce those who would not remove their heads from the sand—or as in 17:23, where it provides mitigation: they were trying to do the right thing, but knew no better.

The speeches of Peter in Acts 3:12–26 and Paul in 17:22–31 demonstrate that Athens and Jerusalem have a good deal in common. (See Table 6.13.) One of them is "ignorance". Both addresses deploy the theme of ignorance to promote what ancient rhetoric called *ethos*, the establishment of a positive relationship with the audience.[211] The speakers do not attack their audiences for their misdeeds. Their object is to move the hearers to repent (3:19; 17:30). When the subjects in question are not in the congregation, so to speak, *ethos* can take a different tack. In Pisidian Antioch (Acts 13:27) Paul urges his hearers not to be as stupid as the people in Jerusalem, whose ignorance is due to their refusal to listen.

Table 6.12: Good Conscience

Pastorals 1 Timothy 1:5, 19; 3:9	Acts Acts 23:1; 24:16	Other Hebrews 13:18
5 τὸ δὲ τέλος τῆς παραγγελίας ἐστὶν ἀγάπη ἐκ καθαρᾶς καρδίας καὶ **συνειδήσεως ἀγαθῆς** καὶ πίστεως ἀνυποκρίτου. But the aim of such instruction is love that comes from a pure heart, a **good conscience**, and sincere faith. 19 ἔχων πίστιν καὶ **ἀγαθὴν συνείδησιν**, ἥν τινες ἀπωσάμενοι περὶ τὴν πίστιν ἐναυάγησαν having faith and a **good conscience**. By rejecting conscience, certain persons have suffered shipwreck in the faith 9 ἔχοντας τὸ μυστήριον τῆς πίστεως ἐν **καθαρᾷ συνειδήσει** they must hold fast to the mystery of the faith with a **clear conscience** 2 Timothy 1:3a Χάριν ἔχω τῷ θεῷ, ᾧ λατρεύω ἀπὸ προγόνων ἐν καθαρᾷ συνειδήσει. I am grateful to God—whom I worship with a **clear conscience**, as my ancestors did	ἀτενίσας δὲ τῷ συνεδρίῳ ὁ Παῦλος εἶπεν, Ἄνδρες ἀδελφοί, ἐγὼ **πάσῃ συνειδήσει ἀγαθῇ** πεπολίτευμαι τῷ θεῷ ἄχρι ταύτης τῆς ἡμέρας While Paul was looking intently at the council he said, "Brothers, up to this day I have lived my life with a **clear conscience** before God." 16 ἐν τούτῳ καὶ αὐτὸς ἀσκῶ **ἀπρόσκοπον συνείδησιν** ἔχειν πρὸς τὸν θεὸν καὶ τοὺς ἀνθρώπους διὰ παντός Therefore I do my best always to have a **clear conscience** toward God and all people	Προσεύχεσθε περὶ ἡμῶν, πειθόμεθα γὰρ ὅτι **καλὴν συνείδησιν** ἔχομεν, ἐν πᾶσιν καλῶς θέλοντες ἀναστρέφεσθαι Pray for us; we are sure that we have a **clear conscience** 1 Peter 3:16, 21 16 ἀλλὰ μετὰ πραΰτητος καὶ φόβου, **συνείδησιν** ἔχοντες **ἀγαθήν** yet do it with gentleness and reverence. Keep your conscience clear, 21 ὃ καὶ ὑμᾶς ἀντίτυπον νῦν σῴζει βάπτισμα, οὐ σαρκὸς ἀπόθεσις ῥύπου ἀλλὰ **συνειδήσεως ἀγαθῆς** ἐπερώτημα εἰς θεόν . . . And baptism, which this prefigured, now saves you—not as a removal of dirt from the body, but as an appeal to God for a **good conscience** 1 Clement 1:3; 41:1; 45:7 γυναιξίν τε ἐν **ἀμώμῳ καὶ σεμνῇ καὶ ἁγνῇ συνειδήσει** πάντα ἐπιτελεῖν παρηγγέλλετε. You instructed your women to do everything with a blameless and **pure conscience** ἕκαστος ἡμῶν, ἀδελφοί, ἐν τῷ ἰδίῳ τάγματι εὐαρεστείτω τῷ θεῷ ἐν **ἀγαθῇ συνειδήσει** ὑπάρχων Each of us, sisters and brothers, in his own rank, must win God's approval and have a **clear conscience**. μὴ εἰδότες, ὅτι ὁ ὕψιστος ὑπέρμαχος καὶ ὑπερασπιστής ἐστιν τῶν ἐν **καθαρᾷ συνειδήσει** λατρευόντων τῷ παναρέτῳ ὀνόματι αὐτοῦ. They failed to realize that the Most High is the champion and defender of those who worship his excellent name with a **pure conscience**.[212] Polycarp *Phil* 5.3 τὰς παρθένους ἐν **ἀμώμῳ καὶ ἁγνῇ συνειδήσει** περιπατεῖν. Unmarried women (virgins) are to conduct themselves with a blameless and **pure conscience**. (cf. **1 Clem** 1:3)

Table 6.13: Vincible Ignorance

Acts I: Jews	Acts II: Gentiles	Other New Testament	Other
3:17 "And now, friends, I know that you acted **in ignorance,** (κατὰ ἄγνοιαν) as did also your rulers. Cf. **13:27** Because the residents of Jerusalem and their leaders did not recognize (ἀγνοήσαντες) him or understand the words of the prophets that are read every sabbath, they fulfilled those words by condemning him	**17:23, 30.** For as I went through the city and looked carefully at the objects of your worship, I found among them an altar with the inscription, 'To an **unknown** god.' (Ἀγνώστῳ θεῷ) What therefore you worship as **unknown,** (ἀγνοοῦντες εὐσεβεῖτε) this I proclaim to you. 30 While God has overlooked the times of human **ignorance** (ἀγνοίας), now he commands all people everywhere to repent	**Ephesians 4:18** They are darkened in their understanding, alienated from the life of God because of their **ignorance** (τὴν ἄγνοιαν τὴν οὖσαν ἐν αὐτοῖς) and hardness of heart **1 Timothy 1:13** . . . even though I was formerly a blasphemer, a persecutor, and a man of violence. But I received mercy because I had acted **ignorantly** (ἀγνοῶν) in unbelief, **1 Peter 1:14** Like obedient children, do not be conformed to the desires that you formerly had in **ignorance** (ἐν τῇ ἀγνοίᾳ) **2 Peter 2:12** These people, however, are like irrational animals, mere creatures of instinct, born to be caught and killed. They slander what they **do not understand,** (ἐν οἷς ἀγνοοῦσιν βλασφημοῦντες)	**Aseneth** 13:11–13 Behold now, all the gods whom I once used to worship in **ignorance:** I have now recognized that they were dumb and dead idols. . . . Yet you rescue me from my many deeds of **ignorance** and pardon me, because I have sinned against you in **ignorance**[213]

REPENTANCE

If Lukan theology exhibits one element on which a consensus exists, it is that repentance is a basic concept.[214] (See Table 6.14.) Repentance is not identical to forgiveness, nor do the two quite fashion a hendiadys. Repentance is the initial act in conversion. Genuine repentance brings forgiveness and manifests itself in the ethical life of believers (Jesus: Luke 5:32; Paul: Acts 26:20). Not all need to repent, at least in theory.[215] Repentance also serves as a bridge for uniting Jews and gentiles and as a bond between past and present (salvation-history), because it is obedience to the constant summons of Law and Prophets. *1 Clement's* understanding of repentance relies heavily on the same conceptions — salvation-historical, ethical, and anthropological — and thus accords it a fundamental place in the scheme of things religious. So strong is the ethical interest in *1 Clement* that repentance in large measure becomes one desirable moral quality among others.[216] Reflection will show that this is not far from the mark for Luke and Acts either, although the situation is masked by the focus upon the role of repentance in the initial conversion. For both Luke and 1 Clement, the redemptive effect of Christ's victory can be described as repentance (Luke 24:47; Acts 5:31; *1 Clement* 7:4). The christological language of the last is notably reminiscent of Acts 20:28: ". . . [S]hepherd the church of God that he obtained with the blood of his own Son."[217]

Even more noteworthy is 62:1–2, which reads like a summary of this entire section[218] (See Table 6.15): Acts and *1 Clement* thus have a similar understanding of repentance, which they tend to associate with ethical qualities A number of the terms used by the writer of the letter from Rome to Corinth to summarize the work belong to the later strata of the New Testament, including Acts. At some point it will be necessary to ask how many swallows *do* make a spring.

Excursus: How Widely was *1 Clement* Known in the Second Century?

Since the letter from the church at Rome to that at Corinth plays a large role in the comparisons that this chapter proposes, it is quite justifiable to inquire about its availability and circulation. Comparisons with an obscure text are not necessarily invalid, but they are different from theories, inferences, or deductions based upon a work of relative popularity. In questions related to intertextuality this question can be crucial. In all cases it is important.[219]

Ignatius of Antioch may well allude to *1 Clement* when he says, in his letter to the Romans, 3:1, that they have taught others. Grant calls this "probable," but it cannot be demonstrated.[220] The current tendency (Lindemann excepted) is to affirm the dependence of Polycarp upon *1 Clement*. At the very least the data indicate the extent to which the works participate in a kindred milieu.[221] Hegesippus and Dionysius of Corinth (both active c. 170) make explicit mention of the letter, which enjoyed great favor at Corinth and was often read.[222] Irenaeus also values the piece, summarizing it in part (*Against Heresies* 3.3.3). For Clement of Alexandria (c. 190) the letter is of considerable importance and the subject of frequent citation.[223] Alexandrian and other Eastern theologians continued to use

Table 6.14: Repentance

Luke	Acts	1 Clement
5:32 οὐκ ἐλήλυθα καλέσαι δικαίους ἀλλὰ ἁμαρτωλοὺς εἰς **μετάνοιαν**[224] I have come to call not the righteous but sinners to **repentance** 15:7. λέγω ὑμῖν ὅτι οὕτως χαρὰ ἐν τῷ οὐρανῷ ἔσται ἐπὶ ἑνὶ ἁμαρτωλῷ **μετανοοῦντι** ἢ ἐπὶ ἐνενήκοντα ἐννέα δικαίοις οἵτινες οὐ χρείαν ἔχουσιν **μετανοίας** Just so, I tell you, there will be more joy in heaven over one sinner who **repents** than over ninety-nine righteous persons who need no **repentance** 24:47 καὶ κηρυχθῆναι ἐπὶ τῷ ὀνόματι αὐτοῦ **μετάνοιαν** καὶ ἄφεσιν ἁμαρτιῶν εἰς πάντα τὰ ἔθνη – ἀρξάμενοι ἀπὸ Ἰερουσαλὴμ **repentance** and forgiveness of sins is to be proclaimed in his name to all nations, beginning from Jerusalem.	5:31 τοῦτον ὁ θεὸς ἀρχηγὸν καὶ σωτῆρα ὕψωσεν τῇ δεξιᾷ αὐτοῦ, δοῦναι **μετάνοιαν** τῷ Ἰσραὴλ καὶ ἄφεσιν ἁμαρτιῶν. [Peter] "God exalted him at his right hand as Leader and Savior that he might give repentance to Israel and forgiveness of sins." 11:18 [Jerusalem believers] Ἄρα καὶ τοῖς ἔθνεσιν ὁ θεὸς τὴν **μετάνοιαν** εἰς ζωὴν ἔδωκεν. "Then God has given even to the Gentiles the **repentance** that leads to life." 20:21 διαμαρτυρόμενος Ἰουδαίοις τε καὶ Ἕλλησιν τὴν εἰς θεὸν **μετάνοιαν** καὶ πίστιν εἰς τὸν κύριον ἡμῶν Ἰησοῦν [Paul] as I testified to both Jews and Greeks about **repentance** toward God and faith toward our Lord Jesus 26:20 ἀλλὰ τοῖς ἐν Δαμασκῷ πρῶτόν τε καὶ Ἱεροσολύμοις, πᾶσάν τε τὴν χώραν τῆς Ἰουδαίας καὶ τοῖς ἔθνεσιν ἀπήγγελλον **μετανοεῖν** καὶ ἐπιστρέφειν ἐπὶ τὸν θεόν, ἄξια τῆς **μετανοίας** ἔργα πράσσοντας. [I Paul] declared first to those in Damascus, then in Jerusalem and throughout the countryside of Judea, and also to the Gentiles, that they should **repent** and turn to God and do deeds consistent with **repentance**	7:4–8:1. Let us fix our eyes on the blood of Christ and let us realize how precious it is to his Father, since it was poured out for our salvation and brought the grace of **repentance** to the whole world (ὡς ἔστιν τίμιον τῷ πατρὶ αὐτοῦ, ὅτι διὰ τὴν ἡμετέραν σωτηρίαν ἐκχυθὲν παντὶ τῷ κόσμῳ μετανοίας χάριν ἐπήνεγκεν). Let us go through all the generations and observe that from one generation to another the Master "has afforded an opportunity of **repentance.** [Wisdom 12:10] to those who are willing to turn to him. Noah preached **repentance** . . . Jonah preached destruction to the Ninevites; and when they had **repented** of their sins . . . 8.1 the ministers of God's grace [prophets] spoke about **repentance** through the Holy Spirit . . . 57:1. . . . You who are responsible for the revolt (στάσις) must submit to the presbyters. You must humble your hearts and be disciplined so that you **repent** 62:1–2 περὶ μὲν τῶν ἀνηκόντων τῇ θρησκείᾳ ἡμῶν καὶ τῶν ὠφελιμωτάτων εἰς ἐνάρετον βίον τοῖς θέλουσιν εὐσεβῶς καὶ δικαίως διευθύνειν, ἱκανῶς ἐπεστείλαμεν ὑμῖν, ἄνδρες ἀδελφοί. περὶ γὰρ πίστεως καὶ **μετανοίας** καὶ γνησίας ἀγάπης καὶ ἐγκρατείας καὶ ὑπομονῆς πάντα τόπον ἐψηλαφήσαμεν, ὑπομιμνήσκοντες δεῖν ὑμᾶς ἐν δικαιοσύνῃ καὶ ἀληθείᾳ καὶ μακροθυμίᾳ. We have written enough to you, sisters and brothers, about what befits our religion and is most helpful to those who want reverently and uprightly to lead a virtuous life. We have, indeed, touched on every topic— faith, **repentance**, genuine love, self-control, sobriety, and patience. We have reminded you that you must reverently please almighty God by your uprightness, truthfulness, and long-suffering . . .[225]

Table 6.15 Virtues

Terms in *1 Clement* 62	Luke and Acts	Other NT
Religion: θρησκεία	1	Col; Jas (2)
*Reverently δικαίως: εὐσεβῶς Justly δικαίως (below) (Faith: πίστις)[226]	4	Pastorals 13; 2 Pet 5
Repentance: μετάνοια	11	Rom; 2 Cor (2); 2 Tim; Heb (3); 2 Pet
Love: ἀγάπη	1	115, lacking only in Mark, Acts, and Jas
Self-control: ἐγκράτεια	1	Gal; 2 Pet (2); Tit
"sobriety": σωφροσύνη	1	1 Tim (2)
patience: ὑπομονή	2	Paul (10); Col (1); 2 Thess (2); Pastorals (3); Heb (2); Jas (3); 2 Pet (2); Rev (13)
*uprightness: δικαιοσύνη	5[227]	Eph (2–3); Pastorals (4); Heb (6); 1 Pet (2); 2 Pet (4); 1 John (3) Rev (2)
truthfulness: ἀλήθεια	1[228]	Rom (2)
long-suffering: μακροθυμία * includes nouns, adjs., advs.	—	Paul (4); Eph; Col (2); Pastorals (3); Heb ; Jas ; 1 Pet ; 2 Pet .

1 Clement into the ninth century. Western use is less frequent.[229] The letter is a part of the New Testament codex Alexandrinus (fourth century), present in numerous Coptic manuscripts, and in a Syriac ms. of the twelfth century (with *2 Clement*, between the catholic epistles and the Pauline letters).[230] This work thus has early and wide attestation—indeed, for the period up to 180, better than that of Acts. For both Polycarp is the earliest witness, although the data for Polycarp's use of *1 Clement* is more substantial than that for his use of Acts.

Ignorance is an important motif in discussions of conversion from polytheism to Judaism or Christianity. A useful illustration is the citation (in Table 6.13) from (*Joseph and*) *Aseneth*, a classic story of conversion from polytheism.[231] The outstanding example, however, of "ignorance" in relation to the conversion of a "heathen" is none other than our Paul. Among the most edifying, if least historically defensible, elements of the post-Pauline construct is the portrayal of "the pre-Christian Paul" as a vicious sinner, the veritable enemy of the people of God, and, more or less, as a gentile. 1 Timothy 1:12–17 is perhaps the most remarkable example of this tendency:

> I am grateful to Christ Jesus our Lord, who has strengthened me, because he judged me faithful and appointed me to his service, even though I was formerly a blasphemer, a persecutor, and a man of violence. But I received mercy because I had acted ignorantly in unbelief, and the grace of our Lord overflowed for me with the faith and love that are in Christ Jesus. The saying is sure and worthy of full acceptance, that Christ Jesus came into the world to save. But for that very reason I received mercy, so that in me, as the foremost, Jesus Christ might display the utmost patience, making me an example to those who would come to believe in him for eternal life. To the King of the ages, immortal, invisible, the only God, be honor and glory forever and ever. Amen.

Of the several terms, only "persecutor" belongs to Paul's self-description.[232] The epithets βλάσφημος and ὑβριστής (blasphemer, violent person, v. 13)[233] do not correspond to Paul's view of his career, nor does he describe himself as the "foremost of sinners" (vv. 15–16). "Ignorance" (verse 13) brings to mind Acts 3:17, 17:30, and Ephesians 4:18, where the term serves to explain, if not to excuse, *gentile* behavior. The pre-conversion Paul of 1 Timothy is as ignorant as the idolatrous Athenians because the contrast between "pagan" and "Christian" Paul is central to the moral teaching of the Pastorals. Paul is the prototypical sinner and therefore the model convert from the orbit of polytheism.

Eph. 2:9

1 Timothy is not the sole witness to this edifying development. The quite assuredly pre-Lukan legend of "The Conversion of Paul" (Acts 9) includes this remarkable phrase: "Who are you, Lord?" (v. 5). Such a question belongs to a polytheistic milieu, in which one needs to know just which particular god's ire has been aroused and the reason for the epiphany. It is therefore quite at home in polytheistic "conversion stories," but scarcely in the present context.[234] Saul was quite aware of whom he was persecuting, nor had he learned at the feet of Gamaliel or elsewhere that there were many true lords. The persecutor presented here is a typical θεόμαχος,[235] the enemy of the people of God, and to all intents and purposes a polytheist sinner.[236] Luke and the Pastorals exhibit a portrait of Paul stemming from a time and a place in which gentile converts were the leading concern. To reiterate: Acts 9:1–19a is in large part pre-Lucan. In his retellings of the story (Acts 22 and 26) Luke, as argued in Chapter Four, thrust it in a different direction. Although pre-Lucan, the story of Acts 9 stems from an entirely gentile milieu.[237]

Behind the dichotomy between "ignorance" (polytheism) and "enlightenment" (conversion) stands the claim of these religions to possess what traditional theology calls "particular/special revelation" (as opposed to "general revelation"). Greco-Roman culture, backward and oppressive as it may have been, accepted and appreciated a great deal of what we call religious pluralism and diversity. The claim of one nation or group to have been honored with *the* truth was generally abhorrent. Related to this is the apparent injustice of condemning persons for sins of which they were not aware. Few will happily pay a $50 fine for parking in a place where there was no indication that parking was forbidden. Luke's common-sense approach to ignorance as mitigation can be seen in the unbeatable example of his expansion of a parable discussed earlier.[238]

> That slave who *knew* what his master wanted, but did not prepare himself or do what was wanted, will receive a severe beating. But the *one who did not know* and did what deserved a beating will receive a light beating. From everyone to whom much has been given, much will be required; and from the one to whom much has been entrusted, even more will be demanded. (Luke 12:47–48)

The issue of fairness had, perforce, to emerge in apologetics, a discipline never divorced from the subject of mission.[239] Apologists tended to invoke a number of arguments. One was, in effect, "You *should* have known better." The world is filled with evidence of religious and moral fireplugs which none can justify blocking. There exists, then, a connection—dare I call it natural—between God and the world that is apparent in nature. "natural theology" is the constant companion of the leading strand of missionary-apologetic discourse; the link is manifest in Paul's address to the Council of the Areopagus in Acts 17.[240]

The importance of this link between "mission" in the broad sense and natural theology is that the essence of apologetics is *reasonableness*. The "excuse" of ignorance is utterly rational and perfectly fair in appearance. It thus forms another prong of the case: "You *could not* have known better."[241] This standard of what is reasonable and fair is, in fact, very much a matter of cultural convention. One need not look back to antiquity to find a culture that believed it was "natural" for women to remain at home to care for house and children. Cultures tend to assume that what is manifestly "right" is rooted in nature. Therein lies the warrant for "an ethic . . . based on common sense, pragmatism, and the natural order of things." This is the ethic of conventional virtues and values that is dominant in Luke, the Pastoral Epistles, *1 Clement*, Polycarp, and other writers of the first third of the second century.[242] I should, however, disagree with Stephen Wilson, whose words are quoted above, on the matter of whether this morality is "In place of an ethic rooted in a theology . . ."[243] It *is* rooted in a theology that is "natural" in several senses.

One ethical implication of the positive valuation of nature and common sense comes to light in discussions of diet, for that debate involved not only disputes over *kashrut,* the applicability of Jewish dietary regulations to (at least gentile) followers of Jesus, but also responses to ascetic demands that were often grounded in antipathy to the natural world.

RITUAL PURITY AND MORAL PURITY

The general tendency to moralize "ritual purity" is manifest is the widespread proverb, "For the (morally) pure everything is (ritually) pure."[244] (See Table 6.16.) This rational/ethical slogan provides a link between the "strong," with whom Paul sided in principle but would not hesitate to oppose in practice, and

Table 6.16: Ritual Purity

Luke 11:41[245]	Titus 1:15	Romans 14:20
πλὴν τὰ ἐνόντα δότε ἐλεημοσύνην, καὶ ἰδοὺ **πάντα καθαρὰ** ὑμῖν ἐστιν So give for alms those things that are within; and see, **everything will be clean** for you	**πάντα καθαρὰ** τοῖς **καθαροῖς**· τοῖς δὲ μεμιαμμένοις καὶ ἀπίστοις οὐδὲν **καθαρόν**, ἀλλὰ μεμίανται αὐτῶν καὶ ὁ νοῦς καὶ ἡ **συνείδησις**. **To the pure all things are pure**, but to the cor-	. . . **πάντα** μὲν **καθαρά**, ἀλλὰ κακὸν τῷ ἀνθρώπῳ τῷ διὰ προσκόμματος ἐσθίοντι **Everything** is indeed **clean**, but it is wrong for you to make others fall by what you eat.
Acts 10:15 Ἃ ὁ θεὸς **ἐκαθάρισεν** σὺ μὴ κοίνου *a voice from heaven said to Peter:* "What God has **made clean**, you must not call profane."	rupt and unbelieving nothing is pure. Their very minds and con- sciences are corrupted **1 Timothy 4:4** ὅτι πᾶν κτίσμα θεοῦ καλόν, καὶ	**Ephesians 5:26** ἵνα αὐτὴν ἁγιάσῃ **καθαρίσας** τῷ λουτρῷ τοῦ ὕδατος ἐν ῥήματι in order to make her [the church] holy by **cleans-**
Acts 10:28 κἀμοὶ ὁ θεὸς ἔδειξεν μηδένα κοινὸν ἢ **ἀκάθαρτον** λέγειν ἄνθρωπον· God has shown me that I should not call anyone profane or **unclean**.	οὐδὲν ἀπόβλητον μετὰ εὐχαριστίας λαμβανόμενον For everything created by God is good, and nothing is to be rejected, provided it is received with thanksgiving	**ing** her with the washing of water by the word **Barnabas 8:3** (In the course of an alle- gorical interpretation of the ceremonies for the Day of Atonement
Acts 15:9 καὶ οὐθὲν διέκρινεν μεταξὺ ἡμῶν τε καὶ αὐτῶν, τῇ πίστει **καθαρίσας** τὰς καρδίας αὐτῶν and in cleansing their hearts by faith he has made no distinction between them and us.		[Numbers 19]) οἱ ῥαντίζοντες παῖδες οἱ εὐαγγελισάμενοι ἡμῖν τὴν ἄφεσιν τῶν ἁμαρτιῶν καὶ τὸν ἁγνισμὸν τῆς καρδίας The children who sprin- kle [the people] are they who proclaimed to us forgiveness of sins and purification of heart.

the "opponents" of the pastor.[246] Unlike Paul, who in effect held that whatever offends "the weak" is "unclean," the Pastor takes the general view that personal character is determinative. When Acts invokes the principle of the goodness of all that God has made in order to justify the abolition of distinctions between Jew and gentile, it is the same principle defended by the Pastor. The historical Paul did not approach the Torah from the perspective that ritual purity was in tension with the goodness of creation.[247] For both Luke (Acts 10) and the Pastor (1 Timothy 4:3–5) the essential goodness and consequent reliability of creation provide, however implicitly, the underpinning of the Christian ethic. Natural theology and ethics "based on . . . the natural order of things" (S. Wilson, above) are not strange bedfellows.

An objection to this is contained in the argument that Luke uses the "goodness of creation" in a salvation-historical context, which the Pastor (and others) later transformed into a weapon against heresy. But although Luke *does* use the argument in a salvation-historical manner, that scarcely makes it an earlier form of that principle, but an adaptation of it. Salvation-history is not natural history. Acts rather uses the natural theology of its time to provide a rational and intelligible explanation of the grounds for setting aside the requirements of the Torah.[248] Luke, Ephesians, and *Barnabas* also show how the concept of "purification" could be "spiritualized" as a once-for-all cleansing. Although the gift of the Spirit provided a concrete demonstration of Cornelius's moral purity, that condition had already been affirmed in the narrative (Acts 10:35).[249] Helmut Koester says, "The Pastoral Epistles mark the end of Christian eschatological ethics and thus prepare the way for Christian apologetics."[250] The observation is just. I should like to extend it to include Luke and Acts, especially the latter, where the relation between natural theology and ethics, a basic feature of apologetics, is more explicit than in the Pastorals.[251] Establishment of that extension has been a leading purpose of this chapter. Despite its dramatic date, Acts presents an understanding of Christian ethics and its theological grounding that is at home in the theological writings and conflicts of the early second century.

DIVINE PROVIDENCE

Acts and *1 Clement* are the two earliest Christian texts to argue in any detail that the benignity of nature presupposes a beneficent God and to deduce consequences from that assertion.[252] The intellectual basis for this view is the Stoic argument for Providence, which both Luke and *1 Clement* have received through the medium of Hellenistic Judaism, wherein the argument had acquired a clearly theocentric thrust.[253] All of these passages in Tables 6.17a-c are examples of *deliberative* rhetoric, efforts to get their audiences to adopt a course of action.[254] In Acts 14 the immediate goal is to dissuade the crowd from offering sacrifice to Barnabas and Paul. In Acts 17 Paul contends that the "unknown god" piously worshiped by the Athenians is actually known and inappropriately worshiped.[255] Their theology wants revision. The purpose of *1 Clement* is to resolve the crisis brought about by a "rebellion." Despite these differences of purpose, all four texts presuppose continuity between the *ordo naturae* and the *ordo salutis*, between the realms of "nature" and "grace." No thoroughly apocalyptic theologian (Paul, e.g.) would assume such continuity.[256] For both Luke and *1 Clement* continuity is fundamental. History—the link between Israel and Christianity, Jewish and gentile communities—is predominant in Luke, but this is not the only sense in which continuity is important to him. God's fingerprints lie not only upon history; they can also be seen in nature. Miracle, a leading subject in Acts 14:8–18, is not in opposition to "science" or laws of nature.[257] *1 Clement* might have proclaimed the normal model of Hellenistic philosophies:

Table 6.17a: Divine Providence

Acts 14:15-17	Acts 17:24-29	1 Clement 20	1 Clement 33:2-8
καὶ λέγοντες, Ἄνδρες,[258] τί ταῦτα ποιεῖτε; καὶ ἡμεῖς ὁμοιοπαθεῖς ἐσμεν ὑμῖν ἄνθρωποι, εὐαγγελιζόμενοι ὑμᾶς ἀπὸ τούτων τῶν ματαίων ἐπιστρέφειν ἐπὶ θεὸν ζῶντα **ὃς ἐποίησεν τὸν οὐρανὸν καὶ τὴν γῆν καὶ τὴν θάλασσαν καὶ πάντα τὰ ἐν αὐτοῖς·** 16 ὃς ἐν ταῖς παρῳχημέναις γενεαῖς εἴασεν πάντα τὰ ἔθνη πορεύεσθαι ταῖς ὁδοῖς αὐτῶν· 17 καίτοι οὐκ ἀμάρτυρον αὑτὸν ἀφῆκεν ἀγαθουργῶν, **οὐρανόθεν ὑμῖν ὑετοὺς διδοὺς καὶ καιροὺς καρποφόρους, ἐμπιπλῶν τροφῆς καὶ εὐφροσύνης τὰς καρδίας ὑμῶν**	**ὁ θεὸς ὁ ποιήσας τὸν κόσμον καὶ πάντα τὰ ἐν αὐτῷ, οὗτος οὐρανοῦ καὶ γῆς ὑπάρχων κύριος** οὐκ ἐν χειροποιήτοις ναοῖς κατοικεῖ 25 οὐδὲ ὑπὸ χειρῶν ἀνθρωπίνων θεραπεύεται προσδεόμενός τινος,[259] αὐτὸς διδοὺς πᾶσι ζωὴν καὶ πνοὴν καὶ τὰ πάντα· 26 ἐποίησέν τε ἐξ ἑνὸς πᾶν ἔθνος ἀνθρώπων κατοικεῖν ἐπὶ παντὸς προσώπου τῆς γῆς, ὁρίσας **προστεταγμένους καιροὺς καὶ τὰς ὁροθεσίας τῆς** κατοικίας αὐτῶν, 27 ζητεῖν τὸν θεὸν εἰ ἄρα γε ψηλαφήσειαν αὐτὸν καὶ εὕροιεν, καί γε οὐ μακρὰν ἀπὸ ἑνὸς ἑκάστου ἡμῶν ὑπάρχοντα. 28 Ἐν	οἱ οὐρανοὶ τῇ διοικήσει αὐτοῦ σαλευόμενοι ἐν εἰρήνῃ ὑποτάσσονται αὐτῷ. Ἡμέρα τε καὶ νὺξ τὸν τεταγμένον ὑπ᾽ αὐτοῦ δρόμον διανύουσιν, μηδὲν ἀλλήλοις ἐμποδίζοντα. Ἥλιός τε καὶ σελήνη, ἀστέρων τε χοροὶ κατὰ τὴν διαταγὴν αὐτοῦ ἐν ὁμονοίᾳ δίχα πάσης παρεκβάσεως ἐξελίσσουσιν τοὺς ἐπιτεταγμένους αὐτοῖς ὁρισμούς. Γῆ κυοφοροῦσα κατὰ τὸ θέλημα αὐτοῦ τοῖς ἰδίοις καιροῖς τὴν παντελῆ ἀνθρώποις τε καὶ θηρσὶν καὶ πᾶσιν τοῖς οὖσιν ἐπ᾽ αὐτῆς ζώοις ἀνατέλλει τροφήν, μὴ διχοστατοῦσα μηδὲ ἀλλοιοῦσα τι τῶν δεδογματισμένων ὑπ᾽ αὐτοῦ. Ἀβύσσων τε ἀνεξιχνίαστα καὶ νερτέρων ἀνεκδιήγητα κρίματα τοῖς αὐτοῖς συνέχεται προστάγμασιν. Τὸ κύτος τῆς ἀπείρου θαλάσσης κατὰ τὴν δημιουργίαν αὐτοῦ συσταθὲν εἰς τὰς συναγωγὰς οὐ παρεκβαίνει τὰ περιτεθειμένα αὐτῇ κλεῖθρα, ἀλλὰ καθὼς διέταξεν αὐτῇ, οὕτως ποιεῖ. Εἶπεν γάρ "Ἕως ὧδε ἥξεις,	αὐτὸς γὰρ ὁ **δημιουργὸς καὶ δεσπότης τῶν ἁπάντων** ἐπὶ τοῖς ἔργοις αὐτοῦ ἀγαλλιᾶται. Τῷ γὰρ παμμεγεθεστάτῳ αὐτοῦ κράτει οὐρανοὺς ἐστήριξεν καὶ τῇ ἀκαταλήμπτῳ αὐτοῦ συνέσει **διεκόσμησεν αὐτούς· γῆν τε διεχώρισεν ἀπὸ τοῦ περιέχοντος αὐτὴν ὕδατος** καὶ ἥδρασεν ἐπὶ τὸν ἀσφαλῆ τοῦ ἰδίου βουλήματος θεμέλιον, τά τε ἐν αὐτῇ ζῷα φοιτῶντα τῇ ἑαυτοῦ διατάξει ἐκέλευσεν εἶναι **θάλασσαν λαὶ τὰ ἐν αὐτῇ ζῷα προετοιμάσας ἐνέκλεισεν τῇ ἑαυτοῦ δυνάμει.** Ἐπὶ πᾶσι τὸ ἐξοχώτατον καὶ παμμέγεθες, ἄνθρωπον, ταῖς ἱεραῖς καὶ ἀμώμοις χερσὶν ἔπλασεν τῆς ἑαυτοῦ εἰκόνος χαρακτῆρα. Οὕτως γάρ φησιν ὁ θεός· Ποιήσωμεν ἄνθρωπον κατ᾽ εἰκόνα καὶ καθ᾽ ὁμοίωσιν ἡμετέραν. Καὶ ἐποίησεν ὁ θεὸς τὸν ἄνθρωπον, ἄρσεν καὶ θῆλυ ἐποίησεν αὐτούς. ταῦτα οὖν πάντα τελειώσας ἐπῄνεσεν

αὐτὰ καὶ ηὐλόγησεν καὶ εἶπεν "Αὐξάνεσθε καὶ πληθύνεσθε." Ἴδωμεν, ὅτι ἐν ἔργοις ἀγαθοῖς πάντες ἐκοσμήθησαν οἱ δίκαιοι, καὶ αὐτὸς δὲ ὁ κύριος ἔργοις ἀγαθοῖς ἑαυτὸν κοσμήσας ἐχάρη. Ἴδωμεν, ὅτι ἐν ἔργοις ἀγαθοῖς πάντες ἐκοσμήθησαν οἱ δίκαιοι, καὶ αὐτὸς δὲ ὁ κύριος ἔργοις ἀγαθοῖς ἑαυτὸν κοσμήσας ἐχάρη. Ἔχοντες οὖν τοῦτον τὸν ὑπογραμμὸν ἀόκνως προσέλθωμεν τῷ θελήματι αὐτοῦ· ἐξ ὅλης τῆς ἰσχύος ἡμῶν ἐργασώμεθα ἔργον δικαιοσύνης.

καὶ τὰ κύματά σου συντριβήσεται. Ὠκεανὸς ἀπέραντος ἀνθρώποις καὶ οἱ μετ' αὐτὸν κόσμοι ταῖς αὐταῖς ταγαῖς τοῦ δεσπότου διευθύνονται. καιροὶ ἐαρινοὶ καὶ μετοπωρινοὶ καὶ χειμερινοὶ ἐν εἰρήνῃ μεταπαραδιδόασιν ἀλλήλοις. Ἀνέμων σταθμοὶ κατὰ τὸν ἴδιον καιρὸν τὴν λειτουργίαν αὐτῶν ἀπροσκόπτως ἐπιτελοῦσιν ἀέναοί τε πηγαί, πρὸς ἀπόλαυσιν καὶ ὑγείαν δημιουργηθεῖσα, δίχα ἐλλείψεως παρέχονται τοὺς πρὸς ζωῆς ἀνθρώποις μαζούς· τά τε ἐλάχιστα τῶν ζῴων τὰς συνελεύσεις αὐτῶν ἐν ὁμονοίᾳ καὶ εἰρήνῃ ποιοῦνται. Ταῦτα πάντα ὁ μέγας δημιουργὸς καὶ δεσπότης τῶν ἁπάντων ἐν εἰρήνῃ καὶ ὁμονοίᾳ προσέταξεν εἶναι, εὐεργετῶν τὰ πάντα, ὑπερεκπερισσῶς δὲ ἡμᾶς τοὺς προσπεφευγότας τοῖς οἰκτιρμοῖς αὐτοῦ διὰ τοῦ κυρίου ἡμῶν Ἰησοῦ Χριστοῦ.

αὐτῷ γὰρ ζῶμεν καὶ κινούμεθα καὶ ἐσμέν, ὡς καί τινες τῶν καθ' ὑμᾶς ποιητῶν εἰρήκασιν, Τοῦ γὰρ καὶ γένος ἐσμέν. 29 γένος οὖν ὑπάρχοντες τοῦ θεοῦ οὐκ ὀφείλομεν νομίζειν χρυσῷ ἢ ἀργύρῳ ἢ λίθῳ, χαράγματι τέχνης καὶ ἐνθυμήσεως ἀνθρώπου, τὸ θεῖον εἶναι ὅμοιον.

Table 6.17b

Acts 14:15–17	Acts 17:24–29	1 Clement 20	Clement 32:2–8
15 "Friends, why are you doing this? We are mortals just like you, and we bring you good news, that you should turn from these worthless things to **the living God, who made the heaven and the earth and the sea and all that is in them.** 16 In past generations he allowed all the nations to follow their own ways; 17 yet he has not left himself without a witness in **doing good—giving you rains from heaven and fruitful seasons, and filling you with food and your hearts with joy."**	Acts 17:24–29 **The God who made the world and everything in it, he who is Lord of heaven and earth,** does not live in shrines made by human hands, 25 nor is he served by human hands, as though he needed anything, since he himself gives to all mortals life and breath and all things. 26 From one ancestor he made all nations to inhabit the whole earth, and **he allotted the times of their existence and the boundaries of the places where they would live,**[260] 27 so that they would search for God and perhaps grope for him and find him—though indeed he is not far from each one of us. 28 For 'In him we live and move and have our being'; as even some of your own poets have said, 'For we too are his	19:2. Let us fix our eyes on the **father and creator of the universe** and cling to his magnificent and excellent gifts of peace and kindness to us. 20.1 the heavens move at his direction and peacefully obey him. Day and night observe the course he has appointed them, without getting in each other's way. The sun and the moon and the choirs of stars roll on harmoniously in their appointed courses at his command, and with never a deviation. By his will and without dissension or altering anything he has decreed **the earth becomes fruitful at the proper seasons and brings forth abundant food for mortal and animals and every living thing upon it.** The unsearchable, abysmal depths and the indescribable regions of the underworld are subject to the same decrees. The basin of the boundless sea is by his arrangement constructed to hold the heaped up waters, so that the sea does not flow beyond the barriers surrounding it, but does just as he bids it. For he said, "thus far you shall come, and your waves shall break within you." (Job 38:11) The ocean which humans cannot pass, and the worlds beyond it, are 1	(33:1 What, then, sisters and brothers ought we do do? Should we grow slack in doing good . . .) For the Creator and Master of the universe himself rejoices in his works. Thus by his almighty power he established the heavens and by his inscrutable wisdom he arranged them. He separated the land from the water surrounding it and fixed it upon the sure foundation of his own will. By his decree he brought into existence the living creatures which roam on it; and after creating the sea and the creatures which inhabit it, he fixed its boundaries by his power. 4. Above all, with his holy and pure hands he formed humanity, his outstanding and greatest achievement, stamped with his own image. For this is what God said: "Let us make humanity in our own image and likeness. And God made humanity: male and female he created them." [Gen 1:26–27] And so, when he had finished all this, he praised it and blessed it and said,

offspring.' 29 Since we are God's offspring, we ought not to think that the deity is like gold, or silver, or stone, an image formed by the art and imagination of mortals.

governed by the same decrees of the Master. **The seasons, spring, summer, autumn, and winter, peacefully give way to each other.** The winds from their different points perform their service at the proper time and without hindrance. Perennial springs, created for enjoyment and health, never fail to offer their life-giving breasts to mortals. The tiniest creatures come together in harmony and peace. All these things the great Creator and Master of the universe ordained to exist in peace and harmony. Thus he showed his benefits on them all, but most abundantly on us who have taken refuge in his compassion through our Lord Jesus Christ. . . .

"Increase and multiply." [Gen 1:28] We should observe that all the righteous have been adorned with good deeds and the very Lord adorns himself with good deeds and rejoices. Since, then, we have this example, we should unhesitatingly give ourselves to his will, and put all our effort into acting uprightly.[261]

Table 6.17c

Acts 14:15; 17:25[262]	Diognetus 3:4	Acts of Paul
ὃς ἐποίησεν τὸν οὐρανὸν καὶ τὴν γῆν καὶ τὴν θάλασσαν καὶ πάντα τὰ ἐν αὐτοῖς· who made the heaven and the earth and the sea and all that is in them. 25 οὐδὲ ὑπὸ χειρῶν ἀνθρωπίνων θεραπεύεται προσδεόμενός τινος, αὐτὸς διδοὺς πᾶσι ζωὴν καὶ πνοὴν καὶ τὰ πάντα· as though he needed anything, since he himself gives to all mortals life and breath and all things. Cf. Acts 4:24 Δέσποτα, σὺ ὁ ποιήσας τὸν οὐρανὸν καὶ τὴν γῆν καὶ τὴν θάλασσαν καὶ πάντα τὰ ἐν αὐτοῖς, 25 ὁ τοῦ πατρὸς ἡμῶν διὰ πνεύματος ἁγίου στόματος Δαυὶδ παιδός σου εἰπών When they heard it, they raised their voices together to God and said, "Sovereign Lord, who made the heaven and the earth, the sea, and everything in them	Ὁ γὰρ ποιήσας τὸν οὐρανὸν καὶ τὴν γῆν καὶ πάντα τὰ ἐν αὐτοῖς For he who made the heaven and the earth and all that is in them, καὶ πᾶσιν ἡμῖν χορηγῶν, ὧν προσδεόμεθα, οὐδενὸς ἂν αὐτὸς προσδέοιτο τούτων ὧν τοῖς οἰομένοις διδόναι παρέχει αὐτός. and provides us with everything we need, can scarcely need any of the things that he himself supplies to those who fancy that they are giving something to him.[263]	8.3.19 (3 Corinthians) λέγοντες μὴ εἶναι τὸν οὐρανὸν καὶ τὴν γῆν καὶ πάντα τὰ ἐν αὐτοῖς ἔργα τοῦ πατρὸς [heretics who] say that heaven and earth and all that is in them are not works of the Father cf. 7.1 (PHamb p.1) 3.24. ἐβόησεν Πάτερ, ὁ ποιήσας τὸν οὐρανὸν καὶ τὴν γῆν, ὁ τοῦ παιδὸς τοῦ υἱοῦ ἀγαπητοῦ σου Ἰησου Χριστοῦ πατήρ [Thecla] cried out: "Father, who made heaven and earth, the Father of the beloved servant and son, Jesus Christ."

"Follow Nature!" The author wants his auditors to follow God, of course; nature reveals that God is interested in *order*. (At times one may wonder if the author believes that this is almost the sole subject of divine interest.) *1 Clement* 31–34 follow the argument of Romans 4–6. After the example/story of Abraham (Romans 4; *1 Clement* 31) comes a statement about justification (Romans 5; *1 Clement* 32). Chapter 33 begins with a paraphrase of Romans 6:1 (sin so that grace may flourish? No!). But, whereas Paul offers a sacramental argument based upon Baptism, (the "early Catholic"!) *1 Clement* reiterates his earlier argu-

ment from creation, which exhibits a pattern of "righteousness." Creation urges
the imitation of God. This is another theme of Greco-Roman philosophy that is
also present in Luke:

> But love your enemies, do good, and lend, expecting nothing in return. Your
> reward will be great, and you will be children of the Most High; for he is kind to
> the ungrateful and the wicked. Be merciful, just as your Father is merciful. (Luke
> 6:35–36)[264]

Mikeal Parsons and I sketched this background and some of its implications
for Luke and Acts.[265] *1 Clement* belongs to the same theological milieu. Both
writers appeal to the parenthood of God and to the creation story in Genesis
to validate their ethical norms and ideas.[266] For Luke, creation in the image
and likeness of God has missionary implications: all can be righteous.[267] For
1 Clement (especially chapter 33) this is the basis of the possibility of righteousness. In theological jargon, possession of the divine image is the indicative
behind the imperative.[268] The structure is Pauline, but the thought is Deutero-
Pauline.[269]

In pursuing their disparate goals these two authors touch upon many of
the same subjects. God has created all that exists. This is "the first and great
commandment."[270] The ultimate source of this material is almost certainly
Hellenistic Judaism, probably the liturgy of the synagogue.

> Christianity is Diaspora-Judaism become universal, *freed of its limitations*, but it
> is also *Diaspora-Judaism* in spite of the removal of its limitations. It continues the
> development which had already successfully begun in Diaspora-Judaism, in the
> same direction . . . When we read I Clement, we are surprised to see that here
> Christianity is hardly anything other than this belief in the one almighty Creator
> God . . . In solemn, choice language, which now and then rises to the level of a
> majestic hymn and which clearly sows the influence of Stoic popular philoso-
> phy which probably had been filtered through Judaism, Clement celebrates this
> Creator God.[271]

Bousset then cites *1 Clement* 19.2 (above), referring to the role of creation
also in many texts under scrutiny here. His proposal that post-apostolic gentile Christianity became more integrated into Greco-Roman culture by taking
up the language of Greek-speaking Jewish worship cannot be proved, as little
remains of this material, but it is so probable that few have even attempted to
refute it.[272] His categories have been superseded, and much work has been done
since, but Bousset apprehended and expounded the key issues with insight and
vigor.[273] Luke and *1 Clement* (among others) perceive the *mirabilia Dei* (God's
mighty acts) on a spectrum from creation to resurrection, Genesis 1 to Judgment
Day. God is "the maker of all things, the judge of all people." The views about
creation and ethics expressed in Luke's books, the Pastorals, and *1 Clement*
(and other writings) fully cohere. The presence of theological inconsistencies
in Luke and Acts is not surprising, nor should it of itself provide an opening

for "Luke-bashing." Inconsistency is all but inevitable in theologies that seek both to comprehend the traditions (about Jesus and of Paul) and to amalgamate these into a broader and more open model. Indeed, it is very nearly correct to say that where in early Christianity theology is absolutely consistent, there is heresy.[274]

I am therefore in disagreement with Jacob Jervell's contention that the speeches of Acts 14:15–18 and 17:16–34 are inconsistent with the New Testament in general and Luke in particular.[275] Despite the numerous proposals about the genre or genres of Luke and Acts or Luke-Acts or of Luke or of Acts, the leading participants in this conversation agree that their subject is "legitimating narrative." The adjective describes the *rhetorical function* of these books; their *literary method* lies enshrined in the noun. Historically, the phrase is a Janus-head. "Legitimating" points to the era of the early Christian Apologists (c. 140–180 CE), who contended that Christianity was a valid religious movement that the ruling powers ought to acknowledge as acceptable.[276] The narrative method of Luke and Acts is essentially that of the Evangelists, who composed a larger story by means of gathering, assembling, composing, and arranging a number of short stories, tales, anecdotes, and the like.[277] This world of "in-between" is where I find the "home" of Luke, chronologically no less than ideologically. In speaking of the sermons of Acts 14 and 17, Robert Grant observes: "The themes of God's universal providence and humanity's search for him are to be found in Stoic sources and in Hellenistic Judaism. They belong to the apologetic tradition, as does the emphasis on creation and resurrection."[278] Apologetic of one sort or another is not time-bound, to be sure, but the apologetic tradition in view here is that of second century Christianity. Among its pre-conditions are sufficient growth to bring the movement to the attention of society in general, and a clear separation from Judaism, which was accepted as an ancient religion and thus enjoyed, at the very least, the right to exist.

Operating on the principle that a work must be dated by reference to its latest identifiable features, this chapter began by resuming the description of Luke's view of church organization, structure, and function. Although he is aware of the "three-fold ministry" of bishops, presbyters, and deacons, Luke is not wedded to that plan. His preference is for functional descriptions of "ministry." The communities Luke envisions are large enough to have distinct groups or bodies of widows, whose needs can create problems of management. As comparisons indicate, this is the church of the first decades of the second century. Primary attention is given to the nurture and protection of stable communities.

Luke and Acts also devote considerable attention to the qualities, duties, and manners of community leaders. The author's distinctive contribution is that church leaders are not to imitate those of the general culture. They are, as Paul said, "managers," not owners, and are therefore to protect and nurture their charges without the expectation of adulation and authority based upon providing goods and services (benefaction). Financial issues, symbolized by the concept of "greed," loom large. Christianity has become sufficiently attractive to appeal to a number of persons of means, as well as those with economic aspirations.

In its procedures the church meets the expectations of Greco-Roman society for the proper and orderly conduct of business in which leaders and people play their appropriate parts. Churches are exemplary civic entities. The anachronistic theme of "Church and State" relates to a revised understanding of eschatology and the place of Christians in the world. Believers can, and should, aspire to "good citizenship," which is both pleasing to God and beneficial to numerical growth. "Good citizenship" has nothing to do with voting in elections and has little in common with the ancient equivalents of careful recycling of waste. Good citizens order their households as miniature models of general society, social entities in which all perform their appropriate functions in their proper place. Entirely consonant with this view of the church in society is a positive emphasis upon creation and a relatively optimistic anthropology. The church can make use of the world's values and institutions. These include not only ethics and structures but also, as Luke and Acts illustrate in detail, "market place" views of persuasion and proof. The criteria for missionary methods come from the general culture. Ready to hand for nearly all of this were examples from Diaspora Judaism, which had faced the same challenges and had devised means for addressing them. Christians could appropriate these, once they were divested of some of their more controversial features, including male circumcision and avoidance of pork. Most particularly, association with rebellious Judea and its allegedly odious Temple cult formed no part of the program, nor, of course, were national or ethnic pride or particularity in this picture. God's old ideal of human unity, about which more than a few poets and philosophers had spoken, could now be realized.

On both textual and typological grounds the trends delineated above belong to the first third of the second century. The next chapter will represent not a new departure, but a continuation of the methods and argument employed in this one, with concentration upon a wide range of frequently detailed philological investigation.

7 Acts among the Apostolic Fathers II

SOME WORDS, TERMS, AND CONCEPTS

In continuation of the work begun in Chapter Six, this chapter will examine a number of words, terms, and concepts that I believe to be illuminating for the date and milieu of Acts. No claims are made for comprehensiveness, adherence to a strictly scientific model, or complete lack of bias. The goal is the identification of data that support further arguments for dating Acts later than the 80s of the first century. Its chief foundation is the postulate that opened the previous chapter: works must be dated by their latest elements. If Acts contains terminology that is more at home in the period c. 100 and later, the case for a later dating is considerably strengthened. Whereas the previous chapter concentrated upon broader theological systems and concepts, attention now turns to individual words. Precision will not be possible, of course, for of none of these words can it be said that they were first used on 15 August 96 CE. Those who regularly read dictionaries may find this chapter easy going; others may not. I am filling a jar with pebbles. What ultimately counts is the total weight, but the value of each pebble needs to be justified.

I make no resort to detailed statistical analyses, not only because of the deficiencies in my knowledge of statistical method but also because, for better or for worse, no issues of the date or sources of Biblical books have ever been absolutely settled by rigorous statistical analyses. The survey that follows is therefore impressionistic and incomplete, but it strives to be honest. The object of this phase of the inquiry is the identification of language and ideas that are at home in "later writings" of the New Testament and in the Apostolic Fathers, with some attention to the earlier Apologists. The center of these probes is the Deutero-Pauline material and its "friends and relations": Colossians, Ephesians, 2 Thessalonians, the Pastorals (1–2 Timothy and Titus), Hebrews, James, *1–2 Clement*, Ignatius of Antioch, Polycarp of Smyrna, 1–2 Peter, and various apologists, particularly Justin.[1] The date of none of these writings is secure, and scholarly opinion varies.[2] Whenever possible, I shall attempt to illustrate a trajectory (or better, some elements of a trajectory) from Paul through the Pastorals and, if appropriate, beyond. A subsidiary goal is to reinforce the extent to which Luke and Acts share—as against Matthew, Mark, and John—the language of Paul. Because the intention is to lend some color to social and theological milieus, concentration lies upon terms and values of theological or moral importance. Just who uses or does not use ὑποστέλλω can be quite significant if one is attempting to prove that Ignatius wrote the epistle of James, but it is not germane to the present survey. No single example of the following brief studies is probative or pretends to be probative. Those that may seem less convincing have been included on the grounds of integrity. As often in this book, the object is to construct a *cumulative* argument. I am, to use a metaphor at once more venerable and weighty than pebbles in a jar, placing one straw after another upon the back of the camel. To avoid making the matter unnecessarily complex or prejudicial, questions of intertextuality are generally left to one side.

Excursus: Two Notes on Method

Readers deserve to know the bases of my method. The origin is unabashedly intuitive. The words considered have come to attention as the result of years of reading Luke, Acts, and other texts. Thereafter came consultation of the various concordances, the relevant lexicons, philological reference works, the specialized dictionaries, and, finally, commentaries upon the several passages. Some may ask about the absence of visible controls, the equivalent of the group that receives a placebo when drugs are tested. In response I observe that what follows is not the same as an appeal to vocabulary and ideas in an attempt to show that Luke wrote the Pastoral Epistles or that he was a physician. This is a quest for affinities, the construction of ever more numerous and increasingly thicker lines that will yield a number of circles with which Luke and Acts intersect—some more than others. Its object is not the exclusion of one or more hypotheses, but the establishment of a network of affinities. This is not, to shift the metaphor, a chain that will be no stronger than its weakest link, because the purpose is to construct not a single chain, but many.

   Some of the following little studies include examples of words that different writers use in distinct senses with variant meanings. Objections may arise, some of which could be valid. I should like to make two important observations. The first is that this criterion may be of great weight in discussions of authorship. If "righteousness," for example, means "doing the right thing" in a particular text rather than a manifestation of divine power, one may ask whether Paul would have made such a shift. In the present instance such changes are quite likely—as the usage of that very word indicates. Writers take up terms from their sources and, intentionally or otherwise, use them according to their own fashion and understanding. The other observation is that even scholars can fall into the trap of appearing to presume that Paul or Luke or Plutarch "thought in English." No one would affirm that proposal, to be sure, but it can lie behind such assertions as "Paul was not talking about correct behavior, i.e. 'works' righteousness,' but about *justification*." That may be, and usually is, perfectly true, but the starting point is one Greek word (δικαιουσύνη), not two English (or German, French, etc.) expressions. What follows is an assembly of Greek terms rather than a detailed analysis of meanings. It is a vocabulary, not a dictionary—even if it often reads like a dictionary.

ἀγνοία ("ignorance").[3] Cf. the synonymous ἀγνωσία. In addition to the passages discussed in the previous chapter,[4] this term as a characteristic of or excuse for gentiles alienated from knowledge of God is found also in Ignatius,

Ephesians, 19:3; the *Preaching of Peter*, fragment 4; *Hermas Mandates* 4.1.5, and regularly in apologetic literature.[5] It comes from the realm of Hellenistic Judaism (see e.g., *3 Maccabees* 5:27), but belongs to the period when Christians have developed an essentially gentile self-consciousness. Ignorance helps to alleviate the problem of particularity. Educated Greco-Roman people took offense at the idea that a good and just God would limit revelation to a particular people.[6]

ἀγαθοεργεῖν ("to do good," "confer benefits") According to BDAG this verb is "quite rare" outside of patristic literature. It occurs but twice in the New Testament: Acts 14:17, as an assertion of God's providing nourishment for humanity, and 1 Timothy 6:18, in an exhortation to the wealthy. The term is quite congenial to the ethical world of Luke and the Pastorals, for it uses the language of benefaction and sets God as the model (Acts) who is to be imitated by fortunate humans (1 Timothy). Semantically related are ἀγαθοποιεῖν ("do good"), and various nouns and adjectives (ἀγαθοποίησις, ἀγαθοποιΐα, ἀγαθοποιός). These appear seven times in 1 Peter, four times in Luke, six times in *Hermas*, four times in *1 Clement*, and once each in *2 Clement* and *Diognetus*. This is evidently a Jewish coinage, long limited to Jewish and Christian writings.[7]

ἀδικία ("unrighteousness"). This is the opposite of δικαιουσύνη (below). In the LXX are 228 appearances.[8] Paul uses this noun eight times, and it appears six times in Luke and Acts.[9] Other occurrences include James, John, 1 John (twice), 2 Thessalonians, 2 Timothy, Hebrews (twice), *1 Clement*, 2 Peter (twice), *Diognetus* (twice), *2 Clement*, *Barnabas*, and Polycarp. Justin finds twenty-one occasions to employ the word, Theophilus four, and Melito two. Here is another example of an abstract noun that can be traced from Paul to the Apologists.[10]

ἀθέμιτος (also ἀθέμιστος) ("what is not allowed," "forbidden.") This is a learned term from the realm of Greek religion and ethics. Although Hellenistic Judaism applied ἀθέμιτος to major violations of Torah, the LXX uses it but four times, in 2 and 3 Maccabees. Josephus uses this adjective about ten times. It belongs to an elevated style of Jewish writing in Greek and is thus suitable for Peter to use with Cornelius (Acts 10:28). The only other New Testament example occurs in 1 Peter 4:3. In early Christian literature the term occurs once in *1 Clement*, the *Didache*, Justin Martyr, *Diognetus*, and Clement of Alexandria. In addition to five instances in Theophilus, the Pseudo-Clementines are fond of this adjective. ἀθέμιτος, then, is a fine example of a "good Greek" word found in Acts that has but one possible late first century attestation (1 Peter) and many from the second.[11]

αἵρεσις ("school," "sect," "faction;" "leading dogmas") Chapter five discussed the use of "sect" in Acts and Josephus. In Galatians 5:20 and 1 Corinthians 11:18–19 Paul effectively opposes *hairesis* to Church.[12] Luke is probably of a similar mind in Acts 24:5, where the followers of Jesus are labeled "the party of the Nazoreans." For Ignatius the idea of a *hairesis* is the antithesis of his view of unity (*Ephesians* 6:2; *Trallians* 6:1). Translators are tempted to render the term as "heresy." Justin attributes the word to Jewish opponents of

Christianity (*Dialogue* 17:1; "the godless sect of the Christians," [αἵρεσιν ἄθεον χριστιανῶν]; 108:2¹³). In Justin's *1 Apology* 26.8 the term effectively means "heresies." 2 Peter 2:1 may have a similar meaning, although it can be translated "destructive opinions." In Titus 3:10 the adjective means "factious." For *Hermas Similitude* 9.23.6 "false opinion" is a sound rendition. No word is more revealing of the ongoing quest for Christian unity than is this term for "school," or "sect." For Paul, who pioneered the pejorative sense of *hairesis*, the word meant "faction." Luke is more conventional, but the term is never fully neutral in his writings. He points the way to the future. By the time of Justin *hairesis* had acquired the meaning of "heresy." Acts belongs on a trajectory between Paul and Justin.¹⁴

αἰσχροκερδής (See also πλεονεξία-εκτης, φιλαργυρία. On these terms for greed see p. 220–25.

ἄλογος ("irrational," "unreasonable.") Festus's statement, "for it seems to me unreasonable to send a prisoner [Paul] without indicating the charges against him." (Acts 25:27) is perfectly reasonable. Yet Luke does invoke the term in an "apologetic" context, and this word is a favorite with apologists, used more than twenty times by Justin, nine times by Athenagoras, and twice each by Melito and Theophilus. The adjective is found once in the *Acts of John*, and more than twenty times in the Pseudo-Clementines, in varied senses. The only other New Testament use is in Jude 10//2 Peter 2:12, where it has the sense of "lacking the capacity to reason," an attribute of animals. Six of eight appearances in the LXX are in works that exist only in Greek, most of which have an apologetic orientation.¹⁵

ἄνδρες ἀδελφοί ("gentlemen and brethren"). On this form of address, found fourteen times in Acts and four times in *1 Clement*, see p. 303.

ἀνόητος, ("foolish") ἄνοια ("folly," "mindless rage"). The adjective appears once in Luke, three times in Paul ("foolish Galatians"), and twice in the Pastorals. The Apostolic Fathers offer three examples from *1 Clement* (two in citations), and one from Hermas. Justin uses the adjective ten times, and three examples come from Theophilus. The noun is found once each in Luke and the Pastorals. It also appears in *2 Clement*, and *3 Corinthians*, five times in Justin, three times in the surviving Greek portions of Irenaeus, and is common in Clement of Alexandria and Origen. In the LXX the adjective appears eleven times, six in works only in Greek. Statistics for the noun are similar: Thirteen total, eight from works in Greek. ἄνοια belongs to the intellectual world and has a slightly philosophical cast, as can be seen in Clement and Origen.¹⁶

ἀρχαῖος ("ancient," in the sense of existing for a very long time) turns up about ten times in the New Testament in reference to genuinely "ancient times." Luke, who can apply the word to the age of the prophets (Luke 9:8, 19), twice avails himself of the opportunity to display this word in Acts to refer to the "early Church." At the "Apostolic Council" Peter can look back to the conversion of Cornelius as an event of the "old days" (15:7; cf. v. 21). The Cypriote Mnason is a disciple of "long standing" (21:16).¹⁷ Luke is obviously seeking to make the Christian movement appear more venerable than it is. Nonetheless, the practice is echoed in *1 Clement*, which quite properly assigns those of the period from Cain to David to the "ancients" (5:1), but which can also refer to the "ancient Church of the Corinthians" (47:6), an epithet also applied by Polycarp to the Church of the Philippians (1:2). This somewhat arcane practice of "instant antiquity" is another characteristic that Luke shares with some of the Apostolic Fathers. The motive for this claim was that the Greco-Roman world tended to approve of, or at least to accept, that which had the aura of antiquity. The older the better.

ascension / *exaltation;*

two ^

The ascension of Christ and the session at the right hand of God become distinct items in the creedal narrative and doctrines of later texts. Early believers used a number of terms and images to characterize the Easter victory of God. The view that God had *exalted* Jesus to a privileged "place in Heaven" does not presume that resurrection and ascension preceded this act. Hebrews prefers the concept of exaltation to resurrection. Therefore Hebrews 4:14 ("Since, then, we have a great high priest who has passed through the heavens, Jesus, the Son of God, let us hold fast to our confession") should not be read as a reference to the ascension in the Lucan sense. John's narrative does speak of ascension (6:62, etc.), which the narrative of chapter 20 integrates into a narrative sequence of resurrection and ascension (20:17), albeit with some tension. 1 Timothy 3:16 should probably be read as describing an ascension. Luke 24:51 and Acts 1:9 are clear narrative descriptions of the physical ascension of a body.[18] One must admit that Ephesians 4:8–10, which also refers to the ascension, can be variously construed.[19]

> Therefore it is said, "When he ascended on high he made captivity itself a captive; he gave gifts to his people." (When it says, "He ascended," what does it mean but that he had also descended into the lower parts of the earth? He who descended is the same one who ascended far above all the heavens, so that he might fill all things.)

Nevertheless, in the light of 1:20 ("God put this power to work in Christ when he raised him from the dead and seated him at his right hand in the heavenly places"), Ephesians appears to share the view that Christ was raised (2:6) and seated at God's right hand. Session at God's right hand is implicit in Acts 2:35 and explicit at 7:55. 1 Peter 3:22 also proclaims the seating of Christ in heaven.[20] Although Luke's narration of the event may strike some readers as a bit crude, his statements show a developing creed that is otherwise (and variously) attested in writings of c. 90 and later.[21]

ἀσκέω ("to discipline oneself") is a verb that long referred to athletic training and eventually yielded the English word "asceticism."[22] The sole New Testament occurrence is in Acts 24:16. Paul's defense speech gains quality and color with this "classy" word. The one example of this verb in the LXX is in 2 Maccabees 15:4.[23] Hans Windisch notes "... [I]n Ep Ar. [*Aristeas*] 168 we have a statement which almost reads like a commentary on Ac. 24:16 in its use of ἀσκεῖν . . . Paul gives us an example of genuine Jewish Hellenism in Acts 24:16 and the whole passage 24:14–18."[24] Outside of the New Testament there are examples of ἀσκέω in Polycarp, *Hermas, 2 Clement,* Justin, Tatian, *Diognetus,* the *Acts of Paul,* and often in the Pseudo-Clementines. Although the word appears but once in Acts, it is a worthy addition to this catalogue of terms that become at home in Christian literature c. 130 CE and thereafter.

ἀσωτία, ἀσώτως ("prodigality," "recklessness," "dissipation"). When imagining Roman "orgies" of the Hollywood variety, this is the verbal stem that will come to the minds of those who think in ancient Greek. "Recklessness" is the root meaning,[25] but moralists routinely used it of immoderate drinking and its putative corollaries: irregular hours, loose companions, wild partying, and sexual promiscuity.[26] Luke aptly illustrates this propensity when he portrays the angry older brother of the "prodigal" (so called for the adverb in Luke 15:13) as complaining that his junior sibling had wasted the family fortune on prostitutes (15:30). Proper reproof of "debauchery" emerges in non-narrative contexts in Ephesians 5:18, 1 Peter 4:4, and Titus 1:6. The next Christian writer to use the word was Justin Martyr, *1 Apology* 62.1. This terminology belongs to the more literary and morally "proper" Christian world of the end of the first century and later.[27]

αὐξάνω ("grow"). Paul popularized the metaphorical application of this word to qualitative and quantitative community growth (1 Corinthians 3:6, 7; 2 Corinthians 9:10; 10:15). This word, with its cognate noun, αὔξησις ("growth"), became popular in the post-Pauline era as part of the language of Christian nurture, i.e., spiritual formation. The words appear seven times in Colossians and Ephesians as well as once each in 1 and 2 Peter. On three important occasions Acts speaks of "the word" growing (6:7; 12:24; 19:20). The phrase is unusual, since "word" seems to be a kind of personification, a "hypostasis." I think it preferable to view this as a kind of metonymy, in which the attribute or cause stands for the effect. It derives from the Pauline view of the church as a creation of the word (Romans 9:8–9).[28] Because Luke focuses upon the empirical, quantitative growth in the face of adversity is his explicit emphasis, but it is reasonable to suppose that he has qualitative growth in mind as well.[29]

ἄφεσις ("forgiveness") This noun commonly has the sense of "forgiveness" in Luke and Acts, eight times with "of sins" (ἁμαρτιῶν), but is not found in Paul.[30] It does emerge in the Deutero-Pauline sphere, however, in Colossians 1:14//Ephesians 1:7, as well as twice in Hebrews.[31] Eleven examples appear in the Apostolic Fathers, two of them in citations. This Lucan usage is thus another indicator of its place within the post-Pauline world. It was a common term used in a specialized sense for the instruction of former polytheists who had to learn of the possibility that one could sin against God and receive forgiveness from God. These notions were not widely held in polytheist culture.[32]

δεσμεύω, δέσμιος, δεσμός ("bind," "prisoner," "bonds/chains"). Cf. συναιχμάλωτος ("fellow prisoner") and φυλακή (in the sense of "custody," "imprisonment"). Five items in the Pauline corpus are written from prison:

Philippians, Philemon, Colossians, Ephesians, and 2 Timothy. Of these only Philippians and tiny Philemon are authentic. Half of the Deutero-Pauline letters, therefore, purport to be written by the imprisoned apostle. Paul's own credentials included the boast that he had been imprisoned "far more" often than any of his rivals (2 Corinthians 11:23). By the end of the first century this Pauline predication seems to have been almost universally accepted, and without a touch of irony. Jail was very much the proper place for an apostle to be. In support of this principle there is a great deal of evidence from the various books of Acts.[33] In the canonical Acts imprisonment leads to much rousing adventure, but pathos is not neglected. And pathos predominates in the letters: "I therefore, the prisoner in the Lord, beg you to lead a life worthy of the calling to which you have been called" (Ephesians 4:1). In 2 Timothy 4:6–18 the Pastor mounts the organ bench to render a piece that requires the full purpureal capacity of every sentimental and pathetic stop. From Acts 21:17 to the end of the book, the picture of Paul the prisoner is present, and often dominant.[34] *1 Clement* also knows of Paul's criminal record: according to 5:6 he was placed in chains a biblically suitable seven times.

Although for both Paul and his later imitators and admirers, imprisonment was a dimension of his suffering in identification with and in the service of Christ, imitation does not provide a comprehensive explanation for the importance of this theme. Jesus, according to the tradition, was arrested but once and incarcerated for less than a day. Acts alone has ample evidence that the idea of the martyr or prisoner as witness *par excellence* has already taken its place in the scale of Christian values. Such discipleship is of the highest type. That the words of prisoners are trustworthy is attested by their fidelity.[35] Just as adventure is important for its inspirational and exemplary value, so pathos has more than sentimental attraction. The appeal of Paul the prisoner is, to be candid, manipulative: who can disregard the wishes of a prisoner on the verge of death? The example of Paul encourages believers not to view imprisonment as a loss of honor and cause of shame (e.g., 2 Timothy 1:8, 16). "Binding" and "prison" can also be symbols of the realm of the dead (1 Peter 3:19; Revelation 2:10; 18:2; 20:7).[36] In some sense the imprisoned apostle of the Deutero-Pauline letters is empowered after his departure to address the entire world. This symbolism possesses universal, eschatological significance. The God who delivers captives from prison (Acts 5:17–21; 12:3–11; 16:19–34) is the one who will deliver believers from the bondage of sin and death.[37] This ultimate eschatological reversal is related to a present eschatological truth, well put by the Pastor: "I suffer hardship, even to the point of being chained like a criminal. But the word of God is not chained" (2 Timothy 2:9).[38] Because captivity was a basic metaphor for the human condition, it could be used in a number of ways; the one emphasized here is the function of the image in the Deutero-Pauline sphere, in particular that of the suffering, absent apostle who still cares for his converts.

δεσπότης ("master," "sovereign" as a designation for God[39]). This term, which can be difficult to distinguish in translations from the more common κύριος, appears ten times in the New Testament. In the Pastorals (four times) and 1 Peter (2:18) the word means "master of slaves" or simply "owner." In Jude 4//2 Peter 2:1 (the latter dependent upon the former) the δεσπότης (i.e., Christ) is "sovereign". In Luke 2:29 (the *Nunc Dimittis*), Acts 4:24, and Revelation 6:10 "sovereign" applies to God. All three occur in prayers. This liturgical usage derives from the later books of the LXX.[40] In the Apostolic Fathers "sovereign" is found more than twenty times in *1 Clement*, a good fifteen times in *Hermas*, twice each in *Diognetus* and *Barnabas*, and once in the *Didache*.[41]

The citations in Table 7.1 purport to show that Luke is familiar with the language of Christian worship of the first decades of the second century. These ascriptions correspond to the standard Jewish prayer after meals, which thank God for bringing forth "bread from the earth" and "wine to gladden our hearts."[42] The eucharistic prayers in the *Didache* represent a rather "pure" form.[43] Acts, *1 Clement*, and *Diognetus* exhibit a "Hellenistic" adaptation that characterizes divine goodness as beneficent/philanthropic and emphasizes the orderliness and regularity of creation. These adaptations conform to popular Greco-Roman political/anthropological values and to philosophical common-places.[44] They represent a step in the direction of apologetic.

διάβολος. The devil you say! I do say that the Devil is a late-comer on the scene.[45] The adversary debuts in the Q Temptation Story (Luke 4:1–13), where eight of the thirty-six New Testament attestations occur. John Kloppenborg makes a convincing case for viewing this story as a late addition to Q, at a time when the sayings gospel was beginning to respond to the tug of the narrative and biographical tendencies that would soon obliterate it.[46] A date c. 90 would not be too late for this addition. Otherwise, Matthew uses the term twice, Luke and Acts three times, John three times, Ephesians twice, the Pastorals four times, Hebrews, James, 1 Peter, and Jude once each, 1 John three times and Revelation five times. About thirty appearances are in the Apostolic Fathers and eighteen in Justin Martyr. Paul does not use this word, which belongs to the later strands of the New Testament and other early Christian literature.[47] "The appearance of the word in Acts may be claimed as evidence that Acts and Ephesians belong to the same period in the development of Christian thought and phraseology . . ."[48]

δικαιοσύνη, δίκαιος (in the sense of proper conduct, "doing the right thing;" "upright," "virtuous"). Chapter six included an examination of the use of this word in Acts, the Pastorals, and *1 Clement*.[49] This view will become domi-nant. "In the majority of cases *dikaiousyne* and *dikaios* denote moral upright-ness."[50] Examples include Acts 13:10, James 5:6, 16; 1 Peter 3:12, 2 Peter 2:7–8; Revelation 22:1; *Barnabas* 1:6; 19:6; Polycarp *Philippians* 9:2, and often in Hermas, which uses these two words more than forty times. For Polycarp, *Philippians* 3:1, "concerning righteousness" introduces an ethical section. This is a precise parallel to Acts 24:25, which it explicates. "Righteousness" can now appear as an item in lists of virtues and, as in Acts and Polycarp, as an expression that

Table 7.1: The Sovereign

Acts 4:24b	1 Clement 20:11	Didache 10:3	Diognetus 8:7
Δέσποτα, σὺ ὁ **ποιήσας** τὸν οὐρανὸν καὶ τὴν γῆν καὶ τὴν θάλασσαν καὶ **πάντα τὰ ἐν** αὐτοῖς **Sovereign Lord**, who made the heaven and the earth, the sea, and everything in them, Cf. 14:15 . . . ὃς ἐποίησεν τὸν οὐρανὸν καὶ τὴν γῆν καὶ τὴν θάλασσαν καὶ πάντα τὰ ἐν αὐτοῖς . . . 17 . . . ἀγαθουργῶν, οὐρανόθεν ὑμῖν ὑετοὺς διδοὺς καὶ καιροὺς καρποφόρους, ἐμπιπλῶν τροφῆς καὶ εὐφροσύνης τὰς καρδίας ὑμῶν. **who made** the heaven and the earth and the sea and **all** that is in them . . . doing good—giving you rains from heaven and fruitful seasons, and filling you with food and your hearts with joy.	Ταῦτα πάντα ὁ μέγας δημιουργὸς καὶ δεσπότης τῶν ἁπάντων ἐν εἰρήνῃ καὶ ὁμονοίᾳ προσέταξεν εἶναι, εὐεργετῶν τὰ πάντα, ὑπερεκπερισσῶς δὲ ἡμᾶς τοὺς προσπεφευγότας τοῖς οἰκτιρμοῖς αὐτοῦ διὰ τοῦ κυρίου ἡμῶν Ἰησοῦ Χριστοῦ. All these things the great Creator and **Sovereign** of the universe ordained to exist in peace and harmony. Thus, he showered his benefits on them all, but most abundantly on us who have taken refuge in his compassion through our Lord Jesus Christ . . .[51] Cf. 33:2 Αὐτὸς γὰρ ὁ δημιουργὸς καὶ **δεσπότης** τῶν ἁπάντων ἐπὶ τοῖς ἔργοις αὐτοῦ ἀγαλλιᾶται For the Creator and Sovereign of the universe himself rejoices in his works.[52]	Σύ, **δέσποτα** παντοκράτορ, ἔκτισας τὰ πάντα ἕνεκεν τοῦ ὀνόματός σου, τροφήν τε καὶ ποτὸν ἔδωκας τοῖς υἱοῖς τῶν ἀνθρώπων εἰς ἀπόλαυσιν, ἵνα σοι εὐχαριστήσωσιν Almighty **Sovereign**, you have created everything for the sake of your name, and have given mortals food and drink to enjoy so that they may thank you.[53]	Ὁ γὰρ **δεσπότης** καὶ δημιουργὸς τῶν ὅλων θεός, ὁ **ποιήσας τὰ πάντα** καὶ κατὰ τάξιν διακρίνας, οὐ μόνον φιλάνθρωπος ἐγένετο ἀλλὰ καὶ μακρόθυμος For God, the **Sovereign** and Maker of the universe, who **made all things** and determined the proper place of each, showed himself to be long-suffering, as well as a true friend of humanity.[54]

encapsulates all of the virtues. This is not Pauline; rather, it is characteristic of the early second century.

δωδεκάφυλος ("the twelve tribes"). This metonymy for the Israelites is of interest simply because, other than two metrically convenient appearances in the *Sibylline Oracles*, it is found only in Acts 26:7, *1 Clement* 55:6, and the *Protevangelium of James* 1:3. The Christian usages suggest that the adjective evidently conveyed a certain literary flair and provided those who so wished with a variant for "Israel," "the Jews," etc.[55]

ἐγκράτεια, ἐγκρατής ("self-control," "disciplined"). Words in ἐγκρατ-, like those in σωφρον-, evolve in Christian usage toward the meaning of sexual continence. The notion that the moral life requires mastery of one's emotions and actions plays a fundamental role in ancient Greek ethics.[56] It is thus not surprising that Philo appreciates the quality and applies it to various types of restraint.[57] The sole LXX use of the noun is in *4 Maccabees*, while all ten occurrences of the adjectival forms are in books not found in the Hebrew Scriptures. Paul includes the noun in a list of virtues (Galatians 5:23) and lays the ground for the later sense of "sexual restraint," i.e., virginity, in 1 Corinthians 7:5, 9, where the verb occurs.[58] The reason for its rarity in biblical writings is that "self-restraint" presumes a "high" anthropology, that is, the conviction that individuals *can* achieve mastery over minds and bodies. The noun is quite properly paired with "righteousness" in Acts 24:25. Forms from this stem also appear once each in Titus, 2 Peter, and *Barnabas*, twice in *2 Clement* and Polycarp, four times in *1 Clement*, and six or seven times in *Hermas*.[59] In *2 Clement* 15 self-control is a suitable term for summarizing the author's moral exhortation.[60] Once again, Acts has a foothold in the sphere of early Christian ethics during its process of transition from an inward and eschatological orientation toward a more rational and outward accommodation to general ethical values. 270

ἐκδικέω, ἐκδίκησις (Verb and noun, "vengeance," "to vindicate," "revenge," and various legal meanings). This word group (and others related to it) is common in the LXX. In the New Testament the words appear twice each in Romans (one a citation) and 2 Corinthians, twice in Revelation, and one time each in 2 Thessalonians, Hebrews (a citation), and 1 Peter. Six examples come from Luke and Acts, with five in Luke, while Philo provides seven and Josephus twenty-four. The verb appears in *Barnabas*, the sole occurrence in the "Apostolic Fathers." From the Apologists there are four instances in Justin Martyr and one in Athenagoras. The New Testament Apocrypha contribute a good twenty-five instances. Luke is noteworthy here in that his use of the verb shows contemporary juridical usage and does not follow the semantics of the LXX.[61] That is the principal reason for including these terms in this catalogue: ἐκδίκησις provides a patina of Hellenism.

ἐκτένεια, *etc.* ("perseverance, " "constancy," resolution," *etc.*). The noun appears in Acts 26:7, the adverb in Luke 22:44; Acts 12:5, 1 Peter 1:22. The adjective turns up 1 Peter 4:8 and as a variant reading for the adverb in Luke and Acts.[62] *1 Clement* uses the adjective three times, the adverb and the noun once each. Ignatius has recourse to the noun on a single occasion. This term often has moral associations, in particular when matters of contribution to civic life and personal relations are in view.[63]

ἔλευσις ("coming"). This rare term—"parousia" is more common—is found in the New Testament only at Acts 7:52 ("the coming of the Righteous One"), where it is associated with a christological title found in later writings.[64] The term is used in other early Christian works of the "first coming" (*1 Clement* 17:1, Polycarp *Philippians* 6:3) and of the "second" (*Acts of Thomas* 28).[65]. In Irenaeus (*Against Heresies* 1.10.1) it is used of both the first and second advents of Christ. ἔλευσις seems to have been in vogue during the second century.

ἐπισκοπή ("visitation," "oversight"). In Luke 19:44, 1 Peter 2:12, and *1 Clement* 50:3 the noun has the sense of "(divine) visitation." Ignatius *Polycarp* 8:3 is somewhat difficult, but "divine care" appears to be the meaning. In 1 Timothy 3:1 and *1 Clement* 44:1, and 3 the meaning is practically "episcopate," which will be its sense in Irenaeus and thereafter.[66] In this light Acts 1:20, "'Let another take his position of overseer,'" although a citation, is interesting. I do not suppose that Luke picked up this verse from the Psalter by casting lots. He used it because it belonged to the emerging technical terminology of Christian leadership.[67] This suggests, as later statements in Acts confirm, that the apostles were engaged in pastoral care and other responsibilities subsequently undertaken by "deacons," "bishops," and presbyters. A kindred conception stands behind *1 Clement* 44.

ἐπιστροφή (in the sense of "conversion"). In Acts 15:3 Luke elects this rather technical word, applied to philosophical "conversion" since Plato and rendered by Cicero with what will become a religious technical term, *conversio*.[68] Although the verb is relatively common, especially in Luke and Acts,[69] this noun form appears nowhere else in the New Testament and among the Apostolic Fathers only at *Barnabas* 11:8 in this sense.[70] Other uses include Justin Martyr (*Dialogue* 30.1, with μετάνοια), several examples in the *Acts of John*, the *Acts of Peter*, frequent appearances in Clement of Alexandria (not always in the sense of "conversion,"), and more than fifty in Origen (with some variation in meaning).[71] In the LXX only Sirach 18:11 has the definite meaning of conversion. At the beginning of what is the watershed and arguably the most important chapter in Acts, Luke chooses to use this rather elegant and "gentile" term. That choice is scarcely inadvertent;[72] hereafter the vocabulary and style of Acts will also make a "turn" toward more literary Greek. With this single word Luke neatly signals that the polytheists have begun to turn toward the Christian message.

Acts 15: change in style

εὐεργεσία, εὐεργετέω, εὐεργέτης, εὐεργετικός ("benefaction," "confer benefit," "benefactor,").[73] In Greco-Roman society the pursuit of wealth was deemed vulgar. Members of the ruling class were nonetheless subject to occasional acquisitive urges. They attempted to see that their money came either from land or in plain brown wrappers. The chief difference from a modern capitalist society is that acquiring wealth was regarded more as the pursuit of honor (φιλοτιμία) than as an end in itself. Benefaction was the means for obtaining honor and therefore a value for which only the elite need apply. The label "benefactor" was but rarely attached to those who dispensed a cup of cold water. In the LXX, God is the only subject of the verb. *1 Clement* upholds this tradition in 19:2; 20:11; 21:1; 23:1; 38:3, and 59:3.[74] *Diognetus* 8:11 and 9:5 also speak of divine benefaction. *Diognetus* 10:5–6 approximates Luke, for the writer urges readers to find satisfaction not through oppressing (καταδυναστεύειν) others but by conferring benefits (εὐεργετεῖν). Those who serve as benefactors will become imitators of God. Ignatius uses the participle once in the sense of "generous treatment" of his guards (who nonetheless remained unresponsive).[75] Luke 22:25 ("The kings of the Gentiles lord it over them; and those in authority over them are called benefactors") has already come under scrutiny.[76] Acts 4:9 applies the term to a healing, while the earthly Jesus is the source of such benefits in 10:38.[77] 1 Timothy 6:2 can be read as a role reversal—slaves as "benefactors" to their masters—but this is far from certain. The very term suggests that the masters are the sources of favor.[78] The word group appears twenty-four times in the LXX, always in the writings, with a substantial majority from books that exist only in Greek.[79] There is no need to argue that the language of benefaction belongs to the civic and moral world of Hellenism. My argument is rather that its appearance in Luke and Acts is characteristic of a later era when Christians were beginning to express their moral convictions in the language of the general culture.[80]

εὐσεβεία ("godliness"). See p. 236–37.

ζῆλος ("zeal," "envy," "rivalry"). In the Greek tradition, as can be seen in Philo, this is essentially a positive quality representative of an ethic of competition.[81] That positive or neutral sense of "zeal" or "ardor" and also the inverse—"jealousy" as a vice—are common in Paul. In Acts 5:17; 13:45 (noun) as well as 7:9; 17:5 (verb) the term is particular, an explanation of the motivation for persecuting the heroes of the faith (Joseph, the apostles, Paul). Persecution is the mainspring of the plot of Acts: representatives of the good are persecuted because their success arouses envy. This is a popular narrative device: "They don't like us because they are jealous." *1 Clement* introduces the same motif to explain the sufferings of Peter and Paul (5:2–5) and is sufficiently fond of this word to use it more than twenty times, presumably because of its value as an insinuation about the grounds of the unpleasantness at Corinth.

1 Clement 4:1–6:4 describes the dangers of jealousy, not excluding persecution and homicide. After parading such ancient heroes as Joseph in chapter 4, the author comes in chapter 5 to Peter and Paul.[82] It is noteworthy that Acts and *1 Clement* take a similar approach to "jealousy" in their models, methods, and techniques. Rhetorical training motivates the author of *1 Clement* to expand a list of vices by illustrating them with examples from both the distant past and more recent times. Rhetorical paradigms inform the author of Acts that it is useful to attribute base motives to those whom one would criticize. Both utilize the timeless and popular device of attributing opposition to jealousy whenever possible.[83]

ἡσυχία-ος. ("peace and quiet"). See p. 232.

θρησκεία. ("worship," "religious observance").[84] Although this word possesses a certain elegance in early Christian literature, it is quite common in Greek and would be one of the candidates for a word meaning "religion."[85] 4 Maccabees and Josephus so use it,[86] as does Acts 26:5, which speaks of "our religion." 1 Clement 45:7 and 62:1 follow the same path.[87] Diognetus 2:8 (verb) and 3:2 are, like Col 2:18, 23, more neutral. James 1:27 ("Religion that is pure and undefiled before God, the Father, is this: to care for orphans and widows in their distress, and to keep oneself unstained by the world") exemplifies the trend toward the "spiritualization" of cultic devotion in the Roman world. θρησκεία is thus yet another instance of the vocabulary of Hellenistic Judaism that assumes a place in the later and more literary works of the New Testament and other early Christian literature.[88]

θύρα ("door"). Although "door" can be used in several metaphorical senses, for Paul and the writer of Colossians the specific meaning is not the "door to God's dominion" but "opportunity for mission."[89] As the examples in Table 7.2 indicate, Paul does not use "door" with a genitive ("of x"). Acts ("door of faith") and Colossians ("door of the word") represent typical Deutero-Pauline constructions. One could certainly make a case for intertextuality here, but doors do open. More cogent, in my view, is the evidence of post-Pauline modifications to a Pauline metaphor. It came to seem desirable to indicate what kind of door was in mind.

καταπονέω ("subdue," "oppress"). This verb occurs but twice in the LXX, both times in 3 Maccabees. In the New Testament it is found at Acts 7:24 (and

Table 7.2: Door of Faith

Acts 14:27	Paul and Deutero-Paul
παραγενόμενοι δὲ καὶ συναγαγόντες τὴν ἐκκλησίαν ἀνήγγελλον ὅσα ἐποίησεν ὁ θεὸς μετ' αὐτῶν καὶ ὅτι **ἤνοιξεν** τοῖς ἔθνεσιν **θύραν** πίστεως. When they arrived, they called the church together and related all that God had done with them, and how he had **opened a door** of faith for the Gentiles	**1 Corinthians 16:9**; **θύρα** γάρ μοι **ἀνέῳγεν** μεγάλη καὶ ἐνεργής for a wide **door** for effective work has **opened** to me, and there are many adversaries. **2 Corinthians 2:12** Ἐλθὼν δὲ εἰς τὴν Τρῳάδα εἰς τὸ εὐαγγέλιον τοῦ Χριστοῦ, καὶ **θύρας** μοι **ἀνεῳγμένης** ἐν κυρίῳ When I came to Troas to proclaim the good news of Christ, a **door was opened** for me in the Lord. **Colossians 4:3** προσευχόμενοι ἅμα καὶ περὶ ἡμῶν, ἵνα ὁ θεὸς **ἀνοίξῃ** ἡμῖν **θύραν** τοῦ λόγου At the same time pray for us as well that God will **open** to us a **door** for the word, that we may declare the mystery of Christ

4:2 as a variant [D]) and 2 Peter 2:7. Examples from the Apostolic Fathers are in *1 Clement* 46:8, *Didache* 5:2 (twice), and *Barnabas* 20:2 (twice). Theophilus of Antioch and Clement of Alexandria also attest this verb. Conclusion: the word is at home in the Christian vocabulary of the second century.

καρδιογνώστης ("One who knows the heart"). This epithet is applied to God in Acts 1:24; 15:8. When Haenchen describes this as "a favorite expression of post-apostolic Christendom," he is correct only in part.[90] The term *does* belong to the post-apostolic era, but it is not especially common. A TLG search for the first two centuries identified fourteen occurrences. Six of these are in Origen and three in Clement of Alexandria. For the present purpose the Pseudo-Clementine *Homilies* 10.13, *Acts of Paul* 3.24, and *Hermas Mandates* 4.3.4 are the most important. The Clementines and the *Acts of Paul* may be dependent upon Acts here (as they are elsewhere), but *Hermas* is not demonstrably familiar with Acts. καρδιογνώστης is otherwise known only in writings of the second and later centuries. This may well be an example of the developing liturgical vocabulary of the period from c. 100 onward.[91]

κλῆρος ("lot," "portion," "position"). Outside of the casting of lots for Jesus's garments, lot appears in Acts 26:18 (above); 1:17, 20; 8:21; Col 1:12 (above); and 1 Peter 5:3. Ignatius uses the word four times, *Diognetus* twice, and Barnabas and the *Martyrdom of Polycarp* once each. In the letter about the *Martyrs of Lyons* the word refers to the fate/reward of the martyrs, while Irenaeus uses it for episcopal succession. The same word is used in conjunction with μερίς ("part") at Acts 8:21 and Colossians 1:12. With these one should compare *1 Clement* 29:2–30:1.[92]

λατρεύω ("serve"). There is absolutely nothing remarkable about this verb, which is used more than 100 times in the LXX, nearly always to translate a single Hebrew verb. In Jewish, then Christian, Greek this verb is restricted to "divine service." The interest here lies in the distribution. λατρεύω appears once in Matthew, three times in Paul, eight times in Luke and Acts, once in the Pastorals, six times in Hebrews, twice in Revelation, once each in Ignatius, Polycarp, and *1 Clement*. Justin makes use of it eight times and the apologist Theophilus thrice. Other occurrences are in the *Preaching of Peter*, and the *Acts of Paul*.[93] This verb is another example of the reception of technical cultic language into a Christian sphere.

λειτουργέω, etc. ("serve," including two nouns and an adjective). Words from the stem λειτουργ- are common in the LXX. Appearing twice in Luke and Acts (Luke 1:23; Acts 13:2), the group is also found seven times in Paul, six in Hebrews, twice in the *Didache*, seventeen times in *1 Clement* and six times in *Hermas*. There is one example each in Justin and Athenagoras. This is yet one more instance of the vocabulary of Hellenistic Judaism that found a place in Paul and later Christian writers.[94]

μαίνομαι, μανία, ἐμμαίνομαι, ("to be insane," "mad,"). "Madness" is the antonym of σωφροσύνη ("reasonableness," below).[95] This term is important in apologetics, as opponents of a religious or intellectual movement often accuse its practitioners of insanity or fanaticism. (Cf. such disparaging expressions as "foaming at the mouth charismatics.") Conversely, persecutors—tyrants and the like, including Saul/Paul—are often described as "mad." As noun and verb it is found eleven times in the LXX, six of which are in books extant only in Greek. In the New Testament the verbs appear once each in John and Paul, and four times in Acts.[96] The noun occurs but once: in Acts (26:24).

In their apologetic writings Philo and Josephus use these terms, Josephus only twice. Among the Christian apologists Justin employs them four times, Athenagoras five, and Theophilus once. The refutation of the charge of "madness," a charge that can include everything from poor taste and lack of decorum to certifiable insanity, was a firm component of the apologetic tradition, as was its application to one's opponents.[97] Acts 26 is at home in the world of apologetics.

μάταιος, *etc.* ("Vain," "useless," etc.) This word-group is represented by more than 150 appearances in the LXX.[98] The single usage in Acts, 14:15, is typical of anti-polytheist propaganda: " you should turn from these worthless things to the living God."[99] Four examples come from Paul, one from Ephesians, three from the Pastoral Epistles, and one each in James, 1 Peter, and 2 Peter. The yield from the Apostolic Fathers is quite rich: three instances from *1 Clement*, five in *Barnabas*, twelve in *Hermas*, two in Ignatius and Polycarp, and one each in Ignatius and *2 Clement*. Justin supplies eight examples of the stem.[100] This word-complex is an additional instance of the language of Hellenistic Judaism derived from the LXX that becomes part of the standard theological vocabulary of early gentile Christianity.[101]

μεγαλειότης ("greatness"[of God], "majesty"). This is a rewarding inquiry. "Divinities coming from the East frequently received the attribute 'great'."[102] The sustained acclamation, "God (or *name* of particular god) is great," which still lives in the Islamic world (*"Allahu akbar"*), is known to most Western Christians through Acts 19: "When they heard this, they were enraged and shouted, 'Great is Artemis of the Ephesians!'"[103] The preceding verse in Acts gives a point to the history-of-religions approach by applying the noun μεγαλειότης to Artemis. Other uses in the literature being examined are Luke 9:43; *1 Clement* 24:5, and 2 Peter 1:16. Here, then, is another specimen of the language of Hellenistic Judaism appropriated by Christians in the post-apostolic era.[104]

μετάνοια ("repentance," "change of mind") and the vocabulary of conversion and initiation.[105] A previous section looked at "repentance" in Acts and *1 Clement*.[106] Both writers tend to "ethicize" the term. The object here is to broaden the range and see how Acts fits into the emerging debate. The range is as follows: this noun occurs once in Mark, twice in Matthew, eleven times in Luke and Acts, three times in Paul, three times in Hebrews, once in the Pastorals and once in 2 Peter. *Hermas* wins the prize, with fifty-six entries; *1 Clement* uses the noun nine times, *2 Clement* twice, while Ignatius, *Barnabas*, and the *Martyrdom of Polycarp* have one occurrence each. Justin Martyr brings this noun into play fourteen times.[107] In the LXX μετάνοια occurs once in the writings included in the Hebrew Bible and six times in books available only in Greek. μετάνοια is at home in the later New Testament writings and subsequent early Christian literature.

At the center of the debate lies what might for convenience be called the distinction between "Sin" and "sins." "Sin" is characteristic of theologians like Paul and John (who are similar here, although not identical). Viewed from a context informed by apocalyptic "Sin" is alienation from God, manifest in people's stance toward God and the world. "Sins," on the other hand, are the failings and misdeeds of human beings. The term "forgiveness" does not really apply to Sin, which can be defeated only through "conversion." Other writers, including Luke, speak more often of "sins," which can be forgiven (at least initially) through repentance.[108] Two important factors require consideration. In the Deutero-Pauline world the notion of "sins" made considerable inroads.[109] Those who attempted to maintain the earlier (Sin) orientation, had to struggle with the problem of "Perfectionism," which held that believers were free from sin. A good deal of contention was aroused by two of the possible applications of the doctrine that believers do not sin: 1) those who sin are not believers and must be expelled, and 2) nothing that believers do is sinful. One can trace this debate most clearly in the Johannine tradition.[110]

Whatever their orientation, writers of the post-apostolic period had to wrestle with the problem of "post-baptismal" sin. In the language of church discipline the problem addressed the issue of what sins can be forgiven and the form (if any) this forgiveness would take. That debate raged in North Africa from the earliest days of Latin Christianity (known through the writings of Tertullian) until the Arab conquest more or less ended the argument by extinguishing Christianity (seventh century and later). Elsewhere the debate played a major role in the Montanist movement (a "charismatic" and strict form of the Christian faith centered in rural Asia Minor in the second half of the second century), and at Rome, which eventually took a pastoral approach that would dominate the West thereafter.

Luke and Acts appear to represent a compromise approach. The Q passages about forgiveness (Luke 12:10, sin against the Holy Spirit; 17:3, "if a sister or brother sins . . .) are retained. The three parables of Luke 15 literally celebrate the possibility of repentance.[111] Acts suggests—but does not state—how repentance functions in community life. Ananias and Sapphira "sin against the Holy Spirit" (5:3) and suffer dire consequences. 19:18–19 describe the behavior of believers who have indulged in magic. They confess their sins, destroy their magical literature, and (presumably) are forgiven. The petition of Simon in 8:24 suggests that ambiguity remains: Peter cannot "absolve" Simon, but believers Lk.12:47f. may pray for him. Luke does not have a division between "venial" and "mortal" sin, but the narrative indicates that some failures can be forgiven by the community, others must be left in the hands of God, and actions like those of Judas and the propertied couple of 5:1–11 place the sinner beyond the bounds of divine forbearance.

For *1 Clement* repentance seems to be an omnipresent opportunity (7:4–8:5). Believers can repent. In *1 Clement* and the Lukan writings a similar anthropology is operative, and their view of repentance is related to this understanding of "human nature." God has endowed human beings with the gifts of reason and insight. They can therefore recognize their failures and repent. For both authors sin (="sins") applies primarily to human failings.[112] Repentance is a human possibility, though it may come but once: Hebrews withdraws the opportunity for a second repentance in the case of apostates (6:1, 6; 12:17). A substantial portion of the sermon known as *2 Clement* is an exhortation to repentance (8–18). As in Luke, Acts, and *1 Clement*, this has a psychological element. It is something to be done whole-heartedly (8:2). Sincerity requires demonstration. The relation to eschatology is often a matter of repenting while there is still time.[113] The book of Revelation takes a similar approach (2:5, 16, 21, 33, etc.). Millennial fears have frequently served as grounds for a summons to repentance. In the second century this stimulus, often coupled with the explicit notion that God grants every generation opportunity for repentance (*1 Clement* 7:5–7), brought forth the conviction that the entire world was now being given one last chance. While showing the influence of such thought, *Hermas* protests against the view of repentance as mere confession of sin and expression of remorse, whether done once or seventy-seven times. For *Hermas* repentance is characteristic of the life-long process of conversion.[114] Behind these diverse developments stands the effort to maintain a vital role for repentance in changed circumstances. From the Hellenistic Jewish background came the idea that God "gives" all an opportunity for repentance. That concept can be used apologetically to reject the notion of exclusivity, as in *1 Clement* 7, or, as in Wisdom 12, to justify slaughtering the inhabitants of Canaan. For the Canaanites the gift of repentance (12:10) was "bad news," for they did not accept the offer. To Israel it was a source of hope (12:19).[115] God's Gift of repentance is apparent in Acts 5:31; *Rom.2:4* 11:18; 2 Timothy 2:25; *1 Clement* 7:4; *Barnabas* 16:9, and *Hermas, Similitude* 8.6:1–2; but it means the gift of an *opportunity* for repentance, which is no longer a direct manifestation of divine power.[116] If some find this development lamentable, it is certainly highly intelligible.

Metanoia is also familiar in the popular philosophical tradition. The *Tabula of Cebes*, a work that probably belongs to the period 50–150 CE, is a catechism presented as an interpretation of a work of art.[117] The figure identified as "Lamentation" (ὀδυρμὸς) is doomed to a miserable life, ". . . unless from her own choice Repentance [μετάνοια] happens to encounter him [lamentation]." She will bring Lamentation relief and arrange the opportunity for a choice between true and false education (παιδεία).[118] In the tradition exemplified by the *Tabula*, as in Luke and Acts, repentance is the preliminary act in "conversion."

For Luke and others attention therefore centers upon the language of *conversion*, often expressed in the vocabulary and symbols of initiation. Acts 26:18, earlier examined from the perspective of intertextuality, is Luke's essen-

Table 7.3: Darkness to Light

Luke and Acts / Other NT	Jewish	Early Christian	Apologists, etc / Polytheist
Luke and Acts Luke 1:77–79 to give knowledge of salvation to his people by the forgiveness of their sins. By the tender mercy of our God, the dawn from on high will break upon us, to give light to those who sit in *darkness* and in the shadow of death . . . Acts 26:18 to open their eyes so that they *may turn from darkness to light* and from the power of Satan to God, so that they may receive forgiveness of sins and a place among those who are sanctified by faith in me.' Luke 2:30–32; for my eyes have seen your salvation . . . a *light* for revelation to the Gentiles and for glory may bring salvation to the ends of the earth.' **Other NT** Colossians 1:13 He has rescued us from the power of *darkness* and transferred us into the kingdom of his beloved Son, Ephesians 1:18 so that, with the *eyes of your heart enlightened,* you may know what is the hope to which *he has called you,* what are the riches of his glorious inheritance among the saints, Eph 5:8 For once you were *darkness,* but now in the Lord you are *light.* 1 Peter 2:9 But you are a chosen race, a royal priesthood, a holy nation, God's own people, in order that you may proclaim the mighty acts of him	**Jewish** Philo, *Virtues* (repentance) 179. All those therefore who, although they did not originally choose to honor the Creator and Father of the universe, have yet changed and done so afterwards, having learnt to prefer to honor a single monarch rather than a number of rulers . . . and we ought to sympathize in joy with and to congratulate them, since even if they were blind previously they have now received their sight, *beholding the most brilliant of all lights instead of the most profound darkness.* *Aseneth* 8.10. The one who made all things alive, and *called from darkness into the light,*	**Early Christian** *1 Clem* 59.2–3. We shall beg . . . that the Creator of the universe will keep intact the precise number of the elect in the whole world, through his beloved child Jesus Christ. It was through him that he *called us from darkness to light,* from ignorance to the recognition of his glorious name, to hope on your name, which is the origin of all creation. You have opened the eyes of our hearts [Eph 1:18] so that we realize. . . .[119] *Odes of Solomon* 14.18–19. And I said, Blessed, O Lord, are they who are planted in the land and who have a place in they paradise; and who grow in the growth	**Apologists, etc** Minucius Felix 1.4 . . . And he did not reject my companionship when I was beginning to rise out of the dispersing mists and the abyss of darkness into the light of true wisdom . . .[120] Melito of Sardis, *On the Passover* 69 This is the one who delivered us from bondage to freedom, *from darkness to light,* from death to life, from tyranny to eternal royalty . . . **Polytheist** *Life of Aesop,* 5 A priestess of Isis concludes her prayer to the goddess" "... for you can bring into the light those things that have fallen into darkness."[121] Apuleius, *Met.* 11:23. (The initiation of

to your people Israel." Acts 13:47 the Lord has commanded us, saying, 'I have set you to be a light for the Gentiles, so that you	*who called you out of darkness into his marvelous light.* Cf. also Hebrews 6:4; 10:32.	and from error into truth, and from death to life. 15.13 Blessed is the Lord God, who sent you *to deliver me from darkness* and to lead me up *into the light.*	*of thy trees, and have passed from darkness into light.*	Lucius into the cult of Isis began at night and ended in the morning) "In the middle of the night I saw the sun flashing with bright light."122 Lucian *Nigrinus* 4. I . . . was glad to be looking up, as it were, out of the murky atmosphere of my past life to a clear sky and a great life.123

tial statement of the nature and meaning of conversion.[124] The metaphor of transferal from darkness (ignorance, sin) to light (knowledge, salvation) has a long history in descriptions of "conversion" to philosophy and of religious transformation.[125] In Christian texts the image characterizes the transformation wrought by baptism.[126]

The purpose of Table 7.3 is to illustrate a "familiar missionary style"[127] in ritual and philosophical contexts, as well as the place of the "darkness to light" motif in Christian writings of the late first and second centuries. Of course, the rich Biblical background of the theme is important to Luke.[128] In Acts 26:18 it becomes his cutting edge: passage from "darkness to light" characterizes radical change. It is especially suitable for polytheists who have come to acknowledge the true God, but it can also serve to praise God for the deliverance of Israel (Melito[129]). *1 Clement* 59 is the opening of the solemn, final prayer. It is highly likely that the author uses familiar liturgical language here.[130] The intellectual milieu is that of Hellenistic Judaism; the literary milieu is that of the post-apostolic, Deutero-Pauline, and later eras.[131]

ESCAPING THE BONDS
OF DEATH: ACTS 12

The story of Peter's delivery from execution, Acts 12:6–11 is rich in paschal and baptismal imagery.[132] The setting is "the days of unleavened bread" (12:3).[133]

> [6]The very night before Herod was going to bring him out, Peter, *bound* with two chains, was *sleeping* between two soldiers, while guards in front of the door were keeping watch over the prison. [7]Suddenly an angel of the Lord appeared and a *light* shone in the cell. He tapped Peter on the side and woke him, saying, "*Get up* quickly." And the *chains fell off* his wrists. [8]The angel said to him, "*Fasten your belt and put on your sandals*." He did so. Then he said to him, "Wrap your cloak around you and follow me." [9]Peter went out and followed him; he did not realize that what was happening with the angel's help was real; he thought he was seeing a vision. [10]After they had passed the first and the second guard, they came before the iron gate leading into the city. It *opened for them of its own accord*, and they went outside and walked along a lane, when suddenly the angel left him. [11]Then Peter came to himself and said, "Now I am sure that *the Lord has sent his angel and rescued me from the hands of Herod* and from all that the Jewish people were expecting."

V.6. The action takes place at *night*, which is the time of Passover and also the normal time of initiation.[134] Bonds are a synecdoche for captivity, the antonym of freedom. The dominant prototype is the captivity of Israel in Egypt. Note Psalm 107:10–14,[135] Isaiah 52:2, and, notably, the citation of Isaiah 61:1–2 in Luke 4:18, the inaugural sermon of Jesus: "The Spirit of the Lord is upon me . . . He has sent me to proclaim release to the captives and recovery of sight to the blind, to let the oppressed go free." Peter is *asleep*. This is a common trope for ignorance and spiritual "blindness," as the frequent exhortation to "stay awake" (for example, Luke 21:34–36) indicates.[136]

V.7. *Light* shines in darkness, a typical item of conversion imagery. "Get up quickly." The Greek word for "wake up" is the same as that for "rising (from the dead): ἀνάστα. The best commentary on this verse in the present connection is Ephesians 5:14: "Sleeper, awake! Rise from the dead, and Christ will shine on you," which is evidently a fragment from a baptismal hymn that has many parallels in the history of religions.[137] The correspondences are "sleep"=(spiritual) death, "waking" as the inauguration of a new and genuine life, and "light"=the illumination of the believer/initiate through knowledge, etc. The awakening of Peter in this instance involves deliverance from bondage. "The chains fell off his wrists," employs the same trope introduced at the beginning.

V.8. The commands to get dressed have two applications. It underscores the paschal setting, echoing the rubrics for the Passover feast: "your loins girded, your sandals on your feet, and your staff in your hand; and you shall eat it hurriedly. It is the passover of the Lord." (Exodus 12:11). The newly baptized would, of course, get dressed, and this concept also has a rich symbolic history.[138] The most relevant here are the Deutero-Pauline developments of the baptismal formula in Galatians 3:27. Whereas Paul wrote of believers having "put on Christ," the writer of Colossians exhorts his hearers: "seeing that you have stripped off the old self with its practices and have clothed yourselves with the new self . . ." (Colossians 3:9–10).[139] Acts 12 makes yet another evident initiatory reference by depicting Peter as a new born babe who must be told by his nurse or mother how to dress himself. The most famous evocation of this imagery of the neophyte is 1 Peter 2:1–2: "Rid yourselves,[140] therefore, of all malice, and all guile, insincerity, envy, and all slander. Like newborn infants, long for the pure, spiritual milk, so that by it you may grow into salvation." The noteworthy use of paschal imagery in 1 Peter is an appropriate example of the theme of this unit, which is the life open to those who have been regenerated (in baptism, 1:3, 23). Metaphorical and literal uses of the expression "dressed for action"[141] (see Table 7.4) are common, with or without paschal symbolism. There is general overlap between Acts 12 and 1 Peter in so insofar as exhortations to be sober, alert, and ready for action have an eschatological orientation, as they have in Luke 12:42–46, and are therefore congruent with paschal imagery.[142]

V.10. Within a paschal framework, the door-miracle and passage from prison intimate the transit of the Red Sea.[143] With the assistance of such passages as Isaiah 42:6–7 and 45:1–2,[144] second century writers developed complex baptismal typologies that in turn had influence upon ceremonies. The same material was applied to the doctrine of Christ's "Harrowing of Hell."[145]

V.11. "The Lord has sent his angel and rescued me from the hands of Herod" (καὶ ἐξείλατό με ἐκ χειρὸς Ἡρῴδου). This is a close evocation of the LXX of Exodus 18:4 "The God of my father was my helper and has rescued me from the hands of Pharaoh" (καὶ ἐξείλατό με ἐκ χειρὸς Φαραω). The purpose of this allusion is to establish "Herod" as a wicked king who slaughters the people of

Table 7.4: Dressed for Success

Exodus 12:11	Luke and Acts	1 Peter and other
οὕτως δὲ φάγεσθε αὐτό· αἱ ὀσφύες ὑμῶν περιεζωσμέναι, καὶ τὰ ὑποδήματα ἐν τοῖς ποσὶν ὑμῶν, καὶ αἱ βακτηρίαι ἐν ταῖς χερσὶν ὑμῶν . . . This is how you shall eat it: *your loins girded*, your sandals on your feet, and your staff in your hand	Luke 12:35 Ἔστωσαν ὑμῶν **αἱ ὀσφύες περιεζωσμέναι** καὶ οἱ λύχνοι καιόμενοι "*Be dressed for action* and have your lamps lit; Acts 12:8 εἶπεν δὲ ὁ ἄγγελος πρὸς αὐτόν, Ζῶσαι καὶ ὑπόδησαι τὰ σανδάλιά σου. The angel said to him, "Fasten your belt and put on your sandals	1:13 Διὸ ἀναζωσάμενοι τὰς ὀσφύας τῆς διανοίας ὑμῶν, νήφοντες, τελείως ἐλπίσατε ἐπὶ τὴν φερομένην ὑμῖν χάριν ἐν ἀποκαλύψει Ἰησοῦ Χριστοῦ Therefore *prepare* your minds *for action*; discipline yourselves; set all your hope on the grace that Jesus Christ will bring you when he is revealed Ephesians 6:14 στῆτε οὖν περιζωσάμενοι τὴν ὀσφὺν ὑμῶν ἐν ἀληθείᾳ, καὶ ἐνδυσάμενοι τὸν θώρακα τῆς δικαιοσύνης Stand therefore, and *fasten the belt of truth around your waist*, and put on the breastplate of righteousness. Polycarp, *Phil* 2:1 Διὸ ἀναζωσάμενοι τὰς ὀσφύας ὑμῶν δουλεύσατε τῷ θεῷ ἐν φόβῳ καὶ ἀληθείᾳ, ἀπολιπόντες τὴν κενὴν ματαιολογίαν καὶ τὴν τῶν πολλῶν πλάνην. Therefore, gird-ing your loins, serve God in fear and in truth, forsaking empty talk-ativeness and the erroneous teach-ing of the crowd . . .[146]

God, and to offer Peter as an example of one liberated from death during the feast of liberation. Through these series of allusions to baptism as resurrection—deliverance from death and the power of Satan—Luke makes the story of Peter applicable to all believers. The density of these associations does ńot conform to the milieu of the 60s, 70s, or 80s of the first century. They are at home in the baptismal thought and scriptural typology of the early second century. Luke may not have endorsed all the theological implications thereof, but he seems to have been conversant with traditions found in writings like *Barnabas* and, quite possibly, to have expected his implied readers to have known them also.

νομοδιδάσκαλος ("Teacher of the Law"). Although this appears to be a perfectly acceptable Jewish term, it is not found in Jewish literature. Other than in Luke 5:17, Acts 5:34, and 1 Tim 1:7, the term appears in Clement *Excerpta ex Theodoto* 5, Irenaeus *Against Heresies* 1.1.5, and Eusebius, *Praise of Constantine* 17. The word reflects a Christian understanding of a particular educational function that was not uncommon in both "orthodox" and "heretical" circles during the second century.[147]

οἰκοδομέω, οἰκοδομή (in the sense of "edify," "edification").[148] This metaphor is very much at home in the Pauline world. The noun and verb, as well as the nearly synonymous ἐποικοδομέω, remained popular in the post-Pauline world: Colossians 2:20; Ephesians 2:20, 21; 4:12, 16, 29; 1 Peter 2:5, 7; Jude 20; Polycarp *Philippians* 3:2. Acts 9:31 and 20:32 correspond to these usages. The former also uses "church" in the universal sense; the latter probably depends upon Ephesians. Later use seems identical to that of Paul. It differs in that the content of what "edifies" has become more definite and circumscribed. For Paul the consumption of meat with a dubious pedigree *may* not be edifying, especially to the "weak" (1 Corinthians 10:1). For Luke the consumption of meat offered to 2 3 ? the gods is not edifying because it violates the rules (Acts 15:29).

οἰκονόμος ("manager"). See p. xxx.

ὄνομα ("name," used as an absolute). Acts 5:41, "As they left the council, they rejoiced that they were considered worthy to suffer dishonor for the sake of the name," is a metonymy of generally clear but specifically uncertain meaning. In varying circumstances "the name" may simply be an abbreviation for "the name of Christ," or, by further extension, refer to the individual Christian or to "the faith," in the sense of "the church."[149] If a Jewish context is preferred, the expression implies a high Christology, since "name" became a circumlocution for "God" in Judaism.[150] Luke's own Christology does not claim that Christ is God. All of the other witnesses for name=church are late: 3 John 7; Ignatius, *Ephesians* 1:2 and five or six other occasions, *Barnabas* 16:8, and Theophilus 1:1. By referring to Christ (or Christianity) as "the Name" Acts uses language of the second century.[151] Note also ὑπὲρ τοῦ ὀνόματος ("in behalf of the name"). This phrase appears five times in Acts (5:41 [above]; 9:16; 15:26; 2:13). Elsewhere it is found in Romans 1:5 and once each in Ignatius (*Ephesians* 1:2) and Hermas (*Similitude* 9.28.2[105]). A TLG search unearthed but two other uses of the phrase, in Dionysius of Halicarnassus, a first-century BCE historian. The particular context in most of these passages is suffering, always in the performance of leadership or mission. As it is used in Acts, the prepositional phrase "in behalf of the name" is a second-century expression.

ὁσιότης ("holiness"). See p. xxx.

παθητός ("capable of suffering")[152] This is a particularly choice word that appears in an apt context at the climax of Paul's speech before King Agrippa II (Acts 26:23). Luke may have overreached himself a bit here, for he evidently wishes to say something like "the Messiah had to die" rather than to affirm the humanity of Jesus.[153] Although the adjective appears but once in Acts, it is worthy of mention because of the important roles it will play in subsequent homiletic and theological discourse. Ignatius uses it in his "creedal antitheses" (*Ephesians* 7:2; *Polycarp* 3:2), while Justin employs the term more than twenty times. παθητός also appears in Athenagoras and is common in Clement of Alexandria. This word, with its philosophical background, was destined to play an important role in second century discussions about Gnosticism and the question of God's "passibility," i. e., liability to suffering.[154] Whether Luke had any inkling of its future significance, his selection of this adjective shows which way the cultural and theological wind was blowing.

παιδεία, παιδευτής, παιδεύω ("education," "culture," "discipline," "corrector" and related verbal meanings, often transliterated in the following as *paideia*.) Those who need or desire a quick—if not painless—course in the educational methods of the biblical world might note that the same verbal stem serves for both "education" and "corporal punishment." When Pilate proposes that he subject the accused to *paideia* before releasing him (παιδεύσας ... ἀπολύσω: Luke 23:16, 22), he does not have in mind requiring Jesus to learn five hundred lines of Homer. At least fourteen of the twenty-one uses of this word group in the New Testament clearly refer to a "discipline" that implies "punishment."[155] Not too many years ago students were still privileged to learn that the tragedian Aeschylus's use of the theme "no pain, no gain" (πάθει μαθεῖν) brought that playwright to the threshold of Christian insight![156]

"Education" in our sense emerged in the Classical Greek world as a primary mark of the truly civilized person—who was, of course, a male member of the aristocracy. Education was extolled as the source of genuine freedom. (Thus the notion of the "liberal arts.") By the middle of the fourth century BCE some, such as the orator Isocrates, saw in *paideia* a ground for uniting all Greeks and, indeed, all persons of culture. Hellenistic Judaism responded to this offer.[157] Two passages in Acts reflect a classical biographical formula: place of birth, place where one was reared, and the nature and location of one's education.[158] According to 7:22, "Moses was *instructed* (ἐπαιδεύθη) in all the wisdom of the Egyptians." To a mob in the temple at Jerusalem Paul proclaims: "I am a Jew, *born* in Tarsus in Cilicia, but *brought up* in this city at the feet of Gamaliel, *educated* (πεπαιδευμένος) strictly according to our ancestral law ..." The first places Moses in the admirable position of assimilating Egyptian *paideia*, widely (and not altogether wrongly) viewed as the fountainhead of Greek learning.[159] In the second, Paul, in some ways a successor of Moses, boasts of his Hebrew erudition in the language of Hellenistic Judaism.

Paul can *tell* about his Jewish learning. Greek *paideia* is a quality that he *shows* throughout the second half of Acts, never more briefly and effectively than in a few words uttered just prior to the verse just quoted: "I am a Jew, from Tarsus in Cilicia, a citizen of an important city" (Acts 21:39). With this sentence the missionary relegates to the realm of absurdity the idea that he could be an Egyptian insurrectionist.[160] And with its assertion that "All scripture is inspired by God and is useful for teaching, for reproof, for correction, and *for training in righteousness* (πρὸς παιδείαν τὴν ἐν δικαιοσύνῃ)," the well-known 2 Timothy 3:16 represents the Hellenistic Jewish view of scripture as the basis of *paideia*, now taken up by Christians and never to be set aside.[161] The goal of education is the moral life, as polytheists had long affirmed.[162] Its textbook is Sacred Scripture. The mellifluous Titus 2:12 views "grace" as the educative force for moral life. These two statements, while not anti-Pauline, show the how Paul's ideas were transcribed for Greco-Roman family and civic life. Of the first (2 Timothy 3:16), Georg Bertram says,

> It might almost seem that here, in contrast to Gl. 3:24, there is set up again a παιδεία νόμου [teaching of the Torah] even after Christ. But the author does not see, and certainly does not intend, any contradiction of Gl. 3:24 or of Paul generally. He has in view the Christian and his nurture.[163]

Ephesians 6:4 (not paralleled in Colossians 3:21) introduces the concept of *paideia* in the sense of the formation of children by parental teaching. Polycarp *Philippians* 4:2 is rather similar, with a view to the role of mothers. *1 Clement* is divided. Of the fifteen uses of the noun and/or verb, a majority (including two citations) refer to punishment. At least six, however, relate to instruction in "Christian culture." *1 Clement* 21:6 is evocative of the Pastorals: "Let us teach (παιδεύσωμεν) the young that learning (παιδείαν) that pertains to the fear of God" in 62:3 is quite similar to 2 Timothy 3:16. The prayer of 59:3 says that through Jesus Christ God has "taught, sanctified, and honored" the faithful (δι' οὗ ἡμᾶς ἐπαίδευσας, ἡγίασας, ἐτίμησας). The middle verb is traditional, while the first and third represent values of Greco-Roman culture—interpreted, certainly, in Jewish and early Christian terms. In one of his last scholarly undertakings, Werner Jaeger, author of a three-volume study of Greek *paideia*, took up the reception of that concept into early Christianity, beginning with *1 Clement*. Before examining that text, however, he reflects about Paul's mission to gentiles in Acts, with particular attention to the Areopagus address (17:16–34). Jaeger finds the author of the *Acts of Philip* an excellent interpreter of Luke, for when he brings his hero to Athens to dispute with philosophers, he has Philip announce that "My Lord has brought a genuinely fresh and original παιδεία into the world.[164] Revelation of the *Paideia* of Christ was, according to Jaeger, "What the author of our [i.e., the canonical] Acts wanted to do."[165] He regards *1 Clement* as "a large expansion of this idea and of its application in Christian life and thought."[166] On a similar note, in the beginning of his first *Apology* Justin calls the son of Antoninus Pius a "lover of culture" (ἐραστῇ παιδείας), presuming that like would appeal to like. Not until Clement of Alexandria would the confrontation between "pagan" and "Christian" *paideia* be overt, but the beginnings of this movement can be seen in Hebrews, Ephesians, the Pastorals, Polycarp, Acts, and *1 Clement*. The latter uses the technical terminology most often, whereas Luke expresses its meaning most daringly in his narrative accounts.[167]

παρατίθημι ("place before") See p. 210.

πατριάρχης ("patriarch," "founding father"). This term appears three times in Acts (2:29, of David; 7:8–9, of the Sons of Jacob). The other New Testament usage is Hebrews 7:4, of Abraham). It appears seven times in the LXX, five of which are in the chronicles, two in 4 Maccabees. "Patriarch" is another term from Jewish Hellenism that Christianity found useful because it supports the antiquity of the faith and its claim to be the legitimate heir of the promises to Israel. Justin cites or uses "patriarch" twenty times in his *Dialogue*, the *Protevangelium of James* twice, Irenaeus once, Clement of Alexandria three times, and Theophilus and Melito (*On the Passover*) twice. Finally, the Pseudo-Clementines were fond enough of the word to employ it twenty-five times.

περιεργάζω, περίεργος ("to be curious," here in negative sense of being a "gossip," "busybody"). As is the case with any good society, Greco-Roman culture vigorously condemned meddlesome behavior and the activities of "moral police," and was no less guilty of these activities than have been many others. Acts 17:21–22 associates the well-known curiosity of the Athenians with their propensity to be "quite religious." The language is rather delicate, for it can also mean that Athenians are given over to gossip and superstition, while their taste inclines toward the merely vogue and ephemeral. Athenian failure to receive the message of Paul will entail no surprise.[168]

In Acts 19:19 the adjective refers to magical practices. This is more of a circumlocution than a euphemism, for practical magic was among the most meddlesome of activities, directed as it usually was toward the manipulation of other people.[169] The philosophical tradition disapproved of meddling and had to defend itself against the same charge. ". . . [T]he slur that they were busybodies meddling in other peoples' affairs was constantly hurled at them."[170] The word group entered into language of popular Jewish moral writings.[171] The writer of 2 Thessalonians associates meddlesome behavior with the "disorderly," those for whose idle hands (and mouths) the Devil has found some employment (2 Thessalonians 3:11). Luke takes note of just such persons in Thessalonica, where they are easy prey for those seeking fodder to foment a riot (Acts 17:5). Although Luke does not care that much for disorder, *1 Clement* should win the prize here: "disorderly" draws perilously close to the sin against the Holy Spirit. The Pastor, too, regards meddlesome gossip as the kind of activity widows of insufficient years are likely to practice (1 Timothy 5:13[172]); indeed, gossip and superstition are vices that men have never hesitated to attribute to women. Because he believed that Paul wrote 1 Timothy and that Acts was written by a companion of Paul, Ceslas Spicq could draw a link between Acts 19:19 and 1 Timothy 5:13. The historical grounds for his observations are tenuous, but his insight into ancient culture is sound.[173]

Disapproval of "curiosity" and meddling doubtless enters Christian writings as a part of the general accommodation to conventional values, as can be seen in the inclusion of a synonym in a catalogue of vicious persons enunciated in 1 Peter 4:15: "But let none of you suffer as a murderer, a thief, a criminal, or even as a mischief maker (ἀλλοτριεπίσκοπος, "minder of someone else's business"). *Hermas* employs both verb and noun with only mild disapproval, or less.[174] Yet Christians were vulnerable to charges of interfering in the lives of others because of their missionary efforts. In the words of a late second century opponent:[175]

In private houses also we see wool-workers, cobblers, laundry-workers, and the
most illiterate and bucolic yokels, who would not dare to say anything at all in
front of their elders and more intelligent masters. But whenever they get hold
of children in private and some stupid women with them, they let out some
astounding statements as, for example, that they must not pay any attention to
their father and school-teachers, but must obey them; they say that these talk
nonsense and have no understanding, and that in reality they neither know nor
are able to do anything good, but are taken up with mere empty chatter. But they
alone, they say, know the right way to live, and if the children would believe
them, they would become happy and make their home happy as well. And if just
as they are speaking they see one of the school-teachers coming, or some intelligent person, or even the father himself, the more cautious of them flee in all direc-
tions; but the more reckless urge the children on to rebel.[176]

For Celsus, the polytheist philosopher who wrote these words, Christian missionaries are the very kind of people the Pastor opposes: meddlers who exploit
those lacking *paideia*. To be sure, Acts pictures the famous Paul practicing a trade
not unlike that of a cobbler, but its account of his missionary work hardly jibes
with Celsus's vituperative portrait of Christian mission. In refuting these and
similar charges, Origen refers to the behavior of Cynic philosophers.[177] For his
part, Justin, taking as it were a leaf from Acts 17, notes that other "philosophers"
have been dragged before judges on the charge of meddling. His example is
Socrates.[178] περίεργος is another indicator of how Acts participates in the moral
world of second-century Christianity and becomes entangled in debates over
what is "good citizenship" and what is unwarranted interference.

πίστις ("trust," "confidence," "the faith"). Occurring 243 times and found
in every book except the Gospel of John, this is far from being a rare noun in
the New Testament.[179] The meaning of πίστις is open to debate in a number of
cases.[180] The present interest is in distinguishing between faith as one virtue
among others and faith as a belief system. Traditional theological jargon contrasts the *fides qua*, faith as gift and quality, as in "the faith by which I live," to
the *fides quae*, faith as creed, "the faith to which I subscribe." On two occasions
in Acts πίστις is evidently a virtue, both times in descriptions of leaders as "full
of faith and holy spirit" (6:5, Stephen; 11:24, Barnabas[181]). Faith is often a virtue
in *1 Clement*, and is acquiring that quality in Ignatius.[182]

More noteworthy is the tendency for Acts (unlike the Gospel of Luke) to
speak of "the faith," almost in the sense of "the church." Among the examples
of this usage are 6:7; 13:8, and 14:22. Schuyler Brown describes the matter as
follows:

The book of Acts reveals a notable shift from "*your* faith" to "*the* faith": πίστις is
objectified, i.e. identified with the Christian kerygma. This objectification entails
an ecclesialization of the notion: the bearer of the faith is not the individual
Christian but the community; the strong faith of the churches (Acts 16,5) takes the
place of the strong faith of the suffering Christian.[183]

Although there are traces of this understanding appear in Paul, it becomes more common and marked in the Deutero-Pauline and other later literature. Examples include Ephesians 4:5, Jude 3//2 Peter 1:1, Jude 20, and in particular, the Pastoral Epistles.[184] Later usage continues this application of the term.[185] Luke's readiness to speak of "the faith" indicates a strong affinity with works of the second century, most notably the Pastorals.

πολιτεύομαι. (in the sense of "lead one's life"). In Acts this verb appears only in Paul's boast to the Sanhedrin (23:1), "up to this day I have lived my life with a clear conscience before God." One may argue that Luke has taken the term from Philippians 1:27, but it also reflects the apologetic language of Hellenistic Judaism appropriated by Christians of the second and third centuries (see below). The term appears eight times in the LXX, once in Esther and the balance in 2–4 Maccabees, where it gives a religious sense to a characteristically Greek metaphor. Luke's Paul uses this word in just that sense ("before God"). No further instances of this verb are to be found in the New Testament.

Philo and Josephus also use this verb in apologetic contexts, as will Justin, Athenagoras, Theophilus, and Origen among Christian apologists. Among the Apostolic Fathers πολιτεύομαι occurs twice in Diognetus, and once each in Polycarp and *Hermas*. Particularly interesting for this study is 1 *Clement*, where the verb appears six times. This is another indicator of the affinity between Acts and 1 *Clement*, one additional instance of their shared interest in the Christian life as an expression of "good citizenship," political and religious.[186]

προπετής ("rash," "impetuous"). 1 *Clement* 1:1 attributes the unpleasantness at Corinth to the behavior of "a few rash (προπετῆ) and self-willed individuals." With the exception of behavior in combat, ancient philosophy strongly disapproved of the "rash," for it implied a lamentable lack of self-control, similar to what we describe as "impulsive behavior."[187] The term enters Jewish wisdom literature in Greek (Proverbs 10:14; 13:3; Sirach 9:18) out of conformity to Hellenistic ethics rather than to scrupulous accuracy in translation.[188] Other than 1 *Clement*, the only other appearances of this term in the New Testament and related literature are Acts 19:36, where it is a part of the "city clerk's" sage advice to the unruly assembly, and 2 Timothy 3:4, where it is one of the qualities of eschatological false teachers.[189] "Rash" is another word of good Greek standing that suits the moral world of Acts, 1 *Clement*, and the Pastoral Epistles, as well as the morals of the general culture.

προσήλυτος ("convert"). The term appears four times in the New Testament: Matthew 23:15; Acts 2:11; 6:5; 13:43.[190] In Matthew and Acts 13:43 the NRSV renders the term "convert." The two other instances prefer "proselyte." Martin Goodman is typical of recent analysts in claiming that Matthew 23:15 ("Woe to you, scribes and Pharisees, hypocrites! For you cross sea and land to make a single convert, and you make the new convert twice as much a child of hell as yourselves.") refers to efforts to bring persons into agreement with the "party line" of the Pharisees.[191] In Acts 2:11, 6:5, and evidently 13:43, it is a technical term for a gentile who has fully converted to the religion of Israel, a usage was not fully established until the second century.[192] Philo uses the term eight times with various meanings, while Josephus avoids it. Not until the second century does the term become common, and then only in Christian writings. The most interesting example is Justin, who uses this noun eleven times in his *Dialogue with Trypho* (a Jew). It is thus possible that the examples in Acts show that it was written when "proselyte" had all but fully acquired its technical meaning. The matter is not certain, but it is clear that Acts cannot be used to prove the meaning of the word in the period c. 75 CE.[193] The more Acts appears to take the meaning of "proselyte" for granted, the later it is likelier to be.

σεμνότης, κ.τ.λ., ("dignity") See p. 236.

συμβιβάζω ("unite," "prove," "instruct"). This rather rare and somewhat *recherché* term appears in 1 Corinthians 2:16 (and Justin, *Dialogue* 50:5) citing Isaiah 40:13–14. Elsewhere in the New Testament συμβιβάζω turns up in Colossians 2:2; 2:19 and its parallel in Ephesians 4:16, as well as in Acts 9:22; 16:10; 19:33. The verb has ten appearances in the LXX (usually in the sense of "instruct" or "guide"). The final Jewish or Christian example up to the end of the second century appears in Clement of Alexandria, *Miscellanies* 1.161.3. These are rather slim pickings, but they do represent a Greek intellectual word with some background in Hellenistic Judaism that except for one quotation is restricted to the Deutero-Pauline realm.[194] συμβιβάζω is not probative, but it is instructive.

συνείδησις ("consciousness," "conscience"). See pp. 240–41.

σωτήρ, (savior) This noun appears 4 times in Luke and Acts.[195] In the undisputed Pauline letters it occurs only in Philippians 3:20, where it refers to a future savior. The word makes a single appearance in John, Ephesians, 1 John, and Jude. In the Pastorals "savior" occurs ten times. 2 Peter has five examples. Ignatius employs the noun five times, and it occurs once each in *1 Clement*, Polycarp, *2 Clement*, *Diognetus*, and the *Martyrdom of Polycarp*. The still valuable excursus on "The Soteriological Terminology of Titus 2:11–14 and 3:4–7" in Dibelius/Conzelmann's commentary elucidates the apparent inconsistencies in this terminology by reference to diverse backgrounds.[196] The Pastor inclines toward the vocabulary of the imperial cult as a means for characterizing the munificent grace of God. Such "borrowing" should not be viewed as the nadir of syncretistic decadence. Christianity frequently collided with the ruler cult, conformity to which became the touchstone for persecutors. Those who would not participate in the cult had done the equivalent of refusing to rise for the national anthem or salute the flag. Competition requires "borrowing;" the stronger the competition, the more extensive the borrowing. More particularly, the customs and apparatus of the royal court had long served as a major source of imagery about "the Heavenly Court," for Israelites no less than others.[197] The soteriology of the Pastorals uses what is today called "relevant language."[198] The adjective σωτήριος ("salvific," "saving") is of particular interest to Luke because of its appearance in Isaiah, especially Isaiah 40:5 (Luke 2:30; 3:6; Acts 28:28). Other uses are Ephesians 6:17 and Titus 2:11. (τὸ σωτήριον is the normal LXX equivalent of σωτηρία, "salvation," the English word normally used to translate it.) *1 Clement* uses the term four times, three in citations, the final time (36:1) in exposition of a citation.[199] "Savior" is another term that shows the desire to speak in terms familiar to the general public.

σοφρωσύνη, σώφρων, σωφρονισμός, σωφρόνως ("reasonableness," "prudent," "self-controlled"). σοφρωσύνη, one of the four cardinal Greek virtues, follows the path of ἐγκράτεια ("self-control") with which it was already associated by Plato (*e.g., Republic* 4, 430E), in that it comes to mean "chastity." In the Greek world this group expressed the ideal of μηδὲν ἄγαν ("nothing in excess"), an ideal that governed almost the entire realm of life and encapsulates the essence of "classicism" in literature and art. In this word the ethical and aesthetic meet. "Good taste" was as much a matter of morals as of aesthetics. In the Hellenistic and Roman eras σοφρωσύνη became the virtue *par excellence* of women, attested in abundant inscriptions, some of which assure the readers that the honoree actually possessed this virtue.[200] In the LXX the word-group is restricted to writings in Greek or under Greek influence. Philo, as might be expected, favors the quality and gives it his own "spin."[201] Acts 26:25 captures the essence of the classical sense, in an appropriate context and at the proper moment: "Paul said, " 'I am not out of my mind, most excellent Festus, but I am speaking the sober truth.'" "Sober truth" is σοφρωσύνη.[202] As noun or adjective the word appears nine times in the Pastorals, four times in *1 Clement*, and once in Ignatius.[203] Although Luke's Paul was claiming no more on the surface than a sound mind, his language shows that he is aware of the important virtues—and thus, by ancient standards, he is a practitioner of them.

ταπεινοφροσύνη ("humility"), cf. ταπεινός, ταπείνος, ταπεινόφρων. Humility was not a Greco-Roman virtue. The root refers to the status of the down-trodden, whose position was neither admirable nor enviable.[204] This noun is an almost exclusively Christian usage.[205] Not found in the LXX, the term occurs in Acts 20:19 and six times in epistles, one of which (Philippians 2:3) is genuinely Pauline. From that slender root grew a good-sized bush. The writer of Colossians took up the word, using it three times.[206] From there it entered Ephesians (4:2) and thence Acts.[207] 1 Peter also admires the term, using it and the related adjective three times. "Humility" quickly gained a proud place in the language of Christian ethics. *1 Clement* finds seven occasions to use the noun, two for the adjective, and 12 for a derived verb, while the noun appears twice in *Hermas* and the adjective once, as well as three uses of ταπεινοφρονεῖν. *Barnabas* and Ignatius employ the adjective once each. In short order the word comes to refer to ascetic discipline and is associated with fasting and self-abasement.[208] Although Luke uses this noun but once, and that in dependence upon Ephesians, he gives it an important place and thus stands within the tradition of post-apostolic Christianity, which was seeking to inculcate a different motivation for ethical behavior. As Luke 22:24–30 says in different words, Christian "benefactors" are to perform their services without arrogance or self-aggrandizement.

τόπος ("place," in the sense of one's destiny[209]). Acts 1:25 plays with two figurative applications: "to take the place (τόπον) in this ministry and apostleship from which Judas turned aside to go to his own place (τόπον)." *1 Clement* 5:4 is quite similar: "... Peter ... went to the glorious place which he merited" (εἰς τὸν ὀφειλόμενον τόπον τῆς δόξης),[210] an assurance that brings to mind the enigmatic statement about Peter in Acts 12:17. Polycarp *Philippians* 9:2 uses the phrase with the same participle. Other related examples are Ignatius *Magnesians* 5:1, and Hermas *Similitudes* 9.4.7; 5.4; 12.4, and 27.3. "Place" in this sense of "place for which one is destined" is an element of the vocabulary of early Christian piety shared by Luke and certain Apostolic Fathers.[211] "Place" meaning "office" (cf. "position"), found in Acts 1:25a, also appears in these writings.[212]

ὑπερήφανος ("haughty," "arrogant"). Other than the famous quote from Proverbs 3:24, shared by James and 1 Peter, this adjective is found once each in Paul, Luke, and 2 Timothy.[213] Four examples appear in *1 Clement* (one a citation), and one each in Ignatius and the *Didache*. Twenty of the forty-one appearances in the LXX are in books not found in Hebrew. This is a relatively minor example of the moral vocabulary of Hellenistic Judaism that is represented in Luke.[214]

ὑπὸ τὸν οὐρανόν ("under heaven"). This phrase appears in Luke 17:24, Acts 2:5, and 4:12. Elsewhere it occurs in Colossians 1:23, twice in *Hermas*, three times in Justin, and twice in Clement of Alexandria.[215] However innocuous or common "under heaven" may seem, it is part of the language of the late first and second century Christianity. For Luke and the writer of Colossians this construction endows the universal mission of Christianity with a poetic touch: "every nation under heaven."

φιλανθρωπία, φιλανθρώπως ("generosity," "kindly"), φίλος ("friend"). φιλανθρωπία was an important civic virtue in the Greco-Roman world.[216] Although "generosity" was a general expectation, it tends to be a virtue of those with more power, ranging from the monarch to a kindly centurion (Acts 27:3) and even to virtue-impaired "barbarians" (Acts 28:2). "Generosity" is a manifestation of benefaction and the related system of reciprocity. The εὐεργέτης ("benefactor") displays φιλανθρωπία. English "philanthropist" is not misleading insofar as the epithet is not routinely applied to people who lob a quarter into the Salvation Army Christmas pail. Philanthropists are persons admired because their generosity is practically a vocation and their means are sufficient to make their gifts important. For the wealthy of antiquity, philanthropy was an *obligation*. " 'Loving kindness' (φιλανθρωπία) is the one virtue typical of the ruler."[217] Its frequent companion is "goodness" (χρηστότης).[218]

Luke's gospel is, among other things, a primer in philanthropy for relatively well-off Christians, many of whom probably belonged to the *nouveaux riches*.[219] Spontaneous generosity marks the opening chapters of Acts, in which those with property liquidate it and hand over the proceeds to the community (2:44–45; 4:34–37). These narratives are not only exemplary for believers; they also show that the followers of Jesus are "good citizens." "Philanthropy" means treating all humanity (ὁ ἄνθρωπος) as a "friend." (φίλος).²²⁰ Friends, after all, share everything, as an enduring Greek proverb has it (κοινὰ τῶν φιλῶν, cf. Acts 4:32). If human instances do not suffice, divine examples can be found, ranging from the "tender mercies of our God" (Luke 1:78) that bring salvation to the universal benefit of the bountiful earth (Acts 14:15–17), to the healing of a suffering individual (Acts 4:9). Greek authors from the early fifth century BCE onward describe the gods as "philanthropic".²²¹ Early Jews²²² and Christians used the specific term reluctantly, although they approved of the concept.²²³

Eighteen of the twenty-nine uses of the term "friend" are in Luke and Acts.²²⁴ At least one of these is antithetical to the reciprocity-based ethic of the Greco-Roman world (Luke 14:12: "Don't invite your friends . . .").²²⁵ Two of the three New Testament uses of the φιλανθρωπ- group appear in the account of Paul's voyage to Rome (Acts 27:3; 28:2), a section in which Luke is at his most Hellenic. This language bears upon the question of whether "The/his friends" in 27:3 is a term for believers. Harnack believes that ". . . Luke with his classical culture has permitted himself this once to use the classical designation."²²⁶ He may be right. The term is not technical, but it conforms to the ethos of this section of Acts. The only other NT use of the group is Titus 3:4, which associates "philanthropy" with "goodness" in the customary manner. Quite similar to this are *Diognetus* 9:2 and Justin, *Dialogue* 47.5. *Diognetus* 8:7 relates the orderliness of creation to God's "kindly" and "long-suffering" nature: "For God, the Sovereign and Maker of the universe, who made all things and determined the proper place of each, showed himself to be long-suffering, as well as a true friend of humanity.²²⁷ His sparing use of this vocabulary is sufficient to support the evidence that Luke is prepared to integrate general ethical values into his narrative world.²²⁸

φόβος ("fear of God/ "to fear God"). Acts 9:31, "Meanwhile the church throughout Judea, Galilee, and Samaria had peace and was built up. Living in the fear of the Lord and in the comfort of the Holy Spirit, it increased in numbers,"²²⁹ represents "fear of God" as the Christian posture. A similar usage ("fear of Christ") appears in Ephesians 5:21 and in a non-Pauline interpolation, 2 Corinthians 7:1.²³⁰ "Fear" without qualification but with the same sense can be found three times in 1 Peter and once in Jude, while the verb is found in Colossians, 1 Peter, and several times in Revelation. In *1 Clement* and *Hermas* this understanding is quite common.²³¹ Once again, Acts shows that it is familiar with the ethics and piety of the post-apostolic era. This Lukan summary has a thoroughly Deutero-Pauline character.²³²

χριστιανός ("Christian"). The emergence of this adjective marks the definite recognition of the followers of Jesus as an organization separate from Judaism. "Christian" is a Greek word of Latin form and semitic background. The stem χριστ- obtains its meaning here as a translation of the Hebrew word for "anointed" ("messiah," in English, a metonymy for monarchs). Most Greek words in -*ian*- are translations that employ their original Latin suffix²³³ to indicate adherents of a person, for example, "the Herodians" (Mark 3:6, 12:13). More often than not such labels were coined by outsiders.²³⁴ Acts 11:26 implies this, or is willing to permit its readers to draw the conclusion that Barnabas's and Paul's missionary labors in Antioch were so successful that the movement became well known. Since neither Paul nor any other writer of the first two generations betrays familiarity with the word, it is rather unlikely that "Christian" first emerged in Antioch during the 30s and 40s of the early first century.

"Christian/Christianity" bursts out in the 90s and later in writings linked in one way or another to Rome, Antioch, or Asia Minor. The earliest datable reference (Rome: early 90s) is Josephus, *Antiquities* 18.64—*if* this is genuine.[235] 1 Peter 4:16, which may be the earliest extant reference, relates to Rome and northern Asia Minor and uses the term in the context of persecution. Persecution also hovers in the background of Acts 26:28. The earliest Latin references all relate to legal process and were written between c. 110–120 by members of the same ruling-class circle.[236] Pliny's account of his actions to suppress Christianity is contemporary, a part of his correspondence with the Emperor Trajan (*Letters* 10.96–97). The other references (Suetonius, *Nero* 16.2; Tacitus *Annals* 15.44) relate a local persecution of Christians at Rome by Nero, a half-century before the time of composition. They agree that Christians constituted a depraved, wicked, and uncontrolled "superstition." These views, of which Pliny was, by direct experience, somewhat disabused, are those attacked by the later apologists. Neither Suetonius nor Tacitus can be invoked as evidence that the word "Christian" was known in Rome c. 64 CE.[237] The designation "Christian," probably had its origin in popular usage and became the official legal designation at some time before 110, quite possibly a good decade earlier. Luke is not unduly enamored of this term. He prefers the word "movement" ("way," e.g., Acts 9:2; 24:22), but is willing to allow that "Christian" is familiar and to place it on the lips of a client king. The appearances in Acts quite conform to the usages of the Latin authors, with the exception that Luke does not, of course, view the designation as opprobrious.[238]

In the *Didache* "Christian" appears but once, in a context devoid of any dishonor. Nor was the word objectionable to Polycarp or to Ignatius, or to the composer of the *Martyrdom of Polycarp*.[239] Ignatius, Bishop of *Antioch* and a writer of letters to communities in Asia Minor, either coins or uses the term χριστιανισμός, "Christianism." This usage, found also in the *Martyrdom of Polycarp*, soon became standard and passed from Tertullian into Latin (and thence into Romance[240]). Whatever the origins of "Christian," "Christianism" is a counter-coinage and antithesis to "Judaism" (Ἰουδαισμός) that proclaims Christianity as a distinct religion. Luke's awareness of the popularity of the adjective "Christian"—not merely of its existence—indicates a time around the close of the first century or later.[241]

SUMMARY

The result of the foregoing data and argumentation is a thick list of affinities among texts, some with Colossians, Ephesians, 1 Peter, Hebrews, James, and 2 Peter, Ignatius of Antioch, the Didache, *Barnabas*, the *Shepherd of Hermas*, and *Diognetus*, but many shared among Luke and Acts, *1 Clement*, the Pastoral

Epistles, and Polycarp of Smyrna. These affinities embrace a number of theological topics, matters of Church Order and community life, stances towards society, and ethics. Some are certainly clearer and more cogent than others. Objections may be raised, and as in the case of the proposed use of Paul's letters, I shall freely and happily consent to removing more than one half of these terms and concepts. That would not alter the result. The collective weight of the data urges the conclusion that Acts belongs to the period between c. 100 and 130 ce. If Acts had appeared fifteen or twenty years earlier than 1 *Clement*, it would have been well ahead of its time in more ways than credibility can reasonably tolerate. According to the criterion of the latest datable material, Acts is close in time to the Pastorals and to Polycarp. In further pursuit of this proposal I shall proceed to an examination of passages often cited in the discussion of possible allusions to Acts in early Christian literature. These do not relate to individual words or concepts, but to phrases or sentences that have strong affinities to Acts.

ALLEGED ALLUSIONS TO ACTS
AS AN INDICATOR OF DATE

Chapter two looked at possible and explicit evidence of familiarity with Acts as one means of determining the *terminus ante quem*. That was a selective examination, focusing upon the more probable instances of dependency. The purpose of the following discussion is to see the extent other texts sometimes advanced as possible indicators of familiarity with Acts appear to stem from a similar environment, including not only possible geographical proximity and potential theological kinship, but, also and most importantly, date.

PSEUDO-MARK 16:9–20

The "Longer Ending" of verses 9–20[242] represents an effort not only to provide Mark with what was regarded as a more suitable ending but also to bridge the gap between the life of Jesus and the mission of the apostles. (See Table 7.5.) The "longer ending" has, therefore, the same object as that pursued by Luke in the book of Acts. The material represents a popular theology that was common in the second century. One may see elements of this theological outlook in the various apocryphal gospels and acts, as well as in the work of Luke. The possible relevance of the "Longer Ending" to the date of Acts is limited by two factors. The first is that it may be dependent upon Acts. Secondly, the date of this piece is itself uncertain.

Although the portion of this passage cited in Table 7.5 has themes in common with Acts, it does not seem to be simply dependent upon it. Verse 19 shows elaboration toward the "Apostles' Creed." The expression "all creation" (πᾶσα κτίσις) is not Lukan.[243] "New tongues" gives the xenoglossia (speaking in foreign languages) of Acts a different eschatological twist—perhaps similar to

Table 7.5: "Mark" 16:15–20

Ps-Mark 16:15–20	Luke, Acts, and Other
15 Πορευθέντες εἰς τὸν κόσμον ἅπαντα **κηρύξατε** τὸ εὐαγγέλιον **πάσῃ τῇ κτίσει** Go into all the world and **proclaim the good news to the whole creation.**	Luke 24:47 καὶ **κηρυχθῆναι** ἐπὶ τῷ ὀνόματι αὐτοῦ μετάνοιαν καὶ ἄφεσιν ἁμαρτιῶν εἰς πάντα τὰ ἔθνη repentance and forgiveness of sins is to be **proclaim**ed in his name to all nations, beginning from Jerusalem. Col. 1:23 . . . τοῦ εὐαγγελίου οὗ ἠκούσατε, τοῦ **κηρυχθέντος** ἐν **πάσῃ κτίσει** τῇ ὑπὸ τὸν οὐρανόν, οὗ ἐγενόμην ἐγὼ Παῦλος διάκονος. the **gospel** that you heard, which has been **proclaimed to every creature** under heaven. V.16 conforms to Acts
16 The one who believes and is baptized will be saved 17 And these signs will accompany (παρακολουθήσει) those who believe: by using my name they will cast out demons; they will speak in new tongues; (γλώσσαις λαλήσουσιν καιναῖς) 18 they will pick up snakes in their hands, and if they drink any deadly thing, it will not hurt them; they will lay their hands on the sick, and they will recover.	17. Verb παρακολουθεῖν Luke 1:3; 1 Tim 4:6; 2 Tim 3:10. Exorcisms: Acts 16:18; Tongues: Acts 2:3–4; 10:46; 19:6; 1 Cor12:28. (But ἑτέραις in 2:3–4, otherwise unmarked.) Pick up snakes: cf. Acts 28:3–5 Poison: Prochorus *Acts of John*; Barsabbas: Eusebius *H.E.* 3.39.9.[244] Healing through imposition of hands: Acts 28:8
19 Ὁ μὲν οὖν κύριος [Ἰησοῦς] μετὰ τὸ λαλῆσαι αὐτοῖς ἀνελήμφθη εἰς τὸν οὐρανὸν καὶ ἐκάθισεν ἐκ δεξιῶν τοῦ θεοῦ. So then the Lord Jesus, after he had spoken to them, was taken up into heaven and sat down at the right hand of God.	V.19. Acts 1:11 . . . ὁ Ἰησοῦς ὁ **ἀναλημφθεὶς** ἀφ' ὑμῶν **εἰς τὸν οὐρανὸν** This Jesus, who has been **taken up** from you **into heaven.**

the views held at Corinth. Papias could have written this passage. That affinity suggests a date c. 125–150 CE. The common themes—universal proclamation of the Christian message, miracle-working apostles, the ascension and session of the risen Lord—are of some value in identifying the milieu of Acts.

EPHESIANS

The affinities between Acts and Ephesians exist at numerous levels, from the verbal and superficial to the thematic and ecclesiastical. Both may derive from the same area, Ephesus. The differences are hardly less deserving of atten-

Table 7.6: Near and Far

Acts 2:39 ὑμῖν γὰρ ἐστιν ἡ ἐπαγγελία καὶ τοῖς τέκνοις ὑμῶν καὶ πᾶσιν **τοῖς εἰς μακρὰν** For the promise is for you, for your children, and for all who are **far away** 10:36 τὸν λόγον [ὃν] ἀπέστειλεν τοῖς υἱοῖς Ἰσραὴλ **εὐαγγελιζόμενος εἰρήνην** διὰ Ἰησοῦ Χριστοῦ the message he sent to the people of Israel, **preaching peace** by Jesus Christ Isaiah 57:19 **εἰρήνην** ἐπ' **εἰρήνην τοῖς μακρὰν** καὶ **τοῖς ἐγγὺς** οὖσιν· καὶ εἶπεν κύριος Ἰάσομαι αὐτούς **Peace, peace, to the far and the near**, says the LORD	Ephesians 2:13, 17: 13. νυνὶ δὲ ἐν Χριστῷ Ἰησοῦ ὑμεῖς οἵ ποτε ὄντες **μακρὰν** ἐγενήθητε **ἐγγὺς** But now in Christ Jesus you who once were **far off** have been brought **near** . . . 17. ἐλθὼν **εὐηγγελίσατο εἰρήνην** ὑμῖν **τοῖς μακρὰν καὶ εἰρήνην τοῖς ἐγγύς** 17 So he came and **proclaimed peace** to you who were **far off** and **peace** to those who were **near**

tion. Ephesians prefers the speculative theology of one branch of the Pauline heritage, is at home with the use of spatial rather than temporal constructs, and views the church as a supernatural body headed by Christ. Equally congenial to Ephesians is the Household Code, in which tradition a sacramental understanding of marriage is coming to fruition. Luke endorses none of these approaches. Ephesians, moreover, has the form of a Pauline letter and reveres Paul as the only apostle worth naming. Acts says nothing about letters from Paul and cannot regard him as an apostle, although Paul gains status from his association with other apostles, Peter in particular. These irreconcilable differences give substantial weight to the similarities. My working hypothesis, enunciated in chapter four, is that Acts knows and uses Ephesians. Yet while literary dependence could be held to account for the similarities, it need not. Indeed, it is unlikely that dependence can explain each and every similarity. The more probable hypothesis is that some of these are due to a common environment.[245] In addition to items discussed in this and previous chapters I offer the following.

Isaiah 57:19 is the source of the imagery in Table 7.6. Ephesians 2:17 is closest to its wording, but Luke and the writer of Ephesians are the only New Testament authors who use "near and far" as tropes for Jews and gentiles. Each can link the image to its own spatial imagery. Ephesians speaks of the earthly and the heavenly, while for Acts the goal is "the ends of the earth" (1:8).[246] If this use of metaphor is independent, it is an unusual coincidence. The choice between intertextuality and the current language of Christian mission is not easy to make.

For Ephesians the reconciliation of Jews and gentiles is the basis for peace in the Church. (See Table 7.7.) Luke does not make much explicit use of the Pauline vocabulary of reconciliation, although the concept is fundamental to his narra-

Table 7.7: Reconciliation

Acts 7:26	Colossians 1:20	Ephesians 2:16–17
τῇ τε ἐπιούσῃ ἡμέρᾳ ὤφθη αὐτοῖς μαχομένοις καὶ **συνήλλασσεν** αὐτοὺς εἰς **εἰρήνην** The next day *Moses* came to some of them as they were quarreling and tried to reconcile them,	καὶ δι' αὐτοῦ **ἀποκαταλλάξαι** τὰ πάντα εἰς αὐτόν, **εἰρηνοποιήσας** διὰ τοῦ αἵματος τοῦ σταυροῦ αὐτοῦ, [δι' αὐτοῦ] εἴτε τὰ ἐπὶ τῆς γῆς εἴτε τὰ ἐν τοῖς οὐρανοῖς.and through him God was pleased to **reconcile** to himself all things, whether on earth or in heaven, by **making peace** through the blood of his cross.	16 καὶ **ἀποκαταλλάξῃ** τοὺς ἀμφοτέρους ἐν ἑνὶ σώματι τῷ θεῷ διὰ τοῦ σταυροῦ, ἀποκτείνας τὴν ἔχθραν ἐν αὐτῷ. 17 καὶ ἐλθὼν εὐηγγελίσατο **εἰρήνην** ὑμῖν . . . and might **reconcile** both groups to God in one body through the cross, thus putting to death that hostility through it. *17* So he came and proclaimed **peace** . . .[247]

tive, as in the story of the "Prodigal" Son (Luke 15:11–32). That he was aware of this imagery is apparent in Stephen's speech, which strongly emphasizes the similarities between the respective careers of Moses and Jesus (Acts 7:20–40). The argument for intertextuality here (See Table 7.7) is rather thin, but the view of Moses's mission as the achievement of peace through reconciliation suggests that Luke viewed the goal of Ephesians with sympathy.[248] The "unnecessary addition" of εἰς εἰρήνην ("in peace," "into peace"),[249] left untranslated by the NRSV, looks like a redundancy that is straining to make the connection with the activity of Jesus in 10:36 (above), as well as with the program of Ephesians.[250]

Leslie Mitton (who was at the time of writing a member of the Methodist clergy) found a "remarkable" resemblance in the suggestion "that there is a certain similarity between a man who is intoxicated and one who is filled with the Holy Spirit."[251] (See Table 7.8.) In fact, the idea of a spiritual eleva-

Table 7.8: High Sobriety

Acts 2:4, 15	Ephesians 5:18–19
4. καὶ **ἐπλήσθησαν** πάντες πνεύματος ἁγίου, καὶ ἤρξαντο λαλεῖν ἑτέραις γλώσσαις . . . All of them were filled with the Holy Spirit and began to speak in other languages . . . 15. οὐ γὰρ ὡς ὑμεῖς ὑπολαμβάνετε οὗτοι **μεθύουσιν**, Indeed, these are not **drunk**, as you suppose	18 καὶ μὴ **μεθύσκεσθε** οἴνῳ, ἐν ᾧ ἐστιν ἀσωτία, ἀλλὰ **πληροῦσθε** ἐν πνεύματι, 19 λαλοῦντες . . . Do not get **drunk** with wine, for that is debauchery; but be filled with the Spirit, speaking . . .

tion that issues in "high sobriety" was part of the intellectual tradition. In a beautiful (and Platonic) rapture Philo says of the soaring mind (νοῦς) ". . . it is seized by a sober intoxication, like those filled with Corybantic frenzy, and is inspired . . ."[252] Philo elsewhere admits that those in a state of ecstasy can resemble persons who have taken a drop or two more than the situation strictly required.[253] The problem arises in Acts 2, for if one person heard a rustic Celt speaking Rumanian—the listener's own native language—while the individual next to him heard the same speech in his ancestral Turkish, the last conclusion to which either of them would leap is that the *speaker* was drunk. At such moments people question their own state of mind—or so one is told.[254]

Mitton's argument that here Ephesians depends upon Acts does not stand. What the passages share is dependence upon a theme used by no other early Christian authors. This is symptomatic of a broadening Christian intellectual horizon. Both authors allude to a commonplace description of religious rapture. Paul's reservations about ecstasy as a missionary instrument (1 Corinthians 12–14) have hardened. Luke does not want Christians to be viewed as rabid fanatics.[255] The author of Ephesians recommends singing "psalms and hymns and spiritual songs" (5:19) for spiritual edification. Another indication of a different environment is the shared expression "filled with (the Holy) Spirit," which is not Pauline. The same language appears in 1 *Clement* 2:2 (on which see below).

The development of a universalistic outlook is vital for Colossians, Ephesians, and Acts. Comparison shows that this viewpoint followed the Pauline use of Abrahamic traditions and drew upon similar scriptural resources. (See Table 7.9.) The basic source of Acts 3:25 is Genesis 22:18 (cf. also Genesis 12:3; 18:18), but the expression in common with Ephesians does not appear in Genesis. The word πατριά ("family") is associated with the gentiles (ἔθνη) in passages from the Psalter. The two references cited speak of gentiles worshipping the God of Israel.[256] Acts and Ephesians appear to share the same exegetical background and tradition, but it was not a general tradition, for this term πατριά appears in no other early Christian writer.[257] In this instance the intertextual solution is not lacking cogency, but it is difficult to explain why Luke or Ephesians would independently choose to borrow these two words. The argument that both reflect a common vocabulary appears to have the stronger case.

Ephesians 4:11 modifies 1 Corinthians 12:28 "And God has appointed in the church first apostles, second prophets, third teachers;" to read "The gifts he gave were that some would be apostles, some prophets, some evangelists, some pastors and teachers." Ephesians has added "evangelists" and "pastors," though "pastors and teachers" evidently refers to the same persons. "Pastor" is the Latin word for "shepherd," found as a verb in Acts 20:28, etc.[258] Acts, Ephesians, the Pastorals, Ignatius, and others assign the *magisterium* (teaching authority) to the pastors or "bishops." "Evangelist" appears only here (4:11), in Acts 21:8 (where it may not be a technical term), and in 2 Timothy 4:5.[259] Acts and Ephesians agree with Paul on the presence of prophets within Christian communities. The extent to which either author saw this office as continuing

Table 7.9: Every Family on Earth

Acts 3:25	Ephesians 3:14–15
ὑμεῖς ἐστε οἱ υἱοὶ τῶν προφητῶν καὶ τῆς διαθήκης ἧς διέθετο ὁ θεὸς πρὸς τοὺς πατέρας ὑμῶν, λέγων πρὸς Ἀβραάμ, Καὶ ἐν τῷ σπέρματί σου ἐνευλογηθήσονται **πᾶσαι αἱ πατριαὶ τῆς γῆς**. You are the descendants of the prophets and of the covenant that God gave to your ancestors, saying to Abraham, 'And in your descendants **all the families of the earth** shall be blessed.' Genesis 22:18 καὶ *ἐνευλογηθήσονται ἐν τῷ σπέρματί σου* **πάντα** τὰ ἔθνη **τῆς γῆς** . . . and by your offspring shall **all the nations of the earth** gain blessing for themselves . . . Psalm 21 (22):[260] 28 μνησθήσονται καὶ ἐπιστραφήσονται πρὸς κύριον πάντα τὰ πέρατα **τῆς γῆς** καὶ προσκυνήσουσιν ἐνώπιόν σου **πᾶσαι αἱ πατριαὶ** τῶν ἐθνῶν. All the ends of the earth shall remember and turn to the LORD; and **all the families of the nations** shall worship before him. Psalm 95 (96):7 ἐνέγκατε τῷ κυρίῳ, αἱ **πατριαὶ** τῶν ἐθνῶν, ἐνέγκατε τῷ κυρίῳ δόξαν καὶ τιμήν Ascribe to the LORD, **O families of the people**s, ascribe to the LORD glory and strength	Τούτου χάριν κάμπτω τὰ γόνατά μου πρὸς τὸν πατέρα, 15 ἐξ οὗ **πᾶσα πατριὰ** ἐν οὐρανοῖς καὶ ἐπὶ **γῆς** ὀνομάζεται For this reason I bow my knees before the Father, from whom **every family** in heaven and **on earth** takes its name

is not explicit, but although their number in proto-orthodox circles was not large,[261] one can find plenty of evidence for the continuing presence of prophets in Asia Minor from Revelation to the late second century. Unlike Acts, however, Ephesians does not countenance presbyters.

The concept of a divine plan is not common in the New Testament. Luke and Acts speak of God's βουλή on at least five occasions.[262] The only other examples are Ephesians 1:11 and Hebrews 6:17. Ephesians also uses προορίζω ("foresee," often with a sense of predestination) there and in 1:5. Ephesians is more evocative of Paul (Romans 8:29–30; 1 Corinthians 2:7) than is Acts 4:28. Acts and Ephesians are two different refractions of ideas related to providence and predestination, both developed from Pauline stock but with deeper roots in Hellenistic Judaism and Greco-Roman thought. In Ephesians, by implication, and with fuller development in Luke/Acts these roots have begun to push forth a stem whose branches will bear the fruit of a Christian theodicy.[263]

Another Pauline theme that Ephesians and Acts strongly support and develop is the goal of unity with peace. Implicit in each is the understanding that unity without peace is no real unity. Angels explain the meaning of Messiah's arrival with these words: "Glory to God in the highest heaven, and on earth peace among those who enjoy divine favor!" (Luke 2:14, my translation). Acts

10:36 summarizes the message of Jesus as "preaching peace."[264] Luke and Acts utilize the word about twenty times, as opposed to nine in Matthew, Mark, and John combined. Outside of initial and final greetings, Ephesians invokes peace five times. Only Romans has more instances among the letters, and Romans is nearly three times the longer of the two. Romans was probably a major source and inspiration for this "peace program." Paul evidently lost his life in an apparently unsuccessful effort to secure some degree of peace and unity among Jewish and gentile believers. Ephesians 2:11–22 speaks of the unification of Jews and gentiles through Christ. The opening verses admonish those of gentile background, intimating that they are insensitive to those of Jewish origin. Acts mirrors this perception. In Acts 15 Peter and James must come to the support of gentile believers. By Chapter 21:18–26, on the other hand, James must demand that Paul show sensitivity to "Jewish-Christians."[265] There is an almost plaintive quality in James's seemingly otiose repetition of the "Apostolic Decree," in 21:25. From Ephesians 2 and Acts 21 one gains more a sense of a "beleaguered" than of a "mighty" minority.[266] The plea of Ephesians 4:1–16 for unity in the community has theological warrants that Luke would not endorse, but the goal is one that he happily shares, as well as a number of expressions and phrases. Acts and Ephesians are two different representatives of a fundamental Deutero-Pauline program: the invocation of apostolic authority in the service of unity and peace.[267]

Leslie Mitton's patient, cautious, and open-minded work upon the relations between Acts and Ephesians exposes the limits of purely intertextual study and speculative historical reconstruction. His work bears some other marks of the "Goodspeed School," specifically a general neglect of theological factors and a positive aversion to the history of religions.[268] No bill of particulars drawn up against Ernst Käsemann (1906–1998) could accuse him of overlooking the history of religions or of not taking theology into account. Käsemann's admiration for Ephesians was not unqualified, and his appreciation of Acts was even more grudging, but appreciation there was.

The late exegete from Tübingen understood what the writers of Acts and Ephesians were trying to achieve. He did not, to reiterate, care very much for their program, but he understood its purpose. While short on sympathy, he did not lack insight. Much of Käsemann's work on the later New Testament writings is now under a cloud because of his antipathy to the specter of "Early Catholicism." In his brief essay "Ephesians and Acts" Käsemann defined that movement as ". . . a step away from early Christianity which understands itself eschatologically and moves toward the early Catholicism which regards itself as a force in history." The next sentence reads: "Ephesians as well as Acts marks the moment of this transition."[269] Although the experience of the Third Reich had pretty successfully vaccinated him against the virus of extolling "forces in history" for their own sake, Käsemann knew that the Christian church was such a force.[270] His objection was to the incorporation of apologies for and expositions of this force into the foundational documents of the Christian faith[271].

For Käsemann, Acts and Ephesians have a similar view of tradition, which is no longer seen as a basis for conversation but as a norm in itself. This leads to an understanding of the church as "the eschatological phenomenon per se."[272] In short, one will not tell the "story of the church" until the church has become a part of the means of salvation (from which it will, in due and precipitous course, degenerate into an institution dispensing salvation). It is therefore important to stress the place of the faith of Israel in the story of salvation. Ephesians states the role of the apostles as the foundation of a unified church (2:20); Acts presents it in narrative form. Their respective views of church organization are quite similar. The theological difference can be summarized in a sentence:

> Ephesians is rooted in the world of Hellenistic mystery-religion piety; in contrast, Luke represents, despite all miracles and various traditional elements, the enlightened—or better, rationalizing—religiosity of Hellenism, without which he could not have written the history of Christianity.[273]

Today one will speak rather of the adaptation of different theological outlooks from Hellenistic Judaism, relate Luke's view of miracles to "rationalizing religiosity," and use such terms as "speculative" and "apologetic"; but Käsemann is essentially correct. He does not allow differences to obscure similarities. "Eph. 1:12b-14 contains in concentrated form the themes which are painted broadly by Acts in the Cornelius story."[274] Acts is a narrative exposition of the ideas set forth by Ephesians in liturgical/propositional language. For both, the preeminent miracle is that gentiles can become part of the people of God. Precisely for this reason Ephesians and Acts insist that the linkage to historical Israel, to the "Bible story," not be allowed to languish and that unity stand as a primary instrument and goal. False teachers threaten unity by despising the historical heritage. Käsemann, who wrote this essay long before sociological analysis came back into the picture, grasped that Ephesians and Acts have an interest in stabilizing and protecting organized communities. This is probably the most penetrating study of the relation between these two books.

I am less certain than was Käsemann that Acts and Ephesians stand "at the moment" of the transition from an understanding of the Jesus movement as an eschatological phenomenon to a recognition of the church as a factor in history. Transitions of this sort are never complete and hence difficult to pinpoint. Both Luke and Deutero-Paul express this modulation from a perspective that has acquired some maturity, and neither has accepted it completely. Each has experienced and understood enough of the change to have reservations about it. The unity of the human race is, after all, an eschatological goal (Galatians 3:26–28).

THE PASTORAL EPISTLES

Abundant affinities between the writings of Luke and the Pastor have been noted in the course of this book. Indeed, some observers have discovered enough likenesses to have proposed that Luke wrote the Pastorals.[275] Others

Table 7.10: A Sports Metaphor

Luke and Acts[276]	Paul	Pastoral Epistles
Acts 13:25 ὡς δὲ **ἐπλήρου** Ἰωάννης **τὸν δρόμον**, as John was **finishing his work** . . . 20:24 ἀλλ᾽ οὐδενὸς λόγου ποιοῦμαι τὴν ψυχὴν τιμίαν ἐμαυτῷ ὡς **τελειώσω τὸν δρόμον** μου . . . But I do not count my life of any value to myself, if only **I may finish my course** . . .	Philippians 2:16–17 λόγον ζωῆς ἐπέχοντες, εἰς καύχημα ἐμοὶ εἰς ἡμέραν Χριστοῦ, ὅτι οὐκ εἰς κενὸν **ἔδραμον** οὐδὲ εἰς κενὸν ἐκοπίασα. 17 ἀλλὰ εἰ καὶ σπένδομαι ἐπὶ τῇ θυσίᾳ καὶ λειτουργίᾳ τῆς πίστεως ὑμῶν, χαίρω καὶ συγχαίρω πᾶσιν ὑμῖν· 16 It is by your holding fast to the word of life that I can boast on the day of Christ that I did **not run** in vain or labor in vain. 17 But even if I am being poured out as a libation over the sacrifice and the offering of your faith, I am glad and rejoice with all of you— 3:12 Οὐχ ὅτι ἤδη ἔλαβον ἢ ἤδη τετελείωμαι, διώκω δὲ εἰ καὶ καταλάβω, ἐφ᾽ ᾧ καὶ κατελήμφθην ὑπὸ Χριστοῦ [Ἰησοῦ].Not that I have already obtained this or have already reached the goal; but I press on to make it my own, because Christ Jesus has made me his own.	2 Timothy 4:6–7 Ἐγὼ γὰρ ἤδη σπένδομαι, καὶ ὁ καιρὸς τῆς ἀναλύσεώς μου ἐφέστηκεν. 7 τὸν καλὸν ἀγῶνα ἠγώνισμαι, τὸν **δρόμον τετέλεκα**, τὴν πίστιν τετήρηκα· As for me, I am already being poured out as a libation, and the time of my departure has come. 7 I have fought the good fight, **I have finished the race**, I have kept the faith.

are content to take note of similarities.[277] One example may be found in Table 7.10. Although this may strain the credulity of some, (male) writers of the Greco-Roman world made frequent use of metaphors derived from the world of sport.[278] Sports-language suited the goals of the popular educational style ("diatribe"), which sought to convey ideas through the use of relevant imagery from daily life. The existential value of this imagery for Paul and others was that sports language depicts life as a struggle that is not yet complete.[279] The death of Paul is the unifying theme of Phil 2:16–17, Acts 20:24, and 2 Timothy 4:6–7. The particular context is martyrdom, often described as an athletic competition.[280] That metaphor is aptly illustrated in 1 Clement 6:2: "By reason of rivalry women were persecuted in the roles of Danaids and Dircae. Victims of dreadful and blasphemous outrages, they ran with sureness the course of faith to the finish, and despite their physical weakness won a notable prize."[281] Rather than propose an intertextual solution, I think that the value of this parallel is to indicate that both Acts and 2 Timothy view the martyrdom of Paul as an accomplished fact.[282] Acts and the Pastorals, like 1 Clement 5, extol Paul as a hero of the faith.

Both Acts 20:17–35 and 2 Timothy 2 are Testaments of Paul delivered to the presbyters in charge of the church at Ephesus, somewhat irregularly in each case, since the speech in Acts is delivered at Miletus, while the Ephesian elders are to receive their instructions through Timothy. This is an interesting coincidence. Lewis Donelson, who points out many parallels between the two texts, suggests a common source.[283] Were there such a source, it could not be earlier than the end of the first century. The more economical alternative is an intertextual solution. Whatever the merits of Donelson's hypothesis, he does help to underscore a common function related to a similar ecclesiastical structure in the same place in response to kindred issues. This high level of similarity deserves no less attention than does the question of source, and surely one should attend carefully to the similarities before arguing for dependence of the one upon the other. When the author of Acts looks to the post-Pauline world, he is so much like the Pastor that it becomes easy to understand why many have identified the two. Their worlds have a great deal in common. Important differences between the two make common authorship all but impossible; a much more likely explanation is proximity in date and time.

I CLEMENT

In the not too distant past it was possible to assume that *1 Clement* knew and used the book of Acts.[284] This is no longer a settled issue.[285] On the question of the saying "It is better to give than to receive" I argued that if an intertextual solution is to be sought, Acts is more likely to be the recipient than the donor.[286] Psalm 89 presents a more difficult case. No other author until Clement of Alexandria cites the passage featured in Table 7.11, and he follows *1 Clement*.[287]

Table 7.11: Psalm 89

Septuagint	Acts 13:22	1 Clement 18:1
Psalm 88:21 (89:20) εὗρον Δαυιδ τὸν δοῦλόν μου, ἐν ἐλαίῳ ἁγίῳ μου ἔχρισα αὐτόν **I have found David, my servant; with my holy oil I have anointed him.**	καὶ μεταστήσας αὐτὸν ἤγειρεν τὸν Δαυὶδ αὐτοῖς εἰς βασιλέα, ᾧ καὶ εἶπεν μαρτυρήσας, **Εὗρον Δαυὶδ** τὸν τοῦ Ἰεσσαί, ἄνδρα κατὰ τὴν καρδίαν μου, ὃς ποιήσει πάντα τὰ θελήματά μου	Τί δὲ εἴπωμεν ἐπὶ τῷ μεμαρτυρημένῳ Δαυίδ, πρὸς ὅν εἶπεν ὁ θεός **Εὗρον ἄνδρα κατὰ τὴν καρδίαν μου, Δαυὶδ** τὸν τοῦ Ἰεσσαί ἐν ἐλέει αἰωνίῳ ἔχρισα αὐτόν.
Jeremiah 3:15. καὶ δώσω ὑμῖν ποιμένας κατὰ τὴν καρδίαν μου . . . I shall give you shepherds *after my heart*	When *God* had removed *Saul*, he made David their king. In his testimony about him he *said*, 'I **have found David,** *son of Jesse, to be a man after my heart,* who will carry out all my wishes.'	And what shall we say of the famous David? God *said* of him, "**I have found** *a man after my heart,* **David,** *son of Jesse:* I have anointed him with eternal mercy."[288]
1 Sam 13:14. καὶ νῦν ἡ βασιλεία σου οὐ στήσεται, καὶ ζητήσει κύριος ἑαυτῷ ἄνθρωπον **κατὰ τὴν καρδίαν** αὐτοῦ . . . but now your kingdom will not continue; the LORD has sought out a man *after his own heart*		

The present interest does not reside in the citation itself, which the two authors use in different contexts (Luke in a summary of salvation history, *1 Clement* as an example of humility), but in the deviations from the received text of the Psalm. Among the explanations are:

1. *1 Clement* has made use of Acts to give David a proper introduction.
2. Acts has borrowed the introduction of David from *1 Clement*.
3. Both Acts and *1 Clement* depend upon Jewish tradition, a tradition also reflected in the Targum of Jonathan.[289] This opens up the possibility of the existence of a collection of "Testimonies," prophetic proofs supporting the Christian viewpoint.[290]

Both authors use the expression "He/God said," which is used in quotations from an authoritative source.[291] The formula is more common in *1 Clement*, but then so are quotations. In the end, none of the explanations is particularly compelling. It is most unlikely that a description of such scribal complexity was "discovered" on more than one occasion. Neither Acts nor *1 Clement* stems from authors or circles enamored of such complex intertextual endeavors. Reliance upon available tradition (3) probably offers the best resolution to this interesting case.

If neither Luke nor the author of *1 Clement* excels at the skillful combination of biblical passages, both are steeped in the language of the Greek Bible and the cultural tradition of imitation, as has been noted on more than one occasion.[292] Both also relate "Bible History" that uses extra-biblical sources and traditions[293] Nowhere is this more striking than in the passages extolling the providential order of nature in Acts 14:15–17, 17:24–29, and *1 Clement* 20, which adapt Greek concepts to biblical language.[294] The works belong to a similar intellectual and cultural milieu. The Apologists will develop these ideas, but the early fondness for "biblical" language will gradually be restricted to the liturgy.

Both Acts and *1 Clement* narrate a "golden age," a period when all were good and all was consequently well.[295] The golden age narrated in Acts 2:42–46 and 4:32–35 truly resembles an ancient utopia, while that of *1 Clement* 1:3–2:8 more approximates the conservative ideal of those good old days when women knew their place and children were (occasionally) seen but not heard; nevertheless, the content and function of these descriptions is quite similar.[296] Both writers evoke the past by means of summary narration. See the common themes in Table 7:12.

Both of these summaries contain implicit exhortation. They set criteria for community health, one sign of which is a "full effusion of the Holy Spirit upon all" (*1 Clement* 2:2; cf. Acts 2:38; 4:31).[297] Each relates the life of the past to the solution of community problems. *1 Clement* presses the Corinthian believers to end their strife and to restore deposed presbyters. The reason for the removal of these officers is not given. When growth and diversity lead to dissatisfaction in Jerusalem (Acts 6:1–7), the result could have been a "revolt" like that at Corinth. Rather than "throw the bums out," the people listen to their leaders' call for the

Table 7.12: The Golden Age

Theme	Acts	1 Clement
1. Fidelity, Piety	2:42, 43	1:2
2. Charity	2:44-45; 4:32-35	2:1 (cf. 1:2, hospitality
3. Prayer, Worship	2:42, 46	2:3
4. Peace and Harmony	4:32	2:2, 6
5. Growth	2:47	cf. 2:4
6. Absence of Division	4:32	2:6

creation of a new group of specialized ministers. The result is further growth. Acts would have provided, from the viewpoint of *1 Clement*, a useful story about conflict management for the Corinthians to ponder.[298] Perhaps removing those in power is not always the most creative solution. *1 Clement* would correct what it regards as an injustice. Acts 6 likewise addresses an alleged injustice. In both writings the focus is not upon seeing that justice is done. (Acts mentions allegations of injustice and allows readers to presume that the occasion for these allegations was removed. The sole injustice noted by *1 Clement* was that done to the leaders.) The explicit goal of both works is the achievement of unity and peace.

Those nurtured in particular views about inspiration may be surprised at the claim of the Roman community to have "written through the Holy Spirit" (*1 Clement* 63.2).[299] Acts 15:28, "For it has seemed good to the Holy Spirit and to us," is equally nonchalant. Such confidence is typical of the era.[300] Similar to Acts 5:29 is the sentiment of *1 Clement* 14:1, which claims that it is better to obey God than (wicked) mortals.[301] That verse contains the address ἄνδρες ἀδελφοί ("gentlemen and brethren"), modeled upon the opening of Attic orations, "Gentlemen of Athens" (17:22). "Gentlemen and brethren" is found fourteen times in Acts, four altogether in *1 Clement*, and elsewhere only in works dependent upon Acts.[302]

Acts 2:17 is a citation of Joel 3:1. (See Table 7.13.) At the conclusion of the speech (2:38), Peter will promise the gift of the Spirit to all who are baptized. This gift is also a consequence of baptism in Titus. R. Knopf saw the gift of the Spirit in *1 Clement* 2:2 as a reward for good conduct and a prime indicator of the work's "moral rationalism."[303] He does not there note 46:6, which views the gift of the Spirit as the ground for Christian existence, but Acts is not, when all is said and done, less "moralistic," nor is Titus, as the context will indicate.[304] All three of these writings are attempting to preserve the Pauline heritage by bringing it up to date—or to maintain it without realizing that they are changing it, if you will. Similar tensions are present in each of them. If, for various reasons, they show diminished interest in certain aspects of Galatians 3:26–28 (no longer slave or free, male and female), they fully agree that "all . . . are one in Christ Jesus." If the ecstasy of Galatians 4:6 is to be tempered or ignored, all three would heartily assent to Galatians 5:22–23: "the fruit of the Spirit is love, joy,

Table 7.13: Effusion of the Spirit

Acts 2:17	1 Clement 2:2	Titus 3:5–6
Καὶ ἔσται ἐν ταῖς ἐσχάταις ἡμέραις, λέγει ὁ θεός, ἐκχεῶ ἀπὸ τοῦ **πνεύματός** μου ἐπὶ πᾶσαν σάρκα . . . 'In the last days it will be, God declares, that I will pour out my **Spirit** upon all flesh. Cf. Joel 3:1 Καὶ ἔσται μετὰ ταῦτα καὶ **ἐκχεῶ** ἀπὸ τοῦ **πνεύματός** μου ἐπὶ **πᾶσαν σάρκα** . . . After these things it shall come to pass that I shall **pour out** my **spirit upon all flesh** . . .	οὕτως εἰρηνη βαθεῖα καὶ λιπαρὰ ἐδεδοτα πᾶσιν καὶ ἀκορεστος πόθος εἰς ἀγαθοποιίαν, καὶ πλήρης **πνεύματος** ἁγίου **ἔκχυσις** ἐπὶ **πάντας** ἐγίνετο. In consequence, [of humility, etc.] you were all granted a profound and rich peace and an insatiable longing to do good, while the **Holy Spirit was** abundantly **poured out** *on* **you all**.[305] Cf. 46:6	. . . **πνεύματος** ἁγίου, 6 οὗ **ἐξέχεεν** ἐφ' ἡμᾶς πλουσίως διὰ Ἰησοῦ Χριστοῦ τοῦ σωτῆρος ἡμῶν . . . . . . This *Spirit* he *poured out* on us richly through Jesus Christ our Savior, . . .

peace, patience, kindness, generosity, faithfulness, gentleness and self-control." *1 Clement* does not seem to have known Galatians, but the author would have no difficulty maintaining that 5:22–23 is an excellent summary of his purpose. Luke and the Pastor, who evidently *did* know Galatians, would have no hesitations about endorsing the sentiment of this "catalogue of virtues" as scholars call it, or list of "spiritual gifts," as Paul understands it.[306]

Other similarities also noted elsewhere include the exhortation to imitate God the creator and redeemer, as in Luke 6:35–36 and *1 Clement* 14:3; 33:1–8.[307] *1 Clement* 29:3 tells of God making a people from the nations, an idea like that of James in Acts 15:17.[308] The Church is the legitimate successor to Israel and Jacob.[309] *1 Clement* 23:5 uses the title "Holy One" of Christ (evidently), reminiscent of Acts 3:14.[310] Luke, following Josephus, as I have argued, can characterize Christianity as a philosophy or philosophical school, as will Justin and other apologists.[311] His preferred term, "the way," suits this understanding. It also suits the view of the church as a *politeia*, which may be rendered as "political body" or as "way of life." *Politeia* is also *1 Clement's* preferred understanding. As verb or noun, the term is found seven times in *1 Clement*, only once in Acts (verb: 23:1), but the importance of the concept resides less in vocabulary than in the civic values so important to each work: orderly community life marked by an absence of faction and sedition, together with the pursuit of unity and concord. *1 Clement* is no advocate of democracy, for, as noted earlier, it opposes the removal of presbyters at Corinth, whose elevation to that office was most probably held to have been the result of an "election." Luke does not depict the election of presbyters by popular vote. The apostles and elders chose the delegates of 15:22–27. The role of the assembly was to ratify this choice.[312] Both writers believe that decency and good order preclude democracy or "mob rule."[313] (Roman aristocrats could not or did not easily distinguish between these two.) For Luke the political-philosophical elements are a kind of icing on the cake. The heart of his ecclesiological understanding is Pauline: the church as a corporate body.[314] If the relationship between Acts and *1 Clement* is literary— one made use of the other—at least as good a case for Acts as dependent upon *1 Clement* can be made as the alternative, but decisions about intertextuality will not exhaust the similarities between these two books.

THE EPISTLE OF BARNABAS

The first parallel reveals shared language of a developing Christian creed. (See Table 7.14.) No valid grounds exist for attempting an intertextual solution. In this instance one need not speculate about "common traditions" and the like, for the tradition is patent.[315] Acts 7:49 (Speech of Stephen), and *Barnabas* 16:2 quote Isaiah 66:1 almost exactly from the LXX. Acts 7:49 served as proof that the temple was not the house of God and would become a regular feature of Christian apologetic.[316] The author of *Barnabas* did not have to turn to Acts to discover this useful verse.

THE DIDACHE

The citations from the *Didache* and *Barnabas* in Table 7.15 are part of a hypothetical early Jewish catechism called "the two ways." Early Christians subsequently took up this catechism for their own use.[317] All three of these passages reflect an early Christian (communitarian) ethical ideal.[318] The catechism is prescriptive, while Acts is descriptive, an entirely genre-appropriate difference.

POLYCARP OF SMYRNA

Polycarp may supply a *terminus ante quem* for Acts, as an earlier review of *Philippians* 1:2 concluded.[319] In addition to that close parallel, a number of other similarities are of interest, however unconvincing most of them are for establishing Polycarp's knowledge of Acts. The affinities exhibited in Table 7.16, some of which are arguably intertextual and discussed elsewhere, indicate that Polycarp and Luke participated in a Christian world that was developing its own creedal expressions while at the same time incorporating into its own self-understanding the terminology used in the Greek Bible to describe the people of God. In the second century ἔλευσις ("coming") will become a fashionable word for the (first or second) advent of Christ.[320] Terms like "lot," "portion," and "inheritance" have come to describe, without the need for argument, the "people of God," i.e., believers in Christ. Supersession is the established order of things.

Table 7.14: Eschatological Judge

Acts 10:42	Barnabas 7:2	Polycarp *Phil.* 2:1	2 *Clement* 1:1
. . . οὗτός ἐστιν ὁ ὡρισμένος ὑπὸ τοῦ θεοῦ κριτὴς ζώντων καὶ νεκρῶν *Christ* is the one ordained by God as **judge of the living and the dead**	εἰ οὖν ὁ υἱὸς τοῦ θεοῦ, ὢν κύριος καὶ μέλλων κρίνειν ζῶντας καὶ νεκρούς. If the the Son of God, although Lord and going to **judge** the **living and** the *dead* **Hegisippus** (Eusebius *H. E.* 3.20.4) ὁπηνίκα ἐλθὼν ἐν δόξῃ **κρινεῖ ζῶντας** καὶ **νεκρούς** When he shall come in glory and **judge the living and** the **dead** *Barnabas* 16:2 λέγει κύριος Ὁ οὐρανός μοι θρόνος, ἡ δὲ γῆ ὑποπόδιον τῶν ποδῶν μου ποῖον οἶκον οἰκοδομήσετέ μοι, ἢ τίς τόπος τῆς καταπαύσεως μου; Isa 66:1 LXX Οὕτως λέγει κύριος Ὁ οὐρανός μοι θρόνος, ἡ δὲ γῆ ὑποπόδιον τῶν ποδῶν μου ποῖον οἶκον οἰκοδομήσετέ μοι; ἢ ποῖος τόπος τῆς καταπαύσεώς μου;	ὃς ἔρχεται **κρίτης ζώντων** **καὶ νεκρῶν** [Christ] who will come as **judge of the living and** *the* **dead** **2 Timothy 4:1** . . . Χριστοῦ Ἰησοῦ, τοῦ *μέλλοντος* *κρίνειν ζῶντας* *καὶ νεκρούς* Christ Jesus, who is to judge the living and the dead **1 Peter 4:5** . . . τῷ ἑτοίμως ἔχοντι **κρῖναι ζῶντας καὶ νεκρούς** to him who stands ready to judge the living and the dead	δεῖ ἡμᾶς φρονεῖν περὶ Ἰησοῦ Χριστοῦ, ὡς ὡς περὶ θεοῦ, ὡς περὶ κριτοῦ ζώντων καὶ νεκρῶν. We ought to think about Jesus Christ as we do about God, as **judge of the living and the dead**
Acts 7:49 Ὁ οὐρανός μοι θρόνος, ἡ δὲ γῆ ὑποπόδιον τῶν ποδῶν μου· ποῖον οἶκον οἰκοδομήσετέ μοι, λέγει κύριος, ἢ τίς τόπος τῆς καταπαύσεώς μου; Heaven is my throne, and the earth is my footstool. What kind of house will you build for me, says the Lord, or what is the place of my rest?			

After noting the parallels with Polycarp, Haenchen concludes that "... Polycarp, despite the numerous echoes, did not use Acts as a source, but ... both he and the author of Acts were working with a stock of contemporary formulae held largely in common."[321] With the possible exception of *Philippians* 1:2, I find this judgment quite sound. *1 Clement* and Polycarp establish a close approximation of the desired "bracket."[322] Acts appears to be later

Table 7.15: All in Common

Acts 4:32	Didache 4:8	Barnabas 19:8
. . . οὐδὲ εἷς τι τῶν ὑπαρχόντων αὐτῷ ἔλεγεν ἴδιον εἶναι, ἀλλ' ἦν αὐτοῖς πάντα κοινά no one **claimed** private ownership of any possessions, but **everything** they owned was held in **common**.	κοινωνήσεις δὲ πάντα τῷ ἀδελφῷ σου καὶ οὐκ ἐρεῖς ἴδια εἶναι *You* **shall share all things with your** sister or brother and **you shall not say that anything is a private possession.**	κοινωνήσεις ἐν πᾶσιν τῷ Πλησίον σοῦ καὶ οὐκ ἐρεῖς ἴδια εἶναι **You shall share all things with your** neighbor *and* **you shall not say that anything is a private possession.**

than *1 Clement*, with which it may be familiar, since Acts appears to know a "fuller" collection of Pauline letters, whereas *1 Clement* knows but two.[323] Acts also has a number of terms, concepts, and themes in common with the Pastorals and with Polycarp, where dependence is possible, if insecure.

The overlap between Polycarp and the Pastorals was sufficiently substantial to lead Campenhausen to propose that the former composed the latter.[324] Few have been convinced by this hypothesis, but he has unequivocally established a close proximity between them.[325] Others have suggested or contended that Luke wrote the Pastorals.[326] Their arguments are not without weaknesses, but the willingness of reputable and eminent scholars to make such cases indicates the presence of important points of similarity and contact among these three authors.[327] Polycarp, who is familiar with the teaching of Marcion, is not to be dated earlier than 130; 135 is a standard calculation. If *1 Clement* is placed at c. 90–100, where most, with good reason, locate it, the range for Acts may be set at c. 100–c. 130.[328] Within that period 110–120 is more likely than 100–110. Against placement in the first decade are the many features shared with the Pastorals and Polycarp. The third (120–130) is somewhat less likely, especially for the Gospel of Luke, which was utilized by Marcion and may have been "the Gospel" of the church at Sinope, in which Marcion was reared.[329]

Chapters One and Two set out the issues and methods, then established c. 130 as a reasonable, but not certain, earliest possible *terminus ad quem*. Through examination of sources in chapters three through five a *terminus a quo* of c. 100 emerged. This and the previous chapter have looked to internal evidence to support and specify this range of c. 100–c. 130. The evidence is confirmatory and the results are stated above, with a preference for 110–120 as the best fit for the data. The final chapter will take up other sorts of data to test the hypothesis that has emerged from the identification of datable sources and the pursuit of a suitable milieu. I shall then examine in detail two of the more substantial proposals of recent decades about the date of Acts before proceeding to the most important aspect of this endeavor: reflection upon the implications of the proposed date for the book of Acts.

Table 7.16: The Coming Inheritance

Acts 7:52	Polycarp *Phil.* 6:3	*1 Clement* 17:1
τίνα τῶν προφητῶν οὐκ ἐδίωξαν οἱ πατέρες ὑμῶν; καὶ ἀπέκτειναν τοὺς προκαταγγείλαντας περὶ τῆς ἐλεύσεως τοῦ δικαίου . . . Which of the prophets did your ancestors not persecute? They killed those who **foretold the coming of the** Righteous One, and now you have become his betrayers and murderers. 8:21 οὐκ ἔστιν σοι μερὶς οὐδὲ κλῆρος ἐν τῷ λόγῳ τούτῳ, 20:32 καὶ τὰ νῦν παρατίθεμαι ὑμᾶς τῷ θεῷ . . . καὶ δοῦναι τὴν *κληρονομίαν ἐν τοῖς ἡγιασμένοις πᾶσιν*. And now I commend you to God and to the message of his grace, a message that is able to build you up and to give you the **inheritance among all who are sanctified**. 26:18[330] ἀνοῖξαι ὀφθαλμοὺς αὐτῶν . . . καὶ κλῆρον ἐν τοῖς ἡγιασμένοις πίστει τῇ εἰς ἐμέ. to open their eyes so that they may turn from darkness to light and from the power of Satan to God, so that they may receive forgiveness of sins and a **place among those who are sanctified** by faith in me.'	εὐαγγελισάμενοι ἡμᾶς ἀπόστολοι καὶ οἱ προφῆται, οἱ προκηρύξαντες τὴν ἔλευσιν τοῦ κυρίου ἡμῶν The apostles who proclaimed the gospel to us and the prophets who **foretold** the **coming of** our Lord. 12: 2 . . . det vobis *sortem et partem inter sanctos suos* May *God* give you a **part and share** among his saints. cf. Col 1:12 εὐχαριστοῦντες τῷ πατρὶ τῷ ἱκανώσαντι ὑμᾶς εἰς τὴν *μερίδα τοῦ κλήρου τῶν ἁγίων ἐν* τῷ φωτί giving thanks to the Father, who has enabled you to share in the inheritance of the saints in the light cf. Deut 33:3–4 . . . καὶ πάντες οἱ ἡγιασμένοι ὑπὸ τὰς χεῖράς σου· καὶ οὗτοι ὑπὸ σέ εἰσιν, καὶ ἐδέξατο ἀπὸ τῶν λόγων αὐτοῦ 4 νόμον, ὃν ἐνετείλατο ἡμῖν Μωϋσῆς, *κληρονομίαν συναγωγαῖς Ιακωβ* **all his holy ones** were in your charge; they accepted direction from you. Moses charged us with the law, as a **possession** for the assembly of Jacob	μιμηταὶ γενώμεθα κἀκείνων, οἵτινες ἐν δέρμασιν αἰγείοις καί μηλοταῖς περιεπάτησαν *κηρύσσοντεσ τὴν ἔλευσιν* του Χριστοῦ Let us also be imitators of those who went about in the skins of goats and sheep, heralding the **coming** of Christ.

Acts as a Writing
of the First Decades
of the Second Century

This penultimate chapter will address various matters relevant to the date of Acts that have not been engaged in the studies of sources and subjects, and will then take up specific arguments about that date. The first task involves what are traditionally referred to as "anachronisms."

POSSIBLE "ANACHRONISMS" AND SIMILAR MATTERS

In the strict sense anachronisms are references to material later than the dramatic date of a work. For Acts this means concepts or institutions that did not appear until after the apparent time of the narrative "events." A scholarly axiom holds that anachronisms increase exponentially with the distance from the dramatic date. I am not aware of any proof of this axiom, reasonable as it certainly appears to be. The axiom itself may be somewhat anachronistic in that it presumes that later writers who wish to be understood as writing at an earlier time avoid anachronism to the best of their ability.[1] Modern scholars are profoundly grateful to the many who do not appear to have made much of an effort in that direction.[2] Furthermore, the term is not quite applicable to Acts, for it does not claim to be contemporaneous with the events narrated. More precisely stated, then, the current subject is the identification of material in Acts that presumes a date later than c. 75–85.

Jewish and Christian texts from the ancient world contain *intentional* or *dogmatic* anachronisms, such as having the Deity rest on the Sabbath after six days devoted to creative labor or placing on the lips of the "historical Jesus" instructions for church discipline[3] These are easily detected and readily intelligible, but many matters of history, such as the specific date of boundary changes or the introduction of a certain office, are highly uncertain. At any time an inscription may come to light that will remove one possible anachronism or expose another. To gain an idea of how complex and uncertain these issues can be, it is profitable to consider the task from the opposite direction: demonstrating that Acts is early on the grounds of names, institutions, and other details. On this project Colin Hemer labored with diligence and skill, but many of his claims are open to challenge or question. Some are much too refined; others are quite circular. His and kindred work often demands more precision of Luke than the text will bear. Nicety of detail and a level of specificity now expected of footnotes were not characteristics of ancient historians, who do not appear to have read the inscriptions now so valued, let alone to have engaged in quantitative studies.[4]

Most of the obvious anachronisms and similar anomalies of Acts do not bear upon the argument of this book, since they may fit a date in the 80s just as well as a date in the 120s. The most egregious historical anachronism in Acts is the reference in 5:36 to the rebellion of Theudas, which took place more than a decade after the dramatic date.[5] This is an error that could probably have been perpetrated in the 60s. The least disputable and most cogent anachronisms in Acts have already been discussed. These relate to community organization: presbyters who can also be called "bishops," individuals who have some of the functions of later deacons, and widows with at least enough organization to make their voice heard.[6] All of these belong to the world of the early second century.

Cultural distance creates some howlers. In 1:19 Peter addresses the faithful shortly after the ascension, saying, "This [the death of Judas and its aftermath] became known to all the residents of Jerusalem, so that the field was called in their language Hakeldama, that is, Field of Blood." His words overlook the fact that his hearers are among those very "residents of Jerusalem" and that the (Aramaic) word he so helpfully glosses for them comes from the very tongue in which the address would have been made.[7] Greater importance attaches to the use of οἱ ἐκ περιτομῆς ("those of the circumcision") in Acts 10:45 and 11:2 in reporting events of a time when (according to Acts) all male believers with Peter or in Jerusalem were circumcised, or the occasions on which Peter, Stephen, or Paul speak of "your forebears" as if they were not themselves Jews (e.g. Acts 3:25; 7:52; 28:25.)[8] Statements like these imply not only a non-Jewish narrator, but a movement that views itself as separate. This understanding of "Christianity" as a distinct "religion" and of Jews as "the other" is appropriate to the period beginning at about the turn of the first century.[9] A great many scholars sense the weight of this distance and regard it as strong evidence against an early date.[10] Raymond E. Brown is typical of those who sense the distance but wish to keep it within limits:

> "Indeed, the relation espoused by the Paul of Acts 28:25–28 between the mission to the Gentiles and the failure of the mission to the Jews is so different from what Paul himself wrote in Rom 9–11 *ca.* 57/58 that it is hard to imagine a date in the early 60s for Acts."[11]

Although Brown regards 100 as too late, he does not take up the discussion of when the distinct separation mirrored in Acts becomes apparent. Those who do seek to pinpoint this shift take into account both the viewpoints reflected in various texts and the transformation within the religion of Israel that will lead to rabbinic Judaism. The crucial period in this development was not the 20s and 30s, when John the Baptizer and Jesus appeared, but the time of Jewish Revolts, from 66–135 CE. One outcome of these struggles was the rise of deep and widespread antipathy to Jews, who became *the* internal enemy to Romans and thus fair game for every slander and all calumny.[12] For Vespasian and his sons, who used their suppression of the first Revolt (66–73/4) to aid in the foundation of a new dynasty, it was expedient to magnify the scope and danger of the revolt, not least by the construction of Judaism as a dangerous threat from which the new ruling family had delivered the Roman people. Judea was a "rogue nation," one of the smaller countries that comprised the first century axis of evil.[13] Luke can trade off the general popular animosity toward "Jews" by making them the villains of his story, while simultaneously stripping them of such religious assets as seemed desirable.[14] Revolts under Trajan (115–117), and the second great Revolt (132–135) solidified matters. The second Revolt evoked harsh and enduring anti-Jewish sentiments.[15] By the last decade of the first century interest in being identified with Jews declined. From the Jewish perspective it was necessary to erect a new foundation and basis.[16] Without the temple and the homeland as bonds and symbols of unity, the pluralism evident in a variety of sects became a deficit. Jews perceived a need to define themselves more closely. As the followers of Jesus became less welcome among Jews, Judaism lost appeal as an umbrella for those believers who identified themselves as Jews in some sense. By the period from c. 115 onward, the approach of Christians to their "Jewish roots" tended to shift focus. Some, including Marcion and various Gnostics, capitalized upon widespread anti-Jewish sentiment that was further exacerbated by the grim events of the Second Revolt. All of these developments took time. The Rabbis did not establish full control for centuries, and some Christian groups remained rather closer to their Jewish heritage than did the majority, while the Christian desire to refute Jewish claims and to appropriate Jewish learning did not disappear with the dawn of the year 100.[17] Acts emerged between these two major revolts. Its approach to the ancestral religion is manifest in Justin, whose *Dialogue* with the Jew Trypho does not include a great deal of genuine conversation. From the crises sparked by the Revolt of 66–73/74 arose two "religions": Judaism as it would become and Christianity in the making. Luke and Acts stem from this time of separation, and not from its preliminary phases.[18]

Acts 10:1 is probably typical of the problems involved in the identification of anachronisms: "In Caesarea there was a man named Cornelius, a centurion of the Italian Cohort, as it was called." The difficulty often alleged is that these Roman troops would not have been in Caesarea during 41–44, when Judea was technically independent and Agrippa had his own troops (Josephus, *Antiquities* 19.365).[19] A more important question is whether such troops would have been garrisoned in Caesarea *prior to* 41, but the entire argument may be a phantom, for Luke does not date the conversion of Cornelius. Therefore, certain knowledge would not shed much light on the date of Acts even if the anachronism could be unequivocally substantiated.[20]

The possibility of a definite and relevant anachronism emerges in Acts 19:35, where the "town clerk" characterizes Ephesus as the universally recognized "temple keeper of the great Artemis" (νεωκόρον οὖσαν τῆς μεγάλης Ἀρτέμιδος). The term *"Neokoros* of Artemis" is probably a dramatic anachronism, since the time in question was c. 55 CE, while the earliest arguable (but not certain) attestation of this term is 65–66, and it was not at all common until the final decade of the first century. Greek cities vied desperately to secure symbolic honors. A *"Neokoros"* was in origin a kind of sexton.[21] In Roman times the label became by metonymy an honorific designation for a city entrusted with a temple of the imperial cult. Discussion about the date of the neokorate show that, although not grossly anachronistic, it savors of a later period and accommodates to a later date for Acts more readily than to an earlier.[22] Little more can be said.

Acts 25:26, in which the perplexed procurator struggles to provide a rationale for sending Paul to Rome, presents a similar case: "But I have nothing definite to write to our sovereign about him." (περὶ οὗ ἀσφαλές τι γράψαι τῷ κυρίῳ οὐκ ἔχω). This is the earliest example of the *absolute* use of *kyrios* ("lord," "sovereign") for the Roman emperor thus far attested. "Lord" as a modifier for the Emperor ("The Lord Titus") appears from the time of Nero onward, but does not proliferate until the end of the century. Absolute "My Lord" does not appear until the second century.[23] This distinction is sometimes neglected—or avoided.[24] Popular usage may well have been looser, but the available evidence points to the next century.[25]

Several passages in Acts may be taken as grounds for assuming that proselytism for converts to Judaism is illegal because Roman law forbids such conversions. One is 16: 21: *The accusers of Paul and Silas* say, "They are advocating customs that are not lawful for us as Romans to adopt or observe." Then in 17:7 *the accusers of Paul and Silas* say, ". . . and Jason has entertained them as guests. They are all acting contrary to the decrees of the emperor, saying that there is another king named Jesus." Last, according to 18:13 *Paul's Jewish accusers said to Gallio,* "This man is persuading people to worship God in ways that are contrary to the law." 16:21 is certainly the strongest of these possible references, but all can be otherwise interpreted.[26] Despite the variety, the recurrence of these vague allegations lends some weight to a possible general understanding of conversion as illegal, and readers in the first half of the second century would have been likely to understand them thus. So far so good, but an even greater difficulty remains: the establishment and dating of legislation or decrees making conversion illegal. Rome was *never* especially tolerant of activities that involved conversion of her citizens to Judaism, and one could contend that believing conversion to be illegal is congenial to any possible date for Acts.[27] Nonetheless, it was not until the last years of Domitian's reign (81–96) that ". . . the 'atheism' involved in conversion to Judaism became a criminal offense."[28] The apparent attitude to Jewish conversions in Acts is thus quite consonant with a date of c. 100, but it will not establish a *terminus a quo.*

In conclusion: The "minor anachronisms" of Acts have produced no conclusive proof that the book was written later than c. 85. They provide no comfort to those who would date the book prior to 80, to be sure, but for those who favor a later date they offer only collateral evidence. The more important anachronisms deal with ecclesiastical matters and are rather weightier, for they envision an organizational structure that did not exist before 100. Acts *is* anachronistic, but its anachronism should be evaluated from its perspective, which is essentially timeless, and from its chronology, which is non-existent. In so far as the perspec-   *Woof* tive is that of a timeless past, Acts is closer in method to the gospels than to the historians. Since internal chronology is quite deficient, a reader who could not look up the dates of Pilate and Festus, i.e., nearly every early reader, would be forgiven for believing that the entire narrative embraced a frame closer to one decade than to three.[29] The chronological data of Acts are incidental. All who seek to provide the narrative with a chronological framework must correlate those incidental data with information from external sources.[30] This approach has its full quota of pitfalls.[31]

Luke's failure to deal with chronology raises a question about genre, for historians were expected to attend to this crucial matter. The closest Luke gets to the traditional approach is the synchronism of Luke 3:1–2, a procedure lamentably lacking in Acts.[32] To remove all hints of malice or opportunities for bias, the notorious skeptic Richard Pervo will step aside to let the redoubtable Lukan apologist Sir William Ramsay speak:

> Luke was deficient in the sense for time; and hence his chronology is bad. It would be quite impossible from *Acts* alone to get a true idea of the lapse of time. That is the fault of his age; Tacitus, writing the biography of Agricola (about 98 A.D.), makes no chronological statement, until in the last paragraph he gives a series of statistics.[33]

One might ask the late Sir William if he would date Acts c. 100. He would not.[34] Moreover, five pages later he suggests that "the failure of chronological data" may be due to the author's death before final revision. He notes that the Gospel of Luke has some good chronology, but Acts does not, "except for the vague 'under Claudius' of XI 28, in itself a striking contrast to 'the fifteenth year of Tiberius,' *Luke* III 1."[35]

That "vague" indicator would not be terribly useful in a text written within a decade of his reign. (Claudius ruled from 41–54.) Indeed, a TLG search revealed that the only occurrence of the phrase in first-century literature is that in Acts. Justin Martyr (c. 160) uses it to locate Simon Magus.[36] Other examples include the historian Cassius Dio in the third century and Dictys Cretensis in the fourth.[37] Perhaps the reference most relevant to Acts is *Acta Alexandrinorum* 8.70 (ἐπὶ τοῦ θεοῦ Κλαυδίου, "under Claudius the god"), the dramatic date of which is prior to 115.[38] One may observe that this phrase is not a solid foundation block, but it does constitute more than an exiguous pebble. C. K. Barrett states: "His reference to Claudius betrays the hand of one who was writing towards the close of the century and could look back to the 'time of Claudius' (fourteen years in fact) as a relatively small period."[39] As the references to Justin and others indicate, one should append "or later" to "the close of the century." Acts seems to modern readers to compress time because of its distance from events. Such impressions are suspect, as they may themselves be anachronistic, but the expression "under Claudius" lends them support.

A similar observation applies to the references to Pilate, Acts 3:13; 4:27, who was, according to the dramatic date of Acts, still in office at that time, but seems, as in 1 Timothy 6:13, to be a figure of the past. Other inferences about the date of composition—imprecise but helpful—come from an examination of the narrator's perspective. The prefaces to Luke and Acts are helpful here.

The anonymous author we call Luke produced two volumes, linked by means of prefaces. This very act is revelatory, for the composition of prefaces exhibits interest in *paideia*, in presenting the Christian movement as not inimical to a society whose conventions the writer both knows and appreciates,[40] while the tradition of anonymity belongs to the sphere of the Gospels and of "Biblical History" in the primary sense (e.g., Genesis-Esther). Anonymity implies timeless and omniscient authority;[41] prefaces suggest a more limited horizon.[42] The form of the preface gives no more than a general clue to the date.[43] The content is more revelatory.

The narrator of Luke's preface appears to stand in the third level or generation. "Since many have undertaken to set down an orderly account of the events that have been fulfilled among us, just as they were handed on to us by those who from the beginning were eyewitnesses and servants of the word, I too decided . . ." (Luke 1:1–3a). In the first group are the eyewitnesses (a qualification for apostles: Acts 1:21–22) and "ministers," a title bestowed upon Paul (Acts 26:16). The first generation thus lasts until c. 60 (in our calculations). Representing the second are those ("many") who prepared earlier accounts. Now it's my turn ("I too).[44] One may see a similar perspective, with different emphases, in 1 *Clement* 42.1–4 and 44:4, passages previously examined.

> The apostles received the gospel for us from the Lord Jesus Christ; Jesus, the Christ, was sent from God. Thus Christ is from God and the apostles from Christ. In both instances the orderly procedure depends on God's will. And so the apostles, after receiving their orders and being fully convinced by the resurrection of our Lord Jesus Christ and assured by God's word, went out in the confidence of the Holy Spirit to preach the good news that God's Kingdom was about to come. They preached in country and city, and appointed their first converts, after testing them by the Spirit, to be the bishops and deacons of future believers . . . Furthermore, they later added a codicil to the effect that, should these die, other approved men should succeed to their ministry.[45]

The first generation is that of the apostles (among whom the author places Paul). Care for the next generation comes from those whom they appointed to serve future believers (as in Acts 20:17–38, especially 28–29). The perspective is quite like that of (Luke and) Acts.[46] After them come appointees of the appointees, as it were.[47] To these last belong, as the context makes clear, the Corinthian presbyters who have been deposed and whose reinstatement *1 Clement* urges. The placement of Luke within the third generation is not a recent discovery. After citing W. Michaelis (1896–1965) for this view, Hans Conzelmann proceeds to say:

> The idea of the third generation was not invented by Luke. It was widespread in many variations. It is presupposed in the Pastoral letters and developed in I Clem. 42. It is so powerful that it dominates whole generations which historically can no longer be counted among the third generation; that is, it is maintained by Polycarp, Papias Quadratus, Irenaeus; and later Eusebius made it the principle for his understanding of church history as a whole.[48]

The third generation is always crucial. A leading psychological factor may be the sense of a living link to the past through one's "grandparents"—i.e., those who told how "in their day" the winters were much fiercer and they had to walk three miles to school through towering drifts of snow, or how, as toddlers, they were taken to view the coffin of Abraham Lincoln on its progress to Springfield, Illinois. Irenaeus says, "The blessed apostles . . . committed into the hands of Linus the office of the episcopate [at Rome]. This man, as he had seen the blessed apostles, and had been conversant with them, might be said to have the preaching of the apostles still echoing [in his ears], and their traditions before his eyes." He identifies this Linus with the sender of greetings in 2 Timothy 4:21. Anacletus followed him, succeeded by Clement. In Clement's time dissension erupted at Corinth.[49] Polycarp, another who had been instructed by the Apostles and appointed by them as Bishop of Smyrna, was a pupil of the long lived "disciple of the Lord," John. In his "early youth" Irenaeus had seen Polycarp. By this stretch the Bishop of Lyons around 180 could claim to stand in a "third generation" from Jesus, a century and a half earlier. It is worth noting that to cover the same period he can list thirteen successive bishops of Rome.[50]

Quadratus wrote, according to Eusebius, a defense of the faith under Hadrian (117–138). His claim to third-generation fame rests upon Eusebius's single extract, in which Quadratus states that he has seen some of those healed or raised by Jesus.[51] Rather more important is that "principle" of Eusebius noted by Conzelmann. Allegedly depending upon Hegesippus, the ancient historian says:

> Until then [106–107] the church remained a pure and uncorrupted virgin, for those who attempted to corrupt the healthful rule of the Saviour's preaching, if they existed at all, lurked in obscure darkness. But when the sacred band of the Apostles *and the generation of those to whom it had been vouchsafed to hear with their own ears the divine wisdom* had reached the several ends of their lives, then the federation of godless error took its beginning through the deceit of false teachers who, seeing that none of the Apostles still remained, barefacedly tried against the preaching of the truth the counter-proclamation of "knowledge falsely so-called."[52]

From the next book of the *Ecclesiastical History* (4.22.4) it is evident that the views expressed above are those of Eusebius, who has generalized a statement that Hegesippus had made about James. The passage is saturated with ideas that emerge in Deutero-Pauline spheres. The image of the church as a pure bride owes a great deal to Ephesians 5:27 (cf. 2 Corinthians 11:2). "Healthful" is a favorite image of the Pastor (see e.g. Titus 2:8).[53] "Those who had heard with their own ears" is reminiscent of the passage from Irenaeus about Clement cited above,[54] while the closing words of the translation quote 1 Timothy 6:20. The chief point, however, is that Eusebius has generalized a dogma given expression in Acts 20:29–30: "I know that after I have gone, savage wolves will come in among you, not sparing the flock. Some even from your own group will come distorting the truth in order to entice the disciples to follow them." The subsequent task was, as Irenaeus and Eusebius reveal, to draw out that "apostolic period" to the greatest extent possible. For openers, they included within it the immediate followers of the apostles and *their* followers. Eusebius' model, which has had a wide impact upon church history, takes its frame from two Lukan concepts: the absence of heresy so long as apostles and their associates lived, and the crucial role of the third generation.[55]

The Pastor presents the Apostle Paul engaged in the responsibility of instructing his followers, Timothy and Titus, on the pastoral care of *their* followers. His explicit framework appears as implicit narrative in 2 Timothy 1:5: "I am reminded of your sincere faith, a faith that lived first in your grandmother Lois and your mother Eunice and now, I am sure, lives in you." The Pastor does not say that three generations were converted at once, but rather that Timothy stands in the third generation of believers. For Jews such a sequence would have been almost too normal (one might say "natural") to merit attention. The least interesting thing about this statement is that it is impossible. Of greater interest is that the "genealogy of faith" descends through women. This might be a reflection of prominence of women among converts.[56] The chief interest, however, is that three generations of faith is a positive thing, exhibiting stability and establishing continuity. The Pastor does not find in "the delay of the Parousia" grounds for even a faint whiff of embarrassment. The longer the "delay," the longer the genealogy of the faithful will become. What Käsemann mourned as the transition from understanding the church as a purely eschatological phenomenon to viewing it as a force in history is for the Pastor a cause of satisfaction.[57] This movement is not like the "the grass of the field, which is alive today and tomorrow is thrown into the oven" (Matthew 6:30).

There lies the fundamental "fact" of the third-generation perspective of Luke, *1 Clement*, and the Pastorals. To stand in the third generation is regrettable in so far as there are no apostles to blast heretics and banish dissent, but it is admirable in that it shows the result of patient endurance and loyalty. Christianity is no flash-in-the-pan aberration or will o' the wisp on the religious horizon. It is here to stay. The "we" narrator of Acts—who is otherwise not readily distinguishable

Here's why it's important [handwritten marginal note]

from the third-person narrator—may have been a "companion" of Paul, but the narrator of the preface to Luke could not have been such a companion—good, fickle, constant, or mediocre—because that narrator looks back upon Paul. One should further note that the dogma of the early church as untroubled by heretics—a view that comes not from Acts 20:29–30 alone, but is also demonstrated by the narrative—will find gratifying new opportunities for growth when the living memory of the controversies of the apostolic age are no longer present as a restraining force.[58]

BARE RUINED CHOIRS

According to Luke Paul left Ephesus after a near riot had threatened to bring grievous consequences. Luke uses this incident to portray the *success* of the mission rather than to recount a setback that many infer to have included imprisonment for Paul.[59] A certain Demetrius set this ball in motion by galvanizing the Ephesian Local of the International Brotherhood of Silver Craftsmen, as it were.[60] This creature Paul's denunciations of idolatry present the ". . . danger not only that this trade of ours may come into disrepute but also that the temple of the great goddess Artemis will be scorned, and she will be deprived of her majesty that brought all Asia and the world to worship her." (Acts 19:27).

Pliny ("the younger") concludes his report to the Emperor Trajan about his activities to suppress Christianity in Bithynia, c. 112, with some comments on the effect of his firm but humane policy:

> . . . [T]here is no doubt that people have begun to throng the temples which had been almost entirely deserted for a long time; the sacred rites which had been allowed to lapse are being performed again, and flesh of sacrificial victims is on sale everywhere, though up till recently scarcely anyone could be found to buy it.[61]

In his laudatory address to the same emperor that very Pliny does not hesitate to suggest that Trajan has relieved Jupiter of some of the stresses involved in day-to-day management of the universe (*Panegyricus* 80.5). That may be a touch of hyperbole (and diligent readers of this lengthy and loyal oration will detect others). Plucked from that same rhetorical tree are, I fear, both the statement of Demetrius and the claims of our Pliny about the socio-religious ravages consequent upon the growth of Christianity. Difficult as this may for some to countenance, it is possible that Pliny wanted his work to appear in a good light, that he wished it understood that he had not been devoting his time to the prosecution of a movement so small that it could meet in a telephone booth, and that he was also willing, if pressed, to admit that his policy has had some salutary effects. Pliny will, then, reluctantly allow that his steps had led to both a revival of the old-time religion and to increased vitality in the local economy. Governors have done worse.

Ben Witherington III agrees that Demetrius is prone to exaggeration. He comments:

> It is true enough that in the second century Pliny the Younger reports that sacrifices were down, as was the buying of sacrificial meat in the nearby area of Pontus and Bithynia, because of the increasing success of Christian evangelism (see *Ep.* 10.96), but that has no relevance here. Demetrius is not being portrayed as a credible speaker.[62]

The last sentence would not have pleased Luke, for he was using the mouth of an opponent to show the degree of Paul's success. Witherington is making use of an *argumentum ad hominem* (appeal to the character of a person as a means of discrediting evidence): Demetrius is a cad, a cynical labor-leader; Pliny is a gentleman whose word is trustworthy.[63] Only a minimum of critical acuity is needed to see that both characters are self-serving. The matter of "relevance" here touches upon the date by which such claims would no longer appear as unlikely as Elvis Presley sightings. The Younger Pliny provides one benchmark: the second decade of the second century.

According to the calculations of Rodney Stark, followed by Keith Hopkins, in 55 CE the followers of Jesus numbered about 1600.[64] By 110, Stark's method proposes, they would have increased to about 10,000.[65] If one supposes that in 55 one quarter of these believers lived in Ephesus—a figure that is certainly much too generous—and that the city then had a population of c. 100,000, which is possibly a bit low, the economic impact of less than one-half of one percent of the population would have been negligible.[66] By 110 the Christian population would have been large enough to notice,[67] and noticed it was.[68] It may be that awareness brought fears of what might happen were this group to proliferate: temples would crumble, public celebrations would languish, and the meat-market, among others, would feel the pinch. In any case, I believe that the undesigned coincidence between the views of Demetrius and Pliny can be introduced into discussions about the date of Acts. The "scenario" they imply certainly indicates a date later than the sixth decade of the first century. The date for Acts is not certain, but Pliny's letter can be assigned a specific date: 110.

For those who are allergic to the quantitative, there follows an attempt to summarize and project the foregoing in qualitative form. Inspired by Plato, I herewith unveil a literary dialogue enhanced by the device of time travel, a conversation between subsequent generations of two Ephesian "men on the street." (Respectable women were not to be found on the street.). Diogenes and Blastus are their names.

Scenario 1: c. 55
    D. These Jesus-people are really weird, man.
    B. Never heard of 'em.

Scenario 2: c. 110 (Their families have gained status.)
    D. I fear that if something is not done about the odious Christians, civi-

lization as we know it will be in danger. Should these abominations be
allowed to propagate unchecked, the market might be depressed.

B. You may have a point there.

Scenario 3: c. 220 (Their families are in slow decline.)

D. The Nile's down; the barbarians are up in arms. The Christians to the
lion, I say.

B. That's your solution for everything. Still, I don't see what harm it could
do.

Scenario 4: c. 440 (Their families are frozen in their occupations as cloth-merchants.)

D. Under the gracious patronage of Our Lady and with the puissant
assistance of St. John the Evangelist, these vile Nestorians will soon be
eradicated.

B. May God grant your reverent wish![69]

APOSTOLIC HEROES

The dogma that a passage of time is required to "idealize" figures of the past
is an important half-truth that one must often resist. The good Parson Weems
(1759–1825) wrote a famous fictionalized biography of George Washington that
first appeared within a year of the death of his subject.[70] Cicero sought in vain
for a contemporary Parson Weems to prepare a laudatory monograph about
his suppression of the Catalinarian conspiracy.[71] Encomiastic rhetoric has long
made substantial contributions to political debate, matched trope for trope by
the rhetoric of defamation. The elucidation of firm criteria for the identification
of later idealization may be impossible; in any case there will be no attempt to
find such criteria here.[72] Once again, the initial technique will be correlation.

The descriptions of Peter and Paul in *1 Clement* 5:4–7, so often cited in this
study, have evoked more comparisons with Acts than any other passage in that
letter.[73]

> Let us set before our eyes the noble apostles: Peter, who by reason of wicked
> jealousy, not only once or twice but frequently endured suffering and thus, bear-
> ing his witness, went to the glorious place which he merited. By reason of rivalry
> and contention Paul showed how to win the prize for patient endurance. Seven
> times he was in chains; he was exiled, stoned, became a herald in East and West,
> and won the noble renown which his faith merited. To the whole world he taught
> righteousness, and reaching the limits of the West he bore his witness before rul-
> ers. And so, released from this world, he was taken up into the holy place and
> became the greatest example of patient endurance.[74]

This is a carefully crafted and well-polished piece of prose, with obvious
parallelism and many rhetorical features.[75] The structural elements delineate
the cause of suffering, a description of it, the subject's conduct, and his ultimate

reward. All of these features are characteristic of a martyrdom-story.[76] The particular features here are also indebted to the Cynic hero and related ancient Greco-Roman ideal types that had been adapted by Hellenistic Judaism (especially 4 Maccabees).[77] They are apparent in the accounts of Jesus' Passion and in the story of Stephen's martyrdom. A closer parallel, however, in scope and wording, is the account of the fate of Judas in Acts 1:16–25.

1. Cause: Greed (v. 18).
2. Suffering: Burst open (v. 18).
3. Conduct: Guide to those who arrested Jesus (v. 16); purchase of property from ill-gotten gains (v. 18).
4. Reward: Went to his own place (πορευθῆναι εἰς τὸν τόπον τὸν ἴδιον).[78] The enrichment of Judas's story through the citation and exposition of biblical prophecies does not make it less of a "passion narrative."

Only in the case of Paul does 1 Clement provide any "biographical" information. Verses 6 and 7 are parallel. The common element is the universal range of Paul's missionary labors. The first summarizes his sufferings: imprisonment, exile, stoning. The second summarizes his message: righteousness.[79] The theme of the benefactor who "conquers" the world by bringing civilization and teaching virtue was popular in the Hellenistic era and, through the model of Alexander the Great, remained potent in the first two and one-half centuries of the Roman Empire.[80]

The next example derives from scholarly hypotheses about the canonical 2 Corinthians, which nearly every critical expositor treats as a composite.[81] The position taken here is that 2 Corinthians is a carefully constructed work based upon a number of pieces of correspondence.[82] A starting point is the observation that a report commencing in 2 Corinthians 2:13, "but my mind could not rest (οὐκ ἔσχηκα ἄνεσιν τῷ πνεύματί μου) because I did not find my brother Titus there. So I said farewell to them and went on to Macedonia (ἐξῆλθον εἰς Μακεδονίαν)" continues in 7:5: "For even when we came into Macedonia (ἐλθόντων ἡμῶν εἰς Μακεδονίαν), our bodies had no rest (οὐδεμίαν ἔσχηκεν ἄνεσιν ἡ σάρξ ἡμῶν), but we were afflicted in every way—disputes without and fears within." The editor has followed a conventional practice of "resumptive repetition," repeating the closing words of a source when it is taken up after the insertion or interpolation of other material. *and lots of it in this case*

2 Corinthians 2:14–7:4 is thus an insertion into another text. That text, labeled, "the letter of reconciliation," (1:1–2:13; 7:5–16; perhaps 13:11–13) was written after the conflict described elsewhere (especially chapters 2:14–7:4 and chapters 10–13) had been resolved.[83] The editor of the text as we have it continues after 2:13: "But thanks be to God, who in Christ always leads us in triumphal procession, and through us spreads in every place the fragrance that comes from knowing him." This verse (2 Corinthians 2:14) is a part of the Thanksgiving that normally comes near the beginning of Pauline letters.[84]

In its current placement the triumphal image is difficult to understand, for Paul portrays himself as the *victim* who will be executed at the end of the ceremonial procession, not as *triumphator*, the victor who is being extolled. This is a typical piece of Pauline irony;[85] he views the apostolic role as suffering imitation of the Lord. The editor, however, viewed this image positively.[86] Paul's missionary travels are a triumphal procession from East to West, here expressed by the passage from "Asia" to "Europe," a crossing also given special attention in Acts (16:6–10). In short, the missionary travels of Paul, however motivated, are part of the glorious progress of the gospel towards Rome (and perhaps points west).[87] The editor's view of "Paul's progress" thus informed the editing of 2 Corinthians. For that editor this view was a firmly fixed presupposition; he and the author of *1 Clement* thus share a very similar idea of the missionary career of Paul. Another who expresses the same concept is the author of Acts. This view could well have arisen before the end of the first century, but it is nonetheless noteworthy that it appears in *1 Clement*, canonical 2 Corinthians (which was not known to *1 Clement*), and Acts.[88] This is one more concurrence that suggests a close agreement in date.

SOME ADDITIONAL
THEOLOGICAL INDICATORS OF DATE

In previous chapters a number of theological issues were identified or examined. At this point I shall introduce some other theological themes, issues, or tendencies that have bearing upon the date of Acts.

Individualized Eschatology. Those who seek to learn "What will happen to me when I die?" may complain that the Bible provides little in the way of an answer. One reason for this perceived lack of clear and reassuring information is that the Biblical writers were not, by and large, very interested in the question. Their paramount concern was the fate of the people of God. Such issues as the end of the world receive attention only in so far as they relate to that fundamental subject. One of the primary achievements of social-scientific exegesis for the United States in particular and Western culture in general has been to disabuse those engaged in biblical studies of the habit of reading the Bible as if its various authors normally and regularly addressed individuals rather than communities.[89]

When the dominant trend is "realized" or "present" eschatology—a focus on the possession of salvation and (many of) its benefits *now*—individualism comes to the fore. This can be seen in even a casual survey of the Fourth Gospel, where the *krisis*, the decisive moment, is not the very public and quite collective "final judgment," but the decision of the individual to join a community of faith. It is also highly apparent in 1 Corinthians, where Paul criticizes an individualism that was linked to a "realized eschatology" and was often indifferent to the needs and feelings of others.[90] Individualistic, realized eschatology will flourish in Gnosticism, where it finds its classic expression in the ancient world.[91]

Over time, future-oriented eschatology also begins to acquire individualistic features. In his letter to the Thessalonians, Paul stresses the unity of the living and the dead rather than the fate of particular persons (1 Thess 4:13–5:11). That focus will eventually shift. The passage of time is the best explanation for this shift of focus to the individual, which, it should be noted, was never the dominant understanding and did not become a prominent concern in the West until the High Middle Ages. A good example of this transition comes from the *Shepherd of Hermas*, a book often discussed from the framework of apocalyptic.[92]

Once upon a time, so to speak, Hermas went out for a stroll in the country. There he saw ". . . dust, reaching as it were up to heaven . . ." As the cloud grew larger and thicker, he suspected that it was a portent.

> The sun shone out a little, and lo! I saw a great beast like some Leviathan, and fiery locusts were going out of his mouth. The beast was in size about a hundred feet and its head was like a piece of pottery. And I began to weep and to pray the Lord to rescue me from it, and I remembered the word which I had heard, "Do not be double-minded, Hermas." Thus, sisters and brothers, clothed in the faith of the Lord and remembering the great things which he had taught me, I took courage and faced the beast. The beast came on with a rush that was sufficient to ravage a city. I came near to it, and the Leviathan for all its size stretched itself out on the ground and put forth nothing except its tongue, and did not move at all until I had passed it by.[93]

This was not your average Sunday afternoon adventure, but neither was Leviathan the typical apocalyptic monstrosity. The individual believer, empowered by the "armor of faith," renders the beast harmless. In his commentary on *Hermas*, Martin Dibelius observed that "The author has individualized apocalyptic horrors . . . This individualizing corresponds to a transformation of Christian hope characteristic of [or "important for"] that time: the interest lies not in the fate of humankind at the end of time but in the fate of the individual at the end of his or her life."[94]

In this forerunner of *Pilgrim's Progress* the author of *Hermas* reveals that he is no hapless denizen of the post-apostolic theological jungle. Believers are not urged to watch the sky or scrutinize the news for signs of the end but to overcome the apocalyptic beast by the power of faith in the course of their daily journey. *Hermas* here is somewhat like 1 John 2:18–23. The focus is upon the present. One difference is that *Hermas* is thoroughly individualistic, whereas 1 John was concerned with the influence of "antichrists" (=false prophets) upon the community.[95]

1 *Clement*'s examples of apostolic perseverance in the face of jealousy include Peter, who ". . . went to the glorious place (τόπος) which he merited" and Paul, who ". . . was taken up into the holy place (τόπος). This is a different kind of individual eschatology: the ultimate reward of martyrs and the future hope of heaven now enjoyed by the faithful departed.[96] Acts 1:25, ". . . [T]his ministry and apostleship from which Judas turned aside to go to his own place (τόπος)"

applies the term to "the other place," as it were.[97] The parables of Luke's Gospel include examples of an individualizing approach to eschatology, as in "the Rich Fool," Luke 12:16–20, and the tale of "Lazarus and the Rich Man," 16:19–31, especially verses 22–23: "The poor man died and was carried away by the angels to be with Abraham. The rich man also died and was buried. In Hades, where he was being tormented, he looked up and saw Abraham far away with Lazarus by his side." Yet these are *stories*, after all. One would be unwise to think, for example, that people who tell a story about members of the Jewish, Protestant, and Roman Catholic clergy appearing before St Peter in Heaven are necessarily expressing their own theological views.

Luke 23:43 is therefore more apposite: "*Jesus said to the thief beside him, 'Truly I tell you, today you will be with me in Paradise.'*" He does not say, "At the resurrection you will be numbered among the just," but speaks of the immediate reward to individuals. The book of Acts contributes the story of Stephen's vision, 7:56, and quotes his prayer in 7:59. The latter is quite like the statement of Jesus in Luke 23:46. The genesis of this development emerges in the promise that Luke's Jesus offers along with his instructions about whom to invite to dinner: "You will be blessed, because they cannot repay you, for you will be repaid at the resurrection of the righteous." (Luke 14:14).[98] "Th[e] general version of the future hope as the hope of individual resurrection is what takes the place of the collective, cosmic early expectation . . ."[99] One response to the loss of a sense of imminence (vulgarly: the world is about to end) is to focus upon one's *individual* hope of reward, whether future, as in Luke 14,[100] or more immediate, as in Luke 23.[101] One dimension of eschatology, teaching about the "last things," is becoming a component of soteriology.[102] Luke's manifest tendency to view "afterlife" from an individual perspective is not sure and certain proof of later date, but it is readily explicable from that perspective—one shared by *1 Clement* rather directly, and supported in a quite different manner by the *Shepherd of Hermas*. Those who wish to argue that Luke is rather early will have a greater challenge than those who see his shifts toward the individualization of eschatology as symptomatic of a later period.

Eschatology and Ethics. A recurring theme of this study has been the reworking of early Christian ethics to suit a third (or later) generation of Christian life. It is largely parody to suggest that the relationship between the indicative of Galatians 5:1 ("For freedom Christ has set us free") and its consequent imperative ("Stand firm, therefore, and do not submit again to a yoke of slavery") has given way to "be good or you will go to Hell," in which the indicative threatens punishment and the imperative becomes a means by which to elude that dire fate. Deutero-Pauline writers continue to maintain that believers are equipped with the armor of initiation and nourished by word and sacrament, but there is no lack of ". . . the use of eschatology to inculcate a morality of steadfastness and temperance . . ."[103] For those who live in a world shaped in so many direct and indirect ways by the Christian (and eventually Muslim) view of a final judgment,[104] an ultimate accounting and permanent reckoning, it is difficult to realize how absurd that idea once seemed.[105] In the long run the most important

to pagans?

effect of the introduction of eschatology was to inculcate the value that nothing is permanent. This notion struck at the heart of ancient scientific and social
thought.[106] Therefore, even when Christian ethics seems to be disappointingly
prosaic and jejune, as in many of the texts brought into purview here, a fundamental difference is ticking away beneath the surface. The impact of eschatology upon ethics has not really disappeared; it has changed. The "political" orientation of Acts and its cognates, a proclivity that takes its departure from Paul,
was collaborative *vis à vis* the authorities, but it did not envision an alliance, let
alone a permanent union, with the civil powers.[107] Augustine did not invent the
notion of a heavenly Jerusalem.

    The Place of Israel in the History of Salvation. Few subjects are more controver-
sial among scholars of Christian background than that of "Luke-Acts and the
Jews." Robert Tannehill completes his two-volume study of Luke and Acts by
reflecting upon an

> . . . unfilled expectation . . . the promise of salvation to the Jewish people. This
> expectation not only requires more time; its realization has become problematic
> because of Jewish rejection. Here lies the real openness of the ending of Acts. The
> narrative provides a basis for completing Paul's personal story, but it does not
> provide a solution to the problem of Jewish rejection.[108]

    I rather think that the narrator has supplied "a solution to the problem of
Jewish rejection," and that this solution is writ large in the text of Luke and
Acts. Acts wishes to demonstrate that the failure of the Jewish people to accept
Jesus as God's promised savior is their own fault, a mistake for which they have
been thoroughly chastised. Despite persecution and rejection, conspiracy and
plot, animosity and intrigue, Paul continued to the end to proclaim the saving
message of God. The aged prophet Simeon exults that he has been privileged
to see God's savior, confirming that in Jesus the hope of the prophets had been
fulfilled (Luke 2:25–32). John's advent fulfilled the promise of Isaiah "All flesh
shall see the salvation (σωτήριον) of God" (Luke 3:6). At the close of Acts Paul
cites Isaiah's prophecy that the people will neither see nor hear (Isaiah 6:9–10//
Acts 28:26–27). He concludes by saying: "Let it be known to you then that this
salvation (σωτήριον) of God has been sent to the Gentiles; they will listen."
(Acts 28:28).[109] No people ever had more opportunities to "get the word." The
blame therefore lies upon the "Jews," a position made clear by God for all to see
through the destruction of the temple, the loss of the homeland, and numerous
other indignities.[110]

    Paul knew about this rejection first hand, but he was convinced that it was
not the final answer. (See Romans 9–11, especially 11:26: "All Israel will be
saved.") For Luke rejection had become the "final answer." Acts presupposes
this answer, just as it reflects widespread animosity toward Jews.[111] In the full-
ness of apologetic perfection the argument goes thus:

> [The Jews], too, to be sure, [once worshiped] our God; He is the God of all. While
> they continued to do this with heart pure, innocent, and devout, while they con-

tinued to be obedient to His salutary commandments, they who were once small in number became countless, once needy they became rich, once slaves they became kings; even as they fled from their pursuers, though not numerous themselves they overwhelmed armed troops, by the command of God and the support of His elements.[112]

The author of the preceding, Minucius Felix, was no contemporary of Luke, for he probably wrote in the first half of the third century. By this time a Christian author is *defending* Jews with regard to their early history and generously agrees that Jews worship "our God." Much earlier Ignatius had written to the Magnesians that "The divine prophets themselves lived Christ Jesus' way. That is why they were persecuted . . . It is monstrous to talk Jesus Christ and to live like a Jew. For Christianity did not believe in Judaism, but Judaism in Christianity."[113] In language highly colored by the concepts and vocabulary of Hellenistic Judaism Ignatius gives Christianity temporal priority. He evidently maintains that the prophets did not keep the Sabbath.[114] Judaism is obliged to give way to Christianity.[115]

In his own way the Bishop of Antioch says what is at very least implicit throughout Luke and Acts. The prophets spoke of the coming of Christ. Those who lack the eyes to see and the ears to hear this — a concern already voiced by Isaiah — have effectively lost title to the claim to be the people of God and to the book of promises. "Acts presents a theology in which the Church has abandoned the people and appropriated the Book."[116] *1 Clement* and the Pastoral Epistles do not so much as use the words "Jew," "Judaism," or "Judaize." For them Christianity is the sole "Biblical religion." *Barnabas* has great admiration for the prophets (e.g., 1:7), for they show that sacrifices and the like have been abolished (chapters 2–3; 13–14). The Covenant is "ours," for the Israelites lost it (4:6–8). All of the rites and ordinances are symbols of great realities (chapters 6–10; 15–16). With the important exception of the explicit allegorization of Scripture, *Barnabas* promotes a view similar to that of Stephen in Acts 7.[117] *Diognetus* agrees with the Jewish belief in the one creator God, but does not hesitate to repudiate Jewish "superstitions" (3–4). For the Didachist, Jews are "hypocrites," and Christians are to structure their lives in distinct and different patterns (*Didache* 8:1–2).

Hebrews also allegorizes Israelite history and worship. In their own ways Matthew and John (which were probably composed in the 90s) distinguish "church" from "synagogue." Acts not only follows the same path, but also seeks to demonstrate that the Jewish people who did not accept the Christian message made an irrational and essentially indefensible choice.[118] Luke thrusts this "bad choice" back into the time of Paul. Although incorrect, this shows that the separation was not a part of the immediate past and that the writer of Acts wished to imbue it with apostolic authority. Acts does not so much as hint that "they will eventually change their minds." "Their" minds are made up.

Virulent anti-Judaism of the type we call "anti-Semitism" thrived in Egypt from c. 40 CE onwards because of substantial conflict between Jews and Greeks in Alexandria, and in Rome after the First Revolt (66–73/4).[119] Menachem Stern's collection of the literature on Jews by Greeks and Romans locates the first truly condemnatory Roman outburst in Seneca, who in the 60s referred to the Jews as "an abominable race" (*sceleratissimae gentis*), followed by Quintilian, who wrote under Domitian (81–96) and calls the Jews a "pernicious race" (*perniciosam ceteris gentem*).[120] Earlier writers may oppose Jewish political power or speak of their odd habits (to a Roman) of abstaining from pork and observing Sabbath, but Seneca and Quintilian sound a new note. That note increases in volume with the historian Tacitus and the satirist Juvenal.[121] Although conservative Romans were never overly fond of any other national groups and had little positive to say about "Oriental Religions," the accusations of unacceptable religious practices and of misanthropy emerge at about the time of the First Jewish Revolt and remain at a high level for at least the first third of the second century. The final work of Josephus, *Against Apionem*, is allegedly a response to critics of his *Antiquities*. Those whom he refutes are not, in fact, quite that recent.[122] In the light of later events, their anti-Jewish works and sentiments had evidently been revived, come "back into print" in response to general interest.

In this milieu Luke could move on more than narrowly "Christian" ground in his attribution of most of the difficulties experienced by "the Way" to one form of Jewish-sponsored wickedness or another.[123] The author of Acts wished to show that responsible Roman officials did not oppose the movement, but this kind of political apologetic did not exhaust his intentions. The Jewish people rejected Jesus and all of their prophets because of the same obstinate malice that had led them to rebel against Rome. When Luke wrote, Jewish opposition to the Christian message could be adduced in favor of the new movement. The recognition and distinction of "Christianity" as a separate religion are not earlier than the end of the first century. Antagonism toward Jews did not abate after suppression of the First Revolt; indeed, it appears to have been on the increase during the 90s. Although Luke writes of events from c. 30–60, his perspective on the movement's ties with its parent religion is manifestly that of the early second century.[124]

The problem was the failure of so many Jews to acknowledge that Jesus of Nazareth was the promised Messiah. The trajectory opens with Paul's confident hope that the promises would be fulfilled, even if matters did not unfold in the expected fashion. By the close of the first century, things had changed. The ruinous failure of the First Jewish Revolt stimulated Christians to usurp the prophetic model and hold that "the Jews" were punished for unbelief.[125] Luke develops this judgment into a theology of Providence that has some tentative links to the philosophical tradition, mediated through Hellenistic Judaism.[126] Quite similar to Luke, if more daring, is 1 Clement, notably 20–26.[127] Both writers ground their view of providence in the doctrine of God as beneficent creator (Acts 14:15–17; 17:24–29; 1 Clement 20), and both make tentative use of a polytheist *praeparatio evangelica* (groundwork for the Gospel). 1 Clement has a more advanced "natural theology," while Luke makes more explicit the role of providence in human affairs. Systematic integration of the philosophical doctrine of providence (largely Stoic in origin) will have to await the efforts of the apologists, but the development is underway in Acts.[128]

As has long been recognized, Luke stands theologically between "the evangelists" and "the apologists."

> When the Areopagus speaker refers to the unity of the human race in its natural kinship to God and to its natural knowledge of God, and when he refers to the altar inscription and to the statements of pagan poets to make this point, he thereby lays claim to pagan history, culture, and religion as the prehistory of Christianity. His distance from Paul is just as clear as his nearness to the apologists.[129]

Reactions against this famous and vigorously stated article of Philip Vielhauer (1914–1977) have sought to reduce the tension between "the Paul of the Epistles" and "The Paul of Acts."[130] They can identify some exaggerations and imbalances, but I am not yet aware of any attempts to address Vielhauer's basic thesis, which is that appreciation of Luke and Acts requires not just backward glances at Mark and Paul and the LXX, but also thoughtful probes toward the Apostolic Fathers and the Apologists. Yet Vielhauer himself seems to deviate from this observation when he describes Luke's "adoptionistic Christology" as closer to that of the earliest Christian communities than the pre-existence Christology of Paul.[131] Still, there is no reason to believe that the Christology of Paul is particularly "late." It cannot, by any standard, be later than a decade before the earliest possible date of Acts.

Adoptionism enjoyed a long if not always pleasant history — at least from the emerging orthodox perspective. One may see developments from essential features of Lukan Christology in the theology of Theophilus of Antioch and thereafter in the "Antiochene" theology that contributed to the sophisticated Christology of Paul of Samosata and eventually gave birth to the views of Nestorius.[132] The ultimate victory of the Alexandrine position has condemned much of the Adoptionist tradition to a fragmentary existence, but it was anything other than primitive.[133] The clear implication of these varied theological arguments is that Acts is at home "between the Evangelists and the Apologists." From the theological perspective a date prior to 100 is quite unlikely. The theology of Acts fits the time between 100 and 140 far more suitably than it corresponds to issues and trends of the time c. 75–90.

SOCIAL AND LEGAL ISSUES

As scholars of various orientations have long observed, the book of Acts shares a number of characteristics with the Christian apologists of the Second Century. Among these are a willingness to ridicule polytheistic practices, refutation of the claims that Christianity is a novel and morally dubious superstition that appeals to the inferior and uneducated, and the plea that authorities abstain from persecuting them.[134] Acts 19:23–40, in which enthusiastic backers of the Ephesian Artemis look dangerously foolish, is an example of the first. Apologists were fond of exposing the improprieties of the gods (e.g., Justin 1 *Apology* 21). Luke's basic theological program, a demonstration of the continuity between Israel and the Church, is a response to the charge of novelty. ". . . [I]nnovation was suspect, for it could be a menace to the established order."[135] Acts spares no pains to emphasize the high social standing of early converts and their leaders, especially Paul.[136] From the intellectual perspective Christianity is best viewed as a philosophy, not a secretive sect.[137]

Persecution permeates Acts. Insofar as this is due to the authority and/or machinations of "the Jews," one need say no more, since everyone knew the enormities of which those people were capable. Luke's basic argument *vis à vis* civic and imperial law is made plain in Gallio's ruling: "If it were a matter of crime or serious villainy, I would be justified in accepting the complaint of you Jews; but since it is a matter of questions about words and names and your own law, see to it yourselves; I do not wish to be a judge of these matters." (18:14–15); that argument plays a dominant role from 21:27 to the close of the book.[138] Throughout these chapters Roman officials (and the client king Agrippa) declare that Paul is, from the perspective of Roman law, innocent. Two examples of this "verdict" are the letter of Claudius Lysias to Felix, the Roman governor (23:26–30) and the statement of his successor, Festus, to King Agrippa (25:14–21). Of the letter Lake and Cadbury say, "The speech of Festus can be grouped with the letter of Claudius Lysias to Felix as representing Luke's attempt to tell the story as he supposed that Roman officials would have told it."[139] It might be preferable to emend "as he supposed" to "as he *wished*. . . ." Luke does not cite a letters attributed to Hadrian and other emperors, as does Justin in 1 *Apology* 68.[140] Instead, he concocts a letter making the desired point.

In his remarks to King Agrippa, the procurator Festus adduces the basic legal right to confront one's accusers face to face.[141] While they do not do so by means of omniscient narration, apologists assert the same right.[142] On all of these matters Luke shares the viewpoint of the later apologists; the difference is that he *shows*, whereas they *tell*. Acts presents in narrative form what the Apologists set forth in rhetorical treatises. Thus Luke says what the apologists will also say, but he does so in the style of an evangelist: by telling stories. Once again Luke stands between the Evangelists and the Apologists.

ARGUMENTS FOR AND
AGAINST A LATE DATE

J. C. O'Neill attempted to date Acts in proximity to Justin Martyr on the grounds of its theological milieu and consequently to argue that it was not written before c. 115.[143] Hans Conzelmann refuted him with arguments that are now familiar.[144] I believe that Conzelmann is essentially correct. Not all of his arguments possess equal relevance or applicability. His first substantive argument addresses the lack of apostolic succession in Acts. The choice is strange, and not simply because neither Ignatius nor the *Didache* nor *Barnabas* nor Polycarp promotes the notion of apostolic succession, but because the idea is not especially prominent in Justin.[145] Another issue raised by Conzelmann is the difference in the manner of debate with Jews. Luke summarizes; Justin develops detailed argumentation. All that this says is that Acts and the *Dialogue* represent different genres. Hebrews and *Barnabas* can be quite detailed, if not as lengthy. No doubt the *Dialogue with Trypho* is later than Acts, but quantity is not convincing proof of a later date.

When Conzelmann says: "Justin looks back to the 'Memoirs of the Apostles' and quotes them," he makes an important observation.[146] Justin belongs to a world more involved in the consolidation and harmonizing of existing materials than in Gospel production. Yet in the first half of the second century, gospels were still being produced as well as edited. The difference between Tatian (a student of Justin who produced a super Gospel out of four or more) and Luke (or Matthew) is that Tatian's work has always been known as a conglomeration, whereas Matthew's and Luke's Gospels were not. Justin knows of more than one Gospel; and, although they are not "canonical," these "apostolic memoirs" are authoritative and are read in addition to or alongside of the biblical prophets. Conzelmann agrees that Justin ". . . reduces the issue between the church and Judaism to the existence of the common Book" but will not accept this for Luke. Once more, I believe that he is largely, but not entirely, correct. He maintains that the Bible is for Luke ". . . the historical source of the first epoch of redemptive history . . ."[147] But that description is also applicable to Justin, even if he does not emphasize it in his apologetic works.[148] Conzelmann's final observation, that Justin makes much greater and deeper use of Greek philosophy than does Luke is certainly indisputable. Justin Martyr appears to be intellectually a good generation later than Luke. His *First Apology* is to be dated about 150–155. To sum up, then, the value and importance of O'Neill's work is not vitiated by the failure of his thesis. The importance of his contribution is that he attempts to date Acts by reference to its latest features and succeeds in showing that Acts is closer to Justin than most would concede.

Jacob Jervell would refute the kind of claims made by O'Neill from another perspective:

> We are far removed from a time and a milieu such as we know from Justin, among others, where Jewish Christians are a contested and barely tolerated group in the church. While Justin is concerned to defend fulfillment of the law on the part of Jewish Christians, the issue for Luke is the minimal demands that can be imposed on Gentile Christians in view of the Jewish law.[149]

Although I agree that a generation separates Luke from Justin—a generation that included the Second Revolt (132–135), which led to stringent sanctions and strong feelings against Jews—Jervell's argument is not without weaknesses. "Time" and "milieu" are not, after all, identical. Jervell overlooks the strong

"Jewish Christianity" represented, for example, in the Pseudo-Clementines. In some areas Christianity of this sort appears to have remained long dominant. Moreover, the gap between Acts and Justin is not so wide as Jervell suggests. As noted elsewhere, in Acts 21:18–25 it is the Torah-observant believers who appear to be on the defensive. Although James repeats the requirements of chapter 15, the narrative of 21 indicates that the tables are turning or have turned.

In *Dialogue* 47 Justin's Jewish interlocutor asks whether those who acknowledge Jesus as the Messiah yet also wish to observe Torah shall be saved. Justin responds that they will receive salvation unless they strongly induce others to observe by claiming that they cannot be saved if they do not follow Torah. This is quite the same issue raised in Acts 15: the question of Torah observance as a soteriological requirement. Jervell is correct in that the situation is now viewed from the perspective of gentile believers, but the same issue is present and the same answer given: Torah-observant believers are acceptable unless they attempt to coerce others to observe or refuse to associate with them. Justin knows of Christians who will have nothing to do with such observant believers. He does not agree with them. Their view is the only "minority opinion" clearly identified as such. Justin rejects two extremes: demand for observance and the excommunication of the observant. The gap between Acts 21 and Justin's *Dialogue* is much narrower than Jervell claims.

John Townsend leaves Justin and O'Neil essentially aside, returning to the argument of John Knox (*Marcion and the New Testament*, 1942).[150] Unlike almost everyone else, Townsend seeks to demonstrate how difficult it is to argue that Acts does *not* date from close to the middle of the second century. He uses the familiar evidence about attestation to establish his point.[151] Townsend reiterates Knox's contention that the Gospel used by Marcion may have antedated canonical Luke. Although few are willing to agree with this assertion, developed in some detail by Knox, it is more or less impossible to disprove and should not be summarily discarded.[152]

In his arguments about the influence of Marcion, Townsend adds little to the earlier reconstruction of Knox. His own particular contribution is to look to another front, the debate with Jewish Christianity, for which he turns to the sources behind the pseudo-Clementine writings.[153] Townsend's leading example is the "Apostolic Decree" of Acts 15. Other than the general question of meat offered to idols, Townsend finds the broadest discussion of the issues addressed in the decrees to be found among Jewish Christian circles around the middle of the second century.[154] After surveying some other areas of concern and offering yet one more refutation of the notion that the "primitive" christological titles of Acts demonstrate an early date, Townsend closes by stating that Acts cannot be dated with certainty, but that ". . . whatever evidence exists is compatible with a date that approaches the middle of the second century."[155] His methodologically adventurous but ultimately cautious essay is another valuable lesson in the danger of establishing the date of Acts—or any work—by arguing for the earliest possible time of origin.

Joseph Tyson points to one passage that could allude to Marcion: Acts 16:6–8, in which the Holy Spirit or the Spirit of Jesus did not permit the missionaries to proclaim their message in Asia and in Bithynia. He notes the proximity of this province to Pontus, which was the homeland of Marcion. "How better to disassociate Paul from Marcion than to say that in the very area where Marcion was born and began his preaching, there had been no Pauline mission, thus no association with earlier Christianity?"[156] This proposal may not be especially compelling, but it does serve to address an opaque moment in Acts; if it is valid, 16:6–8 would not be the first time in which Luke has dealt with a difficult matter by keeping Paul out of the picture.[157]

THE FALL AND RISE OF ACTS

Related concerns emerge in the work of the leading contemporary commentator on Acts. Charles Kingsley Barrett agrees that John Knox made some telling points; he believes, however, that Acts was written c. 85–95.[158] He is troubled by the silence of many authors, Justin in particular, about Acts and grants that

> "It is tempting to draw the conclusion that Acts was written in the middle of
> the century as a mediating and conciliatory work, or at least, with John Knox, to
> think that the double work, Luke-Acts, reached its final form at that time and was
> directed against Marcion."[159]

This is a temptation that Barrett can resist, but he holds as very probable the notion that Acts may have been ignored—not necessarily under a cloud, but neglected—for some time until Marcion raised his challenge, whereupon it ". . . was rediscovered, or perhaps deliberately revived."[160] As both Irenaeus and Tertullian amply confirm, Acts was eminently suitable for the refutation of Marcion, since it shows all of the apostles proclaiming the same message about a god who is both creator and redeemer. Barrett would explain the "long silence" about Acts as due to its irrelevance. He hypothesizes that Marcion's use of Paul brought Acts into the light of day.

This is true in at least some part. Acts *was* attractive to people like Irenaeus in developing criticism of Marcion. Still, this proposal does not explain why Justin, Papias, and especially Hegesippus, who was contemporaneous with Irenaeus, are ignorant of or silent about the book. If Marcion knew and rejected Acts, it is difficult to understand why Justin did not already see its utility: "The enemy of my enemy is my friend." One is reduced to the view that Justin would not hear the name of Paul from any source. Barrett says that Luke became a part of the four-Gospel "canon" ("collection" is a preferable term), but that Acts had no place in which to fit. Those who wanted Paul could take him neat, in the letters. "Did he [a reader] need guidance in regard to moral problems? He could find them discussed explicitly in 1 Corinthians, whereas they scarcely reached the surface in Acts."[161] But on the question of eating meat offered to other gods, for example, the solution presented in Acts 15 was, as elsewhere noted, everywhere preferred in nascent "orthodox" and catholic circles to the convoluted arguments of Paul.[162] For Barrett the "reader" is someone like Irenaeus—who certainly did read Acts—but I think that Barrett's definition is too narrow. Others read Acts, including both those who did not write comments and some whose comments have not survived.

And, as the proliferation of the various Apocryphal Acts from c. 150 onward indicates, less sophisticated folks loved stories of miraculous events and astonishing conversions. Moreover, one finds no evidence for the four-gospel collection before Tatian and Irenaeus. Justin neglected the Gospel of John as carefully as he ignored the letters of Paul. The four-gospel collection became authoritative at Rome sometime around the period of Tatian, roughly 175.[163] The history of the reception of Acts as it is usually studied is largely the history of its use in the more learned and intellectual circles. Once the polemic against Marcion receded, Acts returned to obscurity. Other than the later, short, incisive commentary of Bede, Chrysostom's exposition, which is in the form of sermons to a general audience rather than learned commentary, is the only substantial work on Acts that survives from the first millennium.[164]

When one turns to "popular narrative," however, a very different picture emerges. As indicated in Chapter Two, The *Acts of Paul*, the *Acts of Peter*, the *Acts of John*, the *Acts of Andrew*, the *Acts of Thomas*, the *Pseudo-Clementines*, the *Epistle of the Apostles*, and such hagiographic works as the *Martyrdom of Polycarp* and *The Martyrs of Lyons* abundantly testify to the attractions of such narrative, and, in most of these examples, to a knowledge of the canonical book of Acts. The Fragments of Papias that survive show no knowledge of Acts and differ from it, but they exude interest in utopian fantasy, brave martyrdom, heaven-sent protection for the faithful, and gruesome punishment of the wicked. Acts was popular enough to be revised, imitated, and "corrected." These considerations of reception in less learned circles will move the question back to a date prior to Justin, but not much before 150. I think it is more reasonable to say that the requirements of refuting Marcion caused some theologians to move Acts up to a higher shelf for a period and thus guarantee that it would be listed among the authoritative writings that would eventually constitute a New Testament Canon than it would be to propose that it was rediscovered in an hour of great peril.[165] The question is not whether Marcion rejected Acts as an authoritative text. Acts was not, at that time, an "authoritative text" in any known official circles. Official acceptance and rejection were not issues then pertinent to Acts. It might be argued that Marcion "made" Acts an authoritative text in the circles of his catholic opponents, but one could hardly demonstrate that he had any urgent need to anathematize the work.

The suitability of Acts for refuting Marcion raises another question that cannot advance beyond speculation. That question is whether Marcion's Paulinism was entirely his own discovery or if he had forerunners, radical or consistent interpreters of Paul. John Knox saw the importance of this question and tended

Acts opposes radical Paulinists who were active even before Marcion.

toward a positive answer.[166] He posited the existence of Pauline communities in Greece and Asia Minor, churches in which the apostle's authority remained supreme. The Deutero-Pauline letters support this hypothesis; for all of them Paul is essentially the only apostle. These letters are the products of Pauline circles engaged in interpreting the founder's words for their own time. In those circles lay the motivation for collecting and editing the body of Pauline letters known to Marcion (and to others, including, I have argued, Luke). It is at least permissible to ask whether Marcion learned in his native environment that the entire LXX was authoritative scripture. No justification exists for assuming that the scriptures of Israel held a revered place among all Christians in every place. Ignatius alone gives reasons for caution in this matter. If Marcion's reservations about the utility of scripture for teaching, etc. were deeply shocking to the Pastor (cf. 2 Timothy 3:16), it is also conceivable that he was no less appalled to learn that believers in Christ were urged to grant Jewish scripture an authoritative position. From the more veiled comments of the Pastor and the less vague observations of Polycarp it is apparent that some of Marcion's ideas were current in Asia Minor and Greece c. 130, before he went to Rome.[167]

If Marcion had predecessors in his radical Paulinism, it is quite reasonable to propose that Acts included these among the "rapacious wolves" against which his Paul warns in Acts 20:29–30. Against this speculation is the apparent absence of such "hyper-Paulinists" from the letters of Ignatius—unless, of course, he is counted as one of them. Somewhat in its favor could be the vague false teachings attacked in Revelation 1–3,[168] and later the radical Paulinism of the *Acts of Paul*, a theology that exhibits no marks of recent origin. Silence also makes its contribution. The existence of radical exponents of Paul would also help to account for Luke's utter and absolute neglect of Paul as a letter-writer. One need not date Acts in the middle of the second century to explain its utility as a weapon against Marcion. 130 would suit quite well, while 120 is far from impossible. To be sure, Luke's argument for the continuity of salvation history does not require a corresponding idea of "so what?" or a corresponding celebration of discontinuity, but it is unwise to assume that his sole interest was in refuting outsiders who claimed that the Christian movement lacked links to its parental religious history. Nothing in this proposal can lay claim to anything like certainty, but it is at least as likely as Barrett's theory that Acts unintentionally set forth a picture that would somehow rise from the grave to serve as a key weapon in the anti-Marcionite armory. Barrett wants to have Acts written c. 90 and then left to languish for two generations. If, on the other hand, Acts is close in time to Polycarp and the Pastorals, its attention to matters like radical discontinuity and its strong incompatibility with Docetism are perfectly apt. Of these alternatives—composition c. 90 followed by lengthy neglect, or composition c. 110–120—the latter is stronger because it does not need to claim that Acts was unintentionally pertinent to later issues, but can justifiably claim that these issues were already present in some form. Thus I propound three reasons for rejecting Barrett's solution:

1. His claim that Acts was neglected applies primarily to theological writers like Justin, while overlooking the demotic milieu in which Acts *was*
   read.
2. He cannot clearly explain why Acts happened to be so useful in attacking hyper-Paulinism.
3. The internal data of Acts as well as information from other writings that
   appeared c. 100 and later evince an awareness of and hostility to radical
   Christianity—or, as in the case of the *Acts of Paul*, at least, awareness and
   approval of radical Christianity.

ARGUMENTS FOR AN EARLY DATE

Colin Hemer operates from a different perspective; his method is precisely the
opposite of John Townsend's. Rather than focus upon a *terminus ante quem*, he
wishes to date Acts as early as possible and gives close attention only to obstacles to an early date. In the chapter specifically devoted to this subject, Hemer
does not open with historical arguments.[169] He first takes note of the large
amount of material that, in his estimate, ". . . is not easily explained as the product of reflective editing." The metaphor selected is that of "stones on a beach."
Smooth stones reveal the erosion of "tradition or hearsay." Acts has a number
"which have been freshly broken from the primeval rock." Moving away from
his reflections on the beach, Hemer tackles "the state of the question," beginning with a lengthy inventory of proposed dates for Acts.[170] Thereafter comes
a list of twelve criteria. Contradiction, an example of which is argument for or
against a "persecution setting,"[171] provides some grounds for simplification on
the principle that contradictory arguments cancel one another out.[172]

Hemer then turns to ". . . a case of much more far-reaching import . . . the
recurring claim that Luke depends on Josephus." At this juncture one regrets
the lack of references, for I know of no one who had proposed that view in the
half century and more before Hemer's death.[173] Since the two (Josephus and
Acts) contradict one another, Hemer concludes that this would be a case of
misuse,[174] something that in his view is unthinkable. Having dispensed with
this important criterion, Hemer identifies three groups: those who opt for pre-
70 (a), those who prefer c. 80 (b), and, lastly, those who favor a date close to the
end of the century or later (c). From these come two dichotomies: (a) + (b) vs.
(c). and (a) vs. (b). One notes that (c) does not have a place other than as the
target/opponent of (a) and (b). At the basis of (c) is the requirement of ". . . more
thorough-going redactional approaches" for sufficient time to subject the tradition to radical alteration. Proponents of this group tend to utilize ". . . diverse
and often incompatible specific arguments . . ."[175] The primary issue dividing
the proponents of (a) from the supporters of (b) is the question of whether Luke
reflects the events of 70 CE.

At page 376 Hemer turns to his negative indicators: no mention of the fall of Jerusalem, no hint of the outbreak of the war in 66, no hint of the deterioration of Christian relations with Rome, no knowledge of Paul's letters, and no hint of the death of James.[176] On the positive side the judgment of Gallio in 18:14–17 is still in effect, which would have been less likely after Nero. The prominence of the Sadducees fits pre-70, and sympathy to Pharisees would have been "extremely difficult" at a later time. Similarly, the presence of "God-fearers" in synagogues is more likely pre-70, as proselytism declined soon thereafter. Many details evoke the ". . . cultural milieu of early, even Julio-Claudian" date. Among these are: the prominence of popular assemblies rather than administrative councils in civic matters, the importance of Roman citizenship rather than grades within that citizenship, and the "early phase in the history of Roman provincial administration, exemplified in Paul's trial experiences." In addition one notes "a tone and feel of civic life which finds its nearest parallels in the first century writers Strabo, Josephus, and Dio Chrysostom." Then there are old-fashioned names, a synagogue of "Hellenists," provincial terminology of pre-72 style, "decrees of Caesar" (Acts 17:7), reference to *sicarii*, and episodes that presume that the temple still stands.[177]

Hemer echoes Harnack in claiming that παῖς ("child," "servant") is a "primitive" christological title in Acts (3:13, 26; 4:25, 27, 30).[178] I disagree. This is liturgical, as in *1 Clement* 59:2–4.[179] Harnack was not, it transpires, the last person to examine such titles. In his study of Peter's public speeches in Jerusalem, Richard Zehnle noted and analyzed a number of "unusual" expressions in Acts 3.[180] Among these are the following:

> Acts 3:13: "The God of Abraham and of Isaac and of Jacob" (ὁ θεὸς Ἀβραὰμ καὶ [ὁ θεὸς] Ἰσαὰκ καὶ [ὁ θεὸς] Ἰακώβ).[181] The source of this title is Exodus 3:6, by way of Mark 12:22 (cf. Luke 20:37). The phrase recurs in the speech of Stephen, 7:32. There is nothing primitive about this, for the Markan and, especially the Lukan, contexts reveal that it is understood in terms similar to those of *4 Maccabees* 7:19: that is, as a "proof text" for the doctrine of the immortality of the soul.[182] The expression next appears in Justin Martyr and Valentinus, both of whom wrote well into the middle of the second century.[183]

> Acts 3:13: "The God of our forebears." (ὁ θεὸς τῶν πατέρων ἡμῶν, immediately following the citation above). The phrase recurs in Acts 5:30; 7:32; 22:14, next thereafter in Justin, *1 Apology* 63.[184] These contiguous examples indicate that one may gain the "impression" that Luke's Septuagintal language reflects the uses of primitive Christianity when in fact the data suggest a period closer to 150 CE.

> Acts 3:14: "The holy and righteous one" (ὁ ἅγιος καὶ δίκαιος). The compound is unique. Mark 6:20 applies the two adjectives to John the Baptizer, in reverse order: Mark: "Herod feared John, knowing that he was a righteous and holy man" (ἄνδρα δίκαιον καὶ ἅγιον). The terms there refer to legal innocence and to piety. If this phrase is to be understood as a christological title or titles, it/they have no

Primitive Titles (margin annotation)

claim to be especially early or primitive. "The Holy One" is certainly rare. Justin applies it in his *Dialogue* 116.1.

Acts 3:15: "Author of life" (ἀϱχηγὸς τῆς ζωῆς). The title ἀϱχηγός appears also in Acts 5:31; Hebrews 2:10, 12:2; and 2 *Clement* 20:5. Although its place in the history of religions has been the subject on extensive debate, the idea that it is "primitive" has not been in the center of the debate.[185] Having refuted these claims, I revert to Hemer's arguments.

Hemer next takes up the ending of Acts, which is not, in his view, determinative of the date.[186] He returns to his thesis of "immediacy," with particular attention to Acts 27–28, which ". . . is the extreme converse of the redactional factor." This leads to the conclusion that Acts should be dated c. 62.[187] The next fourteen pages (390–404) deal with the end of Paul's life and seek to establish a chronology that suits the proposed date of Acts, followed by a hypothesis on the process of composition, one more stab at the mysterious ending of Acts, and a summary.[188]

Although he speaks of "rigorous treatment of evidence" and is characterized as a philologist, Hemer seems to have been a romantic at heart.[189] I say this not simply because he elects to open with "stones on the beach," which may have been no more than the residue of the prelude to a lecture, intended to captivate the hearers[190]. For Hemer the terms "redactional" and "redactive" mean rather more than the work of an editor or author as editor shaping the material. "Redactional" means "late;" it is likely to be subservient to one theory or another, a school of thought free from, indeed, indifferent to historical method.[191] Its antonym is "immediate," the unreflective, unstructured, uncensored, all but spontaneous report. When such reports are found, they are historical gold. What is immediate is unedited and therefore the writing of an author who was on the scene and wrote shortly thereafter. One need no more than repeat this implicit syllogism to demonstrate that its logic is faulty.

"Immediacy" is primarily a literary quality that every author must at times employ. It is one component of verisimilitude. Reports written shortly after an event may or may not be immediate, while what is unreflective, etc., may be due to limited competence. For Hemer "immediate" is nothing other than the opposite of "redactional," a quality that he does not admire and is not particularly willing to find in the New Testament. He creates a straw creature and then argues that Luke does not resemble it. Moreover, ancient historians did not admit such "immediate" material into their writings, even when they had been present at the events. Editing ("redaction," if the German word is preferable) is, after all, the essence of authorial activity. Finally, Hemer does not produce for the identification of this immediacy any criteria that go beyond a very general and quite vague contrast of some episodes to others.[192] He believes that the "redactional" view requires time to mature.

In methodological terms what Hemer has in mind is similar to the form criticism of the Hebrew Bible, specifically the work of Herman Gunkel (1862–1932) and his colleagues, who viewed the legends of the Pentateuch as the products of generations of oral usage. Although form criticism of the Gospels (for example, that of Rudolph Bultmann, 1884–1976) took its point of departure from this work, it did not, and could not, appeal to the erosion of generations, but to the change in situation from Jesus to the communities of his followers.

The difficulty of making judgments on the basis of subjective criteria is apparent in Vincent Taylor's great commentary on Mark. Taylor (1887–1968) made use of form criticism. He often argued that passages which he regarded as "formless" were just such "immediate" recollections of Peter. Regarding the powerful story of Jesus in Gethsemane Taylor says:

> The narrative is one of the most vivid in the Passion Narrative and has strong claims to be regarded as Petrine. Only as dependent on the testimony of Peter himself is a story so damaging to his reputation and to that of all the disciples conceivable . . . Close study of the narrative confirms this estimate. Both in the descriptive element and in the words of Jesus, we receive the impression of standing very close to the original facts . . .[193]

This appealing reconstruction has but one small difficulty, one that is grounded in the same appeal to immediacy and spontaneity that Hemer proposes: according to the narrator, Peter slept through most of the scene. Mark 14:32–42 is an example of omniscient narration.[194] Taylor set forth his arguments and reasons, exposing himself to criticism. Hemer does not get much beyond the contrast between rough and smooth pebbles. His argument from "immediacy" is not discussable and is thus no argument at all, but simply a conviction.

Much the same can be said of Hemer's negative indicators. Luke does not extend his narrative into Judea in the 60s. His failure to mention the fall of Jerusalem, etc. is meaningless as a clue for the date. J. A. T. Robinson made lack of overt reference to this event the leading criterion for dating New Testament writings. By this standard James Joyce's *Ulysses* and H. J. Cadbury's *The Style and Literary Method of Luke* must have been issued prior to World War I, an event that both fail to mention.[195] The dramatic date of every book in the New Testament, with the probable exception of Revelation, is prior to the Jewish War. Robinson's principle is a noteworthy example of the difficulties of arguments from silence. It is also an anachronism, for it demands, as Joseph Tyson observes, that Luke (or any other author) ought to have referred to a matter that we regard as important.[196] Luke and Acts are not wanting in covert references to the war and the destruction of Jerusalem, to be sure, but the dramatic date excludes direct references.[197] As observed earlier, I find the argument from lack of knowledge of Paul's letters apt for those who would date the work from c. 80–90, but scarcely convincing for one who would date it in 62 and regard the author as a companion of Paul. To the same category belong his evidence about Jewish sects and the like.

Hemer is on shaky ground when he claims that references to the presence of "God-Fearers" in synagogues do not fit a date after 70 because of the decline of proselytism: this assumes that Jews actively sought converts and that the "God-Fearers" were the product of this activity. Both the nature of Jewish "proselytism" (if it existed) and the meaning of the term "God-Fearer" in Acts are subjects of intense debate.[198] A. T. Kraabel has long argued that the "God-Fearers" of Acts are a Lukan invention.[199] Without entering into that debate, I shall merely observe that what is often held as decisive proof of the existence of the "God-Fearers" is the famous "Aphrodisias Inscription," which appears to be from the third century.[200] Since most of the inscriptional evidence about "God-Fearers" comes from the second century CE and later, it is difficult to adduce those data to support a pre-70 date.

Hemer also makes a questionable assumption concerning the ruling of Gallio in 18:14–15:

> Gallio said to the Jews, "If it were a matter of crime or serious villainy, I would be justified in accepting the complaint of you Jews; but since it is a matter of questions about words and names and your own law, see to it yourselves; I do not wish to be a judge of these matters."

He proposes that it had the force of legal precedent and remained in effect until Nero made Christianity illegal. This assertion is invalid, since there is no historical evidence for either claim.

His examples of a "Julio-Claudian" (14 BCE-68 CE) milieu begin with the "prominence of popular assemblies." The one example is the *ekklesia* of Ephesus in Acts 19. A search of the data base found 543 references to assemblies (ἐκκλησία) in inscriptions of the second century, in comparison with 398 for the first.[201] By this criterion Acts is more likely to date from the second century, but the criterion is faulty because popular assemblies are not prominent in Acts. Hemer deems Acts to be early since it does not mark distinctions among grades of Roman citizens, but views citizenship itself as the privilege. Legal distinction between *honestiores* and *humiliores* (prominent and inferior) citizens is a development of the second century.[202] But this, too, is irrelevant, for Acts deals only with flagrant violations of civic rights.

Matters pertaining to provincial administration are far from transparent. Those who proceed, as does A. N. Sherwin-White, from the perspective of justifying Acts are able to do so, but those who read his carefully phrased descriptions cannot help but see how tentative many of his conclusions are.[203] The formal works on Roman law are later; what is available for the first century comes from sources of other types—including Acts. All of Sherwin-White's findings depend upon the assumption that Acts *intends* to give quite exact and precise data. This is debatable, and not only for Luke. Sherwin-White's knowledge of Roman law and, probably, history went beyond that of H. J. Cadbury, but Sherwin-White was not so astute an historical critic.[204] Let one example suffice: Hemer takes note of the grouping of Cilicia with Syria in Acts 15:23, 41 (noting also 9:30 and Galatians 1:21). This, he observes, reflects the state of affairs before 72. The same matter is somewhat troubling to Sherwin-White when he turns to a passage to which Hemer did not refer, Acts 23:34–35: "*Felix* asked what province *Paul* belonged to, and when he learned that he was from Cilicia, he said, 'I will give you a hearing when your accusers arrive.'"[205] Whatever the outcome of such debates, such information would apply primarily to the *sources* of Acts and not to the establishment of its date.[206] In any case, arguments about Roman law cannot resolve the issues of either the date of Acts or of its accuracy, for developments in Roman laws dealing with civic rights and the like cannot be determined with precision.

Hemer's statement about " a tone and feel of civic life which finds its nearest parallels in the first century writers Strabo, Josephus, and Dio Chrysostom"[207] gives away the store, for although Strabo was an old man in the early years of Tiberius (14–37), Josephus wrote in the late first century and Dio's speeches date from c. 70 to after 100, the vast majority after 80.[208] I happily receive this evidence for the date of Acts. Old-fashioned names and nomenclature bear little weight, as many of these names could derive from sources, and Luke gives every Roman, from Silas to Claudius, a single name, with one partial exception.[209] Edwin A. Judge wrote a piece in 1971 suggesting a specific legal setting for Acts 17:7 "*Paul and Silas* are all acting contrary to the decrees of the emperor, saying that there is another king named Jesus."[210] This admittedly speculative proposal refers to a decree of Augustus in 11 CE and could attest to the historicity of the scene, but it does not bear upon the date of Acts. References to *sicarii* (assassins) and episodes in the temple are also appropriate to the dramatic date of Acts. Hemer could not have expected Luke to place Paul on the site of the temple ruins, after all.

Despite the welcome length and detail of this chapter, Hemer does not make much of a case, if any, for assigning Acts an early date—or any date, for that matter.[211] He undertakes no valid effort to refute arguments for a later date. The empirical core of his case consists of data from Acts that he states apply to an earlier situation. Since Hemer's chief object is to support the claim of Acts to be highly accurate in large and in small, his material pertaining to date is congruent with his views, but it is largely not applicable to that question. Hemer's idea of "immediacy"—that Luke's impressions of the shipwreck were recorded before the sands of time had worn them smooth, for example—would be pertinent if demonstrated, but it is not demonstrated and is probably not demonstrable.

Two fallacies undermine what Hemer purports to be a purely historical approach. The first is the assumption that "vividness" demonstrates personal presence at the events described. Vivid writing is a matter of style.[212] Fiction, including ancient fiction, can produce writing that is no less vivid than any history.[213] The vividness of ancient historians tends to limit itself to stereotyped scenes, such as the horrors of sieges. This may be one reason why some trained in classical philology used to be captivated by the narrative of Acts.[214] It *is* more vivid than the customary specimens of historiography. The second fallacy is like unto the first. This is the assumption that verisimilitude, the creation of a realistic scene with accuracy of detail, is a proof of authenticity. Verisimilitude is also characteristic of fiction, but it does not establish truth, for it is a literary achievement.[215] By seeking to determine the date of Acts through reference to knowledge of events and institutions contemporary with the dramatic date, Hemer violates the fundamental principle of the procedure: that works are to be dated by their latest integral material. Although he does not state in so many words that he is interested only in data that imply an early date, Hemer does not even begin with evidence for the *terminus ante quem*. He has every personal and scholarly right to argue on behalf of an early date, but this right entails the obligation to evaluate claims for later dates and to refute them. Since scorn and dismissal do not constitute scholarly argument, Hemer cannot be said to refute alternatives. His proposal lacks methodological completeness and scholarly objectivity. In short, Hemer has not made an argument nor has he sought to answer a question. He has an answer and a conclusion, in support of which he assembles a multitude of data of quite varied quality.[216]

HOW LATE CAN A GOSPEL BE?

The notion that a book like Luke simply could not be so late as 110, let alone 120, rarely reaches the light of day or the form of print, but it is a powerful conception that helps keep Acts moored at an earlier place on the time-line.[217] Gospels, an unstated thesis runs, belong to the period from 75–90 or 100. After that come the varied literary products of the Apostolic Fathers, followed in due course by Apologists. Against this covert assumption I place in exhibit the first volume of Schneemelcher's *New Testament Apocrypha* and Koester's *Ancient Christian Gospels*. Gospel writing and Gospel revision, as noted previously, went on throughout most of the second century. Around 180 Tatian could still walk in the path of Matthew and Luke by producing a Gospel composed of other Gospels. His project was so successful that centuries would pass before Syrian church leaders could extinguish this *Diatessaron* in favor of what were called "The Separated Gospels." The *Gospel of Thomas* is one example of the continued popularity of types that were more "primitive" than Matthew or Luke. To support this case I shall call but a single witness, the so-called *Infancy Gospel of James*, which might more aptly be titled the "Gospel of/about Mary." This book, which has had an enormous influence upon popular piety, stems from the second half of the second century, but in style and form it differs little from the opening chapters of Matthew or Luke.[218] Discussions of its literary character begin by noting its substantial borrowing from and imitation of the LXX, precisely as is the case with Luke.[219] By the criteria of J. A. T. Robinson, the *Infancy Gospel of James* would be dated prior to 70.[220] Chapter 25, a colophon, supplies the kind of precise information that New Testament scholars long to have: the author's name (James) and an exact date: 4 BCE, just after the death of Herod the Great. Conversely, by the criteria of formal and stylistic comparison, the Gospel of Luke could be dated c. 150, slightly before the *Infancy Gospel of James*. Few prejudices have a firmer foundation in ignorance than does the view that because of its genre Luke could not be much later than 80–90.

ONE LITERARY ANALOGY

The *Kerygma Petri* has much that scholarship loves and hates: it is both obscure and extant only in fragments drawn from later authors who extracted them in accordance with their interests and prejudices—and whose citations may include their own comments or alterations. Its original scope, structure, date, and place of origin are all uncertain.[221] Egypt is the provenance of choice for this work, which appeared in the opening decades of the second century.[222] The *KP*, as it is known to its small band of admirers, is pertinent to the discussion of Acts for two reasons: it is "apocryphal" in form and at least partly apologetic in content. The work purports to be the content of Peter's message. Its original form is unclear. Schneemelcher observes that "It could have shown a certain proximity to the speeches of Acts and to the [Apocryphal Acts], but may also have taken over other forms."[223] Because the work appeared under the name of Peter, it hearkens to the era of the Apostles and Evangelists. Schneemelcher cites with approval the judgment of E. von Dobschütz, written in 1893, that the *KP* "marks the transition from the early Christian to the apologetic literature"—a verdict, he states, that more recent work has confirmed.[224] Still, the *KP* is not an apology like that of Justin, although it is moving in that direction.

> The *KP* is however evidence that we cannot, as so often happens, assume a radical breach between primitive Christian theology and preaching on the one hand and the apologists on the other, but must reckon with connecting lines of many kinds. The significance of the *KP* seems to lie in the fact that here we have a middle term in the preaching tradition between the early Christian missionary preaching, which has left traces for example in Acts, and the Greek apologetic.[225]

My contribution is merely to claim that Acts also belongs to this "middle term," from which Schneemelcher can separate it only by identifying speeches like that of Acts 17 as "early Christian missionary preaching." Yet this kind of preaching is the essence of the "middle term." Like Acts, the extant fragments of *KP* emphasize the unity of God the creator, who will forgive all who repent of what they have done in ignorance (Fragments 2b, 3c). The "Old Testament" is just that: a Christian book (Fragment 2d).

Fragment 3b comes from a post-resurrection speech of Christ:

> I have chosen you twelve because I judged you worthy to be my disciples [whom the Lord wished].[226] And I sent them, of whom I was persuaded that they would be true apostles, into the world to proclaim to people in all the world the joyous message that they may know that there is (only) one God, and to reveal what

future happenings there would be through faith in me, to the end that those who hear and believe may be saved; and that those who believe not may testify that they have heard it and not be able to excuse themselves, saying "We have not heard."[227]

The framework of the *KP* evidently has something in common with Acts as well. Were the entire text available, comparisons might be more compelling; they could also be less so. From what is known, it is reasonable to say that the *KP* stands between the Evangelists and the Apologists: its subject is Peter (and at least to a degree, other apostles) and its setting is in apostolic times, but its contents reflect the view of the later apologists who confront both Judaism and polytheism with rational arguments indebted to philosophy. The posture of Acts is quite similar, as is its position regarding the Jewish heritage and polytheistic society. The analogy of the *KP* underscores the broader agenda of Acts.[228]

I have more in mind than arguing that c. 85 is too early a date for Acts and therefore moving the pin on some color-coded timeline forward thirty years. If date is no more than an ink-spot on some well-designed graphic, one has little reason not to accept the views of J. A. T. Robinson or of Hemer—or those of F. C. Baur. The purpose of trying to discover the date of Acts is to illuminate its meaning and place in early Christian thought and literature. Whatever date is selected will have a bearing upon interpretation. Arguments for a particular date should have the merit of helping to resolve recognized problems or issues in the text—that is, of providing at least as good a solution to difficulties as does any other hypothesis. I have attempted to demonstrate that a later date for Acts fulfills that responsibility. The closing chapter will summarize many of these insights and explanations.

9 Conclusion

This book has argued that the date of the canonical book of Acts is important for both its interpretation and its use as a source for the reconstruction of Christian origins. The current consensus that would date (Luke and) Acts c. 85 represents more of a political compromise than a hypothesis established by rigorously examined and argued criteria. I have proposed that the evidence points to a date c. 115, or 110–120. That evidence is debatable—were it otherwise, the matter of date would have been unimpeachably established long ago—but the data are substantial in quantity, varied in nature, and mutually reinforcing. Furthermore, the debatable character of the information cannot be pressed into service as an argument for an earlier date, especially not when much of the evidence for a very early date is of a type that would support an early date for the *Acts of Paul* and the *Infancy Gospel of James*.

FORMAL, EXTERNAL CRITERIA FOR DATING

Intertextual evidence from datable sources establishes a *terminus a quo* of c. 100. Further strong evidence comes from the extrinsic probability that Luke had access to letters of Paul, supported by the intrinsic evidence for his use of a collection of these epistles. There is no sufficient indicator of the existence of such a collection before 100.[1] Other evidence derives from the good probability that Luke made use of the last volume of the *Antiquities* of Flavius Josephus, which can be dated to 93/94. The most certain *terminus ad quem* is c. 180, for Irenaeus makes explicit use of Luke and Acts. Justin Martyr does not provide anything resembling conclusive proof, but from the (second) letter of Polycarp to Philippi onwards, i.e. c. 130–135, the number of possible hints and allusions indicate that Acts was known by 150, if not a full decade, or perhaps even two decades, earlier.

"SOFTER" CRITERIA

Ecclesiastical Structure and Function

The ecclesiastical, social, and ethical perspective of Acts is very much like that of the Apostolic Fathers and the Pastoral Epistles. From a third-generation perch, Luke looks back to an early Golden Age that is to be the model for subsequent generations. Communities are under the leadership of presbyters, an institution that goes back to the early days of Paul's missionary activities and has corollaries in Jerusalem. Luke is also aware of "bishops," whom he does not wish to see exercising one-man rule, and of deacons, subordinates who perform a ministry of service. Widows are numerous enough to be an organized power bloc. Charity requires an organization, with officials to administer it. These features speak of numerical growth over considerable time. To find parallels to the type(s) of church organization displayed in Acts one will turn to 1 *Clement*, Polycarp, and the Pastorals. Acts shares the ecclesiastical framework of many churches in the period from c. 100–c. 120 and later. The chief function of leaders is to protect their communities from heresy and mismanagement, particularly financial mismanagement. Those roles also emerge in the early second century.

Church and Society

The theoretically discrete realms that people in the western world today refer to as politics, ethics, and social life were much more closely integrated in Greco-Roman society than in our own. Despite, or perhaps because of, the existence of persecution, Acts refuses to take an anti-government stance. The same view emerges in other writers and texts that know of persecution, including 1 *Clement*, 1 Peter, and Polycarp of Smyrna. Followers of Jesus can be good citizens and contribute to the well-being of their communities and of the empire. Luke evidently sought to integrate the ethics of the Jesus tradition with the moral world of the Deutero-Pauline perspective. From the perspective of the undisputed epistles of Paul, the Gospel of Luke is, in our terms, "liberal." Acts is notably less so, for its emphasis upon the social status of converts reveals a conservative viewpoint. Maintenance of the social order demands obedience from the more lowly placed and generosity from those of means.[2] This generosity may derive from ethical norms, but it also represents enlightened self-interest. Jesus issued radical exhortations, and the early community produced some inspiring models, but Luke does not need to be told that universal imitation of Jesus of Nazareth (or Francis of Assisi) would produce chaos. Peter did not impose upon Cornelius liquidation of his property as a pre-condition for baptism, nor is anyone flabbergasted when Acts fails to report that Dionysius the Areopagite sold all that he had and distributed it to the poor.

Theology

Lucan theology has been a matter of substantial controversy for a half a century.[3] A partial explanation of this controversy is, in my view, that Lucan theology is not so consistent as historians of theology would like it to be. Reasons for this may include the composition of two books, perhaps at different times, and whatever human imperfections Luke possessed. The argument that has driven this book is that Luke stands between the Evangelists and the Apologists. Highly consistent theology is not likely to emerge from an author so located. There is much to be said for studies of Lukan theology that take note of ambiguities.[4] Behind Hans Conzelmann's approach to the theology of Luke is the understanding that the author of Luke and Acts stood in between eras. Discussion has focused upon Conzelmann's understanding of salvation history in Luke, rightly so, since this is Conzelmann's leading theme. The implications of this structure are of sufficient importance to survive its demolition.

"Early Catholicism" is illustrative. Arguments have been advanced to claim that Luke was either "for" or "against" the development of institutional structures and doctrinal norms. Rather than choose between the two, I believe that Luke is a collaborator with the emergent catholic church. Since there is no doubt that he is well aware of the structure(s) of the first third of the second century, he is better viewed as one seeking to express some reservations than as a writer for whom these developments are yet no more than distant hints on a broad horizon. A second example appears in the greatly debated question of "the other" in Luke/Acts.

The Other

Definition of "the other" is, to employ contemporary parlance, a way of saying, "Who are the bad guys?" Identification of opponents is one means for determining the temporal, geographical, and social location of an undated writing. If "the others" are Marcionites, Arians, Anglicans, Yankees, or Trotskyites, one will be able to date a work and learn something about its orientation. The leading candidate for the role of "the other" in the Gospel of Luke is the Samaritans. They are not universally friendly (9:52–55), but can receive sympathetic treatment. As representatives of "the other," Samaritans can be grateful (Luke 17:11–17). A famous story suggests the possibility that a Samaritan could be "good" (Luke 10:30–35). By chauvinistic standards a good "other" is an oxymoron. But in Acts, "the other" is "the Jews," who seldom receive sympathetic treatment.[5] Yet, as argued in the comparison with Ephesians above, Luke is insistent upon the validity of the Israelite tradition (as Christians have appropriated it) and is sympathetic to Jews who have affiliated with the church. These persons are not "Jews" and did not wish to be known as "Jewish Christians" or the like. Larry Wills sees both the issues and their implications:

> Some scholars on *Acts* posit an early author who is looking ahead to future missionary successes and is not particularly anti-Jewish, but I am more convinced by those who date *Acts* to a later period (second century) and who envision an author who is looking *back* on a romanticized period of early Christian missionary activity, which was supposedly troubled by Jewish resistance. For the author of *Acts*, the boundary maintenance comes not in insisting that Jews and Christians are separate—that would be boundary formation—but in insisting that Jews were the ones who broke off relations.[6]

"Boundary maintenance" does not belong to the earliest period; it is a dimension of "community protection," and thus a characteristic of the third generation and later. Although I believe that Jack T. Sanders is generally right, he leaves no room for ambiguity.[7] Luke and Acts are anti-Jewish through and through. Joseph B. Tyson's emphasis upon "Images of Judaism" attends to the several issues involved.[8] In the end the question is not whether Luke is "anti-Jewish" (after all, Matthew and John, as well as Luke/Acts may be characterized as strongly "pro-" and pervasively "anti-Jewish") but where Luke and Acts stand in the history of the development of the Christian church. In Matthew and in John the separation is definite but recent and painful. For Luke and Acts the Jews "broke off relations" in the past.

Luke envisions a complex situation. There are four "fronts" on his polemic and apologetic horizon: Judaism, polytheistic religion, "heresies," and Greco-Roman civic life, values, and expectations. If the first two have always "been there," comparison with Paul shows major changes in orientation. Jews are more or less "the enemy;" polytheism is now a target of criticism rather than the past background of converts. False teaching and ambivalent engagement with civic life are new elements in the picture. Even his harshest critics will be compelled to admit that Luke manages this multiplicity of contexts quite adroitly. But it is of at least equal importance to note that the map of the apologists includes these same four provinces, and responds to them in similar ways. Judaism has missed the boat; polytheism is ridiculous, heresy presents strong challenges, and to society the church says "yes, but . . ." This multiplicity of outlook is another factor indicative of a later date.

The burden of this lengthy and multi-faceted argument and the weight of evidence marshaled in its support is that Acts should be dated c. 115. That date also accounts for the various social and ideological orientations of the book. One can better understand Acts as a product of the decade 110–120 than of the decade 80–90. Approximately 115 is therefore the most probable date. Acts is one product of an era and of understandings that lay between the "Evangelists" and the Apologists.[9]

I Scholarship on the Sources of Acts

Appendix

This purpose of this appendix is to review proposals about the sources of Acts and provide a summary, with some evaluation, of much of the discussion since J. Dupont's *The Sources of Acts*, (1964), which serves as a general benchmark, although some earlier proposals will receive consideration.[1] "Sources," for this purpose, are *written* texts of some length, not independent legends or succinct bits of oral tradition. Scholarship of various types and stripes has come to reject the notion that the sources of Acts can be readily be identified by linguistic criteria.[2] Form and content are the determinative factors.

The most widely accepted particular written sources for Acts are an "Antiochene" or "Hellenist" source, including parts of Acts 6–11; (13–14) 15, and one or more accounts of travel, "diaries," embracing elements of chapters 15–21; 27–28. Harnack (1909, 162–189) first proposed the existence of an "Antiochene Source." Because of the relevance of this source to the question of Luke's possible use of Galatians, chapter four included a number of references to this proposal. An important conclusion of that discussion was that Acts 15 appears to be responding to events and issues raised in Galatians rather than to represent an "Antiochene" point of view.[3]

Another suggestion of Harnack, that there was a "Jerusalem Source," no longer finds much support.[4] Torrey contended (1916) for the presence of an Aramaic source for the first half of Acts. While this idea is not linguistically viable and has no qualified current advocates,[5] Max Wilcox has revived it in a modified form.[6] Although many would assent to the notion that some parts of Acts have an Aramaic background, little of this is deemed recoverable and there have been no generally acknowledged proposals attempting to show that Luke had access to (and could understand) these semitic language traditions.[7]

Ernst Haenchen (*Acts*, 1956–, 24–34, 81–90, and 117–120) surveys the history of scholarship. Although renowned for his skepticism, Haenchen believed that Luke had written sources, even that he engaged in research. He envisions the author as visiting various communities, possibly writing letters, and obtaining a diary relating to the collection from Philippi (86–87). Haenchen's example of a seam that shows the use of written sources is 18:18–22. This is a likely looking candidate. Haenchen had an acute editorial eye, as can be seen in his commentaries on John and on the synoptic parallels.[8] His ability to detect seams and identify gaps is an important factor to consider in assessing his understanding of the sources of Acts.

Behind 14:8–18 (healing of a cripple at Lystra) there may be a local legend, but Haenchen observes—rightly—that ". . . information about a given community need not derive from that community itself" (88). In his view two hypothetical sources, the Antiochene source and a travel diary, deserve serious consideration. His criticism of the grounds upon which these sources have been isolated has been quite influential, but has not led to their general abandonment.[9] Haenchen's judgment was not that Luke had no sources, but that these are, by and large, irrecoverable. This opinion has attained the status of critical orthodoxy.

Hans Conzelmann (*Acts*, 1987 [1972], xxxvi-xl) asks whether Luke used extensive sources or "individual traditions." He states that Luke ". . . did not invent his individual stories, he merely put them into narrative form and connected them" The assumption that the first half of Acts is based on lengthy sources is "precarious." Written sources are most evident in the following cases: lists, contradictions, the presence of a Lucan editorial link (such as 18:19–20) or a non-Lucan perspective (Antioch is his example), points where marks of pre-Lucan style emerge (e.g., 12:3–19), and occasions where a narrative has been "mutilated" by placement in its present context (e.g. 19:13–16). The sources are evident but essentially irrecoverable. Conzelmann thinks that there was a collection of stories about the twelve at Jerusalem, and a kind of "Hellenistic" or Antiochene source. The story of Saul's conversion also derives from a source. The balance of his discussion takes up the use of "we" and an "itinerary." Conzelmann inclines to the view that the author has shaped various reports into a travel narrative. The use of "we" remains a mystery, but literary explanations are possible.

Eckhard Plümacher's contribution to the Theologische Realenzklopädie devotes ten important pages to source issues.[10] This includes acute criticism of the "Antiochene Source" (see below) and of the problems of defining the genre and purpose of a "we source." Plümacher finds it more satisfactory to speak of traditions, which he classifies by formal type. Many of the traditional items, however, are no more than bits of individual data. He also investigates and evaluates the "character" of the traditions, recognizing the numerous difficulties. Plümacher thinks that the "we" material derives from an eyewitness. Finally, he discusses the assembly of source material in the light of ancient historiographical practice. Plümacher views the source problem in its entirety and complexity. He asks the right questions and seeks answers with appropriate methods. This scholar does not resolve all of the source problems, nor does he attempt to resolve them; rather he lays out a kind of map. One objection that can be raised is the apparent assumption that every bit of concrete data must be a "tradition"—not that Plümacher says this, but readers may infer it. His article gathers together just about everything in Acts that *could* belong to a source. It is a useful data-base.

Gerhard Schneider (*Apostelgeschichte*, 1980, 1:82–95) supplies a detailed and analytical review of research. His review of the "we" material and diary hypotheses is incisive and includes valuable criticisms of Haenchen. Schneider is inclined to view "we" as the mark of an eyewitness, though by this he does not mean that every use of the first person plural stems from the author of Acts (89–95). On the matter of the Antiochene source he observes that the story of the selection of the Seven (Acts 6:1–6), a common starting point of that hypothetical document, is linked to the story of Stephen by an editorial comment in 6:7 and concludes that the author of Acts is responsible for placing this passage before the stories about Stephen and Philip (6:8–8:40). Schneider does not thereby rule out the possibility of an Antiochene source, but he states that decisions must be made on a passage-by-passage basis (87). That is, in fact, the approach that Gerd Lüdemann carries out with meticulous precision.

Rudolph Pesch (*Die Apostelgeschichte*, 1986, 1:45–51) looks to both "circles" and "centers" of tradents, recognizing the merits of both places and "schools," as it were. This distinction clarifies that terms like "Ephesian Source" may mask the existence of quite divergent views and groups in Ephesus. Having raised the level of complexity, Pesch apparently seeks to find a way out of the controversies about personal authorities by reference to "circles" rather than, say, to Paul or to James. Circles develop their own "stories," and these will defend and reflect their identity. Circles produce legends and "creeds" or platforms.[11] According to Pesch, information deriving from circles—namely Jerusalem and Antioch—tends to predominate in the first half of Acts. He believes that much of 15:35–18:23 (the "second missionary journey") derives from pre-Lucan tradition, the source of which was one of Paul's companions. Pesch also regards the Ephesian material in 18–19 to be based upon tradition, and holds the same view about the story of the collection in 20–21.[12] For him, the story of Paul's trials in 21–26 also has a pre-Lucan background, and Timothy is the authority for the voyage to Rome in Acts 27–28.

As a prolegomenon to his analysis of traditions, Gerd Lüdemann (1989 [1987], 22) identifies at least five sources: an "itinerary supplemented by individual episodes" in 15:40–21:36 (?),[13] an account of the trial before Festus (25), "written traditions from the Hellenist groups" (6–8; 11; 13–14[?]), oral or written stories about Peter (3, 5, and 12, and various oral traditions "from the early period of the Jerusalem community." He is more or less agnostic about the we-passages.

Without question the prize for the most original, and difficult, hypothesis about the sources of Acts goes to Boismard and Lamouille (1990). It must also be said that what they have produced is not a theory about the sources of Acts, but a theory of the development of a work that seeks to account for its sources, the variations in the textual tradition, and stages of editorial activity. Their theory begins with a Proto-Luke (an edition of the Gospel without the Marcan outline), prepared by a Jewish Christian, that included material about the early Church—that is, a "Proto-Luke-Acts." Luke himself produced the second edition, which divided the Gospel from Acts. In the 90s a third version, an anonymous emendation, yielded the text as usually printed today. A number of documents, including a Petrine source and a travel-journal, as well as elements from the *Gospel of Peter*, and a text from the circle of John the Baptizer, contributed to the various stages. These authors make many interesting observations and highlight numerous difficulties, but their theory seems doomed to neglect, for several important reasons:

First, when hypotheses are constructed upon the presumption of the validity of other hypotheses, the result is a house of cards, even if the foundation is considered to be rock rather than sand. Those who do not, for example, accept the arguments of Boismard and Lamouille for the secondary character of the Alexandrian text will not be able to journey down their path.

Second, as Barrett indicates, this theory is irrefutable and therefore not truly discussable.[14] An argument that cannot be falsified—that is, refuted by logic and data—is no argument.

Third, theories based upon successive editings and multiple layers of tradition are quite suitable to a text like the Gospel of John, where the text all but cries out for such solutions. (Luke and) Acts contain some conflicts and infelicities, but the narratives as a whole reveal the hand of a single author in full control (in so far as the use of scrolls allowed) of the text.[15] Boismard and Lamouille do seek to account for some authentic problems, but their elaborate theory is liable to the charge of solving problems that do not, in the judgment of most scholars and readers, exist.

Last, although it is reasonable to maintain that text criticism and source criticism should not take place in separate compartments, this theory often appears to confound the two disciplines rather than correlate them.[16]

Jürgen Becker makes some brief observations about the sources of Acts in his study of the life of Paul.[17] He thinks that the author lived a good generation after Paul. Sources include legends about Paul of various types: biographical, missionary, and miraculous. Luke's methods in rewriting his sources and the lack of comparison make their isolation all but impossible. He is nonetheless confident about "the possibility of an Antiochene source," found piecemeal within Acts 6: 1–15:35, and an itinerary beginning in Acts 13.

F. F. Bruce (*Acts*, 1990, 40–46) begins with the we-material, which he assigns to the author, who was present on those occasions. Other travel documents may have been used. Chapters 1–5 come from a Jerusalem source, written or oral. Chapters 6–8 are from a "Hellenistic source." The conversion of Saul also derives from a source. In addition, "Acts of Peter" appear in 9:32–11:18 and 12:1–24. Chapter 15 is to be attributed to a Jerusalem source. For the second half of Acts matters are more difficult. Luke used neither letters nor Josephus. The major sources here are informants, whose identities remain a matter of conjecture.

Heikki Leppä identifies a fundamental flaw in the claims of F. F. Bruce and Colin Hemer and others who believe that the author of Acts was Luke "the beloved physician" and that he did not have access to the letters of Paul. Information about Luke comes from letters of Paul, in particular Philemon 24, which is undisputed, and Colossians 4:14, which Bruce and Hemer regard as genuine. Those who identify the author of Acts as Luke (the physician) therefore postulate an individual who sent greetings to persons addressed by Paul in a letter but who somehow did not have access to, perhaps not even knowledge of, these letters. Colossians 4:16, which recommends the exchange of letters, is particularly telling, for it refers to the sharing of letters beyond the circle of their original recipients.[18] It is not possible to assert both the traditional Lukan authorship of Acts and that writer's ignorance about the letters of Paul. If the Luke known to Paul wrote Acts, he must, as Ramsay assumed, have known the letters and almost certainly have had access to at least some of them.[19]

Luke T. Johnson (*Acts*, 1992, 3–5) sees little, if any, hope for the detection of sources in Acts. That sources existed, including purveyors of tradition and eyewitnesses, he does not doubt. Johnson is not very confident about the presence of detectable source material for the first twelve chapters. Much of chapters 13–28 seems to come from associates of Paul. The accuracy of this material can be verified from the letters of Paul and other evidence. He is more concerned with the final product than with its sources, but does wish to defend the general reliability of Acts as an historical record.

For Barrett (*Acts*, 1994–98, 1:49–56; 2:xxiv-xxx) source-issues arise from questions raised by the narrative. He does not believe that the problem of gentile inclusion was resolved without great difficulty, nor that movement in this area was uniform. In short, Barrett does not accept the narrative line of Acts. Luke was a collector of "early contacts with Gentiles," garnered from four sources: Philip the Evangelist, Caesarea, Antioch, and information from Paul or Pauline sources (51–52). One will do well to speak of traditions, without specification of from or nature. In general Barrett finds the arguments of Haenchen cogent and specifically approves of his view of how Luke gathered material. In the introduction to his second volume Barrett makes clear his acceptance of an Antiochene source for Acts 6–15. The we-passages and their environs come under close scrutiny, and the conclusion is drawn that the we-passages probably derive from another source, as Barrett does not believe that Acts comes from ". . . one of Paul's immediate circle." (xxviii-xxix). After some speculation he concludes:

> The person responsible for Acts 16–28 must in any case be thought of as a traveller, sufficiently familiar with Corinth and Ephesus, probably with other cities also, to have picked up local traditions and memories of Paul and his missions. Much or all of the contents of chs. 17, 18, 10 will be accounted for in this way, as well as some of the paragraphs inserted into the 'We' passages in chs. 27–28. (p. xxx)

Joseph Fitzmyer (1998, 80–88) also offers a review of research. Although he can be classified as a proponent of the view that Luke "freely composed his accounts" (80),[20] Fitzmyer does believe that Luke had sources. In general he endorses the source analysis of Pierre Benoit.[21] On pages 85–88 Fitzmyer lists in outline fashion the sources for each of 83 passages in Acts. In more than 30 of these "Lucan Composition" is the chief component. In that category are all of the speeches and a number of short summaries. More than 40 are entirely or chiefly attributed to "Palestinian," "Antiochene," or "Pauline" sources. He places the We-passages in a category by themselves.

Ben Witherington III devotes an excursus to sources (*Acts*, 1998, 165–73). He begins with the frequent references to hosts. Use of these names was a mode of recognizing their contributions to Luke's research, an ancient equivalent to the expressions of gratitude now relegated to prefaces.[22] From this it is evident that Witherington is interested in oral information communicated to the author. Rather than conversing about the weather or retailing local gossip, these kind hosts shared with Luke what they knew about the apostles. Limitations upon his availability imposed some restrictions, leading to a "heavy concentration upon Petrine and Pauline material (167)." The author was an occasional companion of Paul on some of his missionary expeditions. Time spent in Jerusalem and Caesarea permitted interviews with Philip, James, Mary the mother of John Mark, the Magdalene, Joanna (who could tell all that one might wish to learn about the Herods) and perhaps also with Mary the mother of Jesus. At Caesarea the story of Cornelius was ripe for the picking. Enforced leisure brought about by the delay in a decision in Paul's legal case gave scope for field work in Joppa and Lydda. "Indeed, he could even have traveled on to Damascus and Antioch during this time . . ." (169). All of which is to say that the author did not have or need "a vast amount of sources to compose Acts as we have it" (170). Substantial consultation with Paul and good use of that down time in Jerusalem and Caesarea, not to mention Miletus, would have done it.

In support of this view is the absence of knowledge of Paul's letters, "with the possible exception of some of the Captivity Epistles . . ." (170). Luke might have known Romans, but none of "the capital Paulines" (171). This rules out a late date and supports the source hypothesis proposed, for it is difficult ". . . to believe in a third-generation Luke who sees Paul as his hero, uses sources extensively, *but can't find any of Paul's main letters to use*" (171). In short, Witherington believes that Luke used sources extensively but did not need or seem to have had a "vast amount" thereof.[23] Witherington's Luke is thus a scholar who engages in extensive field research and related interviews, as many ancient historians claim, often falsely, to have done. Those of a critical orientation are likely to regard his reconstruction as fantastic, for only infrequently does Acts bear any resemblance to material based upon eye-witness reports. Witherington sees little need for written sources. His argument is unfalsifiable and therefore not particularly discussible.

Professor Witherington evidently arrived at his understanding independently of Colin Hemer, who devotes a lengthy chapter to the issues of authorship and sources, two subjects that stand or fall together for Hemer (*Book of Acts*, 308–64).[24] The we-material comes from the author who is Luke, the companion of Paul. When he turns to sources proper—data obtained from others—Hemer brings into consideration what Luke learned from ". . . personal communication with Paul of Tarsus, a person with whom he was in constant and intimate association before and perhaps during the period of the writing . . . ," eyewitness material from others, and a miscellaneous category, which may or may not have been documentary. A specimen of "material from others" is Acts 12, based upon "personal interviews with Peter and with Rhoda."[25] 7:54–8:1 is a good example of what Luke learned from Paul:

> The stoning of Stephen is linked explicitly with the first actual mention of Saul. The implication that Saul was profoundly shaken by his connivance is almost palpable. On a traditional understanding of Luke's association with Paul this looks [like?] an almost paradigmatic case of a pericope derived from Paul, on whom the occasion must have made an unforgettable impact.[26]

I agree that the example is paradigmatic of Hemer's approach to sources. Acts is a canvass. Sources are persons who may be represented by dots. Luke connected these dots to construct his picture of the early Church. Hemer identifies the underlying dots. As in his arguments about date, Hemer often takes a "psychological" approach to sources ("unforgettable impact").

In 1962 Jacob Jervell published an important essay entitled, "The Problem of Traditions in Acts."[27] In this essay Jervell challenged the claim of Dibelius (followed by Haenchen) "that circumstances were very unfavorable for the formation of a tradition about apostolic times" (20). He shows that stories about apostles and about communities formed part of the proclamation. To his examples one might add Paul's efforts to refute stories told about him. Those who read Galatians and 2 Corinthians might reasonably conclude that Paul would have dearly wished that circumstances were very unfavorable for the formation of traditions about apostolic times.[28] In his recent commentary Jervell (*Apostelgeschichte*, 61–72) finds no sustained sources for Acts 1–12. Matters are quite different for chapters 13–28. The we-material marks the presence of the author, who was a companion of Paul. An additional source dealing with Paul's legal travails is not to be confused with a court record. Jervell is skeptical about the use of a diary or itinerary. The limits of this putative source are difficult to establish, as is its character and function. Oral traditions, which served evangelistic and ethical ends, were common. This is not to suggest that the identification of local tradition is simple, but communities did keep track of one another.[29] Jervell does not doubt that Luke wrote the speeches of Acts, but he identifies the presence of traditional elements in them, as well as the possibility of summaries of what Peter or James or Paul said.

Some commentators give but slight attention to source questions. Jürgen Roloff (*Apostlegeschichte*, 1981, 9–10) devotes less than a page to the matter. He does not believe that sources were substantial, especially in the first half. Acts 13–14 probably rest on Antiochene tradition, 16–18 from a diary of the Pauline circle. Luke was personally a part of the delegation bringing the collection, and one or more associates of Paul provided material for chapters 21–28. In addition there may well have been a cycle of legends about Peter and Paul. His contribution to the *Dictionary of Biblical Interpretation*, co-authored with John Hayes, specifies that "most of the material came from oral tradition." He finds "convincing traces" of written sources for some of chapters 13–14, the itinerary for 16–18, some material about Paul in prison in 21–25, and the voyage to Rome, perhaps from Aristarchus. In addition, sixteen verses in 20–21 seem to derive from a report on the collection trip that may have been "an official protocol," and diverse material elsewhere, including legends about individuals, seem to suggest literary sources.[30] Insofar as I can tell the introductions to the short commentaries of Kee (*To Every Nation under Heaven*, 1997), Dunn (*Acts*, 1996), and Walasky (*Acts*, 1998) do not address the subject. In his contribution to the new Tyndale series (*Acts*, 1980, 37–39) I. H. Marshall notes some of the difficulties with the view that the later chapters stem from an eyewitness, but he affirms it and believes that the author (Luke, companion of Paul) obtained information from participants for the earlier sections. Marshall states that the limited scope of his work precludes detailed attention to the use of sources. Gerhard Krodel (*Acts*, 1986, 39) is highly skeptical about written sources, but is confident that the author had traditions and reports, some of which may have been first hand.

This survey has given first attention to commentaries because in them one expects to find up-to-date surveys and evaluation of research, as well as relevant bibliography. Much of the important work on this subject initially appeared in the form of articles and within monographs.[31] Two German dissertations have wrestled with the problem of the "we." One, C.-J. Thornton's *Der Zeuge des Zeugen*, prepared under the supervision of Martin Hengel, defends, with considerable nuance, the traditional view.[32] Jürgen Wehnert looks in a different direction at the Jewish tradition, including not only Ezra-Nehemiah, as did Torrey and others, but also the book of Daniel. Although some scholars have examined this problem from the perspective of Greek and Latin fiction, Wehnert is probably the first to introduce specifically Jewish fictional composition into the discussion.[33] Although the method may be that of Daniel, the content is, Wehnert thinks, based upon an authority. That authority is Silas. In their investigations of Pauline chronology R. Jewett and G. Lüdemann were obliged to wrestle with the issue of the sources of Acts.[34] The important article of P. Benoit has already been recognized.

Martin Hengel long remained a vigorous proponent of an Antiochene Source, although he doubted that its specific contents could be delineated.[35] In what will probably be his final statement on the matter, Hengel withdrew his endorsement:

> Nor can any independent basis be demonstrated for the much discussed 'Antiochene source.' Probably it is based on notes collected by Luke, since if we put together the remains of it, for the most part there is no consecutive 'source.' How this information came to Luke we do not know. What counts most against such a pre-Lukan literary source in Acts is that Luke tells us so little about events

in Antioch. Here the events between Paul's arrival in the city and the Apostolic Council must have been very important. It is not least this sparse information from Antioch which makes it improbable that Luke himself came from the Syrian metropolis, as is reported in later sources from the early church. Probably Luke composed a framework in the form of a memorandum before he wrote Acts, which he then developed.[36]

The reason for so lengthy a citation is that Hengel's concession may mark the death-knell of the "Antiochene Source" as traditionally conceived. The difficulties of attributing Acts 15 to an Antiochene Source came under scrutiny earlier.[37] Hengel's subsequent comments and notes indicate that he now agrees with the conception of Ernst Haenchen about Luke's methods of obtaining data.[38] If I may be permitted to offer a few words of my own at this funeral, I should like to build upon the criticism offered earlier. It seems reasonable to suspect that such a source did exist, and quite possibly at Antioch, but that this putative source was not a "history" of the Antiochene mission. Its subject was rather the origins of "gentile Christianity." Following the hint of Galatians 4:6 and the lead of Acts 10, a source of this nature could be expected to stress the presence of ecstatic phenomena as a mark or "sign" of divine approval. Its beginning would, by this criterion, be found not in Acts 6 or 7, but in 2:1–13, the story of Pentecost. From the same observation it would immediately become clear that Luke has so altered his "underlying source" that almost no certain information beyond the phenomenon of (presumably) group ecstasy could be derived from it.[39] The function of this source (for which Conzelmann's term "Hellenistic" would be a better designation than "Antiochene"[40]) would have been a "foundation story." In the light of later controversies, such as that known from Galatians 2, the dominant party at Antioch could quite justifiably have wished to trace their roots to Jerusalem, to celebrate Peter as the leading agent in a mission to accept gentiles, to emphasize the role of the Spirit in the movement to accept non-Jews, and to portray Barnabas as Paul's predecessor and superior.

All four of these factors are apparent in Acts (2:1–13), 6:1–13:3. Although the first three are fully in tune with Luke's own ideas, the last is not, while the others could once have served different purposes from the uses to which Luke has put them. The proposed source evidently saw its roots in a marked expansion of the Jesus movement toward Greek-speaking Jews of Diaspora background and connections. Stephen and Philip receive honor for their achievements in that endeavor, which opened the door to work among others, possibly some Samaritans and the inhabitants of the coastal regions. Without such a mission there could have been no overture to gentiles. The role of Peter in converting the prominent God-fearer Cornelius permits Luke to demonstrate that Paul did not inaugurate the gentile mission. For Luke that conversion serves to defend both the gentile mission and the person of Paul. Others could have recited the story to show that Peter had been engaged in the business of converting gentiles while Paul was still opposing the movement: Paul did not "invent" the gentile mission; Peter did. Acts 13:1–3 serves to show that the Spirit endorsed a mission carried out by Barnabas and Saul. 11:19–26 is another component in the argument for the priority of Barnabas. He arrived in Antioch as the authorized representative of Jerusalem. While engaged in a vibrant mission Barnabas came up with the notion of enlisting as his aide Saul, who had been languishing at Tarsus. These two passages are excellent candidates for the label "Antiochene traditions." One apparent function would have been to explain why the majority of the community supported Barnabas and Peter against Paul. Such an explanation might well take the following shape: The roots of the movement were in Jerusalem. That contention responds to an important point in the controversy that exploded in Galatia. The winners at Antioch could trumpet, "We can and most emphatically do trace ourselves back to the followers of Jesus in Jerusalem. Thence came Barnabas, and, in due course, Peter, who sided with him. Oh yes, Paul also labored here for a time, under the supervision of Barnabas, from whom he separated." The same data refuted the contention of those who demanded that all believers in Jesus become fully initiated and observant children of the Covenant. With various adjustments and unknown abbreviation and deletion, Luke utilized these traditions for a different purpose. Among those adjustments was removal of the emphasis upon Paul's subordination to Barnabas. Within ten verses of the oracle dedicating Barnabas and Saul to a missionary task Luke can write "Paul and company" (οἱ περὶ Παῦλον, 13:3). The so-called "Antiochene Source" was therefore somewhat anti-Pauline in the matter of his quarrels with Peter and Barnabas, but not anti-Pauline in regard to the validity of the gentile mission.[41]

To return to the primary subject of this appendix, Ernst Haenchen made other contributions to discussions of sources. In addition to his article on the we-material cited earlier, he also raised the question of a Philip-Source.[42] This takes up an oft-mentioned but never fully pursued genre: collections of stories about deeds of individual "apostles." Collections of πράξεις ("deeds") had their inspiration and background in the Jesus-tradition. By analysis of Mark and comparison of Mark to John, scholars have identified pre-Marcan catenae of miracles.[43] Failure to follow up this possibility, which explores a known genre, rather than a hypothetical "chronicle" or "diary," is in part due to the erroneous notion that people in the early church were not interested in stories about apostles.[44]

As is his custom, Walter Schmithals has gone his own way by proposing that the second half of Acts stems from a single, continuous source often modified and altered by Luke.[45] Lewis Donelson has attempted to discover what Luke might have found if he had visited various sites. The leading example is Ephesus, where Acts 20 and 2 Timothy may preserve elements of a common tradition. Donelson does not ask whether both texts may stem from Ephesus, nor does he introduce Acts 19, but his essay does attempt not only to describe Acts in terms of ancient histories, but also to exemplify the practice with detailed examples.[46] In the light of the numerous descriptions of ancient historiographical method in relation to Acts, anyone who actually relates theory to practice must be regarded as both refreshing and innovative.[47]

Stanley Porter devotes several chapters of his investigation of the Paul of Acts to the we-material, which he reconstructs in full.[48] He rejects all of the proposals that attempt to relate this material to Jewish or Graeco-Roman genres. Porter thus concludes that the material is *sui generis* (generically unique). He does not, however, believe that the author of Acts wrote this source. Although he does not claim to have isolated and identified the we-source with precision, Porter argues that he has identified a particular literary structure that differs somewhat from that of Acts. His source includes several such narrative episodes as 20:7–12 (the raising of Eutychus), but does not include the address to the Ephesian elders in 20:18–35. Porter's ultimate goal is to defend the historical reliability of Acts. Since he will accept no analogies that are less than fully satisfactory, he has little difficulty in putting all generic arguments aside. The weakness of this is that Porter does not take note of the contributions of the several proposals, the actual or potential light that they shed in providing a general literary profile. He would have genre abide by rules as precise as those of prescriptive grammar.[49] His universe has little room for shades of gray; yet whatever its limitations, this is the most detailed study of the problem to appear in English in a number of years.

CONCLUSION

Outside of protracted labors yielding divergent results on the problem of the first-person plural, little advance has been made in the study of the sources of Acts during the past generation. Perhaps the most unmistakable indicator of the state of affairs is the remarkable fact that the multi-volume series edited by Bruce Winter, *The Book of Acts in Its First-Century Setting* (a work of conservative orientation and clearly although not explicitly intended to update Jackson and Lake, *The Beginnings of Christianity*) includes no contribution on the sources of Acts. The we-material is more or less inextricably bound up with the issue of authorship. For the rest, literary interests in the text as it stands and (eminently justified) skepticism about the detection of sources dominate the field. The labors required to propose an appropriate literary form for any particular source and to equip that form with a reasonable setting and function, as well as to delineate the apparent scope and boundaries of its contents, evidently seem excessive at the present time. One senses little scholarly anticipation that further refinement of the source question will yield fresh information on Christian origins. Judging from the dearth of serious scholarship on such issues, the possibilities that Luke knew some of Josephus's writings or that he used Pauline correspondence are sufficiently remote to call forth no more than a sentence; point-by-point refutation of these absurd notions seems not to be required.

In the end, Helmut Koester's summary well expresses the results of critical endeavors:

While the sources used for the composition of Luke's Gospel are fairly clear, the sources used in the Book of Acts remain a conundrum. Scholars have tried to identify two different written sources, an "Antiochian Source" for the materials in the first part of the book . . . and a travel narrative, called the "We Source," for the second part . . . Both theories, however, are burdened with considerable difficulties.

Koester notes the problem of finding a genre for the Antiochene Source, which includes a number of formal types. He prefers to attribute the result to the author, who ". . . connected partly legendary traditions with some authentic documents . . ." The search for an Antiochene source is evidently a "futile effort." Koester does not doubt the existence of historical information, giving as examples the lists in Acts 6 and 13 and the martyrdom of Stephen (chapter 7). He also states that "we" is not consistent. Some of the first-person material may derive from a travel report, but other examples of "we" (especially Acts 27–28) are a stylistic device of the author.[50]

A MODEST PROPOSAL

In this book I have sought to advance source proposals that invite and require discussion and refutation. Only one of these possesses even a hint of novelty. It can reasonably be argued that Luke had access to a collection Paul's letters; he might also (at Ephesus?) have read one or more pieces of Pauline correspondence that have not survived. And one has good reason to suspect that Paul wrote a number of short administrative or personal notes or letters that were not deemed collectable or may have quickly disappeared.[51] As John Knox realized many years ago, the most pressing question about Philemon is why it gained a place in the published collection.[52] It was hardly likely to have been the only brief letter that Paul ever wrote.

One candidate for that oft-mentioned source dealing with the Collection for Jerusalem is a letter of Paul to the various contributing communities, explaining the results. An alternative is a letter with the same purpose, written by a colleague of Paul. In such a communication "we" would have been quite appropriate, since the Collection was delivered by a delegation and represented the efforts of a group. This hypothesis is incapable of proof, and thus not a basis upon which to build further speculation, yet it does appeal to a known form, the early Christian letter, and to an example that would have had a quite intelligible purpose. In the light of such passages as 2 Corinthians 8 such an accounting might well be labeled a "necessity." If the Collection was rejected — a likely outcome — the hypothetical letter might have been taken by the delegates who returned the monies (if they could be recovered). The alternative genre, an "itinerary," is also a generally known form, but none of its proponents have been able to mount a generally convincing argument about why such a list of stopping places would have been kept.

Scholarly Estimates
of the Date of Acts
Appendix

The following catalogue of scholarly opinions indicates both the wide range of dates that have been proposed and the emergence of a general consensus in the past few decades. It is based on the catalogue developed by C. J. Hemer in *The Book of Acts in the Setting of Hellenistic History*, 367–370. Items preceded by an asterisk (*) derive from Hemer, where bibliographical information may be found. Not all of these have been verified.[1] For any errors in other entries I am, of course, responsible.[2] In his discussion of the question, Joseph Fitzmyer included a brief list of authorities that advocate a date c. 80. [3] In order to illustrate his claim that the date of Acts is one of the most irascible problems of the discipline, Günther Klein cites one authority each for twelve positions, ranging from 63–140/145.[4] I include some of these, marked with an initial plus-sign (+).

This list is biased toward commentaries and introductory handbooks. Although authors of monographs often have views about the date of Luke or Acts, they rarely present evidence or argument for their views, which often appear only in passing, if at all.[5] Commentators and authors of introductions are expected to have studied the question and to present the evidence.

F. Blass	56 or 60. (*Philology of the Gospels*, 1898, 33–34)[6]
A. J. Maclean	c. 61 ("Acts of the Apostles," 1909, 10)
R. B. Rackham	By 64, probably 64. (*Acts*, 1904, l-lv)
A. v. Harnack	Early 60s. (1911)[7]
A. Steinmann	Early 60s (*Apostelgeschichte*, 1934, 15)
J. Belser	61–62 (*Apostelgeschichte*, 1905, 16–18)
*G. Edmundson	Before 62. (1913)
C. C. Torrey	64 (*Composition and Date*, 1916, 67)
*P. S. Bihel	62+ (1930)
*A. T. Robertson	63 (1939)
E. M. Blaiklock	Early 60s (*Acts*, 1959, 14–15)
*P. Barker	62–63 (1965)
E. R. Goodenough	Early 60s (SLA 1966, 57–58,)
J. Munck	Early 60s (*Acts*, 1967, liv)
*F. V. Filson	Early (prior to Peter's arrival at Rome, 1970)

D. Guthrie	c. 63 (*Introduction*, 1970, 115; 340–348)
*A. J. Mattill	While Paul in Rome (1970)
B. Reicke	62 ("Synoptic Prophecies on the Destruction of Jerusalem," 1972, 134)
C. Hemer	62 (*Book of Acts*, 1989, 408)
J. A. T. Robinson	62– (*Redating*, 1976, 88–92)
*E. F. Harrison	c. 62 (1975)
D. Carson, *et al.*	62–64 (*Introduction*, 1992, 190–194)
E. Jacquier	64 (*Actes*, 1926, cxjx)
R. E. Longenecker	c. 64 ("Acts of the Apostles," 1981, 236–238)
L. McDonald and S. Porter	64–67 (*Early Christianity*, 2000, 295–297)
A. Wikenhauser	after 66/67, the death of Paul (*Apostelgeschichte*, 1956, 21–22, 291)[8]
*J. Finegan	While Paul in Rome (1981)
*H. G. Russell	Before 70 (1955)
C. S. C. Williams	"prefers" c. 66–70 (1957)[9]
*J. Dupont	After death of Paul (1953)
E. E. Ellis	c. 70 (*The Gospel of Luke*, 1974, 55–60)
I. H. Marshall	Towards 70 (*Acts*, 1980, 46–48)
*T. W. Manson	64–70 (1944)
W. Michaelis	late 60s-early 70s (*Einleitung*, 1961, 142)
*A. C. Headlam	Soon after 70 (1900)
+K. Aland	Shortly after 70 (1957)
*J. V. Bartlet	Perhaps 72–74 (1901)
T. Zahn	75 (*Introduction*, 1909, 3:159)
*T. E. Page	After 70 (1900)
*D. J. Williams	c. 75 (1985)
G. Stählin	c. 70–80 (*Apostelgeschichte*, 1962, 9)
W. Neil	70s or 80s (*Acts*, 1973, 24).
E. Freed	70–90 (*New Testament*, 1986, 141)
*W. K. L. Clarke	c. 80 (1922)
A. Plummer	75–80 (*St. Luke*, 1901, xxxi)
W. M. Ramsay	81 or soon thereafter (1896, 387)
F. F. Bruce	Late 70s or early 80s (*Acts*, 1990,18)
F. W. Danker	Late 70s or early 80s (*Jesus and the New Age*, 1988, 18)
B. Witherington	Late 70s or early 80s (*Acts*, 1998, 62)
P. W. Walaskay	75–85 (*Acts*, 1998, 6)
C. C. Hill	after 70 (*Hellenists and Hebrews*, 1992, 19 n.3)
W. H. Willimon	70–100 (*Acts*, 1988, 1)
F. Scott Spencer	70–100 (*Acts*, 1997, 16)
C. F. Evans	75–130 (*Saint Luke*, 1990, 14–15)
*E. Stauffer	c. 80 (1952)

L. T. Johnson	c. 80 (*Luke*, 1991, 1–2).
A. A. T. Ehrhardt	c. 80 (*Acts*, 1965, 4)
A. Morton and G. MacGregor	80 (at earliest, *Structure of Luke and Acts*, 1964, 53)
E. Schweizer	80– (*The Good News according to Luke*, 1984, 6–7)
O. Bauernfeind	c. 80 (*Kommentar*, 1939, 80)
J. Kürzinger	c. 80 (*The Acts of the Apostles*, 1981, 1:xii).
W. Eckey	c. 80 (*Die Apostelgeschichte: Der Weg des Evangeliums von Jerusalem nach Rom*, 2000, 17.)
E. Trocmé	80–85 (*Livre des Actes*, 1957, 71)
M. D. Goulder	80–85 (*Type and History in Acts*, 1964, 14 n.1)
J. M. Creed	c. 80–85 (*Gospel according to St. Luke*, 1930, xxiii, with possibility of "a date somewhat later in the century")
J. D. G. Dunn	80s (*Acts*, 1996, xi)
J. Kilgallen	80s (*A Brief Commentary on the Gospel of Luke*, 1988, 26).
R. P. Martin	80s (*New Testament Foundations*, 1978, 63–67)
*G. H. C. Macgregor	c. 85 (1954)
R. Brown	c. 85 (*Introduction*, 1997, 274)
M. Boismard, A. Lamouille	c. 80 (*Actes*, 1990, 1:43)
J. Price	85–90 (*Interpreting the New Testament*, 1997, 105. This states the most common opinion.)
W. G. Kümmel	80–90 (although 90–100 is possible.) *Introduction to the New Testament*, 1973, 186)
G. Schneider	80–90 (*Apostelgeschichte*, 1980, 1:118–121)
A. Weiser	80–90 (*Die Apostelgeschichte*, 1981, 1:40)
D. Juel	80–90 (*Luke-Acts: The Promise of History*, 1983, 7)
G. A. Krodel	80–90 (*Acts*, 1986, 14)
R. Pesch	80–90 (*Apostelgeschichte*, 1986, 1:28)
J. Jervell	80–90 (*Apostelgeschichte*, 1998, 86)
R. C. Tannehill	80–90 (*Luke*, 1996, 26)
F. Bovon	80–90 (*Luc*, 1991, 28)[10]
G. Lüdemann	80s (70s-90s are possible) "Apostelgeschichte," 1998, 643)
M. Hengel	80–90 (*Acts and the History of Earliest Christianity*; 1980, 63)
N. Perrin and D. Duling	80–90 (*New Testament*, 1982, 294. 85 +/- five years)
R. Maddox	80s or early 90s (*Purpose of Acts*, 1982, 9)

P. Esler	c. 85–early 90s (*Community and Gospel*, 1987, 27–29)
J. W Packer	Late 80s; possibly later (*The Acts of the Apostles*, 1966, 13)
*M. Goguel	85–90 (1949)
R. Spivey and D. M. Smith	80–100 (*Anatomy of the New Testament*, 1969, 139)
B. Gaventa	80–100 (*The Acts of the Apostles*, 2003, 51)
H. Windisch	80s or 90s, but could be 100–110 (*Beg.* 2:308–309, 1922)
E. Plümacher	90 or a few years earlier ("Apostelgeschichte," 1978, 521,)
+H. Hommel	c. 90 (1955)
L. P. Pherigo	c. 90 (1951 278)
C. K. Barrett	Late 80s or early 90s (*Acts*, 1998, 2:xlii)
David L. Barr	Late 80s or early 90s (*New Testament Story*, 1995, 329)
F. J. Foakes Jackson	c. 90 (*Acts*, 1931, ix)
*A. H. McNeile	c. 90 (Introduction, 1952, 36.)
M. Dibelius	c. 90 (*Studies*, 1951, 72)
E. J. Goodspeed	c. 90 (Introduction, 1937, 191–97)
J. Roloff	c. 90 (*Apostelgeschichte*, 1981, 5–6; Hayes and Roloff, 1999, 10).
E. Plümacher	c. 90 (*Lukas*, 1972, 7)
P. Vielhauer	c. 90 (*Geschichte*, 1975, 407)
B. H. Streeter	c. 90–95 (*The Four Gospels*, 1924, 535)
G. Sterling	c. 90 or early 90s (*Historiography*, 1992, 330)
R. R. Williams	Either 62 or c. 95–100, but not c. 70–80 (*Acts of the Apostles*, 1965, 21.)
S. Davies	c. 90 (85–100, *The New Testament*, 1988, 141.
K. Lake	90–100 ("Acts of the Apostles," 1916, 15).
W. Marxen	90–100 (*Introduction*, 1968, 171–72)
H. C. Kee	90s to 100s (*To Every Nation under Heaven*, 1997, 14)
H. Conzelmann	c. 90–100 ("Luke's Place," 1966)
M. Parsons	Late first century ("Acts," 1997, 2)
H. Wendt	c. 95–100 (*Apostelgeschichte*, 1913, 46)
R. P. C. Hanson	Late first or early second century (*Acts*, 1967, 1–2)
*W. Schmithals	90–110 (1980)
+H. von Soden	c. 100 (1931)
E. Lohse	c. 100 (*Formation of the New Testament*, 1981, 162)
M. P. Bonz	c. 100 (*Past as Legacy*, 2000, 25, 163)

F. C. Burkitt	95–105 (*Gospel History and Transmission* 1907, 105–110.
B. Shellard	98–100 (*New Light on Luke*, 2002, 23–31).
G. Bornkamm	c. 100– ("at the earliest toward the end of the first century," *Paul*, 1971, xv)
J. Moffatt	c. 100 (*Introduction*, 1921, 312)
A. Jülicher	100–105 (*Einleitung*, 1921, 395–97)
M. Enslin	c. 100–105 (*Christian Beginnings*, 1938, 422–24)
H. Koester	100–110 (*Introduction*, 2000, 2:314).
*P. W. Schmiedel	105–130 (1899)
J. C. O'Neill	c. 115–130 (*Theology of Acts*, 1961, 21)
J. Drury	c. 115–130 (*Tradition and Design*, 1976, 21–22)
J. Knox	125 at latest ("Acts and the Pauline Letter Corpus," 1966, 286).
C. Mount	Before 130 (*Pauline Christianity*, 2002, 168, n.17.)
+ E. Barnikol	c. 135 (1958)
+P. L Couchoud	135– (1935)
J. Townsend	c. 140– ("The Date of Luke-Acts," 1984)

Absentees: The following authorities did not answer the roll call:

H. J. Cadbury is often cited for giving inner and outer limits to the date of Acts, but he did not himself supply a figure. This is typical of Cadbury.[11]

Ernst Haenchen does not specify a date (or a genre or a provenance) for Acts in the introduction to his magisterial commentary.[12]

Charles H. Talbert will venture no more than ". . . anytime between the early sixties and the early second century."[13]

III Dates of Authors and Texts
Appendix

This appendix is intended to serve as a convenience. When an argument for date has been made in the text, the entry gives a date and provides a reference to the data and argument. Dates should be understood as approximate—sometimes *very* approximate. Detailed arguments for the dates of all of the following persons and texts would require a small monograph in itself. Controversy exists in almost every case. This list will indicate my own views. For the sake of convenience various works and authors cited in the text but not crucial to the date of Acts are included below. The quantity of references and data is directly proportionate to the importance of the date of a particular work to the date of Acts. The arrangement is roughly chronological. An asterisk (*) marks items that have some introduction in the text of this book, especially in Chapter Two.

*Gospel of Mark. 80–85.[1] The importance of the date of Mark for this book is that according to the standard view of sources (to which I adhere), Luke made use of Mark and must therefore be later.

James. 80– (See Brown, *Introduction*, 742).

Colossians. 80–85. Colossians could be somewhat earlier, but the proposed date seems more likely than c. 65–75 (Koester, *Introduction*, 2:268–271; Brown, *Introduction*, 616).

Hebrews. 80 (Attridge, 6–9)

Ephesians. 90–95. (Brown, *Introduction*, 630; Mitton *Epistle*, 260–261[2]). Koester (*Introduction*, 2:271–275), prefers 100–.

2 Thessalonians. 80–90. 2 Thessalonians is difficult to date. Although this piece is late enough to sound the alarm about forged letters (2:2; 3:17), it follows 1 Thessalonians more closely, for example, than Ephesians follows Colossians. Colossians may well be its target.[3]

1 Peter. 90–95. *1 Clement* may have known 1 Peter. Polycarp certainly did know the letter, although he does not identify it by name. 1 Peter is definitely post-70. J. H. Elliott (*1 Peter* 124–38) posits a range of 73–92. P. Achtemeier (*1 Peter* 43–50) gives a range of 80–100, with a preference for earlier over later. P. Vielhauer (*Geschichte*, 587–88) dates the letter c. 100 and H. Koester states that it cannot be later than 100–120 (*Introduction* 2:297). 1 Peter has a number of affinities with Acts (Achtemeier, 14–15). On the grounds of its religious vocabulary, and its understanding of Christian life and practice, I think it unlikely that 1 Peter is earlier than 90.

1 Clement.[4] 95–100. This date of *1 Clement* is generally accepted, albeit often for the wrong reasons. The alleged "persecution of Domitian" (died 96) cannot be used to date this letter. Although Welborn ("On the Date") indicates the difficulties, there are some indicators to narrow the range. *1 Clement* is late enough to know Hebrews and possibly 1 Peter, but not late enough to be aware of the published collection of ten Pauline letters.[5] This establishes a range of 80–100, if not 90–100. Its view of church structure is like that of (Acts and the) Pastorals: there are presbyters and some officers called/also known as "bishops." The presbyterate has been in place for more than one generation.[6] Tradition has become a norm. These and related factors support the traditional date.[7]

The *Corpus Paulinum* (Collection of Paul's Letters) c. 100. "The collected letters of Paul must have been available by the late first century or early in the second. But the first solid evidence of an extensive collection is provided by Marcion near the middle of the second century . . .[8] The basis for Gamble's auxiliary verb "must" are citations from letters of Paul and references to a group of them. The latter emerge quite early and are of quite uncertain meaning.[9] Many of the alleged citations are also disputable. Gamble elsewhere states: "Clement of Rome, Ignatius of Antioch, and Polycarp of Smyrna all attest that Paul's letters were known and used over a broad geographic area by the end of the first and the beginning of the second centuries."[10] 2 Corinthians has been the touchstone for proof of use of a relatively complete edition of Pauline letters in this book,[11] whereas references to Romans or 1 Corinthians have been held to offer no such proof, as these two evidently enjoyed independent circulation.[12] *1 Clement* knows Romans and 1 Corinthians (as well as Hebrews, and, possibly, 1 Peter), but shows no awareness of 2 Corinthians. According to the rigorous standards of "A Committee of the Oxford Society of Historical Theology," Polycarp is the first orthodox witness to 2 Corinthians.[13] This text was in Marcions's collection, which may have antedated Polycarp. Even Ignatius presents no more than a precarious case upon which to demonstrate the existence of a relatively full collection of the Pauline correspondence.[14] The major criticism of the date of c. 100 for the emergence of a collection including ten of the letters known today is that it may be too early.[15]

Barnabas 100–130. Although the reference to building the temple 16:3–5) leads one to place *Barnabas* just before the Second Revolt (132–135), that reference is disputable, and the work may be several decades earlier. Paget (*Epistle of Barnabas*, 9–30) comes down in favor of a date under Nerva (96–98).

The *Didache* 110–120 (Niederwimmer, 53). This work is extremely difficult to date, for it is composed of various elements and was often revised; but none of the material is earlier than the late first century, while its view of church offices seems to be earlier than the mid-second century.

Ignatius of Antioch. 115–125. Ignatius is usually dated late in the reign of Trajan (98–117), but he may have been executed under Hadrian (117–138)[16]

*Shepherd of Hermas.*110–145. *Hermas* is very difficult to date. It is most unlikely that this work was finished in the first century (Osiek, 18–20). The conventional division has posited three sections: "Visions," (*Vis.*), "Parables" (*Sim.*), and "Commandments" (*Mand.*). This is being superseded by a consecutive enumeration of "chapter and verse" segments. I retain the traditional system in references because it is found in most of the texts and translations in general use in English-speaking countries. Osiek's *Hermeneia* commentary provides both, as does the latest edition of Funk-Bihlmeyer.

2 Clement has nothing to do with *1 Clement*. This is an early Christian sermon, probably composed around the middle of the second century (Lindemann, 1992, 195).

*Marcion of Sinope. C. 90 (?)-c. 154 (?).[17] According to his opponents Marcion went to Rome c. 138 and was excommunicated in 144. The traditional, patristic dating of Marcion's ministry is the middle third of the second century. He must have been active in Asia before Polycarp wrote to Philippi. 1 Timothy 6:20 looks very much like a reference to his *Antitheses*. This establishes c. 120–130 as a possible date. John Knox (*Marcion*, 1942) argued for rather earlier dating.[18] R. Joseph Hoffmann has recently reopened the case for an earlier date.[19] If Marcion was active early in the second century, it is possible that the canonical Luke and Acts do represent a revision of Marcion's Gospel, together with an additional volume placing Paul in the desired perspective.[20] Hoffmann has succeeded at least to the extent that debate must now focus upon how much earlier than 130 Marcion's activity is to be dated rather than how much later. In conclusion, it is possible that Marcion's radical Paulinism was on the horizon when Acts was written.

2 Peter. 130–150. Second Peter is the latest work in the New Testament, with the theological vocabulary and intellectual tools of the apologists, an acceptance of authoritative Christian writings, and anti-Gnostic polemic (Koester, *Introduction* 2:298–300). Brown (*Introduction* 766–67) says 130 +/-ten years.

*Papias. 130 (may be as much as two decades earlier).[21]

*Polycarp, *Philippians*. 125–135. This text may well incorporate two letters. Chapter 13 (and part of 14?) come from the time of Ignatius's journey to martyrdom, or not long thereafter.

*Pastoral Epistles (1–2 Timothy, Titus), 125. As noted elsewhere, the Pastorals are close to Polycarp and are therefore dated in proximity to his later letter.[22] (Brown, *Introduction*, 668, says that most scholars date the Pastorals between 80 and 100.)

Hegesippus. (?c. 120–180). Among the vanished books of early Christian literature that historians would love to recover are the five volumes of notes prepared by Hegesippus. Eusebius preserves fragments of this work in his *Ecclesiastical History*. He played an important role in establishing the vital role of Apostolic Succession as a weapon against heresy.

*Justin Martyr, *1–2 Apologies*. 150–160. Justin wrote his apologies during the second half of the reign of Antoninus Pius (138–161) and was executed, according to tradition, during the rule of Marcus Aurelius (161–180). Barnard tentatively dates *1 Apology* 151–155 and says that the second "cannot be long after the first."[23] (The dominant tendency in current scholarship is to view *2 Apology* as an appendix to the major apology rather than a distinct work.)

Martyrdom of Polycarp. 160–. Polycarp, Bishop of Smyrna, died in 155/156 (or later). The *Martyrdom* has been revised and could be from c. 180 in its present form.

Diognetus 150+. This piece, which appears to be composed of two different writings, cannot be dated with any security.

Athenagoras. Second Century. Athenagoras wrote an apology (177) and a work on the resurrection.

*****Tatian** (d. c. 185). Tatian was a Syrian who studied under Justin Martyr at Rome in the mid-second century. In c. 172 he was obliged to leave Rome for alleged heresies. Tatian wrote an atypical apology, the *Oration to the Greeks*, which reveals his antagonism to Hellenism and various theological peculiarities. His *Diatessaron*, a harmony of the four canonical gospels and other material (perhaps the *Gospel of Thomas*) was long the canonical form of the Christian Gospel among Syrian Christians of a more or less catholic orientation.

Theophilus of Antioch. (Late second century). Theophilus was bishop of Antioch, a continuator of Lucan theology, and the author of an apology.

Melito of Sardis. (d. c. 190). Melito was a prolific writer, best known today for his Easter sermon, "On Pascha." Fragments of an apology survive.

Irenaeus of Lyons. C. 130–c. 200. Irenaeus became bishop after 177. His literary activity, especially *Against Heresies*, can be dated close to 180.[24]

*****Clement of Alexandria**. (c. 150–160–c. 215). Little is known of the life and career of this Alexandrian theologian. His surviving writings are to be dated sometime after 180 to c. 200.

The Pseudo-Clementines. Two novels of the fourth century, the *Homilies* and the *Recognitions*, present a form of Jewish Christianity at considerable variance with that found in the New Testament and elsewhere. The sources of this material, which includes prefatory correspondence between James and Peter, have long been disputed. *Recognitions* 1.27–71 probably derives from a second century Hellenistic Jewish-Christian text. The author knew the canonical Acts and reinterpreted it in an anti-Pauline manner.

IV The Diaspora Revolts of 115–117
Appendix

During the last years of the Emperor Trajan (98–117), Jews in Egypt, Cyrene (modern Libya), Mesopotamia (modern Iraq), and Cyprus launched a series of rebellions against Roman rule. Because there is no surviving narrative account of these actions, they remain obscure and have received relatively limited attention.[1] Yet it is arguable that for many outside of Judea and its environs these revolts had a greater impact than those that took place in the Jewish homeland in 66–73/4 and 132–135. The purpose of this Appendix is to show that these years would constitute a highly suitable context for Acts' portrait of the Jews as a subversive, disobedient, and violently obstinate people, and thus to suggest that this portrait did not depend upon animosities aroused by the rebellion of the 60s—antipathies that some might imagine to have faded by the second decade of the second century. I begin with a brief historical sketch.

When Rome absorbed the Hellenistic empires that had arisen in the wake of the conquests of Alexander the Great (d. 323 BCE), it inherited the old struggle between Greece and Persia. Control of the small kingdom of Armenia constituted an enduring source of friction between the Roman and the Arsacid (Parthian, contemporary Iranian) Empires. Both powers agreed that Armenia was to be a buffer state, but each sought to insure that the buffer was softer on its own side of the fence, resulting in competing efforts to make Armenia a quasi-satellite.[2] When the Parthians deposed the current Armenian ruler, Emperor Trajan attacked them in 114. This expedition was successful. Armenia was reduced to the status of a Roman province. The Romans also occupied northern Mesopotamia, which was east of the Euphrates, the traditional border between Rome and Persia). A subsequent campaign in 115 moved further east to Adiabene, generating another new province, Assyria. Trajan again turned south and met with additional success. The days of Iranian power seemed numbered.

Upon his return to this region in 116, Trajan discovered that the Parthians had launched a counter-offensive. The situation was grave. The emperor was not able to recover all of his previous gains. This perilous situation, involving a campaign far from established bases, was made vastly more dangerous and difficult by the need to attend to Jewish uprisings in a number of regions. These revolts threatened lines of supply and communication. They also required the emperor to redeploy some of his best troops and most able generals when he had dire need of their services. Patriotic Romans, of whom the historian Tacitus is the classic example, would not soon forget—and probably never forgive—this disruption of the largest Roman conquest of "civilized" regions in 175 years. For Rome these revolts were a series of momentous and treacherous stabs in the back. Trajan's successor Hadrian (117–138) abandoned the new conquests as untenable. Although modern historians usually agree with his judgment, many at the time did not, while others could argue that these new regions might well have been properly secured had it not been for the perfidious interference of contumacious Jewish rebels.

The spark that set off these explosions is unknown. Perhaps it was an opportunistic attempt to take advantage of the withdrawal of Roman legions for the Eastern campaign. The relatively abundant data from North Africa—Egypt and Cyrene—indicate that the rebellion had a messianic character, and that it evoked and was eventually overcome by a corresponding polytheist holy war.[3] This vicious conflict produced casualties. In the early phases gentiles were massacred, and when the authorities got things in hand, there was a retaliatory slaughter of Jews. Many temples and polytheist shrines were plundered, desecrated, or destroyed by the rebels. The largest synagogue in Alexandria also suffered destruction. The island of Cyprus was the scene of another extremely bloody revolt.[4] It is quite possible that an uprising in Palestine was quashed in its initial stages by prompt Roman intervention. Finally, Jews in Mesopotamia rebelled against Roman rule. These were evidently irredentists seeking the return of Parthian rule. A vastly reduced number of Jews in Alexandria survived, but the Jewry of the Egyptian countryside was nearly eradicated.

Roman subjects in Syria, Asia Minor, and Greece must have thought that the whole surrounding world was ablaze, and this while the Emperor was seeking to salvage a distant and precarious campaign. Many who lived in the Roman East probably cared little whether the borders of the empire advanced a centimeter, but the security of their own homes and cults was not a matter of indifference. To gain some sense of their feelings, one might imagine how American citizens would have regarded a sudden outbreak of hostilities against the U.S. by Mexico and Cuba in 1943. The revolts in the mid-110s would not have endeared Jews—who were exempt from Roman military service—to their gentile neighbors.

Whatever may be said about religious toleration in the Roman world did not apply to Egypt and its environs. Writing of the revolt there John Barclay says, "It is only on the assumption of prolonged and profound social alienation between Jews and non-Jews that we can explain the ferocity of the Jewish uprising in 116–117 CE and its equally ferocious suppression."[5] The Flavian advertisement of Judaism as an unacceptable superstition evidently served not only to exacerbate gentile hostility toward Jews but also to justify an all-out Jewish assault upon polytheism in Greek-speaking North Africa.[6]

Those inclined to date Acts in the second century will regard this period of revolt as part of the milieu for Luke's depiction of the Jews as threats to security and stability. Barclay's words, quoted above, testify that hostility between Jews and others did not appear out of the blue one fine day in the year 115. Rather, what occurred was the eruption of a volcano that had long been belching fire and smoke. In some cities, at least, tensions remained as high in 110 as they had been earlier. Literary evidence for the 90s comes from Josephus, who took care to show that the Jews were not responsible for urban unrest.[7] There follows an examination of some documentary and quasi-literary texts that bear directly upon a hypothetical setting of Acts in the first two decades of the second century.

A few specific instances emerge in the papyri edited by Tcherikover and Fuks (abbreviated CPJ).[8] They note that standard terms for the affair are θόρυβος and τάραχος.[9] A letter written in 117/118, for example, says διὰ τ[οὺ]ς τ[ῶ]ν [Ἰουδαί]ων θορύβους ("because of the Jewish disturbances," CPJ 444.25–26). The same letter refers to a state of insurrection: στάσεως οὔ[σης] (CPJ 444.30). CPJ 449 is an official document from 151, thirty-four years after the revolt. Line 23 notes that land remained untilled because the previous owners perished ἐν τῷ Ἰουδ(αικῷ) ταράχῳ ("in the Jewish uprising").[10] Acts uses the noun θόρυβος in reference to the temple riot in 21:34 and 24:18, as well as of the disturbance in Ephesus, 20:1. The related verb characterizes the results of Jewish intrigue in 17:5.[11] τάραχος also characterizes the unpleasantness at Ephesus (19:23), while the cognate verb ταράσσω and compounds describe Jewish maneuvers at Thessalonica and Berea.[12] στάσις and its cognates were, as has been noted, among the most dreaded terms in the political lexicon of the ruling class.[13] See Luke 23:19, 25 (Barabbas), Acts 19:40 (Ephesus), and 24:5 (Paul as revolutionary agitator).[14] Extreme disorder is also a prominent feature in the deliberations of the Sanhedrin: 23:7, 10.[15] If their most privileged and dignified body cannot meet without rioting, what can one expect of the Jewish rank and file? Luke does not compel his readers to guess about the answer to this question. The book of Acts shows familiarity with the vocabulary utilized in documents to describe the Egyptian rebellion of 115–117.[16] For readers of that period, these terms were not likely to connote political agitation or large demonstrations alone. They rather evoked all of the outrages associated with unbridled civil war.

Another source of contemporary gentile views of the Jews can be found in some of the *Acta Alexandrinorum*, or "Acts of the Pagan Martyrs," as Musurillo entitled them.[17] These "Acts" (in the legal sense i.e., trial reports), showing numerous novelistic features and sometimes resembling mimes, shed interesting literary and ideological light upon the book of Acts. Those who found edification in these reports were the sort who shared the literary tastes of people who read popular novels and works like the various Gospels and Acts. Mary Smallwood, at a loss to explain the revolts of 115–117, opened her discussion by referring to an "... incident at Alexandria only a decade or so before the revolt."[18] Her subject is the *Acta Hermaisci*, Musurillo VIII (=P. Oxy. 1242 =CPJ 157).[19] The surviving fragments tell of a delegation of Alexandrians going to Rome in reference to a conflict with Jews. When the latter learn of this delegation they send representatives of their own. Each party came equipped with its gods. The text is unfortunately broken here, but it later transpires that the Alexandrians brought a bust of Serapis.[20] At first things go badly for the Alexandrians, since Trajan's wife Plotina had persuaded the emperor's council (Senators?[21]) to support the Jews. Hermaiscus boldly resists the tyrant, claiming that his council/senate is filled with Jews. The statue of Serapis opportunely begins to sweat.[22] This epiphany astonished the Emperor and led to a vast public disturbance. The text breaks off with the entire population of Rome fleeing for the hills. Serapis had done rather better than Baal (1 Kings 18:20–40), and this Trajan is most definitely not one of the "five good emperors" about whom one learned in school.

For the purposes of this appendix, three important story elements stand out. The first is the intense hostility toward the "impious Jews."[23] This a sentiment that is more or less ubiquitous in the *Acta Alexandrinorum*. Second is the belief that the Jews have great political power and that many Jews occupy high positions in the imperial court, and third is the view that they exercised this influence through the baleful and irregular interference of a woman.[24] By replacing Plotina with Poppaea (the wife of Nero, known to be pro-Jewish), one could write up the outcome of Paul's trial along similar lines.[25] Alexandrian polytheists were happy to imagine that Jews and their interests controlled the imperial court. This is paranoid fantasy, but it is not 100% paranoid fantasy. At Rome (and elsewhere), Jews were not powerless. More important, it was widely believed that they were *very* powerful. One is assured that Roman emperors, like the Franklin Roosevelt of Nazi propaganda, were misled by Jewish advisers.[26]

In conclusion, this brief survey of material from Egypt indicates that what Acts says about the Jews is quite compatible with the proposed date of c. 115. When Luke took pains to portray the Jewish people as threats to the established order, he was not seeking to promote a hitherto unheard-of idea. The period leading up to and during this Diaspora revolt is at least as suitable as the period from 75 onward. For those who lived around the Aegean Sea this revolt was probably more cogent and threatening than was the earlier rebellion of the 60s.

otes

Chapter One
The Date of Acts and Some of its Sources

1. H. Wendt, *Die Apostelgeschichte.*

2. Haenchen's commentary has been succeeded in turn by the distinctly different contribution of Jacob Jervell.

3. C. Talbert, *Reading Acts,* 2. Insofar as attention to such matters as sources and dates detracts from concern for the author's intention, these activities are worse than fruitless; they are positively counter-productive. Students of Acts are least culpable on this charge. Since the first edition of Haenchen's commentary, if not from the first of Dibelius's essays (1923) and Cadbury's *Making of Luke-Acts,* the purpose and character of the author have been in the forefront of study. In the end, Talbert is evidently willing to date Acts c. 100. See Appendix II.

4. The model takes its name from the German philosopher G.W.F. Hegel (1770–1831).

5. In these two sentences resides the distinction between "popular" (or "journalistic") and "scientific" history. Popular history tends to assume that the questions, issues, and even the values do not change over generations. This approach stems from a naïve cultural centrism.

6. Baur paid a heavy price for his refusal to regard "our" questions as "their" questions. Few theologians of modern times have attracted more enmity.

7. Marcion is a key figure in the discussion about the date(s) of Luke and Acts. See the excursus in chapter two p. 24.

8. Both Marcion and the *Pseudo-Clementines* continue to generate quite different reconstructions and interpretations.

9. An erroneous charge, long used to condemn Baur, is that he took the Hegelian dialectical model and forced the history of early Christianity into its framework. For one fairly recent example of this charge see *ATR* 60 (1978) 222–23.

10. For a succinct and insightful survey of Acts-scholarship in this era see Ernst Haenchen, *The Acts of the Apostles* , 16–32. More detailed and somewhat less insightful is W. Ward Gasque *A History of the Criticism of the Acts of the Apostles,* 21–164. (On which see *ATR* 59 [1977] 108–12.)

11. See also Appendix II.

12. A bit of that sensation is still apparent in Gasque *A History,* 155. Harnack's earlier views evolved from a strong preference for 78+ (1897) to lukewarm support: *The Acts of the Apostles* , 290–97. In 1911 Harnack came down in favor of 62 in *Neue Untersuchungen zur Apostelgeschichte* , 64–65.

13. F. F. Bruce *The Acts of the Apostles* 9–19, citation from 19. The references for the 1951 and 1952 editions are 11–13 and 13, respectively. Other examples are Ben Witherington III, *The Acts of the Apostles: A Socio-Rhetorical Commentary,* 60–62; Raymond E. Brown, *Introduction to the New Testament,* 273–74; Joseph A. Fitzmyer, *The Acts of the Apostles,* 54–55, with a long list of those who support a date of c. 80–90 on 54.

14. G. Sterling, *Historiography and Self-Definition. Josephos, Luke-Acts and Apologetic Historiography,* 329 (A consensus to which Sterling himself does not subscribe). See n. 18. Mark. A. Powell said in his 1991 review, "The great majority of scholars date Acts somewhere around a.d. 80–85, with the admission that this cannot be established with precision," *What Are They Saying about Acts?,* 37.

15. C. K. Barrett, *Acts,* 2:xlii–xliii.

16. Gerhard Schneider, *Die Apostelgeschichte* 1:118–21. The leading exception is Colin Hemer, *The Book of Acts in the Setting of Hellenistic History*, who lavishes 45 pages on the subject (365–410), including a long list of proposed dates (367–70). His work is discussed in chapter eight. (Purely quantitative approaches to this question overlook differences in treatment—for example, whether the question of date is included with observations about early witnesses to the text.)

17. Fitzmyer, *Acts*, 55.

18. The fullest statement of Conzelmann's view about the date of Acts is "Luke's Place in the Development of Early Christianity," SLA 298–316, with a conclusion on p. 309, dating Acts at ". . . roughly speaking, the transition from the first to the second century." Note also Gregory Sterling, *Historiography and Self-Definition*, 330, and Helmut Koester, *Introduction to the New Testament* , 2:314.

19. Brown, *Introduction*, 274.

20. Henry J. Cadbury "The Tradition," *Beg.* 2:260–61; *The Book of Acts in History*, 147–48.

21. Three relatively short studies of ancient historiography in English are Charles William Fornara, *The Nature of History in Ancient Greece and Rome*, Emilio Gabba, "Literature," in M. Crawford, *Sources for Ancient History*, 1–79, and David S. Potter, *Literary Texts and the Roman Historian*.

22. Note Artapanus, Frag. 3.27, in which "the king" requests a sign (σημεῖον).

23. H. J. Cadbury presents a more leisurely and detailed account of this process in his *Making of Luke-Acts*, 155–83.

24. R. Stoops, "Introduction: Apocryphal Acts of the Apostles in Intertextual Perspectives," 1. Note also the various studies in Dennis R. MacDonald, editor, *Mimesis and Intertextuality in Antiquity and Christianity*.

25. The NRSV has been modified to conform to the Septuagint.

26. Trans. Whiston.

27. For some recent work on the sources of Acts see Appendix I.

28. "Synoptic Tradition" refers to the first three Gospels, Matthew, Mark, and Luke, which are similar enough in outline, incident, and wording to require an intertextual solution: one or more of these three used one of more of the other two.

29. *The Sources of Acts*.

30. Dupont, *Sources*, 166–67.

31. *Acts*, 85. Haenchen does not suggest that Luke concocted the entire book. His views are summarized in Appendix I.

32. I write "embodied" to emphasize that Haenchen was not the only person to contribute to this basic shift. He was, nonetheless, the most important but, ironically least recognized for this contribution by many of those who approach Acts as literature. In his *The Narrative Unity of Luke-Acts: A Literary Interpretation* Vol. 2 R. Tannehill refers to Haenchen's commentary at least forty-five times. Three of these references are positive; about ten are neutral; the rest express disagreement. No reader of this book would imagine that Haenchen had blazed the trail that Tannehill follows.

33. As regards the Gospel of John, Haenchen made important contributions to the discussion of sources, producing *John* a two-volume redaction-critical commentary published after his death.

34. For examples of deliberate changes by copyists in NT mss. see Bruce M. Metzger, *The Text of the New Testament: Its Transmission, Corruption, and Restoration*. Bart D. Ehrman reviews doctrinally motivated alterations in *The Orthodox Corruption of Scripture*.

35. On this saying see also pp. 228–29.

36. The "Sermon on the Plain" is the Lucan parallel to Matthew's "Sermon on the Mount." It is, in effect, the Q sermon on discipleship and ethics. Note the passage on "giving" in Luke 6:30–36.

37. To illustrate the difficulty: one could describe Paul's founding of the Christian community at Ephesus so as to "glorify" Ephesus ("We are an apostolic foundation") or to demonstrate the prowess of Paul. Furthermore, stories may be used for different purposes, so that a story once celebrating the origins of Christianity at Ephesus could be included in an account of various exploits of Paul—and vice-versa.

38. Nonetheless—as was always the case in the era before textual standardization, and especially prior to the advent of printing—the particular form of the LXX known to Luke can be uncertain.

39. Biblical scholars and, to an even greater degree, archaeologists of earlier generations were often avid readers of detective novels.

40. This is not to suggest that his methods are inexplicit nor that he is inconsistent in application of them.

41. On these matters, see the more detailed account of theories in Appendix I.

42. Nevertheless, Chapter Four *suggests* the possibility that Luke may have been familiar with no longer extant Pauline correspondence.

43. The leading source for the history of the Roman Empire in the eras of Jesus and Paul is Cornelius Tacitus, who was born c. 56 CE. Another is the biographer Gaius Suetonius Tranquillus, who was born c. 70. Flavius Josephus, the chief authority for the history of Palestine in the time of Jesus, was born in 37 or 38.

44. This is already apparent in the work of "Herodotus," the "Father of [western] history." For Thucydides the view is axiomatic. In the study of Jewish and Christian origins the outstanding example is Josephus, whose object in both cases was to explain the present situation with an eye toward the future.

45. "Gospel according to Luke" and "Acts of the Apostles" are later names for these two anonymous books. Marianne Palmer Bonz compares Luke-Acts to Virgil in *The Past as Legacy*. On p. 153 she states, "Indeed, from a historical critical standpoint, it is much more reasonable to assume that Luke's composition was originally a unity, which very early in its transmission history was split in half."

46. See M. Parsons and R. Pervo, *Rethinking the Unity of Luke and Acts*. Defense of the traditional view appears to have been one motive behind the conference that gave birth to J. Verheyden, ed., *The Unity of Luke-Acts*. The chief exceptions to the prevailing assumption of unity are those who view Acts as a work of history and therefore separable from the Gospel. The *Book of Acts in Its First Century Setting* (BIFCS) series is representative of this perspective.

47. On the use of Mark in Acts, see chapter three.

48. S. G. Wilson, "Lucan Eschatology," 347, commenting upon the lack of imminent expectation of the end in Acts. J. Hawkins's studies led him to the conclusion ". . . that a considerable time must have elapsed between the writing of the two books." *Horae Synopticae*, 177–82, quoting p. 177.

49. Note the comment of R. Maddox, *The Purpose of Luke-Acts*, 9.

50. Ten years would seem to be a reasonable maximum for the interval between the beginning of the composition of Luke and the completion of Acts. This does not mean that the works were written a decade apart, merely that they could have been written over the period of a decade.

51. Such chemical means as carbon-14 analysis continue to improve, but yield too wide a range to determine more than that various manuscripts are not forgeries from a later era. Some manuscripts come with a built-in *terminus a quo* because they were written on the reverse side of datable material. Ancients often "recycled" papyrus by writing on the backs of documents that were no longer needed. If such a document were a tax register of the year 215 CE, for example, the text written on its *verso* would have been copied after 215.

52. The example also suggests difficulties. If a work contained but one such phrase, as well as "neither a borrower nor a lender be," critics could suggest that Shakespeare took the phrase from this source and that the second was already a cliché. Similar problems arise in the case of Acts and other ancient writings.

53. "Dramatic date" refers to a time or era *portrayed* in a work, rather than that of its composition. The dramatic date of Shakespeare's *Julius Caesar* is I BCE.

54. C. Hemer presumes from Tacitus that the term was evidently in use in 64. See Chapter Eight, pp. 334–41.

55. For examples see Chapters Six and Seven.

Chapter Two
Establishing the Range

1. 𝔓 is the symbol for "papyri," and is used because NT manuscripts are classified according to the *medium*, paper made from the papyrus plant. The superscript number is a means for identification, based upon the order of discovery. The very earliest NT mss. are

papyri, but the 𝔓 symbol does not guarantee an early date; indeed, some papyri are as late as 700. (Nor is the date of a ms. a sure indicator of the antiquity of its *text*; late mss. may be quite valuable. For the present purpose, however, the date of the ms. is fundamental.)

2. A convenient survey of the earliest papyri is provided by Barrett, *Acts*, 1:2–3.

3. The rigorous labors of paleographers have yielded a typology based upon the evolution of handwriting style that provides approximate dates, but this method, although useful, is not exact. External citation also entails numerous qualifications. The dates of many texts and authors are known only through deduction and those of some of the earliest, such as the collection known as the Apostolic Fathers, are uncertain and contested. Clement of Alexandria was active in the last decades of the second century (see below). When he refers to an incident in "the Acts of the Apostles" (as he does, e.g., in *Miscellanies* [*Stromata*] 5:12), and this incident is recounted in the text of Acts known today, one can positively affirm the existence of Acts before Clement's time. Other writers, as will be seen, make ostensible allusions to Acts without mentioning the work or acknowledging the existence of a quotation. Those are the most important cases, and they require scholarly investigation and debate.

4. The fullest survey of data up to Irenaeus is that of Cadbury, "The Tradition," *Beg* 2:209–64. Barrett, *Acts*, 1: 30–48, with further judgments in 2:42, is acute. See also Conzelmann, *Acts*, xxvii-xxxii and Haenchen, *Acts*, 3–14, both with judicious comments. Schneider, *Apostelgeschichte*, 1:169–76 has a full set of references, without original texts. Still valuable for its detailed analysis and caution is *The New Testament in the Apostolic Fathers*, prepared by "A Committee of the Oxford Society of Historical Theology." This book introduced the system of letter grades: A-D, representing a scale of high to low probability.

5. Those unfamiliar with ancient languages may wish to skim through this tedious and exacting discussion. (This is not to suggest that they are advised to accept my conclusions sight unseen!)

6. Irenaeus, *Against Heresies* 3.12.11: *ex sermonibus et actibus* apostolorum ("from the speeches and deeds [acts] of the apostles"); 3.13.3, *ex actibus apostolorum* ("from the deeds of the Apostles"); 3.15.1, *de actibus et doctrina apostolorum* ("Concerning the deeds and teaching of the apostles"), and *Lucae de apostolis testificatio* ("the testimony/witness of Luke about the apostles"), 3.13.3. cf. 3.15.1. From 3.3.3 one can date *Against Heresies* to the era when Eleutheros was Bishop of Rome (c. 175–189).

7. Clement *Miscellanies* (*Stromata*) 5.82. ἐν ταῖς πράξεσι τῶν ἀποστόλων ("in the Acts of the Apostles"), etc. Secure biographical data about Clement are almost totally wanting. Conjectural birth dates run c. 150–c. 160, and most posit c. 215 as the time of his death. The *Stromata* (-*eis*) follow his trilogy in time and are thus roughly dated at c. 200.

8. The author may have given Acts no title. The single word "Acts" (πράξεις) is the earliest known designation and found in the earliest mss. "Acts of the Apostles" is certainly later, for, according to Acts, Paul, its chief character, was not an apostle.

9. Tertullian entitles the work as *Acta* (rather than *Actus*) and less formally as *commentarius Lucae* (Memoirs of Luke) (*De Ieiunio* [*On Fasting*]10). The latter is an interesting generic designation, for "commentaries" were often rough-drafts. Caesar used the term for his memoirs of the Gallic Wars, as if they were diaries prepared in camp—an extravagant understatement.

10. For the use of the canonical Acts in these Christian Apocrypha, see the essays of D. MacDonald, R. Pervo, R. Stoops, J. Hills, R. Bauckham, D. Marguerat, C. M. Thomas, C. R. Matthews, And F. S. Jones in R. Stoops, Ed.,*The Apocryphal Acts of the Apostles in Intertextual Perspectives*. If the *Epistle of the Apostles* does not use Acts, it must make use of an *Acts of Paul*, possibly both. Those interested in learning something about these texts should begin with W. Schneemelcher, ed., *New Testament Apocrypha*. Vol. 2.

11. *Pastoral Epistles*, 4. In his commentary on Acts Conzelmann himself says, "It is doubtful that the pastoral Epistles show knowledge of Acts." (xxvii).

12. Ceslas Spicq's eye for pathos surpasses that of the Pastor. His proposal that Timothy really ought to have participated in the stoning of Paul (Acts 14:19–20) and that he may have seen his mother and grandmother care for the injured missionary is a fine bit of romance, *Les épitres pastorales*, 2:782.

13. D. R. MacDonald, *The Legend and the Apostle: The Battle for Paul in Story and Canon*. On 2 Tim 3:11 and Acts see p. 61.

14. R. Bauckham, "The Acts of Paul as a Sequel to Acts," 105–152, 122–130.

15. See also pp. 97, 203. On the difficulties of translating this word see Loveday Alexander, *The Preface to Luke's Gospel*, 127–30.

16. BDAG 767, 3.

17. The phrase in brackets is a marginal gloss inserted in the margins of two Greek mss (K, 181) and one Syriac ms. (Harclean, which often preserves D-text readings).

18. See Barrett, *Acts* 1:34, and Conzelmann, *Acts* xxvii.

19. See also Haenchen, *Acts*, 5.

20. *Introduction*, 2:314.

21. Joseph B. Lightfoot, *The Apostolic Fathers* Part Two Volume 3, 323; F. X. Funk and K. Bihlmeyer, *Die Apostolischen Väter*, 244.

22. Haenchen, 6, calls the resemblance "strikingly close," Conzelmann treats it under formal parallels, xxix, followed evidently, by Bruce, *Acts* 10, while Barrett is cautious and not fully committal, referring to ". . . [A] somewhat stronger case . . . [that] may supply a terminus ante quem for Acts" (*Acts*, 1:36). Fitzmyer, *Acts*, 256, is non-committal.

23. I accept the hypothesis that *Philippians* combines earlier (ch. 13, possibly 14) and later (c. 135) correspondence. For Polycarp's use of 1 Peter see Paul J. Achtemeier, *1 Peter*, 44–45, who is rigorous but concludes that acquaintance is "probable." J. H. Elliott says that use is clear, *I Peter*, 143.

24. Polycarp *Phil* 9.2 contains the famous "*sicut Paulus docet*," ("As Paul teaches") after 1 Cor 4:17, transformed from first to third person. "Paul" evidently refers to an edition of the letters, i.e., a book.

25. P. V. M. Benecke, principal author of the chapter on Polycarp in *The New Testament in the Apostolic Fathers*, 83, judges that "In his undoubted quotations from N. T. we find that, while collections of words are sometimes repeated exactly, in longer passages the order is treated very freely, omissions occur for which no reason can be assigned, and the spirit rather than the actual words is sometimes reproduced. The quotations have the appearance of having been made from memory; rarely, if ever, from a book." *Phil* 1:2 receives a "C" ranking, indicating a "lower degree of probability" (on a scale of A-D), 98.

26. J. B. Lightfoot, *The Apostolic Fathers*, Part Two: 3:323. Hennig Paulsen, in his revision of W. Bauer is perhaps a bit more cautious: ". . . *erinnert an Apg 2, 24* . . ."("Alludes to/reminiscent of Acts 2:24"), (*Die Briefe des Ignatius von Antiochia und der Brief des Polykarp von Smyrna*, 114).

27. On the creedal formula see below.

28. That the reading may be secondary (it appears to assimilate to vv. 27 and 31, where "Hades" is a place) is immaterial.

29. All comments about Polycarp's usage should be qualified by the time-span involved in the two letters, the brevity of this epistle, possible changes introduced by editors, and the fact that only 8+ of 14 short chapters are extant in Greek.

30. The Hebrew alphabet does not, by and large, mark vowels. Points to indicate vocalization were added in late antiquity. (Wrtng wtht vwls s brly pssbl n nglsh. *Wrd*, for example, could be read as "word," "weird," "wired," or "ward," though the solution is very often obvious.)

31. The English translations, given for convenience, are based upon the Hebrew text, which is often at considerable variance from the LXX, which was "the Bible" of early Christians.

32. This is from the Thanksgiving Hymns of the Dead Sea Scrolls, trans. G. Vermes, *The Complete Dead Sea Scrolls in English*, 259. (In earlier editions col. XI was col. III.)

33. Thus C. C. Torrey, *The Composition and Date of Acts*, 28–29, who says "Luke had before him the words *atym yd aylbj arc*, 'loosing the bands of death.'" Cadbury and Lake (*Beg.* 4:23) and Haenchen (*Acts*, 180 n.14) reject this proposal.

34. A second objection is that Acts 2:24b is almost certainly Lucan. The notion of "impossibility" implies "necessity," resonating with the theme of a divine plan introduced in v.23. Furthermore, 24b prepares for the subsequent citation. See below and Richard F. Zehnle, *Peter's Pentecost Discourse*, 34.

35. BDAG 607B. One of these, Aelian *The Nature of Animals*. 12.5, raises questions about the incompetence of the LXX translators: καθημένης δὲ ἐπ᾽ ὠδῖσι τῆς Ἀλκμήνης καὶ τεκεῖν οὐ δυναμένης, τὴν δὲ παραδραμεῖν καὶ τοὺς τῶν ὠδίνων λῦσαι δεσμούς. ὠδίνες may have come to contain the idea of "bonds," perhaps from the "arresting" effect of severe pain. See also the references in Lampe, *s.v.* λύω, 817 B3e, and ὠδίν, 1555, 1B. In

these later writers the phrase is a metonymy for "be born," "give birth." J. Jervell is also hesitant to declare "pangs" an error, *Die Apostelgeschichte*, 146.

36. ὠδίν, κ.τ.λ., *TDNT* 9:667–74, 673. He is followed by W. Radl, EDNT 3:506.

37. "Messianic Woes" are the various tribulations and disasters associated with the end of the world.

38. Barrett, *Acts*, 1:143–44.

39. So Cadbury, Haenchen, Barrett, *et al.* Although Haenchen waves off any link to Col 1:18 ("Firstborn from the dead"), the Greek patristic tradition happily followed this path, especially the Cappadocians. See, for example: Greg. Nyssa, *Con. Eunomium* 3.2.50, Theodoret, *Eranistes* (PG) 261.32, and also his *De Sancta Trin.* 75, and *De Incarnatione* 75, as well as Basil, *Theol. Or.* 31.1684. Schneider says, not without justice, that one cannot be certain of Luke's understanding of the phrase, *Apostelgeschichte* 1:272. In n.77 he considers that Luke may have understood the term in the general sense of "pain" (*Schmerzen*).

40. Acts 3:15; 4:10; 5:30; 10:38–39; 13:33

41. This is a prominent "Peter-Paul parallel."

42. Note that Luke eliminates the final clause of Mark 13:8: ἀρχὴ ὠδίνων ταῦτα.

43. *Apostelgeschichte*, 146. ". . . [V]ersteht die Septuaginta `die Wehen des Todes' als einen geheimnissvollen Ausdruck für die Macht des Todes. Wir haben keine Vorstellung von Christus als vom Tode geboren, denn Gott ist immer der handelnde; Gott hat die Macht des Todes durch die Auferstehung gebrochen, wonach also der Tod mythologisch als Macht verstanden ist . . ."

44. 1 Cor 15:55.

45. On this subject see Susan R. Garrett, *The Demise of the Devil.*

46. So Haenchen, *Acts*, 6; Conzelmann, *Acts*, xxviii-xxix, 20 (with references), Bruce, *Acts*, 10; cf. Barrett, *Acts*, 1:143. The use of relative clauses has been acknowledged as a mark of creedal hymns and kerygmatic formulae since E. Norden's *Agnostos Theos*, 168–76; 201–07. See also L. Schenke, "Die Kontrastformel Apg 4,10b."

47. Haenchen, *Acts*, 6 (". . . [A]n old kerygmatic formula, liturgically amplified."), E. Plümacher, *Lukas als hellenistischer*, 42. "Christ" could have been the subject of the participle.

48. Extant liturgies prefer πατήσας τὸν θάνατον, as in the Liturgy of St. Gregory (PG) 36.724.4–11 For examples of later use see n. 19. (This is, in various forms, the most ecumenical of all Christian Eucharistic Prayers in use. The version in the American *Book of Common Prayer* (1979) reads ". . . [R]ising from the grave, destroyed death, and made the whole creation new" (374).

49. One would think than an opponent of Marcion who admired Paul would have found more than a little useful material in Acts.

50. "Overwhelming evidence" would involve the use of a phrase that is characteristic of Acts, in thought, wording, and form, or at least two of the three.

51. In a recent study of the subject (*Polycarp and the New Testament*, 185) Paul Hartog concludes: "In the final analysis, it appears that Polycarp probably uses Matthew, and perhaps Luke and Acts as well."

52. Papias, *Frag.* 3 relates a different story of the death of Judas from that in Acts (or Matthew). *Frag.* 11.3, unlike Acts 12:2 (but like Mark 10:35–40) states that John the Evangelist and his brother James were killed by the Jews.

53. See W. Schoedel, "Papias," ABD 5:192–95, P. L. Trudinger, "Papias," *Dictionary of Biblical Interpretation*, 2:234–235, and R. Heard, "Papias' Quotations from the New Testament."

54. See the comments of Barrett, *Acts*, 2:lxiv.

55. By tradition the apology of Justin is divided into two works. Current scholarship views the second apology as an appendix to the main work. Citations here follow the conventional division.

56. Scholars use the verb "know" somewhat loosely in this context. It is, of course, all but impossible to prove that someone had never seen or even heard of a particular text. Since Justin does not refer to Acts, the question is whether he had read it in whole or part.

57. So Talbert, *Reading*, 1. Haenchen, *Acts*, 8. Bruce says (*Acts* 11) that this is a summary of Acts 1:1–9. Conzelmann, *Acts*, xxx, is not fully committal, while Barrett, *Acts*, 41–44, seems dubious.

58. Trans. E. R. Hardy, *Early Christian Fathers*, 1953), 274.

59. This follows the D-text, which is preferable here. See M. C. Parsons, *The Departure of Jesus in Luke-Acts*, 29–52.

60. Luke 24:26; 44–46; Acts 3:18; 17:3.

61. Note καὶ εἰς πᾶν γένος ἀνθρωπών, which reverberates with Luke 24:47. See also Justin *1 Apology* 39.3. Irenaeus, *Against Heresies* 3.1.1 is like Justin and may be dependent upon him. The view of these authors has more in common with the idea of the "Apostolic Lottery," as found at the beginning of the *Acts of Thomas* and the *Acts of Andrew and Matthias*, and generally presumed in much early Christian popular thought. See Walter Bauer, "Accounts," in Hennecke-Schneemelcher *New Testament Apocrypha* 2:43–44. (This is not the current edition of "Schneemelcher.") By the time of Eusebius (*Ecclesiastical History* 3.1) this division of the world into specific territories was an accepted fact.

62. "Magus" has effectively become this Simon's last name. The term is pejorative here.

63. This is an egregious historical error. Justin seems to identify Simon with a Sabine god Semo Sancus. An inscription to this god, *Semoni Sanco Deo*, was discovered on an island in the Tiber in the sixteenth century. See L. W. Barnard, *St. Justin Martyr*, 136 n.181 on this statue.

64. Justin would not wish to mention, just here, that women also traveled with Jesus (Luke 8:1–3, etc.) and that he was befriended by a prostitute (Luke 7:36–50).

65. Justin *1 Apol* 26, trans. Hardy (*alt.*), 274. See also 56. One may contrast Irenaeus on this subject: *Against Heresies* 2.32.3. Irenaeus knew Acts.

66. For observations on this material see Pierre Nautin, *Lettres et écrivains chrétiens des IIe et IIIe siècles*, 13–22.

67. Διονύσιος ὁ Ἀρεοπαγίτης ὑπὸ τοῦ ἀποστόλου Παύλου προτραπεὶς ἐπὶ τὴν πίστιν κατὰ τὰ ἐν ταῖς Πράξεσιν δεδηλωμένα, πρῶτος Ἀθήνσι παροικίας τὴν ἐπισκοπὴν ἐγκεχείρωτο. Trans. K. Lake in *Eusebius Ecclesiastical History*, LCL 1:379.

68. In any case he evidently referred to the illustrious founding bishop. Was this a tradition independent of Acts? Another possibility is that the information came from the *Acts of Paul* and that Eusebius mentions "the Acts" without adding, as he usually does, the name Luke.

69. Eusebius, *Ecclesiastical History*, 5.1–2.5 (=Musurillo 82.35–36): καὶ ὑπὲρ τῶν τὰ δεινὰ διατιθέντων ηὔχοντο, καθάπερ Στέφανος ὁ τέλειος μάρτυς· κύριε, μὴ στήσῃς αὐτοῖς τὴν ἁμαρτίαν ταύτην. The translation is that of Herbert Musurillo, *The Acts of the Christian Martyrs*, 83.

70. Acts 7:60: θεὶς δὲ τὰ γόνατα ἔκραξεν φωνῇ μεγάλῃ, Κύριε, μὴ στήσῃς αὐτοῖς ταύτην τὴν ἁμαρτίαν.

71. Musurillo, xxi–xxii.

72. Oskar Skarsaune, *The Proof from Prophecy*, 104–105, finds no real evidence for Justin's use of Acts in his interpretation of scripture passages.

73. Joel B. Green, "Festus," ABD 2:794–95, prefers a later date of 59. Much of his rationale depends upon the precision of Acts as an historical source. See also HJP 1:465–66 n.42 (which opts for 60).

74. On the genre See William S. Kurz, *Farewell Addresses in the New Testament*, 9–32, with a discussion of Acts 20 on pp. 33–51, and Hans-Joachim Michel, *Die Abschiedsrede des Paulus an die Kirche*, 35–72. For the use of Pauline letters in this speech see chapter four.

75. Major discussions include M. D. Goulder, *Type and History in Acts*, C. Talbert, *Literary Patterns, Theological Themes, and the Genre of Luke-Acts*, W. Radl, *Paulus und Jesus im Lucanischen Doppelwerk*, and G. R. Jacobson, "Paul in Luke-Acts: The Savior Who Is Present." Note also the useful cautions in S. M. Praeder, "Jesus-Paul, Peter-Paul, and Jesus-Peter Parallelisms."

76. Traditions of more or less simultaneous martyrdoms of Peter and Paul serve the cause of church unity rather than of sober history. For a relatively recent examination of the historical and legendary material see W. Tajra, *The Martyrdom of St. Paul*.

77. See p. 11–12.

78. See also Chapter Eight.

79. For a detailed study of Justin's gospel material see Helmut Koester, *Ancient Christian Gospels*, 360–402. In *The Theology of Acts in Its Historical Setting*, 28–43. J. C. O'Neill attempts to demonstrate that Justin did not know the Gospel of Luke.

80. Substantial uncertainty and considerable debate about the temporal range of Marcion's activity exist. See Appendix III.

81. A. v. Harnack, *Marcion: Das Evangelium vom fremden Gott*, 73 n.2, 155*–156*. Barrett revisits Harnack's observation in support of his view of Acts (*Acts* 2.lxvii-lxviii): In Marcion's time Acts ". . . was thought of not as a part of the NT as this, consisting of gospels and epistles, was gradually coming into being; it served rather as an introduction to the new collection." I view this notion that an authoritative collection of Christian texts existed c. 140–150 as highly anachronistic.

82. The statements of Tertullian about the non-reception or repudiation of Acts by the Marcionites (*Prescription of Heretics*, 22; *Against Marcion*, 5.2) are not good evidence for the views of Marcion himself.

83. Justin does not refer to individual gospels by name.

84. At one time it was popular to speak of a profound silence about Paul in orthodox circles from c. 140–180. C. K. Barrett endorses the idea that Acts was long neglected. See p. 205.

85. For further comments on the early readership of Acts see p. 16.

86. "Subsidiary Points," *Beg.* 2:358. In 1966 Hans Conzelmann could say ". . . [W]ith regard to date we are not yet beyond the summary given by H. J. Cadbury." ("Luke's Place in the Development of Early Christianity."

87. See, for example, D. R. MacDonald, *The Homeric Epics and the Gospel of Mark*, 8–9. MacDonald there speaks of "mimesis," imitation of one text or author by another, but the criteria apply to all arguments involving intertextual relationships.

88. The term "jargon" is not demeaning. These terms leave room for a more elastic environment than the mechanical "source" and "principle text" often imply.

89. In the case of the Septuagint there is no doubt that it was accessible to the writer of Acts, and few would claim that Mark does not precede Luke. The qualification applies to the *Antiquities* of Josephus and a collection of Pauline letters, both of which appeared later than the conventional date of (Luke and) Acts.

Chapter Three
Acts among the Prophets, Apostles and Evangelists

1. This book does not intend to identify every possible source of Acts. The focus is upon those that help to illuminate its date, with subsidiary attention to sources that bear upon the question of historical data or records available to Luke. One example of a highly likely source (however extensive) that will not be treated in detail is the Homeric epics, written in the second half of the eighth century BCE. In addition, Luke may well have utilized the Jewish historian Artapanus, who wrote in the third or second century BCE, but that case will not be argued here.

2. The term "LXX" derives from a legend that the Torah (Genesis through Deuteronomy) was the product of a translation committee of seventy or seventy-two persons. Nothing like a uniform edition of the Greek "Old Testament" exists, however, for some works appear in quite divergent editions, the number of books varies in lists and mss., and the corpus emerged over more than two centuries. None of the books of the LXX cited or used in Acts is later than 50 CE, however, and the vast majority, if not all, appeared before the common era. For an excellent review of Septuagint studies with substantial bibliography, see Melvin K. H. Peters, "Septuagint," ABD 5, 1093–1104.

3. W. K. L. Clarke lists five "exact quotations," seven exhibiting "substantial agreement," and sixteen "free versions of the LXX" ("The Use of the LXX in Acts,"). The last group may be marked by quotation formulas, as in 1:20 and 2:16–21.

4. The authoritative study from the perspective of Greco-Roman literary culture of Luke as an imitator of the LXX is Eckhard Plümacher, *Lukas als hellenistischer Schriftsteller*, 48–72.

5. At times scholars use the Latin translation of this term, *imitatio*.

6. Consider, for example, the deeply set notion in the U.S. that "Gothic" is the proper style for ecclesiastical architecture and the preference for Greco-Roman "classicism" in public buildings. These styles arose in eras of mimesis (the eighteenth century classical revival and the Gothic revival of the nineteenth) but took on lives of their own, so that few American citizens would remark upon the presence of a courthouse that looked like a Greek temple or marvel that a Methodist Church in the downtown area of a Midwestern

U.S. city has been modeled upon a Gothic cathedral very much like the English edifices from which John Wesley was often excluded.

7. Ancient discussions, which are not devoid of psychological and pedagogical insight, include the *Controversies* of the Elder Seneca, the "Younger" Seneca's *Epistle* 114, and Quintillian *Institutes*, e.g., 10.2. Thomas L. Brodie has made a good general survey oriented toward Luke and Acts, "Greco-Roman Imitation of Texts as a Partial Guide to Luke's Use of Sources.". For a general survey see the various essays in Dennis R. MacDonald, ed., *Mimesis and Intertextuality in Antiquity and Christianity*.

8. Two comments: educated Greeks would view taking the LXX as a model for imitation as a cultural disaster, for its style was often "barbarous." Proper mimesis demanded that one rewrite the LXX in good style. This is what Josephus does in the first thirteen books of his *Antiquities*, as exhibited in table 1.1. Secondly, the practice is by no means restricted to the Greek and Latin spheres, for Jewish writers produced any number of "stylistically improved" texts like *Jubilees* and the so-called *Biblical Antiquities* of Pseudo-Philo. One survey is Daniel Harrington, "The Bible Rewritten," in R. Kraft, G. Nickelsburg, eds., *Early Judaism and its Modern Interpreters*, 239–47, bibliography 255–58.

9. Clarke, "Use of the LXX," 100.

10. So, for example, Thomas L. Brodie, "Luke the Literary Interpreter: Luke-Acts as a Systematic Rewriting and Updating of the Elijah-Elisha Narrative in 1 and 2 Kings," (Diss. Pontifical University of St. Thomas Aquinas, 1981), elements of which have appeared in a number of journal articles. The following pages will provide some examples of his hypotheses.

11. Examples of this quotation formula are Matthew 1:22; 2:5, 15, 17, 23; 3:3; 4:14; 8:17; 12:17; 13:14,35; 21:4; 26:56; 27:9.

12. See R. Pervo, *Profit with Delight*, 65–66, and *Luke's Story of Paul*, 72.

13. The NRSV is acceptable, but euphemistic, in its rendition of ἐπέπεσεν αὐτῷ καὶ συμπεριβαλών. My alteration intends to highlight the parallel.

14. The statement is disputed. Barrett (*Acts* 2:xxvi) says: "*We* continues up to the Christian supper in v. 8, drops out in the story of Eutychus, and is resumed when the voyage is taken up again in v. 13. Does this mean that the miracle story of the raising of Eutychus was drawn from a different source, perhaps not an eye-witness source, a less trustworthy source? It may be so."

15. Dibelius, *Studies*, 17–19.

16. Dennis R. MacDonald, "Luke's Eutychus and Homer's Elpenor: Acts 20:7–12 and *Odyssey*, 10–12."

17. Dibelius, *Studies*, 18.

18. Although he does not say so, I suspect that Dibelius consigned Acts 20:7–12 to the *profan* ("secular") because it lacks several typical features of a biblical resurrection story. One item found in these stories is retardation (see e.g., Mark 5:21–43; John 11:1–44). Acts looks like a sophisticated variant of this. Paul does not raise suspense by stopping for another healing, as in Mark, or in delaying for a few days, as in John, but the narrator leaves the reader in suspense by failing to give an immediate report of the good news in its entirety. Many aspects of 20:7–12 incline one toward viewing it as essentially Lucan composition.

19. See Luke 4:26.

20. 2 Kings 4:34: "Then he got up on the bed and lay upon the child, putting his mouth upon his mouth, his eyes upon his eyes, and his hands upon his hands; and while he lay bent over him, the flesh of the child became warm." This act, more detailed than the description of 1 Kings 17:21, has in its background a kind of "sympathetic magic" in which life is restored by mimicking the action (sexual intercourse) through which it is created. See R. Merkelbach, *Roman und Mysterium*, 86. Bruce, who notes the Elijah/Elisha parallels asks, "Is a form of artificial respiration implied?" (*Acts*, 426). This risible anachronism only supports the history-of-religions interpretation ("sympathetic magic.").

21. For details of the Greek text see Barrett, *Acts* 2: 954–55.

22. See n.20.

23. On Acts 9:38–41 see also p. 218–20.

24. Acts 9:37 and 1 Kings 17:19, 40 and 2 Kings 4:33, 35.

25. So T. L. Brodie, "Towards Unravelling Luke's Uses of the Old Testament: Luke 7:11–17 as *imitatio* of 1 Kgs 17:17–24."

26. Gerd Lüdemann, who is not unwilling to find historical traditions and sources, believes that Luke has used a "secular" source (*Early Christianity*, 221–25). In effect, both Dibelius and Lüdemann provide support for MacDonald's hypothesis, i.e., a "secular" source.

27. See R. Pervo, *Luke's Story*, 72, and L. T. Johnson, *The Acts of the Apostles*, 358.

28. Haenchen, *Acts*, 315. The preceding sentence clarifies "Hellenistic" as ". . . [T]he account which the *Hellenists* handed down . . ."

29. Haenchen, *Acts*, 316. His primary criterion is that of popular miracle-mongering, which he found prevalent in the story of Philip in Samaria and absent in the case of the eunuch. This is a flimsy criterion, but he is right about the differences in style, form, tone, and goal.

30. For examples see C. Martin, "A Chamberlain's Journey and the Challenge of Interpretation for Liberation." A sense of the idealization of Ethiopians, general in Greek poetry since Homer, justifies the setting of Heliodorus's *Ethiopian Story*, one of the most famous, admired, and influential of ancient Greek novels. On the concept of Ethiopia as "the ends of the earth" in the Greco-Roman world, see, for example, James S. Romm, *The Edges of the Earth in Ancient Thought*, 45–60.

31. Beverly R. Gaventa has a good general review of this passage in *From Darkness to Light*, 98–107. The most substantial study of Philip published in English is F. Scott Spencer, *The Portrait of Philip in Acts*. On the passage at hand, see C. R. Matthews, *Philip: Apostle and Evangelist*, 71–90.

32. Joseph Grassi, "Emmaus Revisited (Luke 24, 13–35 and Acts 8:26–40)." See also Witherington, *Acts*, 292.

33. Acts 8:37 is an interpolation that makes the story conform to liturgical practice (believers make a confession of faith at the time of baptism).

34. Of course, composition does not preclude the use of sources. Behind Luke 24:13–35 and John 21:1–14 may be a story about eucharistic recognition. (Note that Luke uses the theme of the miraculous catch in 5:1–11—although John 21 [a later appendix to John] may be written with Luke in mind.) See R. J. Dillon, *From Eyewitnesses to Ministers of the Word*, 69–155; H. D. Betz, "The Origin and Nature of Christian Faith according to the Emmaus Legend (Luke 24:13–32),"), 32–46; A. A. Just, *The Ongoing Feast: Table Fellowship and Eschatology at Emmaus.* ; and G.F. Nuttall, *Moment of Recognition: Luke as Story-Teller.*

35. Verses 30–31. On the quality of the Greek see, Haenchen, *Acts*, 311 and Barrett, *Acts*, 1:428, with the references of each.

36. Even a cursory examination of the Fourth Servant Song (Isa 52:13–53:12) shows that Luke avoids any reference that viewed the death of Jesus as an atoning sacrifice.

37. Cf. Acts 8:4–25.

38. Haenchen, *Acts*, 315. Tannehill notes other parallels with the story of Cornelius, *Narrative Unity* 2:110–11.

39. T. L Brodie, "Toward Unraveling the Rhetorical Imitation of Sources in Acts: 2 Kgs 5 as One Component of Acts 8,9–40."

40. Barrett is straightforward: "One must ask whether a man could be found of whom all these predicates are true: he was an Ethiopian; he was a eunuch; he belonged to the ruling class of his people; he read the Bible; he went on pilgrimage to Jerusalem. He was certainly a rare bird." 1:426.

41. I have omitted Clarke's comparison of Acts 8:39 to Zeph 3:4.

42. See n.28.

43. By the late second century Irenaeus could report that the official became a missionary (*Against Heresies*. 3.12.8). Cf. also Eusebius *Ecclesiastical History* 2.2.13–14.

44. The most thoroughly redaction-critical study of this unit to date is that of Alfons Weiser, *Die Apostelgeschichte*, 1:208–11 who identifies twelve redactional features. Lüdemann, *Early Christianity*, 104–5, extracts these elements: 27b "an Ethiopian, a eunuch;" v. 38, both descend into water; Ethiopian baptized; v. 39 "When they came up out of the water, the Spirit of the Lord snatched Philip away; the eunuch saw him no more. " This is enough, in his view, to identify the passage as a "conversion story." But v. 39, as argued, has nothing to do with a "conversion story." Its proper home is at the conclusion of an epiphany. (cf. Mark 9:8, where the awkward construction reveals an original story ending with "they saw no one," and Luke 24:31. Note also εὑρέθη [was/ was found] in Luke 9:36 and Acts 8:40).

45. Reflection upon the influence of the LXX has become much more methodologically sophisticated since the time of Clarke's essay (1922), and Luke and Acts have been subjected to detailed scrutiny. Examples of a range of approaches include David P. Moessner, *Lord of the Banquet: The literary and Theological Significance of the Lucan Travel Narrative*; C. A. Evans and J. A. Sanders, *Luke and Scripture*; and Robert L. Brawley: *Text to Text Pours Forth Speech: Voices of Scripture in Luke-Acts*.

46. See pp. 185–86.

47. Erich Klostermann (*Das Lukasevangelium*, 204), notes both a conflict with v. 32 and possible christological objections, with a reference to Acts 1:7. One possible "christological" issue is the ignorance of "the Son." J. M. Creed suggested that the omission may reflect that concern, with reference to Acts 1:7 (*The Gospel according to St. Luke*, 258). The question of the possible ignorance of the Son is made more acute by the Q passage, Luke 10:21–22: "All things have been given me by my Father." L. T. Johnson simply notes that Luke eliminates this ignorance (*Luke*, 328. For Conzelmann the Son knows, but we are not to know. See *the Theology of St. Luke*, 131 and 179, with the relevant notes (which refer to Acts 1:7). John Nolland (*Luke 3* 18:35–24:53,1010) states: "Luke makes no use of Mark 13:32. Acts 1:7 may be in his eyes some kind of an equivalent. In any case Luke is likely to feel that Mark 13:32 could only detract from the force that he intends for the preceding verse." This is intelligent.

48. Lake and Cadbury pose this as a question, answered affirmatively in the next sentence (*Beg.* 4: 8). F.F. Bruce refers to Mark, ". . . Which has (significantly) no parallel in Luke 21:29–36, (*Acts* 102). Ernst Haenchen is quite definite: "For this purpose Luke makes use of a logion which he had not taken from Mark into his own gospel but had saved for this passage," *Acts*, 143. Gerhard Schneider is also quite certain, *Apostelgeschichte* 1:202. C.K. Barrett, *Acts* 1:76, views 1:7 as "parallel" to Mark 13:32. On the text see B. M. Metzger, *Textual Commentary*, 243–44.

49. Cf. 1 Thess 5:11 and Schneider, *Apostelgeschichte* 1:202.

50. Some witnesses to Matthew 24:36 and Mark 13:32 also eliminate "not even the son." This is harmonization based upon theological presuppositions.

51. For a similar case contrast Mark 3:27 with Luke 11:21–22.

52. By "tradition" here I mean essentially oral tradition, rather than written "traditions." R. W. Funk provides a literary and theoretical explanation and justification for this assertion about summary and source in his *The Poetics of Biblical Narrative*, 50–52.

53. So, for example, Karl Ludwig Schmidt, *Der Rahmen der Geschichte Jesu*, 105.

54. Mark 1:21–34 is the premier example. Vv. 21–28 report an exorcism, while 29–31 describe a healing. The summary in 32–34 speaks of numerous examples of each. Readers do not require further descriptions to imagine what took place. It is important to note that from the literary perspective such descriptions would be boring.

55. Cadbury's comments may be found in *Beg.* 4:55 (cited above), and in his note on "The Summaries in Acts," *Beg.* 5, 392–402), especially 399, from which the quote is taken. Gerd Lüdemann is blunt: "Verse 15a-b corresponds to Mark 6.56, a passage which the author passes over in the gospel of Luke and inserts." (*Early Christianity*, 67).

56. The term occurs four times in Mark 2:1–12, but not in the parallels (Matthew 9:1–8; Luke 5:17–26), and in 6:55 (but not Matthew 14:34). For Acts see also 9:33.

57. Mark 6:56, incidentally, indicates that the original text of Mark mentioned a fringe, and thus abolishes one of the "minor agreements" of Matthew (9:21) and Luke (8:44).

58. Other instances of healing cloth are Plutarch, *Sulla* 35.3–5 and Athenaeus, *Deipnosophistae*, 5.212F. Note also the mantle of Elijah: 2 Kings 2:8 (and 19:19). Ben Witherington hastens to note that narrator does not claim that "Paul traded in healing handkerchiefs or the like, or that he initiated such practices." *Acts*, 578.

59. The particle is found in this sense only in Mark 5:28; 6:56, Acts 5:15, and 2 Cor 11:16. See BDAG 507.

60. Therein lies, as stated above, the purpose of such summaries.

61. For those requiring reassurance, the D-text makes the matter perfectly clear.

62. C.K. Barrett, *Acts*, 1:276.

63. On this subject see H.D. Betz, *Lukian von Samosata und das Neue Testament*, 151, n.7 and Pieter van der Horst, "Peter's Shadow: The Religio-Historical Background of Acts V.15.". Key parallel passages are quoted by Barrett, *Acts* 1:276–77.

64. Haenchen, *Acts*, 246. Barrett (*Acts* 1:276–77) follows Schneider in affirming that

Haenchen's criticism does not recognize that God is the source of all miraculous power. This sound notion does not quite remove the difficulties of charismatic power that flows without any perceptible human or divine control.

65. The similarity between Acts 5:12–16 and 19:11–12 is not merely formal. Just as the former epitomizes the apex of the mission to Jews in Jerusalem, so does the latter express the high point of Paul's mission to gentiles.

66. If correct, this conclusion would provide some evidence against the hypothesis that the "Great Omission" of Luke is due to the absence of 6:45–8:26 from his edition of Mark. Helmut Koester, *Ancient Christian Gospels*, 284–286, hypothesizes that this material was not an original part of Mark and not in the edition of Mark used by Luke. More substantial though less specific evidence can be seen in the apparent use of Mark 7:1–23 (ritual purity) in Acts 10:1–11:18.

67. So *Beg.* 4:69, and Lüdemann, *Early Christianity*, 81, among others. The latter observes that, presuming the dependence, "[I]t is important to note that Luke did not take up the second part of the false witness in Mark 14.58 . . . Luke is probably deliberately avoiding any statement about the rebuilding of the temple, as he is writing after its destruction." On this passage see also pp. 37–41.

68. On this passage see also pp. 37–41.

69. The "Messianic Secret" is a much-discussed feature of Mark's tendency to portray Jesus as rejecting public disclosure of his status and avoiding publicity based upon miracles. Christopher Tuckett has produced a collection of the classical issues in *The Messianic Secret*

70. Barrett, *Acts*, 1:485, with a review of opinions.

71. Ταβιθα W a r¹; Θαβιτα D; *tabea* e.

72. Note also Acts 13:9: πλησθεὶς πνεύματος ἁγίου ("full of holy spirit") and 10: τὰς ὁδους τοῦ κυρίου ("the ways of the Lord"). The former echoes Luke 4:1, 14. The latter evokes Luke 3:4. For another connection between Mark 1:21–28 see below. On Acts 13:6–12 see also pp. 98, 186.

73. Others could be mentioned. Acts 28:7–10 represents a "new beginning," as it were, of Paul's ministry, with a healing parallel to that of Peter's mother-in-law (Mark 1:29–31; Luke 4:38–39. Acts uses the verb κατάκειμαι ("lie"), which is found in Mark 1:30 and Acts 28:8, but not at Luke 4:38. (Similarly, this verb occurs with κράβαττος ["mat"] only in Mark 2:4 and Acts 9:33.)

74. Drusilla, too, had been previously married, although there is no reason to expect that the implied reader of Acts would know that. ("Frequentative imperfects" refers to one sense of the Greek imperfect tense: repeated or habitual action. If one translated the sentence "While I lived in Lafayette I studied on Saturdays" into Greek, "studied" would be in the imperfect tense. A contrast would be "I studied last Saturday." In Greek this would call for the aorist tense.)

75. The addition in v. 24, included in the translation, is found only in a marginal gloss of the Harclean edition of the Syriac text. The alternate in v. 27 is found there and also in the Greek mss. 614 and 2147. See also R. B. Rackham, *The Acts of the Apostles*, 451

76. For Luke's purpose in constructing this unit see R. Pervo, *Profit*, 77–81.

77. According to Josephus, *Antiquities* 20.143 Drusilla's marriage to Felix was a violation of "the ancestral laws." Felix did not convert to Judaism. Chapter Five will explore the possibility that Luke made use of Josephus in his portrait of Drusilla.

78. See also above.

79. On this usage see Haenchen, *Acts*, 495, G. Bertram, ὕψος, κ.τ.λ., *TDNT* 8:602–20, 614–20, and C. Breytenbach, "Hypsistos," *DDD* 439–43.

80. G. Lüdemann says "The healing story goes back to tradition," *Early Christianity*, 182. His only grounds for this claim is that behind Acts 16:16–18 there "might have been a complete story of an exorcism." He has done no more than to isolate a hypothetical form. That this account has formal elements proves only that Luke was familiar with the conventional features of an exorcism narrative.

81. The verb is used in the (false) charges against Jesus, Luke 23:5. Note also 1 *Clement* 46:9; 47:5.

82. Simon (Acts 8:4–25), the aforementioned Elymas (13:6–12), and the sons of Sceva (19:13–17) show the limits of deceiving prophets in the matter of miracles.

83. On Acts 20:29–30 see pp. 316–17.

84. On the use of Mark 12 here see Lars Aejmelaeus *Die Rezeption der Paulusbriefe in der*

Miletrede (APG 20:18–35), 142–148.

85. On this passage see also pp. 316–17.

86. For the view that Acts 12:4 derives from Mark see *Beg.* 4:134.

87. Cf. also Luke 20:19.

88. See pp. 278–80.

89. There are also a number of brief points of contact. Acts 8:7 is close to such Markan summaries of healings and exorcisms as Mark 1:33–34. Acts 8:39 (discussed above) probably derives from Mark 9:8. Mark 5:39 is the source of Acts 20:10, also discussed above, since θορυβεῖσθε occurs only in these two resurrection stories. These minor parallels add a little weight but have limited effect upon larger hypotheses.

90. I omit the summaries, as there is no substantial doubt that these are, by and large, authorial compositions. The oft-noted summaries in Acts are, however, imitations of the practice first exemplified in Mark.

91. See, for example, Charles H. Talbert, *Literary Patterns*, 17.

92. Worthy of reflection is the possibility that the somewhat vague and indefinite ending of Acts might have been inspired by the quite unsettling ending of Mark. Luke, like Matthew and some later editors of Mark, found Mark 16:8 an unsatisfactory ending for a gospel. Why does the sequel—or second half—lack for some the "sense of an ending" that is so strong at the conclusion of Luke 24?

93. Also Lucan is the notion of Satanic binding of victims (v. 16). Note further the reference to Abraham in v. 16, repeated in v. 28.

94. See above.

95. For details see H. D. Betz, "The Cleansing of the Ten Lepers (Luke 17:11–19)."

96. Non-specialists are reminded that Matthew and Luke would not have had identical copies of Mark before them, for each manuscript varies in details. Most of the extant mss. of Mark are heavily "contaminated" by Matthew—and sometimes Luke. The critical text of Mark printed and translated in contemporary bibles is probably, in some degree, a later edition. On this question see H. Koester, *Early Christian Gospels*, 273–303; he has not evaded any of the problems, even if his own complex theory has not won wide acceptance.

97. For views on the sources of Acts see Appendix I.

98. Evidence of such development is not entirely lacking in the gospel. One may compare Luke 4:16–30 with its presumed source, Mark 6:1–6.

99. Heikki Leppä supports his contention that Luke used Galatians by a study of his transformation of several Markan passages: *Luke's Critical Use of Galatians*, 143–161. His reasoning is sound and his examples are well chosen. Rudolph Pesch, who has written one of the more conservative commentaries on Acts, adduces many examples of the use of Mark as one of its sources: *Die Apostelgeschichte*, 1.24–25 *et passim*.

100. Brown, *Introduction*, 164.

101. This is not based upon an assumption that such prophecies must be *vaticinia ex eventu* (predictions after the fact). Rare indeed is a total absence of prophets of doom. The operative principle is that unsuccessful historical predictions have a reduced chance for survival. People fasten upon those that were, or could be said to be, accurate. A rather typical, if unusually large, collection of portents and prophecies surrounds the last years of the Temple in Josephus *War* 6.288–315.

102. This interpretation is well and clearly stated by Werner Kelber, *The Kingdom in Mark*, especially 87–128.

103. For analysis see J. D. Crossan, *In Parables: the Challenge of the Historical Jesus* (New York: Harper and Row, 1973), 86–96. Crossan's views form the basis of Brandon Scott's interpretation: *Here Then the Parable*, 237–253. See also Crossan's *Four Other Gospels*, 53–62.

104. Thackeray translates the verb as "farm out," with a note on the meaning (*Josephus III*), 567, but "sell" is much more likely. See LSJ *s.v.*, and Martin Goodman, who refers to an article of B. Isaac, n.2 for his contention that the land ". . . [W]as confiscated by Vespasian and sold up to the highest bidder . . ." (*The Ruling Class of Judaea*, 231. Goodman observes that only by an exception was Josephus able to retain his estates (*Life* 422).

105. See E. Mary Smallwood, *The Jews under Roman Rule*, 332–341. She is skeptical about the extent to which this expropriation was applied.

106. 75 is the *earliest* date for Mark. 80 is not unlikely. A gap of five years between the composition of Mark and that of Luke, followed at some point by Acts, is certainly reasonable. I therefore prefer 80, but leave 75 as a firm terminus.

Chapter Four
Acts among the Apostles

1. For bibliography on this subject I am greatly indebted to William O. Walker, Jr.'s "Select Bibliography on the Pauline Letters as Sources for [the] Acts of the Apostles," prepared for the March, 2002 meeting of the Westar Institute's Acts Seminar. Surveys of research include Lars Aejmelaeus, *Die Rezeption der Paulusbriefe in der Miletrede (APG 20:18–35)*, 41–73; Schenk, "Luke as a Reader of Paul: Observations on his Reception," in S. Draisma, ed., *Intertextuality in Biblical Writings: Essays . . . B. van Iersel*, 127–139; Steve Walton, *Leadership and Lifestyle: The Portrait of Paul in the Miletus Speech and I Thessalonians*, 2000), 14–17; and H. Leppä, *Luke's Critical Use*, 13–32.

2. For an encomium to Ramsay see Gasque, *History of the Criticism*, 137–142 and the references at 137 n.2. (The claim that Ramsay once adhered to the views of Baur *et al.* is almost certainly an autobiographical legend. For an outline of its difficulties see *ATR* 59, [1977] 108–112.)

3. Ramsay, *St. Paul the Traveller and Roman Citizen*, 385.

4. Hemer, *Book of Acts*, 245. Notice that "essentially independent" provides a loophole. Bruce concurs with the view that Acts shows no knowledge of the letters. In his comparison of the two he concludes that the letters were not accessible to Luke (*Acts*, 43, 53). For difficulties in the view of Hemer and Bruce see Appendix I.

5. Edgar J. Goodspeed (1871–1962) proposed that the circulation of Acts (c. 90) stimulated interest in Paul, leading to the publication of his letters in a collection headed by Ephesians, which was composed for the occasion as an introductory cover letter. See his *An Introduction to the New Testament*, 191–97. C. L. Mitton has written a good, short summary of the work of the "Goodspeed School" on this problem: *The Formation of the Pauline Corpus of Letters*. John Knox gives a brief, personal summary of Goodspeed's theory and its impact in his contribution to SLA, "Acts and the Pauline Letter Corpus," 279–80. Knox's own response to Goodspeed's proposal, *Marcion and the New Testament*, 114–139, argued that Luke/Acts in its present form stems from the conflicts surrounding Marcion's use of Pauline letters, and dates to near the middle of the second century. Similarly, J. C. O'Neill, *The Theology of Acts in its Historical Setting*, 21, locates Acts between 115–130. Hemer claims the silence about Paul's letters as evidence of an early date: *Book of Acts*, 377, specifically 62, 404.

6. Christopher Mount has been willing to ask whether the assumption that Luke could not have known about Paul without knowing about the letters is due to history or if is based upon the later standing of those letters among authoritative Christian texts in the late second century: *Pauline Christianity: Luke-Acts and the Legacy of Paul*, 57 and n.206. I believe that there is sufficient evidence to answer the question with a negative: Paul and his letters go hand in hand, but it is an important question and Mount has written a valuable study.

7. The classic essay on the subject is Robert W. Funk, "The Apostolic Presence: Paul," in his *Parables and Presence: Forms of the New Testament Tradition*, 81–102 (first published in 1967).

8. *1 Clem* 5.5–7, trans. Holt Graham in R. M. Grant and H. H. Graham, *The Apostolic Fathers*, vol. 2, 25–26. Although this summary shares some features with Acts, it does not derive from Acts, which does not speak of Paul's final "witness before rulers" in Rome. Since *1 Clement* stems from Rome, it could not view that city as the "limits of the west." The text evidently assumes that Paul made the journey to Spain envisioned in Romans 15.

9. *1 Clement* certainly also knows Romans and Hebrews; 1 Peter is a possibility. See Albert E. Barnett, *Paul Becomes a Literary Influence*, 88–104.

10. For the present argument, *3 Corinthians* is probably beyond the relevant date range. *Laodiceans* almost certainly is. Eventually there were more pseudo-Pauline letters than genuine examples.

11. Lindemann advanced this argument in his *Paulus im Ältesten Christentum*, e.g., 36–49. Heikki Leppä crisply summarizes this perspective in *Luke's Critical Use*, 28.

12. Note also the letters of authorization obtained by Paul in Acts 9:2.

13. Knox, *Marcion and the New Testament*, 134–35.

14. Knox apparently had his eye upon 16:1–4, in which Paul and Silas communicate the decrees of the apostles and elders at Jerusalem to believers in the region visited in Acts 14.

But these latter were not addressees of the letter, and Luke refrains from saying that it was formally conveyed to them (Acts 15:30–31 vs. 16:4.)

15. M. S. Enslin, "Once Again, Luke and Paul," 254. Leppä ably summarizes the inadequacies of the traditional view in a section entitled "How could Luke know nothing about Paul's letters?," *Luke's Critical Use*, 20–28. Günther Klein makes no effort to hide his scorn of the idea that Luke had not heard of Paul's letters: *Die Zwölf Apostel*, 189–192.

16. Enslin first addressed the matter of dependence in "'Luke' and Paul."

17. Lars Aejimelaeus pioneered the recent undermining of the dam with his *Die Rezeption der Paulusbriefe* (1987), although Lindemann, as references will indicate, had made cautious proposals in 1979. See also W. Schenk, "Luke as a Reader of Paul: Observations on his Reception"; W. O. Walker, Jr., "Acts and the Pauline Corpus Reconsidered," 3–23; H. Leppä, *Luke's Critical Use*; and other works cited in the following pages. Leppä summarizes this scholarship on pp. 28–32.

18. Literally: "A type of thesis that requires no proof." Enslin, "Once Again," 255. The quote is from an old article of A. Sabatier, used to characterize the assumption of dependence ("L'auteur du livre des Actes des Apôtres a-t-il connu et utilize les épitres de Saint Paul," *Bibliothèque de l' École des Hautes Études, Sciences religieuses* 1, (1899) 205–229, quoting from 206. (Enslin is the source of this information.)

19. One example of each: Luke ignores Mark's story of the execution of John the Baptizer (Mark 6:17–29) and contradicts Mark's claim that the family of Jesus were not followers (Mark 3:20–21; 31–35; cf. Luke 2:51; Acts 1:14). H. Leppä uses comparisons with Luke's use of Mark to support the case for his dependence upon Galatians, *Luke's Critical Use*, 143–161.

20. "Luke the Literary Physician," 143.

21. James expresses this fear in Acts 21:18–25. In retrospect he seems to have been right.

22. This assertion derives from two factors: frequency of citation and editing. For the former see Barnett, *Paul Becomes a Literary Influence*. Different editions of Romans once existed, including at least one that omits "(at) Rome" in 1:7, 15. See H. Gamble, *The Textual History of the Letter to the Romans*, especially 29–33. The address of 1 Cor 1:2 has also been altered to make the text applicable to all believers. See G. Zuntz, *The Text of the Epistles*, 91–92 and G. Sellin, "Hauptprobleme des Ersten Korintherbriefes," *ANRW* 1.25.4, 2940–3044. Finally, Ephesians exists in manuscripts with and without an address (contrast Eph. 1:1 in RSV to NRSV) and was known to Marcion as the letter to the Laodiceans. See Ernest Best, "Recipients and Title of the Letter to the Ephesians: Why and When the Designation 'Ephesians'?" *ANRW* 2.25.4., 3247–79.

23. 1 Cor. 1:10–3:23. On Apollos see below.

24. Two good brief studies of the Deutero-Pauline letters and their worlds are J. Christiaan Beker, *Heirs of Paul: Paul's Legacy in the New Testament and in the Church Today* and Raymond F. Collins, *Letters That Paul Did Not Write*.

25. Each army lost seven thousand in less than one hour in the respective actions, 15% of those mounting the assault at Cold Harbor, 50% in Pickett's attack.

26. Lee was not opposed to slavery, nor was he a political moderate. He attributed the problems of the Democratic Party in 1860 to the failure of Stephen Douglas to withdraw in favor of John Breckinridge, who was the candidate of the breakaway minority that demanded no limitations upon the expansion of slavery.

27. American military leaders, for whom romance is undesirable, never bought this line. Consider the military strategy of the U.S. in the twentieth century. As carried out most successfully in WWII under the leadership of George C. Marshall (a graduate of the Virginia Military Institute where "Stonewall" Jackson once taught and the boys of whose cadet corps covered themselves with glory at New Market in 1864), it has been that of U. S. Grant. And William T. Sherman (whose troops did not slaughter civilians) is another founder of modern warfare, which places high priority upon the destruction of an enemy's resources and the demoralization of its public. This is an unpleasantness by any standard, but it has been the consistent policy of the U.S. in its wars since 1941. For their part, agents of the failing Confederacy likewise exhibited some of the less appealing dimensions of modern conflict, including many of the weapons of the weak, such as plans for or attempts at assassination, kidnapping, urban terrorism, biological warfare, and massacre. As is often the case with failed causes, terrorism continued for some years after the war. The best-known example is the activity of the Ku Klux Klan. Another is the post-war career of Jesse

James. In the quest for reconciliation it became expedient to regard James as a criminal with Robin Hood overtones and John Wilkes Booth as a madman acting on his own. See William A. Tidwell, *Come Retribution: The Confederate Secret Service and the Assassination of Abraham Lincoln*; Bertram Wyatt-Brown, "Anatomy of A Murder," *New York Review of Books*, 24 October 2002, 22–24; and T. J. Stiles, *Jesse James: Last Rebel of the Civil War*.

28. Edward Everett Hale published *The Man without a Country* in 1863. It dealt with an accused traitor whose wish never again to hear the words "the United States" was scrupulously honored in accordance with a judicial order.

29. For a balanced assessment of Lee, see James M. McPherson, "Lee Dissected," *New York Review of Books*, 7 November 1991, 10–14. There is an analysis of the process of revision in Stetson Kennedy, *After Appomattox: How the South Won the War*. Scholarly "correction" of the *Gone with the Wind* view of the Civil War has reached the major media (D. B. Davis, "The Enduring Legacy of the South's Civil War Victory," *New York Times*, 26 August 2001, sec. 4, "The Week in Review"; M. Singer, "Never Surrender," *The New Yorker*, 14 May 2001, 52–57; and J. M. McPherson, "Southern Comfort," *The New York Review of Books*, 12 April 2001, 28–32). Still, Jay Winik's best-seller, *April 1865*, promulgates much of the old view, absent its virulent racism. Its popularity indicates the persistence of the "revisionist history." One of Winik's heroes is R. E. Lee, who declined to convert his army into a guerilla force to avoid surrender and thereby delivered the country from the horrors of such war. One difficulty with this thesis is that hundreds of thousands of Americans (mainly former slaves) did suffer from widespread terrorism.

30. The bill for this unity was paid by the African-American ex-slaves and their descendants. Continued controversy about display of the Confederate flag is a reminder that the discussion is not over. One able recent study is David W. Blight, *Race and Reunion: The Civil War in American Memory*.

31. One defect in Luke's credentials as an historian has been his failure to learn that Paul wrote letters and to seek to discover these and report them.

32. This expression is associated with the *Horae Paulinae* (1790) of William Paley (1743–1805). Paley, a critic of Deism and of David Hume, emphasized detailed investigation of ancient sources. He held that the agreements between Paul's letters and Acts supported the traditional view of Christian origins. A recent example of this orientation is David Wenham, "Acts and the Pauline Corpus II. The Evidence of Parallels," in *Ancient Literary Setting*, 215–258. Other examples include A. Wikenhauser, *Die Apostelgeschichte und ihr Geschichtswert*, 58–62, and C. Hemer, *Book of Acts*, 181–190. Many of Hemer's examples demand tortuous exegesis. For example, he correlates Acts 9:24–25 with 2 Cor 11:33. Noting that Acts attributes the opposition to "the Jews" and Paul to the ethnarch of Aretas, he observes, "It should be unnecessary to point out the possibility that different opponents may make common cause" (182). On 187 he relates Acts 18:18 to the recommendation of Phoebe in Rom. 16:1, though the two verses share only a place name. Acts 24:17 confirms the various epistolary references to the Collection, 189. Hemer chooses to overlook Luke's failure to mention what according to the letters is the purpose for the visit. This is a representative sample. Insofar as these alleged "undesigned coincidences" do not involve special pleading (Acts 9:24–25) or outright contradiction (Acts 24:17), they are likely to juxtapose data that show no more than a tenuous link (Acts 18:18).

33. The anachronism in this instance is the projection into the ancient past of modern standards and values about historical research and practice: "There is a right way to do things. This right way has always existed (and ever shall). Historians of the modern world call this "whiggish history."

34. This is sharply posed by Lindemann: *Paulus*, 172–73.

35. Both Jackson and Lake were born and educated in the United Kingdom before accepting positions at Union and Harvard, while *Beginnings* includes contributors from several nations, but the project was conceived and executed in the U.S.

36. Post-Constantinian Christians are more likely to recall that their faith does, in fact, proclaim that God's victory took place through an emperor who had no clothes, the "crucified Messiah." ("Post-Constantinian" is theological shorthand for the situation of Christianity following the demise of "Christendom" in the wake of World War I. Since that time churches in the western world find themselves in circumstances approximating those of the period before Christianity was given a privileged status.)

37. Even if Luke knew Paul's letters as a collection, it is possible that he also had access (presumably at Ephesus) to some administrative correspondence of Paul that was not incorporated into other letters (such as 2 Cor 8–9; Phil 4:10–20,5:9). This question will reappear later in this chapter. See also Appendix I.   I Cor.

38. To note yet another apparent consensus, ". . . [T]here is broad agreement that a more or less full collection had come into existence by the late years of the first century." H. Gamble, *Books and Readers in the Early Church*, 59. For discussion of this consensus see Appendix III.

39. David Trobisch argues that the collection began at Paul's own initiative and that the first included Romans, 1–2 Corinthians, and Galatians (*Paul's Letter Collection: Tracing the Origins* His thesis is debatable, but he does make a good case for the growth of the collection.

40. See below, p. 137.

41. The public reading of church letters is assumed in Acts 15:31. 1 Thess 5:27 commands public reading of the letter. After the death of Paul the practice expanded. Col 4:16 speaks of an exchange of letters. The Colossians are to read the letter to Laodicea and see to it that the Laodiceans read the epistle directed to Colossae. By c. 80, then, and perhaps a bit earlier, believers were exchanging Paul's letters, which were therefore no longer regarded as occasional missives to people at a particular place at a certain time. Colossians demonstrates the rapid pace of the collection of Pauline letters, the composition of additional letters, and the goal of "universalizing" Paul's message.

42. This speech is quoted below.

43. Dispassionate history cannot really determine whether Luke was too dull to grasp the purpose of the Pauline doctrine of justification nor can it establish Paul's doctrine as the norm by which all others are to be evaluated. There is insufficient data for the former, while the latter depends upon theological values—which, while they have their place, cannot serve as tools for historical analysis. What the data *do* reveal is that, when Acts appeared, the circumstances in which Paul's arguments emerged were no longer applicable.

44. E. Franklin, says that such passages as this "push the Pauline doctrine back firmly into the life of Jesus," *Christ the Lord: A Study in the Purpose and Theology of Luke-Acts*, 183.

45. In his Gospel Luke happily uses and indeed prefers as ethical examples such "outsiders" as the prostitute of 7:36–50; a Samaritan in 10:25–30; the tax-collector here (18:9–14) and in 19:1–10; and for a climax, the "good criminal" on the cross beside Jesus (23:39–43). Sentimentality is a feature of the sort of popular taste that loves "wicked" people with hearts of gold. To be sure, Luke will not reduce everything to sentiment (witness Luke 9:27; 14:15; 23:28), and Acts includes no bad guys with good hearts. After the resurrection harlots and publicans disappear from the stage, to be replaced by widows, businesswomen, centurions, and Roman governors. See Cadbury, *The Making of Luke-Acts*, 255, 272.

46. Readers who think that this toll-collector could return to life as usual until his justification needed topping off will be well advised to consult Luke 19:1–10 (Zacchaeus) and 5:32 (vs. Mark 2:17). Luke may not describe justification as empowerment, but he does expect it to produce change.

47. These two examples lead one to suspect that Luke equated "justification" with "forgiveness of sins" and presumed that it was a consequence of "repentance."

48. On Luke 18 and 13 and their relation to Pauline theology see Andreas Lindemann, *Paulus*, 162–163.

49. Lindemann, *Paulus*, 162–63.

50. Cf. Phil 3:6, where the word occurs in association with the noun δικαιοσύνη, and the parallel ἐν χριστῷ in Gal 2:17.

51. This should be easily distinguishable from the use of italics to clarify quotations, as noted at the close of the Preface.

52. Origen believed that these were two separate incidents. In extracts from his work on Joshua he states, "The apostle was twice saved in a similar manner from his enemies," and quotes from both 2 Corinthians and Acts (*Selecta in Jesum Nave* 12.820.36–43). Although he was guilty here of crude harmonization, Origen was more acute than many subsequent interpreters in that he saw the difficulty of reconciling the two accounts.

53. The most recent study of the subject is Douglas A. Campbell, "An Anchor for

Pauline Chronology: Paul's Flight from 'the Ethnarch of King Aretas,' 2 Cor 11:32–33."
Other discussions about the political situation and other details include Cadbury, *Book*,
19–21 and Victor P. Furnish, *II Corinthians*, 521–523.

54. A realistic account of such an escape appears in Plutarch's life of Aemilius Paulus,
26.2. His admiral, Gnaeus Octavius, allowed the defeated Macedonian king Persius asylum
on Samothrace, but guarded against escape by sea. Perseus, however, ". . . suffered pitiful-
ly in letting himself down through a narrow window in the fortress, together with his wife
and little children, who were unacquainted with wandering and hardships. . . ." (trans.
Bernadotte Perrin, *Plutarch's Lives* VI, LCL, 423). Note also Athenaeus, *Deipnosophistae* 5.52
(from Posidonius?), describing the flight of many Athenians "down from the walls" at
night to escape from guarded gates.

55. The Roman award was the *corona militaris* (military crown).

56. R. Pervo, *Profit*, 149 n.63. (Much of the two preceding paragraphs is adopted from
pp. 30–31 of that work, to which I hold copyright.) This conjecture was probably inspired
by the argument of O. Linton, "The Third Aspect: A Neglected Point of View. A Study in
Gal. 1–22 and Acts ix and xv."

57. See also Charles Masson, "À propos de Act. 9:19b-25. Note sur l'utilisation de
Galatians et de 2 Cor. Par l'auteur des Actes," 161–166; M. Enslin, " 'Luke' and Paul," 88,
"Once Again," 265; W. Walker, "Acts and the Pauline Corpus Reconsidered," 9; Blassi,
Making Charisma: The Social Construction of Paul's Public Image, 52–53; Lindemann, *Paulus*,
155, 167; and Leppä, *Luke's Critical Use*, 82–85. An argument against dependence upon 2
Corinthians is made by C. Burchard, *Dreizehnte*, 152–53, on which see Lars Aejmelaeus, *Die
Rezeption*, 52–53.

58. In place of the homey σαργάνη, which is evidently part of the satire, Acts uses
σπυρίς, "hamper." Wilfred Knox (*The Acts of the Apostles*, 29) says that the ". . . story of the
escape from Damascus agrees almost verbatim with 2 Cor. xi.33 except that a rather more
classical σπυρίς is substituted for the Pauline σαργάνη. Luke may have read the passage
in 2 Cor, but it is equally likely that he had often heard Paul 'glorying in his infirmities.' "
The second half of this sentence is unlikely for several reasons. Beside my doubts that
Luke was an auditor of Paul, it is improbable that Paul would have "often" given such
performances. Had he done so, the oral account would almost certainly have been a good
deal more elaborate. This story is much more likely the derivative of an available written
text than a summary of an oral account that fortuitously preserves a particular structure
and word choice.

59. Jack Sanders, *The Jews in Luke-Acts*, 254, agrees that Acts 9 is dependent upon 2
Corinthians.

60. For data on the earliest attestation of 2 Corinthians see Furnish, *II Corinthians*,
29–30. Marcion knew, and prized, this letter in its present form. Polycarp knew the Pauline
corpus and his writings include a number of possible allusions to 2 Corinthians, although
none of them are certain. See also P. V. M. Benecke, *New Testament in the Apostolic Fathers*,
91. Furnish notes that Marcion's collection may well antedate Polycarp's *Philippians*.
Indeed, this seems quite probable.

61. Failure to consider such broader issues as the great utility 2 Corinthians would
have possessed for *1 Clement* is a weakness of narrowly philological projects like *The New
Testament in the Apostolic Fathers* and Barnett's *Paul Becomes a Literary Influence*. It is certainly appropriate to apply quantitative linguistic tools in a sterile environment, but research
cannot stop at that point. It is not likely that *1 Clement* would gather a single crumb from
2 Corinthians yet ignore the vast array of fresh and wholesome loaves that it provides to
sustain the argument for authority.

62. Our 2 Corinthians is a composite text based upon at least two and more probably five
pieces of Pauline correspondence and at least one non-Pauline fragment. Fundamental to
recent discussion is the contribution of G. Bornkamm, "Die Vorgeschichte des sogenannten
Zweiten Korintherbriefes,", developed by his student Dieter Georgi, *Remembering the Poor:
The History of Paul's Collection for Jerusalem*. I further developed and refined their arguments
in a paper entitled "Romans and 2 Corinthians as Early Patristic Texts," presented to the
Annual Meeting of the North American Patristics Society at Loyola University, Chicago,
Illinois, 28 May 1992. Hans Dieter Betz includes a full review of scholarship through
1984 in *2 Corinthians 8 and 9* 1985), 3–35. The standard history of research is Gerhard
Dautzenberg, "Der Zweite Korintherbrief als Briefsammlung: Zur Frage der literarischen

Einheitlichkeit und des theologischen Gefüges von 2 Kor 1–8," *ANRW* 2.25.4, (1987) 3045–66. Other implications of the composite nature of 2 Corinthians receive attention on p. 320.

63. Lindemann, *Paulus*, 167 n.130, also sees this possibility.

64. The evidence for use of other parts of 2 Cor is not strong. See pp. 116–17 for another possible reference. One possible explanation is that very little in 2 Corinthians would appeal to Luke, for on a number of important points his views approximate those of Paul's opponents. Luke has repressed the idea that Paul had to contend with opposition among fellow believers and that some of his converts rebelled against his authority. In those circumstances little of 2 Corinthians remains to work with.

65. On this passage see also p. 319.

66. See p. 194.

67. The term can mean "confinements."

68. "Imprisonments" is not identical to being placed in bonds. Acts enumerates other occasions on which Paul was apprehended or arrested, such as 17:5–10; 17:18; and 18:12 (?).

69. Section numbers of those found in W. Schneemelcher, *New Testament Apocrypha*, 2.237–70. Paul was arrested on other occasions.

70. In a lost incident that was recounted later (7) Paul baptized a lion.

71. Most early readers would have taken this catalogue at face value, as do most modern readers. Although I should not be prepared to wager that this list contains no hyperbole or invention, it is here assumed that the data are essentially "historical."

72. See p. 315.

73. 2 Cor 11:24 is a mystery for exegetes. If Paul were a missionary to the gentiles, why did he so often become embroiled with Jewish officials?

74. The term translated "thieves" in Luke 18:11 is the same as that translated "robbers" in 1 Cor 6:10.

75. See Schenk, "Luke as Reader," 133–135, who provides detailed arguments and references to scholarly opinion.

76. "Luke as Reader,"134.

77. Major discussions with bibliographical references include Bruce Metzger, *A Textual Commentary on the Greek New Testament*, 148–150, with a full display of evidence; I. Howard Marshall, *Commentary on Luke*, 799–800, with a full bibliography; and Joseph A. Fitzmyer, *The Gospel according to Luke X–XXIV*, 1387–90, with bibliography 1405–06.

78. Yet one must also introduce the matter of liturgical practice here. See, for example, the formula in Justin, *1 Apology* 66.3, which follows a discussion of the Real Presence: οἱ γὰρ ἀπόστολοι ἐν τοῖς γενομένοις ὑπ' αὐτῶν ἀπομνημονεύμασιν, ἃ καλεῖται εὐαγγέλια, οὕτως παρέδωκαν ἐντετάλθαι αὐτοῖς τὸν Ἰησοῦν λαβόντα ἄρτον εὐχαριστήσαντα εἰπεῖν τοῦτο ποιεῖτε εἰς τὴν ἀνάμνησίν μου, τοῦτ' ἐστι τὸ σῶμα μου καὶ τὸ ποτήριον ὁμοίως λαβόντα καὶ εὐχαριστήσαντα εἰπεῖν· τοῦτο ἐστι τὸ αἷμα μου· καὶ μόνοις αὐτοῖς μεταδοῦναι. For the apostles in the memoirs composed by them, which are called Gospels, thus handed down what was commanded them: that Jesus, taking bread and having given thanks, said, "Do this for my memorial, this is my body"; and likewise taking the cup and giving thanks he said, "this is my blood"; and gave it to them alone (trans. E. R. Hardy, *Early Christian Fathers*, 286). Justin attributes this to "the Gospels," but it seems to be a liturgical formula that incorporates "Marcan" and "Pauline" elements. It would be unwise to list Justin as a witness for the longer text of Luke.

79. Enslin, "Once Again," 265, is also hesitant about the longer text of Luke, but does take note of 1 Corinthians 10.

80. M. Goulder, "Did Luke Know any of the Pauline Letters?," 106. He also suggests, quite tentatively, that the treachery of Judas is moved to the end of the passage as an example of unworthy reception. *… under influence of 1 Cor. 11:27–32 ? (Lk. has*

81. The adjective occurs in a positive sense in *1 Clem* 45:1. *Judas dying by accident, not*

82. Note that the Greek text of each citation is abbreviated. *suicide.)*

83. See R. Bultmann, μεριμνάω, κ.τ.λ., *TDNT* 4:589–93, who twice links the two passages, 591 and 592.

84. For connections with the wisdom tradition see D. Zeller μέριμνα, *EDNT* 2:408; Bultmann (previous n.) canvasses the philosophical tradition.

85. Evidently, young male students in the Greco-Roman world were often assigned

essays giving arguments for and against marriage. The most famous product of this tradition is Juvenal's Sixth Satire, usually glossed "Against Women," because it is essentially an attack upon married women. (Note that Luke does not describe either Mary or Martha as married; i.e., he does not oppose Paul's views about marriage here.)

86. Turid Seim, *The Double Message*, 97–107.

87. So, Enslin, "Once Again" 262; Walker "Acts . . . Reconsidered," 13; Blassi, *Making Charisma*, 53–54; and Schenk, "Luke as Reader," 134.

88. The application of an historical criterion to this practice, i.e., holding that it is more or less acceptable to compose a fictitious "parable" but not a narrative incident such as Luke 10:38–42, is misplaced. Luke could appeal to the example of Jesus, who also communicated his views by telling fictitious stories.

89. Walker, "Acts . . . Reconsidered," 13. See also Schenk, "Luke as Reader," 133.

90. See the full discussion, with references, in Hans Dieter Betz, *The Sermon on the Mount*, 592–95.

91. James M. Robinson *et al.*, *Critical Edition of Q*, 56–57. John Kloppenborg does not include this portion of the text, nor does he mention any proponents, *Q-Parallels*, 28–31. The references in this and the previous note mask differences among scholars. Betz works with the notion of a self-standing "Sermon on the Plain," while Walker (and Enslin) do not accept the Q hypothesis.

92. Robinson *et al.*, *Critical Edition*, enclose this phrase in [[ ]], indicating that the material is probably, but not certainly, Q.

93. "Acts . . . Reconsidered," 13–14. Although I accept the Q hypothesis—that Matthew and Luke made independent use of a collection of Jesus' teachings—I agree that the arguments of Michael D. Goulder, "Did Luke Know any of the Pauline Letters?", merit serious consideration.

94. The preceding chapter called attention to two episodes of the "L Tradition" (13:10–17 and 17:11–17) that may well be Lukan compositions inspired by Mark. 7:11–17 exhibits, like 17:11–17, strong influence from LXX. "L" denotes material found in Luke but not in Matthew, Mark (or John); it is what remains after Mark and Q have been extracted. L is not a known proposed source for Luke, as is Mark, nor even a hypothetical proposed source, such as Q. The quest for diverse origins of its contents is therefore quite appropriate.

95. "Did Luke Know any of the Pauline Letters?," 97–112, 106.

96. The *Thesaurus Linguae Graecae*, produced by the University of California at Irvine, provides a searchable data base for ancient Greek literature.

97. In his report on the Jesus Seminar's study of John, W. Barnes Tatum indicates a rating of .27, well in the "gray" range. Only six percent of the voters judged the saying "authentic." *John the Baptist and Jesus: A Report of the Jesus Seminar*, 134.

98. On John's speech in Luke 3:10–14 see also pp. 183–84.

99. Like many other scholars, I think that the story of the Transfiguration (Mark 9:2–8), which includes Peter, James, and John, was at one time a resurrection appearance.

100. "Luke as Reader," 136–37.

101. Anthony J. Blassi, *Making Charisma*, 47–59, identifies a number of Lukan passages that may reflect Pauline influence, including 1 Cor 15 (51–52). See below for a summary and critique of his work on the influence of the letters upon Acts.

102. See, for example, G. Lüdemann, *Early Christianity*, 65.

103. "For the destruction of the flesh," 5:5. What this phrase may have meant—let alone its puzzling sequel—is not the present concern. The question here is how an early reader may have understood the passage. For the problems of interpretation in 1 Cor 5 and possible backgrounds see A. Y. Collins, "The Function of Excommunication in Paul," 251–263.

104. On double dreams see R. Pervo, *Profit with Delight*, 73, and the references there.

105. This oxymoron refers to later additions to NT texts.

106. Jerome, *On Famous Men* (De Vir. Ill.) 2.

107. See Spicq, *Theological Lexicon*, 2:546–47, and the note of Cadbury in *Beg.* 4:50 (a "rather obscure word").

108. Τί ὠλέθρευσας ἡμᾶς; ἐξολεθρεῦσαι σε κύριος καθὰ καὶ σήμερον. Cf. Acts 5:3, 9.

109. Joshua does not include burial of the victim. Josephus, *Ant.* 5:44 mentions the burial of Achan, but this conclusion is probably coincidental.

110. Chapter Three discussed Luke's use of the LXX.

111. *Early Christianity*, 65. Theissen describes "rule miracles" in *The Miracle Stories of the Early Christian Tradition*, 106–112. Anton Weiser develops this line of interpretation in *Die Apostelgeschichte,*, 1:138–48. Barrett, *Acts* 1:263, approves.

112. H. Leppä discusses Luke 13:1–9 as a revision of Mark 11:12–14, 20–21 in *Luke's Critical Use*, 143–47.

113. Yarbro Collins supplies references to magical papyri in "Excommunication," 255–56.

114. The D-text of Acts makes a number of alterations to magnify the place of Peter. For examples see R. Pervo, "Social and Religious Aspects of the Western Text,", 229–41, and the references there.

115. On the meaning see P. Menoud, "Le sens du verbe πορθεῖν, Galatians I, 13, 23; Act. IX, 21," 178–86.

116. Cf. also the Authorized ("King James"), Version, the New American Bible, the New Jerusalem Bible, the New International Version and other modern translations.

117. Ceslas Spicq states that Philo often uses the verb metaphorically, *Theological Lexicon*, 2:142.

118. So Enslin, "Once Again," 262; Masson, "À propos," 163–64; and Leppä, *Luke's Critical Use*, 40–44. The last offers the most detailed study.

119. ἐλυμαίνετο ("ravaging"), a NT *hapax*, is a synonym for πορθεῖν. ("*Hapax*" ["once"] is used to designate a word that appears but once in a particular author or work.)

120. Additional assistance may have been provided by 3 *Macc* 3:25 "Therefore we have given orders that, as soon as this letter arrives, you are to send to us those who live among you, together with their wives and children, with insulting and harsh treatment, and bound securely with iron fetters, to suffer the sure and shameful death that befits enemies." Cf. also 2 Macc 8:10–11.

121. Leppä also appears to believe that Luke constructed his picture of Paul the persecutor from Galatians: *Critical Use*, 69–76.

122. Enslin, "Once Again," 258, points to the identical phrases. See also Leppä, *Luke's Critical Use*, 44–47.

123. Charles Masson, "À propos de Act. 9:19b-25," 161–66.

124. The closest approximation to an exception is Acts 13:32b-33: ". . . what God promised to our ancestors he has fulfilled for us, their children, by raising Jesus" . . . "You are my Son; today I have begotten you." Masson did not mention Acts 7:56, in which "Son of God" is a variant to the usually accepted "Son of Man."

125. Lüdemann, *Paul the Founder of Christianity*, 35.

126. Little weight should attach to the adverb εὐθέως, "immediately," although this is its only appearance in the Pauline corpus. Acts uses it nine times (three of which fall in this chapter). It may be noteworthy that only here does it directly modify a verb.

127. See below for more observations upon Luke's use of Paul's story of his "conversion."

128. See J. Schniewind and G. Friedrich, ἐπαγγέλλω, κ.τ.λ., *TDNT* 2:576–86.

129. See E. Käsemann, "Ephesians and Acts," *SLA*, 288–97, 295.

130. Acts 13:38–39 mentions the law of Moses in the context of a negative comparison.

131. This point is taken by Chrysostom, at the beginning of *Homily* 16 on Acts, MPG 9:147.

132. See Barrett, *Acts* 1:378, who cites Exod 33:2 and discusses other passages. A longer list appears in *Beg.* 4:78, and a good discussion in Bruce, *Acts*, 209.

133. Fitzmyer, *Acts* 386.

134. Dependence is also argued by Enslin, "Once Again," 62, and Leppä, *Luke's Critical Use*, 57–59.

135. According to Harnack, *Marcion*, 71*, Gal 3:15–25 was not in Marcion's edition of the letter.

136. If so intended, Luke succeeded well beyond his wildest dreams. Not only was this model of reading the letters *via* Acts implemented (in part) by Irenaeus and his successors, but it became "canonical" to the extent that Acts precedes the letters of Paul in the standard arrangement of NT books. Those who read the NT in course will be rewarded by finding Paul, at the end of Acts, in Rome. On the next page begins the letter to the Romans.

137. This influence is inevitable because nearly every Christian scholar to date who

works with the material comes to know Paul first from the stories in Acts, in most cases from Sunday School stories or Bible histories.

138. To which one might add the articles, etc., to which commentators refer. Jervell, *Apostelgeschichte*, 326–29, has a full and current bibliography. He agrees that money may have been sent, but not through the agency of Paul at a time prior to or during the reign of Agrippa I (41–44). Barrett, *Acts*, 1:558–60, contends that this is the same historical visit also narrated in Acts 15 and Gal 2:1–10. See also Haenchen *Acts*, 375–79, who has many sharp comments and some cloudy judgments. Identification of Acts 11:27–30 with Gal 2:1–10 is also pressed by some conservative scholars, who can then maintain that Acts 15 deals with a later meeting. So contend Ramsay, *St. Paul the Traveller*, 46–47, and Hemer, *Book of Acts*, 266–67. Bruce, *Acts*, 278, rejects the view that Acts 11 is a doublet of that reported in chapter 15.

139. On Luke's silence about Paul's Collection for Jerusalem see below.

140. In addition to the two from Acts and Gal 2:10 these are 1 Cor 11:23; 15:1, 3; cf. Phil 2:5.

141. One might classify Acts 26:10 as "a touch of Pauline style." On this see also Leppä, *Luke's Critical Use*, 54, who notes that Acts 11:29–30 and Gal 2:9–10 share the mention of Barnabas and Saul/Paul. He further observes that both of the references to this collection in Acts, 11:27–30 and 12:25 have links to Gal 2.

142. Charles Cousar surveys the issues in "Jerusalem, Council of," *ABD* 3:766–68, together with standard bibliography. See also Barrett, *Acts* 2:605, 707–09 for further bibliography.

143. Paul prefers to use (a grecized spelling of) the Aramaic nickname, "Rock," more often found in a Greek translation, *petros*, or in its anglicized form, Peter. (As yet, no evidence exists for the use of "Peter" as a proper name before the rise of Christianity.)

144. J. B. Lightfoot, *St Paul's Epistle to the Galatians*, 123–24. For the weaknesses of Lightfoot's attempt both to sustain the identity of the meetings and defend the credibility of Acts see W. Knox, *Acts of the Apostles*, 42.

145. As Dibelius noted (*Studies*, 99), the so-called "Apostolic Council" of Acts 15 deserves this title because of the formality with which Luke invests the proceedings.

146. Galatians 2:11–14. A good, objective discussion of this meeting appears in Bengt Holmberg, *Paul and Power*, 46–56. For a perspective from the reconstructed view of James, see John Painter, *Just James: the Brother of Jesus in History and Tradition*, especially 58–78. Recent scholarship rejects the view, once popular in some circles, that James (through his representatives) acted in bad faith, while Peter was, at best, a hypocrite.

147. Had Paul accepted and promulgated the "Apostolic Decree" of Acts 15:23–29, he would have had no need to write 1 Cor 8 and 10:23–11:1, which wrestle with the issue of "meat sacrificed to idols." Acts 15:29 simply forbids such food.

148. Numerous minor variations and variations within the traditions have been omitted. Details may be found in a critical edition. See the detailed discussion and full bibliography in B. Metzger, *A Textual Commentary*, 376–86. See also W.A. Strange, *The Problem of the Text of Acts*, 87–93, 133–44. On pages 87–88 Strange sets out the full range of data. Six forms of this "decree" exist.

149. For examples of these changes and alterations see Paul F. Bradshaw *et al.* eds., *The Apostolic Tradition*. See also n.168.

150. Cf. 1 Cor 7:8, 20, 24, and 40.

151. Michael Goulder indicates how Luke or someone else could have extracted the "Apostolic Decree" from a reading of 1 Corinthians, "Did Luke Know any of the Pauline Letters?," 104–05.

152. Evidently the D-text identified these persons as believing Pharisees in 15:1 but did not repeat the information in v. 5. See the note of J. H. Ropes, *Beg.*, 3:140.

153. The "standard text" does not report the visitors as demanding that believers must be circumcised *and* keep the Torah, whereas it is a part of the demand in v. 5. (Since the expression "be circumcised by the custom of Moses" (τῷ ἔθει Μωυσέως) is quite unusual, the D-text may be more original (with some confusion generated by περιτμηθῆτε/περιπατῆτε, "circumcise," "walk"?) The important difference, however, is that 15:1 makes this observance a soteriological requirement: "you cannot be *saved*." The "Christian Pharisees" of 15:5 reiterate the demand but do not introduce soteriology. (Soteriology is the branch of theology that deals with the means, etc., of salvation.) By overlooking this

omission—which reduces the entire question to a matter of practice—the D-text negates a key Lukan point. (The textual differences in chap. 15 raise considerable obstacles to any attempts to assign both forms of the text of Acts to the same author.)

154. Ropes, *Beg.*, 3:138.

155. Gal 2:2. There is no necessary conflict between this "revelation" and a request or order from some human authority.

156. Together, "circumcise" and "circumcision" occur thirteen times in Galatians.

157. On this interpretation see below.

158. On the subject of circumcision see also Table 4.17 and comments.

159. A modern proponent of this interpretation is Johannes Munck: *Paul and the Salvation of Mankind*, 100–103. See also below.

160. The similarity in phrasing has long been noted. See, for example, Enslin, "Once Again," 258.

161. Acts uses this verb to describe the activities of "rabble-rousers": 17:8 and 13.

162. See also p. 170.

163. One might otherwise wonder why Paul does not challenge them with statements to the effect that he, too, is a Pharisee and punctilious in observance (23:6; 26:5).

164. W. O. Walker, Jr., "The Timothy-Titus Problem Reconsidered," 231–35. H. Leppä devastates the arguments for the historicity of this episode, *Luke's Critical Use*, 145–150.

165. For more details see Walker, "Timothy-Titus Problem," 233–34. Dixon Slingerland makes a strong case for the non-historical character of Acts 16:1–3 in his "'The Jews' in the Pauline Portion of Acts," 308–312.

166. *Beg.* 4:184.

167. This interpretation is not dependent upon Greek philology or textual variation. The earliest evidence for it is, however, textual: the omission of the negative οὐδέ in v. 5. Without a negative the verse would mean: "We submitted to them for a while . . ." This omission, limited to Latin witnesses of the D-text, has little claim to originality. It is probably based upon an attempt to harmonize these two passages. The discussion in J. B. Lightfoot, *Galatians*, 122–23 is still worthy of consultation.

168. On the early history of this interpretation see, in particular, Cohen (n. 162); M. Wiles, *The Divine Apostle*, 19, 70–71; and A. Souter, *The Earliest Latin Commentaries on the Epistles of St. Paul*, 15, 19, 24, 63, and 223–24. For more recent examples of this interpretation see D. Betz, *Galatians*, 89 n.298.

169. Walker, "The Timothy-Titus Problem," 234.

170. One of the more perplexing questions of Acts is whether the narrator understands Timothy to be a Jew or a gentile. Shaye Cohen presents cogent arguments in favor of the view that Luke did not regard Timothy as Jewish. This is certainly the plainest reading of the text. See "Was Timothy Jewish?," Appendix D of *The Beginnings of Jewishness*, 363–377. (This is a revision of his article in JBL 105, [1985] 251–68.) Cohen also discusses the interpretation, including patristic and later comments, of Galatians 2:3–5. It is anachronistic to evoke the matrilineal principle, a feature of Roman law that was not normative among the Jews until the Mishnaic period (third century). Lawrence Schiffman ("At the Crossroads: Tannaitic Perspectives on the Jewish-Christian Schism," in E. P. Sanders *et al.*, eds., *Jewish and Christian Self-Definition*, vol. 2: *Aspects of Judaism in the Greco-Roman Period* 115–156, 117–22) argues that the matrilineal principle appeared at an early date, but his method is flawed, since he dates rabbinic texts by reference to the named authorities. This is equivalent to dating an early Christian saying to c. 30 CE because it is attributed to Jesus.

171. This tendency is, regrettably, not confined to more primitive times nor limited to the realm of religion.

172. John is the third of the "pillars" named in Gal 2:9. See the excursus in D. Betz, *Galatians*, 101.

173. There are other and numerous differences in tone and point of view.

174. Rudolf Bultmann, in his 1959 critique of Haenchen's approach to source questions, made Acts 15 his primary case, "Zur Frage nach den Quellen der Apostelgeschichte," *Exegetica*, 415–18. He focuses upon the Decree, making a number of apposite observations. Gerd Lüdemann is convinced that tradition underlies the account, but he finds it difficult "to extract any consecutive source" in chap. 15 (169). That is, nonetheless, what he does, 170–71. His criteria are ". . . [C]oncreteness and—more important—agreement with the

course of the conference as it can be reconstructed from Gal. 2." (*Early Christianity* 169–71). The second merely begs the question, while the first proves nothing. On the matter of the sources of Acts, see Appendix I.

175. Lüdemann, *Early Christianity*, 166; Barrett *Acts*, 2:696. The "revelation" of Galatians 2:2 could have taken a form like the oracle of Acts 13:1–3, where the presence of Antiochene tradition is quite arguable. (Luke does have, for whatever reason, a "revelation" motivating the journey of Barnabas and Saul to Jerusalem in Acts 11: the oracle of Agabus about the coming famine, 11:27–28.)

176. The (second century) *Didache* begins: "The teaching of the Lord through the Twelve Apostles to the gentiles." This association continues with the (later) title, "The teaching of the Lord through the Twelve Apostles to the gentiles." This claim that church rules were promulgated by apostles continues with the (later) *Didascalia*, and the still later *Apostolic Constitutions*.

177. Although, as the D-text indicates, the commands were given "moral" interpretations later in the second century, the prohibition against eating meat sacrificed to idols long endured. See, for example, Justin *Dial.* 35:1; Irenaeus *Against Heresies* 1.6.3; 1.24.5; 1.26.3; 1.28.2; Eusebius *Ecclesiastical History* 4.7.7; 5.1.26;; Hippolytus *Against Heresies* 7.36; Epiphanius *Panarion* 26.9.2; *Did* 6:3; Minucius Felix *Octavius* 30; Tertullian *Apology* 9; the Pseudo-Clementine *Letter on Virginity* 2.5.2; and Thom 14.

178. Gal 2:2 stresses the private character of the consultation, Acts 15 its public nature. The latter is characteristic of Luke, who rejects the notion that Paul taught in private (Acts 20:20).

179. *Studies*, 93–101, with conclusion on 99.

180. This is the view of Enslin among others ("Once Again," 258), fully developed by Leppä, 93–101.

181. Leppä, *Luke's Critical Use*, 35–37. I had come to the same conclusion before reading his study.

182. Greeks and Romans seem to have viewed male circumcision as mutilation and to have regarded it with a revulsion similar to that modern Western people have toward so-called "female circumcision."

183. For data see Leppä, *Luke's Critical Use*, 38, as well as his discussion, 37–39, which refers also to the Helsinki dissertation of Kalervo Salo.

184. The other NT examples are Pauline (sixteen times) and Deutero-Pauline (three occurrences).

185. Leppä, *Luke's Critical Use*, 55.

186. The LXX has four examples.

187. The definite article τῆς, which is not uniformly attested in the manuscript tradition, distinguishes this usage slightly from the others.

188. Weizsacker, *The Apostolic Age of the Christian Church*, vol. I, 211–12.

189. M.-E. Boismard, "Le 'concile' de Jérusalem (Act 15, 1–33). Essai de critique Littéraire,"; F. Refoulé, "Le discours de Pierre à l'assemblée de Jérusalem," W. Walker, "Acts and the Pauline Corpus Revisited: Peter's Speech at the Jerusalem Conference," in R. P. Thompson and T. E. Philips, eds., *Literary Studies in Luke-Acts*: FS Joseph B. Tyson, 77–86; and H. Leppä, *Luke's Critical Use*, 119–25, which provides a full summary and discussion.

190. This is the dramatic effect of the "vain repetition" in 15:2 and 7: γενομένης δὲ στάσεως καὶ ζητήσεως οὐκ ὀλίγης . . . πολλῆς δὲ ζητήσεως γενομένης (There was conflict and not inconsiderable debate . . . there was much debate).

191. Literally, "those of (the) circumcision," οἱ ἐκ (τῆς) περιτομῆς. On this metonymy see also Table 4.19. In Acts 10:45 it may stand for "Jews" in contrast to the uncircumcised Cornelius, but in 11:2 that is nearly impossible, for Jews alone were present. Those who do not know Paul will find this expression in Acts 11 perplexing.

192. In fairness it should be noted that Jews would have agreed. The issue for them would have been whether the obligations of the Covenant—a gift of grace—remained in effect for the people of the Covenant.

193. Walker, "Acts . . . Revisited," 79.

194. The construction ὁ λόγος τοῦ εὐαγγελίου (gospel message) is without exact parallel. It approaches the Deutero-Pauline world, as in Col 1: 5 ἐν τῷ λόγῳ τῆς ἀληθείας τοῦ εὐαγγελίου, which can be translated in various ways.

195. See also Table 4.28 and the discussion below.

196. In religious and educational contexts "yoke" was not a necessarily negative term. Note, in particular, Matthew 11:29–30: the yoke of Jesus is not oppressive, as is that of others (23:4). Cf. also Sirach 6:24–30; 51:26 and *Aboth* 3:6. See G. Bertram and K. H. Rengstorf, ζύγος, *TDNT* 2:896–901, and Leppä, *Luke's Critical Use*, 52–53. J. Nolland, "A Fresh Look at Acts 15.10," 105–15, wishes to set aside the interpretation given here on the grounds that yoke was not always a negative image. Jews agreed that Torah was a yoke and could be burdensome, but did not agree that it was impossible to fulfill. Nolland's harmonization must ignore the final part of Peter's statement, which is a typically gentile view of Torah observance.

197. Barrett, *Acts*, 2:719: "He is described here as something of a Paulinist, though the Paulinism is not accurately portrayed."

198. Barrett, *Acts*, 2:719.

199. Walker, "Acts . . . Revisited," 82. This summarizes and builds upon his arguments on pp. 80–82.

200. Walker, "Acts . . . Revisited," 83.

201. James does not, however, endorse Peter's view of Torah as an impossible burden; chapter 21:18–25 can speak of "myriads" of observant followers of Jesus.

202. On Peter, or perhaps better the *figure* of Peter, as an agent and symbol of ecclesial comprehension see Pheme Perkins, *Peter: Apostle for the Whole Church*, 9–14 *et passim*.

203. "Le discours de Pierre à l'assemblée de Jérusalem," especially 244–47.

204. See below, p. 266.

205. Not all so understood Galatians., of course, most notably Marcion.

206. The verb σώζειν (save) does not occur in Gal. It is found thirteen times in Acts, in the present context most notably in 15:1 and 11. For another parallel with Eph. 2:7–8 see Acts 16:31.

207. For the use of Gal 2:1–10 to refute the idea of a fundamental disagreement between Peter and Paul see Refoulé, "Discours," 240.

208. Few subjects raised more difficulties for patristic interpreters—and generated more creative solutions—than the conflict of Gal. 2:15–18. See Maurice Wiles, *The Divine Apostle*, 22, 25, and 71. In the *Letter of Peter to James* 2.3–4, which is a part of the Pseudo-Clementines, Peter expressly rejects the views attributed to him in Acts 15.

209. See Leppä, *Critical Use*, 113.

210. From the logic of Gal 5:3, circumcision obliged observance of the entire Torah. The observant could not therefore associate with (celebrate the eucharist together with) non-observant gentiles. In this light the charges of Acts 21:21, that Paul taught Jewish believers not to circumcise their male children or to follow Torah, are true. Luke, however, understood Paul in the light of the more irenic Romans—not to mention the ever useful "all things to all people" passage (1 Cor 9:19–23) with its particular reference to "becoming a Jew to Jews."

211. Anthony J. Blassi, *Making Charisma*, 40.

212. Blassi, *Making Charisma*, 41.

213. *Making Charisma*, 43. Blassi also says (42) that use of "we" for events that he did not witness would have undermined Luke's credibility. This is a modern standard. More decisively, it neglects the anonymity of (Luke and) Acts.

214. One example is that the "in order" of Luke 1:3 means "reasonable narrative order" rather than "strictly chronological and historical order". The same term (καθεξῆς) appears in Acts 11:4, in the beginning of a speech that exhibits divergences from the account it summarizes (10:1–48).

215. Blassi, *Making Charisma*, 45.

216. Whereas qualitative research, which is general in the humanities, tends to focus upon *the* appropriate method or theory and its application, social scientists, who use quantitative research, are more likely to seek independent confirmation of their findings from different methods and disciplines.

217. This assertion coheres with the prevalent picture of Pauline chronology. There are dissenters, among whom Gerd Lüdemann is prominent (*Paul, Apostle to the Gentiles: Studies in Chronology*). Rainer Riesner reviews the various theories in *Paul's Early Period*, 1–28.

218. Calculation of the elapsed time is vexing. Is one to add the "three years" of

Galatians 1:17 to the "fourteen" of Galatians 2:1? The temporal preposition in the latter is unusual. Furthermore, ancient reckoning was often "inclusive." We, for example, would say that Easter comes two days after Good Friday, but NT writers speak of "after three days" or "on the third day."

219. See R. Pervo, *Profit with Delight*, 55. On this episode see also p. 186.

220. Conzelmann, *Acts*, 98.

221. So Enslin, "Once Again," 258–60.

222. For his part, Paul does not point out that Barnabas was his colleague, and initially, at least, his superior in this mission. Note also that Paul says nothing of missionary labors in south-central Asia Minor. Has Luke transferred these from his independent period to an earlier time?

223. When Luke has no sources he can create some of his most brilliant and dramatic scenes.

224. Johnson, *Acts* 318.

225. If, as seems likely, the list of Acts 20:4 comes from a source, such as a no longer extant administrative letter of Paul, Luke could have learned about, or deduced, missions to Berea and Derbe from that source.

226. Paphos was the site of the confrontation between Paul and the magus, followed by the conversion of the latter's one-time protégé; but for all the reader of Acts knows, their encounter took place in a back alley.

227. Those who inquire how the author learned that there was a synagogue at Antioch may be referred to Luke 4:16–30, a leading candidate for the source of this story.

228. The account of the healing of the cripple at Lystra has been so closely conformed to the similar healing by another pair (Peter and John) in Acts 3 that no source can be recovered.

229. Lüdemann, who diligently seeks traditions, finds no traditions pertaining to Paul in Acts 13:6–12, assigns 13:13–14, 50–51 to "traditions," and posits other traditions in 14:19–20a *Early Christianity* 148–66.

230. Despite most translations, Paul does not say that he has "preached" or "proclaimed" the message from Jerusalem to Illyricum.

231. The reference to "Dalmatia" (S. Illyricum) in 2 Tim 4:10 could derive from Romans.

232. For a detailed comparison of Paul's itineraries in the epistles with those in Acts see Table 4.48.

233. On these very difficult expressions see Barrett, *Acts* 2:766–69, 881–82, who sums up a good deal of evidence and argument. Acts 18:23 presumes that the area had already been evangelized. There is no reason to suspect that Luke subscribed to the "South Galatian" hypothesis (the view that Galatians was written to cities visited by Paul in Acts 13–14), but it is equally true that the hypothesis owes its very existence to Acts.

234. According to Col 2:1 Paul did not visit that city. (Eph is very similar: 1:15; 3:2, and its original title is uncertain.)

235. Rom 16:5, 1 Cor 16:19, and 2 Cor 1:8.

236. Rom 15:26; 1 Cor 16:15; 2 Cor 9:2.

237. Rom 15:25; 1 Cor 16:5; 2 Cor 1:16; 2:13; 7:5, 8:1; 11:9; Phil 4:15; 1 Thess 1:7–8.

238. It is very apparent that Luke has a better understanding of geography and local color in the cities around the Aegean Sea than with the hinterland of Asia Minor (modern Turkey). This understanding is very likely based upon familiarity with that region. It does not necessarily mean that Luke had better sources for Corinth or Ephesus than for Iconium, although this may have been the case. Likewise, the extant letters of Paul deal with places in the Aegean area.

239. *Making Charisma*, 39–73. The tables are found on 64–67.

240. This category most closely approaches that of traditional NT scholarship.

241. Blassi holds that Luke did not have access to Rom 16, which he regards as a distinct letter (63), noting that Erastus, "the city treasurer" of Corinth would have been difficult for Luke to resist, since he is a person of high status (66). This is to be expected, as early editions of Rom, including the collection known to Marcion, ended with chap. 14, sometimes chap. 15. See H. Gamble, *Textual History*. It does, however, seem probable that Luke was familiar with Rom 15, as will be proposed below. Because Romans and 1 Corinthians long circulated as individual texts, it is unwise to use evidence from them to formulate conclusions about a collection of Pauline letters.

242. On this subject compare Blassi, *Making Charisma*, 65–66.

243. It is erroneous to assume that his letters reveal "the complete Paul." We cannot learn from them whether Paul knew Hebrew, or Aramaic, for example, and they are confined, in the view of most, to a relatively short period of his life.

244. For Gamaliel as the teacher of Paul, see also p. 410. ?

245. Acts 9:1–19a, the first account of Paul's "conversion," evidently derives in-good-part from a source, since the repetitions of this story in Acts 22 and 26 show how Luke would have written the story had he composed it from scratch. The reference to Paul as a "Tarsian" in 9:11 is a surprise, as readers would assume, as does the balance of Acts, that Paul lived in Jerusalem. It is not impossible that the source of Acts 9 derived "Tarsus" from Galatians 1:21, but this may be independent. On the reports of Paul's "conversion" in Acts see Table 4.29, below, and the attendant comments.

246. Ephebes were cadet citizens-in-training. Male citizens normally had to pass through the ephebate.

247. For a defense of the possibility that Paul was a citizen of Tarsus see Brian Rapske, *Paul in Roman Custody*, 72–83. The few examples, none earlier than the end of the second century CE, reflect persons of considerable wealth. A recent discussion is John M. G. Barclay, *Jews in the Mediterranean Diaspora*. See the index, 492, under "Citizenship (Greek)." Other studies include Mary Smallwood, *The Jews in the Roman World*, index, 579, under "citizenship" and "civic status." For her most recent views see her article, "The Diaspora in the Roman period before CE 70," in W. Horbury *et al.*, eds., *The Cambridge History of Judaism, vol. 3,*, 168–91. Note also the two articles of S. Applebaum in *CRINT* 1.1 listed in the bibliography.

248. Rapske, *Roman Custody*, admits the difficulties. The most substantial argument against Roman citizenship is W. Stegemann, "War der Apostel Paulus ein römisher Bürger?" On both matters see also Lentz, *Luke's Portrait*, 23–61. Most supporters of Paul's Roman citizenship do not take up the case of Silas, another Roman citizen from Jerusalem, according to Acts 16:37. Rainer Riesner has an excursus on the question of Paul's Roman citizenship, *Paul's Early Period*, 147–57, on which see the excursus at the close of this chapter.

249. Ronald Hock, *The Social Context of Paul's Ministry*, 20–25, argues that the term has wider application and prefers "leather worker."

250. From that source Luke did not learn that Aquila was originally from Pontus and that the couple had been expelled from Rome. (Rom 16:3–5 would contribute to this subject, if Luke knew of it.)

251. Acts 18:22–23 and 19:1a summarize vast amounts of travel and activity in a few general phrases that describe no concrete events. These verses serve no narrative purpose other than to take Paul away from Ephesus for what must have been a lengthy period of time.

252. Another issue is the extent to which this section of Acts treats the presence of a pre-Pauline Christian community in Ephesus. See Lüdemann, *Early Christianity*, 208–09.

253. Bruce, *Acts*, 393 identifies the two, as does G. Fee, *The First Epistle to the Corinthians*, 63.

254. On the latter see R. Pervo, *Profit with Delight*, 77–81.

255. G. Lüdemann, *Early Christianity*, 203. See 199, 203–04. Lüdemann shares his own reconstruction. Because of the high status of synagogue presidents Paul modified his policy of not baptizing converts. This accession started a stampede of sorts. Acts 18:8b is therefore "a historically reliable statement." (204).

256. John Hurd makes a strong case for viewing the report about Corinth in Acts 18 as an amalgam of information about several visits, *The Origin of 1 Corinthians*, 2d. ed., 30–31.

257. Witherington, *Acts*, 170–71.

258. See also Table 4.28, p. 109 for another example.

259. Conzelmann notes that Luke 21:24 does not conform to conventional apocalyptic thought, *Theology of St. Luke*, 188 n.7.

260. See pp. 247–49.

261. F. Büchsel in Büchsel and Herntrich, κρίνω, κ.τ.λ., *TDNT* 3:921–54, 948 says "linguistically, διακρίνεσθαι in the sense of 'to doubt' is a product of Greek-speaking Christianity."

262. The notion that purity was essentially ethical was a commonplace of Hellenistic

and Roman philosophical theology. Within that context the assertions that God is creator of all but that some creatures are impure was seen as a contradiction. Hellenistic Judaism addressed this issue well before the rise of Christianity. See, for example, *Aristeas*, 120–69. By the time of Luke and of the Pastoral Epistles the intra-Christian issue had changed. The existence of loathsome insects and the like was advanced as an argument against the goodness of creation, which heretics would therefore attribute to the activity of an inferior god.

263. See below, pp. 275–76.

264. Lohse provides data on Qumran texts in *Colossians and Philemon*, 37.

265. Note also Luke 1:79. There is further discussion of Acts 26:18 below and pp. 275–78.

266. The Hebrew idiom means "raise the face (of another)," as in "You need not kiss my ring," and thus shows condescension toward a subordinate.

267. Note the final prepositional phrase in each case.

268. Jouette M. Bassler, *Divine Impartiality: Paul and a Theological Axiom*, 176–78, citation from 176. A general overview appears on 171–83.

269. These include *Didache* 4:10//*Barnabas* 19:7 (slavery), *Didache* 4:3//*Barnabas* 19:4, Polycarp *Phil.* 6:1, 1 Peter 1:17; James 2:21, and *1 Clem.* 1:3, all ethical. See also E. Lohse, πρόσωπον, κ.τ.λ., *TDNT* 6:768–80, especially 179–80, and K. Berger, *EDNT* 3:179–80.

270. See pp. 108–9.

271. Other examples of thrice-told (or summarized) matters are the conversion of Cornelius, 10:1–47; 11:4–17; and 15:7–9, the "Apostolic Decree," 15:19–20, 28–29; 21:25, and the decision of Paul to turn his missionary attentions toward the gentiles: 13:46; 18:6, and 28:28. A useful survey of the stories in Acts is G. Lohfink, *The Conversion of St. Paul: Narrative and History in Acts,*. See also B. R. Gaventa, *From Darkness to Light*, 52–95.

272. Further discussion of "Paul the Persecutor" appears on p. 246.

273. For data see H. D. Betz, *Galatians*, 69–70.

274. Robert Tannehill takes note of many of the prophetic allusions in Acts 22:16–18 in *Narrative Unity* 2:222–25. See also Bruce, *Acts*, 501–02.

275. Haenchen offers some reflections upon the literary and theological implications of omitting Ananias from Acts 26 in *Acts*, 690–91. Bruce (*Acts* 501) attributes the omission to tactics: "Agrippa would not be so interested as the hostile Jerusalem crowd was in the part played by this 'devout man according to the law' (22:12)." However, the characterization of Agrippa in the speech refutes this proposal.

276. In chapter 22 this shift is underway. Although Ananias makes his visit, the gentile commission proper comes from a revelation of Christ in the temple (22:21).

277. Acts 9 does not even hint that the agency of Ananias detracted from the legitimacy of Paul's mission—unlike the charges that would appear to stand behind Galatians. The commission to preach to Jews and gentiles takes the form of an oracle of the heavenly Lord—to Ananias. Acts does not, however, narrate the recitation of this oracle to Paul by Ananias.

278. C.H. Dodd, *The Apostolic Preaching and Its Developments*, 18.

279. ". . . [A] stronger case for Luke's knowledge of the Pauline epistles, or some of them, can be made here than anywhere else in Acts." So Barrett (who does not believe that Luke knew any epistles) in *Acts*, 2:964, with some data. Similarly, Witherington: "If there is a case to be made that Luke knew Paul's letters . . . it must be made in the main on the basis of the Miletus speech" (*Acts* 610). On the following page, n.212, he states, "[T]he attempt to make this speech the linchpin of an argument to prove that Luke knew Paul's letters places far too many eggs into one basket." How this mixture of metaphoric proposals coheres with the thesis of p. 610 is not clear. Witherington proceeds to observe: "If Luke knew Paul's letters, many of Luke's omissions and observations in Acts become virtually inexplicable, especially in regard to the way he treats Paul's apostleship, his coworkers, and, most importantly Paul's letter writing itself, *which Luke never mentions*." He nonetheless holds that the speech is "Pauline" rather than "Paulinist," 611. These statements notwithstanding, on p. 170 Witherington allows that Paul may have been familiar with Romans and allows knowledge of the "captivity epistles," Phil, Phlm, Col, and Eph., regarding Luke's authorship of Colossians as "a distinct possibility" (170, n.25). He repeats and develops knowledge of these five letters in his argument for date, 171.

280. Colin Hemer (below) argues that the speech reflects actual experience. In the 1951 edition of his commentary F. F. Bruce suggested that Luke might have "taken notes," 377. The final edition states more cautiously that, because of its placement within a "we" narra-

tive, ". . . [O]ne would naturally infer that Luke had heard it himself." (429). Witherington, *Acts*, 610–11, provides a table of parallels intended to demonstrate "authentic" Pauline themes. Steve Walton is content to underscore the authenticity of its "Pauline" thought (*Leadership*).

281. Dibelius, *Studies*, 156 n.43, with no detail and an appeal to the general situation. Haenchen avoids any mention of source material, *Acts* 590–98, while Conzelmann views the speech as a Lukan composition in its entirety, *Acts* 173. Lüdemann, *Early Christianity*, 238–39, makes some general and some specific proposals.

282. C. Leslie Mitton (*The Epistle to the Ephesians*, 211–12) considers that the writer of Ephesians used Acts, although he also recognizes that the two may have been independent. Ralph P. Martin, "An Epistle in Search of a Life-Setting,"suggests that the author of Acts wrote Ephesians. A kindred issue is the proposal that Luke composed the Pastoral Epistles, developed most fully in Wilson, *Luke and the Pastoral Epistles*. Lindemann, *Paulus*, 44–49, assumes that Pastorals depend upon Acts.

283. This difference of emphasis and role is one of the reasons why the debate that pits Acts against (or with) the epistles on the question of "the real Paul" is poorly constructed. Each of these sources is limited, the letters by nature, Acts by its form and by choice. The *Acts of Paul* seeks to integrate these two functions, but is not widely viewed as having captured "the real Paul." Community foundation is not Paul's only role in Acts, of course. About six chapters deal with his specific missionary activity (Acts 13–19). Prior to that are a few brief summaries (9:19b-22, 28–29; 11:26). From the middle of chapter 21 through the middle of chapter 28—another six chapters—Paul is a prisoner mainly engaged in self-defense. At 28:23 he resumes his missionary career, which is still going at full force when the book concludes.

284. This is true even of Philemon.

285. "Clergy" would be an anachronistic term, for the idea of the "laity," distinct from clergy, would not emerge until the third century.

286. See R. Pervo, "Romancing an Oft-neglected Stone: The Pastoral Epistles and the Epistolary Novel."

287. On the Testament in Early Christian Literature see H. Koester, *Introduction* 2:138, 303–04. A Jewish example of this developed type, the roots of which are in the Hebrew Bible, is *The Testaments of the Twelve Patriarchs*.

288. See the reference to W.Kurz, p. 379 n. 74. Steve Walton has a good review of the genre discussion, with appropriate cautions, in *Leadership*, 55–65.

289. Walton develops the parallel between Last Supper and Miletus in considerable detail and with many interesting observations: *Leadership*, 99–117.

290. The "Christ-Parallel" also explains why Paul is now a "mild mannered Clark Kent." Like Jesus, he will not, as it were, request nor display wondrous power to deliver him from the cross.

291. *Studies*, 155–58, quoting 155.

292. For a survey of scholarship on the passage see Walton, *Leadership and Lifestyle*. Another excellent review appears in Jan Lambrecht, "Paul's Farewell-Address at Miletus, Acts 20, 17–38," in Kremer, J., ed. *Les Actes de apôtres*, 307–37.

293. Colin Hemer, "The Speeches in Acts I. The Ephesian Elders at Miletus," citing from p. 75.

294. Colin Hemer, "The Speeches in Acts I. The Ephesian Elders at Miletus," citing from p. 79.

295. Hemer misrepresents Dibelius's views on the genre of this speech, claiming that Dibelius called it a biographical encomium for which he could give only one example, the "Testament of Peregrinus" (Lucian *Death of Peregrinus* 32). Dibelius said that Luke sought to achieve for Paul what biographers did with their encomia. Moreover, Dibelius *distinguished* Pergrinus's speech from biographical encomia (*Studies*, 155). One is surprised that Hemer was not aware of the detailed information about such encomia that are available in the ancient rhetorical handbooks. See, for example, Ronald F. Hock, *The Infancy Gospels of James and Thomas. Scholars Bible* 2, 15–20.

296. See Walton's discussion of the structure of 20:17–35, *Leadership*, 66–75.

297. "Ephesian Elders," 81. "Psychology" here does not mean a scientific discipline, but rather the practice of explaining (away) problems in texts by suggesting that the author was troubled or upset. Critical scholarship rejects this approach, not because circumstances

and emotions have no influence upon what one writes, but because such explanations cannot be verified or controlled.

298. The balance of Hemer's article is a denial that Paul refers to his own death and an extended discussion of the saying of Jesus ("more blessed to give") in verse 35. Hemer's literary executors should not have deemed this piece worthy of publication.

299. *Studies*, 156 n.43. Dibelius refers to an article of H. Schulze from 1900.

300. The argument for authorial presence appears with careful nuance and qualification in Steve Walton's *Leadership and Lifestyle*. Walton concludes that Luke either knew Paul personally or that Luke was using Pauline tradition independent of the letters (212). In the end Walton is not far from Dibelius and many others, although he has more overt respect for the ideas of the speech than does, for example, Haenchen (*Acts* 595–98).

301. See Haenchen, *Acts*, 590, as well as Jerome Murphy-O'Connor, *Paul: A Critical Life*, 347.

302. According to the organizational scheme of this book, a discussion of presbyters belongs in Chapter Six, but since the role of these officials is fundamental to the understanding of the Miletus address, it seems preferable to treat the issue here.

303. Julius Wellhausen, *Kritische Analyse der Apostelgeschichte*, 42.

304. Cf. 1 Cor 15:32 and 2 Cor 1:8–10 and p. 182.

305. And at Ephesus Paul's ministry reaches its climax (Acts 19).

306. "Presbyter," the source of the word "priest" in English and many other languages, is a transliteration of Greek πρεσβύτερος, the comparative of an adjective meaning "old." I use it here because both "elder" and "priest" could be misleading renditions.

307. R. Alastair Campbell, *The Elders: Seniority within Earliest Christianity*, 256. Campbell argues against the tradition that sees the eventual three-fold ministry of Bishops, Presbyters, and Deacons as an evolution from diverse forms of church order.

308. Respectively Acts 4:5, 8, 23; 6:12; 23:14; 24:1, and 25:15. (I omit 2:17, where the term means "elderly persons.") Similar references appear in Luke 9:2, 20:1, and 22:52. At Luke 7:3 "presbyters of the Jews" seem to be synagogue leaders (cf. 7:5). Luke 22:66 and Acts 22:5 refer to the "presbytery," the council of presbyters.

309. So also G. Bornkamm: "In Ac. 15; 16:4 the ἀπόστολοι and πρεσβύτεροι clearly function as a supreme court . . . [they] are patterned after the Jewish Sanhedrin . . ." πρέσβυς, κ.τ.λ., *TDNT* 6:651–82, 663.

310. Cf. English "senile"; for "gerousia," cf. "gerontology," the study of aging.

311. For the roles of presbyters in early Judaism see *HJP* III.1:102, and the indices under "elder" and "*presbyteros*," III.2:926 and 978. The situation is far from transparent. Each community apparently had its "elders," but the use of the term for synagogue officials is generally later. To this extent Campbell is probably correct in claiming that Christian presbyters are not simply imitations of the synagogue model, but it is unfortunate that he makes no reference to inscriptional material.

312. Regarding this ceremony, which looks like an ordination, see pp. 214–15. It is not certain that each community had more than one presbyter, but that is a reasonable interpretation.

313. 1 Corinthians 16:19 refers to greetings from "the churches of Asia," which implies a wider region than Ephesus. The one Ephesian house-church mentioned is that in the home of Prisca and Aquila. Doubtless others existed, but none are described as having presbyters.

314. From the account in Acts, a reader would presume that Paul & Co. had chartered the ship, for it seems to stop as desired — at Troas for seven days (20:6), and at Miletus for about the same length of time. Ports of call are determined by Paul (20:16). Luke provides no setting for the speech, other than that it is not on the ship. Readers are free to envision a hall, a large house, or an outdoor scene.

315. Paul addresses his hearers as ἀδελφοί in Pisidian Antioch (13:15, 26, 38), the Temple (22:1), the Sanhedrin (23:1, 5), and at Rome (28:17). Peter uses the word to fellow believers in his speech at the Jerusalem conference (15:7).

316. Acts claims that all the inhabitants of the province had heard the Christian message (19:10). Paul speaks of "the churches of Asia" (1 Corinthians 16:18).

317. The *Testament of Joseph*, for example, devotes chaps. 1–16 to an account of Joseph's experiences in Egypt, with particular attention to the virtue of chastity. 17–18 indicate the rewards of that and other virtues. Chapter 19, which is heavily Christianized, recounts a

dream. The final chapter, 20, begins: "After my death the Egyptians will oppress you."

318. Two monographs (Aejmelaeus, *Rezeption* and Walton, *Leadership*) are entirely devoted to the subject.

319. Comparisons with 1–2 Tim and Tit (as well as Heb) are reserved for Chapter Six.

320. Steve Walton, *Leadership,* includes a lengthy list of authorities upon nearly every verse or issue.

321. The pastoral/pedagogical purpose of these "reminders" is to assure the hearers that they have the resources to deal with the matter themselves. It is somewhat akin to the contemporary exhortation, "Come on, now! You can do it!" Another function, illustrated in the present case and in 1 Thessalonians 1:5, is to build upon shared knowledge and experience. The word forms a bond between writer or speaker and hearer. It is thus an element of rhetorical *pathos.*

322. See, e. g., 1 Thess 2:1, 5, 10, 11; 3:3–4; 4:2; Gal 3:2; 4:13; 1 Cor 6:2; for commentary see Aejmelaeus, *Rezeption,* 98–101 and Walton, *Leadership,* 157–59.

323. Paul could have used the "as you are well aware" motif in his oral communications, but only his writings survive.

324. Searches of the Thesaurus Linguae Graece show appearances of the word or phrase in *literary* texts. They do not include inscriptions and other public or private documents. Unless otherwise noted, the search range is from 2 BCE-CE. I omit all references to *quotations* of the passage by early Christian writers.

325. The anarthrous phrase of Acts appears three times in the Pseudo-Clementines (which know Acts) and twice in the medical writer Galen. Paul's articular phrase occurs sixteen times in various second century medical writers. ("Articular" and "anarthrous" refer to the respective presence or absence of the definite article. Greek has no indefinite article.)

326. Examples include Romans 1:1, Gal 1:10, and Phil 1:1. See also 1 Thess 1:9 (which probably derives from a "pre-Pauline" creedal affirmation), Gal 6:17, and Phil 2:22, among others.

327. For more discussion see Aejmelaeus, *Rezeption,* 102, and Walton, *Leadership,* 186–88.

328. And only in Phil 2:3 in the undisputed letters; otherwise in Col 2:18, 23; 3:12, and Eph 4:2.

329. The adjective πᾶς, "all," "every," occurs about fifty times in the one hundred fifty-four verses of Ephesians.

330. In addition to Mitton, *Epistle,* see, for example, E. Käsemann, "Ephesians and Acts," *SLA,* 298–307.

331. See, for example *Odyssey* 5:82–84 (homesickness).

332. 1 Cor 6:12, 10:23, 12:7; 2 Corinthians 8:10, 12:1. The word also appears in Heb 12:10 and in Matt: 5:29, 30; 18:6; 19:10.

333. "Repentance toward God and faith toward our Lord Jesus" is a Lukan summary of Christian belief. Aejmelaeus, *Rezeption,* 108–12 explores the relation to Pauline texts, with attention to the key Pauline word "faith."

334. Other Pauline uses of the opposition "Jews . . . Greeks" occur in 1 Cor 1:22, 10:32, and Gal 3:28. Cf. also Col 3:11.

335. Josephus uses the phrase once, of a riot in Alexandria (*Ant.* 18.257), while Origen employs it three times, in comments upon Christian texts.

336. See also Table 4.24 and the attendant discussion.

337. Both the Paul of Romans and the Paul of Acts speak of Jewish rejection of Jesus. For Paul this is a temporary rejection, so that gentiles will believe (Romans 11, especially v. 25). In Acts this rejection has a sense of finality (28:25–28).

338. Hendiadys is a figure of speech that in which two words linked by a single conjunction express a single idea. In Acts 1:25, for example, "in this ministry and apostleship" (NRSV) means "apostolic ministry" (so NAB).

339. Aejmelaeus, *Rezeption,* 105–8, has a number of other intertextual proposals regarding Acts 20:20 and 27.

340. Cf. also Table 4.24.

341. Cf. Acts 19:21. Paul resolved in the Spirit to go through Macedonia and Achaia, and then to go on to Jerusalem (πορεύεσθαι εἰς Ιεροσόλυμα). He said, "After I have gone there, I must also see Rome."

342. Romans 15:30–31: I appeal to you, brothers and sisters, by our Lord Jesus Christ and by the love of the Spirit, to join me in earnest prayer to God on my behalf, 31 that I may be rescued from the unbelievers in Judea, and that my ministry to Jerusalem may be acceptable to the saints.

343. The verses say, in effect, "I have no idea what will happen to me in Jerusalem. The only available information forecasts imprisonment, and there is no better authority for this slender datum than repeated messages from the Holy Spirit."

344. See also under verse 24.

345. I have left the NRSV translation "persecution" unaltered, although it is often misleading—certainly misleading if it evokes scenes of cruel officials tossing brave Christians to ravenous lions before cheering crowds. Much of the "persecution" of which Paul speaks is like that experienced by Muslim women in the U.S. because of their dress, or the difficulties strictly observant Jews experience in seeking food when in gentile surroundings, i.e. the experience of "otherness" that is often troubling to the majority culture and leads to various forms of harassment.

346. Acts 14:22; Rom 5:3; 2 Cor 1:4–8; 2:4; 6:4; 7:4; etc.

347. The expression seems to have a slightly different meaning in the two passages, but this does not indicate how Luke might have understood it had he read Philippians.

348. For more discussion see Aejmelaeus, *Rezeption*, 117.

349. Bruce (*Acts*, 433) cites a number of passages: 2 Cor 4:7–11; 6:4–10; 12:9–10; Phil 1:20; 2:17; 3:8; also cf. Col 1:24. Aejmelaeus, whose discussion should be consulted (*Rezeption*, 119–28), pays particular attention to Phil 2:16–17, the structure of which he finds to be parallel to that of Acts 20:24 (122).

350. It is not especially significant that both texts use ψυχή, "life," in this context.

351. Walton, *Leadership*, 178.

352. The image of "table service" is prominent in Luke 10:40 and Acts 6:1; in the latter case it is related to charitable activity as in 11:29; 12:25 (which is Pauline, "the ministry to the saints in Jerusalem," i.e., the Collection). Note also the verb "serve" in Luke 10:40; 12:37; 17:8, and 22:26–27. Acts 1:17, 25 describe the apostleship as "ministry," while 6:4 speaks of a "ministry of the word."

353. Paul's view is close to Mark 10:45 ("The Son of Man did not come to be ministered to but to minister and to give his life . . ."), a verse that Luke did not retain in that form.

354. On the accounts of the conversion see Table 4.29.

355. On Acts 15:7–11 see above,

356. Mark uses the noun seven times, in no case followed by Luke. The use of this word in early Christianity is the subject of pp. 1–48 of H. Koester's *Ancient Christian Gospels*.

357. Elsewhere the expression occurs once in the *Miscellanies* of Clement of Alexandria (3.1.2) and in Origen, *Notes on the Song of Solomon* (Scholia *in Cant. Cant.*) 17.281 (as well as twice in Origen's comments upon Ephesians).

358. Note, however, Acts 14:3: "So they remained for a long time, speaking boldly for the Lord, who testified to the word of his grace" (τῷ λόγῳ τῆς χάριτος αὐτοῦ) . . .

359. For comments on intertextuality here see Aejmelaeus, *Rezeption*, 128–32.

360. See Chapter Six.

361. Luke elsewhere uses the image: Luke 17:7–10. For Paul note also 1 Cor 9:7. The difference is between the occasional employment of metaphors for "pastoral" work and the fixation of these metaphors in titles and structure. Today "pastor" means simply the leader of a religious community, and thus is essentially a dead metaphor.

362. Examples of the expression "Church of God" in Paul include 1 Cor 1:2, 10:32, 11:22; 15:9; 2 Cor 1:1; Gal 1:13.

363. Luke's language is (not for the first or only time) difficult here, resulting in problems of both text and translation. For one review of the problems see Walton, *Leadership*, 94–98, and his references.

364. Aejemelaeus, *Rezeption*, 135.

365. An example is the study of the language and style of Colossians presented by Eduard Lohse, *Colossians and Philemon*, 84–91.

366. Steve Walton, *Leadership*, 173.

367. Note also the remarks of C. Spicq, *Theological Lexicon* 3:100–102.

368. p. 46.

369. For additional arguments see M. Goulder, "Did Luke Know any of the Pauline Letters?," 107–08.

370. For references acknowledging that this is Pauline see Walton, *Leadership*, 161 n.110.

371. Romans 15:14; 1 Corinthians 4:14; Colossians 1:28; 3:16; 1 Thessalonians 5:12, 14 [above], and 2 Thessalonians 3:15.

372. Gal 2:10; Eph 2:11; Col 4:18; 1 Thess 1:3, 2:9 (above); 2 Thess 2:5; 2 Tim 2:8; elsewhere it is found once each in the Synoptics, three times in John, three times each in Hebrews and Revelation.

373. Aejmelaeus examines the phrase in detail, *Rezeption*, 151–53.

374. Cf. Acts 20:28.

375. See also pp. 146–47 below.

376. Haenchen, *Acts*, 595: "This speech also, despite its brevity, gives the reader the impression of a long address. This is partly due to the large number of themes in it."

377. An "exemplarist Christology" views Jesus as an example of the righteous life, one who showed by his actions the path approved by God. An ethical corollary is to approach dilemmas by asking: "What would Jesus do in this situation?" *[handwritten margin note: exemplarist Christology]*

378. Paul uses "night and day" in 1 Thessalonians of his employment. Luke admires the phrase but applies it to pastoral activity, making Paul a pastor who never sleeps. He also works for a living, to be sure, as a means of avoiding imposition upon his charges, and, while he is at it, to support his colleagues.

379. Walton raises this criticism, *Leadership*, 209–10. Against Bruce and Hemer *et al.* one can raise the objection that the "we narrator" whom they presume to be the author of Acts cannot have had much experience with "the pastoral Paul," for that contact was essentially limited to the stops between Philippi and Jerusalem (20:5–21:14 [less 20:13b]).

380. Walton, *Leadership*, 212. My critique of Walton should not be construed as objection to his positive estimation of many of the ideas about leadership promulgated in the Miletus speech.

381. Note that treatment of vv. 29–30 has been reserved for Chapter Six.

382. Ben Witherington seeks to demonstrate the "Pauline" character of the speech with a list of parallels: *Acts* 610. His list does not extend beyond v. 26. Page 611 takes up some issues from vv. 28–30, but not without sufficient detail to constitute argumentation. Steve Walton devotes a chapter to the possible use of Eph and 2 Tim (*Leadership*, 186–98). This amounts to a critique of the work of Mitton and of a rather eccentric theory of Walter Schmithals. Walton too often proceeds as if formulating objections to an argument constitutes its demolition.

383. Farewell speeches and Testaments often deal with the question of succession. I do not wish to suggest that Luke has a concept of succession like that of "apostolic succession," but he does intend to portray an orderly transition of power.

384. See Aejmelaeus, *Rezeption* 158. Other passages include Heb 1:14; 6:12.

385. 1 Corinthians has six occurrences of "edify." "Build" occurs in Rom 15:20 and Gal 2:18 (also 1 Peter 2:5, 7). The use of ἀνοικοδομεῖν in Acts 15:16 is similar. See Walton, *Leadership*, 180–81.

386. Ephesians also uses synonyms: ἐποικοδομεῖν (2:20), and συνοικοδομεῖν (2:22). See O. Michel, οἰκοδομέω,κ.τ.λ., *TDNT* 5:137–48.

387. The perfect participle ἡγιασμένοι, occurs only in these two passages in Acts, as well as 1 Cor 1:2.

388. Cf. also Heb 9:15; 11:8 and 1 Pet 1:4.

389. See, on the Pauline texts, the comments of Rudolf Schnackenburg, *Ephesians: A Commentary*, 222–23.

390. Acts 26:18, alludes to Isa 42:6–7; which is a key lucan passage. Acts 20:32 is partially dependent upon Deut 33:3–4, as shown by Aejmelaeus, *Rezeption*, 162–63.

391. Aejmelaeus has a full and rather balanced discussion of intertextual possibilities, *Rezeption*, 155–66.

392. *The Epistle to the Ephesians*, 214–15.

393. Mitton, *Epistle to the Ephesians*, 213.

394. One does not suspect that Bar-Jesus, a.k.a. Elymas, (13:6–12) was a "tent-making" spiritual director or that the "Sons of Sceva" (19:13–17) performed exorcisms out of a sense of social concern.

395. 1 Thess 2:3–12; 2 Thess 3:7–10; 1 Cor 9:3–18; 2 Cor 4:5; 8–9; 10:1–6; 11:7–11; 12:13.

396. Financial (mis)management will be examined in greater detail in Chapter Six. On this matter see, for example, D. Georgi, *Remembering the Poor*.

397. See pp. 193–94.

398. Walton, *Leadership*, 167–72.

399. Such are the "wolves" of 20:29, who are characterized as βαρεῖς, "fierce," using the same adjective employed by Paul in his claim that he was not a burden upon his charges, although he could "lean on" them (ἐν βάρει). "Oppressive" would not be a bad translation. See also Walton, *Leadership*, 167.

400. The classic study is Abraham J. Malherbe, *Paul and the Popular Philosophers*. On pp. 35–48 he shows that this "apology" is not a defense against specific charges made in Thessalonica. On working teachers see Ron Hock, *Social Context*, 26–65.

401. Conzelmann, *Acts*, 176, on 20:34–35.

402. *Rezeption*, 169. I have supplied the parenthetical expressions to explicate the contexts.

403. The ancient world in general and the Greco-Roman world in particular did not believe that work was "good for you," character-building, or anything of the that sort. When Adam heard "By the sweat of your face you shall eat bread" (Gen 3:19), he was not expected to conclude that he had at last found meaningful work. Underemployment was chronic in many places. Paul urges work as a means of staying out of trouble and avoiding the entanglements that dependence can bring. (Such entanglements could include the expectation of conformity to a patron's religious preferences.)

404. *Acts*, 436.

405. "*Ces mains qui opèrent des miracles (Ac 14,3; 19,11; 28,8) et communiquent le Saint Esprit (19,6) sont aussi les grosses mains d'ouvrier, déformées par un dur labeur.*" *Le discours de Milet. Testament pastoral de Saint Paul (Actes 20,18–36)*, 301.

406. A standard work is G. Agrell, *Work, Toil and Sustenance: An Examination of the View of Work in the New Testament*.

407. Titus 3:14 shows a further shift toward the notion of labor as a value: "And let people learn to devote themselves to good works in order to meet urgent needs, so that they may not be unproductive."

408. See Aejmelaeus, *Rezeption*, 170–71, and Walton, *Leadership*, 171. It is noteworthy that a number of the "Paulinisms" here are found also in 1 Thessalonians.

409. A relevant example is 1 Cor 4:12 καὶ κοπιῶμεν ἐργαζόμενοι ταῖς ἰδίαις χερσίν· λοιδορούμενοι εὐλογοῦμεν, διωκόμενοι ἀνεχόμεθα, ("we grow weary from the work of our own hands.").

410. The only use of "silver and gold" in the undisputed letters is at 1 Corinthians 3:10, and there in a quite different sense. The word ἱματισμός (clothing) is not found in the genuine letters. The verse affirms obedience to the command "Thou shalt not covet thy neighbor's goods." This responds to convention: authentic philosophers/teachers did not practice their profession in order to get rich.

411. Cf. Walton, *Leadership*, 171. Aejmelaeus discusses the background of the saying in full detail: *Rezeption*, 175–83.

412. This comment is not so frivolous as it may seem. Diogenes Laertius's *Lives of the Greek Philosophers* indicates that there was an interest in just such gossip and trivia. Readers discover, for example, that the Stoic Chrysippus was quiet but unsteady on his feet when drunk (7.183).

413. A pertinent example is the proposal of an "itinerary" source behind the journeys of Acts 20–21 and 27:1–28:14 (16). Such a source would explain much, but the absence of a persuasive rationale for it has led many to attribute the information to the author. See Appendix I.

414. This is not to imply that there are no such traditions or that identification of them would not facilitate arguments like these.

415. See pp. 204–8.

416. *Leadership and Lifestyle*, 186–98.

417. Walton, *Leadership and Lifestyle*, 198.

418. If, as most authorities now maintain, Rom. 16 is an integral part of that letter, verses 17–20 must be a subsequent interpolation based upon the conviction of at least some early

Christian editors that *every* letter of Paul must attack false teachings. I presume that Paul would not write his longest extant letter without breathing a hint of the danger of false teachings until the conclusion, where he assigns them three verses sandwiched between his closing greetings and the final blessing.

419. For example, Robert Jewett, *The Thessalonian Correspondence: Pauline Rhetoric and Millenarian Piety.* (Philadelphia: Fortress Press, 1986).

420. See p. 315.

421. See p. 79.

422. Bruce, *Acts*, 480.

423. Bruce, *Acts*, 481.

424. The allegations against Paul are reminiscent of those against Stephen (6:11–14), and for the reader are no less malicious than are charges against Jesus (Luke 23:2).

425. Even though by this time the company of believers is too large for a general community meeting (21:20).

426. On this subject see also A. Lindemann, *Paulus*, 169–70.

427. I do not regard the statement about his "knowing only the baptism of John" (Acts 18:25) as credible. This is a Lucan theme (cf. 19:1–7). Alexandrian Christianity long remained under a cloud; in the circles from which early orthodox Christianity would arise, Alexandrian origin was a red flag. Although Irenaeus mentions orthodox leaders and communities in many regions, Alexandria constitutes a notable exception.

428. Wisdom and eloquence are leading themes in 1 Cor 1–4. Some found Apollos more appealing than Paul (3:1). He "watered" after Paul "planted" (3:6).

429. Knox, "Acts and the Pauline Letter Corpus," *SLA*, 279–87, 284.

430. See pp. 29–30.

431. Knox, "Acts and the Pauline Letter Corpus," 282.

432. Knox, "Acts and the Pauline Letter Corpus," 282.

433. See pp. 60–62.

434. These intuitions and conjectures are no less subject to the influence of prejudice than are any others. The prejudice here is the prevalent view that Luke did not use the letters.

435. This is not to say that Luke is "no longer" a theologian or an historian.

436. There may be/have been an unconscious, certainly unarticulated, assumption that, had Luke known the letters, he would have embraced and espoused their patently superior theology.

437. See Aejmelaeus, *Rezeption*, 56–57, whose arguments I follow and expand.

438. On *1 Clement* see p. 53.

439. For evidence see the thorough discussion by Lindemann, *Paulus*, 240–52.

440. Another late witness is 2 Peter, which can speak of Paul's letters without falling into transports of admiration, 3:15–16.

441. See p. 60–62.

442. I think it unlikely that the self- or posthumously edited collections of letters from antiquity are absolutely complete, even in the case of Cicero, whose collected letters include many minor items. Modern practice suggests that there are two reasons for excluding items from "collected works." One is unworthiness; another is "cannibalism." The latter refers to the practice of incorporating a once independent short story in a larger work, such as a novel. Partition theories related to Pauline letters presume "cannibalization." Having combined parts of other letters to make one, the editors had no interest in retaining the original. "Unworthiness" is an assumption: some of Paul's administrative or personal notes did not merit collection because they lacked importance. Others could have been relegated to oblivion because of their content. The edition of Romans that contained only chaps. 1–14 probably illustrates both. Chapter 16 dealt with personal and local issues, which were of no particular interest and could limit the universal application of the letter. Chapter 15 spoke of Paul's plan to visit Spain, which was not fulfilled, and of his forthcoming delivery of the Collection, which was evidently rejected. When legend filled the vacuum and described the trip to Spain, yet another edition, composed of chaps. 1–15 came into use. The plurality of editions indicates that the sixteen-chapter form, with all of the local addresses and other material, remained in circulation, or at least in existence, although some editions of the Pauline corpus dropped the final two chapters.

443. Not even Marcion would have been interested in retaining evidence of Paul's efforts to make peace with Jerusalem.

444. Acts 21:27–29 attributes the attack on Paul in the Temple to "Asian Jews," presumably Ephesians, for they were said to recognize Trophimus, an Ephesian. For discussion on the rejection of the collection, see J. Painter, *Just James*, 54.

445. Administrative material embedded within Pauline correspondence includes 2 Cor 8, 2 Cor 9, and Phil 4:10–20. 2 Cor 8:20–24 is explicit about the matter of accounting. Since Paul wrote letters in his efforts to raise funds, it is eminently reasonable to think that he might have written letters, or seen to it that others did so, to explain what became of those funds.

446. See pp. 204–5

447. For a survey of the issues associated with the title and destination of Ephesians see E. Best, "Recipients and Title of the Letter to the Ephesians: Why and When the Designation 'Ephesians'?' *ANRW* 2.25.4, 3247–79.

448. Aejmelaeus, *Rezeption* 188 n.3, citing Enslin, " 'Luke' and Paul," 84, with a reference to Walker, "Acts and the Pauline Corpus Reconsidered," 14.

449. On the unity of Luke and Acts see, for example, R. Tannehill, *Narrative Unity*. Cautions about facile generalizations of this unity are raised by M. Parsons and R. Pervo, *Rethinking the Unity of Luke and Acts*. S. Walton, *Leadership*, 40–44, provides a discussion and numerous references.

450. To mention but a few other efforts: the writer of 2 Thessalonians wishes to provide a framework for reading 1 Thessalonians; Ephesians provides a general perspective for understanding Paul. Marcion wrote his *Antitheses* to give a theological groundwork for his "Gospel" and "Apostle" (an edition of Luke and of ten Pauline letters). The author of the Pastoral Epistles provides a conservative Paul as a benchmark. Irenaeus uses a collection including the Pastorals and relies heavily upon the framework established by Luke and Acts.

451. Compare the comments of Barrett, *Acts*, 2:lxvi–lxx.

452. On this connection, see Table 6.6.

453. The text of this passage is disputed. See the discussion above, pp. 66–67.

454. This table closely follows Leppä's outline, *Luke's Critical Use*, 63, with comment 63–66.

455. Paul Wendland was confident that the author of Acts used the letters of Paul and that a collection must have existed when he wrote, *Die Hellenistisch-römische Kultur in ihren Beziehungen zu Judentum und Christentum. Die urchristlichen Literaturformen*, 333. In this, as in many other matters, his views, despite shifts in method, deserve fresh consideration.

456. See the chart in *Making Charisma*, 64–65.

457. See Thomas H. Campbell, "Paul's Missionary Journeys as Reflected in His Letters," and Joseph A. Fitzmyer, "The Pauline Letters and the Lucan Account of Paul's Missionary Journeys," 82–89.

458. I presume that the Galatians to whom Paul wrote were ethnic Galatians (Celts) who dwelt in the Galatian territory. This is the so-called "North Galatian" hypothesis. For more detail see Fitzmyer, "Lucan Account," 83–85.

459. This is the presupposition of the work of F. F. Bruce, as in his *Paul: Apostle of the Heart Set Free*, the grounds for which are set forth in "Is the Paul of Acts the Real Paul?" as well as the research of Colin Hemer (*Book of Acts*) and, in general, the moderate and conservative traditions, represented also by the articles of Campbell and Fitzmyer, cited above. Charles Talbert includes itinerary data on the "historical" side of his Appendix A, "What is Meant by the Historicity of Acts?" (*Reading Acts*, 237–54), 242–43. Campbell's views receive approval from W. G. Kümmel in his *Introduction to the New Testament*, 254. The assumptions challenged here may properly be called "mainstream."

460. For example, Acts 15:36–39 indicates that Luke was aware that Paul left Antioch after the quarrel recorded in Gal 2:11–14 and that he no longer worked with Barnabas. Acts 15:36–39 accords with the location of the split (Antioch) and with the time (following the conference at Jerusalem), but it would be difficult to deduce these facts from Gal 2, for Paul does not describe his career subsequent to the visit of Peter to Antioch. This appears to require the existence of some other source, of whatever nature. Lüdemann, *Early Christianity*, 171, agrees, but does not seek to delineate this tradition. Critical scholarship is in agreement that Luke's explanation of the separation is his own.

461. On this putative source see Appendix I.

462. See George Lyons, *Pauline Autobiography: Toward a New Understanding.*

463. Leppä, *Luke's Critical Use,* 64; M. Enslin, "Once Again," 259–60.

464. Barbara Thiering, "The Acts of the Apostles as Early Christian Art," in *Essays in Honour of Griffithes Wheeler Thatcher,* Ed. E. C. B. MacLaurin, 139–89. Thiering is not hesitant to advance daring hypotheses, but her work lacks methodological rigor. Morton Enslin may have leaned toward the view that Luke lacked other sources, but he did not say so, as Leppä observes in *Luke's Critical Use,* 31.

465. Riesner restricts himself to Roman citizenship, *Paul's Early Period,* 157–66. Rapske deals at some length with Tarsian citizenship also, *Paul in Roman Custody,* 71–112.

466. See above, pp. 100–101

467. The counter-arguments in mind are those of Lentz, *Luke's Portrait of Paul,* 23–61 and W. Stegemann, "War der Apostel Paulus ein römisher Bürger?"

468. See p. 195.

469. Robinson himself exemplifies several of the fallacies identified in this excursus, most notably by claiming that, since he does not accept proofs that *x* is "late," it is therefore early. His discussion of the date of Luke and Acts, for example (*Redating the New Testament,* 88–92), restates the arguments of Harnack. Robinson sees and notes some of the weaknesses of these claims and thus rests his case on the contention that (in his view) no strong arguments can be offered to support an early date for Luke and Acts. His "bottom line" is that whatever cannot to his satisfaction be proven late, is therefore early. Yet, as Tyson insists in his essay "The Date of Acts," Robinson deserves credit for raising the issue of dating and taking the scholarly guild to task for its rather indolent acceptance of received opinions.

Chapter Five
Acts among the Historians

1. See below, n. 260.

2. For a summary of Josephus's life, work, and thought see Harold W. Attridge, "Josephus and His Works," in M. E. Stone, Ed., *Jewish Writings of the Second Temple Period,* CRINT 2.2, 185–232. Note also *Josephus and the New Testament* by Steve Mason, whose proposals will receive further attention below.

3. Cadbury and the Editors, "Subsidiary Points," 355–56. So, for example, B. Niese, the editor of Josephus, could say, in the early twentieth century, "We must regard the evangelist Luke as being the first to make use of his [Josephus's] works, not a few well-attested indications of such dependence being found alike in the third Gospel and in the Acts of the Apostles," "Josephus," in J. Hastings, Ed., *Encyclopedia of Religion and Ethics* 7: 569–79, 577.

4. *Gospel History and Transmission,* 105–10, citing 106. Morton Scott Enslin proposed that Luke had made use of both Josephus and Paul: *Christian Beginnings,* 422–24. Joseph Klausner also maintained, in his once famous *From Jesus to Paul,* 223–30, that the author of Acts used both the letters of Paul and Josephus.

5. Max Krenkel, *Josephus und Lukas: Der schriftstellerische Einfluß des jüdischen Geschichtschreibers auf der christlichen nachgewiesen.*

6. One may also note that Krenkel's study appeared at a time when authorities like Harnack were arguing for an early date for Acts, and the opponents of Tübingen were everywhere triumphant. He could not have selected a less propitious time for publication.

7. H. J. Cadbury and the Editors, "Subsidiary Points," 356. On his own authority, however, Cadbury held in 1933 that "there is exceedingly good ground for thinking that Luke was acquainted with the writings of Josephus," "Roman Law and the Trial of Paul," 328.

8. *Book of Acts,* 372. Heinz Schreckenberg thought that he could, without embarrassment, ignore much of what Krenkel had to say, "Flavius Josephus und die Lucanischen Schriften," in W. Haubeck and H. Bachmann, eds., *Wort in der Zeit,* FS K. H. Rengstorf, 179–209, 193 n.36.

9. W. K. Hobart argued that Luke's vocabulary proved him a physician (*The Medical Language of St. Luke*). This thesis enjoyed three decades of growing popularity before it was shredded by H. J. Cadbury's *The Style and Literary Method of Luke,* 39–72. Hobart showed

that Luke shared much of his vocabulary with medical writers, but neglected to determine whether Luke or those writers shared their vocabulary with other, non-medical, writers.

10. Hemer, *Book of Acts*, 95. An example of that "vogue" is B. H. Streeter, who proposed a sort of compromise: Luke may have heard public readings by Josephus. He sets out this idea in *The Four Gospels: A Study of Origins*, 556–58. Steve Mason hit upon the same idea, apparently independently, *Josephus and the New Testament*, 225, as did, evidently, Barbara Shellard, whose contribution will be discussed at the end of this chapter.

11. Hemer seems content to refer his readers to a two-page refutation by Plummer, from 1901 (95 n.104), although he returns to the subject on p. 372. Other than making assertions and posing rhetorical questions, Plummer lists a number of unremarkable words shared by Luke and Josephus (against the LXX—Krenkel did have at least one control). He does not even touch upon substantive parallels in content. (A. Plummer, *A Critical and Exegetical Commentary upon St Luke*, xxix-xxx). The prevailing view that Luke did not know Josephus is summarized by F. F. Bruce in "The Acts of the Apostles: Historical Record or Theological Reconstruction," *ANRW* II 25.3, 2569–2603, 2590. A good, brief survey of research on the question appears in G. Sterling, *Historiography and Self-Definition*, 365–66. (Sterling did not deem it necessary to examine Krenkel's monograph.)

12. Barbara Shellard holds a view very much like mine: "Although M. Krenkel overstated the case for the dependence of Luke on the *Jewish Antiquities*, with the unfortunate result that many critics have dismissed the evidence he offered altogether, there are nevertheless many significant points of contact between the two texts." *New Light on Luke: Its Purpose, Sources and Literary Context*, 32.

13. Cadbury did not claim that he had "deprived Luke of his doctorate" by proving that he was not a physician, but only that Hobart *et al.* had not demonstrated that "Luke" was a physician.

14. In 1931 Frederick J. Foakes-Jackson felt obliged to devote two pages of his brief introduction to this issue. He concludes that Luke "owes little or nothing" to Josephus, largely on the grounds of errors in Acts 5:36–37 and Luke 3:1: *The Acts of the* Apostles, xv.

15. Steve Mason, *Josephus and the New Testament*, 185–225. This is a handbook in form and therefore lacks the scope for detailed scholarly argument.

16. Style is one of the unwelcome questions that are continually injected into genre discussions. Although style and genre do not enjoy fixed relationships, there are connections. The dogma that a genre required an appropriate style was rather more dominant in antiquity than it is today. Those who want to find Josephus and Luke proximate in genre need to account for differences not only in content but also in matters of style.

17. Gregory E. Sterling, *Historiography and Self-Definition*. "Apologetic Historiography" is Sterling's term for what he considers to be the common genre of Josephus and Luke/Acts. One small difficulty with this well-developed and informative hypothesis is that the contents of Luke's Preface more closely relate to those of Josephus's *War*. In short, the criteria by which Josephus distinguishes his works (see, e.g., *War* 1.17–18) are like those advanced in the preface to Luke, whereas ἀρχαιολογία (*Antiquities*) depends upon older sources and relates events of the distant past. Sterling therefore proposes a Luke who achieves something like the *Antiquities* while claiming to write a work more like the *War*. This difficulty is only partially relieved by Loveday Alexander's demonstration that the prefaces to Luke and Acts do not formally belong to the types found in historical works (*The Preface to Luke's Gospel*).

18. Steve Mason, "Chief Priests, Sadducees, Pharisees and Sanhedrin in Acts," in R. Bauckham, Ed., *The Book of Acts in Its First Century Setting*, vol. 4: *Palestinian Setting*, 115–177.

19. Both make similar truth claims, with similar words. In *Against Apion*, 1.53, defending his *Jewish War* against critics, Josephus says δεῖ τὸν ἄλλοις παράδοσιν πράξεων ἀληθινῶν ὑπισχνούμενον αὐτὸν ἐπίστασθαι ταύτας πρότερον ἀκριβῶς ἢ παρηκολουθηκότα τοῖς γεγονόσιν ἢ παρὰ τῶν εἰδότων πυνθανόμενον. ("Surely they ought to recognize that it is the duty of one who promises to present his readers with actual facts first to obtain an exact knowledge of them himself, either through having been in close touch with the events, or by inquiry from those who knew them." Trans. H. Thackeray, *Josephus* I. LCL, 185. Cf. Luke 1:1–3 . . . πραγμάτων, 2 καθὼς παρέδοσαν ἡμῖν οἱ ἀπ' ἀρχῆς αὐτόπται καὶ ὑπηρέται γενόμενοι τοῦ λόγου, 3 ἔδοξε κἀμοὶ παρηκολουθηκότι ἄνωθεν πᾶσιν ἀκριβῶς καθεξῆς σοι γράψαι . . . (the events just as

they were handed on to us by those who from the beginning were eyewitnesses and servants of the word. I too decided, after investigating everything carefully from the very
first, to write an orderly account for you . . .)

20. *Josephus and the New Testament*, 185–96.

21. *Josephus and the New Testament*, 197–204. Mason succinctly describes one difference:
"Josephus tries to obliterate the equation of 'Jew' with 'rebel,' whereas Luke depends on it
for his appeal." (202).

22. From 6–41 CE Judea proper was supervised by prefects. After Agrippa I (41–44)
these rulers were called "procurators."

23. The conversion of the rulers of Adiabene is discussed below.

24. Alexander was the nephew of Philo Judaeus. Josephus's judgment about the reasons
for his peaceful rule is explicit in *War* 2.220.

25. Since this is a court scene, judicial rhetoric (used in prosecution and defense)
would be appropriate, but this speech is deliberative, the type used for arguing which
alternative is preferable. Other rhetorical flourishes include an A B B A pattern, anaphora,
assonance, variety with reinforcing repetition, and a nicely contrasting pair of closing conditions, the first in the more vague subjunctive, the secondly firmly indicative: if (as some
suppose) . . . if (as it actually is) . . . .

26. Similar sentiment can be found on the lips of an enlightened polytheist, 3 *Macc.* 7:9
and in the rabbinic tradition, *Aboth* 4.14. Gamaliel conforms to Josephus's portrayal of the
Pharisees as Stoic-like believers in Providence (*Ant.* 18.12–15).

27. Some have accepted the challenge. The proposal that Luke offers a summary of
this (and other) speeches is methodologically questionable, for the narrator does not say
"in words to this effect" or the like. If Luke is permitted to summarize without saying so,
permission to invent is also possible. Hemer has this proposal: it is ". . . likely enough in
any case that [Paul] received an account from Gamaliel himself at a time when his mind
was much exercised over the new teaching. He had apparently been close to Gamaliel,
and his teacher's reaction would have made its mark. And Luke, we suppose, was later
close to Paul. Such a reconstruction can only be inferential and speculative, but it is plausible. It might be Paul's first latent imprint on the narrative." (*Book of Acts*, 343 n.72.) Many
things are plausible. It would be more plausible to make Paul the direct source, since
26:10 implies that he was a member of the Sanhedrin. One does not know what kind of a
"mark" Hemer imagines Gamaliel making upon Paul, whose policy was at considerable
variance with that of his "teacher." Witherington concedes that Luke may have concocted
the speech, but allows for the possibility that Paul is the source (234).

28. One potent force driving attempts to redeem Acts 5:34–38 is the nineteenth century
doctrine of Scriptural inerrancy.

29. On the apparently gratuitous defense of Gamaliel's accuracy see the previous note
about the inerrancy of scripture.

30. M. Dibelius, *Studies* 187, endorsed by Haenchen, *Acts*, 252 n.7.

31. Burkitt, *Gospel History*, 107–108.

32. Trans. by William Whiston (1737), *alt.*

33. The references to Pilate, 3:13 and 4:27 are not helpful for fixing the date of the
events in view. At the dramatic date Pilate was still in office, for he held his position from
26–36, but the narrative appears to treat him as a figure of the past.

34. *Acts*, 176

35. Greg Horsley, *NewDoc* 4, (1979) 183–185, citing 183. Horsley's examples are presumably gentiles. On 185 he comes down against the view of Theudas as a hypocorism (nickname). Both Bruce and Hemer (*Book of Acts*, 162 n.5) appeal to Horsley's article, which,
it should be noted, does not support either the claim that Theudas is common and/or a
nickname. (Hemer is much more hesitant than Bruce on this point. He is willing to accept
the possibility of error.) M. H. Williams, "Palestinian Jewish Personal Names in Acts," in
R. Bauckham, ed., *BIFCS* 4, 79–113, finds the name "not much attested among 1st century
Palestinian Jews." She has but one other definite contemporary example, *CIJ* II, 1255.

36. Bruce, *Acts*, 176. (To this one might add *Ant.* 17.285, which speaks of a countryside
brimming with brigandage.)

37. Cf. Richard A. Horsley, with John S. Hanson, *Bandits, Prophets, and Messiahs*, especially 88–189.

38. This same adjective, μέγας, is a variant in 5:36, with strong D-text support.

39. Eusebius, *Ecclesiastical History* 2.11.1–3. φέρε, καὶ τὴν περὶ τούτου παραθώμεωα τοῦ Ιωσήπου γραφήν. ("Well, then. Let's take a look at what Josephus says about this matter.")

40. *War* 2.263. Because Greek numbers were indicated by letters of the alphabet, these data were often altered, confused, or misunderstood. A well-known example is Revelation 13:18 (666 or 616). *Beg.* 4:277 notes the possibility of an "ingenious reconciliation" through confusion of Δ=4 and Λ=30. J. Klausner has some observations on this matter, *From Jesus to Paul*, 27.

41. According to Codex Bezae (without other support) Theudas διελύθη αὐτὸς δι' αὐτοῦ ("He was done away with through his own agency"). This evidently intends to convey that he committed suicide, as had Judas Iscariot.

42. The Christian reader may find irony in the application of ἀνέστη ("rose up") to Theudas and Judas; this is the same verb used for resurrection, e.g. "Jesus rose."

43. For a full discussion of various theories and presentation of the data see HJP 1:399–427, as well as R. Brown, *Birth of the Messiah*, 547–56.

44. So J. Nolland: *Luke 1–9:20*, 99–102, with extensive bibliography 94–96.

45. The name Judas, which belongs to four persons in Acts, was "Enormously popular in 1st-century Palestine," according to Williams, "Palestinian Jewish Personal Names in Acts," 89–90.

46. *Josephus and the New Testament*, 205–08, citing 206. One point of comparison is that in *Histories* 5.9 Tacitus mentions a revolt at the death of Herod, and its suppression by Varus:, ". . . while the Jews were disciplined and divided up into three kingdoms ruled by Herod's sons. In Tiberius' reign all was quiet." (*Tacitus: The Histories*, Trans. K. Wellesley, 276–77). Thus for Tacitus trouble began at the death of Herod (4 BCE).

47. *Josephus and the New Testament*, 208.

48. See Raymond E. Brown, *The Birth of the Messiah*, 35 and Index, 747 s.v. "Herod (the Great)."

49. Dibelius objects to this claim, noting that Judas and/or his sons are not mentioned until sec. 102 (*Studies*, 187). Since fewer than twelve lines of Teubner text separate the end of the Theudas incident from the ref. to Judas, the proximity is rather close.

50. Gerald Downing has made a general and detailed study of similarities between the editorial methods and presuppositions of Josephus and Luke: "Redaction Criticism: Josephus' *Antiquities* and the Synoptic Gospels (II)." Downing has no interest in arguing for Luke's use of Josephus, nor does he claim that Josephus's editorial practices were particularly unusual. The value of his article in the present context is the additional support it provides for general similarities between the methods of Josephus and those of Luke. Among these are such thematic concerns, as their shared "Deuteronomistic" view of law and history and the role played by divine Providence (40, 32). If read from the perspective that Luke may have known Josephus, this article supplies a good deal of support to an hypothesis that was outside of its horizon.

51. The presumption here is that traditional stories may well contain details like "in the days of King Herod" and refer to the birth of someone in a stable or cave, but that specific details like the Proconsulship of Quirinius belong to the realm of literature.

52. Historians since Herodotus have sought to examine "the roots of" major conflicts. This is an important task, even if the efforts more often reveal the biases of the historian than yield a widely accepted theory.

53. Horst Braunert, "Der römische Provinzialzensus und der Schätzungsbericht des Lukas-Evangeliums."

54. Horst Moehring explores the meaning of the census for Luke in "The Census in Luke as an Apologetic Device," in D. E. Aune, Ed., *Studies in New Testament and Early Christian Literature*. FS Wikgren, 144–60.

55. One indication of the deterioration of the consensus that Luke did not use Josephus is the willingness of C. K. Barrett to allow the possibility, *Acts* 1:295.

56. One could argue that Luke's object is not so much the use of a technique of historians as the universalization and hellenization of a prophetic technique. Note in particular, Jer 1:1–2 LXX. See also Isa 6:1.

57. Synchronisms were necessary because ancients used many systems of dating, very few of which were continuous (i.e., starting at year 1) and which began at different times

during the year, according to calendars based upon not only different names and lengths and numbers of months but also upon different (solar, lunar, lunisolar) systems for calibrating a year. A modern example would be, "While Dwight Eisenhower was President of the U.S. and Winston Churchill Prime Minister of Great Britain and Joseph Stalin undisputed head of the Soviet Union . . ." Eisenhower held office from 1953–61. Churchill's second term as Prime Minister was during 1951–55. The time frame is now reduced to less than two years; but since Stalin died in March 1953, this synchronism thus establishes a period of less than two months.

58. For examples and references, as well as a still useful discussion, see E. Klostermann, *Das Lukasevangelium*, 50–51.

59. Joseph A. Fitzmyer, *The Gospel according to Luke I-IX*, 453.

60. Translations obscure the problem: the attested text reads "While Annas and Caiaphas was high priest." Acts 4:6 suggests that "and Caiaphas" is an interpolation designed to correct the error (perhaps influenced by John 18: 13, 24).

61. It also presumes that Luke could readily have put his finger upon the correct information in Josephus. We can do so, because we may consult indices and refer to dates placed in the margin by modern editors, but those who had to struggle with unpaginated and densely written scrolls could have a hard time of it. Cf. Hebr 2:2; 4:6.

62. Plutarch, *Anthony* 36, Cassius Dio 49.32, and Jos. *Ant.* 15.92. The last notes that Antony was crazed with lust and drugs.

63. The inscription is CIG 4521=OGIS 606=IGRR III.1086, the latter two with good notes by Dittenberger and Cagnat, respectively. This inscription refers to a benefactor who describes himself as a former slave of Lysanias the Tetrarch and apparently must be dated to the era of Tiberius. If freed at age 20, he could have been no younger than 70 at the time of his dedication, if it was made at the beginning of Tiberius's reign. *HJP* provides a thorough discussion, 1:567–69. See also Heinz Schreckenberg, "Flavius Josephus und die Lucanischen Schriften," 188–89.

64. H. Schürmann, *Das Lukasevangelium* III, 151.

65. βασιλέα καθίστησιν αὐτὸν τῆς Φιλίππου τετραρχίας δωρησάμενος αὐτῷ καὶ τὴν Λυσανίου τετραρχίαν. The translation is that of L. Feldman in *Josephus IX*, LCL, 143.

66. To make matters interesting, unlike Luke 3:1, this passage does not include Trachonitis in the territories of Philip's dominion, the extent of which Josephus gives in varied form: *Ant.* 18.106, 189, and 319; *War* 2.95. See *HJP* 1:336–38 nn. 1–2 (which also opines that ". . . Luke's statement that Philip also ruled over Iturea is not altogether incorrect. But . . . [t]he Ituraeans proper inhabited the Lebanon . . ."), 338. Nolland (*Luke 1–9:20*, 139) finds that "Iturea is a rather fluid designation." He further notes that Luke omits Perea from the territory of Antipas. Completeness was not Luke's object.

67. Trans. Whiston.

68. The lives of gentiles who transgressed the Temple were forfeit. The Roman government did not dispute summary justice (i.e., lynching) in such cases. Less clear, however, are the legal standing of and jurisdiction over a Jew, such as Paul, who introduced gentiles into a forbidden place.

69. The Greek question, οὐκ ἄρα σὺ εἶ can be construed either as positive—"You are the Egyptian, aren't you?"—or as negative—"You aren't the Egyptian, are you?" The former is grammatically sound, while the context seems to support the latter. See Barrett, *Acts* 2:1024–25.

70. The term is a Latin loan-word, a metonymy derived from the concealed dagger that was their weapon of choice. Josephus is evidently responsible for introducing the word into Greek. It also appears in Rabbinic writings and a few times in patristic sources. Josephus is the probable source of these. See O. Betz, σικάριος, *TDNT*, 7:278–82.

71. Horsley and Hanson discuss their history and goals: *Bandits*, 200–216.

72. Trans. H. St. J. Thackery, *Josephus II*, LCL, 423.

73. Trans. L. H. Feldman, *Josephus IX*, LCL, 479.

74. Mason, *Josephus and the New Testament*, 210.

75. Mason, *Josephus and the New Testament*, 212.

76. Mason, *Josephus and the New Testament*, 209. He refers to *Ant.* 20.160; *War* 2.259; cf. 264.

77. Trans. H. St. J. Thackeray, *Josephus II*. LCL, 423–425, alt.

78. Trans. L. H. Feldman, *Josephus IX* LCL, 477–481. See also *War* 2.261.

79. *Josephus and the New* Testament, 214.

80. See, for example, *War* 1.88–89; 2.8–13; 42–48; 169–74; 223–27; 229–31; 315–20; 406–7; and 449–56.

81. Trans. H. St. J. Thackeray, *Josephus II*. LCL, 327.

82. Note also that the use of two chains in 21:33 establishes a parallel to the experience of Peter, 12:6.

83. D. J. Boorstin offers a good popular survey of the place of memory in learned societies prior to printed books in *The Discoverers*, 480–88, with references on 703.

84. A discussion of the depictions of urban unrest in ancient popular literature appears in R. Pervo, *Profit with Delight*, 34–39.

85. *Josephus and the New Testament*, 214–23.

86. The term αἵρεσις, "the activity of choosing," developed a specialized sense of a group that adhered to the life-style and doctrine of a particular philosophy/philosopher, thus "sect" in the sense of a "school," such as "the school of 'trickle-down' economics." Other meanings are "faction" and "party." The eventually dominant positions in both Early (post 70) Judaism and early Christianity came to reject the very idea of schools and parties, so that the ruling group refused to view itself as a party and labeled minority movements as "heresies.", These were often named, like philosophical schools, for a leader, such as those of Marcion or Valentinus (cf. Plato and Epicurus, whose followers were and are called "Platonists" and "Epicureans." "Lutheran" is a modern religious example, while "Marxist" shows the continuation of the philosophical tradition.). See H. Schlier, αἱρέομαι, κ.τ.λ., *TDNT*, 1:180–185 and G. Baumbach, *EDNT*, 1:40.

87. Prominent examples include the philosopher Justin, who, as I argued in Chapter Two, does not show certain knowledge of Acts;, Irenaeus, who uses succession arguments of the philosophical type that are independent of Acts;, and Tertullian, who knows both Justin and Acts. The projects of Clement of Alexandria and Origen are built upon the same apologetic foundation. Mason is, of course, aware of this apologetic practice: *Josephus and the New Testament*, 224.

88. Luke uses philosophical affinities to place the Jesus movement in a positive light. These are brief, occasional, and far from systematic, such as the sharing of goods, 4:32–35, and allusions to Socrates, 4:29; 17:16–19. A number of concepts, such as the views of providence and creation, have a background in popular philosophical thought. But when, Paul speaks to the Areopagus, he does not say, for example, that Plato had a valid perception of the divine (possibly borrowed from Moses), as Philo and Christian apologists would say or accept, but that even polytheists were aware of an "unknown god" (17:23–24). Paul's appeal is to religious feeling rather than to the results of intellectual reflection. On the Socratic allusions see L. C. A. Alexander, "Acts and Ancient Intellectual Biography," 56–63.

89. *Josephus and the New Testament*, 220. (I would add to "defense" the phrase "and description," as such analogies were [and are] components of the project of translation, which, in a cross-cultural context, usually includes some apologetic features.).

90. *Contemplative Life* 29: ἔστι δὲ αὐτοῖς καὶ συγγράμματα παλαιῶν ἀνδρῶν, οἳ τῆς αἱρέσεως ἀρχηγέται γενόμενοι πολλὰ μνημεῖα τῆς ἐν τοῖς ἀλληγορουμένοις ἰδέας ἀπέλιπον. Colson renders οἳ τῆς αἱρέσεως ἀρχηγέται γενόμενοι as "The founders of their way of thinking" (F.H. Colson, *Philo IX*, LCL, 129). The preceding period (28) speaks of τὴν πάτριον φιλοσοφίαν ("their traditional philosophy"). The two expressions are essentially synonymous. (In *Plant.* 151 Philo uses the term of a Greek philosophical school.)

91. The (status-quo oriented) dominant Greco-Roman tradition viewed political factionalism with horror. See p. 261.

92. In 1 Corinthians Paul uses αἵρεσις as the essential equivalent of σχίσματα (divisions). See Mitchell, *Rhetoric*, 153 and n.523.

93. The same viewpoint may explain Luke's lack of approval for the term "Christian" (11:26; 26:28), since it can be understood as a label: the "Christ party."

94. One of the characteristics of early Rabbinic Judaism is the rejection of sects. See Shaye Cohen, *From the Maccabees to the Mishnah*, 224–28. The process began after the First Revolt, but was not complete for some decades. In the early 90s Josephus found it useful to discuss the various sects, largely in the present tense, as in *Ant.* 20:199–201, cited below.

95. Cf. also the Syriac *Didascalia* 6.5; Ps-Clem. *Hom.* 2.17, 16.21 and *Gospel of Thomas* 16. O. Hofius asserts that this saying (which is embedded in a series of end-time predictions

found in Mark 13 and parallels) derives from 1 Cor 11:18–19 ("Isolated Sayings of Jesus," in W. Schneemelcher, Ed., *New Testament Apocrypha* 1: 87–90, 88.

96. Of αἱρέομαι, H. Schlier, says "The usage in Acts corresponds exactly to that of Josephus and the earlier Rabbis," 182, *TDNT* 1:180–85.

97. The use of the analogy from philosophy is not "natural." *1 Clement*, for example, describes Christianity as a "body politic" (πολιτεία). This is also Luke's apparent preference, although he makes use of the philosophical terminology, especially for Jewish parties. See chapter eight, below.

98. Josephus, *Life*. 191: περὶ τὰ πάτρια νόμιμα δοκοῦσιν τῶν ἄλλων ἀκριβείᾳ διφέρειν. cf. also *War* 1.110; *Antiquities* 17.41.

99. See the previous note for the similarity to the language of Josephus.,

100. Günter Stemberger, *Jewish Contemporaries of Jesus: Pharisees, Sadducees, Essenes*, 90–91.

101. O. Wesley Allen, Jr., *The Death of Herod: The Narrative and Theological Functions of Retribution in Luke-Acts*. For a review see *CBQ* 60, 355–56.

102. During the reign of the second of Vespasian's sons, Domitian (81–96) there was much resistance on the part of intellectuals. A number of philosophers (including the famous Dio of Prusa, "Chrysostom") were exiled; others were executed or elected suicide. See the following note.

103. The epistolary novel *Chion of Heraclea* probably appeared in the late first century as a coded exhortation to staunch resistance. See N. Holzberg, "Letters: Chion," in G. Schmeling, Ed., *The Novel in the Ancient World*, 653. A useful study of resistance activity and literature during the last third of the first century can be found in Ramsay MacMullen, *Enemies of the Roman Order*, 35–40; 61–68.

104. Trans. Whiston, *alt.*

105. Cadbury and Lake: ". . . [T]here can be little doubt that [the author] intended the readers to see in the death of Agrippa divine punishment for his cruelty to the apostles." *Beg.* 4:139. Josephus is quite prepared to view the fate of Herod Antipas's army as divine punishment for his execution of John the Baptizer, *Ant.* 20.119.

106. Source-criticism is not Allen's leading interest. The study of "type-scenes" as he employs and presents it has much in common with form-criticism, (*Death of Herod*, 30–35). The chief differences are that this approach is thoroughly synchronic and thus more amenable to the study of authorial choice and literary development, and that "types" are more linked to specific content than are, for example, apophthegms or parables. Although Allen does not state this, the shift from diachronic (as in "the history of the Synoptic tradition") to synchronic is also a characteristic of more recent form-criticism. See, for example, Gerd Theissen's *The Miracle Stories of the Early Christian Tradition*, and, in general, Klaus Berger, *Formgeschichte des Neuen Testaments*.

107. For contextual differences and other valuable discussion see Allen, *Death of Herod*, 53–56.

108. This gruesome symptom was fitting for one who had so many of his progeny eaten by worms, i.e, put to death.

109. *Antiquities* 17.175 refers to both "innocent" (ἀναιτίοις) and those "considered guilty" (παρεσχηκόσιν αἴτιαν).

110. Those with abiding doubts on this matter may dispel them by consulting his stories of the ends of Jehoram, *Ant.* 9.96–104; Aristobulus, *War* 1.70–84, *Ant.* 13.301–19; and Antiochus IV, *Ant.* 12.354–59., All are summarized by Allen in *Death of Herod*, 46–61.

111. Trans. Feldman, *Josephus IX*, 441, *alt.* (The text seems corrupt here; see 440, nn. 5–6).

112. Feldman, *Josephus IX*, 449.

113. Feldman, *Josephus IX*, 449–451: ἐλέγετο οὖν ὑπὸ τῶν θειαζόντων καὶ οἷς ταῦτα προαποφθέγγεσθαι σοφίᾳ πρόκειται, ποινὴν τοῦ πολλοῦ δυσσεβοῦς ταύτην ὁ θεὸς εἰσπράσσεσθαι παρὰ τοῦ βασιλέως. Feldman's translation is potentially euphemistic. θειάζω refers to inspiration, possession, and/or divination. προαποφθέγγομαι more likely means "announce in advance," "predict." Josephus apparently intends to identify two types of "prophets": those who discern the cause of affairs and those who predict the future outcome of events.

114. The Latin phrase comes from Horace, *Odes* 3.2.13.

115. *Acts*, 288. See also Schneider, *Apostelgeschichte* 2:97.

116. Hemer, *Book of Acts*, 165.

117. Both Antipas and Archelaus used the name "Herod" on coins and elsewhere.

Josephus calls Antipas Herod, but does not apply this name to Archelaus. For the others the epithet is either popular and unofficial or due to confusion. See *HJP*, 1:354. Note the surprising error of Justin, *1 Apol.* 31, who identifies Herod as king at the time of the production of the LXX. This crudity is a useful indicator of the generality of the name. Outright confusion of Herod the Great and Agrippa is apparent at the conclusion of the *Protevangelium of James* and the *Acts of Peter* (on which see Carl Erbe, "Petrus nicht in Rom, sondern in Jerusalem gestorben,"especially 187). In the *Gospel of Peter* King Herod carries out the crucifixion (1.2).

118. Daniel R. Schwartz, *Agrippa I*, 120, n.50, refutes the claim that there is a coin of Agrippa under the name of Herod.

119. So, for example, Witherington, 80, 369. Lake's note, "The Chronology of Acts," *Beg.* 5:445–474, is outdated at points but remains the most detailed study of the question.

120. See Allen, *Death of Herod*, 6–7, which provides a comparative table. (The last of his points of comparison and contrast is contrived.)

121. M. Dibelius, *Studies*, 19–20.

122. This is the shrewd reading of G. Theissen, *The Gospels in Context*, 81–97.

123. Clear evidence for this multiculturalism comes from Agrippa's coinage. In Judea proper he avoids even the emperor's image, while coins from Caesarea include his own. See the comments of A. Reifenberg, *Ancient Jewish Coins*, 20–21 and his catalogue nos. 58–67, pp. 46–47, with Plate 5. In the catalogue of Meshorer (*Jewish Coins of the Second Temple Period*, these are nos. 85–93 (with differences). See also HJP, 1:446–447, which reports the favorable views of the Mishnaic tradition (not all of which are necessarily historical), 451–452 on his philhellenism; and, 451 n.40, on his coins. Josephus says that Agrippa's impending death moved the public to pray for him in sackcloth and ashes (*Ant.* 19.349). Just what populace is in mind is not perfectly clear, for 356–357 report that the death was an occasion of public celebration in Caesarea and Sebaste.

124. In the foregoing account (previous n.) Josephus mentions as one of the chief outrages the sexual abuse of the princesses' statues by soldiers, who transported them to brothels for that purpose. Their conduct was barbarous beyond doubt, but the very existence of such sculpture would have been offensive to the pious. (See Feldman's surprise, *Josephus IX*, 385 n.e.)

125. Consider the enmity Agrippa aroused in Egypt: Philo, *Flacc*, 25–43. Josephus does not describe this incident.

126. The rags-to-riches story of Agrippa reads like a romantic biography, comparable to the hypothetical *Tobiad Romance* and *Royal Family of Adiabene* analyzed by Larry Wills, *The Jewish Novel in the Ancient World*, 185–93, 206–11. D. Schwartz, *Agrippa I*, points to similarities with Jewish fiction about royalty and court figures. Agrippa's coinage suggests a different scenario: examples displayed in Reifenberg 60/Meshorer 89 depict a puny, naked figure receiving a crown from a larger individual. This would seem to portray the great reversal of Agrippa's fortune.

127. Haenchen, *Acts*, 388.

128. Haenchen's rationale conforms more to Josephus's "Greek tragedy" approach than to Luke's account. His insight is apparent in a subsequent comment: "The fact that Josephus presents Herod's death without any miraculous element . . . may be due to his employment of a source which did not wish to show an allegedly popular king as the object of divine wrath." (*Acts*, 388)

129. *Studies*, 19.

130. In his discussion of sources, 169, Witherington states that Joanna could have provided "stories about the Herods." According to Luke 8:3 Joanna was the wife of one of Herod's [Antipas?] managers. In 24:10 she is among the resurrection witnesses. Witherington evidently assumes that she remained in the Jesus community and was available to provide material to the author of Acts a good two decades later. He does not explain how she could have been a source of gossip, etc. about the Herodians for the period after 30 CE, when she had left the court to follow Jesus.

131. For example, Dibelius, Haenchen, and Witherington, as cited. See also Conzelmann, *Acts*, 96; Barrett reports these views without taking a stance, *Acts* 1:589.

132. *Ecclesiastical History* 2.10.1, Trans. K. Lake, 1:129. On this passage see also below.

133. These variants occur in Bezae (D) and Coptic G067, with mixed support from 614 (v. 20) and Latin and Syriac versions.

134. Although these represent an early text type, they can hold scarcely any claim to be original because there is no rationale for explaining why an abbreviator would remove them, and they "work around" difficulties in the text rather than rewriting it. In sum, one can explain the D-text as a revision of the conventional text, but not vice-versa.

135. Wilfred Knox struggles with these questions in *The Acts of the Apostles*, 38 n.1.

136. One does not know what to make of this story. Was Antioch immune from this ecumenical threat? Were these converts so fond of the "Mother Church" that they were willing to sacrifice their own welfare for them? Scholarship trims down this prediction to local famines in the reign of Claudius, firmed up by evidence from Josephus, *Ant.* 20.51–53 and, interestingly, 101, on which see below, Table 5.10 and comment. This is the tactic of Hemer, *Book*, 165, for example. The reader of Acts would, however, be likely to conclude that these events took place during the reign of "Herod," 12:25.

137. Frederick W. Danker has demonstrated the importance of the fundamental Greco-Roman concept of benefaction for Lukan theology. See, for one example, *Jesus and the New Age*.

138. Mark R. Strom reads this passage in the light of Ezekiel 28–32, "An Old Testament Background to Acts 12.20–23." See the critical remarks of Allen, *Death of Herod*, 95–96.

139. The verb θυμομαχεῖν, most often used of physical violence, i.e., warfare, is enhanced here by the noun εἰρήνη, peace. It is unlikely that Acts implies actual war, but it does seek to show violent rage, an emotion quite disapproved by the philosophical tradition, most particularly for rulers. Seneca wrote a three-volume treatise on the subject, which he called "the most pathological and frenzied of all emotions" (*affectum . . . maxime ex omnibus taetrum ac rabidum*), *On Anger* 1.1.1. The "pre-Christian Paul" of Acts is an example of one dominated by undue zeal and uncontrollable rage. See J.C. Lentz, Jr., *Luke's Portrait of Paul*, especially 83–91.

140. For a detailed discussion see pp. 276–80.

141. The portrayal of Herod in Matthew 2 is intriguingly similar.

142. Wilfred Knox (*Acts* 38–39 n.2) worried about the economic information in 12:20. He asked what the nature of a written source might be. "The most obvious kind of document would be a collection of edifying stories of divine punishments for ὕβρις; Philo's *In Flaccum, Leg. Ad Gaium* and his lost tract on Sejanus represent a monstrous writing up of stories with a moral . . . In this case we should be almost compelled to suppose that Luke is responsible for the detail. A good historian might of course have recorded the death of Herod as a punishment for ὕβρις and Luke might have carried over the irrelevant detail, but it is hard to conjecture who this historian can have been." His question is perceptive. Knox's own solution is that the story came from "public knowledge, as interpreted by the oral tradition of the church of Jerusalem," with detail "from his own knowledge." The first part is not unreasonable, but it is vague, while the second is unlikely. How would Luke have known about an otherwise unrecorded inter-urban conflict in Palestine in the early 40s?

143. Careful attention to Luke 1:5 and 3:1, 19–20 distinguishes the king from the tetrarch, but, after 9:7, only "Herod" is used.

144. As such, "Herod" would have the capital jurisdiction indicated in Acts 12:1–23. The historical details are reasonable. On the other hand, Acts has assumed throughout that the Sanhedrin has the authority to command, indeed to administer, capital punishment.

145. So, e. g., Bruce, *Acts*, 288–289, and Fitzmyer, *Acts*, 490.,

146. Haenchen, *Acts*, 388.

147. The language of the three verses is essentially identical: 5:5 . . . ὁ Ἀνανίας . . . πεσὼν ἐξέψυξεν 5:10; . . . ἔπεσεν δὲ παραχρῆμα . . . καὶ ἐξέψυξεν; 12·23 παραχρῆμα . . . ἐξέψυ ξεν. These are the only uses of the verb in the NT.

148. Dibelius, *Studies*, 20.

149. For Eusebius (*Ecclesiastical History* 2.10) Josephus serves once more as proof of the accuracy of Acts. "Even if he seem to some to differ as to the name of the king, nevertheless the date and the events show that he is the same, and either that the name has been changed by some clerical error or that there were two names for the same man, as has happened with many. (Trans. K. Lake, *Beg.* 1:129). In his quotation of this passage from Josephus Eusebius states: "But after a little looking up he saw an angel seated above his head." (*Ibid.* 2.10.6, p. 131). Eusebius, with probable help from Acts, makes the same transformation.

150. Gerd Lüdemann comes to a similar conclusion: "The Lucan version seems to be an abbreviation of that of Josephus." He makes note of the difficulties in arguing from abbreviation of Josephus and/or ". . . a written source," *Early Christianity* 144.

151. However Luke came up with this situation, it fits so conveniently into his literary pattern that if he did not concoct it, he must have altered it considerably.,

152. Mason, *Josephus and the New Testament*, 224.

153. For scholars like Bruce, Hemer, or Witherington, who believe that Luke had oral authorities, among whom were Paul and other figures, these matters are *not* questions. Those who do not accept this approach to the question of sources are the objects of my endeavor, for it does not seem possible (or particularly desirable) to refute the allegation that Luke made use of oral sources, while a late dating makes the use of people mentioned in the NT rather unlikely.

154. At the allegorical level, the servants evidently correspond to followers of Jesus, who will be judged for their deeds. The others are enemies of the Church, and their destruction is a foregone conclusion.

155. For the text see James M. Robinson, *et al.*, Eds., *The Critical Edition of Q*, 524–57. John Kloppenborg gives a catalogue of those who assign the material to Q and those who do not, in *Q Parallels*, 200. Numerous parables deal with masters and slaves, to be sure, including later compositions and such adaptations about absent masters, as Mark 13:33–37 and the parables embedded in Luke 12:35–48.

156. J. Jeremias, *The Parables of Jesus*, 59.

157. See Frank Weinart, "The Parable of the Throne Claimant (Luke 19:12, 14–15, 27), Reconsidered."

158. Scott, *Hear Then*, 223: "The theme of a throne claimant is frequent in oriental literature."

159. This behavior is distinct from exile in another court and the enrollment of allies, something that is common historical stories.

160. C. F. Evans, *Saint Luke*, 668. Others include B. T. D. Smith, *The Parables of the Synoptic Gospels*; J. Jeremias, *Parables*, 59, and Jan Lambrecht, *Once More Astonished*, 174–75. Weinart, in "The Parable of the Throne Claimant," provides a list of adherents to this view.

161. *Antiquities* 17.342 is, to be sure, slightly more vague. We read it in light of the *War*.

162. I. Howard Marshall, who dates Luke (and Acts) c. 70, says, ". . . [T]he story of Archelaus provides the closest parallel to the parable." *The Gospel of Luke*, 35, 704.

163. Jeremias, *Parables*, 59. For a critique, see Evans and Lambrecht, as cited in n.152.

164. The "Parable of the Pounds" rests astride the categories of allegory and example-story. It was, if critical history be the judge, an unsuccessful experiment. In support of the former understanding of the Throne Claimant, allegory tends to emerge whenever Lukan parables closely reflect salvation history, as in 14:15–24 and 20:9–19.,

165. See p. 234.

166. R. Stoops, "Riot and Assembly," 73.

167. R. Pervo, *Profit with Delight*, 34–39; 77–81.

168. For data see Stoops, "Riot," 79–80.

169. Stoops, "Riot," 81.

170. Stoops, "Riot," 80 n.43.

171. Almost exactly the same words were used by M. Krenkel, *Josephus*, 161.

172. Trans. Whiston, *alt.*

173. Stoops does not claim that he has resolved all of the issues and carefully abstains from judgments about historicity. He has undoubtedly put his finger upon the key factor in the matter.

174. A. Loisy, *Actes*, 744–47, 756. (Stoops records this view without comment, "Riot," 75.)

175. The difficulty of locating the provenance of the "imprisonment epistles" (Philippians and Philemon) has led a large number of scholars to the hypothesis that Paul was incarcerated at Ephesus. Key passages include 2 Cor 1:8–11; 6:5; 11:23; and Phil 1:12–26. Two important studies are Wilhelm Michaelis, *Die Gefangenschaft des Paulus in Ephesus*, and George S. Duncan, *St Paul's Ephesian Ministry*, 59–161. For a modern review of the problem, with bibliography, see Koester, *Introduction* 2:135–40.

176. Although Robinson *et al.* reflect the consensus by not even considering the possibility that Luke 3:10–14 derives from Q, a few have done so. Schürmann, *Lukasevangelium*

1:169 believes that Matthew eliminated the passage so as to make Jesus the only source of ethical instruction. Marshall, *Luke*, 142, assigns it to Q on the grounds that Luke's special material has no data about the Baptizer. Both of these commentators wish to minimize the possibility of Lucan composition. See Kloppenborg, *Q Parallels*, 10. On the passage see also Chapter Four.

177. Dio of Prusa speaks of sharing clothes with those who have none (*Oration* 7.61). Contentment with one's pay or resources is a commonplace: Epictetus, *Diss.* 1.1.27; Philippians 4:11; Hebrews 13:6. On v. 14 see table 4.7.

178. The crowds in Acts 2:37 put the same question to Peter. Note also Acts 16:30. Both of these passages precede baptisms.

179. Joseph A. Fitzmyer, *The Gospel according to Luke I-IX*, 465.

180. The question of whether John was a "Hellenistic moralist" received a very negative answer from the Jesus Seminar:, 0.11, black, with no one voting red ("authentic"), according to Tatum, *John the Baptist*, 144.

181. *Antiquities* 18.117, Trans. L. H. Feldman, *Josephus IX* LCL, 83.

182. According to Tacitus, *Annals* 15.44, Nero claimed that followers of Jesus had tried to burn down Rome. The Roman historian does not believe the charge, but he reluctantly concedes that even Nero could occasionally do the right thing for the wrong reason.

183. Jesus: Luke 7:1–10; Peter: Acts 10:1–11:18.

184. Translated L. H. Feldman *Josephus IX*, LCL, 77.

185. Steve Mason summarizes the material about John in Josephus and compares this with the Gospels, *Josephus and the New Testament*, 150–63. Note also A. R. C. Leaney, *The Gospel according to St Luke*, 161.

186. Wills, *The Jewish Novel in the Ancient World*, 8; see also 206–11. For an introduction and fresh translation see his *Ancient Jewish Novels: An Anthology*, 213–25.

187. Paul's teacher in Acts 5 shares the name Ananias.

188. Josephus, *Ant.* 20.41: δυνάμενον δ' αὐτὸν ἔφη καὶ χωρὶς τῆς περιτομῆς τὸ θεῖον σέβειν, εἴγε πάντως κέκρικε ζηλοῦν τὰ πάτρια τῶν Ἰουδαίων: τοῦτ' εἶναι κυριώτερον τοῦ περιτέμνεσθαι.

189. Note the term "strict," ἀκριβής, discussed above as a characteristic of the Pharisees.

190. *Ant.* 20.44–46, trans. L. H. Feldman, *Josephus IX* LCL, 411–13. Feldman's notes on this passage should be consulted.

191. The differences are also characteristic, and instructive. Izates is reading the Torah, while the Ethiopian is studying a scroll of Isaiah. The conversion of Izates is parallel to that of Paul (and of Aseneth), a prelude to a life of conflict in which he succeeds because of divine support. The Ethiopian is sent into the happy ever after.

192. The text here is quite uncertain.

193. Trans. L. Feldman, *Josephus IX* LCL, 465–67, *alt.*

194. Fitzmyer, *Acts*, 739.

195. Suetonius, in the course of reporting that the Emperor Claudius was dominated by his wives and freedmen, has one of the latter, a eunuch, say that Felix was the husband of three "royal personages." ("*regum*," *Claudius* 28). The generally more reliable and even less flattering Tacitus, while speaking of Felix's government of Judea, says that he married Drusilla, the granddaughter of Antony and Cleopatra (*Histories* 5.9). One solution is to hold that two of his three royal brides were named Drusilla, while the name of the third is unknown. It is more likely that there has been a mistake. Josephus is more likely to be correct, as he was closer to the events, but there is no certainty. (Even the *gentilicum* (surname) of Felix is uncertain, *HJP* 1:460 n.19.)

196. A. D. Nock, "Paul and the Magus," *Essays on Religion and the Ancient World*, 308–330, 326. (=*Beg.* 5:164–188).

197. Lüdemann, *Early Christianity*, 149. (See 148–50, where he presents most of the difficulties.)

198. Nock, "Paul and the Magus," 329.

199. Still useful is the discussion of Alfred Wikenhauser, *Die Apostelgeschichte und ihr Geschichtswert*, 396–398. See also Barrett, *Acts*, 1:615–16.

200. See Feldman, *Josephus IX LCL*, 464 n.*e.*

201. A good deal of variation also appears in the form of the name of "Bar-Jesus." See Metzger, *Textual Commentary*, 354–56.

202. On the text of Josephus see also Heinz Schreckenberg, "Flavius Josephus und die Lucanischen Schriften," 198–99.

203. Rackham, *Acts* 198: "Saul emerges as Paul, and as a second Peter binds a second Simon Magus." See also Nock, "Paul and the Magus," 330.

204. H.-J. Klauck (*Magic and Paganism in Early Christianity: The World of the Acts of the Apostles*, 50) reports the speculations of the irrepressible Theodor Zahn: ". . . thanks to Paul's intervention, Bar-Jesus loses his first patron and must look for a new job; in Josephus, we find him at a new low point in his career, because now he has to work a cheap love spell for Felix . . ." (Klauck refers to Zahn's, "Zur Lebensgeschichte des Apostels Paulus," *NKZ* 15 [1904], 23–41; 189–200. The material summarized is on pp.195–200.) Klauck has a number of useful observations, about this passage, 47–55, as does Susan R. Garrett, *The Demise of the Devil: Magic and the Demonic in Luke-Acts*, 79–87.

205. Trans. Ralph Marcus and Allen Wikgren, *Josephus VIII*, LCL, 219–22. The king is Herod the Great. Agrippa is M. Vipsanius Agrippa, the lieutenant of Augustus. The speaker is Nicolas of Damascus. The date is 14 BCE.

206. Trans. Marcus and Wikgren, 415. Varus was the Roman governor of Syria. The King is Herod the Great. The date is c. 4 BCE.

207. See 25:14–22 and, even more notably, 25:24–26:29.

208. Suetonius, *Titus* 7; Tacitus, *Histories*, 2.2; Cassius Dio 56.15, 18; Quintilian, *Institutes* 4.1.19; and Juvenal, *Satires*, 6.156–60. There is a detailed description of her career in Stern, *GLAJJ* 1:514, with references.

209. In his *Life* 49, Josephus refers to Agrippa and Berenice as "monarchs" (βασιλέων). Her presence thus justifies the plural of Acts 9:15.

210. Acts 27:1 picks up the narrative from 25:12. The intervening material does not advance the plot—which is not to imply that it is not important.

211. For another triangle see p. 42.

212. In *Acts*, 679 Haenchen, appears to accept the gossip about Agrippa and Bernice as fact, and also believes that Luke, like "every educated person" knew it also. He thus says that it must remain in the background. His views are quite debatable.

213. Johnson, *Acts*, 428.

214. On this fallacy see pp. 339–40.

215. The parallel account in *War* 1.620–45 is a bit more than one half as long.

216. Accounts of trials and legal actions in ancient fiction and popular literature are generally much closer to those of Acts in length. For some examples see R. Pervo, *Profit with Delight*, 42–48.

217. The text continues by listing slaves who had been examined under torture as well as assorted witnesses.

218. For example, Bruce, *Acts*, 447.

219. W. Ramsay, *Paul the Traveller*, 310–11.

220. Trans. L. Feldman *Josephus IX*, LCL, 353.

221. Trans. Whiston.

222. Elsewhere in the NT found only in 1 Cor 11, where the meaning is somewhat different. (The use of ἵνα with the future indicative in Acts 21:24 is not good Greek.)

223. See the note of Feldman on the passage cited in Table 5.10. The only Greek examples that he identifies are these from Acts 21:24 and Josephus.

224. The strongest evidence against the historicity of the "Nazirite vow" is the text of Acts itself. James could have come to the aid of Paul, and his four fellow devotees could have constituted unimpeachable witnesses in his behalf. Instead they vanish from the narrative as if they had never existed.

225. For a review of some features of the literary character of this episode see R. Pervo, *Profit with Delight*, 32–33.

226. This statement presumes that other traditions about the death of Paul in Rome would be accepted, much as occurred in the case of Peter. In any case, Acts does not report the death of Paul at Rome.

227. Trans. Whiston.

228. See pp. 175–76.

229. Prophetic examples include Isa 8:21; 14:30; Jer 15:2; Ezek 5:17; 14:13. Predictions of famine from Jewish apocalyptic are *1 Enoch* 80:2; *2 Baruch* 27:6, 70:8; *4 Ezra* 6:22; *Jubilees*

23:18; *Sibylline Oracles* 3.540–42. Early Christian examples of this theme include: Mark 13:8//Matt 27:7//Luke 21:11; Rev 6:8, 18:8.

230. For data see *HJP* 1:457; Bruce, *Acts* 276; Barrett, *Acts* 1:562–564;, and their references. Among the important articles are K. S. Gapp, "The Universal Famine under Claudius," J. Dupont, "La famine sous Claude, Actes 11.28," and R. W. Funk, "The Enigma of the Famine Visit."

231. David Aune, *Prophecy in Early Christianity*, 265.

232. See pp. 175–76.

233. Agabus also appears in Acts 21:10–11. Mark 13:8, Matt 24:7, Luke 21:11, and Acts 11:28 all contain the word "famine" (λιμός) and the future of the verb "to be." In Mark 13 and parallels the noun is plural.

234. Claudius is named specifically in *Ant.* 20.37 and 104.

235. See p. 313.

236. For example, the essays in *Beg.* 2 by W. K. L. Clarke, "The Use of the LXX in Acts," 66–105, and F. C. Burkitt, "The Use of Mark in the Gospel according to Luke," 106–120, cited and utilized in chapter three. Clarke had already demonstrated Luke's freedom with sources through applying traditional source-critical methods.

237. *The Acts of the Apostles*, 235–39.

238. Date is probably an implicit agendum, since dependence upon the *Antiquities* would push Acts into the 90s.

239. It is by no means uncharacteristic of Witherington to accuse those he wishes to refute of taking positions that they do not hold. See *JBL* 118, (1999) 364–66. In fact, much of Mason's argument depends upon material where Josephus is anything but "accurate," such as his analyses of Jewish parties as philosophical sects. The strength of Mason's argument resides in his reliance upon subjective material. Witherington is thus 180 degrees off the mark.

240. Witherington does not seem to realize that his strictures about rhetorical historiography apply equally to Luke, since he associates Acts with such writings (2–51).

241. Witherington, *Acts*, 237.

242. Witherington regards the proposition of two rebels named Theudas as a "modest proposal" (239). He invokes F.F. Bruce (*Acts*, 176) on the matter. The proposal is exactly parallel to the postulation of two censuses to explain the problems of Luke 2. That proposal founders, as has been shown, on Acts 5:37. Witherington's second Theudas conflicts with his own thesis that these were major figures.

243. If Witherington and others (such as F. F. Bruce and C. Hemer) really believed that remarks like those of Gamaliel and the Tribune Lysias were accurate quotations, they would have no need to deal with alleged errors: Luke was not responsible for the statements of his characters. Their discomfort with this excuse speaks loudly about their actual views.

244. Witherington got the idea about the Moses parallel from L. T. Johnson (*The Acts of the Apostles*, 99–100). Witherington is also willing to admit "frankly" that Luke made have been mistaken in his reference to Theudas, an error he is able to depict as motivated by Thucydidean historiography (238–39).

245. Such remarks may be apt in reviewing certain works of known genre and stated purpose. One might well, for example, note that a study of Lincoln which neglected to report that he changed his mind about the emigration of freed slaves "should" have done so. One might also state that certain sources "should" have been consulted. The "shoulds" of Witherington amount to no more than what he would have said had he written Acts with Josephus in hand.

246. H. Schreckenberg, "Flavius Josephus und die Lucanischen Schriften," in W. Haubeck and H. Bachmann, Eds., *Wort in der Zeit*, FS K. H. Rengstorf, 179–209. This study includes a useful history of research and concludes with an excellent bibliography.

247. "Flavius Josephus und die Lucanischen Schriften," 192.

248. Further ado may do it. Q, for example, is a hypothetical source, whereas Matthew and Luke are known sources, but most scholars believe that Q existed. Q, one should recall, is deduced from the comparison of two *known* sources (Matthew and Luke) for evidence of a third. This is quite different from the postulation of a hypothetical source from *one* extant text.

249. "Flavius Josephus und die Lucanischen Schriften," 195–98.

250. "Flavius Josephus und die Lucanischen Schriften," 198.

251. A number of the parallels Schreckenberg discusses are quite unlikely, such as the youthful genius revealed by Josephus and Jesus (*Life* 8–9; Luke 2:46–47), 186. His discussion of John the Baptizer omits consideration of Luke 3:10–14, where, as shown above, one may argue for the influence of Josephus. Note also the highly unlikely connection between *Ant.* 18.36–38 and Luke 14:21–24, p. 191.

252. Shellard, *New Light*, 31–34.

253. Shellard, *New Light*, 17–36. For one example of a superficial approach see 18–19.

254. Shellard even devotes eight of her introductory pages to the question of date (23–31).

255. Shellard is inclined to mask her sources under the passive voice (for example, 31–32 n.81) and to refer to "some" or "many" scholars.

256. Shellard, *New Light*, 33. The idea that Luke heard Josephus lecture goes back to Streeter, and is allowed by Mason (above).

257. For example, Shellard points to such place names as Emmaus and Nain, which are found in Josephus but not in the sources of the Synoptic Tradition (31), takes note of the Fall of Jerusalem, and lays particular stress upon such apologetic matters, as the Areopagus Address and Divine Providence.

258. Shellard, *New Light*, 34.

259. A small parallel not taken up by Shellard but illustrative of what detailed investigation might suggestion or reveal is the use of στρατηγός (=Hebrew *sagan*) for the "Captain of the Temple." The term is found in this particular sense only in Josephus (*War* 6.294; *Ant.* 20.131) and the Lukan writings (Luke 22:4, 52; Acts 4:1; 5:24, 26), although both also use the word in the conventional sense (e.g. Josephus *Ant.* 14.247; Acts 16:20). Dependence is far from impossible, and certainly no more improbable than the existence of another source that preserved this title, which is not a "natural" equivalent to its Hebrew prototype. On the term see *HJP* 2.277–78 and the references there.

260. Josephus remarks at the end of the *Antiquities* (20.267) that he is writing in the thirteenth year of Domitian (81–96), and thus in 93 or 94 CE.

261. See Chapter Three.

262. Sterling, *Historiography and Self-Definition*. Josephus himself appears to have patterned his work upon that of Dionysius of Halicarnassus's *Roman Antiquities* (a model and source that, in keeping with the classic tradition, he does not mention).

263. Cadbury includes Josephus among his comparisons, *Making of Luke-Acts*, 196–201. The view that Luke's prefaces are quite similar to those of Josephus (who wrote in three different genres) has been put to rest by Loveday Alexander, *The Preface*. She analyzes those of Josephus on pp. 160–64. Steve Mason examines these prefaces from the perspective of possible imitation, *Josephus and the New Testament*, 186–92.

264. Barbara Shellard vigorously endorses Sterling's view of the genre of Luke/Acts without reflecting upon her own conclusion that Luke utilized Josephus, *New Light*, 17, 31–34.

265. John Squires, *The Plan of God*, is a recent in-depth study of the subject. B. Shellard regards such imitation as probable, *New Light*, 33–34.

266. Gerald Downing's article "Redaction Criticism" contains many subjects for further investigation of these similarities.

267. A number of observations on the relation of these subjects to Hellenistic Judaism appear in Parsons and Pervo, *Rethinking the Unity*, and Stenschke, *Luke's Portrait of Gentiles*.

268. A difficulty with these ideological comparisons is that topics like the role of Providence in history tend to be based upon the entire *Antiquities* or the full corpus of Josephus's works, whereas the hypothesis advanced in this chapter neither requires nor particularly desires the assumption that the author of Acts had all of Josephus's works available.

Chapter Six
Acts among the Apostolic Fathers

1. By "final text" I mean a critically established text from which later emendations and interpolations have been extricated. This qualification can—and does—create loopholes.

2. See p. 260.

3. Both components are important. Seismologists, for example, may say that plate x will move y centimeters in the course of a century. What they cannot predict with much confidence is whether the movement will happen in one short space of time or quite gradually. The former may result in an earthquake. So it is with history. There are earthquakes, such as the Russian Revolution or the emergence of Islam. Other changes, such as the cleavage between Eastern and Western Christianity or the emergence of a French national consciousness, are quite gradual.

4. A corollary to this is the fallacy that "legends take time to develop." Figures of the past are often idealized (or demonized), but it takes no more than thirty seconds to develop or create a legend. People told and embellished, invented and elaborated, stories about Jesus and Paul within their lifetimes. Olof Linton gives some illustrations in his "The Third Aspect: A Neglected Point of View. A Study in Gal. 1–22 and Acts ix and xv."

5. Since this book was written, the Loeb Classical Library has issued a new, 2 vol. edition of *The Apostolic Fathers*, Ed. and Trans. by Bart D. Ehrman. This is a valuable resource, with a current original text, fresh translation, fine introductions, and excellent short bibliographies for this collection and the individual works contained within it.

6. To this one may add that much of the Christian theology seen and heard in contemporary electronic media is quite "primitive." This quality does not seem to serve as a major detraction from its appeal.

7. Harnack, *Neue Untersuchungen*, 72–79.

8. Hemer repeats them, with attribution, *Book of Acts*, 381–82.

9. By "primitive ecclesiology" Witherington has in mind the difference between Luke and the episcopal system of Ignatius of Antioch, which was far from general in 125. I shall propose that Luke may well have known enough about "bishops" to have some misgivings. All criticism of Gnosticism before c. 150 is so vague that scholars argue about what or whom is being attacked. Luke is well aware of some questionable theology (Acts 20:29–30). "Theology of the cross" is associated with Mark and Paul, in particular, both antecedent to Acts. Montanism emerged c.170, later than anyone has dated Acts. All in all, this is not a very coherent objection.

10. Margaret Y. MacDonald, *The Pauline Churches*.

11. Cf. Acts 14:22; 15:41; 18:23. The verb (ἐπι)στηρίζω could almost be rendered as "stabilize" (through strengthening).

12. στάσις in Acts: in addition to 15:2 ; 19:40 (Ephesian assembly); 23:7, 10 (of Sanhedrin in meeting); 24:5 (accusation against Paul). ὁμόνοια is not found in the NT, although there are many synonyms (such as the language of Acts 2:32 and the word ὁμοθυμαδόν, found eleven times in the NT, ten of which are in Acts [although not always of believing groups]). ὁμόνοια occurs fourteen times in 1 *Clement* and is found elsewhere in the "Apostolic Fathers."

13. C. P. Jones, *The Roman World of Dio Chrysostom*, 94. In addition to the speeches of Dio are *Ors.* 23 and 24 of Aelius Aristides. Apollonius of Tyana is shown devoting himself to this task (4.8–9). For examples from historiography and other genres see Margaret M. Mitchell *Paul and the Rhetoric of Reconciliation*, 60–64.

14. On the Corinthian correspondence see M. Mitchell, *Rhetoric*, and L. L. Welborn, *Politics and Rhetoric in the Corinthian Epistles*, 1–42. Barbara E. Bowe discusses 1 *Clement* in *A Church in Crisis*, 7–74. On Ignatius see W. Schoedel, *Ignatius of Antioch*, 16, 21, 22, 52, 53, 55, 74, 76, 104, 105, 112, 114, 116, 117, 129, 130, 148, 198–199, 202, 206, 213, 251–252, 260, 264, 271, 272, 280, and 281. For both of these Apostolic Fathers see J. Rohde, "Häresie und Schisma im ersten Clemensbrief und in den Ignatius-Briefen."

15. The rhetorical tactic is to appeal to the unity and harmony of the "primitive golden age," as, for example, in 1 *Clement* 1–3 (on which see Chapter Eight). Luke provides the narrative "proof" for such exhortation (which has been an enduring phenomenon of Christian history).

16. On the meetings in Acts see R. Pervo, "Meet Right—and Our Bounden Duty,"

17. J. Jeremias, ποιμήν, κ.τ.λ., *TDNT* 6:485–502, who does not include references from Greek culture.

18. 1 Peter 5:2; Acts 20:28, and John 21:16 use the same verb, "shepherd" (ποιμαίνειν), which becomes the operative verb in the prayer for the consecration of a Bishop. Ephesians uses the noun, which is combined with "teachers" (ποιμένας καὶ διδασκάλους). This cor-

responds to Acts and to the Pastorals, where the teaching office is the primary pastoral task.

19. The image is widespread. In Jewish apocalyptic see, e.g., *1 Enoch* 89.13–14; *4 Ezra* 5:18. Epictetus *Diss.* 1.3.7–9 is an example from the philosophical tradition, as is Dio Cassius 56.16.3 on the rapacity of Roman imperial officials. In early Christian literature the epithet is common: *Did* 16.3; *2 Clem* 5.2–4; *IgnPhd* 2.2; Justin *1 Apology* 16.13; *Dialogue* 35.3; 81.2. Matt 7:15 was a popular passage. In *AcPet* 8 Simon is call a "ravaging wolf" (*lupus*). See BDAG 669. The term was applied to Marcion by the orthodox writer Rhodon, according to Eusebius, *Ecclesiastical History*, 5.13.4. For other uses see G. Bornkamm, λύκος, *TDNT* 4:308–311. Note also the comparable image of the lion in 1 Peter 5:8.

20. For an outline of some of the problems at Ephesus in the early second century see Koester, Helmut. "Ephesos in Early Christian Literature," in *idem*, Ed., *Ephesos: Metropolis of Asia*, 119–140. In his "Gnomai Diaphoroi" (Robinson and Koester, *Trajectories*, 154–55) Koester describes Ephesus c. 100 as home to "several rival Christian groups," including "the originally Pauline church, supported by the Qumran-influenced Paulinist who wrote Ephesians, but also represented by the author of Luke-Acts who in his own way accommodated the tradition of the great apostle to the expediencies of the church; a Jewish-Christian 'school' engaging in a daring interpretation of the Old Testament (an early Gnostic like Cerinthus would fit this description rather well); a heretical sect, called the Nicolaitans by the Apocalypse of John (Rev. 2:6); and finally, a Jewish-Christian conventicle which was led by the prophet John . . ."

21. See William Schoedel, *Ignatius*. Further proposals may be found in the classic, if outdated, study of Walter Bauer, *Orthodoxy and Heresy in Earliest Christianity*, Trans. and Ed. R. Kraft and G. Krodel, 61–70; 77–94.

22. For a thorough review of the issues and problems attendant to dating Revelation see R. Brown, *Introduction*, 805–9.

23. Koester, *Introduction* 2:284, opts for the traditional 110–17. W. Schoedel says, "Probably a date between about 105 CE and 135 CE must be allowed as a possibility for the martyrdom of Ignatius and the writing of his letters." ("Ignatius and the Reception of Matthew in Antioch," in D. Balch, Ed., *Social History of the Matthean Community*, 129–186, 130–31 quoted.)

24. Brown, *Introduction*, 639 finds the end of the first century more probable than the early second century. Koester, *Introduction* 2:300–308, gives strong reasons for dating the Pastorals in the reign of Hadrian (117–138). See Appendix III. I believe that the Pastorals must be dated in proximity to Polycarp (c. 130).

25. Polycarp attacks heresy in *Philippians* 7. There is description of and comment upon that heresy in Robinson and Koester, *Trajectories*, 37 and 156.

26. Barrett, *Acts* 2:lxiii; cf. xl-xli.

27. C.H. Talbert's *Luke and the Gnostics* has not received much critical approval, but it does show that enough material from the first third of the second century exists to mount an argument. A few years earlier, Günther Klein had raised and revived arguments about the relation of Luke and Acts to Marcion : *Die Zwölf Apostel: Ursprung und Gehalt einer Idee*. Barbara Shellard is also alert to opposition to "Proto-Gnostic Trends," *New Light on Luke*, 283–86. One matter admits of little doubt: the Gospel of Luke as we have it is a difficult platform upon which to build a theology of docetism (Jesus only seemed to be human) or any speculative theology.

28. So Gregory Sterling, *Historiography and Self-Definition*, 330, who dates Acts c. 90–93 on these grounds. Hemer uses persecution as an argument for dating Acts prior to "the Neronian persecution" (c. 64), *Book of Acts*, 377.

29. See below, p. 230.

30. Even in the fourth and subsequent centuries such Christian bodies as the Donatists (who demanded a "pure" church) and the later Monophysities (opponents of the Council of Chalcedon, 451) vigorously denounced the imperial government—to say nothing of individual believers from the first century to the twenty-first. In the fifth century Salvian (*On the Rule of God*) and Augustine (*The City of God*) took divergent approaches to the decline of the empire in the west. In Salvian the blood of John the writer of Revelation ran true.

31. Translations of *2 Clem*, *IgnPhd*, and *Did* are from C. Richardson, *Early Christian Fathers*, 195, 108, and 178.

32. A primary aim of John 21 was to endorse the model of leadership by human "shepherds" (associated with Peter) without repudiating the alternative symbolized by the "Beloved Disciple."

33. M. Hengel says that James is here portrayed like a prince surrounded by his court (*Between Jesus and Paul*, 108). Note also Acts 2:14.

34. *Against Heresies*, Book 3.

35. Before Irenaeus, Hegesippus had made lists of bishops in various locales.

36. See the Mishnah tractate *Pirqe Aboth* (*Sayings of the Fathers*) 1.1–4, which lists, in philosophical fashion, a succession of teachers from Moses onward.

37. See the list of Roman bishops in Irenaeus, *Against Heresies* 3.3.3. The concept did not grow evenly. Alexandria, for example, does not reveal anything like a strong bishop until the third century. Rome did not have a single bishop until nearly the middle of the second century, various lists notwithstanding.

38. Cf. Acts 14:23.

39. This sentence in *1 Clement* is unclear and susceptible of more than one interpretation.

40. Trans. C. Richardson, *Early Christian Fathers*, 62.

41. See the comments of Robert M. Grant, *The Apostolic Fathers*, vol. II: *First and Second Clement*, 71. Note in particular the reference to the Spirit as a means for verifying suitability.

42. Those who demand proof texts will be satisfied. In the next sentence the letter says: καὶ τοῦτο οὐ καινῶς ἐκ γὰρ δὴ πολλῶν χρόνων ἐγέγραπτο περὶ ἐπισκόπων καὶ διακόνων οὕτως γάρ που λέγει ἡ γραφή Καταστήσω τοὺς ἐπισκόπους αὐτῶν ἐν δικαιοσύνῃ καὶ τοὺς διακόνους αὐτῶν ἐν πίστει. (Nothing novel here, for a good many years ago bishops and deacons were the subject of writing, for scripture says somewhere: "I shall appoint their bishops in righteousness and their deacons in faith.") The "somewhere" is *1 Clement*; the passage in view (cited accurately by Irenaeus *Against Heresies* 4.26.5) is Isa 60:17 LXX: "I shall give your rulers (ἄρχοντας) in peace and your supervisors (ἐπισκόπους) in righteousness."

43. Andreas Lindemann has a valuable commentary on this passage in *Die Clemensbriefe*, 125–135.

44. εἰ δι' ἐμὲ στάσις καὶ ἔρις καὶ σχίσματα, ἐκχωρῶ, ἄπειμι, οὗ ἐὰν βούλησθε, καὶ ποιῶ τὰ προστασσόμενα ὑπὸ τοῦ πλήθους, μόνον τὸ ποίμνιον τοῦ χριστοῦ εἰρηνευέτω μετὰ τῶν καθεσταμένων πρεσβυτέρων (Trans. Richardson, 68). Note the references to "revolt" and "schism." It appears that presbyters are in charge of the "flock," as in Acts 20:28.

45. Charles Talbert, who wishes to read Luke and Acts as the biography of the founder of a school, followed by the stories of his successors, has a different view of this matter. He first set forth this theory in *Literary Patterns, Theological Themes, and the Genre of Luke-Acts* and has subsequently developed it in many of his writings.

46. The translation of διὰ πολλῶν μαρτύρων (through many witnesses) is disputable, but it certainly means that the tradition is not the result of private or secret teaching.

47. Because *1 Clement* is dealing with particular officers, it stresses divine sanction for the persons in office and their succession. The Pastor regards "ordination" as a charism (1 Tim 4:14; 2 Tim 1:6), but also emphasizes the sacred character of the tradition.

48. 1 Tim 6:20; 2 Tim 1:12, 14. See Dibelius/Conzelmann, *The Pastoral Epistles*, 107–8.

49. Steve Walton stresses that Luke and the Pastor use the verb παρατίθημι in different senses (*Leadership and Lifestyle*, 192–193). He is half right. They do use the word in different senses, but each uses the term, and it does belong to the sphere of succession. Note also διατίθημι in Luke 22:29. See C. Maurer, τίθημι, κ.τ.λ., *TDNT* 8:153–168, 162–64.

50. See Chapter Four, p. 122. The participle "tending sheep" (ποιμαίνοντα) is from the same verb used in Acts 20:28.

51. This interpretation is very much indebted to Paul S. Minear, "A Note on Luke 17:7–10."

52. On Luke 10:38–42 see, for example, Turid Seim, *Double Message*, 97–107.

53. On this passage see also pp. 24, 112.

54. A fundamental treatment of the subject is Paul Veyne's *Le pain et le cirque: sociologie historique d'un pluralisme politique*. F. W. Danker provides a collection of inscriptions in his *Benefactor*.

55. See pp. 170–77.

56. For further remarks and references see R. Pervo, "PANTA KOINA: The Feeding Stories in the Light of Economic Data and Social Practice."

57. See below.

58. Heb 13:7, 17, 24; *1 Clem* 1.3.

59. Please note that this *is* a simile. Luke does not say that all will be well if leaders and servants exchange places, but that leadership is to be understood as, and thus to take the form of, service.

60. *Romans* 6:1–3. On the concept of imitation in Ignatius, see the nuanced discussion in W. Schoedel, *Ignatius of Antioch*, 29–31.

61. Bishop: *IgnMag* 6:1 (cf. 2:1); 3:1; *IgnSm* 8:1; *IgnTr* 2:1. Presbyters are always a group, often referred to as "the presbytery." See *IgnMag* 6:1; *IgnTr* 2:2; 3:1; *IgnPhd* 5:1; *IgnSm* 8:1. Ignatius usually refers to deacons as a group. See *IgnMag* 6:1; 7:1; *IgnPhd* 10:2; *IgnSm* 12:2.

62. All of these instances except 21:19, the missionary work of Paul, are discussed elsewhere in this book, especially in Chapter Seven.

63. Although Luke does not suggest that the practice of holding property in common ever ceased, Acts 6 envisions a situation in which only some believers (e.g., widows) were living at community expense.

64. Irenaeus states that Luke reports the ordination of Stephen to the diaconate by the Apostles, *Against Heresies* 3.12; 4.15. In *Church Order in the New Testament*, 74 n.283, E. Schweizer says: "In Acts 6.1–6 the title 'deacon' is lacking, perhaps because Luke knows that this ministry did not originate till later (in Gentile Christian circles?). But the reader must see deacons there."

65. The exception is 11:30, where presbyters alone receive the offering from Antioch. This, as argued above, is one of Luke's ways of showing succession.

66. See pp. 214–15.

67. χειροτονήσαντες δὲ αὐτοῖς κατ ἐκκλησίαν πρεσβυτέρους (after they had appointed elders for them in each church) suggests a plurality; besides, κατ ἐκκλησίαν πρεσβύτερον would have sufficed for "a presbyter in each church."

68. Luke is aware of other titles or possible functionaries. See Chapter Eight. This section does not pretend to be a full discussion of "ministry" in (Luke and) Acts. My primary object is the identification of offices relevant to date and therefore the latest integral material.

69. Luke does not have a purely "secular" or "functional" approach to offices. Acts 20:28 states that the Ephesian leaders are instituted by the Spirit.

70. Protestants usually classify these books as "The Apocrypha," while Roman Catholics regard them as "Deutero-Canonical."

71. This controversy underlined the problem of the biblical Canon. There has never been an agreement among all Christian bodies about the limits of Scripture. The influence of Luther's principle endures in that Lutheranism has never, unlike other confessional bodies, produced a list of the books that constitute the Bible.

72. Roman Catholics and Anglicans might object to some of the tendentious definitions of Early Catholicism offered by its opponents, but they have traditionally viewed such works as Colossians and the Pastorals as confirmation of their understandings of ecclesiology and the right of the Church to create offices and promulgate rules.

73. For a good summary of the topic and basic bibliography see Margaret Y. MacDonald, "Early Catholicism," in R. J. Coggins and J. L. Houlden, Eds., *A Dictionary of Biblical Interpretation*, 182–83. Ecumenism, the development of social-scientific interpretation, and, above all, the appreciation of diversity within the New Testament have moved discussions of Early Catholicism to the periphery. J. Fitzmyer summarizes the relevance of Luke and Acts to these discussions, *Gospel according to Luke I–IX*, 23–27. James D. G. Dunn has a rather sensible approach to the question in his *Unity and Diversity in the New Testament: An Inquiry into the Character of Earliest Christianity*, 2d. ed., 341–66. Dunn attacks three features: the decline of hope for an imminent end, the growth of institutionalization, and the development of fixed forms of the faith (i.e., creedal formulae). Of these the second is the most important, although it is a response to the first, just as the third is a quality of the second. To compress his useful file boxes into a phrase one could define proto-catholicism as one means for adjusting to an indefinite existence in the world. This does

not require that the church be "of the world," for that danger is always present. Some will lament the loss of eschatological consciousness, but existentialism was not yet available to provide alternative categories, and the closest approximation to recategorization led to Gnosticism.

74. In an essay published in 1957 Käsemann said: "Luke is not, as Dibelius still believed, a late pupil of Paul, but the first representative of nascent early catholicism." The basis of this judgment is "His attempt to present the history of the Christian religion . . . as secular history . . ." *New Testament Questions of Today*, 21. See also Haenchen, *Acts*, 48 n.3.

75. See R. Pervo, "Wisdom and Power: Petronius' *Satyricon* and the Social World of Early Christianity," "PANTA KOINA," and the review of W. Countryman, *The Rich Christian in the Church of the Early Empire*, ATR 64 (1982) 238–39.

76. Haenchen, *Acts* 49. Note also Barrett, "The First New Testament?" 99–100, and Bovon, *Luke the Theologian*, 316–17.The latter views Luke as both an adherent of the Pauline conception of the Spirit and as an admirer of "early Catholic" institutions, thus recognizing Luke's ambiguity—or, as some may prefer, his comprehensiveness.

77. Compare Acts 8:4–25 (Samaria: baptism by Philip; Spirit through imposition of apostolic hands) with 10:44–48 (Cornelius; Spirit comes before baptism).

78. David E Aune analyzes Acts 13:1–3 as a prophetic oracle in his *Prophecy in Early Christianity*, 265–66.

79. Note also *1 Clement* 42.3 (above), which speaks of spiritual testing or discernment prior to the appointment of officers. The same verb, δοκιμάζω, is used of deacons in 1 Tim 3:10. On this verb see Spicq, *Theological Lexicon*, 1:353–361 and W. Grundmann, δόκιμος, κ.τ.λ. TDNT 2:255–60.

80. Acts 20:23 mentions revelations "in each city" as if they were no less routine than the ordination of presbyters in Titus 1:5–6, which uses the same prepositional phrase. See, for example, Acts 21:4, 10–11. 20:29–30 makes reference to false prophets.

81. A review of this matter appears in F. Bovon, *Luke the Theologian),* 229–37.

82. On the Household Codes see David Balch, *Let Wives Be Submissive: The Domestic Code in 1 Peter*, David Verner, *The Household of God: The Social World of the Pastoral Epistles*, Koester, *Introduction*, 2:270, 294–295, 304, and 309, Elisabeth Schűssler Fiorenza, *In Memory of Her*, 251–79.

83. "Do you think that I have come to bring peace to the earth? No, I tell you, but rather division! From now on five in one household will be divided, three against two and two against three; they will be divided: father against son and son against father, mother against daughter and daughter against mother, mother-in-law against her daughter-in-law and daughter-in-law against mother-in-law."

84. For Luke's views of marriage, see R. Pervo, *Profit with Delight*, 181 n.179.

85. An additional element of "early catholicism" not stressed by its critics is the attempt to find acceptable compromise and achieve synthesis. With regard to those qualities Luke *can* be labeled "early catholic," but so can Matthew. A consistent feature of the emerging catholic church up to, and often beyond, the fourth century is its preference for the middle rather than the extreme. Both the Ebionite ("Jewish-Christian") and the Marcionite (anti-Jewish-Christian) views were rejected. The "Apostolic Decree" of Acts 15:23–29 is an excellent example of a moderate compromise between competing extremes.

86. On "widows" see also below.

87. On these and other women in (Luke and) Acts see Seim, *Double Message*, and Ivoni Richter Reimer, *Women in the Acts of the Apostles: A Feminist Liberation Perspective*.

88. Advocacy of celibacy can be found in the Apocryphal Acts, the followers of Marcion, and most Gnostics. (The presence of married couples does not mean that a text is unsound on the question of celibacy. When both convert, the couple continue to cohabit, albeit in celibacy, such as Lycomedes and Cleopatra in the *Acts of John*.)

89. In the Pastorals it is noteworthy that "*episkopos*," "bishop," is always singular. The earlier "Bishop-Deacon" scheme is also apparent in that "deacons" are associated with "bishops," but not with presbyters.

90. Hans v. Campenhausen says that the object is "to fuse the two traditions," *Ecclesiastical Authority and Spiritual Power*, 81. Although dated (The German edition appeared in 1953), Campenhausen's essay on "The System of Elders and the Beginnings of Official Authority," 76–123, remains important. Campbell's *The Elders*, while judicious and

scholarly, is something of a tract, since he opposes the World Council of Churches' "Lima Statement," *Baptism, Eucharist, and Ministry.*

91. Wilson, *Luke and the Pastoral Epistles*, 53–68, points to the similarities between the two on the matter of "Church and Ministry." Note his impressive summary, 68. He does not, however, take account of the differences, for he views the Pastorals as a development by the same author of the ideas expressed in Acts.

92. *1 Clement* 50:3 uses the term with regard to the eschatological coming of Christ.

93. "Primitive" is not a valid label for Luke's ecclesiology. See, for example, F. Bovon, *Luke the Theologian*, 290–323.

94. The language continues with little change in the formal style of proposed resolutions: "Whereas . . . be it resolved . . ." Frederick W. Danker discusses the form and its implications in "Reciprocity in the Ancient World and in Acts 15:23–29," in R. J. Cassidy and P. J. Scharper, Eds., *Political Issues in Luke-Acts*, 49–58.

95. Ramsay MacMullen, *Roman Social Relations*, 82.

96. MacMullen, *Roman Social Relations*, 76, with evidence at 178 n.70. One may see something of an analogy in the various fraternal orders that once enjoyed considerable popularity in the U.S. These bodies tended toward punctilious observance of the rules of order and the production of effusive resolutions.

97. See pp. 179–83.

98. Meetings of the Sanhedrin: Acts 4:5–21; 5:21b–40; 6:12–7:60; 22:30–23:10. See R. Pervo, "Meet, Right—and Our Bounden Duty."

99. Chrysostom, *Homily* 14 on Acts.

100. Acts does not identify Dorcas/Tabitha as herself a widow. She certainly appears to be the head of a household.

101. Polycarp's views on widows are almost identical: *Philippians* 4:3.

102. Some data on widows in the Greco-Roman world can be found in R. Pervo, "Aseneth and her Sisters: Women in Jewish Narrative and in the Greek Novels," 155–59.

103. For a brief, semi-popular treatment see Bonnie Bowman Thurston, *The Widows: A Women's Ministry in the Early Church*, 30–34, 39–55. See also ATR 73, (1991) 332–33. Note the excellent article, χήρα, by Gustav Stählin, *TDNT* 9:440–65. Harnack supplies a brief summary, with numerous references to texts, in *The Mission and Expansion of Christianity in the First Three Centuries*, 1:159–60.

104. Acts 2⟨:8–9 notes that Philip had four virgin daughters who were prophets. One might think that one or more of this group could come up with a prophecy suitable for the occasion, but, instead, the honor goes to Agabus, who arrives from Jerusalem for that very purpose: 21:10–11. See R. Pervo, "Four Unmarried Daughters of Philip," in Carol Meyers, Ed., *Women in Scripture*, 467–68. A good general study of women and prophecy in Luke and Acts may be found in T. Seim, *Double Message*, 164–84. Neither Mary nor Elizabeth prophesy when men are present.

105. Cf. Acts 6:3. ("philosophy" is the pursuit of wisdom—*sophia*.)

106. Vasiliki Limberis, "Anna 2," in *Women in Scripture*, 50–51, citing p. 51.

107. See the comments and references of R. Price, *The Widow Traditions in Luke-Acts*, 204.

108. J. Behm, νέος, ἀνανεόω, *TDNT*, 4:896–901, 897, with references. See also Franz Poland, *Geschichte des griechischen Vereinswesens*, 96–97. For a possible Jewish example see *HJP* 3:103.

109. Achtemeier, *1 Peter*, 330–31 is doubtful about the existence of such a body. J. Elliott inclines to view them as more recent converts, *1 Peter*, 836–40. Both of these commentators discuss the issues in detail. The Pastorals are more slightly more amenable to the understanding of the existence of an organized group. See Ceslas Spicq, "La place ou le rôle des jeunes dan certaines communautés néotestamentaires." Haenchen, *Acts* 165, rejects the notion that this refers to a formal group of novices.

110. The sequence from 4:1–6:1 is ourselves [i.e., adult males], our wives, widows, deacons, younger men, presbyters. Bauer/Paulsen, *Polykarpbrief*, 118, refer to 1 Peter 5:5.

111. L. T. Johnson, *The Literary Function of Possessions in Luke-Acts.*

112. James can presume that Paul has the wherewithal to discharge five vows (21:24), while Felix scented enough gold to make himself available to an offer of bribery (24:26)—not to mention the expenses of frequent travel.

113. Jews seeking to maintain a position in the exorcism market also experience their share of discomfort (19:13–17).

114. See G. Delling, πλεονέκτης, κ.τ.λ., *TDNT* 6:266–74; and Spicq, *Theological Lexicon*, 3:117–19.

115. Latin moralists also associate greed with lust, as in Cicero, *De Natura Deorum* 3.71 (*libido, avaritia*). See Delling, πλεονέκτης, 269 for more examples. Polycarp, *Phil.* 11:1 apparently cites Col 3:5.

116. Ancient economic thought, especially in its popular expression, adhered to the doctrine of "limited good": only so much wealth exists; therefore, more for you means less for me. In this atmosphere, the pursuit of wealth always implied exploitation and, in most cases, dishonesty.

117. αἰσχροκερδής: 1 Pet 5:2 (adv.), 1 Tim 3:8; Tit 1:7. ἀφιλάργυρος: 2 Tim 3:3; Heb 13:5; Polycarp *Phil* 5:2; *Did* 15:1;. φιλάργυρος, Luke 16:14; 1 Tim 6:10; 2 *Clem* 4:3; 6:4; Polycarp *Phil* 2:2; 4:1, 3; 6:1; *Did* 3:5. πλεονεξία, κ.τ.λ. appear thirteen times in the Apostolic Fathers. C. Spicq treats ἀφιλάργυρος and αἰσχροκερδής in *Theological Lexicon* 1:245–56 and 1:45–48 respectively. Stephen G. Wilson shows the similarities between Luke and the Pastoral Epistles on this subject in his book of that name, 49–50.

118. So, for example, Philo, *Life of Moses* (Trans. Yonge), 2.212: "Moses intended that devout Israelites would occupy their time wholly to the study of philosophy, not of that sort of philosophy which wordcatchers and sophists, seek to reduce to a system, selling doctrines and reasonings as they would any other vendible thing in the market." In addition to 1 Thess 2:5 see 2 Cor 2:17: "For we are not peddlers of God's word like so many; but in Christ we speak as persons of sincerity, as persons sent from God and standing in his presence." Dibelius has a good collection of texts in his *An die Thessalonicher*, 7–8. Note also A. Malherbe, *Paul and the Popular Philosophers*, passim.

119. See Spicq, *Theological Lexicon* 1:45 n.5. For more detail see his *Les épitres pastorales*, 1:564–65.

120. An analogy from our culture would be such guidelines for job-seekers as dressing appropriately, being punctual, making eye-contact while answering questions clearly and accurately, etc. It is not so much that the Pastor has excessively modest expectations as that he expects Christian leaders to be as respectable as those of other organizations. Those without shirts or shoes will need to seek service elsewhere. For the qualities expected of a general, see the extract from Onosander, in Dibelius/Conzelmann *The Pastoral Epistles*, 158–60.

121. On this passage see pp. 125–30.

122. See 5:1, where the term is included in a catalogue of vices.

123. Cf. also 3:1 in general, and 4:3 concerning widows.

124. Trans. Massey H. Shepherd in Richardson, *Early Christian Fathers*, 133.

125. See also above, pp. 204–6.

126. On this passage see also above, p. 222.

127. Knights (Equestrian class) ranked below the Senatorial order but above the common people. Most knights were, like Decius Mundus, rich.

128. Josephus needs sixteen paragraphs to relate the story of Paulina (*Antiquities* 18:65–80), but is able to dispose of the Fulvia affair in a mere four (81–84). For a recent discussion of these stories see Shelly Matthews, *First Converts*, 10–28. Note also Dieter Georgi, *The Opponents of Paul in Second Corinthians*, 98–102.

129. Justin Martyr, *1 Apology* 21, Trans. E. Hardy, in Richardson, *Early Christian Fathers*, 256. (See 21–25). This denunciation was already old: cf. Plato, *Republic* 2.3.

130. Irenaeus, *Against Heresies*, 1.13.1–7. Cf. also 1.6.3–4.

131. Epiphanius, *Panarion*, 30.16.6–9.

132. On the subject see D. Georgi, *Opponents*, 238–42.

133. *Metamorphoses* (also known as *The Golden Ass*) 8.25–30.

134. See the comments of Lightfoot, *Apostolic Fathers* 3.2.2:340–42 and Bauer/Paulsen *Die Briefe*, 123–24.

135. An interesting fictional example is John 12:6, "*Judas* said this not because he cared about the poor, but because he was a thief; he kept the common purse and used to steal what was put into it.)" This reflects the practice of a common fund and the fear of misuse. Note also 2 Thess 3:10, which presumes the presence of a communal charitable fund. Both of these texts date from around the close of the first century CE. J. Albert Harrill discusses the place of a common fund in ancient associations in his *The Manumission of Slaves in Early Christianity*, 129–57. On Valens see Harry O. Maier, "Purity and Danger in Polycarp's

Epistle to the Philippians: The Sin of Valens in Social Perspective," who has many useful observations about the role of wealth in the moral world of Polycarp and the Pastoral
Epistles.

136. Michael D. Goulder, "Did Luke Know any of the Pauline Letters?," 99–101.

137. See above on benefactors. The "Rich Fool" (Luke 12:16–20) is an object lesson in the
rewards of greed.

138. The NRSV wisely adapts the translation "manager" for most uses of οἰκονόμος,
for this is what "stewards" were: subordinates with responsibilities but without authority.
One can appreciate the desire to avoid the expression "managers of the mysteries of God."

139. This portion of *To Polycarp* is clearly addressed to the entire community.

140. The secondary (Lucan) character of "manager" in 12:42 becomes clear in v. 44, for it
promises a position that the manager already holds.

141. See pp. 210–18.

142. Luke Timothy Johnson says: "This interjection by Peter is found only in Luke, and
it serves a critical redactional function, making the *following* parable apply to the future
leadership of the people, using the image of household management as the metaphor
for authority," *The Gospel of Luke*, 204. So also, e.g., Howard Marshall, *Luke*, 540, 544; B.
B. Scott, *Hear Then*, 209; and Charles H. Talbert, *Reading Luke: A Literary and Theological
Commentary on the Third Gospel*, 143.

143. J. M. Creed, *The Gospel according to St. Luke*, 178, notes that the servants in these two
verses are in a different situation. He suggests that "Perhaps Luke intends to carry on the
thought of the responsibility of the leaders of the Church."

144. Twenty-six verses earlier Luke also spoke of "eating and drinking." These activities
were part of the plan of the "rich fool." He is a "servant" who imagines that he is in charge
of his life.

145. Trans. C. Richardson, *Early Christian Fathers*, 119.

146. Robinson *et al.* do not include Luke 12:37, 47–48 in *Q, Critical Edition*, 358–375. For
discussion and various views see Kloppenborg, *Q Parallels*, 236–240.

147. To be clear: Jesus does speak in Acts 1:4–8 and in revelations such as 9:4, etc, but
"quotation" here refers to the explicit use of his words by another character.

148. See H. Koester, *Ancient Christian Gospels*, 63, 66, and J. M. Robinson and H. Koester,
Trajectories through Early Christianity, 96–97.

149. Koester, *Ancient Christian Gospels*, 66, with n.5.

150. *Ancient Christian Gospels*, 63.

151. Eckhard Plümacher is willing to propose that Thucydides is Luke's source: "Eine
Thukydidesreminiszenz in der Apostelgeschichte (Act 20,33–35 — Thuk. 11 97.3f.)." This
does not seem likely.

152. The most complete list of parallels, mostly Greek, is in Barrett, *Acts* 2:983–84, with a
sound discussion. See also Haenchen, *Acts* 594 n.5.

153. Aejemelaeus, *Rezeption*, 175–83. He makes use of the manuscript dissertation of
Rainer Reuter on the use of Ignatius and *1 Clement* in Luke and Acts (Göttingen, 1985).
This is not available to me.

154. Trans. Richardson, *Early Christian Fathers*, 44. (I have substituted the technical "sayings" for "words.")

155. On giving see above. With regard to humility note, for example, Luke 14:11 (=18:14).
For Christ as the model of humility see also the citation of Isa 53:8 in Acts 8:33.

156. See L. Welborn, "Clement, First Epistle of," *ABD*, 1:1055–60 and the excursus on p.
243.

157. See, e. g., Grant and Graham, *First and Second Clement*, 103.

158. Although one individual probably had primary authority for drafting *1 Clement*, its
stated author is the Roman community. "Clement" is traditional.

159. See p. 169.

160. The word μακάριος ("blessed"), for example, occurs ten times in *1 Clem*, compared
with seventeen uses in Luke and Acts, which is twice the length of *1 Clem*. Instances of
long biblical quotes include chapter 22 and 56:6–15.

161. Trans. Richardson, *Early Christian Fathers*, 44.

162. Cf. also *Did* 4:5. The intertextual field of *Did* 1 is so dense that it is best called a jungle. In addition to the synoptic parallels that come prior to the above citation is the close

parallel to 1:5 in *HermMan* 2.4–6. See the commentary of Kurt Niederwimmer, *The Didache*, 69–83.

163. Koester observes that since neither *1 Clem* nor *Did* attributes this saying to Jesus, neither could be dependent upon Acts: *Synoptische Überlieferung bei den apostolischen Vätern*, 233–34.

164. Although these words are not hyperbolic, they do lack nuance. The sands of Egypt have yielded numerous complaints and protests from persons of modest means—not the poorest of the poor, but not the rich. Sometimes these protests achieved their goals, but their very existence indicates the scope of the problem. Rulers had also to be sensitive to the needs and the views of large urban populations. The story of the choice between Jesus and Barabbas (Mark 15:6–14 and parallels) may well be fictitious, but it shows how the mobs could gain their way.

165. Dibelius-Conzelmann discuss Jewish and Christian prayer for polytheist rulers in their commentary on *The Pastoral Epistles*, 37–38. See also the material assembled by Knopf, *Clemensbriefe*, 146–47.

166. Acts 24:2 and 14 offer good, and mercifully brief, examples of these rhetorical ploys.

167. See above, p. 169.

168. Justin, *1 Apology*, 12.1; 17.3, Trans. E. Fairweather in Richardson, *Early Christian Fathers*, 247, 253.

169. The Jesus Seminar determined that Mark 8:34–35 is Christian, i.e., not a saying of the historical Jesus. Verse 36 (and 37) are adaptations of traditional wisdom that Jesus might have endorsed. See Robert W. Funk, Roy W. Hoover, *et al.*, *The Five Gospels*, 78–79.

170. This citation of 2 Tim 2:17–18 changes the word order, but not the meaning.

171. Trans. C. Richardson, *Early Christian Fathers*, 73.

172. Susan Garrett relates this adjective to the concept of a "rule of life" (not her words). See "Beloved Physician of the Soul? Luke as Advocate for Ascetic Practice," in L. E. Vaage and V. L. Wimbush, Eds., *Asceticism and the New Testament*, 71–95, 86–87.

173. It would not be fair to cast upon Luke the blame for the utter trivialization of the metaphor in U.S. culture, where the "cross" one "just has to bear" may be no more than a difficult supervisor or acne.

174. The first two petitions, "Hallowed be Thy Name," and "Thy Kingdom come" are clearly eschatological, as is the (poorly translated) "Lead us not into temptation." According to Robinson *et al.*, *Critical Edition of Q*, the most likely Q text of the "bread" petition is that found in Matthew.

175. The quotation is from S. Wilson, *Luke and the Pastoral Epistles*, 47.

176. Dibelius/Conzelmann (*The Pastoral Epistles*, 39–41) provides an important excursus on "The Ideal of Good Christian Citizenship." The phrases in quotation marks are from p. 40. Conzelmann took note of the similarities to Luke and Acts, but Dibelius is responsible for the thesis.

177. R. Pervo, *Profit with Delight*, 79. See pp. 77–81 and the references therein adduced.

178. On this passage see also pp. 183–84.

179. Possession of two outer garments would place one a cut or two above "the Joneses."

180. See pp. 130–31.

181. Although the direct evidence is fairly conclusive, one should also note that the two share a background in popular ethics.

182. Luke does not regard "magic" as a sham. It is genuine power that Christ can overcome. See S. Garrett, *Demise of the Devil*. Ignatius expresses a similar view: "Thence [by the incarnation] was destroyed all magic, and every bond vanished." (*Ephesians* 19:3, Trans. W. Schoedel, *Ignatius of Antioch*, 87.)

183. *Pro Flacco* (*In Defense of Flaccus*). Translations are from the Loeb version of C. MacDonald, *Cicero X*. For more on this subject see R. Pervo, "Meet Right."

184. Had it not been nipped in the bud, the uproar in the Ephesian assembly (*ekklesia*) described in Acts 19:21–40 would serve as an excellent specimen of the kind of "futile revolt" so abhorrent to *1 Clem* 61 (above).

185. See p. 52.

186. There is a good brief introduction to this development in Harry Y. Gamble, *The New Testament Canon: Its Making and Meaning*, 35–46. See also Appendix III, "*Corpus Paulinum*."

187. On the importance of the universality of Paul's teaching, see pp. 294–95.

188. Greek has no specific word for "religion," but this noun, εὐσεβεία, is one candidate for the honor.

189. Noun: Acts 3:12; 1 Tim 2:2; 3:16; 4:7, 8; 6:3, 5, 6, 11; 2 Tim 3:5; Tit 1:1; 2 Pet 1:3, 6, 7; 3:11. Verb: Acts 17:23; 1 Tim 5:4. Adjective: Acts 10:2, 7; 2 Pet 2:9. Adverb: 2 Tim 3:12; Tit 2:12. 2 Pet is, according to the critical consensus, the latest writing in the New Testament. Raymond Brown places it at c. 130 (*Introduction*, 767).

190. 2 *Clem* has nothing in common with 1 *Clem* . It is a sermon of unknown provenance probably written between 120 and 140.

191. One of these, Isaiah 33:6, is uncertain.

192. See the article of P. Fiedler in *EDNT*, 2:83–85, as well as Dibelius/Conzelmann, *Pastoral Epistles*, 39, and Werner Foerster, σέβομαι, κ.τ.λ., *TDNT* 7:168–96, 175–85. The last points to the particularity of the stem: "What evokes εὐσεβεῖν [to be reverent] is not a personal entity but a vast order. It is not ὁ θεός [God] but τὸ θεῖον [the divine]."

193. Although the allied noun σεμνότης ("dignity"), is not found in Acts, it helps to fill in the picture. All four NT uses are in the Pastorals. The *Shepherd of Hermas* finds about ten uses for this noun, 1 *Clem* one.

194. See Gottfried Quell and Gottlob Schrenk, δίκη, κ.τ.λ., *TDNT* 2:174–224. (The article [almost all of which was written by Schrenk] is oriented toward the Pauline view, which is understood to be the norm against which deviations may be judged, and is thus skewed.)

195. In 1 Tim 6:11 it is followed by εὐσεβεία ("godliness"). See above.

196. οὐκ ἐξ ἔργων τῶν ἐν δικαιοσύνῃ ἃ ἐποιήσαμεν ἡμεῖς ἀλλὰ κατὰ τὸ αὐτοῦ ἔλεος ἔσωσεν ἡμᾶς διὰ λουτροῦ παλιγγενεσίας καὶ ἀνακαινώσεως πνεύματος ἁγίου, 6 οὗ ἐξέχεεν ἐφ' ἡμᾶς πλουσίως διὰ Ἰησοῦ Χριστοῦ τοῦ σωτῆρος ἡμῶν, 7 ἵνα δικαιωθέντες τῇ ἐκείνου χάριτι κληρονόμοι γενηθῶμεν κατ' ἐλπίδα ζωῆς αἰωνίου.

197. See Dibelius/Conzelmann, *Pastoral Epistles*, 148–50, especially 150, and, on the entire subject of "justification" in Luke and the Pastorals, S. Wilson, *Luke and the Pastoral Epistles*, 24–27.

198. Dibelius/Conzelmann, *Pastoral Epistles*, 88.

199. See p. 61.

200. The next verse (11:1) says that Lot was saved because of his hospitality and piety (εὐσεβεία).

201. ὑπομονή ("endurance) is associated with "righteousness" also in 1 Tim 6:11 (above). S. Wilson discusses the place of ὑπομονή in *Luke and the Pastoral Epistles*, 48.

202. Trans. C. Richardson, *Early Christian Fathers*, 58, alt., with omission of closing doxology. καὶ ἡμεῖς οὖν, διὰ θελήματος αὐτοῦ ἐν Χριστῷ Ἰησοῦ κληθέντες, οὐ δι' ἑαυτῶν δικαιούμεθα οὐδὲ διὰ τῆς ἡμετέρας σοφίας ἢ συνέσεως ἢ εὐσεβείας ἢ ἔργων ὧν κατειργασάμεθα ἐν ὁσιότητι καρδίας, ἀλλὰ διὰ τῆς πίστεως, δι' ἧς πάντας τοὺς ἀπ' αἰῶνος ὁ παντοκράτωρ θεὸς ἐδικαίωσεν.

203. Cf. Lindemann, *Clemensbriefe*, 100 (who also notes the numerous contacts with the Pauline tradition).

204. See Table 6.15, below.

205. BDAG 728, which provides numerous references, and n.186 above.

206. See F. Hauck, ὅσιος, κ.τ.λ., *TDNT* 5:489–93. ὅσιος appears eight times in the canonical NT, five in citations. In 1 *Clem* it (or the adverb) occurs fifteen times, in 2 *Clem* three. In addition to the citation above, from 48:4, 1 *Clement* employs ὁσιότης at 29:1; 32:4; and 60:2. Bultmann (*Theology of the New* Testament, 2:213) says "Particularly characteristic is the combining of 'uprightness,' 'upright' or 'uprightly' with ὅσιος ('devout,' 'pious") or its datives."

207. The NRSV has been adopted here to reflect the LXX.

208. Trans. C. Richardson, *Early Christian Fathers*, 66, alt.

209. Eight of fourteen references are in 1 Cor 8:7–13; 10:25–30.

210. See the excursus in Dibelius/Conzelmann, *Pastoral Epistles*, 18–20, and C. Maurer, συνοίδα, κ.τ.λ., *TDNT*, 7:898–919; both include other references to the Apostolic Fathers.

211. Rhetorical *ethos* has two goals: to get the audience to like/trust/agree with the speaker and to "feel good" about themselves and thus, to complete the circle, to have positive feelings about the speaker.

212. Trans. C. Richardson, alt., *Early Christian Fathers*, 43, 62, and 64.

213. Trans. Christoph Burchard, "Joseph and Aseneth," in J. Charlesworth, editor, *The Old Testament Pseudepigrapha*, 2 vols., 2:177–247, 223.

214. See, for example, H. Conzelmann, *The Theology of St Luke*, 228–30; F. Bovon, *Luke the Theologian*, 275–89; David Moessner, "Paul in Acts: Preacher of Eschatological Repentance to Israel," ; and the articles of Christoph Stenschke ("The Need for Salvation") and Hans F. Bayer ("The Preaching of Peter in Acts") in I. H. Marshall and David Peterson, Eds., *Witness to the Gospel: The Theology of Acts*, 128–144 and 257–74. See also Stenschke's monograph, *Luke's Portrait of Gentiles Prior to Their Coming to Faith*, 457, *s. v.*, "repentance."

215. Luke 15:7 states the theory: "Just so, I tell you, there will be more joy in heaven over one sinner who repents than over ninety-nine righteous persons who need no repentance." In practice the Ethiopian official was not instructed to repent (Acts 8:26–39), nor were Cornelius and his people (10:45–48). His righteousness is noted in 10:2 and 35.

216. This does not mean that *1 Clement* either "moralizes Christianity" or reduces faith to moralism, a criticism often made against it and rightly rejected by Lindemann, *Clemensbriefe*, 21.

217. Cf. also 1 Pet 1:19 "but with the *precious blood* of Christ, like that of a lamb without defect or blemish."

218. See also the commentary of Lindemann, *Clemensbriefe*, 176–77.

219. For discussion about the reception of *1 Clem*, see Lightfoot, *Apostolic Fathers*, 1.1–149–200; Grant and Graham in Grant, Ed., *Apostolic Fathers*, 2:5–8; Lindemann, *Clemensbriefe*, 11–12; and, most recently and thoroughly, Lona, *Clemensbrief*, 89–110.

220. Grant, *Apostolic Fathers*, 5. See also Bauer/Paulsen, *Briefe des Ignatius*, 72.

221. H. Koester, *Introduction*, 2:309, is confident that Polycarp ". . . knows and uses *1 Clement* . . ." He bases his argument in part upon Polycarp's correction of *1 Clem* 13:2 to conform to Matt and Luke (*Phil* 2:3). This is a strong argument. Lona views the use of *1 Clem* by Polycarp as beyond question, *Clemensbrief*, 90–92. There are almost forty parallels to be taken into consideration. Lona regards nine as decisive.

222. Eusebius, *Ecclesiastical History* 4.22.1 and 4.23.11.

223. Lightfoot, *Apostolic Fathers*, 158–160; Grant, 5–6; Lona 93–104.

224. The prepositional phrase "to repentance" is a Lukan addition to Mark 2:17.

225. Trans. C. Richardson, *Early Christian Fathers*, 47, 69, and 73, *alt.*

226. "Faith" is too complex for analysis here, for even when restricted to the concept of a virtue, as here in *1 Clement*, it has too many meanings. I therefore omit it.

227. In the sense of a virtue, rather than "justification."

228. This term is difficult. I have taken a strict construction of "truthfulness" (rather than "truth"). This meaning is possible in Acts 26:25, where it appears in conjunction with σωφροσύνη.

229. Lightfoot, 161–200.

230. For these data I rely upon Lindemann, *Clemensbriefe*, 11.

231. *Aseneth* is difficult to date, because it was often revised. C. 100–150 is quite likely. Edith M. Humphrey, *Joseph and Aseneth,* is a good brief and general introduction to the issues. Quite thorough, and against the grain, is Ross Shepherd Kraemer, *When Aseneth Met Joseph.*

232. Gal 1:13, 23; Phil 3:6.

233. On these terms see Dibelius/Conzelmann, *The Pastoral Epistles*, 27–28, G. Bertram, ὕβρις, κ.τ.λ., *TDNT* 8:295–307, esp. 306; H.W. Beyer, βλασφημέω, κ.τ.λ., *TDNT*, 1:621–25, esp. 624; and, most fully, C. Spicq. *Épitres Pastorales*, 341–42. Spicq supports his acceptance of the authenticity of these terms as self-designations of Paul by references to Acts.

234. One model available to Luke was the story of Heliodorus in 2 Macc 3. A polytheist example is Homeric Hymn 7, "To Dionysus," 16–21. With this contrast John 21:4–7.

235. Acts 5:39. In the background is the futility—and fatality—of human opposition to the triumphant march of Dionysos. The term appears in Euripides's *Bacchae*, 45, 325, and 1255 (cf. 635).

236. Paul's Jewish past is an issue about which the writer of the Pastorals is silent.

237. See pp. 108–11.

238. See p. 225.

239. So, for example Justin, *1 Apol* 7:5; 12:11; 61:10; *2 Apol* 14:1; Aristides, *Apol* 17.4; Athenagoras, *Legatio* 28.4. Other examples are *HermSim* 5.7.4; *AcPet* 2.21–25; *AcJohn* 107.14–15.

240. Another approach appears to be the diametrical opposite. "Ignorance" is the human condition prior to revelation. This view is highly developed in Gnosticism, which tends to

view nature as the deceiving creation of inferior gods rather than a witness to the true god.

241. On "ignorance" here, see Spicq, *Épitres pastorales*, 1:642.

242. Paul was, to be sure, often conventional and pragmatic in his ethical views and thus often surprised at the ethical implications drawn from his theology by some of his converts (1 Cor), but he did not ground these values in a natural theology. (The exception, 1 Cor 11:14, proves the rule.)

243. S. Wilson, *Luke and the Pastoral Epistles*, 47. The full quote is "In place of an ethic rooted in a theology we have one based on common sense, pragmatism, and the natural order of things."

244. Spicq gives many examples, *Épitres pastorales*, 2:612–13. The issue also arises in Judaism. The classical position is that Torah is binding upon Jews only, that gentiles are not held accountable for ritual violations. *Aristeas* (a defense of Jewish identity that supports coexistence with others) affirms the goodness of creation and presents the ritual laws as pointers to moral verities—without thereby becoming purely "symbolic." Both *Aristeas* and the first-century Jewish philosopher Philo (*Special Laws* 3.208–9) stress the importance of relations: contact with the unclean makes one unclean.

245. A discussion of intertextual relations among Luke 11:41, Acts 10, and Romans 14 appears in Chapter Four, p. 106.

246. 1 Cor 8 shows Paul agreeing with the theological views of "the strong" about meat offered to gods who do not exist but disagreeing with their practice when it manifested harmful insensitivity to the "superstitions" of "the weak." Much of 1 Cor 1–9 is based upon the notion that the truly "strong" are strong enough to forego their rights.

p. 249   247. Marcion and others had no difficulty in discovering a tension between nature and grace and Paul. In response to this understanding, second-century writers had to demonstrate that the two were not in opposition.

248. Similarly, the requirements of the "Apostolic Decree" are clear, sensible, and moderate—and were soon modified in a wholly moralizing fashion. See above, p. 235.

249. Note the comment of Conzelmann, *Theology of St Luke*, 226: ". . . Luke does not describe the Christian life in pneumatic, but in ethical categories." See also n.2 on that page.

250. Koester, *Introduction* 2:305.

251. One can argue for elements of "Christian eschatological ethics" in Luke, of course, but these are tempered by other elements and should not be treated in isolation.

252. The Hebrew Bible often speaks about the wonders of creation, as in Psalms 19, 145, and 148, which were used by Hellenistic Jewish and early Christian writers, including those under investigation. These are doxological, expressing praise of God rather than proof for the existence of God. The Q tradition exhibits a kind of popular belief in providence (e.g., Luke 12:6; 22–32), but such views needed no argument, for they were part of the "social construction of reality."

253. The argument of "Hellenism vs. Judaism" is especially pointless in this context. This is a flaw of Bertil Gärtner's *The Areopagus Speech and Natural Revelation*, which nonetheless has many useful references and valuable observations. A recent study concerned with primary sources but also containing references to the most important secondary studies is David L. Balch, "The Areopagus Speech: An Appeal to the Stoic Historian Posidonius against Later Stoics and the Epicureans," in D. Balch *et al.* Eds., *Greeks, Romans, and Christians: Essays in Honor of Abraham J. Malherbe*, 52–79. On *1 Clement* see Lindemann, *Die Clemensbriefe*, 76–77. The most important philosophical source is Cicero, *De Natura Deorum* (*On the Nature of the Gods*), 2:76–154, to which Pease's commentary contributes a host of primary sources and parallels. Also important is the Pseudo-Aristotelian *De Mundo* (*On the Universe*), especially chapters 3 and 5.

254. The citations from the *Acts of Paul* (Table 6.17c) show the broader range. A third, not cited, is from a speech delivered to a polytheist crowd at Ephesus. The text is quite fragmentary, but indicates that it included an appeal to recognize the creator god. Thecla uses the phrase in a prayer, just as in Acts 4:24. The citation from *3 Corinthians* exhibits this creedal formula in a different context. Rather than challenge polytheism, the claim now bolsters opposition to those (such as Marcion and various Gnostics) who separate the creator god from the true God.

255. There is a gap between Acts 17:23 and 24, since v. 23 promises the announcement of an unknown God while v. 24 assumes the existence of that God. Readers of the book do

not usually notice this gap, because it has been filled by 14:15–17, which proclaims that the true God is revealed in creation.

256. Resurrection illustrates this contrast. From the natural perspective, when you die, you're dead. Resurrection claims that God supersedes (or transforms) nature. Paul does not suggest that the vindicated Christ had an earthly body (Gal 1:15–17). Luke establishes continuity: the risen Christ not only has a body, he eats (Luke 24:41–43; cf. Acts 1:3; 10:41. For Luke grace reverses but does not eliminate nature.

257. This issue is discussed in M. Parsons and R. Pervo, *Rethinking the Unity*, 90–101.

258. God needs nothing: cf. also *1 Clem* 52:1.

259. Space requirements dictate that text and translation must be placed in separate tables.

260. On the boundaries of nations see also *1 Clem* 29:2.

261. Trans. C. Richardson, *Early Christian Fathers*, 58–59.

262. This passage from *Diognetus* is distinguished from others because of the possibility—not certainty—of intertextuality. Even if *Diognetus* is dependent upon Acts here, the usage would show how thoroughly these themes of God as creator and benefactor who lacks nothing are at home in the apologetic world. For an elaboration of the nature of creation see *Diognetus* 7:2.

263. Trans. E. R. Fairweather, in C. Richardson, *Early Christian Fathers*, 215.

264. Note the exhortation to generosity and benefaction, discussed above. (Note also that v. 35 has no parallel in Matthew.)

265. Parsons and Pervo, *Rethinking*, especially 101 and 105 n.90.

266. Notice the use of ποιεῖν ("make") of the creation of Adam (Gen 1:26–27) in Acts 17:24 (and Luke 11:3; Acts 14:15; 17:21, 26). Although *1 Clem* 33:4 speaks of εἰκόνος χαρακτῆρα ("stamp of an image"), probably under the influence of Hebr 1:3, his interest, like Luke's, is in the term ὁμοίωσις ("likeness"), which opens a path to ancient discussions of the imitation of God. Further details appear in Parsons and Pervo, *Rethinking*, 105 n.90.

267. Note, yet once more, Cornelius, Acts 10:35.

268. The language comes from Rudolph Bultmann, who found the "uniqueness" in Pauline ethics to reside in such "indicatives" of salvation. Many have said, "Do not sin." Paul (and others) said, in effect: "Christ has freed you from the power of sin." That is the "indicative," the "creed." Because of one's status as a member of the community of the saved, the command to abstain from sin can now be obeyed. In contemporary jargon, the "Indicative/Imperative" refers to "empowerment."

269. *Diognetus* 10:4, 6 also stress the imitation of God, with reference to care for the needy.

270. *HermMan* 1.1 (26.1.); cf. also *Diognetus* 3.3–5.

271. Wilhelm Bousset, *Kyrios Christos*: 370–71. The last revision of the German edition appeared in 1921. 370 n.73 cites Acts 17:24, 26; *HermVis* 1.1; *HermMan* 12.4.2; *2 Clem* 15:2; *Did* 10:3; 1 Tim 6:13.

272. See the thorough examination of the vocabulary of *1 Clem* by Lona, *Clemensbrief*, 30–35, who concludes, 35, that the work belongs to an environment strongly colored by the language of Hellenistic Judaism, especially the LXX. This conclusion, he notes, is reinforced by the occurrence of fifty-nine words found in Hellenistic Jewish writings but neither in the LXX nor the NT.

273. In this mature work of the "History of Religions School" lies the foundation of Part IV, "The Development toward the Ancient Church," of Bultmann's *Theology of the New Testament*, 95–236) and the roots of Helmut Koester's *Introduction*, esp. 2:151–349.

274. Docetism dealt with the apparent difficulties of a divine being who was also human by eliminating the humanity. Marcion was as consistent a Paulinist as has ever appeared. Gnosis cleaned up all the untidy inconsistencies between creation and redemption.

275. J. Jervell, *Apostelgeschichte*, 452: His argument occupies pp. 452–455 and is well worth reading.

276. An excellent survey of these writers is Robert M. Grant, *Greek Apologists of the Second Century*.

277. Although highly compressed, this description has validity. In the book of Acts, Luke, the most literarily sophisticated of the evangelists, has almost abandoned this technique, but his style continues to be episodic.

278. Grant, *Greek Apologists*, 24.

Chapter Seven
Acts among the Apostolic Fathers II

1. A primary occupation with the Pauline world means that Matt and John will receive relatively little attention, although both are probably later than Colossians.

2. See Appendix III.

3. Footnote references to (Luke and) Acts will lump together different parts of speech; in this case see Acts 3:17; 13:27; 17:23; 17:30.

4. See pp. 240–42.

5. Justin uses the term in *1 Apol.* 61.10 and four other times in his two apologies. It appears six times in writings wrongly attributed to Justin, and in Athenagoras, *Legation*, 21.6 and 28.7, as well as in Frag 1 of Melito's *Apology*. On the subject see Bultmann, ἀγνοέω, κ.τ.λ., *TDNT* 1:116–21.

6. See p. 246.

7. See Spicq, *Theological Lexicon* 1:1–4.

8. Most of the data in this chapter about LXX usage come from Lust *et al.*, *A Greek-English Lexicon of the Septuagint*. This work includes data by divisions of the Bible, such as the Pentateuch and the Prophets. That most often cited is the final category: books extant only in Greek.

9. Luke 13:27; 16:8, 9; 18:6; Acts 1:18; 8:23.

10. Luke likes to use this noun in the genitive, giving it a "biblical" flavor. That practice does not separate him from the realm of Greco-Roman moral language.

11. See Alfred Oepke, ἀθέμιτος, *TDNT* 1:166.

12. This is not "church" as opposed to "sect," but the entire body in opposition to factions or interest groups. (For the period from about the fourth century onwards historians assume that "sects" are a reaction to "the church" and "heresy" a reaction to "orthodoxy." This generally valid assumption is quite erroneous in reference to early Church history, which begins with a "sect" or "sects" and in which "orthodoxy" was a reaction to "heresy.")

13. The charge of "atheism"—failure to participate in civic cults—was made against Christians by polytheists. "Atheism" was unpatriotic, an assault on the bonds that held society together. (A modern parallel from U.S. history was the insertion of "under God" into the Pledge of Allegiance in the early 1950s. This was a Cold-War tactic designed to exclude "godless communists" rather than an affirmation of particular religious belief.)

14. See Heinrich Schlier, αἱρέομαι, κ.τ.λ., *TDNT* 1:180–85. On the development of heresy as a formal concept consult Robert M. Grant, *Heresy and Criticism*.

15. See Gerhard Kittel, ἄλογος, *TDNT* 4:441.

16. Origen uses the adjective more than 100 times.

17. In Acts 21:16 the term might mean "original."

18. The text of Luke 24:51 is probable, but not certain.

19. The verb for "he ascended" is ἀνέβη. Considered independently, Eph 4:8–10 presents a view of the descending and ascending redeemer like that of John. The same may be said of Acts 2:32–35, which also employs two "Johannine" verbs: ὑψοῦν and ἀναβαίνειν.

20. The session of Christ at God's right hand (Psalm 110 is in the background; cf. also 1 Kgs 2:19) appears in Rom 8:34, in the sequence, died, rose, is seated. Note Acts 7:55–56; Col 3:1; Heb 1:3; 8:1; 10:12. On the concept of the *sessio ad dextram* (seating at right hand of God) see E. Franklin, *Christ the Lord*, 29–41.

21. Those who find daunting or confusing the notion of ascension distinct from exaltation and resurrection may appreciate the concise summary of Charles Talbert, *Reading Acts*, 22–23, who supplies many references to early Christian writings.

22. Hans Windisch has a succinct outline of the history of usage, ἀσκέω, *TDNT* 1:494–96.

23. Two related nouns appear in *4 Macc.*

24. Windisch, ἀσκέω, 495. The subject of *Aristeas* 168 is "justice." The clause concludes that the purpose of Torah is to enable Jews to *"practice* (ἀσκῶμεν) justice to all in their lives and actions."

25. Its base is the Greek "root" σω-, "save," "be well," to which is prefixed an alpha privative, which negates, as in "amoral" vs. "moral."

26. For examples see Spicq, *Theological Lexicon*, 1:220–22. In the *Tabula of Cebes* 28.3 this word is paired with ἀκρασία.

27. A TLG search revealed fifty-six occurrences in 1 BCE-1 CE, ten in Philo, two in Josephus, twenty-eight in Plutarch, and six in Dio of Prusa.

28. See Daniel Marguerat, *La première histoire du christianisme: les actes des apôtres*, 57–58, and his references.

29. Tertullian was not the first to argue "*sanguis martyrum semen ecclesiae*" ("the blood of the martyrs is the seed [growth force] of the church"). This becomes clear in the actual words of *Apology* 50.13 "*Plures efficimus quoties metimur a vobis, semen est sanguis Christianorum*" ("The more you mow us down, the more we grow; the seed is the blood of Christians").

30. Matt has one instance, Mark two.

31. The double front slash (//) indicates a parallel text. When Eph clearly imitates Col, I do not claim two distinctly separate attestations.

32. For the background and meaning of this word see R. Bultmann, ἀφίημι, κ.τ.λ., *TDNT* 1:509–12. Spicq, *Theological Lexicon*, 1:238–44, suggests that ἄφεσις belongs to the realm of early Christian catechesis. This is a wise conjecture.

33. Representative evidence is listed by R. Pervo, *Profit with Delight*, 18–24.

34. Acts 23:18, 29; 25:14, 27; 26:29; 28:16–17. cf. 21:23; 22:4.

35. This theme can be no less at home in works that tend toward a "theology of glory," such as Acts, than in those more oriented toward the Pauline "theology of the cross." (In a theology of glory the disciple imitates Jesus by working miracles; the theology of the cross stresses heroic suffering as the primary earthly form of imitating Christ.)

36. See G. Bertram, φυλάσσς, φυλακή, *TDNT* 236–44, 244.

37. This symbolism is apparent in Acts 12, on which see the extensive summary beginning at p. 278.

38. See also G. Kittel, δεσμός, δέσμιος, *TDNT* 2:43, and F. Staudinger, *EDNT* 1:288–90.

39. I have altered translations so that "sovereign" is the consistent rendering.

40. K. H. Rengstorf, δεσπότης, κ.τ.λ., *TDNT* 2:44–49, 47. The word is not generally common in the Greek Old Testament. Thirty-six of sixty occurrences are in books available only in Greek and fifty are in these books and the Writings (less 1–2 Chr). "The Writings" constitute the third part of the Hebrew Bible, after "the Torah" and "the Prophets." The Writings include the poetic and wisdom literature as well as some books that Christians classify as "history," (1–2 Chr) or prophecy (Dan).

41. For comparison, Philo uses the word more than 250 times, Josephus more than 150, according to a TLG search. Other early Christian texts in which this noun appears include Justin, *InJas*, and the *Acts of John*. See BDAG, 220 and G. Lampe, *Patristic Greek Lexicon*, 339.

42. On the *Birkat-Ha-Mazon* see K Niederwimmer, *Didache*, 155–57.

43. The liturgical traditions of the *Didache* are among its oldest elements, probably late first century. See Niederwimmer, *Didache* 52.

44. Note Lona's useful and insightful excursus on predications applied to God in *1 Clement*, *Clemensbrief*, 181–85.

45. "Devil" in the strictly lexicographical sense, i.e., not comprising "Satan," "Beliar," "Beelzebul," etc., but this word (which means "adversary" in Greek) only.

46. John S. Kloppenborg, *The Formation of Q*, 246–62.

47. See W. Foerster, διάβολος, *TDNT* 2:71–81. (Foerster does not limit his study to this word, but to the concept of the great adversary of God.) Twenty-two uses appear in the LXX, with a number of different meanings; eighteen of them belong to the Writings. "Devil" is an exceptional meaning there.

48. C. L. Mitton *The Epistle to the Ephesians*, 209.

49. See pp. 238–39.

50. R. Bultmann, *Theology of the New Testament*, 2:212. See the full discussion on pp. 212–13.

51. Trans. Richardson, *Early Christian Fathers*, 54, alt.

52. Trans. Richardson, *Early Christian Fathers*, 58, alt.

53. Trans. Richardson, *Early Christian Fathers*, 175, alt.

54. Trans. Fairweather, in Richardson, *Early Christian Fathers*, 220, alt.

55. There is no early evidence for this word in Jewish circles. For a non-Jewish (or Christian) instance see SEG 14.883, *l.* 1. On the number in general, see the article by K. Rengstorf on δώκεκα, κ.τ.λ. in *TDNT* 2:321–28.

56. Walter Grundmann, ἐγκράτεια, κ.τ.λ., *TDNT* 2:339–42, especially 340–41. See also

the apposite remarks of R. Bultmann (*Theology*, 2:221), who observes, "Nevertheless, a pre-eminent importance is ascribed to it [ἐγκράτεια] when according to Acts 24:25 the moving theme of Paul's address before Felix and Drusilla is 'righteousness and self-control.'"

57. According to a TLG search, the stem is found seventy-four times in the writings of Philo.

58. Cf. the *Acts of Paul* 3.5, 6, where the word means "virginity."

59. The negatives, ἀκρασία, ἀκρατής occur once each in Matt, 1 Cor, 2 Tim, and *Hermas*.

60. Holt Graham in Grant and Graham, *The Apostolic Fathers* 2:129.

61. See W. Schrenck, ἐκδικέω, κ.τ.λ., *TDNT* 2:442–46, 444.

62. The variant readings in Acts 12:5 (ἐκτενῶς, ἐκτενής, ἐν ἐκτενείᾳ), indicate that the usages are synonymous.

63. See the article of Spicq, *Theological Lexicon*, 1:455–61.

64. See p. 335.

65. Note that the term appears in Codex Bezae at Luke 21:7; 23:42 in place of the more common "parousia." These might be original readings, but they are more likely examples of second-century taste. Cf. also the *Acts of Paul* 8:23.

66. For example, Irenaeus, *Against Heresies* 3.2 and 4.6. The word is not common before Origen. Epictetus, *Dissertations*, 3.22.97 provides a philosophical specimen.

67. See pages 122 and 208.

68. Plato, *Republic* 518D; Cicero, *On the Nature of the Gods*, 1.77.

69. Note Acts 15:19, closely parallel to 15:3.

70. *1 Clem* 1:1 is different.

71. Most of the appearances in Irenaeus come from Valentinian usage ("the repentance of Sophia", for example, *Against Heresies* 1.4.5.) See Lampe, 536. Irenaeus opposed the Gnostic theology of Valentinus.

72. On the subject and term see A. D. Nock, *Conversion*, 179 and 296 as well as Bertram, στρέφω, κ.τ.λ., *TDNT* 7:714–29, 722–29. Early Judaism and primitive Christianity tended to prefer, even substitute, μετανοέω/μετάνοια, etc. for ἐπιστρέφω/ἐπιστροφή.

73. See pp. 217 and 288 on Luke 22:24–30 and also under "philanthropy," below.

74. The text of *1 Clem* 59:3 is disputed. For "benefactor" see Lona, *Clemensbrief*, 594, and Lindemann, *Clemensbriefe*, 169. "Benefactor" is the reading of Funk-Bihlmeyer and all recent commentators.

75. Justin uses the participle once, ironically referring to those who would be benefactors of Christians by freeing them from the pain of existence, *1 Apol.* 57.3.

76. See p. 214.

77. For Christ as benefactor see the *Euchologion/Sacramentary of Serapion*, 5:11. This work probably belongs to the third century.

78. On slaves as benefactors see Spicq, *Theological Lexicon* 2:109. So also NRSV and most translations. Dibelius-Conzelmann, *Pastoral Epistles*, 82, give strong reasons for relating the clause to the owners.

79. In addition to the items cited above, are Spicq *Theological Lexicon* 2:107–13 and the concise treatment by G. Bertram, εὐεργετέω, κ.τ.λ., *TDNT* 2:654–55.

80. The realm of benefaction aptly shows that such adaptation did not involve simple assimilation. In Christian usage these values always experienced some alteration and change.

81. Albrecht Stumpff's article, ζῆλος, κ.τ.λ., *TDNT* 2:877–88, well illustrates the range of meanings (although I disagree with his proposal that the passages in Acts have to do with a kind of righteous ardor, 878).

82. R. Grant, *Apostolic Fathers*, 2:23 and 25 discusses the relation between *1 Clem* and Acts on this matter, concluding that *1 Clem* probably used Acts.

83. See R. Pervo, *Profit with Delight*, 27–28 and the references there.

84. See K. L. Schmidt, θρησκεία, κ.τ.λ., *TDNT* 3:155–59 and Spicq, *Theological Lexicon* 2:200–204.

85. Spicq, *Theological Lexicon* 2: 202, observes that θρησκεία often appears in combination with εὐσέβεια.

86. For Josephus see Schmidt, θρησκεία 156 and Spicq, *Theological Lexicon* 2: 203.

87. In Acts 26:5 "our religion" has parties. Paul speaks as a Jew. In *1 Clement* "our religion" is "Christianity."

88. Common enough in Philo and Josephus, θρησκεία appears four times in the LXX, all in books known only in Greek. The parent verb appears twice, in the same group.
89. J. Jeremias, θύρα, *TDNT* 3:173–80, 173–75; *BDAG* 462; and R. Kratz, *EDNT* 2:160–61.
90. Haenchen, *Acts* 162 and n.3.
91. So *Beg.* 4:15, with examples. Blassi, *Making Charisma*, 55, relates the expression "God knows (γινώσκει) your hearts" in Luke 16:15 to Romans 8:27.
92. An important biblical prototype is Isa 57:6: ἐκείνη σου ἡ μερίς, οὗτός σου ὁ κλῆρος, ("Among the smooth stones of the valley is your *portion*; they, they, are your *lot*").
93. Note also the related noun. See H. Strathmann, λατρεύω, λατρεία, *TDNT* 4:58–65.
94. See H. Strathmann and R. Meyer, λειτουργέω, κ.τ.λ., *TDNT* 4:215–31 and Spicq, *Theological Lexicon*, 2:378–84.
95. The opposition between these two terms can be traced back as far as Plato, *Phaedrus* 244A and *Protagoras* 323B. Note also Xenophon, *Memorabilia* 1.1.6.
96. Acts 12:15; 26:24, 25; 26:11, uses ἐμμαίνομαι.
97. See under σωφροσύνη, below, Spicq, *Theological Lexicon* 2:430–31; H. Preisker, μαίνομαι *TDNT* 4:360–61; and A. Malherbe, *Paul and the Popular Philosophers*, 159–60. Pliny, *Letter* 10.96.4, characterizes Christianity as *amentia*, "madness." Betty Radice translates this as "fanatical" in *Pliny: Letters and Panegyricus* II LCL, 287.
98. Otto Bauernfeind, μάταιος, κ.τ.λ., *TDNT* 4:519–24.
99. An equally valid alternative translation is "worthless beings," i.e., the gods of polytheism; note BDAG, 621, which treats the participle as masculine.
100. Particularly close to Acts 14:15 is Justin, *Dialogue with Trypho* 91.3: οἱ ἐκ πάντων τῶν ἐθνῶν διὰ τούτου τοῦ μυστηρίου εἰς τὴν θεοσέβειαν ἐτράπησαν ἀπὸ τῶν ματαίων εἰδώλων καὶ δαιμόνων, ("those from all the gentiles who have turned, through this mystery, from idols and demons to God-worship").
101. An interesting instance from the literature of Hellenistic Judaism appears in *Aristeas* 111.
102. Dibelius/Conzelmann, *Pastoral Epistles*, 144.
103. Acts 19:28. Cf. also 19:27, 34, and 35.
104. A good example of Jewish use is Josephus, *Ant.* 1:24, which states that Torah contains nothing incongruous with "the greatness of God and God's affection for humanity" (οὐδὲν οὔτ' ἄλογον αὐτοῖς οὔτε πρὸς τὴν μεγαλειότητα τοῦ θεοῦ καὶ τὴν φιλανθρωπίαν ἀνάρμοστον). On "philanthropy" see below.
105. On the term see Spicq, *Theological* Lexicon 2:471–77, and Behm and Würthwein, μετανοέω, μετάνοια *TDNT* 4:975–1008.
106. See p. 243.
107. The verb, μετανοέω, which is not the subject of this inquiry, occurs five times in Matthew, twice in Mark, fifteen times in Luke and Acts, once in Paul, and about a dozen times in Revelation. There are thus differences, but the Lukan preference remains prominent.
108. Luke 1:77; 3:3 (John the Baptizer); 24:47; Acts 2:38; 5:31; 10:43; 13:38; 26:18. cf. Col 1:14//Eph 1:7.
109. See the previous note and 1 Tim 5:22, 24; 2 Tim 3:6.
110. Note, in particular, the addition of the story of the woman taken in adultery found in some manuscripts of John at 7:53–8:11 (For John, Sin is the state of unbelievers) and the apparently contradictory statements of 1 John, such as 1:10 and 3:6. Cf. also 5:16–21 and see J. Bogart, *Orthodox and Heretical Perfectionism in the Johannine Community*.
111. Note also Luke 13:3.
112. See A. Lindemann, *Clemensbriefe*, 20–22.
113. On the psychological quality of repentance in Luke and Acts see Conzelmann, *Theology of St. Luke*, 100.
114. Carolyn Osiek, *Shepherd of Hermas*, 28–30. She most often translates μετάνοια as "conversion."
115. See also *Sibylline Oracles* 4:168–169.
116. Conzelmann, *Theology of St. Luke*, 101; Dibelius/Conzelmann, *Pastoral Epistles*, 113–114. The authors in question would not hesitate to ascribe the gift of repentance ultimately to divine favor.
117. See the text and translation by J. T. Fitzgerald and L. L. White, *The Tabula of Cebes*; on the date see 1–4.

118. 10:4–11:1, Trans. Fitzgerald and White, 79. For the use of repentance in Stoic and Cynic thought see their n.40, p. 144. Note also Nock, *Conversion*, 179–80. On *paideia* see also below.

119. Trans. Richardson, *Early Christian Fathers*, 71, alt.

120. Trans. Clarke, 51.

121. Trans. L. M. Wills, *The Quest for the Historical Gospel*, 182. This prayer effects the miraculous restoration of voice to Aesop, enabling him to become a sage. On the *Aesop-Romance* see also R. Pervo, "A Nihilist Fabula: Introducing the *Life of Aesop*."

122. Trans. J. Arthur Hanson, *Apuleius Metamorphoses*, LCL, 2:341.

123. Trans. Harmon, *Lucian I* LCL, 105.

124. See also p. 107.

125. See the almost exhaustive study of Hans Conzelmann, φῶς, κ.τ.λ., *TDNT*. 9: 310–58, with large bibliography. Note also Spicq, *Theological Lexicon*, 3:470–91. There are references to philosophical and patristic usage in G. W. Clarke, *The Octavius of Minucius Felix*, 167–68, n.8.

126. See the full-length study (*The Role and Function of Repentance in Luke-Acts*) by Guy D. Nave, who approaches the subject from a literary critical perspective and takes into account a number of Hellenistic Jewish and early Christian writings.

127. Conzelmann, φῶς, 345.

128. B. R. Gaventa says of 26:18, "Thus, Luke may be drawing on stereotypical conversion language as much as he is on Isaiah [42:16]" (*From Darkness to Light*, 87).

129. See the references in S. G. Hall, *Melito of Sardis*, 37 n.34.

130. See A. Lona, *Clemensbrief*, 613–19 and A. Lindemann, *Clemensbriefe*, 164–68. Lona discusses in detail 2 Macc 1:24–29; 3 Macc 2:2–20, and 6:2–15.

131. By the time of Justin φωτισμός ("enlightenment") has become a term for baptism. See Schnackenburg, *Ephesians*, 222–23. Note also the expression ὁ υἱὸς τῆς ἀγάπης αὐτοῦ (lit., "the son of his [God's] love"), Col 1:13, which is the equivalent of "beloved son" in Mark 1:11. This evokes the baptism of Jesus and confirms that baptism is the locus of the translation of believers from darkness to light. *1 Clem* links the adjective "beloved" with παῖς ("son"), 59.2, 3.

132. Susan R Garrett, "Exodus from Bondage," esp. 670–677, identifies most of these. Note also the earlier study of August Strobel, "Passa-Symbolik und Passa-Wunder in Act XII. 3ff.," 210–15. Allen provides a thorough discussion with many references, *Death of Herod*, 98–107.

133. In Chapter Three, p. 76 and Table 3.11, I show that Luke took the idea of delaying the execution from Mark 14:2, transferring a theme from one "passion narrative" to another.

134. Cf., for example, *The Apostolic Tradition* 20.9–10. Night was also the time at which Lucius received initiation into the mysteries of Isis: Apuleius, *Metamorphoses* 11.23

135. "Some sat in darkness and in gloom, prisoners in misery and in irons, Then they cried to the Lord in their trouble, and he saved them from their distress; he brought them out of darkness and gloom, and broke their bonds asunder."

136. The term will have a particularly rich history in Gnosticism and related texts. For some examples see W. Foerster, *Gnosis*, 2:325, index *s.v.* "awaken."

137. See R. Schnackenburg, *Ephesians*, 228–29.

138. An example is the "Hymn of the Pearl," *Acts of Thomas* 111–12, lines 72–78 (associated with the symbol of awakening). For the symbol of clothing in mystery religions see Karl Kerenyi, *Die griechisch-orientalische Romanliteratur*, 144.

139. Note in addition Rom 12:13–14. On the image in Colossians see E. Schweizer, *The Letter to the Colossians*, 195–96.

140. This term, ἀποθέμενοι, is similar in meaning to "put/take off" in Colossians and Ephesians.

141. To "gird (up) one's loins" has the same meaning as "hike up/hitch up your skirts," for it refers to the full-length outer robe belted at the waist. When engaged in physical labor, slaves and others would blouse this long robe over the belt, raising the hem of their garment to the knees or higher to permit freedom of movement. Mosaics of Roman times show servants with garments raised to their hips carrying food trays and the like.

142. A number of proposals have linked 1 Peter 1:13 with Luke 12:35–48, esp. vv. 42–46. Achtemeier (*1Peter*, 118) is skeptical, and not without reason.

143. On door miracles see Reinhard Kratz, *Rettungswunder: Motiv-, traditions- und formkritische Aufarbeitung einer biblischen Gattung*; for Acts 12 in particular see 351–451.

144. Isa 42:6–7 (First "Servant Song"): "I am the LORD, I have called you in righteousness, I have taken you by the hand and kept you; I have given you as a covenant to the people, a *light* to the nations, 7 to open the eyes that are blind, to *bring out the prisoners from the dungeon, from the prison those who sit in darkness.* (LXX of v. 7: ἀνοῖξαι ὀφθαλμοὺς τυφλῶν, ἐξαγαγεῖν ἐκ δεσμῶν δεδεμένους καὶ ἐξ οἴκου φυλακῆς καθημένους ἐν σκότει.) Isa 45:1–2 Thus says the LORD to his anointed (τῷ χριστῷ μου), to Cyrus, whose right hand I have grasped to subdue nations before him and strip kings of their robes, *to open doors* before him—and the gates shall not be closed: 2 I will go before you and level the mountains, I will break in pieces the *doors* of bronze and cut through the *bars of iron.*"

145. Note the application of Isa 45:2–3 to baptism in *Barn* 11:4 and the citation of Isa 42:6–7; 49:6–7; 61:1–2 in 11:7–8 and the exegesis of "milk and honey" in 6:7–19. These images are important in the *Odes of Solomon*, for example Odes 24, 17:10–12 and 42:10–17. The relation of these texts to baptism has generated considerable discussion. For the various views see the commentary of J. H. Charlesworth, *The Odes of Solomon.* Still useful for the theology of baptism in the second century is André Benoit, *Le baptême chrétien au second siècle.* On the development of the doctrine of the "descent into hell" and its place in the creed, see J. N. D. Kelly, *Early Christian Creeds*, 378–83.

146. Trans. M. Shepherd, in C. Richardson, *Early Christian Fathers*, 131.

147. K. H. Rengstorf says the word is ". . . a Christian construction designed to mark off Jewish from Christian teachers at the decisive point, namely the absolutising of the νόμος." (*TDNT* 2:159).

148. See also pp. 126–27.

149. For discussions see W. Schoedel, *Ignatius of Antioch*, 104–105; H. Bietenhard, ὄνομα, κ.τ.λ., *TDNT* 5:242–83, 272–73; L. Hartmann, *EDNT* 2:519–22, R. Schnackenburg, *The Johannine Epistles* , 295 n.121; and esp. R. Brown, *The Epistles of John*, 302–3 and 711–12.

150. See Barrett, *Acts*, 1:300–301.

151. Brown (*Epistles of John*, 101) dates 3 John 100–110. The Latin term *nomen*, "name," played and plays an important part in the discussion of official persecution of believers. The term already appears in Pliny's famous letter 10.96.2: Is the "mere name" (*nomen ipsum*), i.e., being a Christian, sufficient grounds for execution?

152. See W. Michaelis, πάσχω, κ.τ.λ., *TDNT* 5:904–39, 924.

153. Compare the uses of the verb πάσχω in Luke 24:26, 46; Acts 3:18; 17:3.

154. See Lampe, *Patristic Greek Lexicon*, 991–92.

155. This includes the book more marked by "Greek *paideia*" than any other in the NT: Heb, which uses the word group eight times, always to mean "discipline" in the sense of "punishment."

156. Aeschylus, *Agamemnon* 177.

157. Bertram offers a good overview in παιδεύω, κ.τ.λ., *TDNT* 5:596–625. For a summary of early Jewish views see 612–18.

158. The traditional approach focused upon one's family. The significance of the formula in question is that it gave priority to education over ancestry. A classic study of the formula is W. C. van Unnik's, *Tarsus or Jerusalem.*

159. Neither Philo nor Josephus was willing to boast of Moses's Egyptian educational credentials.

160. Henry J. Cadbury presents an apt description of Paul's Greek *paideia* in *The Book of Acts in History*, 32–57.

161. For references to Hellenistic Judaism see Spicq, *Épitres pastorales*, 2:789.

162. Epictetus, *Dissertations* 3.21.15, makes a very similar statement about the moral and educational merits of the Eleusinian mysteries.

163. Bertram, παιδεύω, κ.τ.λ., 624.

164. *Acts of Philip* 2.3.12.

165. W. Jaeger, *Early Christianity and Greek Paideia*, 12. (Jaeger says nothing about the fresh and original character of this *paideia* here, and wisely so, for Luke would not have accepted that claim in its totality.)

166. *Early Christianity*, 118. Jaeger's remarks about *1 Clem* can be found on 12–26, with notes on 113–18. See also the commentary of H. Lona, *Clemensbrief*, 280–81.

167. It is characteristic that the "unlearned," ἀπαίδευτοι are those with incorrect views rather than insufficient general education: 2 Tim 2:23; *1 Clem* 39:1.

168. The other side of Athenian curiosity emerges in Chariton's novel *Callirhoe*, 1.11.6.

A band of pirates, led by one Theron, has captured the heroine and wish to convert her into cash: "Sailing to Athens appealed to them all. But Theron did not like the inquisitive nature (περιεργία) of the city. 'Are you the only ones,' he asked, 'who have not heard [cf. Luke 24:18] what busybodies the Athenians are? They are a talkative lot and fond of litigation, and in the harbor scores of troublemakers will ask who we are and where we got this cargo.'" *Chariton Callirhoe,* LCL, 69.

169. On these associations see A. Deissmann, *Bible Studies,* 323 n.5.

170. A. Malherbe, *Letters to the Thessalonians,* 453, with discussion and numerous references.

171. E. G., Sirach 3:23; 41:24. The group is common in the T12Pat: *T. Reuben* 3:4, 10; *T. Issacher* 3:5, 5:1; *T. Gad* 6:5; *T. Joseph* 6:2. Philo tends to link "meddling" with serious vice, as in *Opif. Mundi (Creation of the World)* 164; *Leg. All. (Allegorical Laws)* 3.140, 143.

172. 2 Thess 3:11 and 1 Tim 5:13 engage in similar wordplays involving the stem of περιεργία, ἐργ-, "work."

173. Spicq, *Épitres pastorales,* 1:537. The conventional theme of the interplay between curiosity and magic serves high literary and philosophical art in Apuleius's *Metamorphoses (Golden Ass).*

174. *HermSim* 9.2.7; *HermVis* 4.3.1.

175. Celsus, the author of the *True Doctrine* was evidently a Middle Platonic philosopher who composed his critique of Christianity c.175–181.

176. Celsus, in *Origen: Contra* Celsum (3.55), Trans. Chadwick, 165–66.

177. *C. Celsum* 3.50–51.

178. Justin, *2 Apol.* 10.4.

179. The LXX has fifty-nine examples, twenty-six from books extant only in Greek. Meanings include "faith," "faithfulness," and "honesty."

180. See BDAG 818–20, and the large bibliography there. Standard studies include R. Bultmann and A. Weiser, πιστεύω, κ.τ.λ., *TDNT* 6:174–228, G. Barth, *EDNT* 3:91–97 (with a substantial bibliography); and Spicq, *Theological Lexicon,* 3:110–16.

181. The NRSV debatably renders this expression as "the Holy Spirit." Note 11:24, which characterizes Barnabas as "*good* man, full . . ." (ἀνὴρ ἀγαθὸς καὶ πλήρης πνεύματος ἁγίου καὶ πίστεως). The adjective "good" suggests that the two nouns denote moral qualities.

182. On *1 Clement* note 1:2, 3:4; 12:1, 8; 64, etc. This is not the only use. In 5:6 and 58:2 the word means *fides qua,* in the Pauline sense. Of Ignatius, William Schoedel says, "Faith, in short, begins to take on more clearly the characteristics of a virtue" (*Ignatius of Antioch,* 26).

183. S. Brown, *Apostasy and Perseverance in the Theology of Luke,* 146.

184. Bultmann and Weiser, πιστεύω, κ.τ.λ., *TDNT* 6:213. On the Pastorals see also S. Wilson (*Luke and the Pastoral Epistles,* 29–30), who compares their usage with Acts. Examples include 1 Tim 1:19; 4:1, 6; 6:10 (cf. v. 21); 2 Tim 2:18; 4:7; Tit 3:5.

185. So, for example, IgnMag 1:1; Athenagoras 8:1; Irenaeus *Against Heresies* 1.10.2.

186. H. Strathmann, πόλις, κ.τ.λ., *TDNT* 6:516–35, esp. 525–26, 534–35; and Spicq, *Theological Lexicon* 3:131–33.

187. Two examples are Epictetus, *Dissertations* 4.13.5 and Josephus, *Life* 170. The first is relevant to Acts 19:36, as it speaks of "bad-mouthing" Caesar. The second contrasts rashness with self-control. For other examples see Spicq, *Theological Lexicon,* 3:189–90.

188. Spicq, *Theological Lexicon,* 3:189.

189. This adjective does not appear again until Clement of Alexandria, who uses it about seven times.

190. *Barn* 6:3 has προσήλυτοι as a variant for ἐπήλυτοι, which has the same meaning but is the "more difficult" reading.

191. Martin Goodman, *Mission and Conversion,* 69–72. He does not deal with the question of the "scribes."

192. Goodman, *Mission and Conversion,* 72–74. Prior to the second century the term was as ambiguous as "God-fearer."

193. See Karl Georg Kuhn, προσήλυτος *TDNT* 6: 727–44; he assumes that the term was established in Hellenistic Judaism but avoided by Philo in part and Josephus *in toto* because it was obscure and inelegant. H. Kuhli, *EDNT* 3:170–71, has a similar view, a good bibliography of recent literature, and a brief summary of the problems raised by Acts 13:43.

194. See G. Delling, συμβιβάζω, *TDNT* 7:763–66.

195. Luke 1:47; 2:11; Acts 5:31; 18:23.

196. Dibelius/Conzelmann, *Pastoral Epistles*, 144–47.

197. To cite but one example, the *Venite*: "For the Lord is a great God, and a great King above all gods" (Ps 95:3). God is, like the Persian emperor (Ezra 7:12), "king of kings and lord of lords." That expression is not applied to God in the Hebrew Bible (unless *The Messiah* of Handel so qualifies). It is, however, used in 1 Tim 6:15. Most interesting, in this context (cf. also Acts 17:16–34), is Philo, *On the Cherubim*, 99–100: "For if when we are about to receive kings, we prepare our houses to wear a more magnificent appearance, neglecting nothing which may give them ornament, but using every thing in a liberal and unsparing manner, having for our object that they shall have an abode pleasant to them, and in all respects suitable to their majesty; what sort of habitation ought we to prepare for the King of kings, for God the ruler of the whole universe, condescending in his mercy and lovingkindness for man to visit the beings whom he has created, and to come down from the borders of heaven to the lowest regions of the earth, for the purpose of benefiting our race? (100) Shall we prepare him a house of stone or of wooden materials? Away! Such an idea is not holy even to utter; for not even if the whole earth were to change its nature and to become on a sudden gold, or something more valuable than gold, and if it were then to be wholly consumed by the skill of workmen, who should make it into porticoes and vestibules, and chambers, and precincts, and temples—not even then could it be a place worthy for his feet to tread upon, but a pious soul is his fitting abode." (Trans. Yonge).

198. Any who might find Martin Dibelius and Hans Conzelmann dubious witnesses are invited to consult Spicq's *Theological Lexicon*, for example 3:352–53: "All the same, 'savior' in the official and functional titles of sovereigns is not unimportant for understanding the language of the NT, esp. when the Roman emperor is described as 'savior and benefactor,' which are divine attributes." See nn. 41–42 there, as well as 3:443 and n.10. The basic resource is G. Fohrer and W. Foerster, σώτηρ *TDNT* 8:1003–1021 (part of a larger article).

199. See Spicq, *Theological Lexicon*, 3:356–57.

200. In his article on this word group Spicq (*Theological Lexicon* 3:359–65) displays all of *his* virtues, skillfully integrating the documentary and the literary. Ulrich Luck, σώφρων, κ.τ.λ., *TDNT* 7:1097–1104, is especially good on the classical background.

201. Luck, 1101–2. For the general ethical sense Spicq cites *Special Laws* 2.62, p. 363.

202. The literal opposition between "madness" and "sanity" can be seen in Mark 5:15// Luke 8:35. Note also 2 Cor 5:13.

203. Note also Justin, *1 Apology* 13.2–4.

204. See W. Grundmann, ταπεινός, κ.τ.λ., *TDNT* 8:1–27. Note also Spicq, *Theological Lexicon*, 3:369–71, and H. Giesen ταπεινοφροσύνη, *EDNT* 3:333–34.

205. The exceptions are Epictetus, *Diss.* 3.24, 56, where it has a pejorative meaning, and one usage, negative, in Josephus, *War* 4.494.

206. One of these instances (Col 2:18) is of uncertain meaning.

207. I believe that Acts 20:19 is dependent upon Ephesians. See pp. 116–17.

208. Despite Grundmann, ταπεινός, 27, there is no good reason to deny an ascetic sense to Acts 20:19.

209. The expression is evidently a (euphemistic) synecdoche that substitutes the general (place) for the particular (hell, heaven). John 14:2–3 is an example. Cf. also Luke 16:28 (the place of torment).

210. Trans. Richardson, *Early Christian Fathers*, 46.

211. "The phrase was evidently in common use." Barrett, *Acts*, 1:35.

212. See H. Koester, τόπος, *TDNT* 8:187–208, especially 207–208.

213. Luke 1:51; Rom 1:30; 2 Tim 3:2; Jas 4:6 (*cit*); 1 Pet 5:5 (*cit*).

214. The related noun, ὑπερηφανία, is not in Luke or Acts and but once in the NT, though it appears several times in the Apostolic Fathers and the Apologists. See G. Bertram, ὑπερήφανος, ὑπερηφανία, *TDNT* 8:525–29.

215. Nine of the twenty occurrences between 2 BCE and 3 CE are in Origen.

216. See Spicq, *Theological Lexicon* 3:440–45, and U. Luck, φιλανθρωπία, κ.τ.λ., *TDNT* 9:107–12. I use "civic" advisedly, for the term was not common in philosophical discussions. Bruce Winter seeks to find the roots of subsequent Christian views in the undisputed Pauline literature: *Seek the Welfare of the City*.

217. Dibelius/Conzelmann, *Pastoral Epistles*, 144, with references in n.23.

218. *Ibid.* and Spciq, *Theological Lexicon*, 3:442.

219. See R. Pervo, "Wisdom and Power."

220. On the subject see the various essays in John Fitzgerald, Ed., _Greco-Roman Perspectives on Friendship._

221. Aeschylus, _Prometheus Bound,_ 10–11, 28.

222. In the LXX only one of thirteen occurrences of the group involves a translation from the Hebrew Bible, and that is Greek Esther 8:13. _Aristeas_ 207–208 is particularly instructive.

223. Luck, _TDNT_ 9, 111. This may be due to hesitations about appropriating the specific language of "friendship." For data see Adolf Harnack, _The Mission and Expansion of Christianity in the First Three Centuries,_ 1:410–21 and G. Stählin, φιλέω, κ.τ.λ., _TDNT_ 9:113–71.

224. The term appears six times in John and twice in 3 John, referring to believers.

225. On the application of the succeeding parable to its social context see Richard Rohrbaugh, "The Pre-Industrial City in Luke-Acts: Urban Social Relations," in J. Neyrey, Ed., _The Social World of Luke-Acts,_ 125–50, 137–47.

226. _Mission and Expansion_ 1:421. _Beg._ 4:326 and H. J. Cadbury, "Names for Christians and Christianity in Acts," _Beg._ 5:375–392, 379–380, both incline this way. Barrett, _Acts_ 2:1183, says that "these would naturally be Christians," but does not think that the term is technical. (But see 19:31, where Paul's friends the Asiarchs were not believers.) See also BDAG 2 A α, 1059.

227. For the Greek text see table 7.1. Note also Josephus, _Ant._ 1:24, cited in n. 124.

228. J. C. Lentz offers a thorough and insightful study of Luke's use of the ethical tradition to promote his construction of Paul in _Luke's Portrait of Paul,_ 62–104.

229. Ἡ μὲν οὖν ἐκκλησία καθ' ὅλης τῆς Ἰουδαίας καὶ Γαλιλαίας καὶ Σαμαρείας εἶχεν εἰρήνην, οἰκοδομουμένη καὶ πορευομένη τῷ φόβῳ τοῦ κυρίου, καὶ τῇ παρακλήσει τοῦ ἁγίου πνεύματος ἐπληθύνετο.

230. 2 Cor 6:14–7:1 is very probably a non-Pauline insertion into the text. This interpolation was evidently made by the editor of the composite text, thus quite possibly in Ephesus c. 100. See V. Furnish, _II Corinthians,_ 371–83.

231. R. Bultmann, _Theology_ 2:213–14. See also Balz in _TDNT_ 9:189–219, 217–18.

232. For further parallels between Acts 9:31 and later writings see p. 290.

233. Walter Grundmann _et al.,_ χρίω, κ.τ.λ., _TDNT_ 9:493–580, 537 n.298.

234. See A. Harnack, _Mission and Expansion_ 1:410–14.

235. Josephus's two-paragraph account of Jesus (_Ant._ 18.63–64) has stimulated much debate. The final sentence: "And the tribe of the Christians, so called after him, has still to this day not disappeared" (εἰς ἔτι τε νῦν τῶν Χριστιανῶν ἀπὸ τοῦδε ὠνομασμένον οὐκ ἐπέλιπε τὸ φῦλον) would be a bit more clever than many forgeries. The translation is that of L. H. Feldman, _Josephus IX_ LCL, 51.

236. For links among Suetonius, the Younger Pliny, and Tacitus see D. Georgi, _Opponents of Paul,_ 356–58. Robert Wilken summarizes the backgrounds of and connections between Pliny and Tacitus in _The Christians as the Romans Saw Them,_ 1–30, 48–62. See also P. de Labriolle, _la Réaction païenne,_ 28–45.

237. Such uncritical acceptance of Tacitus is common; see, e.g., Hemer, _Book of Acts_ 177. Wilken, _op. cit._ 49, has a critical perspective: "Tacitus's account tells us more about Roman attitudes in his own time, the early second century, than it does about the misfortunes of Christians during Nero's reign."

238. Lucian (c. 120–c. 185) is the first Greek polytheist author of the second century to use the term.

239. _1 Clement,_ among others, does not use the word, but. it is extremely common in _Diognetus,_ appearing fourteen times.

240. This is the normal word for "Christianity" in French, Italian, and Spanish, for example.

241. Among the commentaries note, in particular, Haenchen, _Acts,_ 367–68 n.3 and Barrett, _Acts,_ 1:556–57.

242. Mark 16:9–20 are found in A C D L W 1, most of the later uncials, the great majority of minuscules, most of the Old Latin and Vulgate mss., and some Syriac and Coptic witnesses. The earliest datable witnesses to this text are Irenaeus and the _Diatessaron,_ c. 180. For details and analysis see Metzger, _Textual Commentary,_ 102–7.

243. The phrase can be found in Rom 8:22; Col 1:15 (constantly cited by patristic authorities); 1 Pet 2:13, three times in _1 Clement,_ nine times in _Hermas,_ and elsewhere (_Martyrdom of Polycarp,_ Theophilus of Antioch, _Acts of Justin_).

244. The *Acts of John* by Ps.-Prochorus belongs to the sixth century; this passage does not occur in the second century *Acts of John*. Eusebius attributes the story about Barsabbas to Papias. Vincent Taylor, *Gospel according to St. Mark*, 613, says, "Here, without doubt, is the atmosphere of A.D. 100–40."

245. Elements and aspects of this background are glimpsed from a distance by Clinton E. Arnold, *Ephesians: Power and Magic*. E. Käsemann, "Ephesians and Acts," is both general and polemical, but very insightful.

246. Cf. Acts 22:21.

247. See table 7.6.

248. Paul prefers the simpler καταλάσσω (Rom 5:10; 2 Cor 5:18–20), while Colossians uses ἀποκαταλάσσω. The terms are essentially synonymous. See F. Büchsel, ἀλάσσω, κ.τ.λ., *TDNT* 1:251–59, 258.

249. The quoted words are those of Barrett, *Acts*, 1:358.

250. Luke shies away from the cosmic ideas promoted by Colossians. It is quite likely that this speculative approach greatly stimulated radical interpreters of Paul. Ephesians seeks to redirect these notions. Luke excludes them.

251. *The Epistle to the Ephesians*, 205. On a more sober note, Mitton (Preface, vi) notes that he was a circuit rider. His ability to produce scholarly works under those conditions commands admiration.

252. Philo *Opif.* (*On the Creation*) 71, Trans. F.H. Colson and G. H. Whitaker, *Philo I*, LCL, 57 (μέθη νηφαλίῳ κατασχεθεὶς ὥσπερ οἱ κορυβαντιῶντες ἐνθουσιᾷ). See also *Life of Moses* 1.187, *Every Good Person*, 12–13, *Contemplative* Life, 89, *Allegorical Laws* 1.82 and 3.82. The last speaks of "divine drunkenness." "Sober Drunkenness" (νηφάλιος μέθη) is a term of which Philo was quite fond. See Schnackenburg, *Ephesians*, 236–37 and H. Preisker, μέθη, *TDNT* 4:545–47. The basic work on this subject is Hans Lewy, *Sobria Ebrietas: Untersuchungen zur Geschicthe der antiken Mystik.*

253. *Sobriety*, 147–48. The subject is the prayer of Hannah in 1 Sam. 1:12–14.

254. Luke appears, not for the first time, to be savoring the taste of some cake that yet remains upon the shelf. While fully dissociating Pentecost from any tinge of unruly ecstasy, the author nonetheless gives Peter a chance (Acts 2:15) to draw a conventional philosophical conclusion: this is "high sobriety"—even if his claim that the sun is still above the yard-arm seems unconvincing.

255. See p. 213.

256. Psalm 22 is a major source of traditions about the Passion of Jesus in the gospels. V. 27 is central to Lucan thought ("the ends of the earth"). See W. Schrenk, πατρία, *TDNT* 5:1016–18.

257. Cf. also Luke 2:4. I do not agree that the writer of Ephesians selected this term to create a word-play with πατήρ. More than paronomasia is at issue—in particular the daring substitution of "is named" for "will be blessed."

258. See pp. 204–6.

259. On Acts 21:8 and the term "evangelist" see Barrett, *Acts* 2:993. See also Spicq, *Theological Lexicon*, 2:91–92.

260. Psalm numbers in parentheses are those of the Hebrew (masoretic) text. The LXX enumeration is often one number lower.

261. G. Friedrich has a concise survey in H. Kraemer *et al.*, προφήτης, *TDNT* 6:781–861, 848, 854, 859–60.

262. The number is six if one includes Acts 5:38–39, where it is not restated in the second hypothetical clause.

263. A brief discussion of the importance of divine providence in Acts appears in the subsequent chapter.

264. Rackham, *The Acts of the Apostles*, 157 n.4 says that Eph 2:11–22 is the best commentary on Acts 10:36.

265. Luke's support for these believers shows that he does not associate them with "the Jews," who are religious and political opponents.

266. "Mighty Minority" refers to an essay by Jacob Jervell in *The Unknown Paul*, 26–51. He makes a number of important observations: "Jewish-Christianity" is, to a substantial degree, a response to "gentile Christianity," a movement (better, movements) that became organized *after* the meeting in Jerusalem. At different junctures accessions of Jews joined Christian communities—as well as continuing "Jewish-Christian" bodies. The alleg-

edly "more Jewish" texts in the NT are closer to 100 than to 70, found notably in James, Ephesians, and Matthew. To this list one may add the Gospel of John. Ephesians has at least as many points of contact with the language and thought preserved in the Dead Sea Scrolls as does any other early Christian text. Conflict over Jewish identity, exacerbated by the requirement for payment of the old Temple tax to Rome, seems to have produced a number of apostates. Some of those who no longer wished to be known as "Jews" may have found spiritual homes in Christian communities, where they were not always welcomed as privileged representatives of the parental faith. Not all of these theoretical converts might have regretted the absence of Torah-observance in that new home—and degrees of observance greatly varied among Jews—but some were likely to have done so. A decisive factor for date is that the circumstances envision the possibility that "Jews" could become "Christians" rather than affiliate with a different Jewish sect. They were two distinct "religions."

267. *1 Clem* is has the same program, but reveals no concerns about "Jewish-Christians." Matters at Rome and Ephesus may have been different.

268. John Knox, it should be noted, was a student of Goodspeed who did attend to theology.

269. "Ephesians and Acts," 290.

270. Käsemann was jailed for preaching an anti-Nazi sermon in 1938. Like others, he found in military service an eventual refuge from the Gestapo.

271. The place of the Christian movement in world history is a leading element in Lucan apologetic. The mission is a public phenomenon (from Pentecost, with its thousands of witnesses and participants), and much of its history takes place before persons of high status and imposing rank. See the remarks of Haenchen, *Acts*, 691–92, and the essay of Malherbe, "Not in a Corner," in *Paul and the Popular Philosophers*, 147–163.

272. "Ephesians and Acts," 290.

273. "Ephesians and Acts," 293. Echoes of Bousset (see p. 255) reverberate throughout this sentence.

274. "Ephesians and Acts," 293. The text of Eph 1:12b-14 reads, "so that we, who were the first to set our hope on Christ, might live for the praise of his glory. In him you also, when you had heard the word of truth, the gospel of your salvation, and had believed in him, were marked with the seal of the promised Holy Spirit; this is the pledge of our inheritance toward redemption as God's own people, to the praise of his glory."

275. See below, n. 326.

276. On Acts 20:24 see also pp. 120–21.

277. For example, Charles Talbert, *Reading* Acts, 189.

278. Perhaps out of deference to less appreciative ears, NRSV obliterates the imagery at Acts 13:25. See, for example, 1 Cor 9:24–26; Gal 2:2; 5:7, and Heb 12:1. Examples from Philo are *Agric.* 112, 119, *Praem.* (*Rewards and Punishments*) 5, *Migr. Abr.* (*Departure of Abraham*) 133; and, from polytheist philosophy, Epictetus *Diss.* 3.25.1–4. For Paul see the study of V. C. Pfitzner, *Paul and the Agon Motif,* and in general, E. Stauffer, ἀγών, κ.τ.λ., *TDNT* 1:134–60.

279. The technical term is "agonistic language," from the term for an athletic competition, ἀγών. It is fashionable and far from misleading to describe Greek and Hellenistic culture in general as agonistic, i. e., competitive.

280. *4 Macc* 17:10, 12, 17. A famous Christian example is the vision of Perpetua, *Martyrdom of Perpetua and Felicity*, 10.

281. Trans. Richardson, *Early Christian Fathers*, 46. The now offensive reference to female fragility is typical. Many references to women in ancient literature are directed toward male problems and issues. See Lona, *Clemensbrief*, 171–72, and Lindemann, *Clemensbriefe*, 41–42.

282. Aejmelaeus examines the intertextual relations on pp. 119–22.

283. L. R. Donelson, "Cult Histories and the Sources of Acts," *Biblica* 68 (1987) 1–21.

284. For example, Cadbury, *Beg.* 4:152, with his usual caution; Grant and Graham, *Apostolic Fathers* 2: 25, 103–4; and D. S. Hagner, *The Use of the Old and New Testaments in Clement of Rome*, 271. Hagner's study contains much of value, but it is methodologically flawed in that it assumes the Christian (Protestant) Canon as a norm against which to measure *1 Clement*. He presupposes that the entire NT antedates *1 Clement* and therefore that the category "Non-canonical Quotations" (68) is appropriate.

285. A. Lindemann, *Clemensbriefe*, 18. Lona speaks of shared traditions, *Clemensbrief*, 57.

286. See pp. 228–29.

287. According to the *Biblia Patristica* 1:195.

288. Trans. Richardson, *Early Christian Fathers*, 52, altered to conform with NRSV.

289. See Bruce, *Acts* 305–306 and Barrett, *Acts* 1:636;

290. On this matter see *Beg.* 4:152, Conzelmann, *Acts*, 104, and J. Jervell, *Apostelgeschichte*, 355. Honor for introducing this hypothesis belongs to J. Rendel Harris (1852–1941). Although often pronounced dead, the idea of a "Testimony Book" keeps slipping out of the morgue.

291. For Acts note also 7:3, 7, (and 33), all from the speech of Stephen. Examples from *1 Clem* include 4:4; 10:4, 6; and 35:7.

292. See pp. 7–8, 29.

293. Acts 7:2–53; 13:16–23; *1 Clem* 12; 43; 55.

294. See Lona, *Clemensbrief*, 42–48, especially his comments on the extent to which the author is steeped in "biblical language," 46–47, with examples.

295. *1 Clem* and Acts represent the first written examples of an enduring theme in Christian history: implicit or explicit appeal to the example of "the primitive church" as a model for the present.

296. For some of the affinities of the summaries in Acts 2 and 4 to ancient utopian thought see R. Pervo, *Profit with Delight*, 69–70, 163. It may come as a disappointment to some to observe that for *1 Clement* the golden age is identical to conformity with the "Household Codes," but these, too, had philosophical warrant. See p. 216, above. Gregory Sterling views the utopian descriptions of community life in Acts as an apologetic feature of the book, "Athletes of Virtue," 696.

297. In Acts the gift of the Spirit can be a sign of, or reward for, virtue or divine favor. The story of Cornelius (10:44) closely approximates the view of the Holy Spirit in *1 Clem* 2:2.

298. If the author of *1 Clem* knew Acts, he missed a good opportunity here.

299. Cf. also 59:1.

300. Note the D-text conclusion to the letter in Acts 15:29: ... πράξατε φερόμενοι ἐν τῷ ἁγίῳ πνεύματι ("do well, being guided by the Holy Spirit"). (On φερόμενοι in this context see 2 Pet 1:21.) Codex Bezae adds "full of Holy Spirit" in v. 32. The difficulty of establishing inspiration as a criterion for canonicity is that it was far too general until 180 and not unusual thereafter.

301. Cf. also *2 Clem* 14:4 (and the comments of Haenchen, *Acts*, 6).

302. Four times in the *Acts of Paul*, which is dependent upon Acts, and once in the *Acts of John*, which takes it from Acts or the *Acts of Paul*.

303. Knopf, *Die Lehre*, 46.

304. On *1 Clem* 46:6, Knopf refers only to parallel passages, *Die Lehre* 121–22. For the relation between the gift of the Spirit and moral behavior in Acts see p. 249 on 10:44.

305. Trans. Richardson, *Early Christian Fathers*, 44.

306. A review of Christian history indicates that more or less everyone is at least ostensibly in favor of "love, joy, and peace." The difficulty seems to arise in the exercise of "patience, kindness, generosity, faithfulness, gentleness and self-control" when confronted with others' wrong-headed notions of what the first three might entail in specific situations.

307. See p. 255.

308. *1 Clem* claims to be citing Scripture, but no passage has just these words.

309. Grant and Graham, *Apostolic Fathers*, 2:55.

310. Note also John 6:69.

311. See pp. 168–69.

312. The community did, however, nominate or choose the seven of 6:1–7.

313. See p. 234.

314. Luke does not call the church the Body of Christ, probably because of the kind of speculation represented by Colossians. The nearest approximation to that view is Acts 9:4, which comes from a source.

315. The phrase "... judge both the living and the dead" is found in both the western "Apostles' Creed" and the ecumenical "Nicene Creed."

316. Matthew 5:34–35 is quite different from the citations in Acts and Barn. Note also Justin *1 Apol.* 37; *Dial.* 22:11; and Athenagoras, *Legatio* 9.10.

cf. 23:21

317. Kurt Niederwimmer discusses this question in *The Didache*, 30–41.

318. See also above, on the "utopian community" of Jerusalem according to Acts.

319. See pp. 17–20.

320. This noun also appears in Luke 21:7 and 23:42; in the text of Codex Bezae; the *Acts of Paul*; and *3 Cor* 2:3.

321. Haenchen, *Acts*, 7. Barrett, *Acts* 1:36, finds the case for dependence "somewhat stronger."

322. For this analogy from gunnery, see p. 12.

323. See also the discussion of Acts 20:35//1*Clement* 13:1, pp. 228–29.

324. Hans v. Campenhausen, "Polykarp von Smyrna und die Pastoralbriefe," *Aus der Frühzeit des Christentums*, 197–252.

325. Helmut Koester says that Polycarp is the only known church leader of the era who fits the requirements for authorship of the Pastorals, *Introduction* 2:307–8. (In a Spring Semester 1973 classroom lecture at Harvard, Koester said, "Either Polycarp or someone *very like* Polycarp composed the Pastoral Epistles.")

326. Wilson, *Luke and the Pastoral Epistles*, C. F. D. Moule, "The Problem of the Pastoral Epistles: A Reappraisal," and A. Strobel, "Schreiben des Lukas? Zum sprachlichen Problem der Pastoralbriefe" 191–210. The hypothesis is an old one, already refuted in its earlier forms by v. Campenhausen. "Polykarp von Smyrna und die Pastoralbriefe," 245–46 n.207. For an evaluation of this hypothesis see R. Pervo, "Romancing an Oft-neglected Stone."

327. For one critical flaw in the argument regarding Luke and the Pastorals, see p. 216 on the subject of marriage.

328. On the date of Polycarp's *Letter to the Philippians* and of *1 Clement*, see Appendix III.

329. This study does not assume that Luke and Acts were written in immediate sequence. Acts may have been later, perhaps as much as a decade. It should also be noted that the contents of the Gospel of Luke known to Marcion are not certain. The hypothesis that Marcion possessed a copy of the Gospel essentially the same as that printed in modern editions is no less a speculation than are alternatives. See Chapter Eight.

330. On 26:18 see also pp. 275–78.

Chapter Eight
Acts as a Writing of the First Decades of the Second Century

1. Those who examine a work like *Jubilees*, or even the book of Daniel, are likely to conclude that, rather than a failure to be avoided, anachronism was an object to be pursued.

2. The standard reference on the subject is W. Speyer's, *Die literarische Falschung im hiednischen und christlichen Ältertum*.

3. Gen 2:2; Matt 15: 15–18.

4. At the end of this chapter is a summary and evaluation of Hemer's arguments regarding the date of Acts.

5. See pp. 152–60.

6. See pp. 212–13, 219.

7. Witherington, without a scintilla of justification, assures his audience that this comment is an "aside" by the narrator, *Acts*, 121.

8. In nearly all of the applicable cases, some manuscript witnesses "correct" the pronoun to "our."

9. See R. Pervo, "Israel's Heritage and Claims upon the Genre(s) of Luke and Acts," 137–38.

10. See, for example, Wolfgang Stegemann, *Zwischen Synagoge und Obrigkeit. Zur historischen Situation der lukanischen Christen*. Stegemann dates Acts in the 90s, under Domitian (81–96). He argues that Lukan believers were, to paraphrase his title, caught "between the Synagogue and the government." Despite many useful observations, he views Lucan hostility to the Jews as based upon a common Jewish practice of denouncing Christians to the officials. This stereotyped charge continues to recur, as in the *Martyrdom of Polycarp* 12, where it is the result of later editing. Stegemann may be too credulous about the accounts of Jewish opposition to Paul and others in Acts. In any case these stories do not speak against a date under Trajan (98–117). See also Appendix IV.

11. R. Brown, *Introduction*, 273–74, quoting 273.

12. For partial analogies one might think of the long conflict between France and Britain (omitting the Middle Ages!) that stretched from the late seventeenth century until the end of the Napoleonic era (c. 1815), or of the struggles between France and Germany from 1870 to 1945. From these hostilities arose animosities that have not yet entirely disappeared.

13. Martin Goodman offers a political explanation of the Flavian (69–96) policy and its implications for Jewish identity in *Mission and Conversion*, 42–48.

14. This case will be argued in detail later in the chapter.

15. See Appendix IV.

16. For a good, readable summary of this process see Shaye Cohen, *From the Maccabees to the Mishnah*, esp. 13–26, 214–31.

17. For Josephus (c. 90) the Christians were of minimal importance. Christians probably did not outnumber Jews until the last third of the third century.

18. Luke is not alone here. Both Matt and John also reflect this separation. See Chapter Nine.

19. So concludes, quite trenchantly, *HJP* 1:365. See also T. R. S. Broughton, "The Roman Army," in *Beg.* 5:427–45, 431–43. (Note that Hemer, *Book of Acts*, 164 evades the issue.)

20. See n.24, below. *HJP* 1:365 doubts the presence a Roman unit in Caesarea before 41. If this view is correct, Acts 10:1 is an anachronism by any light. This should be qualified by the possibility that Luke invented the name of the unit, a possibility the authorities do not even consider.

21. Cf., e. g., "chamberlain," which originally referred to the individual responsible for maintaining the monarch's bed-chamber and eventually came to refer to the holder of a high office.

22. See L. Michael White, "Urban Development and Social Change in Imperial Ephesos," 37, and Steven Friesen, "The Cult of the Roman Emperors in Ephesos," 231–32, both with numerous references. Colin Hemer (*Book of Acts*, 122) notes this datum as an example of Luke's knowledge of specifics. The inscription he cites in support (I. Eph. 300) dates from the reign of Septimius Severus (193–211).

23. W. Foerster, κύριος, κ.τ.λ., *TDNT* 3: 1055–56.

24. Examples of this lack of specificity are Bruce, *Acts* 494–95, Hemer, *Book of Acts*, 131, 180, and Witherington, *Acts* 733 n.400.

25. The title ἡγεμών assigned to Felix in Acts 23:24 is anachronistic for pre-70 CE, but this would have bearing only upon those who wish to date Acts before 70.

26. The citizens of the Roman colonies of Philippi and Corinth would have been subject to Roman law. (Few early Christians were citizens of these colonies. Most of them were residents only.)

27. So, for example, the expulsion of Jews from Rome in 19 CE, discussed on p. 224. On the difficult question of when and if proselytism was made illegal, see Dio Cassius 67.14.12, and Barrett, *Acts* 2:873.

28. M. Smallwood, *The Jews under Roman Rule*, 379. See her discussion, 379–81.

29. "Pilate" is not a bad example. One would probably infer, from Acts 3:13 and 4:27, that Pilate was still in office. (cf. also 13:28.) *i.e. one of Lk's 1st readers*

30. For one example see C. Hemer, *Book of Acts*, 51–54. A more thorough examination with similar results is F. F. Bruce, "Chronological Questions in the Acts of the Apostles." That Lake's study, "The Chronology of Acts" in *Beg.* 5:445–74 is still of merit indicates that the same data are still being subjected to the same methods, with differing conclusions but no consensus. The caution of Barrett, *Acts* 2:liv-lxi is justifiable.

31. To give a specific authority to an example already discussed, Haenchen, not one readily beguiled by Luke, regards the "Italic Cohort" in which Cornelius served as an anachronism (*Acts* 346, n.2), because Roman soldiers would not have been stationed in Caesarea during the reign of Agrippa I (41–44). This conclusion derives from Acts 12:1 ("At about that time") and presumes both that the "Herod" of Acts 12 is Agrippa I and that the conversion of Cornelius must have taken place during his reign. Both assumptions rely on the notion that Acts narrates in chronological sequence. See also above.

32. See pp. 160–61 for a discussion of the synchronism.

33. W. Ramsay, *St. Paul the Traveller*, 18.

34. Ramsay suggested that Acts was written in the "years immediately following" 81 CE, *St. Paul the Traveller*, 387.

35. *St. Paul the Traveller*, 23. Cadbury sees the matter differently: "He [Luke] had neither the facilities nor the desire to make the laborious calculations such as would verify synchronism or detect anachronism." *The Making of Luke-Acts*, 327.

36. *1 Apol.* 26.

37. Dio 59.15.5, in his discussion of Corbulo. Dictys Cretensis is a fictional "eye-witness" account of the Trojan War. The phrase occurs in his story of the discovery of a lost book, (*Test.* 1a 49 T.26).

38. On this text see Appendix IV.

39. Barrett, *Acts*, 1:559

40. Henry Cadbury says: "It is in the bare fact of his using a preface rather than in its details that Luke's relation to literature is apparent." He immediately quotes Franz Overbeck: "In fact the preface of Luke is the one place of the New Testament whereof one may say that in it the world shines through most plainly." (*The Making of Luke-Acts*, 196, citing Overbeck's *Christentum und Kultur*, 79.)

41. A statement like the following: "In the beginning when God created the heavens and the earth, the earth was a formless void and darkness covered the face of the deep" (Gen 1:1–2a) would not be enhanced if issued under the name of a mortal author, for some carping critic would no doubt be moved to ask, "How do *you* know? Were you there taking notes?"

42. Thus the extradiegetic ("outside of the story") narrator of the prefaces to Luke and Acts is not identical to the narrator of the body of the text. The latter is omniscient and unlimited; the former is circumscribed.

43. Loveday Alexander, *The Preface*, 147, finds the closest parallels to Luke's prefaces in Hero of Alexandria, who may have been writing c. 70, or later (225).

44. For this reading of the preface to Luke, see, among many, H. J. Cadbury, "Commentary on the Preface of Luke," 497. See also Luke 12:38, which may imply that the hearers are now in the "third watch" (of either three or four in total).

45. Trans. C. Richardson, *Early Christian Fathers*, 62

46. A. Lindemann, *Clemensbriefe*, 126–27.

47. On the various issues raised by this verse see Lona, *Clemensbrief*, 456–459. (The passage is a battleground in the discussion of "Apostolic Succession.")

48. Conzelmann "Luke's Place," 305.

49. Irenaeus does not claim here that Clement wrote *1 Clement*. Rather than appeal to the example of those whose words were echoing in his ears, the author of *1 Clement* views the apostles as residents of the distant past.

50. Irenaeus, *Against Heresies*, 3.3.3–4, Trans. and Ed. A. Roberts and J. Donaldson in *The Ante-Nicene Fathers* I, 416.

51. Eusebius, *Ecclesiastical History*, 4.3. The calculations would run like this: if Quadratus wrote c. 120, at the conventional arbitrary age of forty, he would have been born c. 80, at which time those raised or healed by Jesus as children (e.g., Mark 5:21–43; 9:14–29) would have been in their seventies.

52. Eusebius, *Ecclesiastical History*, 3.32.7–8, trans. K. Lake. LCL, 1:277 (emphasis supplied).

53. The verb appears eight times in the Pastorals. On the imagery see A. Malherbe, *Paul and the Popular Philosophers*, 121–36.

54. Cf. also 1 John 1:1 "We declare to you what was from the beginning, what we have heard . . ."

55. Western Christianity has tended to treat Eusebius's model dynamically and dialectically. The model has remained vital in Protestant traditions, especially those more conservative groups that labor to demonstrate that the NT is without spot of error or blemish of inconsistency, but view all non-canonical writings as fair game for every type of criticism (and deprecation). The basic theological problem inherent in this view—aside, of course, from the image of the "pure virgin"—is that it begins with perfection, from which condition the church may do no better than hold its ground. The image eliminates the possibility of growth. By obvious associations the Apostolic Church becomes a garden populated by the perfect couple, who can either "fall" or remain unchanging. Progress is excluded. (This is one reason for the current admiration of Irenaeus by Western Christians. He believed that God placed Adam and Eve in the garden with the expectation of growth.)

56. It may also be linked to Acts 16:1, although the grandparent could have been identi-

fied as a man. Spicq has a number of observations and speculations about the matter in *Épitres pastorales*, 2:706.

57. E. Käsemann, "Ephesians and Acts," 290. See above, pp. 298–99.

58. Acts 15 may look like an exception, but Luke does not identify the visitors to Antioch in 15:1 as believers. 15:5 does speak of believing Pharisees, but they do not claim that circumcision is a soteriological necessity. See p. 134.

59. See p. 182.

60. An inscription from the first century testifies to the existence of τὸ ἱερὸν συνέδριον τῶν ἀργυροκόπων, "The Sacred Council of the Silverworkers," I. Eph. 636.9–10.

61. *Certe satis constat prope iam desolata templa coepisse celebrari, et sacra sollemnia diu intermissa repeti passimque uenire <carnem> uictimarum, cuius adhuc rarissimus emptor inueniebatur.* Pliny, *Letters*, 10.96.10,. Trans. Betty Radice, *Pliny Letters and Panegyricus* LCL, 2:291.

62. Witherington, *Acts*, 592. The "relevance" he would deny may be that proposed by Conzelmann, *Acts*, 165, who cites Pliny.

63. Witherington devotes a note (*Acts*, 585 n.112) to a defense of the historicity of Acts 19:23–40. He says, "Demetrius emerges an an artisan who is no rhetor and therefore does not understand how to persuade the audience forcefully when he is standing in front of a large crowd. This portrait of such a person is quite believable, as he would not be a person likely to have had the educational training in oratory required to make the most of the occasion." How can he make such a statement when Demetrius's agitation was so manifestly successful? Witherington evidently imagines that Demetrius addressed the assembly without effect. Luke neither says this nor implies it; indeed, he would not wish it to be implied, for his object is to depict chaos generated by a wily agitator.

64. Rodney Stark, *The Rise of Christianity*, Table 1.1, p. 7; Keith Hopkins, "Christian Number and Its Implications," figure 1, page 193, (pp. 189–91 treat the Pliny-Trajan correspondence).

65. Stark posits a growth of 40% *average* per decade. He supports this statistical standard, which derives from the measurable growth of new religions in more recent times, with confirmatory data from other sources, including the production of literature, archaeology, and the conjectures of scholars.

66. The impact will decrease when one considers that the economic power of the Jesus-people was probably below average and that businesses like that of Demetrius would have garnered much of their revenue from visitors. Wise statisticians will also make a small deduction based upon the assumption that some of these believers had been Jews or "God-Fearers," persons who contributed nothing to the cult of Artemis.

67. On the population of Ephesus during the early empire see L. Michael White, "Urban Development," 40–49. Estimates for this period range from c. 50,000 to c. 175,000.

68. See pp. 291, 317.

69. Nestorius advocated a Christology that was condemned at the Council of Ephesus in 431. Legend held that the disciple John, author of the Fourth Gospel, had moved to Ephesus, taking with him the mother of Jesus (cf. John 19:25–27).

70. To be sure, this improved with time. A slightly later edition included the famous story of the cherry tree.

71. *Ad Fam.* (*Letters to His Friends*), 5.12.

72. For an overview of the possibilities see W. Bauer, "The Picture of the Apostle in Early Christian Tradition: 1. Accounts," in W. Schneemelcher, Ed. Trans. ed. R. McL. Wilson, *New Testament Apocrypha*, 2:35–74. (This is from the earlier "Hennecke-Schneemelcher," not in the current edition or translation of the Christian Apocrypha.)

73. Cf. also p. 62 and below.

74. Trans. C. Richardson, *Early Christian Fathers*, 46.

75. These are elucidated by Lona, *Clemensbrief*, 159–67. See also 38–40.

76. See 2 Macc 7.

77. See Grant, *Apostolic Fathers*, 2:25; Beyschlag, *Clemens Romanus* 207–328; and Lindemann, *Clemensbriefe*, 40.

78. See also below, where these passages from Acts and *1 Clement* are examined from the perspective of eschatology.

79. Both of these verses have been great stimuli to scholarship, with particular regard to *1 Clement's* sources.

80. See Ragnar Höistad, *Cynic Hero and Cynic King.* Over the course of time the travels

of Alexander extended throughout the known world, and beyond, as the various editions of the *Alexander-Romance*, re-edited into the Middle Ages, and beyond, indicate. See R. Stoneman, "The Metamorphoses of the *Alexander Romance*," as well as Stoneman's other works listed in the bibliography.

81. Nearly every is not every. Jan Lambrecht, *Second Corinthians*, opts for treating the letter as a unity in the two pages (7–9) he devotes to the subject. Two of Lambrecht's points deserve comment. The first is that no manuscript evidence supports partition. To this one may respond that no manuscript evidence argues the contrary. All manuscript data are too late to resolve the question. Secondly, he states that partition theories require hypotheses. They do, but this requirement is also incumbent upon theories of unity. Immediately after entering his objection to hypotheses, Lambrecht offers some of his own: Paul may not have been so consistent. The time required for composition is unknown. Paul's mood may have changed (p. 9). These hypotheses have the merit of being irrefutable. There are no means for determining how long Paul took in writing this letter, and no accurate record of his mood swings exists. The difficulty with the hypotheses of Bruce or Barrett or Bornkamm is that they are contestable. For that very reason they are scholarly; Lambrecht's hypotheses are not.

82. See p. 62.

83. Those who do not wish to accept this partition must regard the intervening material in chaps. 2–7 as a rather lengthy excursus—and justify this hypothesis.

84. Cf. Rom 1:8–17; 1 Cor 1:4–9; 1 Thess 1:2–12.

85. Cf. 1 Cor 4:9–10.

86. Another example is Col 2:15, which is also Deutero-Pauline.

87. See Bornkamm, *"Vorgeschichte,"* 30, and Robinson and Koester, *Trajectories*, 153. See the lengthy discussion of "triumph" in V. P. Furnish, *II Corinthians*, 174–75. *Acts of Paul* 7 contains a cogent parallel concerning Paul in Ephesus: ὅτι ἐθριαμβεύετο ὑπὸ τῆς πόλεως, "because he was led in triumph by the city."

88. For the importance of *1 Clement* in dating the appearance of canonical 2 Corinthians see p. 58.

89. U.S. society is probably the most individualistic culture in the world. Individualism, whether rugged or of a smoother variety, has brought into currency such concepts as "Jesus Christ as your personal Savior."

90. Raymond Brown presents a cautious and general survey of the issues in his *Introduction*, 515–38. Helmut Koester is more pointed and succinct: *Introduction* 2:126–31.

91. All approaches to eschatology in early Christianity contain some present and some future elements. This includes Gnostic formulations. In short: eschatology is never black or white, although it may claim to be so.

92. See Osiek, *Shepherd of Hermas*, 10–12.

93. *HermVis* 4.1. 5–9, Trans. K Lake, *Apostolic Fathers* 2: 61–63, *alt.*

94. ". . . der Autor apokalyptische Schrecknisse individualisiert hat . . . Diese Individualisierung entspricht der fur jene Zeit bezeichnenden Umwandlung der christlichen Hoffnung: nicht das Schicksal der Menschen am Ende der Tage, sonder das Schicksal des Einzelnen am Ende seines Lebens zieht das Interesse auf sich." *Der Hirt des Hermas*, 485–86. This is not to propose that *Hermas* has lost sight of the communal or that the ethics of the piece are oriented primarily toward the individual. See Osiek, *Shepherd of Hermas*, 30.

95. The author of 1 John "demythologizes" the antichrist by identifying the concept with historical persons. *Hermas* "demythologizes" by transforming the beast into a symbol of the temptations met in the course of the individual's spiritual journey.

96. See Lona, *Clemensbrief*, 161 and especially Lindemann, *Clemensbriefe*, 38.

97. K. Beyschlag reflects on the terminology of *1 Clement* 5 and Acts 1:25; 12:17 in *Clemens Romanus*, 326–28.

98. This promise is in the second person singular, as is the entire unit (Luke 14:7–14), which is peculiar to Luke and not, with the exception of v.11, a part of Q. See Kloppenborg, *Q Parallels*, 162 and Robinson, *et al.*, *Critical Edition*, 430.

99. Hans Conzelmann, *Theology of St. Luke*, 110, and see his references there.

100. See also Luke 16:9.

101. The eschatological use of "reward" is common in Matt (e.g. 10:41), where the tendency is evident, but not so developed as in Luke and Acts.

102. For the views of various scholars, including G. Schneider and J. Dupont, on indi-

vidualization in Lukan eschatology, see F. Bovon, *Luke the Theologian*, 61 and 63.

103. J. C. O'Neill, *The Theology of Acts in Its Historical Setting*, 9.

104. The subject in mind is less "the end of the world" than the ways in which the sense of ultimacy has provided a moral structure to Western life; but as the fears that surrounded the advent of the year 2000 demonstrated, anxiety about "the end" is deeply rooted in Western culture.

105. See Tertullian *Apology* 47.12:. "So comes it that we are laughed at for proclaiming that God will be judge," Trans. T. R. Glover, *Tertullian: Apology; De Spectaculis* LCL, 211. From his perspective Acts 17:32 is "wrong." Resurrection would have presented less of an obstacle than final judgment. See also Wayne Meeks, *The Origins of Christian Morality*, 85 and 177.

106. The idea of change has also hindered Christian mission in civilizations that have tended to presume that society was essentially changeless, e.g., in India and China until the mid-twentieth century, at least.

107. See p. 230 on Romans 13:1–7 (and the qualifications there expressed).

108. Tannehill, *Narrative Unity*, 2:356–57.

109. His words also echo the first missionary speech of Peter in Acts 2:14: "let this be known to you" (τοῦτο ὑμῖν γνωστὸν ἔστω). Acts 28:28 γνωστὸν οὖν ἔστω ὑμῖν.

110. Tannehill summarizes Acts 28:30–31 by saying that Paul continues his work ". . . by welcoming all, both Jews and Gentiles . . ." "Both Jews and Gentiles" is Tannehill's own addition to the text.

111. This claim does not stand against the importance of continuity for Luke. Continuity is all the more important to one susceptible of charges that he is seeking to hijack the Israelite tradition and heritage: continuity supports the claim that, on the contrary, the Jews failed to make the right turn and ended up in a ditch.

112. Minucius Felix, *Octavius*, 33.2–3, Trans. Clarke, 113–14. The text continues with an appeal to read Jewish authors, including Josephus. (The [] supply a supposed lacuna without altering the meaning.)

113. *IgnMag* 8:2; 10:3, trans. C. Richardson, *Early Christian Fathers*, 96–97. Οἱ γὰρ θειότατοι προφῆται κατὰ Χριστὸν Ἰησοῦν ἔζησαν. Διὰ τοῦτο καὶ ἐδιώχθησαν . . . Ὁ γὰρ χριστιανισμὸς οὐκ εἰς Ἰουδαισμὸν ἐπίστευσεν, ἀλλ Ἰουδαισμὸς εἰς χριστιανισμόν.

114. W. Schoedel, *Ignatius of Antioch*, 119.

115. Schoedel, *Ignatius of Antioch*, 126, says, "Here Ignatius comes closest to recognizing 'Judaism' as a legitimate stage in the unfolding of the divine plan."

116. O'Neill, *Theology of Acts*, 90.

117. Stephen's speech in Acts 7 has such clear affinities with the method and view of *Barnabas* that intertextuality has been suggested. For a judicious analysis see James C. Paget, *The Epistle of Barnabas*, 200–207.

118. The existence of multitudes of believers among the Jews in Jerusalem (see esp. 21:20) and elsewhere is not evidence to the contrary. Jews are welcome to "convert," i.e., abandon their old religion and adopt the new.

119. A survey of political history can be found in Mary Smallwood, *The Jews*, 220–55; 356–88.

120. Seneca, *De Superstitione* F145R and Quintilian, *Institutes* 3.7.21, in Menachem Stern. *Greek and Latin Authors on Jews and Judaism* (=*GLAJJ*), 1:431 and 513.

121. *GLAJJ* 1:274–320, 2:1–107.

122. Manetho flourished in the early third century BCE, Chaeremon and Apion c. 40–50 CE.

123. For examples see R. Pervo, *Profit with Delight*, *passim*.

124. See also Appendix IV, which takes up the events of the Jewish revolt of c. 115–117.

125. With this judgment the early Rabbis did not disagree, although they did not see conversion to Christianity as the proper remedy.

126. A recent study of the subject is John T. Squires, *The Plan of God in Luke-Acts*. Note also G. Sterling, *Apologetic Historiography*. For aspects of the popular presentation of this idea see R. Pervo, *Profit with Delight*, 74. If, as seems likely, Luke made use of Josephus, it will no longer be possible to use Josephus as an independent parallel to Luke's thought. On Providence see also J. Behm, προνοέω, πρόνοια, TDNT 4:1009–17.

127. On Providence in *1 Clement* see Grant, *Apostolic Fathers* 2:42–44; Lindemann, *Clemensbriefe*, 20–22; and Lona, *Clemensbrief*, 301–2.

128. Behm, προνοέω, 1017.

129. Philipp Vielhauer, "On the 'Paulinism' of Acts," *SLA*, 33–51, 37. (The German original of this article was published in 1950.)

130. See, for example, F. F. Bruce, "Is the Paul of Acts the Real Paul?" and Hemer, *Book of Acts* 245–47. Stanley Porter has restated the arguments against Vielhauer in *The Paul of Acts*, 187–206.

131. "Paulinism," 44–45. (Current investigation is raising doubts about Paul's adherence to a Christology of pre-existence.)

132. On Theophilus see R. Grant (*Jesus after the Gospels*, 68–82), who is attentive to his Lukan elements.

133. There is a very cursory summary of Adoptionism in the first volume of Pelikan's history of dogma, *The Emergence of the Catholic Tradition (100–600)*, 175–176.

134. Detailed references to and discussion of these matters can be found in A. Malherbe's essay, "'Not in a corner': Early Christian Apologetic in Acts 26:26."

135. Malherbe, "Not in a Corner," 151–152. See his references in n.29.

136. R. Pervo, *Profit with Delight*, 77–81. Note also Malherbe, "Not in a Corner," 150 and n.16.

137. See p. 168, and Malherbe, "Not in a Corner," 152–163.

138. A recent study of this material is Matthew L. Skinner, *Locating Paul*.

139. *Beg.* 4:311.

140. These rescripts do not appear to be forgeries, for they demand no more than the observance of proper legal procedures. In any case, Justin believed that they were genuine.

141. On this principle see the (later) statement of Ulpian, *Digest* (of Roman law) 48.17.1, and the comment of Appian *Civil Wars* 3.54.222 (written c. 140).

142. Justin *1 Apology* 3; Athenagoras *Legatio* 3, and Tertullian *Apology* 1.3; 2.2.

143. Like everyone else, O'Neill had a predecessor: Franz Overbeck, "Über das Verhältniss Justins des Märtyrers zur Apostelgeschichte."

144. Conzelmann, "Luke's Place," 303–04, 309.

145. On the development of the concept and doctrine of Apostolic Succession see pp. 126 and 208.

146. 304. Conzelmann has *1 Apol.* 67 in mind.

147. Both citations are from p. 309.

148. Cf., for example, *1 Apol.* 32 and 61. It is quite reasonable to suppose that Justin addressed Israelite history in his (now lost) writing against Marcion.

149. Jervell, *Luke and the People of God*, 175.

150. Townsend, "The Date of Luke-Acts," in C. Talbert, Ed., *Luke-Acts: New Perspectives from the Society of Biblical Literature Seminar*, 47–62.

151. See Chapter 2.

152. The point here is the contrast between Marcion's "Apostle," which is universally accepted as an edition of the letters of Paul with a number of passages deleted, and his "Gospel," which, if based upon canonical Luke, would have required much more drastic surgery, notably the deletion of chaps. 1–3.

153. For more recent work on this material see F. Stanley Jones, "An Ancient Jewish Christian Rejoinder to Luke's Acts of the Apostles," "The Apocryphal Acts of the Apostles in Intertextual Perspectives," and *An Ancient Jewish Christian Source on the History of Christianity: Pseudo-Clementine Recognitions 1.21–27*.

154. "Date," 49–52.

155. "Date," 58.

156. Tyson, "Date of Acts," 18.

157. For Asia see also Apollos, 18:23–28, and the riot in chapter 19:21–40, in which Paul plays no personal role.

158. Barrett, *Acts* 2:xlii-xliii.

159. Barrett, *Acts*, 2:lxvi.

160. Barrett, *Acts*, 2:lxvi.

161. Barrett, *Acts*, 2:lxix.

162. On meat sacrificed to idols, see p. 89.

163. The basis for this assertion is that, although Tatian seems never to have encountered a stream against which he would not swim, he could still find four gospels as three too many and produce his own unified work. Works viewed as "Canonical" are not available for such treatment.

164. For the sake of completeness one might add the very brief comments of Ephraem (c.306–373) and the sixth-century metrical elaboration of Aratus.

165. The history of reception also shows that no one prior to Irenaeus shows the least recognition of a unity of Luke and Acts.

166. J. Knox, *Marcion and the New Testament*, 14–18.

167. On the date of Marcion, see Appendix III.

168. E. g., the consumption of idol-meat at Pergamum and Thyatira (Rev 2:14, 20). Leppä, *Critical Use*, 171–73, points to the affinities between the views of Paul and those criticized in Rev 2.

169. *Book of Acts*, 365–410; this is the lengthiest study of the subject to appear in the last fifteen years.

170. *Book of Acts*, 367–70 (the basis for Appendix II in this book).

171. *Book of Acts*, 371–72.

172. This claim may seem weighty, but it involves a logical fallacy: the importation of mathematical standards into a sphere not governed by mathematical rules. The issues here deal with qualitative rather than quantitative research. For example, if one person argues that Goethe was fundamentally and profoundly Christian while another maintains that he was hostile to Christianity, the existence of opposing views does not prove that Goethe was indifferent to religion.

173. Subsequently S. Mason and Barbara Shellard have given more positive answers to the question of the possible use of Josephus by Luke. Hemer died in the Spring of 1987.

174. *Book of Acts*, 371–72. A study of ancient historians and their relatives rather tends to indicate that writers so regularly "misused" their sources that such "misuse" is no grounds for arguing against dependence. See Chapter Five.

175. *Book of Acts*, 373.

176. *Book of Acts*, 376–78.

177. *Book of Acts*, 378–81. Many of these points come from the work of Sherwin-White.

178. *Book of Acts*, 381.

179. Cf. also *Did* 9:2–3; 10:2–3; *Martyrdom of Polycarp* 14:1, 3; Irenaeus, *Demonstration* 88, *Against Heresies* 4.33.13, and *Apostolic Tradition* 3–4. On the same grounds one could call *Diognetus* "primitive" (note 8:9, and 8:11, which use the expression "beloved child").

180. Zehnle, *Peter's Pentecost Address*, 44–53.

181. Textual problems arise here, relating to whether the word "God" should be repeated before each proper name. Nestle-Aland[27] includes the repeated noun in brackets. Threefold use of "God" conforms to the LXX of Exod 3:6 and is probably secondary. NRSV includes the triple use.

182. See Parsons and Pervo, *Rethinking the Unity*, 101.

183. Justin, *1 Apology*, 63.7, 11, 17; *Dialogue* 59.2. According to Hippolytus, *Against Heresies*, 6.31, Valentinus made use of this formula. See Zehnle, *Pentecost Discourse*, 45–46.

184. Zehnle, *Pentecost Discourse*, 46–47. His discussion indicates that Justin is not dependent upon Acts.

185. For references see Barrett, *Acts* 1:197–98.

186. Most of those who have argued for an early date have emphasized that the conclusion of Acts indicates that it was written about two years after Paul reached Rome, i.e., c. 60–62. It is important that Hemer finds this quite unpersuasive.

187. *Book of Acts*, 388–90.

188. *Book of Acts*, 404–10.

189. On "rigorous treatment of evidence" see 375 n.26. I. H. Marshall describes Hemer's background in his preface to *The Book of Acts*, vii. On this "romantic" approach to critical problems see also his description of the Miletus speech, p. 113.

190. *The Book of Acts* is a posthumous work, based upon an unfinished draft. I suspect that it contains a number of statements that an author like Colin Hemer would have excised from a final draft.

191. Hans Conzelmann and Ernst Haenchen are the unnamed villains here. Hemer evidently takes his terminology from Martin Hengel.

192. On p. 389 Hemer says that accounts like those of the Areopagus and Ephesus are "vivid, but not 'immediate.'" He allows that the difference is subtle. He is also willing to turn the tables: on p. 246 he finds that the alleged theological differences between Paul and Acts are ". . . often a matter of impression . . ."

193. Vincent. Taylor, *The Gospel according to St. Mark,* 551.

194. Omniscience is blatant in v. 40. Furthermore, the scene is well-crafted, following the "rule of three." It reads like a parody of a miracle story in reverse, with three visits and petitions. In short, Mark 14:32–42 is anything but naïve and formless.

195. *Ulysses* is apt for several reasons. The precise date of publication is known: 2 February 1922. The same applies to the dramatic date: 16 June 1904. The colophon reads: "Trieste, Zürich, Paris, 1914–21." Joyce had to leave Trieste because, as a British subject, he was an enemy alien during WWI. Cadbury's *Style* appeared in 1920. The preface bears the date "December 1919." Cadbury was driven out of his position at Haverford College because of his protest against Germanophobia during World War I.

196. J. Tyson, "The Date of Acts: A Reconsideration," 5.

197. See, for example, Luke 19:41–44; 21:20–24; 23:27–31.

198. Louis Feldman, for example, supports the idea that Jews actively sought converts (*Jew and Gentile in the Ancient World*); Martin Goodman, *Mission and Conversion,* represents the opposite view.

199. Kraabel opened the debate with his article "The Disappearance of the God-Fearers."

200. This inscription was published by J. Reynolds and R. Tannenbaum in *Jews and Godfearers at Aphrodisias.* Its meaning is the source of much disagreement—largely, in my view, because "God-Fearer" had many different meanings. See S. Cohen, *The Beginnings of Jewishness,* 168–74.

201. Because the increase of prosperity in the Greek East led to more inscriptional activity, these figures do not prove that assemblies were more common in the second century, but certainly show that they had not fallen into desuetude.

202. On these distinctions see J. A. Crook, *Law and Life of Rome,* 272–75. On the great value of Roman citizenship for high-status Greeks in the Roman East into the second century see G. Bowersock, *Greek Sophists in the Roman Empire.*

203. Sherwin-White, *Roman Law and Roman Society in the New Testament,* 48–70; 108–19.

204. See Cadbury's "Roman Law and the Trial of Paul," *Beg.* 5:297–338.

205. *Roman Law,* 55–57. Sherwin-White is cognizant of several difficulties in this passage.

206. At this point circularity arrives on stage. Those who wish that Acts was written by a companion of Paul quite reasonably view accurate knowledge as the product of an *immediate* source, proof that Luke was on the scene.

207. *Book of Acts,* 380.

208. C. P. Jones constructs a chronology of Dio's orations in *The Roman World of Dio Chrysostom,* 133–140

209. 23:26: Claudius Lysias (otherwise Lysias).

210. Judge, "The Decrees of Caesar at Thessalonica." .

211. A qualification is in order: this assumes that attempts to date Luke (and thus Acts) before 70 are almost completely out of favor. Any who hold that position will object that Hemer does make a case, or at least restate one.

212. In ancient rhetoric vividness is classed among "emotive figures oriented toward the matter." See H. Lausberg, *Handbook of Literary Rhetoric,* 359–61. The goal of vividness in narration is to enhance its appeal through clarity and probability. Among the examples offered are the building of a town, the capture of a town, a storm at sea, religious celebrations, and epidemics.

213. A pertinent example is the description of a civic assembly in Dio's *Oration 7,* 22–63.

214. William Ramsay is the most obvious example. A lesser-known representative of this tradition is E. M. Blaiklock, a Professor of Classics who produced an earlier edition of the Tyndale Commentary on Acts. This is a short work of splendid clarity and fine style, steeped in the history and culture of the Greco-Roman world. Blaiklock's initial argument for an early (60s) date of Acts is ". . . the fresh and vivid writing of the biographical portions of the book . . . It does not seem reasonable to suppose that such passages were written long after the events described." (*The Acts of the Apostles,* 16.)

215. See the criticisms of Hemer by an admirer, I. H. Marshall, in *The Acts of the Apostles* 88–90, who notes that accuracy in detail does not mean historicity (89), observing that novelists can be meticulous about such details. Refutation of the idea that verisimilitude=verity is a component of the argument of R. Pervo, *Profit with Delight* (who also asks whether the unusual vividness of Acts supports viewing it as a type of historiography).

216. The wealth of data, or at least much of it, makes the work valuable. Scholars will gratefully continue to consult Hemer for many years.

217. Chapter One therefore followed the common path and did not take evidence for the existence of Luke into account when seeking the earliest clear proof of the use of Acts.

218. The work cannot be dated later than 200 CE because it was evidently known to Clement of Alexandria (*Stromata* 7.16.93). It is unlikely to be earlier than 150 because the author makes use of at least three canonical Gospels (Matt, Luke, and John). For a current discussion see Ronald F. Hock, *The Infancy Gospels of James and Thomas*, 11–12, and his references. Provenance is difficult to detect (*ibid.*, 12–13.) A full critical edition and commentary appears in B. Beyers and J. Gijsel, *Libri de Nativitate Mariae.*

219. Hock, *Infancy Gospels*, 21–27.

220. John A. T. Robinson claimed that failure to make explicit mention of the destruction of Jerusalem and the temple was solid grounds for dating a work prior to 70 (*Redating the New Testament*, 21 *et passim*).

221. See Schneemelcher ("The *Kerygma Petri*"), who summarizes the scholarly debate, and provides a translation of the fragments. To his bibliography add A. Malherbe, "The Apologetic Theology of the *Preaching of Peter*."

222. Schneemelcher, "The *Kerygma Petri*," 34.

223. Schneemelcher, 35.

224. Schneemelcher, 36, citing Dobschütz, *Das Kerygma Petri kritisch untersucht*, 66.

225. Schneemelcher, 36.

226. The relative clause in brackets is an observation of Clement of Alexandria, from whose *Stromata* (*Miscellanies*) the undisputed fragments derive.

227. This translation of 3b is slightly altered from that of Wilson, in Schneemelcher, 39.

228. Eduard Norden sensed the relevance of this text in his *Agnostos Theos*, 4, 7.

Chapter Nine
Conclusion

1. On the date of the *Corpus Paulinum* see Appendix III.

2. The provision of "Bread and Circuses" did not make the Roman Imperial Government a liberal organization. Social programs that helped maintain the status quo were supported by wise conservatives. A. Harrill, *The Manumission of Slaves*, offers a good corrective on these matters.

3. Not all agree that it is possible to speak of "Lukan theology." Colin Hemer devotes but two pages (*Book of Acts*, 245–47) to the subject. For him the question related to different viewpoints within the "essential unity" of the NT. While engaged in the preparation of his *Redating the New Testament*, J. A. T. Robinson visited the U.S. In a conversation with graduate students at Harvard in 1973 or 1974 he deprecated the idea that NT authors, with the probable exception of Paul and the likely exception of John, had distinct theologies.

4. Examples include F. Bovon, *Luke the Theologian* and D. Marguerat, *La première histoire.*

5. See R. Pervo, "Israel's Heritage," 137–38 for references.

6. Wills, *Jewish Novel*, 209 n.46. See also his "The Depiction of the Jews in Acts."

7. J. T. Sanders, *The Jews in Luke-Acts.*

8. J. B. Tyson, *Images of Judaism in Luke-Acts*. One should note that those who view Luke as "Pro-Jewish" wish to oppose Christian anti-Semitism. This is a laudable goal. The requirement that this view be explicit in Christian scripture is anachronistic. Quantitatively speaking, Christians c. 100 CE numbered in the thousands, Jews in the millions. Faulting Christians for their hostility at that time is akin to chastising seventeenth century Baptists for their lack of ecumenical sensitivity toward the Church of England. The view that anti-Semitism is wrong and that Luke *must* therefore not be anti-Jewish has no place in historical scholarship.

9. I quite endorse the view of John T. Squires, who concludes his study of a philosophical component of Lucan thought with these comments: "Although it is not the case that Luke presents a fully fledged Christian apologetic in the style of second-century writers, nevertheless it is clear that Luke-Acts includes elements which would later become

identified with Christian apologetic." (*The Plan of God in Luke-Acts*, 193). Cf. also Gregory
Sterling, who observes that the portrayal of community life ". . . is an example of the anticipation of later Christian apologetic in Luke-Acts" ("Athletes of Virtue," 696).

Appendix I
Scholarship on the Sources of Acts

1. This survey is not complete, but it does seek to be representative.
2. Lüdemann (*Early Christianity*) is an exception, but he is not engaged in the isolation
of sources so much as the identification and evaluation of traditions.
3. See, in particular, pp. 79–95.
4. See Barrett, *Acts*, 1:53–55, and Schneider, *Apostelgeschichte* 1:85–89. Harnack also proposed a source originating in Caesarea. This hypothetical source has been all but forgotten.
Harnack's theories are found in *The Acts of the Apostles*, 162–202.
5. Fitzmyer, *Acts*, 81–82. Discoveries from Qumran (Dead Sea Scrolls) and elsewhere
show that first century Palestinian Aramaic differed from Torrey's reconstructions. For literature on the subject up to c. 1980 see Schneider, *Apostelgeschichte* 1:84–85.
6. Wilcox, *The Semitisms of Acts*. See the comments of M. A. Powell in his review of
source theories, *What Are They Saying about Acts?*, 28–29.
7. English-speaking readers are familiar with Harnack's view of sources because of its
influence upon *Beg*. See, for example, Jackson and Lake, "The Internal Evidence of Acts,"
Beg. 2:121–124, as well as the commentary (vol. 4). The endurance of the understanding
that Acts 1–14 is a compilation of Aramaic and other sources is evident in the intelligent
treatment of the subject by W. Knox, *Acts of the Apostles*, 16–39. While accepting the existence of Aramaic sources, Knox rebuts many of Torrey's claims for translation Greek and,
in the end, accepts a sustained source for Acts 1–5 only.
8. The latter appears in *Der Weg Jesu*.
9. See also his "'We' in Acts and the Itinerary." Haenchen believes that 27:1–44 (the voyage to Rome) derives from an eyewitness source, which may have been oral (*Acts* 87, 709).
10. "Apostelgeschichte," *Theologische Realenzyklopädie*, 491–501.
11. The foregoing three sentences represent *my* understanding of the implication of
Pesch's terminology.
12. Note that this view, which is quite common, assumes that the source spoke of the
collection for Jerusalem but that Luke repressed its purpose.
13. Question marks (?) represent Lüdemann's uncertainties about the boundaries of a
unit or section.
14. *Acts* 2:xxxi.
15. The parenthesis makes an important technological observation. Even today it is difficult to achieve editorial perfection. In an era when editors had to move back and forth
between or among costly scrolls in poor light with quills that needed frequent replenish-
ment of ink and regular sharpening, consistency really was a hobgoblin.
16. For a brief summary of this difficult hypothesis, see Fitzmyer, *Acts*, 84–85 and 102–3.
17. Becker, *Paul: Apostle to the Gentiles*, 14–15.
18. H. Leppa, *Luke's Critical Use*, 17–19.
19. For the views of Ramsay, Hemer, and Bruce see pp. 51–52.
20. For evidence of that classification, please see p. 8.
21. P. Benoit, "La deuxième visite de Saint Paul à Jérusalem."
22. Witherington offers no evidence from ancient literature to support this contention.
23. Some may take exception to his exclusion of Romans from the "main letters" of
Paul, but that is not relevant to the question at hand.
24. See also "First Person Narrative in Acts 27–28."
25. *Book of Acts*, 336.
26. *Book of Acts*, 344. For other examples, including an analysis of the transfiguration of
Jesus in Luke 9:28–36, of which Hemer was particularly proud, see R. Pervo, "My Happy
Home," 31 n.4.
27. This is now the first chapter in his *Luke and the People of God: A New Look at Luke-
Acts*. The citation comes from this collection.

28. Olaf Linton, "The Third Aspect," had already made this point. (It should also be noted that Haenchen agreed with Linton, but did not use his observations to question his own theory: *Acts*, 88–89.)

29. Jervell notes the letters in Rev 2–3. One could add the Johannine epistles, the Deutero-Paulines, Ignatius, *1 Clement*, and so forth. The idea that early Christian communities were in frequent communication is one of the themes driving the essays in R. Bauckham, Ed., *The Gospels for All Christians*.

30. J. H. Hayes and J. Roloff, "Acts of the Apostles," 1:10.

31. The most recent review in the *Theologische Rundschau*, by Eckhard Plümacher, "Acta-Forschung 1974–1982 (Fortsetzung und Schluss) " *ThR* 49 (1984) treats sources on 120–38. Erich Grässer's earlier contributions in that journal may now be found in his *Forschungen zur Apostelgeschichte*, 91–96; 179–88.

32. See the summary and critique by Barrett, *Acts* 2:xxvii-xxviii.

33. J. Wehnert, *Die Wir-Passagen der Apostelgeschicht*. Cf. also Vernon Robbins, "By Land and by Sea." In addition note E. Plümacher, "Wirklichkeitserfahrung und Geschicthschreibung bei Lukas" as well as Susan Marie Praeder, "Acts 27:1–28:16," and in particular "The Problem of First person Narration in Acts."

34. R. Jewett, *A Chronology of Paul's Life* and Gerd Luedemann, *Paul Apostle to the Gentiles*.

35. M. Hengel, *Acts and the History of Earliest Christianity*, 65–66, and *Between Jesus and Paul*, 4. See also Craig C. Hill, *Hellenists and Hebrews*, 92–95.

36. M. Hengel and Anna Maria Schwemer, *Paul between Damascus and Antioch*, 19.

37. See p. 348.

38. From n.77, p. 330, it would seem that C. K. Barrett convinced Hengel that Haenchen was on the right track. (Hengel had very little use for Haenchen, who was, in his view, the veritable antichrist of radical modern skepticism about Acts.)

39. See R. Pervo, "My Happy Home," 47–48. M. Hengel, *Between Jesus and Paul* 4, allows that this source may have begun with the story of the gift of languages.

40. Conzelmann, *Acts*, xxxviii.

41. I think it unlikely that the story of Paul's "Conversion" emanates from this source.

42. "Simon Magus in der Apostelgeschichte."

43. Paul J. Achtemeier has studied these pre-Marcan collections in "Toward the Isolation of Pre-Markan Miracle Catenae" and "The Origin and Function of the Pre-Marcan Miracle Catenae. Bovon identifies the gospel tradition as the motive for the various Acts in"The Synoptic Gospels and the non-canonical acts of the apostles."

44. On this idea see J. Tyson, "Date of Acts," 9.

45. See Plümacher, "*Acta Forschung*," 125–27.

46. Lewis R. Donelson, "Cult Histories and the Sources of Acts." This study includes a useful discussion of ancient historiographical theory and practice, as well as some of the views of present-day analysts. One example will suffice. Donelson summarizes the claims of Diodorus of Sicily, then adds: "Having set these rather high standards and having laid claim to the aura of factual truth, Diodorus begins his history with an account of the origin of the gods." (7)

47. For example: W. J. McCoy contributed a twenty-page essay, "In the Shadow of Thucydides," to the collection edited by Ben Witherington, III, *History, Literature and Society in the Book of Acts*. To this the editor kindly supplied a nine-page addendum intended to clarify a few matters about the book of Acts. A major concern is the oft-discussed passage in Thucydides 1.22.3–4. Since McCoy's own discussion of the speeches in Thucydides (pp. 12–16) evidently left a good deal to be desired, Witherington stresses that Thucydides does not contradict himself and that his speeches are generally reliable. Witherington appeals to C. W. Fornara (*The Nature of History in Greece and Rome*, 154–55) to support his assertion that "... *there was no convention in antiquity that a historian should compose speeches for a historical work*"(24). It is in the nature of conventions that they need not be stated, for everyone is supposed to understand them. Conventions are discovered by observation. In any case, Fornara's dogmatic statement is erroneous. In his famous essay on historiography, Lucian of Samosata repeatedly invokes the practice of Thucydides against contemporary historians. Toward the end of the essay Lucian comes to the subject of speeches: "If a person has to be introduced to make a speech, above all let his language suit his person and his subject, and next let these also be as clear as possible. It is then, however, that you can

play the orator and show your eloquence"(The last sentence reads: πλὴν ἐφεῖταί σοι τότε καὶ ῥητορεῦσαι καὶ ἐπιδεῖξαι τὴν τῶν λόγων δεινότητα.). *How to Write History* 58, trans. K. Kilburn, *Lucian VI*. LCL, 71. Despite his hard-nosed posture (and pose), Lucian assumes without argument the right of authors to invent speeches. They should be well-written and appropriate. In par. 26 he gives an example of an inappropriate oration. For insight into what can be said about Thucydides's composition of speeches, I recommend the real McCoy.

48. *The Paul of Acts*, 1–66. On pp. 42–46 Porter offers his reconstruction of the source.

49. Opponents of form criticism are prone to speak of "the rules/laws of form criticism." This is a straw person, for the study of forms and genres works with general proclivities and principles, not with "rules" of the scientific type. The "rule of three" (the shoe fits the third sister), for example, is not to be compared with the law of the conservation of matter. Much of the value of this method comes not from the impossibility of "breaking the rules" (which are regularly "broken"), but from observing such non-conformities as a fourth woman at the trial fitting.

50. Koester, *Introduction* 2:50.

51. H. D. Betz, *2 Corinthians 8 and 9*, 139.

52. To answer that question he wrote a charming little book, *Philemon among the Letters of Paul*, admired by all and endorsed by few. A more mundane and probable explanation is that Philemon, which is not, in fact, addressed to an individual, but to a community, was collected as a companion to Colossians, both presumably addressed to the same community. So H. Gamble, *Books and Readers*, 61.

Appendix II
Scholarly Estimates of the Date of Acts

1. Hemer's interests in an early date are quite apparent in this catalogue. N.9 below is an example of this tendency. (The ms. had not been corrected at the time of his death.) Some of his entries have been omitted. Those that I have verified or corrected are not marked with an *.

2. Authors cited only here may not be listed in the bibliography.

3. Fitzmyer, *Acts*, 54.

4. "Nun ist die Datierung der Apg freilich eine der schwierigsten Fragen der nt-lichen Einleitungswissenschaft." *Die Zwölf Apostel*, 190. His catalogue may be found on 190–91.

5. For an example see J. T. Squires's valuable study of providence, *The Plan of God in Luke-Acts*. Although Squires often speaks about Luke's time and circumstances (e.g., pp. 7, 12, and 194), I have not been able to find an indication of date or provenance beyond the assumption that the writings belong to the first century (14) and a possible endorsement of the late first century (14 n.74). The date and situation of Acts are nonetheless crucial to the interpretations Squires proposes.

6. The alternative depends upon the date at which Festus took office.

7. For Harnack's views on the date of Acts see p. 4.

8. Wikenhauser's views evolved in the direction of a later date. Consult the various editions of his *Introduction to the New Testament* (the last of which was revised by Schmid and places Acts in the 80s, according to Fitzmyer, *Acts*, 54).

9. The quotation is from Hemer. In his contribution to the Harper's/Black's series, *The Acts of the Apostles*, 15, Williams is not nearly so definite. He allows for either c. 66–70 or c. 80–85.

10. In his Hermeneia commentary, a translation from his German work in progress, Bovon does not give a date, but states that the author belonged to the second or third generation, 11.

11. In his reviews of Haenchen, *Die Apostelgeschichte . JBL* 76 1957: 65–66, and of O'Neill, *The Theology of Acts*. *JBL*. 81 1962: 197–98 it appears that the later Cadbury inclined to view the author of Acts as a companion of Paul. From this conclusion it would seem that Cadbury would not date Luke and Acts later than 90 and, more probably, c. 80. His article in IDB ("Acts of the Apostles," 1:28–42, 39–40) is remarkably indecisive.

12. On p. 86 of his *Acts* Haenchen says, in a parenthetical remark, "if he was preparing Acts about the year 75…" This is hypothetical. Page 164 suggests a date c. 80, reinforced in

his discussion of 5:12b, where Haenchen says that "the Temple had been destroyed for a decade" (*Acts*, 244–245), suggesting c. 80 for the composition of Acts. On p. 257 Haenchen places the census "some *eighty* years distant from Acts," which suggests a date c. 85. Haenchen does not argue a "late date" for Acts. Although he is not entirely consistent, he does not depart from the "consensus."

13. See page 1. Yet, when in Appendix A he comes to discuss the historicity of Acts, Talbert suggests that the book was written c. 100, *Reading Acts*, 237.

Appendix III
Dates of Authors and Texts

1. See p. 49.

2. Mitton finds 87–92 as a probable range. This is based upon the view that Ephesians made use of Acts and that the latter is to be dated c. 85.

3. See Frank Witt Hughes, *Early Christian Rhetoric and 2 Thessalonians* for a profile of this letter in its polemical context. Pauline authorship is also defended, most recently by A. Malherbe, *The Letters to the Thessalonians*. Brown, *Introduction*, 590–98, gives a survey of views.

4. Those unfamiliar with the writings known as the "Apostolic Fathers" may appreciate the handbook of Clayton N. Jefford *et al.*, *Reading the Apostolic Fathers*.

5. See p. 62.

6. See pp. 314–15.

7. See Lindemann, *Clemensbriefe*, 12 and Lona, 75–78.

8. H. Gamble, *New Testament Canon*, 41. Pages 36–41 give a succinct review of various theories about the formation of the collection.

9. Cf. 2 Thess. 3:17; 2 Pet 3:16; Ign*Eph* 12:2.

10. *Books and Readers*, 58.

11. It seems highly likely that at least three editions of the collected letters of Paul circulated in the second century. Gamble summarizes the contents of these editions in *Books and Readers*, 59–61.

12. See p. 52.

13. *The New Testament in the Apostolic Fathers*, 137. None of the possible allusions receives a higher rating than B. V. P. Furnish is also uncertain, regarding Marcion as the first witness, *II Corinthians*, 29.

14. Both *The New Testament in the Apostolic Fathers*, 38, and Schoedel, *Ignatius*, 9, state that certainty is possible only for 1 Corinthians. The latter states, on the ground of *Eph.* 12:2 that greater generosity may be desirable.

15. These ten include all of those in the NT except the 1–2 Timothy and Titus, which were not in Marcion's collection and were not included in the earliest manuscript, P[46]. The earliest edition may have arranged these as seven letters to seven churches. O'Neil, *Theology of Acts*, 26, argues that Luke could have written between 115–130 without knowledge of the *corpus Paulinum*. This is unlikely.

16. See p. 204.

17. See also the excursus, pp. 24–25.

18. Note, however, *Marcion and the New Testament*, 139 n.6. Knox tied Luke and Acts to the date of Marcion.

19. His *Marcion: On the Restitution of Christianity,* 44–74 concludes that Marcion was active in Asia c. 110–150 and never went to Rome. Hoffmann's proposals in general have not gone without critical objection. See the list of reviews in his "How then Know This Troublous Teacher?" (173–191, 180 n.30), as well as Gerhard May, "Ein neues Marcionbild?"

20. Please note that I am not advocating that hypothesis here.

21. See p. 20.

22. See p. 307.

23. L. W. Barnard, *St. Justin Martyr: The First and Second Apologies,* 11. R. Grant, *Greek Apologists of the Second Century,* 52, dates the work(s) "after 147."

24. For the date of Irenaeus see p. 376 n. 6.

Appendix IV
The Diaspora Revolts of 115–117

1. For narrative summaries of these events and literature to date see Mary Smallwood, *The Jews under Roman Rule*, 389–427 and Shim'on Applebaum, *Jews and Greeks in Ancient Cyrene*, 261–344. A concise account can be found in Schürer, *A History of the Jewish People in the Time of Jesus Christ*, 1:529–534. Even more concise, but with important interpretation and references is John M. G. Barclay, *Jews in the Mediterranean Diaspora*, 78–81; 240–42, on Egypt and Cyrene. (Barclay had read the ms. of W. Horbury, "The Jewish Revolts under Trajan and Hadrian," scheduled for vol. 4 of *The Cambridge History of Judaism*, which has not yet appeared.) The documentary material edited by Tcherikover and Fuks, *Corpus Papyrorum Judaicarum* (vol. II, 225–260) illuminates in scattered lightning-flashes the extent of the horror and ruin in Egypt. For the revolt in Cyrene see Shim'on Applebaum, *Jews and Greeks in Ancient Cyrene*, 269–94, who devotes particular attention to inscriptional evidence. The chief literary sources are Appian: *Civil Wars* 2.90, *Historia Augusta, Vita Hadriani* 5; Cassius Dio: 68.32, 69.8; Eusebius: *Ecclesiastical History* 4.2–3; Orosius: *Against the Pagans*, 7.12. 80.

2. M. Rostovtzeff summarizes the place of Armenia in Roman-Parthian relations in his "The Sarmatae and Parthians," in S. A. Cook *et al.*, Eds., *The Cambridge Ancient History*, vol. XI, 91–130, 106–9.

3. For the religious motivation of the war see David Frankfurter, "Lest Egypt's City be Deserted."

4. For the revolt in Cyprus see Applebaum, *Jews and Greeks in Ancient Cyrene*, 297–99.

5. Barclay, *Jews in the Mediterranean Diaspora*, 78.

6. Juvenal describes a battle over religious matters between two Egyptian villages in *Satire* 15, which can be dated 127–130. This conflict, which did not involve Jews or Judaism, resulted in cannibalism, according to Juvenal. Similar statements were made about the revolt in Cyrene: Cassius Dio 68.32.

7. See pp. 179–82.

8. In these citations brackets [ ] refer to restorations of missing portions of the document by modern editors. Parentheses ( ) indicate ancient abbreviations filled out for convenience.

9. CPJ 2:396 n.16.

10. See CPJ 2:257 for discussion.

11. The other use is of different meaning: 20:10 (cf. Mark 5:39).

12. In Acts 12:18 τάραχος refers to a different sort of tumult. The verb can mean "harangue," "agitate," as in 15:24 (cf. Gal 1:7; 5:10). Note also 16:20, where gentile agitators are the subject.

13. See pp. 168, 203, and 423 n. 12. On στάσις see also Wills, "Depiction of the Jews," 637–38.

14. These terms also occur in the Letter of Claudius to the Alexandrians, 41 CE (=P. Lond. 1912 =CPJ 153 =Hunt Edgar, *Select Papyri* [Loeb Classical Library] 212), where the Jews are victims of ταραχὴ καὶ στάσις (1.73), which Claudius says should be called "warfare."

15. According to Acts 15:1, the Judean visitors to Antioch set off στάσις by demanding circumcision and full observance of Torah. Luke thereby characterizes them as dangerous outside agitators. There was, however, no disorder at Jerusalem (15:7).

16. This is not to suggest that such terminology was not used earlier.

17. Herbert A. Musurillo, *The Acts of the Pagan Martyrs*.

18. Smallwood, *The Jews under Roman Rule*, 389. Musurillo, *Acts of the Pagan Martyrs* 164–68, is uncertain about the dramatic date, other than it is prior to 113.

19. For text and translation see Musurillo 44–48, with commentary 161–68. Tcherikover and Fuks provide text, translation and comments in CPJ 2:82–87.

20. Editors (see Musurillo, 174–75) assume that the Jews brought a Torah scroll. Another possibility is that this is a joke: the Jews had no "gods" to bring because they are "godless" or "atheists." ("Atheists" were persons who did not observe the civic cults.)

21. The word is συνέδριον, the meaning of which is disputed. See CPJ 2:86 on 1.42.

22. For some data on sweating or bleeding statues, a phenomenon that is still attested, see Musurillo, 163 and CPJ 2:87 on l.52.

23. This adjective, ἀνόσιοι, (l.43) is the standard epithet for Jews in the papyri that deal with the Jewish revolt in N. Africa. See CPJ 2:87.

24. Other features that shed light on Acts but are less germane to this study include the vindication of the Alexandrian cause by miracle, the boldness of Hermaiscus in the face of a tyrant (cf., e.g., Acts 4:13; 5:29; 23:1–3), and the crowd scene that concludes the fragment. The Jewish delegation numbers 7 (cf. Acts 6:1–7; 20:4). Each side brings a trained orator to state its case (cf. Acts 24:1). The delegations arrive at Rome after winter (cf. Acts 27–28).

25. Luke knows of influential Jewish women, such as Drusilla (Acts 24:24) and Bernice (Acts 25:13)—as well as the nefarious Herodias (Luke 3:19).

26. The dates of the surviving fragments show that this anti-Jewish propaganda continued to attract readers for a good century after the final revolt, which ended in 135.

Works Consulted

Not included in the following entries are volumes from the Loeb Classical Library (LCL) and some other sources of translations, as well as articles in EDNT. Full data for these references appear in the relevant notes.

Achtemeier, Paul J., *1 Peter*. Hermeneia. Minneapolis: Fortress Press, 1996.

———, "The Origin and Function of the Pre-Marcan Miracle Catenae," *Journal of Biblical Literature* 91 (1972) 198–221.

———, "Toward the Isolation of Pre-Markan Miracle Catenae," *Journal of Biblical Literature* 89 (1970) 265–291.

Aejmelaeus, Lars, *Die Rezeption der Paulusbriefe in der Miletrede (APG 20:18–35)*. Helsinki: Suomalainen Tiedeakatemia, 1987.

Africa, Thomas, "Worms and the Death of Kings: A Cautionary Note on Disease and History," *Classical Antiquity* 1 (1982) 1–17.

Agrell, G., *Work, Toil and Sustenance: An Examination of the View of Work in the New Testament*. Lund: Verbum Hakan Ohlssons, 1976.

Alexander, Loveday, "Acts and Ancient Intellectual Biography," in Bruce W. Winter and A. D. Clarke, Eds., *The Book of Acts in Its Ancient Literary Setting* BIFCS 1 (Grand Rapids: William B. Eerdmans, 1993), 31–63.

———, *The Preface to Luke's Gospel: Literary Convention and Social Context in Luke 1.1–4 and Acts 1.1*. SNTSMS 78. Cambridge: The University Press, 1993.

Allen, O. Wesley Jr., *The Death of Herod: The Narrative and Theological Functions of Retribution in Luke-Acts* SBLDS 158; Atlanta: Scholars, 1997.

Applebaum, S., "The Legal Status of the Jewish Communities in the Diaspora," in S. Safrai, *et al.*, Eds., *The Jewish People in the First Century*. CRINT 1.1. Assen: Van Gorcum & Comp., 1974, 420–63.

———, "The Organization of the Jewish Communities in the Diaspora," in S. Safrai, *et al.*, Eds., *The Jewish People in the First Century*. CRINT 1.1. Assen: Van Gorcum & Comp., 1974, 464–503.

Arnold, Clinton E., *Ephesians: Power and Magic. The Concept of Power in Ephesians in Light of Its Historical Setting*. Grand Rapids: Baker, 1992.

Attridge, Harold W., "Josephus and His Works," in M. E. Stone, Ed., *Jewish Writings of the Second Temple Period*, CRINT 2.2 Philadelphia: Fortress, 1984, 185–232.

Aune, David E., *Prophecy in Early Christianity*. Grand Rapids: William B. Eerdmans, 1983.

Balch, David L., "The Areopagus Speech: An Appeal to the Stoic Historian Posidonius against Later Stoics and the Epicureans," in *idem. et al.* Eds., *Greeks, Romans, and Christians: Essays in Honor of Abraham J. Malherbe*. Minneapolis: Fortress Press, 1990, 52–79.

———, *Let Wives Be Submissive: The Domestic Code in 1 Peter*. SBLMS 26. Scholars: Chico, CA, 1981.

Balz, Horst and Wanke, Günther, φοβέω, κ.τ.λ., *TDNT* 9:189–219.

Barclay, John M. G., *Jews in the Mediterranean Diaspora from Alexander to Trajan (323 BCE–117 CE)*. Berkeley: University of California Press, 1996.

Barnard, Leslie W., *St. Justin Martyr: The First and Second Apologies. ACW* 56. New York: Paulist, 1997.

Barnett, Albert E., *Paul Becomes a Literary Influence*. Chicago: University of Chicago Press, 1941.

Barr, David L., *New Testament Story: An Introduction*. 2nd Ed.. Belmont California: Wadsworth, 1995.

Barrett, Charles Kingsley, *The Acts of the* Apostles. ICC. 2 vols. Edinburgh: T&T Clark, 1994, 1998.

———, "The First New Testament?" *Novum Testamentum* 38 [1996] 94–104.

Bassler, Jouette M., *Divine Impartiality: Paul and a Theological Axiom* SBLDS 59. Chico, CA: Scholars, 1979.

Bauckham, Richard, "The Acts of Paul as a Sequel to Acts," in B.W. Winter and A.D. Clarke Eds., BIFCS. Vol. 1. *Ancient Literary Setting* (Grand Rapids, Michigan: William B. Eerdmans, 1993), 105–152.

———, Ed., *The Gospels for All Christians: Rethinking the Gospel Audiences*. Grand Rapids: William B. Eerdmans, 1998.

Bauer, Walter, and Paulsen, Henning, *Die Briefe des Ignatius von Antiochia und der Polykarperbrief. HNT* 18. Tübingen: Mohr/Siebeck, 1985.

———, *A Greek-English Lexicon of the New Testament and other Early Christian Literature*. 3rd Ed.. Rev. and Ed. By F. W. Danker. Chicago: University of Chicago Press, 2000.

———, "The Picture of the Apostle in Early Christian Tradition: 1. Accounts," in W. Schneemelcher, Ed. Trans. Ed. R. McL. Wilson, *New Testament Apocrypha*. 2 vols. Philadelphia: Westminster Press, 1965, 2:35–74.

———, *Orthodoxy and Heresy in Earliest Christianity*. Trans. Ed. By R. Kraft and G. Krodel. Philadelphia: Fortress, 1971.

Bauernfeind, Otto, *Kommentar und Studien zur Apostelgeschichte*. Tübingen: Mohr (Siebeck), 1980.

———, μάταιος, κ.τ.λ., *TDNT* 4:519–524.

Bayer, Hans. F., "The Preaching of Peter in Acts," in I. H. Marshall and David Peterson, Eds. *Witness to the Gospel: The Theology of Acts*. Grand Rapids: William B. Eerdmans, 1998, 257–74.

Becker, Jürgen, *Paul: Apostle to the Gentiles*. Translated by O. C. Dean, Jr. Louisville, Kentucky: Westminster/John Knox, 1993.

Behm, J. νέος, ἀνανεόω, *TDNT* 4: 896–901.

———, προνοέω, πρόνοια, *TDNT* 4:1009–17.

Behm, J, and Würthwein, E., μετανοέω, μετάνοια *TDNT* 4:975–1008.

Beker, J. Christiaan, *Heirs of Paul. Paul's Legacy in the New Testament and in the Church Today*. Minneapolis: Fortress Press, 1991.

Belser, Johannes E., *Die Apostelgeschichte*. Wien: Mayer & Co., 1905

Benoit, André, *Le baptême chrétien au second siècle*. Paris: Presses universitaires de France, 1953.

Benoit, Pierre, "La deuxième visite de Saint Paul à Jérusalem," *Biblica* 40 (1959) 778–792.

Berger, Klaus, *Formgeschichte des Neuen Testaments* Heidelberg: Quelle und Meyer, 1984.

Bertram, Georg, ζύγος, *TDNT* 2:896–901.

———, στρέφω, κ.τ.λ., *TDNT* 7:714–29.

———, εὐεργετέω, κ.τ.λ., *TDNT* 2:654–55.

———, παιδεύω, κ.τ.λ., *TDNT* 5:596–625.

———, ὕβρίς, κ.τ.λ., *TDNT* 8:295–307.

———, ὑπερήφανος, ὑπερηφανία, *TDNT* 8:525–529.

———, ὕψσος, κ.τ.λ., *TDNT* 8:602–20.

———, φυλάσσω, φυλακή, *TDNT* 236–44.

Best, Ernest, "Recipients and Title of the Letter to the Ephesians: Why and When the Designation 'Ephesians'?" *ANRW* 2.25.4. 3247–79.

Betz, H. D., "The Cleansing of the Ten Lepers (Luke 17:11–19)," *Journal of Biblical Literature* 90 (1971) 314–328.

———, *2 Corinthians 8 and 9*. Hermeneia. Philadelphia: Fortress, 1985.

———, *Galatians*. Hermeneia. Philadelphia: Fortress Press, 1979.

———, *Lukian von Samosata und das Neue Testament*. TU 76. Berlin: Akademie Verlag, 1961.

———, "The Origin and Nature of Christian Faith according to the Emmaus Legend (Luke 24:13–32) *Interpretation* 23 (1969) 32–46.

———, *The Sermon on the Mount*. Hermeneia. Minneapolis: Fortress Press, 1995.

Betz, O., σικάριος, *TDNT* 7:278–282.

Beyer, H. W., βλασφημέω, κ.τ.λ., *TDNT* 1:621–625.

Beyers, R. and Gijsel, J. *Libri de Nativitate Mariae* CCSA 9–10. Turnhout: Brepols, 1997.

Beyschlag, K., *Clemens Romanus und der Frühkatholizismus*. BHT 35. Tübingen: Mohr/ Siebeck, 1966.

Biblia Patristica I. Des origins à Clément d'Alexandrie et Tertullien. Centre d'analyse et de documentation patristiques. Paris: Éditions du center national de la recherché scientifique, 1975.

Bietenhard, Hans, ὄνομα, κ.τ.λ., *TDNT* 5:242–283.

Blaiklock, E. M., *The Acts of the Apostles*. Tyndale New Testament Commentaries. Grand Rapids: William B. Eerdmans, 1959.

Blass, Friedrich, *Philology of the Gospels*. London: MacMillan and Co., 1898.

Blight, David W., *Race and Reunion: The Civil War in American Memory*. Cambridge: Belknap/Harvard University Press, 2002.

Bogart, J. *Orthodox and Heretical Perfectionism in the Johannine Community as Evident in the First Epistle of John* SBLDS 33; Missoula, MT: Scholars, 1977.

Boismard, M.-E., "Le 'concile' de Jérusalem (Act 15, 1–33). Essai de critique Littéaire, *Ephemerides theologicae lovanienses* 64 (1988) 433–440.

———, and Lamouille, A., *Les Actes des deux Apôtres*. 3 Vols. Paris: Gabalda, 1990.

Bonz, Maianne Palmer, *The Past as Legacy: Luke-Acts and Ancient Epic*. Minneapolis: Fortress Press, 2000.

Boorstin, Daniel J., *The Discoverers: A History of Man's Search to Know His World and Himself*. New York: Vintage, 1983.

Bornkamm, Gunther, λύκος, *TDNT* 4:308–311.

———, *Paul*. Translated D. M. G. Stalker. New York: Harper & Row, 1971.

———, πρέσβυς, κ.τ.λ., *TDNT* 6:651–682.

———, "Die Vorgeschichte des sogenannten Zweiten Korintherbriefes," *Geschichte und Glaube. Gesammelte Aufsätze* IV. Munich: Chr. Kaiser, 1971, 162–194.

Bousset, Wilhelm, *Kyrios Christos: A History of the Belief in Christ from the Beginnings of Christianity to Irenaeus*. Trans John Steely. Nashville: Abingdon, 1970), 370–371.

Bovon, Francois, *L'Evangile de Luc. Commentaire du Nouveau Testament* IIIa. Geneva: Labor et Fides, 1991.

———, *Luke I*. Translated C. Thomas. Hermeneia. Minneapolis: Augsburg Fortress, 2002.

———, *Luke the Theologian: Thirty-three Years of Research (1950–1983)*. Trans K. McKinney. Allison Park, PA: Pickwick Publications, 1987.

Bowe, Barbara, *A Church in Crisis*. HDR 23. Minneapolis: Fortress Press, 1988.

Bowersock, Glenn, *Greek Sophists in the Roman Empire*. New York: Oxford University Press, 1969.

Bradshaw, Paul F., Johnson, Maxwell E., and Phillips, L. Edward, *The Apostolic Tradition*. Hermeneia. Minneapolis: Augsburg Fortress, 2002.

Bratcher, R. G., "Having Loosed the Pangs of Death," *The Bible Translator* 10 (1959) 18–20.

Braunert, Horst, "Der römische Provinzialzensus und der Schätzungsbericht des Lukas-Evangeliums," *Historia* 6 (1957) 192–214.

Brawley, Robert L., *Luke-Acts and the Jews: Conflict, Apology, and Conciliation*. SBLMS Atlanta: Scholars, 1987.

———, *Text to Text Pours Forth Speech: Voices of Scripture in Luke-Acts*. Bloomington: Indiana University Press, 1995.

Bringeland, Hans, "Dibelius, Martin," in John H. Hayes, Ed., *Dictionary of Biblical Interpretation*. Nashville: Abingdon, 1992, 1:296–297.

Brodie, T. L., "Greco-Roman Imitation of Texts as a Partial Guide to Luke's Use of Sources," in C. H. Talbert, Ed., *Luke-Acts: New Perspective from the Society of Biblical Literature Seminar*. New York: Crossroad, 1984, 17–46.

———"Towards Unraveling Luke's Uses of the Old Testament: Luke 7:11–17 as *imitatio* of 1 Kgs 17:17–24*," New Testament Studies* 32 (1986) 247–267

———, "Towards Unraveling the Rhetorical Imitation of Sources in Acts: 2 Kings 5 as one Component of Acts 8, 9–40." *Biblica* 67 (1986) 41–67.

Broughton, T. R. S., "The Roman Army," *Beg.* 5:427–445.

Brown, Raymond E. *The Birth of the Messiah*. ABRL. Rev. Ed. New York: Doubleday, 1993.

———, *The Epistles of John*. AB 30. Garden City, New York: Doubleday, 1982.

———, *Introduction to the New Testament*. New York: Doubleday, 1997.

Brown, Schuyler, *Apostasy and Perseverance in the Theology of Luke*. Analecta Biblica 36. Rome: Pontifical Biblical Institute, 1969.

Bruce, Frederick F., *The Acts of the Apostles*. 3ʳᵈ Ed.. Grand Rapids: William B. Eerdmans, 1990.

———, "The Acts of the Apostles: Historical Record or Theological Reconstruction" *ANRW* II 25.3 2569–2603.

———, Chronological Questions in the Acts of the Apostles," *Bulletin of the John Rylands Library* 68 (1985–86) 273–295.

———, "Is the Paul of Acts the Real Paul?" *Bulletin of the John Rylands Library* 58 1976: 282–305.

———, *Paul: Apostle of the Heart Set Free*. Exeter: Paternoster, 1977.

Büchsel, Friedrich, ἀλάσσω, κ.τ.λ., *TDNT* 1:251–259.

———, and Herntrich, Volkmar, κρίνω, κ.τ.λ., *TDNT* 3:921–954

Bultmann, Rudolf. ἀγνοέω, κ.τ.λ., *TDNT* 1:116–121.

———, ἀφίημι, κ.τ.λ., *TDNT* 1:509–512.

———, *Exegetica*. Tübingen: Mohr/Siebeck, 1967.

———, μεριμνάω, κ.τ.λ., *TDNT* 4:589–593.

———, and A. Weiser, πιστεύω, κ.τ.λ., *TDNT* 6:174–228.

———, *Theology of the New Testament*. Trans. K. Grobel. 2 vols. New York: Charles Scribner's Sons, 1951–55.

Burchard, Christoph, *Der dreizehnte Zeuge*. FRLANT 103. Göttingen: Vandenhoeck & Ruprecht, 1970.

———, "Joseph and Aseneth," in J. Charlesworth, Ed., *The Old Testament Pseudepigrapha*. 2 vols. Garden City, NY: 1985, 2:177–247.

Burkitt, Francis Crawford, *Gospel History and Transmission*. Edinburgh: T&T Clark, 1907.

———, The Use of Mark in the Gospel according to Luke," *Beg* 2:106–20.

Cadbury, Henry J., "Acts of the Apostles," *Interpreters Dictionary of the Bible*. Nashville: Abingdon, 1962, 1:28–42.

———, *The Book of Acts in History*. New York: Harper & Bros., 1955.

———, "Commentary on the Preface of Luke," *Beg.* 2:489–510.

———, *The Making of Luke-Acts*. London: SPCK, 1958 (Original, 1927).

———, "Names for Christians and Christianity in Acts," *Beg.* 5:375–92.

———, "Roman Law and the Trial of Paul," *Beg.* 5:297–338.

———, *The Style and Literary Method of Luke* HTS 6. Cambridge: Harvard University Press, 1920.

———, "The Summaries in Acts," *Beg.* 5:392–402.

———, "The Tradition," *Beg.* 2:209–64.

———, and the Editors, "Subsidiary Points," *Beg.* 2:349–59 (1922).

Campbell, Douglas A., "An Anchor for Pauline Chronology: Paul's Flight from `the Ethnarch of King Aretas,' 2 Cor 11:32–33," *Journal of Biblical Literature* 121 (2002) 279–302.

Campbell, R. Alastair, *The Elders: Seniority within Earliest Christianity.* Edinburgh: T&T Clark, 1994.

Campbell, Thomas H., "Paul's Missionary Journeys as Reflected in His Letters," *Journal of Biblical Literature* 74 (1955) 80–87.

Von Campenhausen Hans, *Ecclesiastical Authority and Spiritual Power.* trans J. A. Baker. Stanford: Stanford University Press, 1969.

———, "Polykarp von Smyrna und die Pastoralbriefe," *Aus der Frühzeit des Christentums.* Tübingen: Mohr/Siebeck, 1963, 197–252.

Carson, Donald A., Moo, D. J., and Morris, Leon. *An Introduction to the New Testament.* Grand Rapids, Michigan: Zondervan, 1992.

Charlesworth, James H., *The Odes of Solomon. SBLTT.* Scholars: Missoula, Montana: 1977.

Clarke, W. K. L., "The Use of the LXX in Acts," *Beg.* 2:66–105.

Cohen, Shaye, *The Beginnings of Jewishness: Boundaries, Varieties, Uncertainties.* Berkeley: University of California Press, 1999.

———, *From the Maccabees to the Mishnah. LEC* 8. Philadelphia: Westminster Press, 1987.

Collins, Adela Yarbro, "The Function of Excommunication in Paul," *Harvard Theological Review* 73 (1980) 251–63.

Collins, Raymond F., *Letters That Paul Did Not Write.* Wilmington: Michael Glazier, 1988.

Conzelmann, Hans, *Acts of the Apostles,* Trans. and Ed. E.J. Epp with C. Matthews. Hermeneia. Philadelphia: Fortress Press, 1987.

———, "Luke's Place in the Development of Early Christianity," *SLA* 298–316.

———, *The Theology of St Luke.* Trans. G. Buswell. New York: Harper & Row, 1960.

———, φῶς, κ.τ.λ., *TDNT.* 9: 310–58.

Creed, John Martin, *The Gospel according to St. Luke.* New York: St. Martin's, 1930.

Crook, J. A., *Law and Life of Rome: 90B.C.-A.D. 212.* Ithaca: Cornell University Press, 1967.

Crossan, John D., *In Parables: the Challenge of the Historical Jesus* (New York: Harper and Row, 1973), 86–96.

Cousar, Charles, "Jerusalem, Council of," *ABD* 3:766–68.

Danker, Frederick W., *Benefactor: Epigraphic Study of A Graeco-Roman and New Testament Semantic Field.* St. Louis: Clayton, 1982.

———, *Jesus and the New Age.* 2nd Ed.. Philadelphia: Fortress Press, 1988.

———, "Reciprocity in the Ancient World and in Acts 15:23–29," in R. J. Cassidy and P. J. Scharper, Eds., *Political Issues in Luke-Acts.* Maryknoll, New York: Orbis Books, 1983, 49–58.

Dautzenberg, Gerhard, "Der Zweite Korintherbrief als Briefsammlung: Zur Frage der literischen Einheitlichkeit und des theologischen Gefüges von 2 Kor 1–8," *ANRW* 2.25.4 (1987) 3045–66.

Davies, Stevan L., *The New Testament: A Contemporary Introduction.* San Francisco: Harper & Row, 1988.

Davis, D. B., "The Enduring Legacy of the South's Civil War Victory," *New York Times,* 26 August 2001, sec. 4, "The Week in Review."

Deissmann, Adolph, *Bible Studies.* Trans. A. Grieve. Edinburgh: T. & T. Clark, 1901.

Delling, Gerhard, πλεονέκτης, κ.τ.λ., *TDNT* 6:266–274.

———, συμβιβάζω, *TDNT* 7:763–766.

Dibelius, Martin, *An die Thessalonicher I-II; an Die Philipper.* Zweite Auflage. *HNT* 11. Tübingen: Mohr/Siebeck, 1923.

———, *Aufsätze zur Apostlegeschichte.* Ed. H. Greeven. Göttingen: Vandenhoeck & Ruprecht, 1953. Translated as *Studies in the Acts of the Apostles.* London: SCM, 1956.

————, *Der Hirt des Hermas, HNT. Apostolischen Vater* IV. Tübingen: Mohr/Siebeck, 1923.
————, and Conzelmann, Hans, *The Pastoral Epistles*. Trans P. Buttolph and A. Yarbro. Hermeneia. Philadelphia: Fortress Press: 1972.
R. J. Dillon, R. J., *From Eyewitnesses to Ministers of the Word: Tradition and Composition in Luke* 24. Rome: Pontifical Biblical Institute, 1978.
Dodd, C. H., *The Apostolic Preaching and Its* Developments. London: Hodder & Stoughton, 1936.
Donelson, Lewis R., "Cult Histories and the Sources of Acts," *Biblica* 68 (1987) 1–21.
Downing, F. Gerald, "Common Ground with Paganism in Luke and Josephus," *New Testament Studies* 28 (1982) 546–559.
Drury, John. *Tradition and Design in Luke's Gospel*. Atlanta: John Knox, 1976.
Downing, F. Gerald, "Redaction Criticism: Josephus' *Antiquities* and the Synoptic Gospels (II)," *Journal for the Study of the New Testament* 9 (1980) 29–48.
Duncan, George S., *St Paul's Ephesian Ministry: A Reconstruction with Special Reference to the Ephesian Origin of the Imprisonment Epistles*. New York: Charles Scribner's Sons, 1930.
Dunn, J. D. G., *The Acts of the Apostles*. Peterborough: Epworth, 1996.
————, *Unity and Diversity in the New Testament: An Inquiry into the Character of Earliest Christianity* 2nd ed.. Philadelphia: Trinity, 1990.
Dupont, Jacques, *Le discours de Milet. Testament pastoral de Saint Paul (Actes 20,18–36)* Paris: Cerf: 1962.
————, "La famine sous Claude, Actes 11.28," *Revue Biblique* 62 (1955) 52–55.
————, *The Sources of Acts*. Trans. K. Pond. New York: Herder & Herder, 1964.
Eckey, Wilfried, *Die Apostelgeschichte: Der Weg des Evangeliums von Jerusalem nach Rom*. Neukirch: Neukirchener Verlag, 2000.
Ehrhardt, A., *The Acts of the Apostles: Ten Lectures*. Manchester: Manchester University Press, 1969.
Ehrman, Bart D., *The Apostolic Fathers*, editor and translator. LCL. 2 vols. Cambridge: Harvard University Press, 2003.
————, *The Orthodox Corruption of Scripture: The Effect of Early Christological Controversies on the Text of the New Testament*. New York: Oxford University Press, 1993.
Elliott, John H., *1 Peter* AB37b. New York: Doubleday, 2000.
Ellis, E. Earle, *The Gospel of Luke*. NCB. Rev. Ed.. London: Oliphants, 1974.
Eltester W., and F. Kettler, Eds. *Apophoreta*, FS E. Haenchen. Berlin: Topelman, 1964.
Enslin, Morton, S., *Christian Beginnings*. Fourth Ed.. New York: Harper and Brothers, 1938.
"'Luke' and Paul," *Journal of the American Oriental Society* 58 (1938) 81–91.
————, "Luke the Literary Physician," in D. E. Aune, Ed., *Studies in New Testament and Early Christian Literature*. FS Wikgren. SNT 33. Leiden: E.J. Brill, 1972, 135–143.
————, "Once Again, Luke and Paul," *Zeitschrift für die neutestamentliche Wissenschaft und die Kunde der älteren Kirche* 61 (1970) 253–271.
Erbe, Carl, "Petrus nicht in Rom, sondern in Jerusalem gestorben," *Zeitschrift fur Kirchengeschicthe* 22 (1901) 1–47; 161–224.
Esler, Philip Francis, *Community and gospel in Luke-Acts: The Social and Political Motivations of Lucan Theology*. SNTSMS 57. Cambridge: Cambridge University Press, 1987.
Eusebius, *Ecclesiastical History*. Trans. K. Lake. LCL. 2 vols. Cambridge: Harvard University Press, 1926.
Evans, C. F., *Saint* Luke Philadelphia: Trinity Press International, 1990.
Fee, Gordon, D., *The First Epistle to the Corinthians*. NICNT. Grand Rapids: William B. Eerdmans, 1987.
Feldman, Louis H., *Jew and Gentile in the Ancient World*. Princeton: Princeton University Press, 1993.

Fiorenza, Elisabeth Schüssler, *In Memory of Her: A Feminist Theological Reconstruction of Christian Origins*. New York: Crossroads, 1983.

Fitzgerald, John, *Cracks in an Earthen Vessel: An Examination of the Catalogues of Hardships in the Corinthian Correspondence*. SBLDS 99 Atlanta: Scholars, 1988.

———, Ed., *Greco-Roman Perspectives on Friendship*. Atlanta: Scholars Press, 1997.

———, and White, L. Michael. *The Tabula of Cebes*. SBLTT. Chico, CA: Scholars, 1983.

Fitzmyer, Joseph A., *The Acts of the Apostles*. AB 31. New York: Doubleday: 1998.

———, *The Gospel according to Luke*. 2 vols AB 28/28a Garden City: Doubleday & Company, 1981 and 1985.

———, "The Pauline Letters and the Lucan Account of Paul's Missionary Journeys," SBLSP 1988, D. J. Lull, editor. Atlanta: Scholars Press, 1988, 82–89.

Foerster, Werner, διάβολος, *TDNT* 2:71–81.

———, *Gnosis*. 2 vols. Trans. Ed. R. McL. Wilson. Oxford: Clarendon, 1974.

———, κύριος, κ.τ.λ., *TDNT* 3: 1055–56.

———, σέβομαι, κ.τ.λ., *TDNT* 7:168–196.

Fohrer, G., and Foerster, W. σώτηρ, *TDNT* 8:1003–1021.

Fornara, Charles William, *The Nature of History in Ancient Greece and Rome* Berkeley: University of California Press, 1983.

Franklin, Eric, *Christ the Lord: A Study in the Purpose and Theology of Luke-Acts*. Philadelphia: The Westminster Press, 1975.

Freed, Edwin D., *The New Testament: A Critical Introduction*. Belmont, California: Wadsworth, 1986.

Friesen, Steven, "The Cult of the Roman Emperors in Ephesos," in H. Koester, Ed. *Ephesos: Metropolis of Asia*. HTS 41 Valley Forge: Trinity Press International, 1995, 229–50.

Funk, F. X. and Bihlmeyer, K., *Die Apostolischen Väter*. Tübingen: Mohr/Siebeck, 1924.

Funk, Robert W., Hoover, Roy W., *et al.*, *The Five Gospels: The Search for the Authentic Words of Jesus*. New York: Macmillan, 1993.

———, "The Enigma of the Famine Visit," *Journal of Biblical Literature* 75 (1956) 130–36.

———, *Parables and Presence: Forms of the New Testament Tradition*. Philadelphia: Fortress Press, 1982.

———, *The Poetics of Biblical Narrative*. Sonoma, CA: Polebridge, 1988.

Furnish, Victor P., *II Corinthians*. AB 32a. Garden City: Doubleday & Company, 1984.

Gabba, Emilio, "Literature," in M. Crawford, *Sources for Ancient History* Cambridge: Cambridge University Press, 1983, 1–79.

Gamble, Harry, Y., *Books and Readers in the Early Church*. New Haven: Yale University Press, 1995.

———, *The New Testament Canon: Its Making and Meaning*. Philadelphia: Fortress Press, 1985.

———, *The Textual History of the Letter to the Romans*. SD 42. Grand Rapids: Eerdmans, 1977.

Gapp, K. S., "The Universal Famine under Claudius," *Harvard Theological Review* 28 (1935) 258–265.

Garrett, Susan R., "Beloved Physician of the Soul? Luke as Advocate for Ascetic Practice," in L. E. Vaage and V. L. Wimbush, Eds., *Asceticism and the New Testament*. London: Routledge, 1999, 71–95.

———, *The Demise of the Devil: Magic and the Demonic in Luke-Acts*. Minneapolis, Minnesota: Fortress, 1989.

———, "Exodus from Bondage: Luke 9:31 and Acts 12:1–24," *Catholic Biblical Quarterly* 52 (1990) 656–689.

Gärtner, Bertil, *The Areopagus Speech and Natural Revelation*. ASNU 21. Uppsala: C. W. K. Gleerup, 1955.

Gasque, W. Ward, *A History of the Criticism of the Acts of the Apostles* Grand Rapids: Wm.

B. Eerdmans, 1975

Gaventa, Beverly R., *The Acts of the Apostles. Abingdon New Testament Commentaries*. Nashville: Abingdon, 2003.

———, *From Darkness to Light: Aspects of Conversion in the New Testament*. OBT. Philadelphia: Fortress Press, 1986.

Georgi, Dieter, *The Opponents of Paul in Second Corinthians*. Philadelphia: Fortress Press, 1986.

———, *Remembering the Poor: The History of Paul's Collection for Jerusalem*. Nashville: Abingdon, 1992.

Goodenough, Erwin R., "The Perspective of Acts," *SLA* 51–59.

Goodman, Martin, *Mission and Conversion: Proselytizing in the Religious History of the Roman Empire*. Oxford: Clarendon, 1994.

Goodspeed, Edgar J., *An Introduction to the New Testament* Chicago: University of Chicago Press, 1937.

Goulder, Michael D., "Did Luke Know any of the Pauline Letters?," *Perspectives in Religious Studies* 13 (1986) 97–112.

———, *Type and History in Acts*. London: SPCK, 1964.

Grant, Robert M. and Graham, Holt H., *The Apostolic Fathers*. Vol. 2. *First and Second Clement*. New York: Thomas Nelson & Sons, 1965.

Grant, Robert M., *Greek Apologists of the Second Century*. Philadelphia: Westminster, 1988.

———, *Heresy and Criticism*. Louisville: Westminster/John Knox, 1993.

———, *Jesus after the Gospels: The Christ of the Second Century*. Louisville: Westminster/John Knox, 1990.

———, *Theophilus of Antioch. Ad Autolycum*. Oxford: Clarendon, 1970.

Grässer, Erich, *Forschungen zur Apostelgeschichte. WUNT* 137. Tübingen: Mohr Siebeck, 2001.

Grassi, Joseph, "Emmaus Revisited (Luke 24, 13–35 and Acts 8:26–40)," *Catholic Biblical Quarterly* 26 (1964) 463–467.

Green, Joel B., "Festus," *ABD* 2:794–95.

Grundmann, Walter, δόκιμος, κ.τ.λ., *TDNT* 2:255–260.

———, ἐγκράτεια, κ.τ.λ., *TDNT* 2:339–342.

———, ταπεινός, κ.τ.λ., *TDNT* 8:1–26.

———, *et al.*, χρίω, κ.τ.λ., *TDNT* 9:493–580.

Guthrie, Donald, *New Testament Introduction*. 3rd Ed.. Downers Grove, Illinois: Intervarsity Press, 1970.

Haenchen, Ernst, *The Acts of the Apostles*. Trans. Ed. R. McL. Wilson. Philadelphia: Westminster, 1971.

———, *John*. Hermeneia. 2 vols, trans. and Ed. R. Funk *et al*. Philadelphia: Fortress Press, 1984.

———, "Simon Magus in der Apostelgeschichte." In *Gnosis und das Neues Testament*, Ed. K. W. Tröger. Gütersloh: Mohn, 1973, 267–79.

———, " 'We' in Acts and the Itinerary." *Journal for Theology and Church* 1 1965: 65–99.

———, *Der Weg Jesu: Eine Erklärung des Markus-Evangeliums und seiner kanonischen Parallelen*. Berlin: W. De Gruyter, 1966.

Hagner, Donald S., *The Use of the Old and New Testaments in Clement of Rome. NTSuppl.* 34. Leiden: E.J. Brill, 1973.

Hall, Stuart, G., *Melito of Sardis*. Oxford: Clarendon, 1979.

Hanson, Richard P. C., *The Acts in the RSV*. Oxford: Clarendon, 1967.

Harnack, Adolph, *The Acts of the Apostles*. Trans J. R. Wilkinson. New York: G. P. Putnam's Sons, 1909.

———, *Marcion: Das Evangelium vom fremden Gott*. Leipzig: J.C. Hinrichs, 1921.

———, *The Mission and Expansion of Christianity in the First Three Centuries*. 2 vols. Trans. J. Moffatt. New York: G. P. Putnam's Sons, 1908.

————, *Neue Untersuchungen zur Apostelgeschichte.* Leipzig: J. C. Hinrichs, 1911.

Harrill, J. Albert, *The Manumission of Slaves in Early Christianity* HUT 32. Tübingen: Mohr/Siebeck, 1995.

Harrington, Daniel, "The Bible Rewritten," in R. Kraft, G. Nickelsburg, Eds., *Early Judaism and its Modern Interpreters.* Atlanta: Scholars, 1986, 239–47.

Hartog, Paul, *Polycarp and the New Testament: The Occasion, Rhetoric, Theme and Unity of the Epistle to the Philippians and Its Allusions to New Testament Literature.* WUNT 134 Tübingen: Mohr Siebeck, 2002.

Hauck, Friedrich, ὅσιος, κ.τ.λ., *TDNT* 5:489–493.

Hawkins, John C., *Horae Synopticae.* Grand Rapids: Baker, 1968 (reprint of the 2nd ed. of 1909).

Hayes, J. H., and Roloff, J., "Acts of the Apostles, Book of the," *Dictionary of Biblical Interpretation*, 1:4–13.

Heard, R., "Papias' Quotations from the New Testament," *New Testament Studies* 1 (1954–55) 130–34.

Hemer, Colin, *The Book of Acts in the Setting of Hellenistic History.* Ed. C. J. Gempf. Winona Lake, Indiana: Eisenbrauns, 1990.

————, "First Person Narrative in Acts 27–28," *Tyndale Bulletin* 36 (1985) 79–109.

————, "The Speeches in Acts I. The Ephesian Elders at Miletus," *Tyndale Bulletin* 40 (1989) 77–85.

Hengel, Martin, *Acts and the History of Earliest Christianity.* Trans. J. Bowden. Philadelphia: Fortress Press, 1979.

————, *Between Jesus and Paul: Studies in the History of Earliest Christianity.* Trans. J. Bowden. Philadelphia: Fortress Press, 1983.

————, and Schwemer, Anna Maria, *Paul between Damascus and Antioch: The Unknown Years.* Trans. J. Bowden. Louisville: Westminster/John Knox, 1997.

Hill, Craig C., *Hellenists and Hebrews: Reappraising Division with the Earliest Church.* Minneapolis: Fortress, 1992.

Hobart, W. K., *The Medical Language of St. Luke* London: Longmans, Green & Co., 1882.

Hock, Ronald F., *The Infancy Gospels of James and Thomas. Scholars Bible* 2. Santa Rosa, CA: Polebridge Press, 1995.

Hoffmann, R. Joseph, "How then Know This Troublous Teacher? Further Reflections on Marcion and his Church," *SecCent* 6 (1987) 173–191.

————, *Marcion: On the Restitution of Christianity: An Essay on the Development of Radical Paulinist Theology in the Second Century.* AARAS 46. Chico:CA: Scholars, 1984.

Höistad, Ragnar, *Cynic Hero and Cynic King.* Uppsala: N.P., 1948.

Holmberg, Bengt, *Paul and Power. The Structure of Authority in the Primitive Church as Reflected in the Pauline Epistles.* Philadelphia: Fortress Press, 1980.

Holzberg, Niklas, "Letters: *Chion,*" in G. Schmeling, Ed., *The Novel in the Ancient World.* Leiden: Brill, 1996, 645–53.

Hopkins, Keith, "Christian Number and Its Implications," *Journal of Early Christian Studies* 6 (1998) 185–226.

Horsley, Richard A. with Hanson, John S., *Bandits, Prophets, and Messiahs.* San Francisco: Harper & Row, 1985.

Hughes, Frank Witt, *Early Christian Rhetoric and 2 Thessalonians.* JSNTS 30. Sheffield: Sheffield Academic Press, 1989,

Humphrey, Edith M., *Joseph and Aseneth.* Sheffield: Sheffield Academic Press, 2000.

Hurd, John C. Jr., *The Origin of 1 Corinthians.* 2nd ed. Macon, Georgia: Mercer University Press, 1983.

Jackson, Frederick J. Foakes, *The Acts of the Apostles.* Moffat. New York: Harper and Brothers, 1931.

————, and Lake, Kirsopp, Eds. *The Beginnings of Christianity.* Part I. 5 vols. New York: Macmillan Co., 1920–33.

———, et al., "The Internal Evidence of Acts," *Beg.* 2:121–204.

Jacobson, G.R., "Paul in Luke-Acts: The Savior Who Is Present," *SBLSP* 1983, Ed. K.H. Richards. Chico, California: Scholars Press, 131–46.

Jacquier, E., *Les Acts des apôtres.* Deuxième ed. EB. Paris: Gabalda, 1926.

Jaeger, Werner, *Early Christianity and Greek Paideia.* Oxford: Oxford University Press, 1969.

Jefford, Clayton N. *et al., Reading the Apostolic Fathers: An Introduction.* Peabody MA: Hendrickson, 1996.

Jeremias, Joachim, θύρα, *TDNT* 3:173–80.

———, *The Parables of Jesus* Trans. S.H. Hooke New York: Charles Scribner's Sons, 1963.

———, ποιμήν, κ.τ.λ., *TDNT* 6:485–502.

Jervell, Jacob, *Die Apostelgeschichte KEK.* Göttingen: Vandenhoeck & Ruprecht, 1998.

———, *Luke and the People of God: A New Look at Luke-Acts.* Minneapolis: Augsburg, 1972.

———, *The Theology of Acts.* New Testament Theology. Cambridge: Cambridge University Press, 1996.

———, *The Unknown Paul: Essays on Luke-Acts and Early Christian History.* Minneapolis: Augsburg, 1984.

Jewett, Robert, *The Thessalonian Correspondence: Pauline Rhetoric and Millenarian Piety.* Philadelphia: Fortress Press, 1986.

Johnson, Luke Timothy, *The Acts of the Apostles.* SP. Collegeville, Minnesota: Liturgical Press, 1992.

———, *The Gospel of Luke.* SP. Collegeville, Minnesota: Liturgical Press, 1991.

———, *The Literary Function of Possessions in Luke-Acts.* SBLDS 39. Missoula: Scholars Press, 1977

Jones, C. P., *The Roman World of Dio Chrysostom.* Cambridge: Harvard University Press, 1978.

Jones, F. Stanley, *An Ancient Jewish Christian Source on the History of Christianity: Pseudo-Clementine Recognitions 1.21–27.* SBLTT 37 Atlanta: Scholars, 1995.

Judge, Edwin A., "The Decrees of Caesar at Thessalonica," *Reformed Theological Review* 30 (1971) 1–7.

Juel. Donald, *Luke-Acts: The Promise of History.* Atlanta: John Knox, 1983.

Jülicher, Adolf, *Einleitung in das Neue Testament.* Fünfte und sechste Auflage. Tübingen: Mohr/Siebeck, 1921.

Just, A. A., *The Ongoing Feast: Table Fellowship and Eschatology at Emmaus.* Collegeville, Minnesota: Liturgical Press, 1993.

Käsemann, Ernst, "Ephesians and Acts," *SLA,* 288–297.

———, *New Testament Questions of Today.* Trans W. J. Montague. London: SCM, 1969.

Kee, Howard C., *To Every Nation under Heaven.* Harrisburg, Pennsylvania: Trinity Press International.

Kelber, Werner, *The Kingdom in Mark.* Philadelphia: Fortress Press, 1974.

Kelly, J. N. D., *Early Christian Creeds.* 3rd Ed. London: Longman, 1972.

Kennedy, Stetson, *After Appomattox: How the South Won the War.* Gainesville: University Press of Florida, 1995.

Kerenyi, Karl, *Die griechisch-orientalische Romanliteratur.* Darmstadt: Wissenschaftliche Buchgesellschaft, 1962 (Reprint of 1927 original).

Kilgallen, John J., *A Brief Commentary on the Gospel of Luke.* Mahwah, New Jersey: Paulist Press, 1988.

Kittel, Gerhard, ἄλογος, *TDNT* 4:441.

———, δεσμός, δέσμιος, *TDNT* 2:43.

Klauck, Hans-Josef, *Magic and Paganism in Early Christianity: The World of the Acts of the Apostles.* Trans. B. McNeil. Edinburgh: T&T Clark. 2000.

Klausner, Joseph, *From Jesus to Paul.* Translated by W. F. Stinespring. New York: Macmillan, 1944 (1925).

Klein, Günther, *Die Zwölf Apostel: Ursprung und Gehalt einer Idee*. FRLANT. Göttingen: Vandenhoeck & Ruprecht, 1961.

Kloppenborg, John S., *The Formation of Q: Trajectories in Ancient Wisdom Collections*. Philadelphia: Fortress Press, 1987.

———, *Q Parallels*. Sonoma, CA: Polebridge Press, 1988.

Klostermann, Erich, *Das Lukasevangelium*. HNT 5. 2nd Ed. Tübingen: Mohr/Siebeck, 1929.

Knopf, Rudolf, Die *Lehre der zwölf Apostel. Die Zwei Clemensbriefe. HNT*. Tübingen: Mohr/Siebeck, 1920.

Knox, John, "Acts and the Pauline Letter Corpus," *SLA*, 279–87

———, *Marcion and the New Testament*. Chicago: University of Chicago Press, 1942.

———, *Philemon among the Letters of Paul*. 2nd ed. Nashville: Abingdon, 1959.

Knox, Wilfred L., *The Acts of the Apostles*. Cambridge: the University Press, 1948.

Koester, Helmut, *Ancient Christian Gospels: Their History and Development*. Philadelphia: Trinity Press International, 1990.

———, "Ephesos in Early Christian Literature," in *ibid.*, Ed., *Ephesos: Metropolis of Asia*. HTS 41. Valley Forge: Trinity Press International, 1995, 119–40.

———, *Introduction to the New Testament*. 2 vols. New York: Walter de Gruyter, 1995–2000.

———, *Synoptische Überlieferung bei den apostolischen Vätern*. TU 65 Berlin: Akademie Verlag, 1957.

———, τόπος, *TDNT* 8:187–208.

Kraabel, A. T., "The Disappearance of the God-Fearers," *Numen* 28 (1981): 113–26.

Kraemer, H., *et al.*, προφήτης, *TDNT* 6:781–861.

Kraemer, Ross Shepherd, *When Aseneth Met Joseph*. New York: Oxford University Press, 1998.

Kraft, Robert A., and Nickelsburg, G. W. E, Eds., *Early Judaism and its Modern Interpreters*. Atlanta: Scholars Press, 1986.

Kratz, Reinhard, *Rettungswunder: Motiv-, traditions- und formkritische Aufarbeitung einer biblischen Gattung*. Frankfurt: Peter Language, 1970.

Krenkel, Max, *Josephus und Lukas: Der schriftstellerische Einfluß des jüdischen Geschichtschreibers auf der christlichen nachgewiesen*. Leipzig: H. Hässel, 1894.

Krodel, Gerhard A., *Acts*. ACNT. Minneapolis: Augsburg, 1986.

Kümmel, W. G., *Introduction to the New Testament*. Trans. H. C. Kee Nashville: Abingdon, 1973.

Kürzinger, Josef, *The Acts of the Apostles*. Translated Anthony N. Fuerst. 2 vols. Crossroad: New York, 1981.

Kuhn, Karl Georg, προσήλυτος *TDNT* 6: 727–744.

Kurz, William S., *Farewell Addresses in the New Testament*. Collegeville: Liturgical Press, 1990.

de Labriolle, Pierre, *La réaction paienne: etude sur la polémique antichrétienne du Ier au Ve siècle*. Paris: l'artisan du livre, 1934.

Ladouceur, D.J., "The Death of Herod the Great," *Classical Philology* 76 (1981) 25–34.

Lake, Kirsopp, "Acts of the Apostles," in J. Hastings, editor, *Dictionary of the Apostolic Church*. 2 vols. New York: Charles Scribner's Sons, 1916, 1:15–29.

———, "The Chronology of Acts," *Beg.* 5:445–474.

Lambrecht, Jan, *Once More Astonished*. New York: Crossroad, 1981.

———, *Second Corinthians*. SP 8. Collegeville, Minnesota: Liturgical Press, 1999.

———, "Paul's Farewell-Address at Miletus, Acts 20, 17–38," in J. Kremer, Ed. *Les Actes de apôtres*. BETL 46. Louvain: Louvain University Press, 1979, 307–37.

Lampe, G. W. H., *Patristic Greek Lexicon*. Oxford: Clarendon, 1961.

Lausberg, Heinrich, *Handbook of Literary Rhetoric*. Trans. Ed. D. Orton and R. Anderson. Leiden: E. J. Brill, 1998.

Leaney, A. R. C., *The Gospel according to St Luke*. Harper's/Blacks. London: Adam &

Charles Black, 1958.

Lentz, John C. Jr., *Luke's Portrait of Paul. SNTSMS 77.* Cambridge: Cambridge University Press, 1993.

Leppä, Heikki, *Luke's Critical Use of Galatians.* Vantaa, Finland: Dark Oy, 2002.

Lewy, Hans, *Sobria Ebrietas: Untersuchungen zur Geschicthe der antiken Mystik* Giessen: A. Töpelmann, 1929.

Lightfoot, Joseph B., *The Apostolic Fathers.* 5 vols. in two parts. New York: Macmillan, 1889–90.

Limberis, Vasiliki, "Anna 2," in Carol Meyers, Ed., *Women in Scripture.* New York: Houghton Mifflin, 2000, 50–51.

Lindemann, Andreas, *Die Clemensbriefe.* HNT 17 Tübingen: Mohr/Siebeck, 1992.

———, *Paulus im Ältesten Christentum.* BHT 58. Tübingen: J.C.B. Mohr (Paul Siebeck), 1979.

Linton, Olof. "The Third Aspect: A Neglected Point of View. A Study in Gal. 1–22 and Acts ix and xv." *Studia Theologica* 3 (1951) 79–95.

Lohfink, Gerhard, *The Conversion of St. Paul: Narrative and History in Acts.* Trans. B. J. Malina. Chicago: Franciscan Herald, 1976.

Lohse, Eduard, *Colossians and Philemon.* Trans. W. Poehlmann and R. J. Karris. Hermeneia. Fortress Press: Philadelphia: 1971.

———, *The Formation of the New Testament.* Translated M. E. Boring. Nashville: Abingdon, 1981.

———, πρόσωπον, κ.τ.λ.," *TDNT* 6:768–80.

Loisy, Alfred, *Les Actes des apôtres.* Paris: E. Nourry, 1920.

Lona, Horacio E., *Der erste Clemensbrief. KAV.* Göttingen: Vandenhoeck & Ruprecht, 1998.

Longenecker, Richard N., "The Acts of the Apostles," in F. E. Gaebelein, General Editor, *The Expositor's Bible Commentary* vol. 9. Grand Rapids: Zondervan, 1981, 207–523.

Luck,Ulrich. σώφρων, κ.τ.λ., *TDNT* 7:1097–1104.

———, φιλανθρωπία, κ.τ.λ., *TDNT* 9:107–12.

Lüdemann, Gerd, "Apostelgeschichte," in H. D. Betz *et al.*, editors, Die *Religion in Geschichte und Gegenwart*[4]. Tübingen: Mohr (Siebeck), 1998, 1:642–648.

———, *Early Christianity according to the Traditions in Acts.* Trans J. Bowden. Philadelphia: Fortress, 1989.

———, *Paul Apostle to the Gentiles: Studies in Chronology.* Trans. F. Stanley Jones. Philadelphia: Fortress Press, 1984.

———, *Paul the Founder of Christianity.* Amherst, New York: Prometheus, 2002.

Lust, J., Eynikel, E., and Hauspie, K., *A Greek-English Lexicon of the Septuagint.* 2 vols. Stuttgart: Deutsche Bibelgesellschaft, 1992.

Lyons, George, *Pauline Autobiography: Toward a New Understanding.* Atlanta: Scholars, 1985.

MacDonald, Dennis R., *Does the New Testament Imitate Homer: Four Cases from the Acts of the Apostles.* New Haven: Yale University Press, 2003.

———, *The Homeric Epics and the Gospel of Mark.* New Haven: Yale University Press, 2000.

———, *The Legend and the Apostle: The Battle for Paul in Story and Canon* Philadelphia: Westminster Press, 1983.

———, "Luke's Eutychus and Homer's Elpenor: Acts 20:7–12 and *Odyssey*, 10–12," *Journal of Historical Criticism,* 1 (1994) 5–24.

———, Ed., *Mimesis and Intertextuality in Antiquity and Christianity.* Harrisburg, Penna: Trinity Press International, 2001.

MacDonald, Margaret Y., "Early Catholicism," in R. J. Coggins and J. L. Houlden, Eds., *A Dictionary of Biblical Interpretation.* Philadelphia: Trinity Press, 1990, 182–83.

———, *The Pauline Churches.* SNTSMS 60. Cambridge: Cambridge University Press, 1988.

Maclean, A. J., "Acts of the Apostles," in James Hastings, editor, *Dictionary of the Bible.* New York: Charles Scribner's Sons, 1909, 8–10.

MacMullen, Ramsey, *Enemies of the Roman Order*. Cambridge: Harvard University Press, 1966.

———, *Roman Social Relations: 50 B.C. to A.D. 284*. New Haven: Yale University Press, 1974.

Maddox, Robert, *The Purpose of Luke-Acts*. Edinburgh: T. & T. Clark, 1982.

Maier, Harry O., "Purity and Danger in Polycarp's Epistle to the Philippians: The Sin of Valens in Social Perspective," *Journal of Early Christian Studies* 1 (1993) 229–247.

Malherbe, Abraham J., "Hellenistic Moralists and the New Testament," *ANRW* II 26:3.267–333, 1992.

———, *The Letters to the Thessalonians*. AB 32b. New York: Doubleday, 2000.

———, *Paul and the Popular Philosophers*. Minneapolis: Fortress, 1989.

Marguerat, Daniel, *La première histoire du christianisme: les actes des apôtres* Paris: Cerf, 1999.

Marshall, I. Howard, *The Acts of the Apostles*. Sheffield: Sheffield Academic Press, 1992.

———, *Commentary on Luke*. NIGTC Grand Rapids: William B. Eerdmans, 1978.

———, and Peterson, David, Eds. *Witness to the Gospel: The Theology of Acts*. Grand Rapids: William B. Eerdmans, 1998.

———, "Luke as theologian," *ABD* 4: 402–3.

Martin, Clarice, "A Chamberlain's Journey and the Challenge of Interpretation for Liberation," *Semeia* 47 (1989) 105–35.

Martin, Ralph P., "An Epistle in Search of a Life-Setting," *Expository Times* 79 (1967) 296–302.

———, *New Testament Foundations: a Guide for Christian Students*. Vol.2. Grand Rapids, William B. Eerdmans, 1978.

Marxen, Willi, *Introduction to the New Testament*. Translated G. Buswell. Philadelphia: Fortress Press, 1968.

Mason, Steve, "Chief Priests, Sadducees, Pharisees and Sanhedrin in Acts," in R. Bauckham, Ed., BIFCS. Vol. 4: *Palestinian Setting*. Wm. B. Eerdmans: Grand Rapids, 1995, 115–77.

———, *Josephus and the New Testament*. Peabody, MA: Hendrickson, 1992.

Masson, Charles, "À propos de Act. 9:19b-25. Note sur l'utilisation de Gal et de 2 Cor. Par l'auteur des Actes," *Theologische Zeitschrift* 18 (1962) 161–66.

Matthews, Christopher R., *Philip: Apostle and Evangelist*. SNT 105 Leiden: E. J. Brill, 2002.

Matthews, Shelley, *First Converts: Rich Pagan Women and the Rhetoric of Mission in Early Judaism and Christianity*. Stanford: Stanford University Press, 2001.

Maurer,C. συνοίδα, κ.τ.λ., *TDNT* 7:898–919.

———, τίθημι, κ.τ.λ., *TDNT* 8:153–68.

May, Gerhard, "Ein neues Marcionbild?" *Theologische Rundschau* 51 (1986) 404–18.

———, "Marcion in Contemporary Views: Results and Open Questions," *Second Century* 6 (1987) 129–51.

McCoy, W. J., "In the Shadow of Thucydides," in Witherington, Ed., *History, Literature and Society in the Book of Acts*, 3–23.

McDonald, Lee M. and Porter, Stanley E., *Early Christianity and Its Sacred Literature*. Peabody, Mass: Hendrickson, 2000.

McNeile, A. H., *Introduction to the New Testament*. 2nd ed., rev. by C. S. C. Williams. Oxford: Clarendon, 1952.

McPherson, James. M., "Lee Dissected," *New York Review of Books*, 7 November 1991, 10–14.

———, "Southern Comfort," *The New York Review of Books*, 12 April 2001, 28–32.

Meeks, Wayne A., *The Origins of Christian Morality: The First Two Centuries*. New Haven: Yale University Press, 1993.

Merkelbach, Reinhold, *Roman und Mysterium*. Berlin: Walter de Gruyter, 1962.

Meshorer, A., *Jewish Coins of the Second Temple Period*. Tel Aviv: Am Hasefer, 1967.

Metzger, Bruce M., *The Text of the New Testament: Its Transmission, Corruption, and Restoration.* 3rd Ed. New York: Oxford University Press, 1992.

———, *A Textual Commentary on the Greek New Testament.* 2nd Ed. New York: American Bible Society, 1994.

Michaelis, Wilhelm, *Einleitung in das Neue Testament.* dritte Auflage. Bern: Berchtold Haller, 1961.

———, *Die Gefangenschaft des Paulus in Ephesus und das Itinerar des Timotheus.* Gütersloh: Bertelsmann, 1925.

———, πάσχω, κ.τ.λ., *TDNT* 5:904–939.

Michel, Hans-Joachim, *Die Abschiedsrede des Paulus an die Kirche Apg 20, 17–38: Motivgeschichte und theologische Bedeutung.* SANT 35. München: Kösel, 1973.

Michel, O., οἶκος, κ.τ.λ., *TDNT* 5:119–159.

Mitchell, Margaret M. *,Paul and the Rhetoric of Reconciliation.* Louisville: Westminster/ John Knox, 1991.

Minear, Paul S., "A Note on Luke 17:7–10," *Journal of Biblical Literature* 93 (1974) 82–87.

Mitton, C. Leslie, *The Epistle to the Ephesians: Its Authorship, Origin and Purpose.* Oxford: Clarendon Press, 1951.

———, *The Formation of the Pauline Corpus of Letters.* London: Epworth, 1955.

Moehring, H. R., "The Census in Luke as an Apologetic Device," in D. E. Aune, Ed., *Studies in New Testament and Early Christian Literature.* FS Wikgren. SNT 33. Leiden: E.J. Brill, 1972, 144–60.

Moessner, David, "Paul in Acts: Preacher of Eschatological Repentance to Israel," *New Testament Studies* 34 (1988) 96–104.

Moffatt, James, *An Introduction to the Literature of the New Testament.* New York: Scribners, 1921.

Morgenthaler, Robert, *Statistik des neutestamentlichen Wortschatzes.* Zürich: Gotthelf, 1958.

Morton, A. Q., and MacGregor, G. H. C., *The Structure of Luke and Acts.* New York: Harper & Row, 1964.

Moule, C. F. D., "The Problem of the Pastoral Epistles: A Reappraisal," *Bulletin of the John Rylands Library* 47 (1965) 430–52.

Moulton, W. F., A. S. Geden, and H. K. Moulton, Eds., *A Concordance to the Greek Testament.* Fifth Ed.. Edinburgh: T. & T. Clark, 1978.

Mount, Christopher, *Pauline Christianity: Luke-Acts and the Legacy of Paul.* SNT 104. Leiden: E. J. Brill, 2002.

Munck, Johannes, *The Acts of the Apostles.* A B. Garden City, New York: Doubleday, 1967.

———, *Paul and the Salvation of Mankind.* Richmond: John Knox, 1959.

Murphy-O'Connor, Jerome, *Paul: A Critical Life.* Oxford: Clarendon Press, 1996.

Musurillo, Herbert, *The Acts of the Christian Martyrs.* Oxford: Clarendon Press, 1972.

———, *The Acts of the Pagan Martyrs.* Oxford: Oxford University Press, 1954.

Nautin, Pierre, *Lettres et écrivains chrétiens des IIᵉ et IIIᵉ siècles.* Paris: Cerf, 1961.

The New Testament in the Apostolic Fathers. By A committee of the Oxford Society of Historical Theology. Oxford: Clarendon, 1905.

Nave, Guy D., Jr., *The Role and Function of Repentance in Luke-Acts* Atlanta: Society of Biblical Literature, 2002.

Neil, William, *The Acts of the Apostles.* NCB. London: Oliphants, 1973.

Niederwimmer, Kurt, *The Didache.* Trans. L. M. Maloney. Hermeneia. Minneapolis: Fortress Press, 1998.

Niese, Benedictus, "Josephus," in J. Hastings, Ed. *Encyclopedia of Religion and Ethics.* New York: Charles Scribner's Sons, 1928, vol. 7: 569–79.

Nock, Arthur Darby, *Conversion: The Old and the New in Religion from Alexander the Great to Augustine of Hippo.* London: Oxford University Press, 1933.

———, *Essays on Religion and the Ancient World.* 2 vols. Ed. Z. Stewart. Cambridge: Harvard University Press, 1972.

Nolland, J. Nolland, "A Fresh Look at Acts 15.10," *New Testament Studies* 27 (1980) 105–15.

――――, *Luke 1–9:20* WBC 35a. Dallas: Word, 1989.

Norden, Eduard, *Agnostos Theos*. Leipzig: Teubner, 1912.

Nuttall, G.F., *Moment of Recognition: Luke as Story-Teller*. London: Athlone, 1978.

Oepke, A. ἀθέμιτος *TDNT* 1:166.

O'Neill, J. C., *The Theology of Acts in Its Historical Setting*. London: SPCK, 1961.

Osiek, Carolyn, *The Shepherd of Hermas*. Hermeneia. Minneapolis: Fortress, 1999.

O'Toole, Robert F., *The Unity of Luke's Theology: An Analysis of Luke-Acts*. GNS 9. Wilmington: Michael Glazier, 1984.

Overbeck, Franz, "Über das Verhältniss Justins des Märtyrers zur Apostelgeschichte," *Zeitschrift für wissenschaftliche Theologie* 15 (1872) 305–49.

Packer, J. W., *The Acts of the Apostles*. Cambridge Bible Commentary. Cambridge: University Press, 1966.

Paget, James Carleton, *The Epistle of Barnabas*. WUNT 64. Tübingen: Mohr/Siebeck, 1994.

Painter, John, *Just James: the Brother of Jesus in History and Tradition*. Columbia, South Carolina: The University of South Carolina Press, 1997.

Parsons, Mikeal C., "Acts," in W. E. Mills, *et al.*, Eds., *Mercer Commentary on the Bible*. Vol. 7: *Acts and Pauline Writings*, Macon, Georgia: Mercer University Press, 1997, 1–64.

――――, *The Departure of Jesus in Luke-Acts. The Ascension Narratives in Context*. JSNTS 21. Sheffield Academic Press, 1987.

――――, and Pervo, Richard I., *Rethinking the Unity of Luke and Acts*. Minneapolis: Fortress, 1993.

Paulsen, Hennig and Bauer, W., *Die Briefe des Ignatius von Antiochia und der Brief des Polykarp von Smyrna*. HNT 18 Tübingen: Mohr/Siebeck, 1985.

Pease, Stanley, Ed., *M. Tulli Ciceronis De Natura Deorum*. 2 vols. Cambridge: Harvard University Press, 1958.

Pelikan, Jaroslav, *The Christian Tradition: A History of the Development of Doctrine. The Emergence of the Catholic Tradition (100–600)*. Chicago: University of Chicago Press, 1971.

Perkins, Pheme, *Peter: Apostle for the Whole Church*. Columbia: University of South Carolina Press, 1994.

Perrin, Norman, and Duling, Dennis, *The New Testament: an Introduction*. 2nd ed.. New York: Harcourt Brace Jovanovich, 1982.

Pervo, Richard I., "Aseneth and her Sisters: Women in Jewish Narrative and in the Greek Novels." In Amy-Jill Levine, Ed. *"Women like This." New Perspectives on Jewish Women in the Greco-Roman World*. Atlanta: Scholars Press, 1991, 145–160.

――――, "Four Unmarried Daughters of Philip," in Carol Meyers, Ed., *Women in Scripture*. New York: Houghton Mifflin, 2000, 467–68.

――――, "A Hard Act to Follow: *The Acts of Paul* and the Canonical Acts," *Journal of Higher Criticism* 2 (1995) 3–32.

――――, "Israel's Heritage and Claims upon the Genre(s) of Luke and Acts: The Problems of a History," in D. P. Moessner, Ed., *Jesus and the Heritage of Israel: Luke's Narrative Claim upon Israel's Legacy*. Harrisburg, PA: Trinity Press International, 1999, 127–43.

――――, *Luke's Story of Paul*. Minneapolis, Fortress Press, 1990.

――――, "Meet Right—and Our Bounden Duty: Meetings and Assemblies in Acts." *Forum* N.S. 4.1, 2001, 45–62.

――――, My Happy Home: The Role of Jerusalem in Acts 1–7, *Forum* N.S. 3.1 (2000) 31–55.

――――, A Nihilist Fabula: Introducing the *Life of Aesop*," in R.F. Hock, J. Chance, and J. Perkins, editors, *Ancient Fiction and Early Christian Narrative*. SBLSS 6. Atlanta: Scholars Press, 1998, 177–200.

――――, "PANTA KOINA: The Feeding Stories in the Light of Economic Data and Social

Practice," in L. Bormann et al. Eds., *Religious Propaganda and Missionary Competition in the New Testament World.* FS Dieter Georgi. Leiden: E.J. Brill, 1994, 164–94.

———, *Profit with Delight: The Literary Genre of the Acts of the Apostles* Philadelphia: Fortress Press, 1987.

———, "Romancing an Oft-neglected Stone: The Pastoral Epistles and the Epistolary Novel." *Journal of Higher Criticism* 1 (1994) 25–47.

———, "Social and Religious Aspects of the Western Text," in D. Groh and R. Jewett, Eds., *The Living Text,* E.W. Saunders FS. Ann Arbor: University Press of America, 1985, 229–41.

———, "Wisdom and Power: Petronius' *Satyricon* and the Social World of Early Christianity," *Anglican Theological Review* 67 (1985) 307–25.

Pesch, Rudolph, *Die Apostelgeschichte. EKK.* 2 vols. Zürich: Benziger, 1986

Peters, Melvin K. H., "Septuagint," *ABD* 5:1093–1104.

Pfitzner, Victor C., *Paul and the Agon Motif.* SNTS 16; Leiden: E. J. Brill, 1967.

Pherigo, P., "Paul's Life after the Close of Acts," *Journal of Biblical Literature* 70 (1951), 277–284.

Plümacher, Eckhard, "Acta-Forschung 1974–1982 (Fortsetzung und Schluss) " *Theologische Rundschau* 49 (1984) 105–79.

———, "Apostelgeschichte," G. Krause *et al.*, Eds., Theologische *Realenzyklopädie.* Berlin: Walter de Gruyter, 1978, 3: 483–528

———, "Eine Thukydidesreminiszenz in der Apostelgeschichte (Act 20,33–35 — Thuk. 11 97.3f)?," *Zeitschrift für die neutestamentliche Wissenschaft und die Kunde der älteren Kirche* 83 (1992) 270–75.

———, *Lukas als hellenistischer Schriftsteller.* SUNT 9. Göttingen: Vandenhoeck & Ruprecht, 1972.

———, "Luke as Historian," *ABD* 4: 398–402.

———, Wirklichkeitserfahrung und Geschichtschreibung bei Lukas: Erwägungen zu den Wir-Stücken der Apostelgeschichte, *Zeitschrift für die neutestamentliche Wissenschaft und die Kunde der älteren Kirche* 68 (1977) 2–22.

Plummer, Alfred, A., *A Critical and Exegetical Commentary upon St Luke. ICC* 4th ed.. Edinburgh: T.&T. Clark, 1901.

Pokorny, Petr, "Christologie et Baptême à l'Epoque du Christianisme Primitif," *New Testament Studies* 27 (1980–81) 370.

———, *Theologie der lukanischen Schriften. FRLANT* 174. Göttingen: Vandenhoeck & Ruprecht, 1998.

Poland, Franz, *Geschichte des griechischen Vereinswesens.* Leipzig: Teubner, 1909.

Polhill, John B., *Acts. NAC* 26. Nashville: Broadman Press, 1992.

Porter, Stanley, *The Paul of Acts. WUNT* 115. Tübingen: Mohr/Siebeck, 1999.

Potter, David S., *Literary Texts and the Roman Historian Approaching the Ancient World.* London: Routledge, 1999.

Powell, Mark Allan, *What Are They Saying about Acts?* Mahwah, New Jersey: Paulist, 1991.

Praeder, Susan M., "Acts 27:1–28:16: Sea Voyages in Ancient Literature and the Theology of Luke-Acts." *Catholic Biblical Quarterly* 46 (1984) 683–706.

———, "Jesus-Paul, Peter-Paul, and Jesus-Peter Parallelisms, *SBLSP* 1984. Chico, California: Scholars Press, 1984, 23–39.

———, "The Problem of First person Narration in Acts, *Novum Testamentum* 39 (1987) 193–218.

Prast, Franz, *Presbyter und Evangelium in nachapostolischer Zeit.* Stuttgart: Verlag Katholisches Bibelwerk, 1979.

Preisker, H., μαίνομαι *TDNT* 4:360–361.

———, μέθη, *TDNT* 4:545–547.

Price, James L., *Interpreting the New Testament*. 2nd ed. New York: Holt, Rinehart & Winston, 1997.

Price, Robert, *The Widow Traditions in Luke-Acts: A Feminist-Critical Scrutiny*. SBLDS 155. Atlanta: Scholars Press, 1997.

Quell, Gottfried, and Schrenk, Gottlob, δίκη, κ.τ.λ., *TDNT* 2:174–224.

Rackham, R. B., *The Acts of the Apostles*. 2nd ed.. London: Methuen & Co., 1904.

Radl, Walter, *Paulus und Jesus im Lucanischen Doppelwerk: Untersuchungen zu Parallelmotiven im Lukasevangelium und in der Apostelgeschichte*. Bern: Peter Lang, 1975.

Ramsay, William M., *St. Paul the Traveller and Roman Citizen*. London: Hodder and Stoughton, 1897.

Reese, M., Alttestamentliche Motive in der Christologie der Lukas, 105–7.

Refoulé, F., "Le discours de Pierre à l'assemblée de Jérusalem," *Revue Biblique* 100 (1993) 239–51.

Reicke, Bo, "Synoptic Prophecies on the Destruction of Jerusalem," in D. E. Aune, Ed., *Studies in New Testament and Early Christian Literature*. FS Wikgren. SNT 33. Leiden: E.J. Brill, 1972, 121–34.

Reifenberg, A., *Ancient Jewish Coins*. Jerusalem: Rubin Mass, 1973.

Reimer, Ivoni Richter, *Women in the Acts of the Apostles: A Feminist Liberation Perspective*. Trans. L. M. Maloney. Minneapolis: Fortress, 1995.

Rengstorf, Karl Heinreich, δεσπότης, κ.τ.λ., *TDNT* 2:44–49.

———, δώκεκα, κ.τ.λ. *TDNT* 2:321–328.

———, νομοδιδάσκαλος, *TDNT* 2:159.

Reynolds, J., and Tannenbaum, R., *Jews and Godfearers at Aphrodisias*. Cambridge Philological Society. Supp. 12. Cambridge: Cambridge University Press, 1987.

Richardson, Cyril C., Ed. *Early Christian Fathers. Library of Christian Classics I*. Philadelphia: Westminster, 1953.

Riesner, Rainer, *Paul's Early Period: Chronology, Mission Strategy, Theology*. Trans. D. Stott. Grand Rapids: William B. Eerdmans, 1998.

Robbins, V., "By Land and by Sea." In C. Talbert, Ed., *Perspectives on Luke-Acts* Danville, Va.: National Association of Baptist Professors of Religion, 1978, 215–42.

Robert, A. and Feuillet, A. *Introduction to the New Testament*. Trans. P. W. Skehan *et al.* New York: Desclee, 1965.

Roberts, A., and Donaldson, J., Eds. Rev. by A. C. Coxe, *The Ante-Nicene Fathers* Grand Rapids: William B. Eerdmans, 1973 (reprint of 1885 original).

Robinson, James M., *et al.*, Eds., *The Critical Ed. of Q*. Hermeneia. Minneapolis: Fortress Press, 2000.

———, and Koester, H. *Trajectories through Early Christianity*. Philadelphia: Fortress, 1971.

Robinson, J. A. T., *Redating the New Testament*. Philadelphia: Westminster Press, 1976.

Rohrbaugh, Richard L., "The Pre-Industrial City in Luke-Acts: Urban Social Relations," in J. Neyrey, Ed., *The Social World of Luke-Acts: Models for Interpretation*. Peabody, MA: Hendrickson, 1991, 125–50.

Roloff, Jürgen, *Die Apostelgeschichte*. NTD 5. Göttingen: Vandenhoeck & Ruprecht, 1981.

Romm, James S., *The Edges of the Earth in Ancient Thought*. Princeton: Princeton University Press, 1992.

Ropes, James Hardy, *The Text of Acts*. Beg. 3. 1926.

Rostovtzeff, M., "The Sarmatae and Parthians," in S. A. Cook *et al.*, editors, *The Cambridge Ancient History* vol. XI. Cambridge: Cambridge University Press, 1936, 91–130.

Sanders, Jack T., *The Jews in Luke-Acts*. Philadelphia: Fortress Press, 1987.

Schenk, Wolfgang, "Luke as Reader of Paul: Observations on his Reception." In *Intertextuality in Biblical Writings*. FS Bas van Iersel, Sipke Draisma, Ed. Kampen: J. H. Kok, 1989), 127–39.

———, *Die Philipperbriefe des Paulus. Kommentar*. Stuttgart: W. Kohlhammer, 1984.
Schencke, H.-M., "Das Weiterwirken des Paulus und die Pflege seines Erbe durch die Paulusschule," *New Testament Studies* 21 (1975), 505–518.
Schlier, Heinrich, αἱϱέομαι, κ.τ.λ., *TDNT* 1:180–185.
———, ἀποστασία, *TDNT* 1:513–514.
Schrenk, W. and Quell, G. πατήϱ, κ.τ.λ., *TDNT* 5:945–1021.
Schrenk, W., ἐκδικέω, κ.τ.λ., *TDNT* 2:442–446.
Schürer, E., *A History of the Jewish People in the Time of Jesus Christ*. Rev. and Ed. G. Vermes, F. Millar *et al*. 3 vols. Edinburgh: T. & T. Clark, 1973–87.
Schmidt, Karl Ludwig, θϱησκεία, κ.τ.λ., *TDNT* 3:155–159.
———, *Der Rahmen der Geschichte Jesu* Darmstadt: Wissentschaftliche Buchgesellschaft, 1964 (reprint of 1919).
Schmitt, Tassilo, *Paroikie und Oikoumene: Sozial- und mentalitätsgeschichtliche Untersuchungen zum 1. Clemensbrief*. Beihefte zur Zeitschrift für die neutestamentliche Wissenschaft und die Kunde der älteren Kirche 110. Berlin: Walter de Gruyter, 2002.
Schneemelcher, Wilhelm, Ed., *New Testament Apocrypha*. Vol. 2. Trans. and Ed. R. M. Wilson *et al*. Philadelphia: Westminster Press, 1992.
Schenke, L., "Die Kontrastformel Apg 4,10b," *Biblische Zeitschrift* 26 (1982) 1–20.
Schiffman, Lawrence H., "At the Crossroads: Tannaitic Perspectives on the Jewish-Christian Schism," in E. P. Sanders *et al*., Eds, *Jewish and Christian Self-Definition*. Vol. 2: *Aspects of Judaism in the Greco-Roman Period*. Philadelphia: Fortress Press, 1981, 115–56.
Schnackenburg, Rudolf, *Ephesians: A Commentary*. Trans. H. Heron. Edinburgh: T&T Clark, 1991.
———, *The Johannine Epistles*. Trans. R. and I. Fuller. New York: Crossroad, 1992.
Schneider, Gerhard, *Die Apostelgeschichte*. HTK. 2 vols. Freiberg: Herder, 1980, 1982.
Schniewind, J. and Friedrich, G., ἐπαγγέλω, κ.τ.λ., *TDNT* 2:576–586.
Schoedel, William, "Ignatius and the Reception of Matthew in Antioch," in D. Balch, Ed., *Social History of the Matthean Community*. Minneapolis: Fortress, 1991, 129–86.
———, *Ignatius of Antioch*. Hermeneia. Philadelphia: Fortress Press, 1985.
———, "Papias," *ABD* 5:192–95.
Schreckenberg, H., "Flavius Josephus und die Lucanischen Schriften," in W. Haubeck and H. Bachmann, Eds. *Wort in der Zeit*. FS K. H. Rengstorf. E.J. Brill: Leiden, 1980, 179–209.
Schürmann, Heinz, Das *Lukasevangelium*. HTK. Vol. 1. Greiburg: Herder, 1969.
Schwartz, Daniel R., *Agrippa I. The Last King of Judaea*. Tübingen: Mohr/Siebeck, 1990.
Schweizer, Eduard, *Church Order in the New Testament*. Trans F. Clarke. Naperville: IL: Allenson, 1961.
———, *The Good News according to Luke*. Trans. D. E. Green Atlanta: John Knox, 1984.
———, *The Letter to the Colossians*. Trans. A. Chester. Minneapolis: Augsburg, 1982.
Scott, Bernard B., *Hear Then the Parable*. Minneapolis: Fortress Press, 1989.
Seim, Turid, *The Double Message: Patterns of Gender in Luke and Acts*. Nashville: Abingdon, 1994.
Sellin, G., "Hauptprobleme des Ersten Korintherbriefes," *ANRW* 1.25.4 2940–3044.
Shellard, Barbara, *New Light on Luke: Its Purpose, Sources and Literary Context*. JSNTS 215. Sheffield: Sheffield Academic Press, 2002.
Sherwin-White, A. N., *Roman Law and Roman Society in the New Testament*. Oxford: Oxford University Press, 1968.
Singer, Marc, "Never Surrender," *The New Yorker*, 14 May 2001, 52–57.
Skarsaune, Oskar, *The Proof from Prophecy* Suppl NT 56. Leiden: E.J. Brill, 1987.
Skinner, Matthew L., *Locating Paul: Places of Custody as Narrative Settings in Acts 21–28*. SBL Academia Biblica 13. Atlanta: Society of Biblical Literature, 2003.
Slingerland, Dixon, "'The Jews' in the Pauline Portion of Acts," *Journal of the American*

Academy of Religion 54 (1986) 305–21.
Smallwood, E. Mary, "The Diaspora in the Roman period before CE 70," in W. Horbury *et al.*, Eds., *The Cambridge History of Judaism*. Vol. 3: *The Early Roman Period*. Cambridge: Cambridge University Press, 1999, 168–91.
———, *The Jews under Roman Rule*. Leiden: E.J. Brill, 1981.
Smith, B.T.D., *The Parables of the Synoptic Gospels* Cambridge: Cambridge University Press, 1937.
Souter, Alexander, *The Earliest Latin Commentaries on the Epistles of St. Paul* Oxford: Clarendon, 1927.
Spencer, F. Scott, *Acts*. Sheffield: Sheffield Academic Press, 1997.
———, *The Portrait of Philip in Acts*. JSNTSMS. Sheffield: JSOT Press, 1992.
Speyer, Wolfgang, *Die literarische Falschung im hiednischen und christlichen Ältertum: ein Versuch ihrer Deutung*. Handbuch der Altertumswissenschaft, 1.2. München: Beck, 1971.
Spicq, Ceslas, *Les épitres pastorales*. Quatrième ed. refondue. Paris: Galbalda, 1969.
———, "La place ou le rôle des jeunes dan certaines communautés néotestamentaires," *Revue Biblique* 76 (1969) 508–27.
———, *Theological Lexicon of the New Testament*. Trans. and Ed. J. D. Ernest. 3 vols. Peabody, MA: Hendrickson, 1994.
Spivey, Robert A, and Smith, D. Moody, *Anatomy of the New Testament*. London: MacMillan, 1969.
Squires, John T., *The Plan of God in Luke-Acts*. SNTSMS 76. Cambridge: Cambridge University Press, 1993.
Stählin, Gustav, *Die Apostelgeschichte* NTD 5 Göttingen: Vandenhoeck & Ruprecht, 1962.
———, φιλέω, κ.τ.λ., *TDNT* 9:113–171.
———, χήρα, *TDNT* 9:440–465.
Stark, Rodney, *The Rise of Christianity: a Sociologist Reconsiders History*. Princeton: Princeton University Press, 1996.
Stauffer, Ethelbert, ἀγών, κ.τ.λ., *TDNT* 1:134–160.
Stegemann, Wolfgang, "War der Apostel Paulus ein römisher Bürger?," *Zeitschrift für die neutestamentliche Wissenschaft und die Kunde der älteren Kirche* 87 (1987) 200–229.
———, *Zwischen Synagoge und Obrigkeit. Zur historischen Situation der lukanischen Christen*. FRLANT 152. Göttingen: Vandenhoeck & Ruprecht, 1991.
Steinmann, A., *Die Apostelgeschichte*. Die Heilige Schrift des Neuen Testamentes 4. 4th Ed.. Bonn: Peter Hanstein, 1934.
Stemberger, Gunther, *Jewish Contemporaries of Jesus: Pharisees, Sadducees, Essenes*. Trans. A.W. Mahnke. Minneapolis: Fortress Press, 1995.
Stenschke, Christoph, *Luke's Portrait of Gentiles Prior to Their Coming to Faith*. WUNT 108. Tübingen: Mohr/Siebeck, 1999.
———, "The Need for Salvation," in I. H. Marshall and David Peterson, Eds. *Witness to the Gospel: The Theology of Acts*. Grand Rapids: William B. Eerdmans, 1998, 128–44.
Sterling, Gregory, E., "Athletes of Virtue": An Analysis of the Summaries in Acts (2:41–47; 4:32–34; 5:12–16)," *Journal of Biblical Literature* 113 (1994) 679–96.
———, *Historiography and Self-Definition. Josephos, Luke-Acts and Apologetic Historiography*. SuppNovTest 64. Leiden: E.J. Brill, 1992.
Stern, Menachem, *Greek and Latin Authors on Jews and Judaism*. 3 Vols. Jerusalem: Israel Academy of Sciences and Humanities, 1974–1984.
Stoneman, Richard, *The Greek Alexander Romance*. London: Penguin, 1991.
———, *Legends of Alexander the Great*. Everyman. London: J. P Dent, 1994.
———, " The Metamorphoses of the *Alexander Romance*," in G. Schmeling, Ed., *The Novel in the Ancient World*. Leiden: Brill, 1996), 601–12.
Stoops, Robert F., Jr., Ed., *Semeia* 80 (1997): *The Apocryphal Acts of the Apostles in*

Intertextual Perspectives.

———, "Riot and Assembly: The Social Context of Acts 19:23–41," *Journal of Biblical Literature* 108 (1989) 73–91.

Strange, M. A., *The Problem of the Text of Acts.* SNTSM 71. Cambridge: Cambridge University Press, 1992.

Strathmann, H., λατρεύω, λατρεία, *TDNT* 4:58–65.

———, πόλις, κ.τ.λ., *TDNT* 6:516–35.

Streeter, Burnett H., *The Four Gospels: A Study of Origins.* London: Macmillan, 1924.

Strobel, August, "Passa-Symbolik und Passa-Wunder in Act XII. 3ff.," *New Testament Studies* 4 (1957–58) 210–215.

———, "Schreiben des Lukas? Zum sprachlichen Problem der Pastoralbriefe," *New Testament Studies* 15 (1969) 191–210.

Strom, Mark R.,"An Old Testament Background to Acts 12.20–23," *New Testament Studies* 32 (1986) 289–92.

Stumpff, Albrecht, ζῆλος, κ.τ.λ., *TDNT* 2:877–88.

Tajra, W., *The Martyrdom of St. Paul: Historical and Judicial Context, Traditions, and Legends* WUNT 2/67. Tübingen: Mohr/Siebeck, 1994.

Talbert, Charles, H., *Literary Patterns, Theological Themes, and the Genre of Luke-Acts.* SBLMS 20. Missoula, Mont.: Scholars Press, 1974.

———, *Reading Acts: A Literary and Theological Commentary on the Acts of the Apostles.* Reading The New Testament Series; New York: Crossroad, 1997.

———, *Reading Luke: A Literary and Theological Commentary on the Third Gospel.* New York: Crossroad, 1982.

Tannehill, Robert, C. *Luke* ANTC Nashville: Abingdon, 1996.

———, *The Narrative Unity of Luke-Acts: A Literary Interpretation.* 2 vols. Minneapolis: Fortress Press, 1986, 1990.

Tatum, W. Barnes, *John the Baptist and Jesus: A Report of the Jesus Seminar.* Sonoma, CA: Polebridge, 1994.

Taylor, Vincent, *The Gospel according to St. Mark.* London: Macmillan & Co., 1953.

Theissen, Gerd, *The Gospels in Context: Social and Political History in the Synoptic Tradition.* Trans. L.M. Maloney. Minneapolis: Fortress Press, 1991.

———, *The Miracle Stories of the Early Christian Tradition.* Trans. F. McDonagh: Ed. J. Riches. Philadelphia: Fortress Press, 1983.

Thiering, Barbara, "The Acts of the Apostles as Early Christian Art," in *Essays in Honour of Griffithes Wheeler Thatcher,* E. C. B. MacLaurin, editor. Sydney: Sydney University Press, 1967, 139–89.

Thornton, C.-J., *Der Zeuge des Zeugen.* Tübingen: Mohr/Siebeck, 1991.

Thurston, Bonnie Bowman, *The Widows: A Women's Ministry in the Early Church.* Minneapolis: Fortress Press, 1989.

Tidwell, William A., *Come Retribution: The Confederate Secret Service and the Assassination of Abraham Lincoln.* Oxford: University Press of Mississippi, 1988.

Torrey, C. C., *The Composition and Date of Acts.* HTS 1. Cambridge: Harvard University Press, 1916.

Townsend, John, "The Date of Luke-Acts," in C. Talbert, Ed., *Luke-Acts: New Perspectives from the Society of Biblical Literature Seminar.* New York: Crossroads, 1984, 47–62.

Trocmé, Étienne, *Le libre des Actes et l'histoire.* Paris: Presses Universitaires de France, 1957.

Trudinger, P. L., "Papias," in John H. Hayes, Ed., *Dictionary of Biblical Interpretation* (Nashville: Abingdon, 1992) 2:234–35.

Tuckett, Christopher, Ed. *The Messianic Secret.* IRT 1. Philadelphia: Fortress Press, 1983.

Tyson, Joseph B., "The Date of Acts: A Reconsideration," a paper prepared for the March 2002 Meeting of the Acts Seminar, Santa Rosa, California.

———, *Images of Judaism in Luke-Acts.* Columbia: University of South Carolina Press,

1992.

———, Ed., *Luke-Acts and the Jewish People: Eight Critical Perspectives*. Minneapolis: Augsburg, 1988.

Unnik, W. C. van, *Tarsus or Jerusalem*. Trans. G. Ogg. Naperville, Ill.: Alec R. Allenson, 1962.

van der Horst, Pieter, "Peter's Shadow: The Religio-Historical Background of Acts V.15," *New Testament Studies* 23 (1976–77) 204–12.

Verheyden, J., Ed., *The Unity of Luke-Acts*. BETL 112. Leuven: University Press, 1999.

Vermes, Geza, *The Complete Dead Sea Scrolls in English*. New York: Penguin, 1997.

Verner, David C., *The Household of God: The Social World of the Pastoral Epistles*. SBLDS 71. Chico, CA: Scholars, 1983.

Veyne, Paul, *Le pain et le cirque: sociologie historique d'un pluralisme politique*. Paris: Seuil, 1976.

Vielhauer, Philipp, *Geschichte der urchristlichen Literatur*. Berlin: Walter de Gruyter, 1975.

———, "On the `Paulinism' of Acts," *SLA*, 33–51.

Walaskay, Paul W., *Acts*. WBC. Louisville: John Knox, 1998.

Walker, William O., Jr., "Acts and the Pauline Corpus Reconsidered," *Journal for the Study of the New Testament* 24 (1985) 3–23.

———, "Acts and the Pauline Corpus Revisited: Peter's Speech at the Jerusalem Conference," in R. P. Thompson and T. E. Philips, Eds., *Literary Studies in Luke-Acts*. FS Joseph B. Tyson. Macon, GA: Mercer University Press, 1998, 77–86.

———, "Select Bibliography on the Pauline Letters as Sources for [the] Acts of the Apostles," a paper prepared for the October, 2002 meeting of the Acts Seminar, Santa Rosa California.

———, "The Timothy-Titus Problem Reconsidered," *Expository Times* 92 (1980–81) 231–235.

Walton, Steve, *Leadership and Lifestyle: The Portrait of Paul in the Miletus Speech and I Thessalonians*. SNTSMS 108. Cambridge: Cambridge University Press, 2000.

Wehnert, Jürgen, *Die Wir-Passagen der Apostelgeschichte*. Göttingen: Vandenhoeck & Ruprecht, 1989.

Weinart, Frank, "The Parable of the Throne Claimant (Luke 19:12, 14–15, 27), Reconsidered," *Catholic Biblical Quarterly* 39 (1977) 505–14.

Weiser, Alfons, *Die Apostelgeschichte*. ÖTKNT 5.1/2. Gütersloh: Gütersloher Verlagshaus Gerd Mohn, 1981, 1985.

Weizsacker, Carl v., *The Apostolic Age of the Christian Church* Trans. J. Millar. vol. I. New York: G. P. Putnam's Sons, 1894.

Welborn, L. L., "On the Date of First Clement," *Biblical Research* 29: 35–54.

———, *Paul's Letter of Reconciliation in 2 Corinthians*. Ph.D. diss. Chicago.

———, *Politics and Rhetoric in the Corinthian Epistles*. Macon, Ga: Mercer University Press, 1997

Wellhausen, Julius, *Kritische Analyse der Apostelgeschichte*. AGG n.s. 15.2. Berlin: Topelman, 1914.

Wendland, Paul, *Die Hellenistisch-römische Kultur in ihren Beziehungen zu Judentum und Christentum. Die urchristlichen Literaturformen*. HNT 1, 2–3. 2nd/3rd Ed.. Tübingen: Mohr/Siebeck, 1912.

Wendt, Hans H., *Die Apostelgeschichte*. KEK Göttingen: Vandenhoeck & Ruprecht, 1913.

Wenham, David, "Acts and the Pauline Corpus II. The Evidence of Parallels," in B. W. Winter and A. D. Clarke, Eds., BIFCS 1. *Ancient Literary Setting* (1993), 215–58.

White, L. Michael, "Urban Development and Social Change in Imperial Ephesos," in H. Koester, Ed. *Ephesos: Metropolis of Asia*. HTS 41. Valley Forge: Trinity Press International, 1995, 27–79.

Wilcox, Max, *The Semitisms of Acts*. Oxford: Clarendon, 1965.

Wilken, Robert L., *The Christians as the Romans Saw Them*. New Haven: Yale University

Press, 1984.

Wikenhauser, Alfred, *Die Apostelgeschichte. Regensburger Neues Testament*. Dritte Auflage. Regensburg: Friedrich Pustet, 1956.

———, *Die Apostelgeschichte und ihr Geschichtswert*. Münster: Aschendorff, 1921.

Wiles, Maurice F., *The Divine Apostle: The Interpretation of St Paul's Epistles in the Early Church*. Cambridge: Cambridge University Press, 1967.

Willimon, William H., *Acts*. Interpretation. Atlanta: John Knox, 1988.

Williams, C. S. C., *The Acts of the Apostles*. Harper's. New York: Harper and Brothers, 1957.

Williams, M.H., "Palestinian Jewish Personal Names in Acts," in R. Bauckham, Ed., *BIFCS* 4, 79–113.

Williams, R. R., *Acts of the Apostles*. Torch. London: SCM, 1965.

Wills, Lawrence M., Ed. and Trans. *Ancient Jewish Novels: An Anthology*. New York: Oxford University Press, 2002.

———, "The Depiction of the Jews in Acts," *Journal of Biblical Literature* 110 (1991) 631–54.

———, *The Jewish Novel in the Ancient World*. Ithaca: Cornell University Press, 1995.

———, *The Quest of the Historical Gospel: Mark, John, and the Origins of the Gospel Genre*. London: Routledge, 1997.

Wilson, Stephen G., "Lucan Eschatology," *New Testament Studies* 14 (1970–71) 330–47.

———, *Luke and the Law*. SNTSMS 50. Cambridge: Cambridge University Press, 1983.

———, *Luke and the Pastoral Epistles*. London: SPCK, 1979.

Windisch, Hans, ἀσκέω, *TDNT* 1:494–96.

———, "The Case against the Tradition," *Beg.* 2:298–348.

Winik, Jay, *April 1865*. New York: HarperCollins, 2001.

Winter, Bruce C., *Seek the Welfare of the City: Christians as Benefactors and Citizens*. Grand Rapids: William B. Eerdmans, 1994.

Witherington Ben III,_The Acts of the Apostles: A Socio-Rhetorical Commentary. Grand Rapids/Cambridge, U. K. Eerdmans; Carlisle: Paternoster, 1998.

———, Ed., *History, Literature and Society in the Book of Acts*. Cambridge: Cambridge University Press, 1996.

Wyatt-Brown, Bertram, "Anatomy of A Murder," *New York Review of Books*, 24 October 2002, 22–24.

Xavier, Jacques, *Lists of New Testament Words Sharing Common Elements*. Rome: Pontifical Biblical Institute Press, 1969.

Zahn, Theodor, *Introduction to the New Testament*. Trans. Ed. M. W. Jacobus. Vol. III. Edinburgh: T. & T. Clark, 1909.

Zehnle, Richard F., *Peter's Pentecost Discourse: Tradition and Lucan Reinterpretation in Peter's Speeches of Acts 2 and 3*. SBLMS 15. Nashville: Abingdon Press, 1971.

Zuntz, G., *The Text of the Epistles*. London: Oxford University Press, 1953.

Index of Ancient Authorities

1–2 Chronicles, 56

1 Clement, 53, 62, 137, 168, 205, 208, 236, 237,
243–44, 255, 268, 284, 288, 344, 386 n.9, 414 n.95,
423 n.12, 430 n.160, 431 n.163, 432 n.193, 433
n.215, 435 n.272, 438 n.87, 441 n.166, 444 n.243,
446 n.267, 452 n.88, 453 n.127

1–3	423 n.15
1:1	286, 438 n.70
1:2	442 n.182
1:3	241, 400 n.269, 426 n.58
1:3–2:8	302
2:1	229b
2:2	296, 302–3, 447 n.297
3:4	442 n.182
4:1–6:4	270
4:4	447 n.291
5	300, 322, 452 n.97
5:1	263
5:2–5	270
5:4	289
5:5–7	62, 319
5:6	265, 442 n.182
6:2	300
7:4	243–44
7:4–8:5	275
7:5–7	275
8:1	121, 244
10:4, 6	447 n.291
10:6, 7	237
12	447 n.293
12:1, 8	442 n.182
13:1–2	228–29, 433 n.221, 448 n.323
14:1	303
14:3	304
16:1	204
17:1	269, 308
18:1	301
19:2	255, 270
20	250, 302, 326
20–26	326
20:11	267, 270
21:1	270
21:6	283

22	430 n.160
23:5	304
24:5	273
29:1	432 n.206
29:2	435 n.260
29:2–30:1	272
29:3	304, 447 n.308
31–24	254
31:2	238
32:4	238, 432 n.206
33:1–8	250, 304
33:2	266
33:4	435 n.266
35:7	447 n.291
36:1	288
38:3	270
39:1	441 n.167
41:1	241
42:1–4	208, 314–15, 427 n.79
43	447 n.293
44:1	269
44:1	217
44:3	204, 208–9, 217, 269
44:4	314
45.1	391 n.81
45:7	241, 271
46:6	303, 447 n.304
46:7–8	228–29, 272
46:9	384 n.81
47:5	384 n.81
47:6	263
48:4	239
50:3	269, 428 n.92
52:1	435 n.258
54:2	204, 209
55	447 n.293
55:3	121
55:6	268
56:6–15	430 n.160
57:1	244
57:2	204
58:2	442 n.182
59	276

Note: This index does not include the persons and texts listed in Appendix III, nor the citations in general or summary tables.

Acts

Acts

I ndex of Modern Authorities

Note: This index does not include references to Appendix II

508

Richard I. Pervo has devoted more than thirty years to studying the interaction of early Jewish and Christian writings with ancient popular literature. His New Testament specialization is the book of Acts, on which he has published three books, including *Profit with Delight: The Literary Genre of the Acts of the Apostles* (Fortress, 1987), *Luke's Story of Paul* (Fortress, 1990) and (with Mikeal Parsons) *Rethinking the Unity of Luke and Acts* (Fortress, 1993). He is currently writing a commentary on Acts for the Hermeneia Commentary Series.

verisimilitude & verisimilitude 339f.